TRADITION
IN AN AGE
OF REFORM

TRADITION IN AN AGE OF REFORM

The Religious Philosophy of Samson Raphael Hirsch

NOAH H. ROSENBLOOM

Philadelphia

THE JEWISH PUBLICATION SOCIETY OF AMERICA

frontispiece portrait of Samson Raphael Hirsch
courtesy of Jewish Division,
New York Public Library,
Astor, Lenox, and Tilden Foundations

לזכר אבי ואמי
מיכאל ושרה לאה
שהועלו בסערה השמימה

Contents

Preface

Of the vast number of philosophers, theologians, and scholars who revolutionized Jewish life and thought in the nineteenth century, few have exerted a more distinctive and continuing influence than Samson Raphael Hirsch (1808–1888). To this day his religious Weltanschauung intrigues many and enjoys considerable popularity in various Jewish circles.

Since ours is a period of mercurial fluctuations, social paroxysms, and intellectual ferment, the fact that his outlook has survived is astonishing. The present generation is profoundly distrustful of metaphysics, theology, theonomic morality, sacral ritualism, and religious formalism. In this climate of widespread disbelief in which absolutes are relativized, certainties dissolved, and religion ignored, this continued interest in Hirsch's theocentric and theonomic viewpoint is most remarkable.

Although Hirsch addressed himself to his contemporaries in German, current interest in his ideas transcends the geographic and linguistic boundaries for which these ideas were originally intended. His works, heretofore the exclusive domain of German-speaking Jews, are now rendered into various languages and accessible to readers in many countries. Numerous monographs, studies, and articles dealing with various aspects of Hirsch's life, views, activities, and influences appear in many lands in many languages.

This renewed interest in Hirsch makes one wonder whether it emanates from the intellectual strength of Hirsch's world view or from the psychological weakness of the modern Jew in his quest for an ideational terra firma. In brief—are we witnessing a genuine interest in Hirsch's outlook or an amorphous fascination with the Hirsch mystique?

This question is neither simple nor easy to resolve, for the modern Jew, like modern man in general, has yet to disentangle his reason from his emotions. Rationally, he appears to have extricated himself from the centuries-old orthodoxy and even from religion per se; but emotionally he is still attracted to it and occasionally even nostalgic.

This rational-emotional paradox and ambivalent complexity, so characteristic of many modern Jews and non-Jews, renders difficult any present-day inquiry into a traditionalist religious outlook. One tends to suspect that the modern Jew's interest in Hirsch is motivated by the same urge that prompts his non-Jewish contemporary to explore the writings of Karl Barth or Jacques Maritain. Both sets of moderns seek in these traditionalist-oriented works a glimmer of salvation in a time aptly termed the Age of Anxiety. Like the sightless Samson at Gaza, many bewildered Jews and non-Jews face extinction beneath the crumbling temple; only today it is the world that is collapsing and they are not endowed with Samson's courage.

Disenchanted with a way of life that has transformed the world into a wasteland and humanity into ciphers, many search for a meaningful faith—not only the Jewish neo-Hirschians but Catholic neo-Thomists and Protestant neo-Reformationists as well. Differences notwithstanding, they share a common mistrust of the liberal theologians who endeavor to re-create God in their own image, who restructure religious values to meet the exigencies of the times, and who tailor ethics to suit whimsical demands and unpredictable situations.

Hirsch seems also to intrigue the modern, acculturated, observant Jew who turns to him for solutions to the multifaceted problems arising from a dual loyalty to the Torah and to the Western mode of life, particularly secular education. While many modern observant Jews seem to have adopted Richelieu's maxim of "acting in matters of State as if one were not a cardinal and in matters of religion as if one were not a statesman," those who are more sophisticated consider this expedient compartmentalization distasteful. The latter prefer to seek out in Hirsch's writings a validating rationale for their traditional commitment in terms of the contemporary universe of discourse.

In view of this widespread interest in and fascination with Hirsch, one wonders at the lack of a comprehensive exposition of Hirsch's thought, which seems long overdue.

This study doesn't propose to analyze the underlying sociopsychological motives that may account for this fascination with Hirsch's personality and/or Weltanschauung. Its aim, rather, is to present an objective, critical exposition of his views on Judaism in the light of his sociocultural milieu and in the context of the Jewish and non-Jewish intellectual currents of his time.

A study of Hirsch's ideational world presents certain problems. Studying his voluminous works written in the course of a half-century is a formidable task. His ornate, grandiloquent style interwoven with Hebrew quotations from biblical, talmudic, and rabbinic sources, and his complex exegesis encumbered with his speculative etymology and rendered in a convoluted German idiom—all this makes for anything but easy reading. Nor do the existing translations help. With some exceptions, most translations slavishly follow not only the German text but its indigenous idiom and syntax as well, thus compounding the difficulties and further beclouding the meaning. Whether this literalism was motivated by a reverence or a faithfulness to the master's word or by other human frailties, it is advisable when reading most translations of Hirsch to consult the German original, despite its strictures.

A more serious problem is gauging Hirsch's ideas, which are frequently buried under such heavy layers of rhetoric that the contemporary reader seeking the ideational kernel is smothered beneath a blanket of embellishment.

None of these problems, however, is unique to the study of Hirsch. Every historian and critic encounters similar or greater obstacles in probing the views of earlier thinkers and restructuring them in the modern idiom. The scholar is usually compensated for the pains of his labor by the calm detachment and dispassion that surround his subject cleared of the mist that might have enveloped it in an earlier period and bereft of the emotive factors which prevent an objective analysis and evaluation. However, this is not so in the case of Hirsch, whose legacy—and the sensibilities of many contemporaries to this legacy—still endure. Hirsch continues to excite a vast ambit of controversy and his views still evoke conflicting emotions. Indeed, although the heat generated in his polemics with the Jewish Reformers of his age has cooled considerably, the residual embers smolder on. Thus, an objective study of Hirsch's religious philosophy, while no longer impossible, is problematic within this century. Somehow, the ideological heirs of the nineteenth-century religious conflict are still sensitive to Hirsch, and feel obligated either to attack or defend him. As a result, the objective discussion of Hirsch's viewpoint that true scholarship demands may still be unsafe, since it may provide too much ammunition to his detractors and too little to his admirers. Thus, an endeavor to indicate Hirsch's indebtedness to the intellectual currents of his time may displease those claiming that he was intellectually self-sufficient. Paradoxically, no such claim was ever advanced with regard to the greatest Jewish philosophers from Saadia to Rosenzweig. That such a claim is not only absurd but even an insult to Hirsch's intelligence is completely ignored by his overzealous admirers.

Foreseen and unforeseen problems notwithstanding, the intent of this study is to pursue its avowed course while resisting the gravitational pull from either right or left. Avoiding polemics and apologetics, it will endeavor to present Hirsch's religious philosophy as he intended to convey it in his time. It was therefore necessary to eschew a substantial part of the existent *Kampfsliteratur* of his epigones who are still engaged in the master's vendetta and to be guided by Hirsch's views alone.

Hirsch's advice on how to read the Bible proves a useful and effective guide to a critical and objective study of his own writings: "May you forget all the annoyance which the reading of these writings caused you in your youth; forget all the prejudices which you may have imbibed from different sources against these writings. Let us read them as though we had never read them; as though we have never heard of them."*

Most of Hirsch's writings stem from two periods in his rabbinic career: his first post in Oldenburg (1830–1841) and his last post in

* *The Nineteen Letters of Ben Uziel,* trans. Bernard Drachman (New York, 1942), p. 16.

Frankfurt am Main (1851–1888); yet there is a marked difference between them. Those from Oldenburg are predominantly philosophical and theological, while those from Frankfurt are mostly polemic and exegetic.

Interestingly, the works dating from the Oldenburg period, written while Hirsch was young, show more restraint, moderation, and conciliation than do those written years later in Frankfurt. Apparently in his Oldenburg period Hirsch addressed himself to all German Jews, traditionalists and nontraditionalists alike, in an effort to bridge the widening religious chasm in the Jewish community. His works from the Frankfurt period are controversial, belligerent, and militant, advocating separation of traditionalists from the nontraditionalists. Ostensibly, Hirsch no longer hoped to build a bridge between these polarized segments in the Jewish community, but rather labored to erect a barrier, making rapprochement virtually impossible.

Since this book is concerned with Hirsch's world of ideas, special attention is given to his works of a philosophical-theological nature, particularly to his interpretation of the commandments. Hirsch's interest in this area continued throughout his life, even after he had abandoned his early ambition to formulate a comprehensive philosophy of Judaism. Impelled by a new insight or new exigencies, he expanded upon, elaborated, and modified many a rationale he had proposed in his earlier works.

Regrettably, unlike his Oldenburg period, where Hirsch collected his interpretations of the commandments into one book, *Horeb*, his subsequent interpretations are scattered throughout his voluminous writings. It was therefore imperative in this study to collect and collate the later interpretations and, when necessary, to indicate the changes and modifications in his rationale of given commandments. To facilitate this task it was found most appropriate to apply the classification Hirsch employed in his *Horeb*. The reader must therefore realize that while the part of the present book dealing with the interpretation of the commandments follows the classification of the *Horeb*, the similarity is only in the formal outline; in content it goes far beyond Hirsch's early handbook. The present analysis encompasses Hirsch's views on this subject as contained in all his works from Oldenburg through Frankfurt am Main.

To enable the reader to orient himself, abbreviated references to the early and later sources are given in parentheses in the text. Most of Hirsch's works are still available only in the original German and where necessary my references relate to German editions; however, where English translations are available I have made use of them. By quoting from existing English translations I hoped to make it possible for readers unfamiliar with German to consult Hirsch's works.

Grateful acknowledgment is made to the scholarly magazines *Historia Judaica, Revue des Études Juives, Jewish Social Studies,* and *Sura Institute for Research* for permission to use my articles on Hirsch which originally appeared there and were substantially revised in form and content to become part of the present work.

I also wish to thank the following publishers for granting me permission to quote from material published by them:

Clarendon Press for Georg Wilhelm Friedrich Hegel, *Philosophy of Right,* trans. T. M. Knox (London, 1942); Hebrew Publishing Company for Moses Maimonides, *Guide of the Perplexed,* trans. Michael Friedländer (New York, 1946); Judaica Press for *The Pentateuch Translated and Explained by Samson Raphael Hirsch,* trans. Isaac Levy (London, 1958–62); KTAV Publishing House for David Philipson, *The Reform Movement in Judaism* (New York, 1967); Leo Baeck Institute for *Leo Baeck Institute Year Books* (London, 1956–68); Philipp Feldheim, Inc., for Samson Raphael Hirsch, *The Nineteen Letters of Ben Uziel,* trans. Bernard Drachman (New York, 1942); Schocken Books, Inc., for Moses Mendelssohn, *Jerusalem,* trans. Alfred Jospe (New York, 1969); Soncino Press, Limited, for Samson Raphael Hirsch, *Horeb: Philosophy of Jewish Laws and Observances,* trans. I. Grunfeld, 2 vols. (London, 1962), and for Hirsch, *Judaism Eternal: Selected Essays from the Writings of S. R. Hirsch,* trans. and annotated by I. Grunfeld, 2 vols. (London, 1956); World Union for Progressive Judaism, Ltd. for W. Gunther Plaut, *The Rise of Reform Judaism* (New York, 1963), and for Jakob J. Petuchowski, *Prayerbook Reform in Europe* (New York, 1968).

In conclusion, I wish to express my gratitude to the Memorial Foundation for Jewish Culture for their fellowship grant; to Dr. Samuel Belkin, president of Yeshiva University, for his long abiding friendship since my student days; to Professor David Mirsky, vice-president of Yeshiva University and dean of Stern College, for providing me with clerical assistance to proofread this manuscript; to Mrs. Sofie Laufer, German Department, Stern College, for proofreading the German phrases and references; above all to my wife and my children for what words cannot express.

N. H. R.

הושענא רבה

תשל"ו

Abbreviations Used in Citations

The following abbreviations are used in all parenthetical citations within the text as well as in the relevant entries in the notes. Note that the numbers appearing in these citations refer to pages—with the exceptions of Hirsch's commentaries on the Pentateuch and the Psalms, where numbers refer to the chapter and verse under discussion, and the *Horeb*, where numbers refer to paragraphs.

C . . . Hirsch's commentary in *The Pentateuch Translated and Ex-*
(*CG,* *plained by Samson Raphael Hirsch,* trans. Isaac Levy (Lon-
CE, don, 1958–62), 5 vols., and *The Psalms Translated and Ex-*
etc.) *plained by Samson Raphael Hirsch,* trans. with commentary
by Gertrude Hirschler (New York, 1960–66), 2 vols.

CCARYB Central Conference of American Rabbis Yearbook (Cincinnati).

G Moses Maimonides, *Guide of the Perplexed,* trans. Michael
Friedländer (New York, 1946).

H Samson Raphael Hirsch, *Horeb,* trans. I. Grunfeld (London,
1962), 2 vols.

HJ Historia Judaica (New York).

JE Samson Raphael Hirsch, *Judaism Eternal: Selected Essays
from the Writings of S. R. Hirsch,* trans. and annotated with
an introduction by I. Grunfeld (London, 1956), 2 vols.

JJLG Jahrbuch der jüdisch-literarischen Gesellschaft (Frankfurt
am Main).

JQR Jewish Quarterly Review (Philadelphia).

LBYB   *Leo Baeck Institute Year Book* (Leo Baeck Institute, 1956–68).

MGWJ   *Monatsschrift für Geschichte und Wissenschaft des Judentums* (Breslau).

NB   *"Neunzehn Briefe"*: Samson Raphael Hirsch, *Igrot Tzafon: Neunzehn Briefe über Judentum von Ben Usiel* (Altona, 1836).

NL   "Nineteen Letters": Samson Raphael Hirsch, *Igrot Tzafon: The Nineteen Letters of Ben Uziel*, trans. Bernard Drachman (New York, 1942).

PR   Georg Wilhelm Friedrich Hegel, *Philosophy of Right*, trans. with notes by T. M. Knox (London, 1942).

PT   Moses Mendelssohn of Hamburg [Moses Frankfurter], *Penei Tevel* (Amsterdam, 1872).

S   Samson Raphael Hirsch, *Gesammelte Schriften*, ed. N. Hirsch (Frankfurt am Main, 1908–12), 6 vols.

Part One

HIRSCH IN THE CONTEXT OF HIS AGE

1

The Intellectual Temper

In the Aftermath of the Revolution

To study Samson Raphael Hirsch apart from the nineteenth-century Reform movement in Judaism is to miss his importance. Paradoxically, it was this movement which Hirsch so vehemently fought that provided him his raison d'être and assured him his place in history. In its absence, Hirsch might have dutifully fulfilled his parent's wishes of becoming a successful merchant.[1] Similarly, to study his Weltanschauung outside the context of Reform would be equally meaningless. Were it not for the philosophical and theological challenge of Reform, Hirsch's religious outlook would have at best been amorphous. On the other hand, to regard Hirsch's interpretation of Judaism as a mere counterstroke to Reform is to miss its singularity. Notwithstanding its dialogical and polemical nature, it has an inner consistency and a dynamic dialectic of its own that merit special attention.

Significant as these two aspects are to the study of Hirsch, there is yet a third aspect to be considered which relates both the Hirschian and Reform Weltanschauungen to the spirit of their time and to the sociopolitical factors that spawned them. Affected by the lingering animus of their polemics, we tend to view the battle as that between Esau and Jacob, forgetting that both emerged from the same womb; differences notwithstanding, both were conceived by the same mother and begotten by the same father.

3

Like the aforementioned twins, Hirsch and the Reformers were born into a confused and unstructured world, exposed to a strange new universe of discourse evolved over a century of revolution and war. Their mentors, likewise, were as wholesome and self-sacrificing as Isaac but, regrettably, equally myopic and irresolute. Like Esau and Jacob, Hirsch and the Reformers had to proceed independently along different roads to attain by different means the same end—the birthright and their father's blessing.

The roots of Hirsch's traditionalism and his opponents' desire for reform are deeply embedded in earlier strata of Jewish history;[2] their immediate origin was the French Revolution and the complexities and transformations resulting from its bloody aftermath. It was this cataclysmic event that shattered the heretofore insular religious-ethnic Jewish world in which Jews had lived for centuries. Isolated and surrounded by Gentile hostility, the Jews had developed a tendency toward exclusivity and separatism. They had transformed the ghetto into a religious-cultural and socioeconomic state-within-a-state; as a result, the ghetto, confined geographically and functionally, acquired all the characteristics of a distinct civilization.

The French Revolution abruptly and unexpectedly upset this exclusiveness and loosened the ethnocentric ties. The egalitarian forces unleashed by this social cataclysm breached not only the Bastille, but also the similarly impregnable walls of the Jewish ghettos inside and outside France's frontiers. As a result, the Jews were catapulted from their physical and spiritual isolation into the seething caldron of western Europe. The events resulting from this colossal upheaval proceeded with such maddening rapidity that within a short period of time painstaking efforts on behalf of Jewish Emancipation became superfluous. Imposed by the bayonets of the French armies rather than by morality and goodwill, Emancipation came sooner than the most enlightened liberals had dared dream. The sudden dissolution of the Jewish socioreligious corporate pattern, beneficial as it was to many Jews, had disastrous consequences for Judaism, however. The unexpected entry of the Jews into the mainstream of Western life did not allow for a period of intellectual gestation which might have eased the cultural shock. Thus, the encounter between Judaism and Occidental thought took place at a time when the Jews were neither intellectually nor psychologically prepared for it.

Although encounters between Judaism and unfamiliar, even antithetical, philosophies and cultures had been numerous in the past, none had been marked by the unexpected swiftness of the emancipation process inaugurated at the end of the eighteenth century. The Jews of ancient Alexandria had time gradually to assimilate some of the Hellenistic ideas of their milieu and weave them into their theological fabric.[3] Similarly, the Jews of medieval Spain, having been exposed for a considerable time to the Kalam, Neoplatonism, and Aristotelianism, incorporated some of these concepts into their own expositions of Judaism.[4] Thus, time was a major factor in mitigating the discordant elements in the encounters of Judaism with other schools of thought.

The unprecedented suddenness of the encounter between Judaism and Occidental culture at the end of the eighteenth century brought about a collision between the two with devastating results for Jews and for Judaism. Within a relatively short period of time, the denizens of the ghetto came to the agonizing realization that the world from which they were geographically separated only by inches was—intellectually and culturally—centuries apart. Suddenly they saw themselves denuded of all the religious and intellectual vestments of which they had been so proud and were overcome by an unusual embarrassment over their "inferiority." The Jew "awoke suddenly to a Copernican astronomy and a Newtonian physics, to the skepticism, the materialism, the deism, and the romantic German pantheism of the eighteenth and early nineteenth centuries. Each of these streams of thought beat against the bases of his Weltanschauung."[5]

Had the acculturation process been gradual, it might have been possible for the Jew to accept the new Occidental influences without unduly disturbing his intellectual and emotional equilibrium or destroying his religious and ethical values. As in the past, some gifted men might have been able to develop a Jewish world view compatible with this new culture. However, the abruptness of the encounter precluded all such possibilities, transforming the blessing of Emancipation into a malediction for the Jewish religion, no matter how undeniably beneficial it was for Jews as individuals. For Judaism, the fall of the ghetto walls was as devastating as was the fall of the Bastille for the ancien régime. Socially, the Emancipation proved even more destructive to the Jewish community, which heretofore had served as a minor interterritorial, nonpolitical state. The destruction of the ghetto accelerated the dissolution of its intricate socioreligious order, and with it the entire ethnocultural pattern of Jewish life.

The rise of capitalism, the expansion of commerce, the intensification of industrialization and urbanization, the progress of political emancipation, and the steady inroads of secularism further widened the gap between life and Law and thus strengthened heterodox sentiments. This was particularly true in the purely juridical domain, where Jewish law regulated the socioeconomic relationships between man and man. A religious-juridical system consisting of ancient biblical and talmudic laws hardly seemed attractive to a generation of disaffiliating Jews preparing to enter the mainstream of European culture and aspiring to social equality, economic integration, and cultural amalgamation.

Unable to cope with the situation, many post-Emancipation Jews became agnostics, latitudinarians, or deists, while others embraced Christianity; some, like Israel Jacobson and Jacob Beer, motivated by practical rather than theological considerations, set out to reform Judaism.

Impelled by the urge to prove themselves worthy of the boon of Emancipation, they began to modernize the synagogue and reform the religious services to appeal to the religious and aesthetic sensibilities of their Christian compatriots. The pre-Emancipation Haskalah endeavor to improve the Jew's image by acculturating him through the slow process of education and the Westernization of his appearance no longer sufficed for the early advocates of Reform. They insisted on improving the Jew's image by improving Judaism's image through the Westernization of its most visible manifestation, the synagogue. This meant the "de-Orientalization" of the religious service, abridgment of the prayer book, elimination of cantillation, and similar practices. They erected Reform temples in Seesen, Berlin, and Hamburg in the style of Protestant churches, dressed their rabbis like Protestant pastors, modeled their sermons after those of the Protestants, installed organ music, composed hymns in German, and published prayer books in which transliterations gradually replaced the Hebrew.[6]

As these haphazard innovations gained momentum, their exponents were soon caught in the maelstrom of unforeseen implications. The principle of change proved extremely catalytic, challenging the validity of the Bible as much as the authority of the Talmud and the rabbinic codes of law. It undermined ethical axioms as it had legal and ritualistic practices. The Reformers soon found that many biblical laws and instructions were as much out of harmony with the modern age as were those of the later Rabbis. This discovery frightened them. They dared not admit that biblical laws were a product of temporal and environmental conditions and hence subject to abrogation. Lacking the courage to destroy the very foundations of Judaism, yet reluctant to abandon their new approach, they adopted a policy of expediency, disregarding biblical laws which conflicted with the spirit of the time while retaining those of ethical significance. Eventually, even some of the Ten Commandments, notably the one pertaining to the Sabbath, seemed irrelevant and oppressive.

Radical and outrageous as these reforms appeared to the traditionalists, they failed to satisfy the more thoughtful, intellectual Westernized Jews who sought meaning rather than accommodations. Unless Judaism were made meaningful, the Reform temple would remain a beautiful mausoleum, or at best a museum housing a petrified mummy, Judaism.

With no one to uphold it and fewer now to validate it, normative Judaism was dying. What was needed was an interpretation of Judaism which would make its norms not only obligatory but reasonable and relevant as well. But such an interpretation was nowhere in sight. The traditionalist rabbis and scholars who were deeply distressed by the initial steps of Reform provided more heat than light and could not meet the challenge presented by the swift-moving events.

The traditionalists, who were least aware of the transformations and fluctuations in the outside world, did not know what these social changes meant to the inner Jewish community. They lived in a static world, believing the outer world to be static as well. They presumed the relationship between the communities was the same as if the tenuous balance had not been disturbed. They did not perceive in the agitation of the early Reformers and defectors on the perimeter of the Jewish community, the symptoms of a multidimensional revolt which had already convulsed the non-Jewish world. They dismissed it as rumblings of dissenters, schismatics, or apostates—malcontents who had always existed in Jewish history but had failed to alter its course.

Assured that nothing extraordinary had occurred, the traditionalists believed that measures employed against such heterodox groups in the past would prove equally effective in the present: condemnation, castigation, and litigation would correct the backslidings of the latitudinarians and Reformers and deter the dissemination of their pernicious views.

Contrary to this misapprehension, the situation was radically different, and nothing in the experience of the traditionalists was equal to meet this challenge. In their fool's paradise they failed to realize the need for new solutions. The temper of the times required either a Maimonides to guide the perplexed or a Saadia to polemicize with the dissidents. The traditionalists in Germany had neither. The four most eminent rabbis of the era, Moses Sofer, Mordecai Benet, Akiba Eger, and Jacob Lorbeerbaum, were in their declining years. They were men of great talmudic erudition, unqualified piety, and high moral principle. Nothing in their background or experience, however, qualified them for the new Kulturkampf, fought on an alien sociointellectual terrain, with weapons and rules they did not comprehend. As a result, the majority of the traditionalists in Germany yielded after a few skirmishes and recoiled behind the walls of spiritual isolation.[7]

Mendelssohn's Normativism

In these circumstances there was dire need of a religious guide to orient the Jews in the new cultural milieu without compromising Judaism. He had to be a person of integrity and intellect, possessing a comprehensive knowledge of Judaism and Western thought and strongly committed to both—in brief, a new Maimonides to guide the numerous perplexed of that bewildered generation.

Unable to find a guide in their own generation, some turned to Moses Mendelssohn, who had lived in a previous generation. The fact that Mendelssohn was able to live as both a Jew and a Western man at the same time confirmed their belief that he could serve as the modern Maimonides. This view, held by the last remnants of the Haskalah, the Hebrew Enlightenment,[8] was not shared by the wider Westernized Jewish circles in Germany. The latter realized that in spite of the relatively short time since Mendelssohn's death, the political, social, and cultural climate had undergone such a radical metamorphosis that Mendelssohn's views, crystallized and articulated in the prerevolutionary era, were no longer cogent or relevant.

Mendelssohn himself never hoped or pretended to be a Maimonides.[9] There is no evidence that he ever felt the necessity for evolving a philosophy of Judaism compatible with the Occidental temper, since few of his contemporary coreligionists were beset with the conflicts arising from a polarity of faith and reason.

Mendelssohn's view on Judaism was similar to that of Baruch Spinoza, who emphasized its legal aspects. He rejected, however, Spinoza's contention that its laws were applicable only to the Jewish Commonwealth of antiquity and lacked validity in the present exilic era. Mendelssohn maintained that Jewish laws, being of divine origin, had an external mandatory quality rendering them unalterable and obligatory. But although Mendelssohn's views on the positive quality of nomistic Judaism retained an aura of erudite respectability if not credibility in the eighteenth century, they were summarily rejected in the nineteenth.

Mendelssohn's concept of Judaism, expounded in *Jerusalem* (1783), seemed inadequate for the post-Emancipation Jews who sought a positive rationale for the maintenance of their ancestral faith. Instead of a vigorous defense of Judaism, *Jerusalem* offered them a feeble apology endeavoring to prove Judaism's unobtrusive nonassertiveness toward world affairs. This quality of nonaggressiveness, accentuated by Mendelssohn in order to make the Jews politically palatable to the Christians, could not raise Judaism's prestige in Jewish eyes. Whether the Jews at the beginning of the nineteenth century realized the underlying reason for Mendelssohn's pallid presentation of Judaism or not, the fact remains that they accepted his views at face value and found them unappealing. Mendelssohn had deliberately understated the dynamic factor of religion in the Jews' lives in order to make Judaism itself seem least obstructive to their emancipation. Since *Jerusalem* was fundamentally a plea for Jewish acceptance into a Christian-controlled state, Mendelssohn minimized the role of Judaism to the point where it would seem inconsequential if not nonexistent.

After Mendelssohn's death, *Jerusalem* was found wanting because it lacked a positive exposition of Judaism; many were repelled by its apologetic tone and the ancillary role it assigned to Judaism.

Having accepted Mendelssohn's view about the dual aspect of Judaism—universal verities common to all men and particular norms limited to Jews only—the Jews in the nineteenth century failed to comply with the latter exposition. They did not quarrel with the universal aspect of Judaism which was confined to certain metaphysical and ethical concepts but was not specifically Jewish. However, Mendelssohn did not offer any plausible rationale for the normative aspect of Judaism which provided the Jewish religion its uniqueness.

Furthermore, Mendelssohn had also deprived Judaism of its redemptive quality—salvation. Throughout the traditional literature, beginning with the Bible, the observance of the Law implied a promise of salvation. Reward and punishment had always been the respective corollaries of compliance and disobedience. The talmudic sage Rabbi Tarfon echoed the prevailing view when he stated, "Faithful is thy employer to pay thee the reward of thy labor, and know that the grant of the reward of the righteous will be the future life."[10] Even Antigonos of Socho, who seemed to advocate a more sublime attitude by teaching that one should not serve the master for the sake of receiving a reward,[11] did not deny that a reward—or in case of noncompliance, a punishment—follows adherence (or nonadherence) to the laws of Judaism. Mendelssohn, however, rejected this traditional view. Whether he did so out of a philosophic conviction that a benevolent God would not punish, or out of political consideration—refusing to give religion, and hence the Church, the power of intimidation—or to legitimize the practice of Judaism in a non-Jewish state, the fact remains that he made normativism seem inane. Thus Judaism became completely meaningless. It neither revealed any truth otherwise unknown nor promised salvation to its adherents that was inaccessible to others. It had no means of enforcement by punishing for its violation. Small wonder that in the light of such an analysis many Jews in the post-Emancipation era failed to comprehend why they were duty bound to comply with the complex juridical-ceremonial regimen of Judaism.

Mendelssohn's claim that the Jews' obligation to obey the Law and perform its rites was based on a specific revelation which ordered them to do so failed to impress the subsequent generation. His ingeniously designed shift from revealed truth, *geoffenbarte Religion*, to revealed Law, *geoffenbarte Gesetze*,[12] might be considered sound rationalistic philosophy, having excluded universal verities from creedal limitations. It might even be considered good politics, having deprived the Church of its very foundation. It was, however, poor Jewish theology. Not only did it obviate the Law, it also deprecated revelation. Revelation, considered always the cornerstone of Judaism—God's unqualified communication of truth and ethics to mankind through Israel—was reduced to a set of legalistic, ritualistic formulas which were designed for one people only and whose performance was neither important to God nor meaningful to man. Furthermore, deprecating the universal and redemptive quality of revelation reduced the Jews' unique theological position as the chosen people to the level of the insignificant and the foolhardy.[13]

As a result of Mendelssohn's pragmatic attenuation of Judaism, *Jerusalem* became an intellectual liability instead of a political asset. In the subsequent generation the Jews who turned to it to vindicate their faith found very little to sustain them. Even when contrasted with Christianity, Judaism appeared lusterless, pallid, and anemic. Its superiority rested not on what it affirmed, but rather on what it negated. Its merit lay not in what it did, but in what it refrained from doing. Its distinction was not its insistence upon deeds, but its lack of insistence on faith.[14]

By denying Judaism its unique prerogatives to metaphysical truth and salvation, Mendelssohn deprived Judaism of its very essence and its adherents of their source of spiritual affirmation. It placed the Jews in a grotesque position, dooming them to perform meaningless rituals from which other people were absolved. Judaism thus became a punishment for the Jews, who were obliged to abide by laws from which all the rest of mankind was exempt. This yoke of the Law seemed not only burdensome but arbitrary. That these laws, unreasonable as they were, should be immutable only added to the perplexity and chagrin of Mendelssohn's successors, a confusion compounded by Mendelssohn's paradoxical view that the validity and immutability of these laws precluded their enforceability.

The new generation, though but a few years removed from Mendelssohn, could no longer comprehend the subtle motives that had compelled him to promulgate such an ingenious if tenuous concept, since they failed to comprehend the complexity of the sociopolitical factors in the pre-Emancipation era.[15] To say to the new generation that a law was devoid of universal sanction was tantamount to a tacit admission of its invalidity. Furthermore, to accept Spinoza's premise of the origin of the Jewish laws while rejecting his conclusion about their present defunct character seemed sheer sophistry. If, as Spinoza maintained and Mendelssohn concurred, the juridical-ritualistic aspect of Judaism was inherent in the theocratic Jewish state, it followed that with the destruction of that state these ancient laws should no longer be mandatory. Mendelssohn, however, using reasons no longer cogent to his successors, insisted that the laws' validity transcended time and space and coupled this view with his own admission of their eventual revocation. This implication of contingency and marginality made Mendelssohn's view of the Law seem incongruous and untenable. In sum, Mendelssohn's philosophic legacy of *Jerusalem* made Judaism a burden rather than an inspiration. By accentuating law rather than faith, and rituals instead of ideals—without even explaining their meaning—he transformed Judaism into a kind of mechanism conforming to irrelevant laws and performing incomprehensible ceremonies which interfered with life, hindered commerce, and dampened all joy. While such a mode of life might be tolerated in the ghetto, it was certainly discordant in the climate of the freedom newly gained after the French Revolution.

In the Shadow of Kant

Mendelssohn's philosophy of Judaism was even further undermined by the radical transformation of Germany's intellectual climate at the end of the eighteenth century. This transformation affected the very foundation of his philosophy. The source of Mendelssohn's Weltanschauung was the Leibnizian-Wolffian philosophic system which dominated German thought during the greater part of that century. This philosophy, which served as the intellectual cornerstone of the Aufklärung, the German Enlightenment, was challenged by a variety of intellectual currents: the faith philosophers, the neo-Spinozists, and Immanuel Kant. Each current had its exponents: the views of the faith philosophers were expounded by Johann Georg Hamann, Johann Caspar Lavater, and Friedrich Heinrich Jacobi; the neo-Spinozists were admirably represented by Gotthold Ephraim Lessing, Johann Gottfried Herder, and Johann Wolfgang von Goethe. Influential as these exponents were, none posed as formidable a challenge to the Leibnizian-Wolffian system as did Kant, whose philosophy finally toppled it.[16] With the collapse of the Leibniz-Wolff universe of discourse, Mendelssohn's Weltanschauung too lay in shambles.[17] Little wonder that Mendelssohn called Kant *der Allzermalmende,* the all-destroyer. But if Kant's views seemed destructive to Mendelssohn's general philosophic outlook, they proved disastrous to his view of Judaism.

Ironically, Kant, who negated Mendelssohn's general philosophic world view, accepted his view on Judaism and considered *Jerusalem* to be *"ein unwiderlegbares Buch,"*[18] an irrefutable book. Kant concurred that the specificity of Judaism lies in its nomistic aspect, a view already expressed by Spinoza but criticized for its excessive legalism and statutoriness.[19] In accepting this Spinozistic-Mendelssohnian view, Kant went beyond them, for they never denied that Judaism contained purely religious and ethical elements in addition to its legal aspect. Kant, however, considered it exclusively statutory and devoid of any religious or ethical value. This extreme attitude is attributable largely to Kant's insistence upon the absolute autonomy of the will in what he defines as ethics. Any action motivated or conditioned by somebody or something external to the individual cannot be considered ethical. The moral value of an action is contingent on its being done for the sake of duty and not to satisfy any external pressure or will, sublime as it may be.[20] As a result, actions dictated by religion cannot be viewed as ethical since a theological basis for action is no more ethical than a social, political, economic, or psychological basis. Duty must not spring from any tangible or intangible authority. Judaism as a theonomic religion could not, therefore, produce an autonomous ethic. Moreover, by addressing itself to external behavior, it further demonstrated its lack of ethicality. At best, it could be presented as a historical juridical-political system, but it could claim no universal ethical-religious content.

Small wonder that the Jews, while they may have dismissed criticism leveled against Judaism by clerics and anti-Semites, could not ignore the same coming from Kant and carrying the aura of objectivity and credibility. The fact that Kant's basic premise about the statutory character of Judaism was grounded in Mendelssohn's *Jerusalem* lent his criticism even more credibility and rendered Mendelssohn's exposition even less acceptable.

Kant's views on Judaism must have been especially agonizing for the Jewish intellectuals of that period. Not only did Judaism fail to compare favorably with Christianity, it was inferior even to polytheism and idolatry. Its contributions were held in contempt. Jewish monotheism was deprecated, the value of Ten Commandments was minimized, the Jewish God was seen as immoral, and Judaism itself was condemned as a tribal, unethical religion which fostered separation and evoked justifiable hatred. Nor did Judaism compensate its adherents with a promise of immortality. Even the Jewish hope for messianic redemption was reduced from a universal idea to a mere parochial, nationalistic aspiration.[21]

Overawed by Kant's stature and prestige, many Jews saw in him a veritable intellectual Goliath whom they revered despite his blasphemy. Since there was no David in their midst, they agonizingly acquiesced to his derogatory remarks on Judaism. It took over a century of intellectual gestation and psychological maturation for this awe to subside, enabling Hermann Cohen to confront Kantian philosophy with Judaism as an equal colloquium. In *Religion der Vernunft aus den Quellen des Judentums*, published posthumously in 1919, Cohen set out to prove that such a colloquium was possible.

However, prior to Cohen's vigorous endeavor, Jewish thought as reflected in nineteenth-century literature is marked by a disturbing uneasiness. Fearing to engage in a direct polemic with the views of the man they deified, Jewish intellectuals attempted indirectly to redefine Judaism in a manner that would avoid conflict with Kant's philosophic outlook. Since Kant had attacked Judaism as being *statutarisch* and *frommes Spielwerk*, concerned only with external laws and meaningless ceremonies, these intellectu-

als constantly accentuated its ethical aspect. The unusually excessive stress on ethics found in the works of Samuel David Luzzatto,
Solomon Ludwig Steinheim. Heymann Steinthal, Moritz Lazarus,
and others betrays this uneasiness.[22] Though they do not polemicize with Kant, they engage him in an indirect dialogue. Wherever and whenever possible, they underscore the ethical nature
of Judaism and interpret its laws, rites, and ceremonies as motiva-
tional means or educational media geared to attain a moral end.

As a result of the uneasiness induced by Kant, a complete reversal of emphasis took place from that of Mendelssohn's time.
Whereas before, the specificity of Judaism expressed itself in the
juridical-ceremonial aspect, its singularity in the post-Kantian period was reflected in its religious-ethical aspect. There was a conscious effort to shift Judaism's center of gravity from the Mendelssohnian *Legalität* to the Kantian *Moralität*. However, Kant posed
a threat not only to the ethical elements of Judaism but to its
metaphysical foundations as well. Having excluded any possibility
of the noumenal realm being reached by man's ratioempirical
means, Kant seemed to have placed Mendelssohn's universal
metaphysical verities outside the ken of human knowledge altogether. Consequently, not only the legal aspect of Judaism but
also its metaphysical basis, considered by Mendelssohn as self-
evident, was no longer tenable.[23]

Judaism was thus undermined by Kant as a religion per se on
metaphysical grounds, and as the Jewish religion on ethical
grounds. Disturbing as this was to many Jewish intellectuals whose
interest in Judaism was only peripheral, it was a source of profound chagrin to the second-generation Reformers[24] to whom it
was fundamental. The latter refused to accept Kant's condemnation of Judaism; at the same time, however, they dared not challenge his contentions.

This tension between emotional loyalty to Judaism and Kantian
intellectual honesty characterized the state of mind of many Jewish illuminati of this period. It superseded the tension between
Mensch and *Jew* typical of the Mendelssohnian era. This tension
is particularly evident in the Reform movement literature of the
second generation. A substantial part of it can be understood only
when we consider that it was written under the mighty shadow of
Kant, whose views on Judaism many exponents of Reform could

neither accept nor dare to reject. An almost neurotic ambivalence marked their attitude toward both Judaism and Kant representing love and fear, both attraction and repulsion. They were eager to uphold Judaism yet they feared the censure of the Kantians; they venerated Kant but could not accept his views on Judaism. As a result, they oscillated between *Kant* and *Tnak*— to borrow a play on words (Kant backwards spells *Tnak* or Bible) made by S. D. Luzzatto in a letter to Leopold Zunz[25]—with unsatisfactory consequences for both. Few exponents of the Reform movement had the courage to reject Kant in favor of Judaism or vice versa. This intellectual and psychological ambivalence gave rise to a host of haphazard theological accommodations and religious innovations which satisfied neither the philosopher nor the theologian since they were prompted by expediency rather than by philosophic consistency or religious integrity.

The position of the second-generation Reformers was far from enviable. Unlike their predecessors, whose general erudition had been as meager as their Jewish scholarship, the younger Reformers were men of vast Jewish and secular knowledge; many had been educated in the foremost German universities, and some had attained a high level of scholastic standing. They could not, therefore, escape Kant's opinions and views, which reigned supreme in the academia, nor overlook the implications these views held for their ancestral faith. Unlike their forerunners, the younger Reformers recognized that external palliatives were not sufficient to solve the intellectual crisis that the new philosophy portended for Judaism. As a result, a muffled, subdued, indirect colloquium with Kant exists in the writings of Abraham Geiger, Samuel Holdheim, and others less prominent in the Reform movement.[26]

Lacking the courage to defend Judaism in its totality over Kant's objections, the Reform theologians seemed willing to concede that it contained elements of statutoriness that needed abrogation. However, unlike Kant, who considered the Law an intrinsic characteristic of Judaism, they deemed it merely accidental and contingent and therefore transitory. In this respect, the exponents of the Reform movement differed from both the Mendelssohnian and Kantian conceptions of Judaism as the apotheosis of Law which were current at the end of the eighteenth century. They rejected the identification of Judaism with the statutoriness of

Kant and the obligatoriness of the legal aspect advocated by Mendelssohn. They were, therefore, much closer to Spinoza's view, which limited the specific nomistic aspect to the temporal existence of the Jewish state, adopting the notion that the end of the Jewish Commonwealth terminated the validity of the Law.

Holdheim's criticism of rabbinic Judaism essentially qualified Kant's. Whereas Kant considered Judaism synonymous with law in its entirety, Holdheim merely limited this characteristic to rabbinic Judaism, thus exonerating parts of biblical Judaism or Mosaism. Holdheim was no less acrimonious in his condemnation of rabbinic Judaism than Kant was of Judaism per se; he blamed the Rabbis for perpetuating the temporal aspects of Judaism and the residual elements of the ancient Jewish theocracy while neglecting its universal and eternal purpose.[27]

Similar antirabbinic and antinomian views were expressed by Abraham Geiger, David Einhorn, Ludwig Philippson, Leopold Stein, Samuel Hirsch, Abraham Adler, Samuel Adler, Joseph Aub, and others.[28] Apparently, by making rabbinic Judaism the culprit of legalism, these men hoped to vindicate Mosaism as a universal and ethical force, as required by Kant. Having conceded the legal aspect of Judaism, *statutarisch* in the Kantian sense, they showed an unusual preoccupation with the ethicization of its nonlegalistic aspects. Furtively and surreptitiously, they aligned these aspects with corresponding elements of Kantian philosophy and ethics.

This view was further strengthened by the rise and popularity of the historical-evolution school, which when applied to Judaism revealed a constant and enduring moral quality. The historical school not only indicated the ethical progression of Judaism, but also further validated the new antinomian tendencies that the Reform theologians fervently expounded. There was no need to deny that Judaism had once contained legal elements which it had shed in the course of its historical development. This factor also enhanced its ethical posture, since it demonstrated that these legal aspects were merely the external shell of Judaism while its ethical core remained intact, and that with the continuous progress of mankind Judaism could divest itself of its legal externals and appear in all its ethical purity. Without polemicizing with the many detractors of Judaism and by avoiding any confrontation with Kant, the younger Reformers seemed to imply that the latter had mistaken the external for the internal, thus rendering negative views on Judaism open for reconsideration. However, while tactfully implying that Kant may have erred in his judgment of Judaism, they explicitly rejected Mendelssohn's view concerning the applicability of the revealed Law. The nomistic aspect of Judaism was only one of many historical stages and as such was transitory and replaceable, they contended. Each historical stage had its necessary appurtenances through which it related the universal ideas of truth and morality. However, while the universal and ethical ideas and values were eternal, the historical appurtenances were merely contingent and inconsequential. Thus, Holdheim did not deny the validity of the Talmud to legislate for the immediate postexilic era of Judaism, he merely contested its contemporary validity: "The Talmud speaks with the ideology of its own time, and for that time it was right. I speak from the higher ideology of my time, and for this age I am right."[29]

Theological Accommodations

The Reform movement constituted a greater revolt against Mendelssohnian Judaism than against traditional Jewish faith. Traditional Judaism, though unacceptable, possessed noble simplicity, unsophisticated trust, and spiritual sublimity—elements that could still evoke some sympathy in the afterglow of the Sturm und Drang era. No such redeeming features existed in the arid, rationalistic-nomistic reformulation of Mendelssohn's Judaism.

In reality, the Reformers rejected only half of Mendelssohn's interpretation. They objected to his premise that the specificity of Judaism lay in its nomistic aspect but concurred with his premise that Judaism had no monopoly on universal truths. Eternal verities, they maintained, could be freely arrived at and were therefore not the exclusive province of Judaism. While this view seemed intellectually commendable, it made the theological position of the Reformers untenable. By accepting the premise that Judaism had no exclusive intimation of universal truth, the Reformers, like Mendelssohn, deprived it of its metaphysical importance. On the other hand, by rejecting its nomistic specificity they abandoned the last stronghold that Mendelssohn had striven to maintain. Thus, the very raison d'être for the Reform movement seemed to vanish, and its continuation as a distinct confessional group appeared problematic if not indefensible.

Professing to adhere to a Jewish religion conceived differently from that of the traditionalists or the Mendelssohnians, the Reformers were obliged to defend its uniqueness. This was apparently no easy task. Like all revolutionary movements, the Reform movement too seemed better qualified to proclaim what it rejected rather than what it affirmed. Thus, the existing works of the Reform theologians and rabbis are most eloquent when elaborating on the negative aspect of traditional Judaism but remarkably reticent in expressing their own positive views. In discussing the aspects of their own exposition, they are at best nebulous and ethereal. Determined to universalize and ethicize the Jewish religion, the leaders of the Reform movement tended to transform it into a new manifestation of deism no longer popular in the nineteenth century. Moreover, their vague and obscure concept of Judaism seemed to obliterate the ill-defined demarcation line that separated it from other ethical-monotheistic religions, notably Christianity. That such a demarcation line was imperative at this time of social and intellectual ferment is obvious. The very emergence of the Reform movement has often been likened to and justified as a barrier halting the defection of non-Orthodox and nonobservant Jews from the fold. The erosion of this boundary line seemed to challenge the rationale for the entire movement.

Indeed, the overwhelming majority of Reform ideologists continued to assert the uniqueness of Judaism and insist upon the special role it was destined to play in man's advancement; but as this uniqueness faded, its posture vis-à-vis Christianity became highly questionable. This made Reform Judaism almost indistinguishable from liberal Christianity, a fact that might delight only the minority of Reform extremists while proving unacceptable to the majority. However, not all the Reformers desired the eventual blurring of distinctions between Judaism and Christianity, nor did they hope for a state of confessional nirvana. Their universalistic aspirations notwithstanding, many of them had reservations about Christianity.[30]

The need for the validation of Judaism on positive grounds—making it universal without sacrificing its uniqueness and reject-

ing its nomistic quality without confusing it with deism or Christianity—necessitated a new approach to the old concept of revelation. Despite misgivings about revelation during the Enlightenment and Kantian eras, the Reformers formed it as the core of
their evolving theology. Unlike Mendelssohn, who had minimized
its importance, the Reform theologians made revelation again the
cornerstone of Judaism vis-à-vis the other religions. Accordingly,
it was revelation that lent Judaism its uniqueness and preeminence over other religions, including Christianity.

This seeming regression on the part of the Reformers, who were
always eager to synchronize Judaism with the Zeitgeist, rested
upon semantics. They merely retained the nomenclature of revelation while changing its meaning. Like many Christian theologians, they rehabilitated the repudiated concept of revelation by
retaining the form while transforming the content. The Christian
theologians paid dearly for making revelation acceptable in non-
theological circles. The Jewish Reformers, impelled by the necessity of providing a raison d'être for their antinomian form of Judaism, did likewise. They, too, stripped this time-honored concept of
its traditional connotation and replaced it with some nebulous
ambiguities that rendered it less dogmatically odious.[31] Such
deliberate ambiguities provoked the ire not only of the conservative elements but also of some liberals as well.

Despite all criticism, the Jewish Reform theologians, like their
liberal Protestant counterparts, considered their usage of *revelation* and its cognate term, *Mosaism*, legitimate. Though it lacked
traditional connotation, it was justified on the grounds that it signified a certain religious apprehension and an immediate primal
cognition of the Divine. According to Friedrich Schleiermacher,
who became the uncrowned theologian of the Jewish Reform
movement, "the contemplation of the pious is the immediate consciousness of the universal existence of all finite things in and
through the Infinite, and of all temporal things in and through the
Eternal."[32] Revelation was, therefore, not a noumenal concept
that was metarational and paralogical, to be dismissed as unascer-
tainable by man's modes of cognition; on the contrary, revelation
was an element of *Gefühl*, which was neither esoteric nor metaphysical but a basic part of man's awareness.

While the concept of revelation was now elevated to the level of respectability, it still needed a justification to explain why it is exclusive to the Jewish people only. Reluctant to subscribe to the traditional covenantal theory, the exponents of Reform needed a new and more adequate rationalization to link revelation with Judaism. Such an answer, seemingly compatible with the spirit of the age, had been provided by Herder. As a romanticist, he was able to operate with ideas that did not have to pass the bar of reason or judgment. He could, therefore, posit views without having to justify them on rational, empirical, or even historical grounds. In the atmosphere that prevailed during the Sturm und Drang era, such suprarational views were readily accepted. Herder seemed to combine an all-embracing monistic view with a simultaneous sense of the preeminence of distinctiveness and individuality. To him, all of nature and history manifest one whole exemplifying law and order. At the same time, both nature and history reveal vast variety and uniqueness. In nature, this is evident in variegated forms of flora and fauna as well as in distinct manifestations; in history, the diversity of talent and creativity is evident in man. This is marked by uniqueness and differences not only in individual man but in the distinctive national cultures as well. Each culture appearing at a given moment in the flux of history reveals an aspect of mankind's final goal.

This concept of national uniqueness and mission to exemplify it was not limited to Herder or to any one philosophical school. It was widespread, and not infrequently crossed invisible demarcation lines otherwise zealously guarded by their respective exponents.[33] This uniqueness, which is supposedly evident in every national culture, cannot be explained in rational terms but is attributable to *génie*, analogous to what the Cartesians termed "irrational" and the "genius," defying any attempts at analysis.[34] Vague and nebulous as this idea of genius or *génie* was, it was considered real by that generation of romantics who sentimentalized it.

It was this mystical idea of genius that some of the Reform theologians employed to explain why revelation and prophecy appeared among the Jews and not among other nations. For some unknown and inexplicable reason, the people of Israel, they claimed, showed a propensity for this kind of divine intimation. They manifested a genius for religion just as the Greeks demonstrated a genius for art and the Romans for law. These unusual manifestations could not be explained by rational or empirical factors, nor by any particular historical or psychological link. Nevertheless, it was an incontrovertible fact that these remarkable phenomena of national genius existed in these people and, though inexplicable, had to be accepted.

This concept of *génie* is dwelt upon extensively by Geiger. At the outset he distinguishes between talent and genius, which to him differ not merely in degree but in essence. Unlike talent, genius cannot be cultivated. Neither effort nor diligence enables man to acquire it. Genius is a freely bestowed favor upon man which he cannot acquire on his own.[35] Accepting the verity of this enigmatic and semiesoteric phenomenon of genius, as evidenced in various nations, Geiger maintains that the Jewish people, too, have been endowed with such a remarkable gift. The inexplicable "breakthrough," *Durchbruch,* which bestowed upon the Greeks their indigenous proclivity for art and science, gave the Jews the unique *génie* for religion. Indeed, other peoples also professed religion, but to them it was merely a talent, whereas with the Jews it was an expression of genius.

The gift of genius was not necessarily manifest in all Jews. Just as not all Greeks had the ability of a Phidias or a Praxiteles, not all Jews had the religious insight of Moses or the prophets.

It is apparent that although like some German theologians, Geiger saw in genius a phenomenon of the spirit, it was nevertheless inextricably bound up with a biological entity or *Volk.* Each *Volk,* Jews included, exhibited a certain *génie* in given areas. Conceding that not every Jew was a religious genius just as not every Greek was an artist, Geiger still proclaimed a kind of mystical psychosomatic relationship, since only the Jews could bring forth prophets, just as only the Greeks could give rise to artists; revelation was thus an inherent Jewish quality.[36]

In terms reminiscent of the Lurianic Cabala, which he undoubtedly dismissed, Geiger spoke of scattered sparks that united and irradiated a light which illuminated the world. These prophets were selected "instruments" through which this light flowed. This term, *instruments of light,* once again seems to recall the Lurianic vessels of emanation. They resemble scattered sparks of light fusing together into a bright flame emanating from a people with a unique predisposition for the extraordinary gift of prophecy.[37]

The fact that the Jewish people disclosed such a mysterious propensity for religion enabled the exponents of Reform theology to advance the idea of mission. It was, however, inherent in the premise of the psychosomatic link of genius and *Volk*, which the Reform theologians could not, wished not, and dared not sever. In this respect, the Reform theologians showed a remarkable affinity to the romantics' notion of *Volksgeist*, the authentic and pristine culture of a people before it became tainted with the syncretism of foreign sources. Influenced by Moser, Herder, Burke, Savigny, and Grimm, this mystical concept of *Volksgeist* was elevated to the level of a dominating entelechy. Herder was particularly lavish in "his invocations of the *Nationalgeist*— an expression probably coined by Karl Friedrich von Moser—and of its many aliases —the *Geist des Volkes, Seele des Volkes, Geist der Nation, Genius des Volkes*, and the more empirical *Nationalcharacter.*"[38] As a people endowed with such unique genius it was the Jews' task to retain the ethnic identity which embodied their spiritual distinctions. Here, the Reformers seem to accept the Mendelssohnian view of the importance of survival. Paradoxically, Mendelssohn in his concern with the sociopolitical rights of the Jews stressed the need for the survival of Judaism, while the Reform theologians in their concern with religion emphasized the need for the survival of the Jews. In Mendelssohn's view, the eternal verities will exist with or without the Jews. The latter are needed merely to retain the harmless externalities of their respective religions. The Reform theologians believed that the eternal verities are intrinsically bound up with the people of Israel and that the absence of Jews would deprive mankind of the *génie* of religious insight and creativity.

It is interesting to note that the concept of intuitive apprehension of the Divine, almost analogous to the idea of genius, had already been expressed by Judah Halevi, who posited the existence of an "inner eye" *(ayin nisteret)* that transcends the faculty of reason: "To the chosen among His creatures He has given *an inner eye* which sees things as they really are, without any alteration."[39] However, considering the spirit of the age, Herder's, Lessing's, and even Lavater's views carried considerably greater weight, prestige, and credibility than the medieval traditionalist Halevi's did.

Having linked the phenomenon of revelation with the people of Israel, the exponents of Reform reshaped it so as to retain the nomenclature yet transform its content. In this new context, revelation assumed a larger dimension. For the Reform theologians, the new concept of revelation transcended a singular divine manifestion and became a continuous process anteceding Sinai and continuing through the present into the distant future. This concept of revelation as a continuous dynamic process within the mainstream of history did not originate with the Reform theologians; they merely attempted to validate the traditional Jewish term in the context of the Zeitgeist. It was Lessing who had transformed the concept of revelation from a static phenomenon into a dynamic process. God, the author of revelation, was not conceived as a rigid legist imposing His laws upon humanity or a segment thereof. Lessing considered God a gentle pedagogue who educated mankind gradually, imparting to it knowledge and truth in accordance with its ability to comprehend. As a result of this continuous educational process and corollary intellectual elevation, God was conceived of differently by different generations. These differences did not reflect any changes or fluctuations in the divine essence, nor did these seemingly different revelations contradict one another. They merely mirrored the conceptual transformations of mankind at various stages of its development. Lessing thus seems to raise Rousseau's psychological concept of éducation progressive to a historical-theological level, which he embodied in his work, Die Erziehung des Menschengeschlechtes, published in 1780, eighteen years after the appearance of Émile.

It is interesting to note that the exponents of Reform who revolted against Mendelssohn's reinterpretation of Judaism eagerly embraced Lessing's concept of progressive revelation which Mendelssohn rejected.[40] This preference for Lessing's view was not motivated by objective inquiry but by theological expediency and accommodation—the prospect it contained to liberalize theology. It also explains why many Reform theologians with a keen understanding of history could accept Lessing's pseudoscientific theory —they were theologians first and historians second, and the need for a change in theology was overriding. Consequently they were determined to employ history, even pseudohistory, to legitimize a new theology. From a practical point of view, therefore, Lessing's theory, regardless of how valid it was, seemed more adequate to the cause of the Reform movement than did Mendelssohn's. To the latter, revelation in its normative aspect implied a static state whose obligatoriness could not change, while Lessing's view legitimized change as an inherent element in divine revelation.[41]

The shift from the Mendelssohnian view of revelation as a static state to Lessing's as a dynamic process had far-reaching consequences for Reform theology. It retained the idea of divine intimation but did not require any fixity of norms. A distinction was made between two aspects of Judaism, the internal and the external. The internal was the intangible element of divine revelation, however conceived; the external was the particular manifestation contingent upon the historic period of development. This manifestation is known as tradition, which due to its dynamic nature is constantly modified by change. As a result, the Reform theologians could accept the Talmud as a stage in the dynamic evolution of Judaism while rejecting its applicability to the present. Holdheim asserted that "der Talmud spricht aus seinem Zeitbewusstsein und für dasselbe hatte er Recht; ich spreche aus einem höheren Bewusstsein meiner Zeit und für dasselbe habe ich Recht."[42] This assertion, for all its radicalism, merely sets the Talmud in a historic context subject to the historic process of continuous change. Its temporal characteristic, defined as a stage in the chain of history, signified its mutability and evanescence. Furthermore, the Talmud per se seemed to legitimize such methodological transformations in the ever-evolving or ever-changing external manifestations of tradition. The fact that Holdheim considered his views more authoritative for his contemporaries than the Talmud's and the superciliousness implicit in his assertion were undoubtedly connected with his optimistic belief in the correlation between progress and time.

By distinguishing between internal revelation and external tradition, the Reform theologians attempted to preserve the preeminence of Judaism as divinely inspired in a general sense. At the same time, they rejected Mendelssohn's insistence upon the immutability of the Law, which they considered tradition and hence contingent upon and subject to change. Geiger asserted that in addition to the eras of revelation and tradition, the Jewish religion also underwent a period of legalism which summarized the older transmitted traditions. This, however, did not constitute a new element in his view of Judaism, but merely implied an arrested stage in the history of Judaism, when due to the convergence of constraining forces the free internal creativity of revelation and the external molding of tradition became petrified.

In light of this reinterpreted concept of revelation, the Reformers could suggest a new period in the history of Judaism or, as Geiger termed it, the era of critical study that would reopen the stream of revelation so that it could course through time and revitalize the Jewish religion as it had in the past. This flow of history would sweep away the last vestiges of legalism and rabbinism and leave authentic ethical-monotheistic Judaism distinctive and pure.

Hegelian Propensities

Most of the interpretative endeavors of the early nineteenth-century Jewish intellectuals with Reform leanings were limited to fragmentary aspects of Judaism. The reasons for this limitation ranged from sheer expediency and pragmatism to honest recognition of intellectual shortcomings. Regardless of the causes, there seemed to prevail a unanimous admission that Judaism in its entirety could not be reconciled with modern thought and that only certain spiritual and ethical fragments might be saved. As a result, the exponents of the Reform movement were critical of many traditional elements in the Jewish religion, particularly those with normative and ritualistic connotations.

As far as philosophy was concerned, most Jewish intellectuals were consistently inconsistent; they were remarkably eclectic and hardly made any attempts to reinterpret Judaism in an allcomprehensive spirit. Consequently, it was not uncommon to find writings about Judaism in which Spinozistic, Kantian, Hegelian, Fichtean, and Schellingian ideas commingled and were underpinned by views culled from Herder, Lessing, Schleiermacher, and a host of others. An amazing disarray of rationalistic, romantic, deistic, idealistic, and materialistic ideas were compelled to coexist in one framework in an attempt, however vain, to link Judaism to modern times.

Amid these eclectic ventures a serious endeavor was made at the beginning of the nineteenth century by a small group of young Jewish intellectuals who proceeded to reformulate Judaism, not by haphazard means but by a single-minded attempt to discover its indigenous spirit. They hoped to attain this aim by a methodological dialectic similar to that of Georg Wilhelm Friedrich Hegel. Although Kant's philosophy was at its zenith at the beginning of the nineteenth century and commanded the respect and admiration of all, Hegel's theories began to attract many young intellectuals and scholars. There were many factors that brought about this fascination. The most impressive was the comprehensiveness of Hegel's philosophic system and its profound dialectic. The influence of this modern Aristotle was soon felt in all fields of intellectual endeavor. Fourteen years after Kant's death, Hegel accepted the chair of philosophy at the University of Berlin and held it until his death in 1831. During this period, he was the unrivaled master in the world of philosophy in Germany. However, despite the great popularity Hegel enjoyed among men of unrelated disciplines, his philosophy was basically religious and his systematic logic very much a rational theology.[43] Hegel himself considered his logic to be "the exposition of God as He is in His eternal essence before the creation of the world and man."[44]

Hegel's critics, too, considered his philosophy a religious exposition. Ludwig Feuerbach regarded Hegel as the last of the great Christian apologists, a thinker who employed all his ingenuity to defend Christian thought and tradition.[45] Bruno Bauer thought that Hegel's philosophy was inextricably tied to Christian theology neatly dressed in its terminological frills and lace.[46] As a result, Hegel's philosophy intrigued many Christian theologians, who saw in its author, prosaic as he may have appeared to Friedrich Hölderlin,[47] a new Augustine or a Protestant Thomas Aquinas. His thought stimulated a strong reorientation in Protestant theology and an unusual productivity in this genre of literature. Thus, Karl Daub, professor of theology at Heidelberg and at first an avowed Schellingian, began to reformulate Protestant theology in accord with the Hegelian dialectic. A similar attempt was made by Phillip Konrad Marheinecke, professor of theology at Berlin, in his posthumously published *System of Christian Dogmatics.* Karl Friedrich Goschel and Karl Ludwig Michelet reinterpreted the supernatural and esoteric dogmas of Christianity in

Hegelian terms, making them synonymous.

Hegel's attitude toward Christianity underwent a radical change during his early years, but his views on Judaism were modified much later in life. As a young man, he shared Hölderlin's enthusiasm for the gods of Greece. Under the influence of Kant, he thought it would be fun to disturb the theologians as much as possible[48] and therefore enjoyed Kant's castigation of clericalism and institutionalized religion.[49] During this period, Hegel wrote *The Positivity of the Christian Religion* (1795), which reflected an extraordinary hostility to Christian teachings and institutions.[50] However, this attitude toward Christianity was radically altered the following year. His essay entitled *The Spirit of Christianity* disclosed a new attitude toward Christianity so different in content from the previous one that it is almost incredible that both works were written by the same author.[51]

Hegel's attitude toward Judaism remained consistent throughout his early years, when, while still strongly under Kant's influence, he seemed to project not only the main features of Kant's critical philosophy but also his outlook on Judaism. Like Kant, he considered Mendelssohn's *Jerusalem* an authentic and authoritative interpretation of Judaism. This interpretation, besides coinciding with the Kantian view, also fell within the mainstream of the Pauline-Spinozistic tradition, which constituted an integral part of Hegel's background. Mendelssohn's *Jerusalem* was not only the source of Hegel's knowledge of Judaism but, as in Kant's case, motivated his criticism of it.[52]

It was only with maturity, with the development of his philosophic system and the attainment of perspective, that Hegel conceded that Judaism possessed spirituality and "sublimity."[53] Although this view represented a radical shift from that of his youth and represented a marked departure from Kant, Judaism to Hegel was still inferior to Christianity. This "religion of sublimity," *Religion der Erhabenheit,* was to Hegel not the highest ideal of religion but merely one of its stages in his dialectic scheme. Sublimity implied God's remoteness from the world, negating the dominion of nature and making it subject to God.[54] The highest ideal of religion was Protestantism, which constituted the embodiment of truth. Since it constituted a higher rung in the dialectical ladder, it transcended the particularity of Judaism and superseded it. Judaism thus became dissolved and synthesized into Protestant Christianity, which was seen as the culmination of the entire developmental process. Hegel's views on Judaism, extrinsically and intrinsically, seemed to hold little promise for the intellectual reconstruction of the Jewish religion.[55] Even in the middle of the nineteenth century when an attempt was made by Samuel Hirsch in his *Religionsphilosophie der Juden* to force a confrontation with Hegel, it ended in failure.[56] It is doubtful whether a similar endeavor at the beginning of the century might have been more successful, yet just such an endeavor was made by a small group of young Jewish intellectuals in Berlin who formed an association that became known as the Verein für Cultur und Wissenschaft des Judentums (Culturverein, for short). Its leading members had strong Hegelian leanings. Notable among them were Leopold Zunz, Edward Gans, Heinrich Heine, Ludwig Markus, Immanuel Wohlwill, Moses Moser, and Markus Jost, men who in the course of time made distinct contributions in many fields of intellectual endeavor.

Though no more religiously observant than their Kantian and Reform contemporaries, the members of the Culturverein appeared to be dissatisfied with external adjustments in Judaism. They too were motivated by political, social, and economic considerations, but at the initial stages of their association they displayed a deep sense of integrity and intellectual honesty. More basic and profound changes were needed to make Judaism meaningful than those brought about by mere external conformity and expediency. The members of the Culturverein wanted to study Judaism in all its ramifications and thus comprehend its inner spirit scientifically, historically, and objectively. Accepting the fundamental view that Judaism was a religion of the spirit, they hoped to search for and discover its essence. The acceptance of this Hegelian premise did not imply that they also subscribed to the place Hegel had assigned it in his dialectical scheme. What seems to have impressed them most was Hegel's methodology, which they hoped to apply to the analysis of Judaism. By following this methodology they hoped to discover the fundamental idea of their religion and thereby also discover themselves.

This historical-theological-philosophical comprehension was considered to have sociopolitical and cultural implications since it might have made possible the integration of the Jews into European society.[57] By applying the scientific methodology to Judaism, the exponents of the *Wissenschaft des Judentums* expected to discover its essence in its pristine purity which discovery would enable them to harmonize their religion with the spirit of the age.[58] The members of the Culturverein thus preferred a scientific to the eclectic approach that had governed early Reform theology and practice. Influenced by Hegel, they advocated the organic method: the whole must be apprehended first, for only then is it possible to understand the parts. The whole is the absolute in all its complexity, and only its knowledge reveals the truth.

This approach, which is fundamental in Hegel's thought, became the basis for the Culturverein and is reflected in its programmatic outline, entitled "Über eine Wissenschaft des Judentums." It was published in the first issue of the *Zeitschrift für die Wissenschaft des Judentums* in 1822 by Immanuel Wohlwill, who used the pen name of Immanuel Wolf. Wohlwill was a member of the faculty of the Israelite Free School in Hamburg and subsequently became the director of the Jacobson School in Seesen. This programmatic outline undoubtedly represented not only the views of Wohlwill but also the collective manifesto and the fundamental guidelines of the Culturverein, arrived at after extensive deliberations.[59] Careful analysis of this manifesto discloses basic Hegelian elements.

Great emphasis was placed upon the need for studying Judaism as a whole. Judaism, the manifesto said, must be conceived as an autonomous metaphysical idea in an organic sense. Only when treated as a whole would its component parts—appearing externally in disarray and as incomprehensible—assume meaning and significance: "In order to comprehend the *whole*, one must know the *whole*, the parts, and their characteristics. A thing or a being exists 'in and for itself' because its asserted independence is the result grown out of its nature."[60]

Applying this Hegelian organic principle to Judaism, Wohlwill projected its analysis "in its comprehensive sense—as the essence of all the circumstances, characteristics, and achievements of the Jews in relation to religion, philosophy, history, law, literature in general, civil life and all the affairs of man."[61] The projected science of Judaism must not confine itself exclusively to pure religion because religious ideas are not always discernible to the untrained eye. They may be present in other, seemingly unrelated areas. The religious idea, fundamental as it is, has a tendency to penetrate all manifestations of life and combine with them to the point that it cannot be easily recognized. If this is true in religion in general, it is even more so in Judaism, where "the influence of the basic religious idea is visible in all circumstances of human life."

The fact that Judaism was a distinct idea and an organic whole explained its ability to survive and resist the syncretistic tendencies which might have contaminated it in the course of time. Stated Wohlwill: "For a period of at least three millennia, Judaism has preserved itself as a characteristic and independent whole." Flowing through history as it did, Judaism could not have been so closed to any alien influences as to bar them completely. Those influences, however, which were absorbed in the course of time "had to submit to the fundamental idea of Judaism in order to assimilate themselves to it and become one with it."

Analogous to a living organism that expels an invading foreign body, Judaism rejected any concept or practice not in accord with its fundamental idea, which was, in the Hegelian sense, characterized by simplicity. It was expressed in one word, the Tetragrammaton, "which signifies indeed the living unity of all being in eternity, the absolute being outside defined time and space." This idea of divine unity and universality was beyond the comprehension of ancient man. Initially, only a few gifted and remarkable individuals could conceive it. However, since it was important that this idea should gradually become universal, it was necessary to accommodate it in such a manner that it could exert its influence on mankind, albeit in an anthropomorphic form. The idea of God "had to be clothed in a body and thus brought nearer to human understanding. In this way, Judaism intimately united the world of the spiritual and the divine with the world of human life."

Wohlwill continued to expound Jewish history along Hegelian lines, showing its ideational unity and distinctiveness from the beginning of Judaism on. As a spirit, Judaism displayed its characteristic dynamism and restlessness to strive forward for its continuous enfoldment. "Peace and permanence are alien to the realm of the spirit, which is truly living. It is in the nature of the spiritual

world to be in constant motion and never to cease development."
Consonant with the dialectic of history, this spirit formed a thesis
which set in motion an antithesis—the state. Eventually it was
resolved in the synthesis, the Second Jewish Commonwealth:
"The struggle of the idea had nearly ceased internally; the Jews
had come to terms with the true spirit of their laws in which the
political and moral principles were bound into an indissoluble
unity by the religious principle, and had thereby become incapable of ever again falling away from the fundamental idea of Judaism."

The clash between Judaism and Hellenism, during the era of the
Second Jewish Commonwealth, was interpreted as a conflict between two contradictory ideas: "In Judaism the divine idea is
present as a given, revealed idea. In Hellenism all knowledge has
developed from the human spirit itself." Viewed in terms of the
Hegelian dialectic, the encounter between these two antithetical
phenomena should have resulted in a new synthesis transcending
and superseding them. The reason that this did not occur and that
Judaism triumphed over Hellenism was due to the disparity of
forces at the time the clash occurred. Judaism was in its natural
habitat and pure, whereas Hellenism, far from its native land, was
adulterated and therefore compelled to yield.

The collapse of the Jewish state in the great war with Rome did
not affect Judaism. Its mentors made every possible effort to align
their beliefs with their life. They interwove the spirit of Judaism
into the complex fabric of life. In the absence of political sovereignty, the Rabbis endeavored to infuse every aspect of domestic
life with the spirit of religion. Thus the Rabbis of the Talmud by
their insistence on Law and ceremonies proved themselves farsighted men, finally responsible for the preservation of the inner
spirit of Judaism. The juridical-ceremonial aspect of Judaism, so
severely maligned by the followers of the Kantian school, was
considered to have been a fence guarding the intrinsic spirit of
religion. Furthermore, these seemingly restrictive, nonethical,
nonreligious rules and rites were impregnated with the true religious and ethical spirit of Judaism.

Normative Judaism was not an impediment to the Jews. They
were not hindered by their juridical-ceremonial system during
the Middle Ages. Though committed to the nomistic aspect of

their religion, the Jews exerted a powerful influence upon the emergence of Islam and transmitted the heritage of Greece to the Western world. The strictures evident in Jewish life were not the result of normativism, but of the outer pressures and persecutions that became intensified during the era of the Crusades and continued for many centuries. These harassments proved unbearable even for the Jews imbued with the dynamic spirit of Judaism: "In the end the spirit, too, had necessarily to succumb to the fetters which deprived the body of freedom of movement." Excluded from all fields of creative endeavor, the Jews recoiled into their inner world. Life became constricted, impeding the freedom of the living spirit. All these constrictions and impediments notwithstanding, Judaism still demonstrated ineradicable traces of its unique and vital idea and continued to serve as an influential factor in the historical development of the human spirit.

If one looks at history neither with preconceived notions nor as a haphazard aggregate of unrelated events and disjointed phenomena, but as a manifestation of the unfolding spirit, Judaism, too, assumes new significance. Wohlwill suggested three principles to serve as criteria for the new scientific approach to Judaism:

1. Judaism must no longer be studied in a fragmentary or eclectic manner. Being an idea which has been developing in the course of history, it must be treated as an organic whole and comprehended in the fullest scope.
2. This scientific approach "unfolds Judaism in accordance with its essence and describes it systematically, always relating individual features to the fundamental principle of the *whole.*"
3. This approach "treats the object of study *in and for itself,* for its own sake, and not for any special purpose or definite intention. It begins without any preconceived opinion and is not concerned with the final result. Its aim is neither to put its object in a favorable, nor in an unfavorable light, in relation to prevailing views, but to show it as it is."

Great emphasis was placed upon the textual study of Judaism, which reflected its inner idea and revealed the profound connection between the seemingly unrelated externalities and the fundamental intrinsic spirit. Such a comprehensive study was not to be motivated by a mere antiquarian interest, but rather by a genuine sense of relevance to the present: "Judaism is not only of historical interest. It is not a principle that belongs to the past, that has already lived and is now preserved merely in the pages of history. It lives on, acknowledged by a not inconsiderable portion of humanity." In conclusion, the manifesto declared, it would be the science of Judaism that would give the objective answer as to the possibility of the Jews taking their place in the Western world, and this by revealing its deeper relationship to the world at large.

Wohlwill's manifesto reflected a new, significant trend in the approach to Judaism, representing an attempt by a few young men to search and investigate the total spirit of Judaism without indiscriminately paring away parts for the sake of convenience, expediency, and accommodation. Indeed, few were the contemporaries who comprehended and valued this effort by the members of the Culturverein. Besides the fact that they were considered too young and inexperienced to deal with such a problem, their project suggested a multitude of unforeseen consequences. Furthermore, though both Kant's and Hegel's philosophies seemed perplexing to the nonphilosophical Jews, Kant's ethics seemed more accessible to the mentality of the average Jew than did Hegel's dialectic. In addition, the latter was associated with the state philosophy and Protestant theology, and therefore only a few Jews in the early nineteenth century saw any possibilities of reinterpreting Judaism in Hegelian terms.

The Culturverein was of short duration; its members were beset by the personal problems that frustrated the lives of all young intellectual Jews in Germany. All avenues for social and economic advancement were closed to them, nor could they find satisfaction within the limited confines of Jewish life. They were too Westernized for the Jews and too Jewish for the Christians. They were therefore viewed by the notables of the Jewish community with distrust and misgiving. Their ideas and views were partly misunderstood and partly misinterpreted. Misunderstood by the Jews and rejected by the non-Jews, the members of Culturverein were overcome by a sense of defeat and frustration. Barred from without and unable to advance within, they became disillusioned; some defected from the very religion they had attempted to reconstruct.

It is possible to argue that Hegel's views on Judaism may have been responsible for these conversions, taking into consideration the absorption of Judaism into the greater whole that, for Hegel, was Christianity. However, the socioeconomic pressures upon these young men were powerful enough to render a philosophical or theological rationalization unacceptable. Beneath the Hegelian dialectic and sophisticated theology operated powerful mundane, materialistic factors. There is, however, no doubt that Judaism's hold on the members of Culturverein was not a sufficient deterrent to their acceptance of Christianity, which in the words of Heine, was a ticket of admission to European culture.

The failure of the Culturverein did not imply the disappearance of the dream shared by many other Jews who also wished to interpret Judaism along Hegelian lines, or at least using Hegelian methodology. Thus in 1832, Berthold Auerbach stated that he hoped to effect a synthesis between Hegelian philosophy and Mosaism similar to attempts by Christian theologians to effect a synthesis between Hegelianism and Christianity. Auerbach, a student of David Friedrich Strauss, was undoubtedly moved by the Hegelian ferment taking place at the time. Among the foremost mentors who attempted an exposition of Judaism according to Hegelian dialectic was Samuel Hirsch in his book *Die Religionsphilosophie der Juden*, which appeared in 1842.

But these were not the only men drawn to Hegel. There were some Hegelians who were marginal Jews and some Jews who were superficial Hegelians. Hegel's philosophy, for all its intricacies and difficulties, somehow kindled the imagination of liberals and conservatives alike. Paradoxical as it may seem, men of the most radically opposed and antithetical outlooks found a place in his system, which lent itself to numerous contradictory interpretations. Not infrequently, these men became disenchanted with Hegel when they realized that Hegelianism was not what they had assumed it to be. Occasionally, views were expressed and opinions formulated that could not be substantiated in Hegel's works. This undoubtedly occurred among

Christians as well as among Jews. That Hegel at the beginning
of the nineteenth century should have fascinated some traditional Jewish thinkers searching for a rational normative Judaism could have been easily foreseen; one of the most outstanding of these was Samson Raphael Hirsch.

2
The Enlightenment Tradition

A Terrain of Conflicts

The Jewish community of Hamburg, one of the newest in Germany, had become one of its largest and most affluent by the time of Samson Raphael Hirsch's birth there in 1808. Its population exceeded that of the older Jewish communities of Berlin and Frankfurt am Main,[1] and its heterogeneity presented a polychromatic microcosm of German Jewry as a whole. It seems that nearly all the religious, social, and intellectual tremors that occurred even in remote places registered seismographically in Hamburg and affected its Jewish community. The heterogeneous nature of its Jewish population, its economic affluence, the cosmopolitan character of the city together with Jewish theological disputes and socioreligious conflicts caused the enfeeblement of Jewish communal cohesion and the breakdown of rabbinic authority. This combination of factors made Hamburg during Hirsch's boyhood one of the leading centers of the Reform movement in Germany, which threatened Judaism with a sectarianism unknown since the Karaite schism eleven hundred years before.

The first Jews to settle clandestinely in Hamburg were Portuguese Marranos. They constituted a small segment of the vast Marrano dispersion throughout the world at the end of the sixteenth century, reaching as far as the newly discovered Americas. The favorable geographic position of Hamburg at the mouth of the

Elbe River in proximity to the North Sea made it one of the most important commercial seaports of Europe. Because of the city's prosperity and international contacts, Hamburg's citizens were more concerned with trade and shipping than with theological sophistry, and were therefore less xenophobic than most other Germans. When prudence and interest dictated the admission of foreigners, the city, although fundamentally Lutheran, opened its gates to Flemings, Walloons, Portuguese, and Huguenots. This tolerant attitude enabled newcomers to develop their potentialities and in return to contribute greatly to the city's economic growth.

A number of crypto-Jews also entered Hamburg disguised as Portuguese. By the time their religion was discovered, their economic importance to this Hanseatic city had outweighed the theological considerations which might have caused their expulsion. While their dominant role in the promotion of capitalism in Hamburg may be disputed, their importance to the economy of the city cannot. They monopolized the import of tobacco, cotton, spices, and certain other aspects of trade.[2] A short time after their arrival at the end of the sixteenth century, the first Jewish settlers had attained a high economic level; a few decades later, some of them were shareholders of the Bank of Hamburg, Germany's most prominent banking institution of international stature of that time.[3]

The ranks of the Jewish settlers from Portugal were soon swelled by Jews coming from other parts of Germany who were either attracted by Hamburg's economic opportunities or compelled by the fratricidal carnage of the Thirty Years' War to flee their homes. Hamburg, having escaped the devastation of other German cities, attracted many of these refugees. Political and legal limitations notwithstanding, it was to them a veritable "little Jerusalem."[4] The draconian laws and regulations contrived to strangle the Jews politically, socially, and economically were less zealously enforced in Hamburg than in any other part of Germany.

To these first two strata of Jewish settlers and a small number of Jews forced to seek refuge from the war between Sweden and Denmark, a third stratum was subsequently added from Poland. Paradoxically, the year 1648, which with the Peace of Westphalia terminated the sufferings of German Jewry by ending three decades of destruction, also marked the beginning of a period of persecution for the Polish Jews. It was the year of the outbreak of the Chmielnicki rebellion and its concomitant horrors. Many of the new Polish refugees were descendants of German Jews who a few centuries earlier had fled to Poland to escape the fury of the Crusaders. The intervening centuries of life in Poland, however, had so profoundly altered their character and life style that upon their return to Germany in the seventeenth century they appeared foreign and strange to their indigenous German coreligionists.

Thus, the Jewish community of Hamburg in the seventeenth century constituted a microcosm of German Jewry at large. The religious, social, economic, cultural, and linguistic differences among its various segments were wider than the interests they had in common. Gradually, the German Ashkenazic Jews rose up the economic and cultural ladder until, like their Portuguese Sephardic brethren, they came to be considered a necessary evil. The inherent differences between the three segments of Hamburg Jewry were never completely obliterated, and although various elements commingled in the course of time, they never fused into a socially, culturally, or even religiously homogeneous community. The Portuguese Jews were not only the most affluent but also the most educated, enlightened, and progressive. Some were shipowners, bankers, physicians, and scientists of note. The fact that the municipal authorities singled out the Portuguese Jews for greater privileges only deepened the cleavage between the various segments of early Hamburg Jewry. Not even the unification of Hamburg's Jewish community with those of neighboring Altona and Wandsbeck under the jurisdiction of a single chief rabbi brought about a sociocultural amalgam.

Hamburg's non-Jewish citizenry was equally religiously, socially, and economically variegated. International trade and foreign visitors gave the city its cosmopolitan character and opened it to the intellectual and cultural breezes blowing in from neighboring France, England, Denmark, Sweden, the Netherlands, and, of course, the rest of Germany. Intellectual convulsions and theological paroxysms seem to have afflicted the Hamburg Jewish community to an extraordinary degree. Paradoxically, the same Jewish settlers who had sought refuge because of religious intoler-

ance and theological disputes elsewhere became strongly involved in doctrinal debates of their own here. The small community of Portuguese Jews was soon rent by an acrimonious theological polemic initiated by Uriel da Costa, himself a former
Portuguese Marrano, during his stay in Hamburg in 1616.[5] It is not
known why da Costa decided to launch his assault on traditional
Judaism in the city where he was a newcomer and where his
brothers were respected businessmen and members of the Jewish
community. Despite a strong refutation by Samuel da Silva, a
prominent Portuguese Jewish physician, the criticism of Judaism
by another Portuguese Jew was a source of deep chagrin to all. The
fact that one of their compatriots had dared denigrate Judaism was
painful; that he was excommunicated by the rabbinical court of
Venice was humiliating; that he died an ignominious death by
suicide must have been shocking.

Outwardly, at least, the da Costa affair, agonizing at it was, had
no major consequences. The seeds of heresy and antinomianism
da Costa had sown did not blossom forth immediately, although
they might have remained deeply imbedded in the minds of some
of his coreligionists in Hamburg whose faith had been weakened
by relentless persecution.[6] The extent of his influence is unknown,
but half a century after the da Costa theological controversy the
Hamburg Jewish community was embroiled in another whose
reverberations continued for almost a century: a controversy over
Sabbateanism, representing the first and most serious revolution
in Judaism since the Middle Ages.[7]

The meteoric rise of Sabbatai Zevi from the remote Turkish
town of Smyrna to worldwide prominence by proclaiming himself
the long-awaited Messiah captured the imagination of Jews and
non-Jews the world over. This messianic movement had its roots
in Jewish tradition and apocalyptic, cabalistic literature. The cata-
strophic events of the Jewish expulsion from Spain and the
Chmielnicki persecutions in Poland gave impetus to—though
they may not have precipitated—this most dangerous and explosive heresy in Judaism. Hamburg was not the only Jewish community to be swept up on the tide of mystical frenzy, and the force
of this emotional impact was strongly felt by its inhabitants.
Strangely enough, the progressive, enterprising, and practical
Jews of this community were no less intoxicated by the new mes-

sianic expectations than were their brethren in the backward lands. Scholars and businessmen, Sephardic and Ashkenazic Jews in this cosmopolitan city were as zealous in their faith in Sabbatai Zevi as were the Jews in the Near East or eastern Europe. "Many people sold their homes, hearth and everything they possessed awaiting redemption,"[8] when Sabbatai Zevi would enter Jerusalem as a king.[9] Few could resist the mass hysteria that gripped world Jewry. Even fewer dared express their reservations and misgivings in public. Open dissent with Sabbateanism, even the suspicion of harboring such sentiments, was dangerous; such suspects were dealt with harshly and threatened with violence.[10]

Nevertheless, Hamburg was also the domicile of the strongest opponent of Sabbateanism. At the height of the mystic entrancement of Hamburg Jewry in the autumn of 1665, Jacob Sasportas came from England to settle in the city.[11] Sasportas, whom some call a "Jewish inquisitor,"[12] soon became one of the most outspoken critics and opponents of the Sabbatean movement.[13] His opposition, overt or covert, made Hamburg a focal point in the war between the proponents and opponents of Sabbateanism.[14] The controversy became particularly bitter after Sabbatai Zevi's conversion to Islam, which enabled Sasportas to excommunicate him openly,[15] in spite of many who still retained their faith in him.[16]

The disillusionment of Hamburg Jews, which they shared with world Jewry in the aftermath of Sabbateanism, was again followed by a new theological controversy—the Emden-Eibeschütz dispute. Sabbateanism had originated in the East and subsequently spread to Hamburg; the new dispute began here but stirred up even distant Jewish communities. The heresy-hunting activities in which Sasportas had engaged in the seventeenth century were continued by Jacob Emden in the eighteenth. Far more erudite than Sasportas, he had a similar "inquisitorial" personality, albeit with a glimmer of liberalism, which can be found in his writings.[17] In 1751, he accused Jonathan Eibeschütz—the newly elected rabbi of Hamburg, Altona, and Wandsbeck—of adherence to Sabbateanism.[18] Emden alleged that Eibeschütz had earlier distributed amulets in his former rabbinic post, Metz, which contained references to the apostate "Messiah."[19] The vituperations, invective, and excommunications exchanged by renowned rabbinic and communal leaders scandalized all, particularly the sensitive and the young. In this venomous atmosphere the entire socioreligious fabric of the Jewish community disintegrated. The views of its leaders were discounted and the decisions of its rabbis ignored.[20]

The Hebrew Enlightenment or Haskalah dawned on a Hamburg exhausted by religious controversy. The last one in particular, the Emden-Eibeschütz embroilment, had left the community in a state of utter confusion and bewilderment, with the credibility of the rabbis shaken and their authority undermined, and the people polarized and too weary to embark on a new battle—which is why the Haskalah was not resisted as vigorously in Hamburg as it was in the other Jewish communities. Moreover, while the Haskalah's emphasis on ethics and aesthetics may have been viewed with suspicion, the movement seemed at first neither ominous nor heretical enough to warrant sharp conflict. It had many followers and sympathizers in Hamburg, and some of its leading mentors had personal roots in this city. Mendelssohn's wife, Fromet Guggenheim, and Naphtali Hartwig Wessely, the most renowned Hebrew poet of his time, exegete, and educational theoretician, were both Hamburgians. Even some writers for the Haskalah magazine *Ha-Meassef* were either natives or residents of Hamburg.[21]

While the Haskalah did not evoke any strong condemnation, the traditionalists' attitude toward it was nevertheless marked by reservation toward the Maskilim (enlightened ones). When Eibeschütz was requested by Abraham Guggenheim to grant the title *ḥaver* to his future son-in-law, Moses Mendelssohn, the rabbi tactfully declined.[22] It is probable that after Eibeschütz's traumatic experience in the ill-fated controversy with Emden over the former's alleged Sabbateanism, he avoided entanglements with anybody or anything not universally acknowledged as Orthodox. Emden's attitude toward Mendelssohn was more candid. Mendelssohn's respect for Emden notwithstanding,[23] the latter remained distrustful and did not conceal the suspicion with which Mendelssohn was viewed.[24]

Despite the comparative calm with which the Haskalah was received in Hamburg, it too soon became a source of contention. The new conflict was caused by Mendelssohn's German translation of the Bible and his commentary, known as the *Biur*. Among its most severe critics was Raphael Cohen, who succeeded Eibe-schütz as rabbi of Hamburg.[25] Apprehensive of the possible deleterious influence of the new commentary, Cohen banned its reading. It is possible that he would have taken even stronger measures had he not feared antagonizing the king of Denmark, who had in the meantime become a subscriber to the *Biur*.[26]

Fortunately for the cause of peace, Rabbi Cohen's distrust of the Enlightenment and his ban of the *Biur* did not evoke any strong reaction in the Hamburg Jewish community; apparently the issue was not of overriding importance, nor were the early German Maskilim as bellicose as their more radical colleagues in eastern Europe. Furthermore, excommunication, so excessively em-ployed in earlier conflicts, probably also lost the implicit terror it had had in the past. But the relative peace which settled over the Hamburg Jewish community was soon shattered in 1818 with the erection of the Reform temple, which demonstrated that the old antinomian aspirations of Sabbateanism were not dead but merely dormant and awaiting the opportunity to reemerge. The relation-ship between Reform and Sabbatean aspirations, differences not-withstanding, is evidenced by the fact that in the beginning of the nineteenth century former centers of Sabbateanism became cen-ters of the Reform movement.[27] Hamburg, a former Sabbatean stronghold, was therefore eminently qualified to become a center of Reform.

The lingering residue of Sabbateanism, however, was only one of the factors responsible for the Reform movement in Hamburg. The century and a half between the zenith of Sabbateanism and the dedication of the Reform temple in that city included many events that made Reform possible. By the time one of the first Reformist preachers, Eduard Kley, arrived from Berlin, he found Hamburg a fertile terrain for religious innovation and experimen-tation and receptive to new views and opinions. The erection of the Reform temple and subsequent publication of the reformed prayer book sparked a conflict matched only by the previous Sab-batean heresy. These events galvanized the members of the com-munity to action even as they polarized them. The gathering storm split not only the local community but all Jewry.

Hamburg was only the locus of the conflict—the animosity it engendered threatened all Judaism. Those for and against the

Reform temple solidified into rigid parties of Orthodox and Reform and launched a fratricidal war. Both groups solicited the aid of leading figures outside of Hamburg, including such renowned rabbis as Akiba Eger of Posen, Moses Sofer of Pressburg, Mordecai Benet of Nikolsburg, Eleazer Fleckeles of Prague, and Jacob Lorbeerbaum of Lissa, who threw their support to the Orthodox. The Reformers could not match such august authorities and received backing from some little-known rabbis of radical leanings in Italy and Hungary.

Erleuchtet Religiös

When the Reform temple was dedicated in Hamburg, Hirsch was ten years old. He never recorded the impression this event made upon him. His parents, who were traditionalists, were undoubtedly opposed to the temple. In one of his rare references to his parents, Hirsch described them as *erleuchtet religiös*,[28] "enlightened-religious." The importance of this description has been overlooked, since the phrase has been considered merely one of Hirsch's rhetorical ornamentations. However, in this case he was being remarkably succinct and precise. Wishing to convey the spirit of religious moderation that characterized his parents and the atmosphere in which he grew up, he deliberately employed two terms which, at the time he wrote the *Neunzehn Briefe* (1836), constituted a *contradictio in adjecto*.

The new religious crisis revived dormant fears and old antagonisms. The specter of a new heresy looming on the horizon beclouded reason and heightened emotions. The fact that the Reform temple attracted Jews whose affiliation with the Jewish community was marginal exacerbated existing suspicions. The infractions of Halakhah and disregard for traditional practices alarmed the traditionalists beyond anything since the conflict over Sabbateanism. As a result, the Jewish community in Hamburg and in all Germany became fragmented ideologically and religiously, and its members could now be classified into two groups, *erleuchtet* or *religiös*, with a chasm between them that neither could traverse with impunity.

Only one small group managed to retain the precarious intellectual equilibrium between the two factions. It consisted primarily of middle-class Jews who preferred to pursue a peaceful and serene life, *still und ruhig Leben*, free from political, religious, or social disturbance. They were not formally affiliated with any particular faction, but shared the outlook of the conservative Maskilim of the Mendelssohn-Wessely era. While religious in spirit and practice, they were at the same time *erleuchtet*, enlightened, equivalent to the Hebrew *maskil*. The Torah remained their absolute religious authority, but they conceded that the times necessitated moderate accommodations.

The Haskalah as a Weltanschauung had more followers than it did as a movement. As far back as the eighteenth century such famous rabbis as Eibeschütz[29] and Emden[30] considered some secular knowledge beneficial. Their reservations about Mendelssohn may have been motivated by far more serious suspicions than the fact that he was knowledgeable in secular subjects. The aftermath of the French Revolution, the Napoleonic invasion of Hamburg, the economic blockade of its port, the furor over the Grand Sanhedrin, and, finally, the controversy over the Reform temple and its new prayer book polarized the community and disturbed the quiet life of these moderate and enlightened Jews. Sober and reasonable, they now found themselves in a most unenviable position, isolated from the Orthodox as too *erleuchtet* and from the Reform as too *religiös*. To this minority, juxtaposed between two hostile camps, the temperate Weltanschauung of Mendelssohn and Wessely personified the height of wisdom. Living in the afterglow of the Age of Reason, deeply rooted in Judaism, they venerated those who represented a coalition of both. Thus they could admire and emulate Moses Maimonides and Moses Mendelssohn. Maimonides's *Moreh Nevukhim* and Mendelssohn's *Biur* were studied assiduously, while the Cabala and Hasidic works were dismissed as harmfully obscurantist. Although opposed to reforms in the Jewish religion, the enlightened-religious Jews were incensed and repelled by the disorder and misconduct common to German Orthodox synagogues and advocated decorum, cleanliness, cultivation of good manners, and a simple but impressive religious service.

Though the Haskalah in Germany was short-lived and its endeavors proved abortive, still many of its salient ideas engaged the moderates. They hoped that the egalitarian forces operating in the new era would eventually realize Mendelssohn's wish for religious freedom and tolerance between Jews and non-Jews. Although the coexistence Mendelssohn hoped for—emancipation and acculturization—harbored dangers for Judaism, it also opened new vistas for Jews, and moderate, religiously enlightened Jews therefore viewed these new opportunities with concern but not with anxiety.

Erleuchtet religiös Jews believed that harmonious coexistence between Jews and non-Jews could be reached only through a reorientation in the education of the young. Jewish children had to be directed as early as possible toward the symbiosis of the domains of *Mensch*— man—and Jew. Every effort was to be made to emphasize the universal, cosmopolitan, and humanitarian elements within Judaism. Confessional singularity did not have to imply social, economic, or cultural exclusiveness.

Wessely tied this new orientation in education into the well-known talmudic dictum *Torah im derekh eretz*, religion combined with worldly occupation. Wessely's motto was merely a Hebrew rendition of Mendelssohn's symbiosis of Jew and *Mensch*, just as his distinction between *torat Elohim*, divine study, and *torat ha-adam*, human study,[31] merely paraphrased Mendelssohn's "revealed law" and "innate natural law." This new approach in education clothed in the old talmudic dictum was, however, particularly pleasing to the enlightened-religious Jews since it seemed to sanction their efforts for modernization with traditional authority. The interpretation of the term *derekh eretz* as connoting secular subjects necessary for the functioning of Jews in a modern world had already been expressed and permitted within certain limitations by some well-known rabbis.

Wessely, however, gave the term a far more liberal meaning than they ever intended. To the enlightened, it seemed necessary for children to study the Hebrew language and its grammar as well as other secular subjects so that they might better understand the text and the religious, moral, and aesthetic values of the Bible, which in their view had primacy. The Talmud's importance was lessened and the time allotted for its study curtailed. "We were not all born to be talmudic scholars,"[32] Wessely maintained. Only when a pupil was proficient in Hebrew and the Bible would he be admitted to the study of the Talmud. This differed sharply from the practice of the Orthodox, who introduced children to the Talmud at a tender age without any adequate preparation or knowledge of either Hebrew or the Bible. To the Orthodox, the Talmud with its codes and its commentaries constituted the alpha and omega of Jewish education.

The enlightened-religious Jews in the early part of the nineteenth century shared Mendelssohn's and Wessely's disdain for Yiddish. A chief reason for this was that to non-Jews Yiddish sounded like a corrupt German dialect. Exceedingly concerned with social acceptability, the enlightened Jews felt that Yiddish not only corrupted the purity of German but also corrupted the Jews intellectually, psychologically, aesthetically, and even morally. Such opinions were expressed not by any anti-Semite or extremist, but by the calm, reserved, rational Mendelssohn—and echoed with ill-tempered irrationality by his colleagues and followers.[33]

The *melamdim* (teachers) who came from Poland were held in similar contempt. Many sins were attributed to them, with the speaking of Yiddish one of the most cardinal. The affluent Jewish German bourgeois despised them as much for their poverty, lack of education, poor manners, Polish background, and religious extremism as for their Yiddish jargon. They were also severely criticized for their dialectical explication of the Talmud known as *pilpul.* Paradoxically, this methodology had its roots in Germany, whence it was exported to Poland in the sixteenth century, only to return to Germany three centuries later via the Polish *melamdim.* Many German Jews subsequently resented and disclaimed their native product.

Jews were generally patriotic throughout Germany. In Hamburg, where the Jews had achieved such economic success, their loyalty to the German authorities was particularly strong. Pleased with this progress, they discounted the existing political disabilities and preferred to live quietly, prudently, and unobtrusively. The loyalty of the Hamburg Jews in general, and of the enlightened-religious in particular, was especially evident during the French invasion of the city. Even though the French occupation forces compelled the Hamburg authorities to grant equality to the Jews and to admit them to seats in the civic council,[34] Jewish enthusiasm for the French was less than anticipated. While many leading Germans enthusiastically greeted Napoleon as the prince of peace *(Friedensfürst)*,[35] many Jews remained cool and even hostile. The latter may have sensed that French rule in Hamburg would be only temporary. Although grateful for the favors, they may have been afraid to display Francophilic sentiments for fear of subsequent reprisals. The economic hardships caused by the war and blockade affected the commerce-oriented Jews of Hamburg and may also have accounted for their resentment.[36] By and large, however, the Jews were prompted by a sense of loyalty and of genuine German patriotism that at times exceeded that of their non-Jewish compatriots. They felt a strong kinship to the native population and a sense of gratitude toward the German authorities. Despite the restrictions that they had been forced to endure, they firmly believed that brotherhood between Jews and Germans would eventually prevail.

Haskalah Antecedents

Hirsch's voluminous writings are virtually devoid of personal data and biographical references; except for the description *erleuchtet religiös*, he offered little information about his parents. Heinrich Graetz, who met Hirsch's father, Raphael (1777–1857), during his stay in Oldenburg, described him as "a pleasant and good-natured person."[37] Besides this vague description, little else is known about him. The fact that he presented Graetz with a new edition of *The Kuzari*[38] may indicate his *erleuchtet* proclivity. Orthodox Jews preferred rabbinic works to philosophic ones, even when written by such an impeccable traditionalist as Judah Halevi. Like all those influenced by the Haskalah spirit, the elder Hirsch loved the study of the Bible. In an essay "Aus einem Briefwechsel über die Psalmen," Samson Raphael Hirsch sentimentally recalled Bible discussions with his father in the evening hours after business; the son presented his observations and comments and eagerly awaited his father's opinions. The Bible was his father's second nature, *zweite Seele*, and he showed great insight and sensitivity to its truth and beauty, "für die Wahrheiten und Schönheiten der heiligen Schriften."[39] Indeed, Orthodox Jews had always displayed appreciation for the truth of the Bible, but to love its beauty and show concern for its aesthetics was characteristic of the

Maskilim. Moreover, since the Orthodox devoted little time to the study of the Bible and much to the Talmud, serious students of the Bible were suspect as Maskilim. The fact that Raphael was clean-shaven,[40] an appearance strongly condemned by the rabbis,[41] further attests to his liberal rather than Orthodox demeanor.

Raphael must have been a modestly prosperous man. Prior to the French occupation he manufactured lace; afterward, he was engaged in money exchange,[42] ostensibly a lucrative business in a teeming port city like Hamburg.

Meager as the information about Hirsch's father is, even less is known about his mother, Gella (1786–1860). She came from a well-known Hamburg family: Herz, previously called Hildesheimer.[43] Like Raphael's, Gella's ancestors had deep roots in the Hamburg community, where they had lived since the seventeenth century.[44] Many were actively engaged in the three communities of Hamburg, Altona, and Wandsbeck.[45] Hirsch belonged to the tenth generation of Jews living in the Hamburg-Altona area. There is a reference to Hirsch's first forebears to settle in the region in the memoirs of the well-known Glueckel of Hameln. Glueckel, a native of Hamburg, was the granddaughter of Hirsch's ancestors Nathan Melrich (d. 1638) and Mattie Melrich (d. 1656). Judging from the name, the family must have originally hailed from Melrichstadt in Bavaria. Nathan was a "wealthy upstanding man who lived in Detmold and when expelled from there moved with his family to Altona at the same time when there were not ten Jews living there."[46] He was reputedly very rich; an eyewitness told Glueckel that Nathan brought with him to Altona "boxes full of golden chains and jewels and bags full of pearls so that for more than a hundred miles around there was no one as rich as he."[47] Glueckel described Nathan's wife, Mattie, as "a clever, pious woman whose equal may not be readily found."[48] Their descendants were mostly traders and merchants, some of them affluent, many occupying important positions in the leadership of the Jewish community, thus directing its social, religious, charitable, and educational institutions.[49] Their wealth, prominence, and putative scholarship made them worthy of contracting marriages with families equally respected for their social status and erudition. Some married young men of outstanding scholarship, among them Jonathan Eibeschütz.[50]

More particulars are known about Hirsch's paternal grandfather, Mendel Frankfurter (1742–1823). As a young man he studied under Eibeschütz,[51] who was, at the time, the rabbi of his community. Although erudite and qualified, Frankfurter refused to enter the rabbinate. Only in his declining years did he reluctantly consent to serve briefly as *dayyan* in Altona—without remuneration;[52] any money paid him for rabbinic duties was assigned to charity. Even so, after a short period he resigned his post and returned to Hamburg.[53] This episode attests to Frankfurter's stature and erudition. No man of mediocre scholarship could have occupied a rabbinic post in Altona, a city in which the memory of scholars like Eibeschütz and Emden was still alive. Probably it was the trauma of the agonizing controversy between these two men which haunted Frankfurter, making the rabbinate distasteful.

A far more important factor which might have made Frankfurter eschew the rabbinate was his former association with Mendelssohn. During his stay in Berlin he frequently visited Mendelssohn and dined at his house. Both men studied daily under Rabbi Hirschel Lewin.[54] These visits brought Frankfurter into contact with many of the Berlin Maskilim, who shared his admiration for Mendelssohn. Had he actively assumed a rabbinic post, Frankfurter's association with the Maskilim might have made him a vulnerable target for criticism. He was undoubtedly aware of Jonathan Eibeschütz's reservations, Jacob Emden's suspicions, Ezekiel Landau's objections, and Raphael Cohen's antagonisms concerning Mendelssohn and the *Biur*. All this, however, did not prevent Frankfurter from maintaining his friendship with and esteem for Mendelssohn. The pride he later took in the memory of this association is in itself an indication that Frankfurter belonged to the *erleuchtet religiös* with Haskalah leanings rather than to the intransigent Orthodox elements of his time.

Frankfurter's inclination toward the Haskalah is also evident from his great admiration for Wessely, his fellow Hamburgian and Eibeschütz's former student. The extent of this esteem can be ascertained in his last will to his children, where Frankfurter saw fit to include a paragraph sanctioning the reading of Wessely's works.[55] Only an ardent admirer of the Haskalah would consider such a provision important enough to include in so solemn a document. Frankfurter's penchant for the Haskalah and his admiration for Mendelssohn and Wessely shed some light on his modest attempt to reform Jewish education. In 1805, the year of Wessely's death, Frankfurter organized a Talmud Torah for the poor children of Hamburg. Traditionalist in outlook and content, the curriculum also included secular subjects in Wessely's spirit of *Torah im derekh eretz*. It was a revolutionary move at the time, considering that thirty-eight of the existing thirty-nine *hadarim* devoted their time exclusively to the Talmud. Only one gave some rudimentary instruction in a foreign language.[56] The aim of the Talmud Torah as formulated by Frankfurter and reported in the Haskalah organ *Ha-Meassef* had unmistakable Wesselyan overtones. It intended to teach the students Jewish religion, Bible, ethics, and good manners and to prepare them for business or a trade. The decision whether to continue to study, engage in business, or pursue a trade was to be reached by the pupils themselves.[57] In 1809, provisions were made for some vocational training for properly qualified students[58] in the utilitarian spirit of the Haskalah. Frankfurter thus endeavored to implement Wessely's idea of *Torah im derekh eretz* three years before the birth of his grandson, Samson Raphael Hirsch, who appropriated Wessely's motto as his slogan.

Hirsch's grandfather was not the only member of the family favorably inclined to the Haskalah. His great-uncle Loeb Frankfurter, Mendel's brother, shared his views and, like him, maintained a close association with Mendelssohn.[59] Similarly, Loeb's work *Ha-Rekhasim le-Bikah*[60] reflects Haskalah values and tendencies. His biblical exegesis was not based, as in traditional exegesis, on talmudic and midrashic interpretations, but rather on grammar, syntax, linguistical comparisons, morphology, and analogies to German. All this was in the spirit of the Maskilim and particularly of Wessely and other coexegetes of the *Biur*. Like the contemporary Maskilim, Loeb Frankfurter exhibited an excessive sensitivity to the purity of the Hebrew language, exactness of expression, and grammatical precision. Like them, he was, therefore, critical of the medieval *paitanim* who violated these rules in their liturgical poetry, particularly by their neologisms. Although some scholars recognized the merit of some of the *piyyutim*,[61] Loeb Frankfurter was not that tolerant. As a purist, he could not forgive the medieval liturgical poets their corruption of the Hebrew language and disregard for its grammar. No poetic insight, quality, or euphony could outweigh such infractions.[62]

The spirit of the Haskalah was most prominently exemplified by

Hirsch's uncle, Mendel Frankfurter's son Moses (1780–1861). Moses's ardor for the Enlightenment is reflected in the name he selected for himself—"Moses Mendelssohn of Hamburg." The name of the city was added to distinguish him from his illustrious namesake of Dessau. The fact that he preferred the name Mendelssohn to Frankfurter, the name by which his family was known, signifies his emotional and ideational kinship with the reputed mentor of the Haskalah.

As in the case of Hirsch's father, there seems to be a tendency on the part of Hirsch's biographers to minimize Moses's connections with the Haskalah. Accordingly, Moses was merely "engaged in literature and was a great lover of Hebrew."[63] This nondescript phrase seems intentionally designed to conceal the fact that the uncle of the champion of modern Orthodoxy was one of the leading Maskilim in Germany. Like his father, Mendel Frankfurter, and like his uncle Loeb, Moses greatly admired Mendelssohn and Wessely. Moses hailed Mendelssohn's *Biur* as a remarkable achievement enhancing Judaism, and considered the rabbis grossly mistaken in their criticism of it.[64] He was also exceptionally proud that Wessely guided him and commended his literary endeavors.[65] His literary contributions appeared in *Ha-Meassef* and in other publications.[66] Like most Maskilim, he was eager to spread secular knowledge among the Jews, and therefore translated Campe's book about the discovery of America, *Die Entdeckung Americas,* into Hebrew.[67]

Moses Frankfurter's most important contribution to Hebrew literature was his book, *Penei Tevel* written in the style of the medieval *maqammas* of Judah al-Ḥarizi and Immanuel of Rome. It reflects the usual Haskalah values: modernization of education, decorum in the synagogue, and aversion to *pilpul*, mysticism, and Hasidism. Though moderate in outlook, Moses's satire and sarcasm is reminiscent of the radical Maskilim of the caliber of Joseph Perl and Isaac Erter in his denunciations and castigations of the ultra-traditionalists for their fanaticism, obscurantism, hypocrisy, and, above all, their opposition to the Haskalah.[68] Moses may have been the most outspoken Maskil of his family, but he certainly was not the only one. He reflected the family's strong Haskalah leanings which Hirsch euphemistically termed *erleuchtet religiös*. Judging from what is known of his close relatives, it is clear that Hirsch hailed from a religious Maskilic family, which due to the changes in climate of opinion was caught in the middle between two extremes.

Secular-Religious Education

The cultural milieu of Hirsch's family sheds some light on the problem posed by Hirsch's early education. Even his admirers are puzzled by the fact that the future champion of Orthodoxy was sent to a non-Jewish school in his formative years, a most extraordinary phenomenon among pious Jews of that era.[69] The apologetic explanation, that Hirsch's parents were prompted to send their young son to a German grammar school because of his "extraordinary gifts,"[70] is nowhere documented and hardly seems justified. Moreover, Orthodox parents fearful of the deleterious effects of the non-Jewish environment ordinarily endeavored to shelter their children from outside influences, and gifted Orthodox children were sent to *yeshivot* to pursue their talmudic studies with diligence. Indeed, some affluent traditionalists, prompted by utilitarian considerations to supplement their children's predominantly religious education with practical secular subjects, engaged private tutors rather than deliberately expose them to a non-Jewish environment.

Nor could the lack of Jewish schools account for Hirsch's parents' decision. In spite of the decline in Jewish education in Germany, there were still some religious schools in Hamburg which Hirsch might have attended. Of the thirty-nine *hadarim* in that city toward the end of the eighteenth century,[71] some must still have been in existence at the time Hirsch was of school age. The fact remains, however, that his parents preferred the dangers inherent in the non-Jewish school to the substandard educational level of the existing *heder* or Talmud Torah.

The extent of his parents' objection to the traditional educational system may be gauged from the fact that they did not even send Hirsch to the Hamburg Talmud Torah organized by his grandfather Mendel Frankfurter. Though comparatively more modern than the other *hadarim*, it apparently did not meet their standards. The curriculum of that Talmud Torah, which also included some secular subjects, was neither far-reaching nor progressive enough to please them. Indeed, it is possible to argue that the reluctance of Hirsch's parents to send him to his grandfather's institution was motivated by socioeconomic factors. Being modestly prosperous, they would not have been inclined to send their son to a school primarily designed for the poor. Should this argument be valid, it would further prove that religious values were less decisive for Hirsch's parents than social and economic considerations. Had it been otherwise, the low economic status of the students attending the Hamburg Talmud Torah would not have been a sufficient deterrent. Orthodox parents would have unreservedly preferred to compromise social status rather than religious spirit.[72]

Hirsch's elementary education is most revealing of his parents' Haskalah orientation. Their religiosity notwithstanding, they valued their son's secular education so highly that it outweighed their apprehension of the deleterious effect of the non-Jewish school. It is possible that had there been a middle-class Haskalah-oriented school with a high-standard dual curriculum of Torah and *derekh eretz* subjects equally taught, Hirsch might have attended it. Such a school, however, did not exist. Even with Frankfurter's modest changes, the Hamburg Talmud Torah was too far to the right and the Reform-oriented *Freischule*[73] too far to the left. Both were educational institutions for poor children, making them socially as well as educationally unacceptable to those such as the Hirschs.

It is hard to tell which factor was more decisive in their consideration—the attractiveness of the German grammar school or the dissatisfaction with the *Winkelschule,* as the *ḥeder* was called. The dissatisfaction was certainly important. Like the Maskilim, Hirsch's parents may have considered the *ḥeder* potentially crippling to the child mentally, physically, and morally. They may have been offended by the *melamdim's* dress, speech, manners, Yiddish, and *pilpul,* and the disciplining of pupils by corporal punishment. Hirsch's grandfather and uncle were critical of these faults in traditionalist education; there is no reason to assume that Hirsch's parents were more tolerant, particularly where their own son was concerned. Thus confronted with a choice between the *ḥeder* and the German grammar school, they, like other enlightened middle-class Jews,[74] opted for the latter. The fact that Hirsch's parents expected him to pursue a business career may have also tipped the scales in favor of the German school.

Hirsch's subsequent call for coequality of religious and secular education, a dual curriculum of Torah and *derekh eretz* subjects, high educational standards, qualified teachers, and linguistic purity may have had its roots in his parents' attitude and the Maskilic sentiments of his family. Even his contempt for the *polnische Leitung,*[75] the Polish management—as Hirsch termed the traditional educational system dominated by eastern European *melamdim*— may be traced back to his Haskalah-oriented family.

Hirsch's secular education was undoubtedly supplemented by a religious education at home, a practice common among many well-to-do enlightened Jewish families, patterned along Wesselyan lines approved of by the conservative Maskilim. In the *Neunzehn Briefe,* Hirsch refers to his early Jewish education: "Reared by enlightened but God-fearing parents, the voices of Tenakh [*Bible*] early spoke to my spirit, and, of my own free will, when my intelligence had already matured, I permitted the Tenakh to lead me to Gemara" (*NL* 9).*

This simple statement is significant because it reflects the Haskalah values in Hirsch's early upbringing. Ostensibly, his parents exposed him to the religious, ethical, and aesthetic elements of the Bible before he was introduced to the study of the Talmud. Moreover, only when he was proficient in Bible and considered himself sufficiently mature, interested, and willing to pursue the study of the Talmud did he undertake it on his own. Such freedom with regard to the study of the Talmud, the exclusive goal in Jewish education at the time, could have only been tolerated in a Maskilic home; no such freedom existed among Orthodox families.

Hirsch apparently never regretted his parents' Haskalah approach to his Jewish education.[76] In later years he advocated it as most rational, effective, and beneficial: "With the Bible the beginning should be made, its language should first be comprehended, and then out of the spirit of the speech the spirit of the speakers should be inferred" (*NL* 197). Then and only then, when the Bible is fully mastered and understood, should the Talmud be intro-

*See pages xvii–xviii for the key to abbreviations.

duced. The Talmud would, thereby, become a natural extension, amplifying the biblical text (*NL* 198).

We have no information about Hirsch's teachers or whether they taught him in the manner he later advocated. Nor do we know their respective influence upon him or the extent of their knowledge of Judaism. We may assume, however, that in view of the long hours spent at the non-Jewish school, his talmudic studies at that time could not have been too extensive. They had to be limited; and considering the fact that a great deal of the time allotted for his Jewish studies was devoted to Bible and Hebrew language, his talmudic knowledge could not have been profound.

Advanced Education

In 1821, the year of Hirsch's bar mitzvah, Isaac Bernays became rabbi of Hamburg. Bernays has been credited with exerting an enormous influence upon the young, alert, and impressionable Hirsch. This influence may have been predominantly psychological rather than philosophic or theological. To the young Hirsch, Bernays may have represented the ideal spiritual leader, suited for his time. He seemed to be the fulfillment of a hope eagerly anticipated by many *erleuchtet religiös* Jews, including members of Hirsch's family. Bernays was a native of Germany and the first traditionalist rabbi with an extensive secular education.[77] The fact that he attended the University of Würzburg may not have endeared him to the extremely Orthodox, but he was warmly welcomed by the enlightened traditionalists.[78] Paradoxically, it was Bernays's secular education rather than his talmudic erudition that won for him the rabbinic post of Hamburg. With the exception of an intransigent minority, most traditionalists realized that the era of excommunications was over. To combat the insurgent Reformers and the newly established Reform temple required a traditionalist rabbi whose background and secular education would command the respect of the illuminati.[79]

Bernays appealed to such enlightened traditionalists as Hirsch's uncle, who in his initial enthusiasm for Bernays dedicated a poem of praise to him.[80] The new rabbi was ideologically close to the traditionalist Maskilim. Although a critic of Mendelssohn,[81] he approved of Wessely[82] and followed many of the latter's ideas in the field of education. Bernays set out to introduce many constructive innovations in the Hamburg Talmud Torah, thus continuing the work of Hirsch's grandfather. The curriculum was expanded to include additional secular subjects.[83] Although careful not to antagonize the Orthodox, Bernays was courageous enough to advocate, in the Wesselyan spirit, the beginning of talmudic studies at the age of thirteen.[84] Like Hirsch after him and the Maskilim before him, Bernays was unalterably opposed to *pilpul*.[85]

Bernays preached in German, an innovation heretofore associated with Reform. His sermons marked a change from the traditionalists not only in language, but also in content. Unlike the traditional *derashah*, they were saturated with subtle ideas culled from philosophy, literature, and even mythology,[86] which, much to the chagrin of his untutored congregation, were beyond their comprehension.[87] The sermons may, however, have impressed the intellectuals.[88]

How much Jewish learning Hirsch was able to gain from *Ḥakham* Bernays,[89] who enjoyed no special reputation in talmudic and rabbinic scholarship, cannot be ascertained. Considering the numerous duties which devolved upon Bernays as rabbi of Hamburg—his battle against the Reform movement, his supervision of the religious school, and much else—his time for study with Hirsch must have been very limited. Moreover, during the years of his association with Bernays, Hirsch was an apprentice in a business[90] and could not have devoted too much time to a study as time-consuming as the Talmud.

The allegation regarding Hirsch that "neither the influence of his pious parents nor that of the scholarly members of the older generation of his family can be compared to the powerful impact of *Ḥakham* Isaac Bernays"[91] is nowhere documented, nor is the assumption that Hirsch's allusion to the "only one star" (*NL* 214) who guided him in his initial steps refers to Bernays.[92] A study comparing Bernays's philosophy and theology with Hirsch's fails to substantiate any significant similarities.[93] The two were rather different in personality, attitudes, thought, and action.[94] Bernays's scant literary legacy, the authorship of which he disclaimed,[95] is hardly an adequate basis for judgment or comparison. The fact remains that only in a very few instances is Bernays ever quoted

in Hirsch's voluminous writings, and these quotes are neither philosophical nor theological but merely exegetical in nature.[96] Such
parsimony of gratitude for a teacher whose influence was supposedly decisive is unlikely even for Hirsch, whose frugality in
crediting his mentors is well known. There is, therefore, no reason
to doubt Hirsch's integrity when he denied the allegations of Bernays's influence.[97]

We may, therefore, assume that Bernays's philosophical and
theological impact on Hirsch has been overrated and exaggerated.
The assertion that with the exception of Bernays nobody among
traditionalist contemporaries was qualified to influence Hirsch[98] is
a dubious argument. Such similarities as appreciation of Hebrew
grammar and rejection of *pilpul* are not necessarily related to
Bernays's influence.[99] As already indicated, these attitudes were
conditioned by the Haskalah spirit which permeated Hirsch's
family; nor can Hirsch's opposition to the Reform movement be
attributed to Bernays.[100] Bernays did not initiate that opposition;
rather, he was brought to Hamburg by the already-existing opponents of Reform to assist in combating it. Bernays's opposition to
Maimonides and Mendelssohn[101] was not shared by Hirsch, despite the latter's criticism of them. As to symbolism and speculative etymology employed by Hirsch in his later works,[102] there is
insufficient evidence to prove Bernays's influence. Many men attempted to construct linguistic theories and grapple with the mysteries of symbolism: Herder, Humboldt, Creuzer, and von
Görres,[103] to mention a few. Hirsch, who read and studied a great
deal on his own, may have been familiar with some of these speculations independently of Bernays. Whatever Bernays's influence
upon Hirsch might have been, it seems that the latter's secular
education took precedence over his religious one. In 1826 at the
age of eighteen, Hirsch entered the Gymnasium rather than a
yeshivah. The role that Bernays played in this decision, if any, is
unknown.

In 1828, Hirsch left for Mannheim to study under Rabbi Jacob
Ettlinger. Whether this move signified Hirsch's decision to prepare for the rabbinate or merely to deepen his knowledge of the
Talmud is unknown. His decision to study under Ettlinger is significant in itself; however, more significant is the fact that he did
not go to any of the institutions of higher talmudic learning in

Germany or its environs. Though such academies were on the decline in Germany, there were still a few of high scholastic repute such as the one in Posen under the direction of Rabbi Akiba Eger, with an enrollment of over fifteen hundred students.[104] There is no evidence that Hirsch wanted to study in any of the prominent *yeshivot* or under the guidance of any of the famous talmudic scholars outside Germany.

There may have been a number of reasons for Hirsch's lack of interest in entering a prominent *yeshivah*. His weak foundation in Talmud might have made it embarrassing for him to attend a *yeshivah* at the age of twenty with students who were younger and scholastically superior. The eastern European spirit dominating those talmudic academies was hardly appealing to his Occidental taste and Maskilic conditioning. Nor could Hirsch appreciate the ingenuity and subtlety of the talmudic expositions of the eastern European masters, whose methodology he sharply criticized a few years later:

The Jewish spirit, in its most recent form, was chiefly devoted to abstract and abstruse speculation; a vivid consciousness of the real world was lacking, and therefore, the object of study was not what it should chiefly have been, the attainment of knowledge of duty, for use in the world and in life. Study became the end instead of the means, the subject of investigation became a matter of indifference, the dialectic subtleties thereof the chief concern. (*NL* 147–48)

Lacking the background of the *ḥeder* and *yeshivah*, reared in a liberal atmosphere, exposed to general culture, and trained in a secular educational system, Hirsch could not share in the admiration of an educational system which he deplored as parochial, constrictive, and unproductive. While praising the Talmud, he condemned the way it was taught at those institutions: "A dull and prosaic dialectic had reduced to merest mummies laws full to overflowing of life and spirit" (*NL* 99). Furthermore, Hirsch might have already decided to continue his studies at the university, which he did the following year, a step which might have caused his expulsion from a traditional *yeshivah*.

Hirsch may have preferred to study under Ettlinger, who was a young native German rabbi only ten years older than Hirsch and aware of the problems that agitated young German Jews. That Ettlinger had an academic background may have further enhanced his prestige in Hirsch's eyes. Ettlinger was a distinguished talmudic scholar; in course of time, his responsa, commentaries, and particularly his *Arukh la-Ner* gained him great fame even among the noted talmudists of eastern Europe. Unlike them, however, he was no *pilpulist*. For Hirsch, these considerations more than compensated for the stature and reputation of the older and more prominent eastern European rabbis and talmudic scholars of his times.

Though an avowed traditionalist, Ettlinger, like Bernays and Nathan Marcus Adler, the subsequent chief rabbi of Great Britain, was a harbinger of a new *erleuchtet religiös* type of rabbi in Germany. Like them, he had studied under Rabbi Abraham Bing in Würzburg while attending the university.[105] Ettlinger showed a great interest in the modernization of traditionalist education and had an understanding of the Zeitgeist. We may assume, therefore, that Bernays recommended Ettlinger to Hirsch. Aware of the views and ability of his colleague and the inclinations of his student, Bernays saw an affinity between them.

The extent of Hirsch's progress in talmudic and rabbinic studies under Ettlinger's tutelage is unknown; only one of Hirsch's queries concerning ritual is quoted in any of Ettlinger's works.[106] But as already noted, Hirsch's reluctance to reveal anything about his background or his educational and intellectual indebtedness is characteristic. It is hard to believe that Hirsch's limited talmudic knowledge, gained haphazardly from private instruction, could have impressed an outstanding scholar like Ettlinger. Even in later years, when Hirsch's piety and sincerity were no longer questioned by the traditionalists, he was taunted as an *am ha-aretz* and a *siddur lamdan*— an ignoramus and a "prayer book scholar":[107] "Hirsch's comparative lack of rabbinical learning made him the inferior of many men who were to look to him for guidance. The mantle of the great legists of an older generation was oppressively heavy for his occidental shoulders."[108]

That Ettlinger might have ordained him—a question to be dealt with later—is a reflection of the sad conditions prevailing among German Jewry rather than a testimony to Hirsch's scholarship, as argued by his admirers.[109] The disarray in the Jewish community in general and among traditionalists in particular, the menace of Reform expansion, and fear of disaffected youth made any talented young man, meager as his Jewish scholarship might be, a desirable candidate for the rabbinate. The very fact that Hirsch was not one of the "Polish teachers" or their apprentices but hailed from an old, prominent, well-to-do German family and was willing to serve as a traditionalist rabbi was sufficient for Ettlinger to ordain him. With Jewish education at low ebb and ignorance in religious matters widespread, the young, sincere, and idealistic Hirsch was eminently qualified to lead a community whose members were far less knowledgeable and certainly less observant than he.

During the period of his studies with Ettlinger, Hirsch met his future ideological opponent, Abraham Geiger, who also contemplated entering the rabbinate. Hirsch's outlook at that time could not have been partisan if, on the eve of his career as traditionalist rabbi, he was able to maintain amicable relations with the man who subsequently became the champion of the Reform movement. It is noteworthy that in spite of the temple controversy that stirred all Germany and particularly Hamburg, Hirsch in his youth had no bitterness against those with Reform leanings. Nor did he exhibit any of the flamboyantly antagonistic sentiments of his subsequent years. He maintained friendly relations with men whose views were Reform-oriented and liberal. It should be noted that nowhere at this time do we find him maintaining similar relations with men further to the right. Apparently, his background and education predisposed him to associate with the more progressive rather than the more conservative. It seems that while he may have differed with the former, he ignored the latter—or perhaps they ignored him.

Soon thereafter, Hirsch and Geiger left to attend the university in Bonn. In their free time together, they studied the Talmud and homiletics.[110] Hirsch was undoubtedly aware of Geiger's views, which, if not as radical as those he expressed later, could not have been excessively Orthodox. Together with his future opponent he organized a debating society in which Jewish students, many of them preparing for the rabbinate, discussed problems of mutual concern. There was apparently sufficient common ground for Hirsch and Geiger to maintain a dialogue. Both men agreed that changes were necessary and that the challenges presented by the spirit of the time had to be met. Consequently, their mutual aims were more important at this time than the differences in method that subsequently divided them. Their friendship continued for a long time, even after Geiger had become one of the most vocal spokesman for Reform. It was only after Geiger had criticized Hirsch's *Neunzehn Briefe* that the latter felt offended; then their friendship ended[111] over personal rather than theological and ideological differences.

Geiger continued his studies at the University of Bonn, published his prize-winning essay "Was hat Mohammed aus dem Judentum aufgenommen," and subsequently received his doctorate from the University of Marburg. However, Hirsch left the university after only a year and a half; what prompted him to interrupt his studies is not known. There is, however, nothing to support the sanctimonious contention that Hirsch wanted merely "a savoring of the spiritual life of the Gentile sages."[112] Given Hirsch's personality and outlook, nothing could be more incongruous. It seems more plausible that Hirsch was sidetracked from pursuing his university education by the offer made to him in 1830 to become the *Landesrabbiner*—chief rabbi—of the Duchy of Oldenburg. This post was then held by Nathan Marcus Adler, who had been installed there only a short time before. Compelled by circumstances to accept his father's post at Hannover, he recommended Hirsch as his successor in Oldenburg.[113]

Ironically, the opportunity to become rabbi of Oldenburg may not have only interrupted Hirsch's academic career but may have interfered with his studies leading to ordination. It seems rather unlikely that a renowned talmudic scholar like Ettlinger would have hastily conferred the title of rabbi upon a student whose talmudic knowledge was unimpressive after one and a half years of study. This suspicion becomes even stronger when we read Adler's letter to the Oldenburg authorities recommending Hirsch for the rabbinic position.[114] Although Adler tried to enhance Hirsch's prestige by praising his character, demeanor, scholastic ability, proficiency in German, and skill in homiletics, he strangely failed to mention his ordination. Moreover, Adler referred to Hirsch as "the young man" rather than by the title rabbi that ordination confers and which was warranted by the occasion.

Adler mentioned that Hirsch had attended a Jewish theological institute at Mannheim for one and a half years, a fact apparently of interest to the Oldenburg government; but he did not indicate whether Hirsch had completed his studies there or whether he was ordained.

Nor was ordination mentioned in the letter of the Oldenburg consul at Hamburg, Schmidt, from whom his government solicited information concerning Hirsch.[115] The consul concurred with Adler in all respects. However, he, too, referred to Hirsch merely as a "young man" without the title rabbi; and although he included details about his character, views, background, and education, there was no reference to his ordination. It is hardly conceivable that, had Hirsch been ordained at that time, Adler or the consul would have deliberately omitted such a salient fact about a candidate for the rabbinic post of Oldenburg. This does not exclude the possibility that Hirsch might have been ordained subsequently while serving as rabbi.

In this connection, it is worthwhile to point out a statement by the Oldenburg consul, included in that letter, concerning Hirsch's views at the time. Apparently, on the basis of the information he had obtained, Hirsch was a traditionalist by upbringing who had come under the "prevalent mild views"—*herrschenden gelinden Ansichten*—of the University of Bonn. As such, he continued, Hirsch would be successful in uniting the divergent elements in the community.[116]

The call to Oldenburg cannot be interpreted as any great recognition of Hirsch by the German Orthodox community, nor can it be attributed to his reputation.[117] Such claims are exaggerated and unfounded. At twenty-two, Hirsch had a reputation neither as a scholar nor as a spokesman for Orthodoxy. Hirsch's weak talmudic foundation would not have overwhelmed the traditionalists, nor would his limited academic education have impressed the liberals. Similarly, his *erleuchtet religiös* background and his amiable relations with the Reform elements might have made him suspect in the eyes of the Orthodox—just as his religious observance made him unacceptable to the radicals.

It is more likely that Adler recommended Hirsch because he, Adler, shared the same background and views as Ettlinger and Bernays and felt that Hirsch, as a student of both, held moderate, liberal views. Adler saw him as a worthy successor. The Jewish community of the city of Oldenburg in the Duchy of Oldenburg was small and not excessively observant.[118] The fact that Adler had to employ sanctions to force his congregation to attend Sabbath, holiday, and fast-day services[119] reflects the prevailing religious climate there. Such a community was hardly sufficiently concerned or capable of judging the scholarship and theological views of their prospective rabbi.

Furthermore, it was not the Jewish community but the grand duke of Oldenburg who was anxious for the appointment of a *Landesrabbiner*. According to a regulation of August 14, 1827, a chief rabbi had to be appointed to supervise the synagogues and Jewish schools of the grand duchy.[120] This arose out of the grand duke's concern to keep the Jews of the duchy loyal to the government by insulating them from the radical influences and subversive trends rife during that period. The rabbi was designated to serve as a responsible government officer under the civil service law, and was obliged to send in a periodical report.[121] It is possible that the Jews' apathy regarding the *Landesrabbiner* was largely due to his official status. They probably considered him someone appointed to keep them within their limited boundaries rather than one who would promote their welfare.[122] These were the qualities the grand duke of Oldenburg had sought in a Jewish spiritual leader for his duchy when he had considered Hirsch's predecessor, Adler: "The duke was anxious to obtain a *Landesrabbiner* who was devout, loyal and obedient. He was soon satisfied that Dr. Adler was precisely his man. His academic qualifications were excellent, his experience nil—with the help of the government officers as guides—his office, it was hoped, would soon train him."[123]

Though the grand duke died soon after Adler's appointment, there is no reason to assume that there was any change of policy during the short period of time leading up to Hirsch's inauguration. There is more reason to assume that knowing the government's requirements, Adler suggested the candidacy of a man who would fulfill them. Indeed, Hirsch's academic attainments were not as impressive as those of Adler, who had studied at the famous universities of Göttingen and Würzburg and had been the recipient of a doctorate in philosophy from the University of Erlangen.

However, Hirsch's qualifications were adequate to satisfy the duchy's political interests: his German was impeccable, his loyalty unquestionable, and he was just as inexperienced as had been his predecessor.

Hirsch had to make an instant decision, since great pressure was being brought upon Adler to assume his rabbinic duties at Hannover. For Hirsch, this was an unusual opportunity, since he lacked the scholarship to aspire to a traditionalist post in a more knowledgeable community. Moreover, considering his liberal inclinations at this stage of his development, such a post would not have suited his views. His academic learning was far too limited for a Reform post, nor would he ever consider one. To succeed Adler, a scion of one of the most prominent rabbinic families in Germany, was for young Hirsch a rare honor and opportunity. Whether or not he considered Oldenburg a mere stepping-stone to more important things, the offer was sufficient motivation for him to discontinue his studies at Bonn.

Hirsch's inaugural address delivered on Rosh Hashanah sounded more like a Reform sermon than a traditional *derashah* preached by Orthodox rabbis on such a solemn occasion.[124] Its style and content resembled that used by Reform rabbis who patterned themselves after their Christian counterparts.[125] It was generally similar to one of Adler's sermons: "It was couched in a well-chosen language of noble sentiment not devoid of platitudes. It was never scholarly; it never informed; it always preached and it was in pure German throughout."[126]

3
Rabbinic Profile

Oldenburg

The grand duchy of Oldenburg in northwestern Germany had at the time Hirsch arrived there about seven hundred Jews scattered throughout many small communities.[1] The Jews of the city of Oldenburg proper were religiously apathetic and indifferent to Jewish community concerns.[2] It is not known whether Hirsch, like Adler before him, endeavored to enforce religious observances by coercive measures. Young Heinrich Graetz, the future great Jewish historian, who substituted for Hirsch during the latter's occasional absences from Oldenburg, once found that there was no *minyan* in the synagogue on an important fast day,[3] which is a sufficient indication of the religious atmosphere in the community.

In Oldenburg Hirsch was generally moderate in his conduct and inclined toward liberalization, at least in matters of religious externalities. His attire hardly differed from that of the Reform rabbis. In contrast to Bernays and Ettlinger, "Hirsch wore a rabbinical gown with white bands; . . . an engraving made in Oldenburg . . . shows him in this gown, without a beard and without head covering."[4] If shaving was an indication of liberal tendencies in the case of his father, then certainly for Hirsch, an Orthodox rabbi in nineteenth-century Germany, going clean-shaven and bareheaded shows an inexcusable lack of concern for tradition. His attire was patterned after the Reform rabbis, who took their

66

model from the vestments of the Christian clergy. The fact that this was allowed to occur also attests to the indifference of his congregation. Jews in other German communities were neither as tolerant nor as docile. This is best illustrated in the case of Hirsch's friend, Abraham Geiger, who dared to don special robes of office and caused such a storm in Breslau that it necessitated the intervention of the Prussian ministry. Despite the fact that Geiger's robes differed from those of the Catholic and Protestant clergy, he was summarily ordered by the Breslau authorities to dispense with them.[5] Hirsch apparently had no such opposition from the members of his community or from the governmental authorities of Oldenburg.

His relationship with the latter was apparently not marked by any difficulties. Hirsch understood the role the government wanted him to play, and he seemed able to perform it splendidly. The sole concern of the authorities was to keep their Jews insulated from exposure to the radical influences of the post-Napoleonic era. Apprehension about French revolutionary and egalitarian ideas was still very real in Oldenburg and in many other parts of Germany. The chief rabbi was, therefore, more important to the government of Oldenburg than to its apathetic Jewish community. His task was to keep the Jews of the grand duchy calm, obedient, and submissive. Hirsch, like Mendelssohn, was content to render unto Caesar what belonged to Caesar and to God what belonged to God.[6]

In accord with this philosophy, acquiescence presented no problem; Hirsch exhorted the Jews to submit absolutely to the will of the government. In the *Horeb,* his compendium of Jewish laws written during his stay in Oldenburg, Hirsch stated categorically that every Jew was obligated "to be loyal to the state with heart and mind, loyal to the kings, to guard the honor of the state with love and pride, to strive with enthusiasm wherever and whenever you can so that the nation's institutions shall prosper, so that every aim which your country has set as its national goal shall be achieved and furthered" (*H* 609). Hirsch made no distinction between ethical or nonethical pursuits of government. Right or wrong, legal or criminal, progressive or draconian, the laws of government must be unconditionally, even enthusiastically, executed. Compliance with the dictates of an autocratic, oppressive, and even anti-Semitic government was not merely a matter of practical prudence or hopeless resignation, but a religious mandate: "This duty is an unconditional duty and not dependent upon whether the state is kindly intentioned toward you or is harsh. Even should it deny your right to be a human being and to develop a lawful human life upon the soil which bore you—*you* shall not neglect your duty" (*H* 609).[7] This compliance with the arbitrary demands of government ought not to express itself merely in outward submission and perfunctory performance. It must be accompanied by an inner zeal and unreserved commitment: "This outward obedience to the laws must be joined by the inner obedience" (*H* 609).

Such unreserved surrender to tyrannical authority was not only a product of the political reality of the era but an integral part of Hirsch's view on the Jews' mission of salvation in the Diaspora (*NL* 80–81). It was part of a larger divine scheme for the destiny of Israel and the redemption of mankind. Such obsequiousness and servility by the chief rabbi could not have displeased the political authorities of Oldenburg.

Unopposed by either the government or his congregation, Hirsch ventured to introduce some innovations which in more traditionally oriented communities would have caused considerable protest. These innovations were primarily of an aesthetic nature. Conservative Maskilim were already critical of the lack of decorum in the synagogue, the abstruse *derashah*, and the Yiddish spoken by the rabbis. Hirsch replaced the *derashah* with the modern *Predigt*, thus substituting idiomatic, cultured German for the Judeo-German dialect. Even if exception is taken to the assertion that his sermon was "patterned very much after Christian models,"[8] it certainly did not resemble those of the leading Orthodox rabbis in Germany.

Among Hirsch's modest innovations was the introduction of a choir to accompany the synagogue service. This practice was frowned upon not only by the Orthodox elements in Germany but even by the liberal-minded Leopold Zunz.[9] Although the choir was an imitation of the Christian church that had caused consternation among traditionalists everywhere and had been one of the principal innovations of the Reform temple in Hamburg, Hirsch did not consider these sufficient reasons to reject the practice. But

the most radical step taken by Hirsch in Oldenburg was the abolition of Kol Nidre. It appears that this act finally stirred his apathetic community to harbor some ill feeling toward him.[10] Although Kol Nidre is of neither biblical nor talmudic origin, it is
rooted in custom hallowed by time and sentiment which few
dared to disregard. Its origin dates back to the Gaonic period in
the eighth century, and although some persons objected to its
recitation, it nevertheless became widespread in Jewish communities.[11] It is therefore astonishing that Hirsch should have abolished
Kol Nidre despite the fact that it was an age-old custom and,
therefore, according to his own view, obligatory, since it possessed
the characteristics of a communal vow (*H* 474.) Hirsch's abrogation of Kol Nidre was unprecedented and audacious and cannot be
explained away as a whimsical or capricious gesture. Though Kol
Nidre is lacking in halakhic sanction and its text might even be
regarded as subversive by the state, no traditionally oriented rabbi
had suggested its elimination. Even the lay members of the Jewish
community resisted its abolition and defied government intervention. When Mendel Hess, the radical Reform district rabbi of Saxe-
Weimar,[12] induced the grand duke of that duchy to order the
abolition of Kol Nidre in 1823, the move was strongly resisted in
the Jewish community and could not be implemented. As late as
1844, five or six years after Hirsch had eliminated Kol Nidre in
Oldenburg, the synod of Reform rabbis at Brunswick were still
grappling with the problem of choosing between sentiment and
practicality.[13]

It is noteworthy that Kol Nidre was not the only popular custom
dismissed by Hirsch as irrelevant. Similar customs such as *kapparot, tashlikh, ḥibbut aravah,*[14] to list but a few, were not even
deemed important enough to mention in the *Horeb.* Unlike Kol
Nidre, the other customs had no political or social implications, so
their omission could not be justified on such grounds. The fact that
Hirsch deliberately omitted Kol Nidre in a manual intended for all
German Jews renders the contention of his well-intentioned
apologists meaningless. Apparently, Hirsch's abolition of Kol
Nidre was merely a temporary measure dictated by the then prevailing circumstances at Oldenburg.[15]

A more plausible explanation for Hirsch's diregard for these
popular customs, including Kol Nidre, may be his "enlightened"

background and aesthetic sensibilities. The Maskilim had always strongly objected to these customs as psychologically harmful, educationally deleterious, and politically unwise. Notwithstanding popular sentiment, or perhaps because of it, they viewed these customs as superstitious and unaesthetic. However, the Maskilim had no opportunity to eliminate them; Hirsch, as a rabbi in a community which showed no sign that it might resist change, attempted to do so. Kol Nidre was particularly distasteful to him since it also served as a source for deliberate misinterpretation by anti-Semites who could use it to accuse the Jews of perfidy and perjury, alleging that it absolved the Jews from their oaths and promises and made them untrustworthy. Hirsch apparently did not feel that this custom warranted such risks. Many traditionalists in Hamburg, Hirsch's native city, were disturbed by his high-handed actions and felt confirmed in their suspicions of Hirsch's piety.[16] Nor did his treatment of these accepted customs advance his popularity in the Orthodox communities of Germany. While not sufficient to identify him with the Reformers, these minor reforms seemed to alienate him from the Orthodox.

However, the decade of isolation that Hirsch spent in Oldenburg was the most fruitful and creative in his life. It is apparent from his prolific writings of this period that he must have worked diligently to make up for the deficiencies in his fragmentary, unsystematic higher education. His responsibilities to the Jewish community were not time-consuming, and he had sufficient time to study, think, and write, but Oldenburg hardly represented an intellectual challenge. Besides his wife, Johanna, whom he had married in 1831, there was no one with whom he could discuss the problems and issues that agitated him. While Johanna was well versed in the Bible and in Schiller's poetry, both highly valued by Hirsch,[17] he would have preferred a more intellectual companion. He was therefore delighted when in 1837 young Heinrich Graetz requested permission to come to Oldenburg as his disciple.

Graetz was attracted to Hirsch after reading his *Neunzehn Briefe über Judentum,* which appeared in 1836. The future historian, then nineteen years old, was in the throes of an intellectual and spiritual crisis. Exposed to a host of contradictory views and ideas, he was confused and perplexed along with many other young men of his generation. Graetz was too earnest and deeply

religious to be satisfied with palliative reforms. He already possessed sufficient insight to realize that arbitrary and expedient
omission of certain laws would eventually bring about the abrogation of all law. Pragmatic tamperings by exponents of Reform did
more harm than good.[18] He was, therefore, delighted when he
read Hirsch's *Neunzehn Briefe,* which purported to offer a new
rationale for Judaism that would anchor it safely in the turbulent
waters of the new era.

The impact of Hirsch's book on the young, perplexed Graetz
was immense and electrifying.[19] It seemed to endow him with the
regenerative powers to resolve his crushing inner conflicts. It was
a religious experience analogous to a reconversion. Graetz described these feelings in his diary:

With avidity I devoured every word. Disloyal though I had been
to the Talmud, this book reconciled me with it. I returned to it as
to a mistress deemed faithless and proved true, and determined
to use my utmost effort to pierce to its depths, acquire a philosophical knowledge thereof, and as many would have me believe that
I might become a so-called "rabbi-doctor of theology" [*studirter
Rabbiner*], publicly demonstrate its truth and utility. I set about
my task at once, beginning with the first folio, *Berakhot,* and the
first book of Moses. I dwelt upon every point with pleasure, treating them not as remnants of antiquity but as books containing
divine help for mankind.[20]

Hirsch must have been delighted to receive Graetz's enthusiastic letter and flattered by the frank veneration of a self-styled
truth-thirsty youth. In his letter, Graetz referred to Hirsch in the
most worshipful terms: "ein helles Sonnenlicht, das mir die Dun-
kelheit erleuchtet" ("a bright sunlight that illuminates my darkness"), "Esro unserer Geistes-Golus" ("the Ezra of our spiritual
exile"), "der grosse Mann und der echteste Jude unserer Generation" ("the most genuine Jew of our generation").[21] Hirsch's
avowed aim was to turn the tide of disaffection from Judaism by
offering a new approach; the adoration of the young, gifted, and
scholarly Graetz substantiated his hopes. In his letter, Graetz had
stated that every line of the *Neunzehn Briefe,* in his words, "divine letters" *(göttliche Epistel),* had melted away the ice of skepticism that had frozen his heart.[22]

Above all, Hirsch was happy about the promised companionship of this young student who would relieve his boredom in the intellectual desert of Oldenburg. He hoped to share with Graetz the ideas which he had been developing in solitude. Hirsch invited Graetz to join him, and revealed his own eagerness by quoting the rabbinic dictum: "More than the calf will suck, the cow desires to suckle."[23] It should be pointed out that Hirsch, taking note of Graetz's exuberance and excitable imagination, attempted to subdue the young man's ardor and expectations by suggesting that Graetz reduce his image of Hirsch to its proper dimension in order to forestall any subsequent disillusionment. Hirsch candidly admitted to Graetz that he was not yet an accomplished master but a man who was groping and searching.[24]

The notes in Graetz's diary concerning his stay in Oldenburg reflect as much about Hirsch as about the diarist. Of interest is the intensive plan of study that Hirsch presented to his student soon after his arrival. It was an unusually heavy schedule: nineteen hours long, from four in the morning to eleven at night—broken only by an hour for lunch and an hour for supper. Significantly, the plan called for time equally divided between Torah subjects and secular, *derekh eretz*, subjects: from 4:00 to 6:00 A.M., Talmud and *Oraḥ Ḥayyim;* 6:00 to 8:00 A.M., prayer, Bible, and breakfast; 8:00 to 10:00 A.M., again Talmud; 10:00 A.M. until noon, Greek; 1:00 to 3:00 P.M., history, Latin, or physics; 3:00 to 5:00 P.M., mathematics and geography; 6:00 to 8:00 P.M., codes and Bible; and the last two hours at night were set aside for alternate readings in Hebrew, German, French, and Latin.[25]

This was essentially the plan Hirsch had outlined in the *Horeb* for Jewish education in general (*H* 553). Since Graetz was intellectually mature, his plan of study was somewhat more intensive and of a higher level than the one suggested in the *Horeb*. Basically, the plan was patterned after the one proposed by Wessely in his *Divrei Shalom ve-Emet;*[26] however, it went beyond the modest requirements set down by Wessely and the conservative Maskilim who advocated practical subjects as necessitated by social and economic considerations. Hirsch, who appreciated the humanistic spirit which permeated the German cultural climate, considered Greek and Latin important and included classical languages in Graetz's plan. Similarly, he set a high value on mathematics, natural sciences, history, and geography.[27]

Despite Hirsch's liberalism in matters of culture and education, he was as critical as Wessely and the other conservative Maskilim of literature that he considered offensive from a religious or moral standpoint. Thus, while reading *Der Salon* by Heine with Graetz, he grew so highly incensed by its blasphemous expressions that he wanted to burn the book and compensate the library for its destruction.[28] The fact that *Der Salon* was written by an apostate did not prevent Hirsch from undertaking to read it. Hirsch voiced similar displeasure when he found Graetz reading the works of Bayle, which Hirsch considered "a treasure of erudition" but still immoral and consequently "contaminated and contaminating."[29]

Hirsch and Graetz got along well. Graetz accompanied Hirsch on some of his visits to the small communities of the grand duchy.[30] Hirsch had enough confidence in his disciple to permit him to render ritual decisions. He also must have appreciated Graetz's literary ability, for he asked him to make the final corrections on the last part of the *Horeb*.[31] But three years after Graetz's arrival in Oldenburg, the cordial relations between the master and the disciple suffered a marked change. Aside from the minor frictions between Graetz and the lady of the house which became a source of irritation,[32] Graetz was somewhat disenchanted with Hirsch himself. Accompanying the chief rabbi in January 1840 on one of his inspection visits, he blamed Hirsch for the lack of decorum in the synagogues and for his failure to abolish the incomprehensible *piyyutim* that the worshippers recited without understanding their meaning.[33]

Graetz was also critical of Hirsch's narrow-minded legalism or, as he termed it, *bornierter Schulchan-Aruchanismus*.[34] He chided Hirsch for being overscrupulous in some of his religious observances such as not drinking milk purchased from non-Jews and refraining from carrying objects on the Sabbath, despite the fact that some rabbinic authorities advocated a more lenient approach to these matters.[35] Though his criticisms concerned matters of a halakhic nature, they were basically personal. Like many young intellectual Jews of his era, Graetz was wary of the petty subtleties and the sham dialectics *(Kleinigkeitsgrübelei und Disputationsflitterware)*[36] which had characterized Jewish learning; still, his criticisms of his master were harsh.

It is possible that Graetz, who had been intoxicated with the promise of a new approach to Judaism as outlined in the *Neunzehn Briefe*, now felt cheated. He had expected—as he had intimated in his first letter to Hirsch—to be guided in the true ideas of Judaism and talmudic exegesis. He had hoped to be introduced to a new, all-encompassing Weltanschauung which would reilluminate Judaism. Much to his chagrin, his hopes had not been fulfilled. Hirsch, who had previously appeared to him like an angel of the Lord,[37] was now reduced in his eyes to a frail mortal; most contemptible of all, he seemed "like a Polish scholar."[38] What had appeared so scintillating from a distance now looked drab close up. Proximity and familiarity made Graetz contemptuous of Hirsch, among whose shortcomings was a weakness in Jewish history, which only added to the future historian's general disappointment.[39]

It is difficult to ascertain whether Graetz's disillusionment was the result of normal maturation or overblown expectations. It is clear that the young man realized that he had overrated Hirsch in many respects. Despite this intellectual disappointment, however, Graetz endeavored to persuade Hirsch to leave Oldenburg and settle in a larger community where he could exert more influence. Having heard that the rabbinic post of Posen was vacant due to the death of Rabbi Akiba Eger, Graetz attempted to promote Hirsch's candidacy.[40] Similarly, upon the demise of Rabbi Samuel Somwel Munk of Wollstein, Graetz tried to persuade that community to elect Hirsch as Munk's successor.[41]

Graetz's disenchantment with Hirsch and his endeavors to place him in a more suitable rabbinic position should not be viewed as contradictory. Though disenchanted with Hirsch intellectually, Graetz was convinced that Hirsch could be of benefit to a Jewish community more dynamic than Oldenburg. For all his shortcomings, Graetz felt, Hirsch was still superior to the other Orthodox rabbis, who were oblivious to the needs of the time.

Much to Graetz's chagrin, Hirsch was hesitant to leave Oldenburg, and his temporizing compounded Graetz's disappointment in him not only as an intellectual but also as a human being. Graetz realized that economy was the determining factor in Hirsch's reluctance to leave Oldenburg. Born to a poor family, the idealistic Graetz could not understand the importance that the economic factor had for Hirsch, who had been brought up with middle-class standards and now had a family to support. He was therefore appalled by what he considered Hirsch's pettiness *(Kleingeistkrämer)*, an attitude unbecoming a man with high aspirations.[42]

Though economic considerations played an important role in Hirsch's decision, there was another factor which Graetz may not have realized: Hirsch was aware of his own shortcomings. Much more pragmatic than Graetz, he knew that his deficiencies in the Talmud and rabbinics rendered him inadequate to assume the mantle of such an eminent scholar as Rabbi Akiba Eger. Nor did he consider himself able to contest the latter's son, Solomon, a man of great talmudic erudition. The location of Wollstein may have caused Hirsch some anxiety, too. Unlike Oldenburg, which was situated in northwestern Germany, where Jewish knowledge was at a low ebb, Posen and Wollstein were in eastern Germany, where high scholastic standards were still maintained for the rabbinate. The Jewish populations of Posen and Wollstein each exceeded that of Oldenburg.[43]

Under the influence of Rabbis Eger and Munk, the Jews of Posen and Wollstein were probably more religiously oriented, more discerning, and more knowledgeable than those of Oldenburg. For Hirsch, who needed time for preparation and maturation, the rabbinate of either Posen or Wollstein might have presented enormous difficulties. We may therefore assume that these psychological considerations played as great a role as the monetary ones in formulating Hirsch's decision.

The strained relations between master and disciple continued for another few months. Their friendship cooled as their respect for each other waned. On June 26, 1840, Graetz wrote in his diary that he could expect little from Hirsch, adding sarcastically in French: "Il a peu de connaissance hors de ses enormes livres poskim" ("Except for his big ritualistic books, he knows nothing").[44] Little did he realize that Hirsch feared that his knowledge of the *poskim* was insufficient for positions in Posen or Wollstein.

On July 26, 1840, Graetz left Oldenburg. The following year, Hirsch accepted the rabbinic post of East Friesland. This new position, unlike that in Posen or Wollstein, was not radically different from the one he had held in Oldenburg. Ironically, Hirsch was succeeded in Oldenburg by Bernhard Wechsler, a radical Reform rabbi, a fact which indicates that Hirsch's traditionalist influence upon his first community was hardly impressive.

East Friesland

The immediate cause or causes prompting Hirsch's departure from Oldenburg, while unknown, can be readily understood. As already indicated, this lethargic and religiously apathetic community had little intellectually to offer to the alert, concerned, talented, and energetic young rabbi. Although Hirsch had used his stay in Oldenburg most advantageously to crystallize and articulate his views, the community was too limited and its opportunities too constrictive for Hirsch, who was only in his early thirties and felt that he could play a more important role than serving as spiritual leader of the Oldenburg Jews. Less understandable is his acceptance of the rabbinical post of East Friesland. With the exception of geographical proximity to his former position, it is difficult to see what might have induced Hirsch to accept the new one.

Hirsch's new position embraced the Jewish communities in the districts ceded to the Hannoverian Kingdom by Prussia in the territorial rearrangements which followed the diplomatic maneuverings of the Congress of Vienna in 1815. It consisted of East Friesland with the port city of Emden and the northern part of Westphalia, including Osnabruck. The political climate in these districts was unlikely to attract Hirsch, since under Hannoverian dominion it was far less hospitable than the one in Oldenburg. While in the latter the liberal influence of nearby Denmark continued to prevail, Hannover in contradistinction was then riding the crest of reaction in Germany. Its king, Ernest August, was reputed to be a most reactionary and autocratic ruler.[45]

Judging from the content of Hirsch's letter of May 30, 1841, addressed to the Royal Hannoverian *Landdrostei* or district at Aurich,[46] the new post hardly improved his economic situation. Unlike Oldenburg, where he was economically independent of the Jewish community and his salary was assured by the government, Hirsch's income in East Friesland came from the Jewish communities. Two-thirds of his salary was paid by the largest and more affluent community of Emden, and the other third had to be contributed by the smaller Jewish communities of the district.[47]

This arrangement did not augur a happy relationship between the rabbi and the community leaders. Facing financial difficulties, the latter were frequently disinclined to meet their assessed contributions to the rabbi's salary. Even Emden, the largest community in the district, considered the chief rabbi a luxury which they could not afford. Some Emden Jews were content with the religious ministrations offered by one of their local residents.[48] The Jewish community of Osnabruck refused to recognize the authority of the chief rabbi or to to contribute to his maintenance. It was the government that finally compelled the Osnabruck Jewish community in 1844, three years after Hirsch had assumed his post there, to acknowledge his authority.[49]

There is no reason to assume that the Jews of East Friesland were more tradition-oriented, more concerned with or more knowledgeable of Judaism, than the Oldenburg Jews. The fact that one of the candidates for the post of chief rabbi of East Friesland was Levi Herzfeld of Brunswick,[50] a leading figure of the Reform movement, is a sufficient indication that the community was not excessively Orthodox.

Most puzzling of all is the fact that Hirsch was eager to exchange the peaceful community of Oldenburg for the strife-torn community of East Friesland. Inner discord and rivalry had prevented the election of a new chief rabbi for two years after the post became vacant with the demise of Rabbi Abraham Levi Loewenstamm in 1839. Even the rabbi's residence was a source of contention between the Jews of East Friesland's capital, Aurich, and those of Emden.[51] Each community claimed this prerogative for itself. Only the direct and vigorous intervention of the government put an end to those quarrels. It insisted on elections in 1841 and decided in favor of Emden as the seat of the *Landesrabbiner*. This concession, however, failed to appease the leaders of the Emden Jewish community, who boycotted the election. They protested that Emden, although it was the largest Jewish community of East Friesland and contributed the largest part of the rabbi's salary, was given only one vote instead of three on the electoral committee.[52] It is quite possible that had Emden received a proportional number of representatives on the electoral committee, Hirsch might not have been elected *Landesrabbiner*. Thus the possibility cannot be excluded that the reluctance of the Emden Jewish community to pay Hirsch's salary was not motivated by financial hardships only. The dissatisfaction with Hirsch may have been an important consideration in this respect.

As already indicated, Hirsch was not the only candidate for this post; two others, Levi Herzfeld of Brunswick and Gabriel Lippmann of Trier, were also under consideration.[53] In addition, the son of the late Rabbi Loewenstamm had his followers. Although the latter's inadequate secular background prevented him from being an official candidate, some saw in him the heir-apparent to this rabbinic office.

That Hirsch was disturbed by the uncooperative attitude of the Emden Jewish community can be seen from the aforementioned letter to the *Landdrostei*. He voiced his apprehension that the lack of respect from the leaders of the community would destroy his effectiveness and leadership. He was particularly chagrined by the fact that this unfavorable attitude was displayed by the leaders of the community he had to reside in. Such an attitude, he asserted, was contagious and could poison his entire relationship with the rest of the Jews in East Friesland.

It is interesting to note the *Landdrostei* 's reply, dated June 5, 1841.[54] In it the authorities advise Hirsch to make every effort to win the respect and cooperation of his congregants by kindness, patience, and love. Such counsel was sound, but Hirsch may not have found it easy. He was accustomed to the conditions of Oldenburg, where he was totally independent of the Jewish community and could ignore their wishes. Indeed, he paid a price for this inattentiveness, becoming more and more isolated. However, deference to the wishes of the community was not characteristic of Hirsch. The fact that he complained to the authorities about the lack of cooperation of the Emden community instead of approaching his congregants directly indicates that he had expected the government to obtain it for him, if necessary by an unmistakable directive. It is not difficult to imagine that Hirsch's attitude hardly endeared him to the Jews of East Friesland.

Hirsch's activities in East Friesland were primarily administrative. He inspected the synagogues, examined the children of the religious schools, and certified documents, sealing them with the prestigious seal of the *Landesrabbiner*. He meticulously reported everything to the government as dutifully as he did in Oldenburg and published instructions for the community leaders advising them in administrative problems.[55] Thus, Hirsch executed eminently his obligations of *Landesrabbiner* vis-à-vis the government of East Friesland; his accomplishments for the Jewish community there were less satisfactory. As a result, two years after his assumption of the post of chief rabbi of East Friesland Hirsch was eager to leave it for another post: that of chief rabbi of London, which in 1842 became vacant with the demise of Rabbi Solomon Hirschel. After protracted deliberations, the selection committee presented four rabbinic candidates from Germany: Adler, Auerbach, H. Hirschfeld, and Hirsch. Apparently, Hirsch now considered himself important enough to compete with Adler for this promising position. It seems, however, that the selection committee failed to share Hirsch's opinion of himself, for Adler was elected by an overwhelming majority. This defeat must have rankled Hirsh's pride severely. Not only had he failed to obtain this high office, but only 2 out of the 134 votes had been cast for him, while Adler received 127.[56] Hirsch was thus compelled to remain in East Friesland until 1847, when he left for Nikolsburg to become the chief rabbi of Moravia and Austrian Silesia.

The six years that Hirsch spent in East Friesland were years of great ferment and agitation for German Jewry. The Reform movement became more assertive and aggressive in its demands for change, aiming to supersede traditional Judaism. Its spokesmen became emboldened to such an extent that they claimed to be the leaders and mentors of German Jewry. The conflict between Hirsch's former colleague Abraham Geiger and Rabbi Solomon T. Tiktin rent the Jewish community of Breslau. Geiger led the Reform faction of that community and challenged Tiktin, its traditionalist rabbi. Some liberal laymen organized themselves into societies advocating extreme reform of the Jewish religion. These included the Culturverein in Berlin, the Lesegesellschaft zur aufgehenden Morgenröthe, and the Verein der Reformfreunde in Frankfurt am Main. These sentiments were finally expressed in three successive synods of Reform rabbis which convened from 1844 to 1846 in Brunswick, Frankfurt, and Breslau. The issues discussed and the tenor of the discussions revealed that the Reform movement was now on a collision course with traditional

Judaism, and that the changes it advocated intended to transform Judaism in a most radical manner.

Unlike the endeavors by the early Reformers, the second-generation Reformers did not shrink from tampering with such fundamental laws as those regarding the Sabbath, circumcision, marriage, divorce, and even intermarriage. Theological concepts such as the belief in the coming of the Messiah, resurrection, and the return to Zion were considered anachronistic; Hebrew as the language of common prayer was all but eliminated. The shock and consternation caused by the synods was not limited to Orthodox circles. Even liberal Jews were overwhelmed by the extremism of the Reform leaders, and a wave of protest arose inside and outside of Germany.

The radicalization of the Reform movement extinguished the hopes of the more moderate to steer a middle course between Orthodoxy and Reform. Even Zachariah Frankel, rabbi of Dresden and one of the leading scholars of the time, whose progressive but moderate views were well known, was compelled to protest against the new trend of the Reform movement.

It is understandable that those with *erleuchtet religiös* leanings were forced to abandon their moderate positions and assume a more conservative and even militant posture. The radicalism of the Reformers convinced them that there was no longer room for moderation, dialogue, or colloquium, but that they had to align themselves with either the Orthodox or the Reform. Unable to accept the Reform position, they were compelled to side with the ultra-Orthodox in condemning the Reform propositions. They realized that the Reformers had gone too far to make any compromise possible.

Hirsch, too, could no longer maintain the aloofness and isolation he had assumed at Oldenburg. Thus, we find him at this period of his stay in East Friesland speaking out against the view of the Verein der Reformfreunde in Frankfurt and just as vigorously denouncing the synods, particularly the first, which convened at Brunswick. While his literary activity during his second post was limited, the little he wrote was no longer of a philosophical but rather of a polemic nature. During that period he published *Zweite Mitteilungen aus einem Briefwechsel über die neueste jüdische Literatur* (1844).[57] In it, Hirsch took issue with Samuel Holdheim's views as set forth in the treatise *Über die Autonomie der Rabbinen und das Prinzip der jüdischen Ehe: Ein Beitrag zur Verständigung über einige das Judentum betreffende Zeitfragen* (1843).[58] In this work, Holdheim argued that the law of the land must replace rabbinic jurisdiction based upon biblical and talmudic legislation even in matters of marriage and inheritance, which heretofore had fallen within the domain of the rabbis. He insisted that the rabbis confine themselves exclusively to the spiritual aspects of Judaism. Marriage, being a civil act, therefore came within the jurisdiction of the state. Employing the talmudic dictum *dina de-malkhuta dina*—the law of the government is binding and supersedes Jewish law in civil matters—Holdheim broadened it to eliminate Jewish law altogether. He demanded in most vigorous manner the denationalization of the Jewish religion and the extinction of any trace of particularism it may have contained.

Holdheim's *Autonomie* presented a challenge as well as a danger to traditional Judaism, which was already embattled from within and without. Indeed, it can be noted from Hirsch's polemic tone that he was deeply stirred by the *Autonomie*. He no longer preserved his former composure and tact in dealing with those with whom he disagreed. He avoided the mention of Holdheim's name and referred to him anonymously as the *Verfasser* (author). Furthermore, Hirsch compared Holdheim to the idolatrous and secessionist King Jeroboam I, who had brought disaster upon the Jewish people. Holdheim, like the Jeroboam of antiquity, aspired to confine Judaism to worship and matters of the spirit, thereby causing its disintegration, Hirsch opined.

Hirsch argued passionately that Judaism did not interfere with the Jews' loyalty to the state. On the contrary, Judaism demanded absolute compliance with the laws of the land. Indeed, the Jewish religion occasionally prevented a Jew from enjoying the advantages a state offered its citizens. Thus, a Jew may not be able to aspire to a governmental post that involved the violation of the Sabbath or of any other religious laws. This, however, did not adversely affect the state, but rather the Jew, and was, therefore, inconsequential. If the Jew's performance of a given task affected the vital interests of the state, as in the case of war or a similar national emergency, then the Jew was not only permitted to break the religious law but obliged to do so.

Hirsch's apologetic argument may not have displeased the

reactionaries, such as Ernest August, who were bent upon the constriction of rights for Jews. It is difficult to understand how young Jews desiring political, social, and economic freedom could accept Hirsch's viewpoint. Actually, Hirsch presented Judaism as a congenital disease that the Jew had to bear bravely while it prevented him from overexercising his abilities. He compared the Jews' inability to perform certain tasks or assume certain posts to a disabled or crippled person who was "more to be pitied than scorned." The state, Hirsch contended, should consider the fact that the Jew had not chosen his religion but been born into it and was therefore helpless to alter the situation.[59] That this view placed the Jew in a disadvantageous position is self-evident. It automatically closed to him all the avenues to political advancement, social progress, and economic improvement. Since Hirsch did not dare advocate that the government make accommodation for Jews whose religious observance may have conflicted with the careers they pursued, he condemned the Jews to perpetual de facto second-class citizenship by virtue of their religion.

Hirsch rejected Holdheim's contention that rabbinic juridicial autonomy be abolished. He dismissed the view that this case presented a conflict between Judaism and the non-Jewish state. Ordinarily, such conflict was nonexistent. Should, however, such conflict arise and the government decide to abolish this autonomy, the dictum of *dina de-malkhuta dina* would sanction the latter religiously.[60] Thus, the differences between Hirsch and Holdheim in this respect became a matter of semantics. While Holdheim wanted this principle to be employed by Jews internally and thus replace talmudic legislation by state law, Hirsch accepted it only when imposed by the government externally, by coercion. Strangely enough, Hirsch did not realize that his view entailed a grave danger, since it could have served as a strong argument for any reactionary government to abolish rabbinic autonomy and impose its will and laws upon the Jews by force. The apparently internal polemic blinded him to the dangers from the reactionary forces outside the Jewish community.

Moravia and Austrian Silesia

Hirsch's assumption of the post of chief rabbi of Moravia in 1847 could not have taken place at a less auspicious period in the history of this community. Shortly after his installation, the entire Austro-Hungarian Empire of which Moravia was part was convulsed by bloody revolts. Between January and April of 1848, most of Europe was rocked by a series of insurrections that threatened the political, social, and economic stability of the governing regimes. The thrones of the great empires, with the exception of Russia and Great Britain, quaked and tottered on the brink of collapse. The uprising of the people of Palermo against their ruler was followed by the successful revolt in Paris against Louis Philippe, which in turn sparked a chain reaction in other countries in which grievances had long been suppressed and discontent mounting. In the Habsburg Austro-Hungarian Empire, which constituted a conglomerate of diverse and multilingual nationalities, the revolutionary spark kindled outside its borders caused a veritable conflagration.

Within a short time this heretofore impregnable, solid, absolutist empire, so adroitly and ingeniously molded and dominated by Metternich, proved a combustible keg of powder from which its own architect was forced to flee. At first, certain palliatives were attempted by the imperial government ruled by conservative statesmen. When these proved limited and unsatisfactory, a general uprising broke out, compelling the emperor to flee Vienna and abandon it to the revolutionaries. To prevent an all-out explosion, or rather in an attempt to gain time, the government consented to convoke a Constituent Assembly to formulate a liberal constitution and institute a series of reforms. Soon, however, the conservatives vitiated all these liberal plans by having General Windischgrätz occupy Vienna, execute many of the radical leaders, and banish the Constituent Assembly to Kremsier, a town in Moravia. To mollify the rising acrimony, the epileptic and feebleminded Emperor Ferdinand I was forced to become the sacrificial lamb and abdicate in favor of his nephew, Francis Joseph I. With the accession to the throne of the new emperor, hopes rose anew in many circles, although the radicals and revolutionaries seemed more realistic and hence remained pessimistic. Indeed,

Francis Joseph did not immediately dissolve the Constituent Assembly at Kremsier. Its members continued their deliberations, worked on liberal legislation, and drew up a constitution. By March 1849, the conservatives under the leadership of Prince Felix zu Schwarzenberg felt themselves sufficiently entrenched to dissolve the Constituent Assembly at Kremsier and put an end to many hopes for progressive legislative reforms.

Needless to say, the Jews were among the most oppressed and discriminated-against minorities in the Habsburg Empire. Indeed, the *Toleranzpatent* (Edict of Toleration) issued in 1781 by Emperor Joseph II was never abrogated. This edict, which had lifted certain restrictions harking back to the Middle Ages, led some enlightened Jews, notably Wessely, to believe that a new era was about to begin for the Jews in the Austrian Empire. This new era, however, was slow in coming. Metternich's attitude toward the Jews was closer to that of Empress Maria Theresa than to that of Joseph II.[61] The Jews' domicile remained curtailed and circumscribed, and in Moravian cities such as Brün and Olmütz they were only permitted to stay overnight. Ghettos and *Judenstrassen* existed everywhere, special taxation on Jews was most oppressive, and there was hardly a move, transaction, or purchase that was not taxable. Most humiliating and inhumane of all was the law restricting marriages among Jews. Like Pharaoh of old, the Austrian rulers were concerned lest the Jews increase, and the law decreed that only the eldest son of a family could get married.

Indeed, not all Jews in the Habsburg Empire, particularly in Moravia, had been grateful to Joseph II for his *Toleranzpatent*, especially for the provision on education which they considered deleterious, since it paved the way for their acculturation and eventual assimilation. The Orthodox elements at that time, as in Hirsch's time, had been resolutely opposed to this dubious privilege. However, they had all been crushed by the oppressive legislation, humiliating restrictions, and burdensome taxations. It was therefore to be expected that some Jews, particularly the acculturated and educated, should become leading spokesmen for the revolt in Vienna. The liberal Rabbi Isaac Noah Mannheimer together with members of the Catholic and Protestant clergy eulogized the victims, many Jews among them, who perished in the revolt. The Reichstag meeting at Vienna in July 1848 included

some Jewish deputies: Adolf Fischhof, Joseph Goldmark, Mannheimer, Ignatz Kuranda, and Moritz Hartmann. Understandably,
when the Constituent Assembly was moved to Kremsier it had on
its agenda the issue of Jewish emancipation, civil rights, and liberties. Among the members of the Constituent Assembly at Kremsier were five Jews: Fischhof, Goldmark, Mannheimer, Abraham
Halpern, and Rabbi Dov Baer Meisels. Although the Constituent
Assembly of Kremsier was dissolved and the constitution it had
drawn rejected, the new emperor residing at Olmütz granted
equal political and civil rights to all citizens of the realm, including
Jews.

The data about the extent of Hirsch's involvement in the events
of those turbulent days in Moravia are sketchy and dubious. According to his biographers, he presented a memorandum demanding the abolition of the restrictions on Jews. With characteristic
hyperbole and simplistic overstatement, one biographer claims
that "it was mainly through this memorandum, which Hirsch put
before the Reichsrat, that Jewish emancipation was secured in
Austria."[62] It was Hirsch who addressed Emperor Francis Joseph
I for granting equal rights to the Austrian Jews, and "the new
monarch was deeply moved by Hirsch's address."[63]

That this is an exaggeration needs no elaboration. One has only
to consider that when this upheaval was rocking the Austrian
Empire, Hirsch was practically a newcomer from another country,
making his revolutionary activities highly improbable. Furthermore, judging from his docility toward the governmental authorities in other places, such sudden audacity and daring hardly seems
consistent with his character. Nor must one forget that he was the
nominal head of an ultraconservative community who was walk-
ing gingerly with the authorities and anxious to avoid all possible
entanglements. As the chief rabbi of such a constituency, Hirsch
could hardly afford to become the champion of liberalism. Considering Hirsch's attitude objectively, it appears that he viewed the
Constituent Assembly at Kremsier as he did emancipation in general, namely, beneficial to Jews provided they did not misuse the
privilege. Undoubtedly Hirsch was no revolutionary, and since the
parliament at Kremsier was initially tolerated by the emperor, he
had no qualms about presenting a memorandum on behalf of the
Jews. There was nothing improper about the tone of the memo-

randum. It was so plaintive, imploring, and beseeching that even the most absolutist monarch could hardly have misconstrued it as rebellious or demanding. As far back as March 1848 Hirsch had addressed an "appeal to his Christian brothers of the same mother-land," *Ein Wort zur Zeit an unsere christlichen Brüder im gemein-samen Vaterland,*[64] to include their Jewish compatriots in their quest for freedom and equality. This appeal was likewise written in a most suppliant and solicitous manner that was intended to evoke sympathy and compassion.

Hirsch's timidity and subservience to the emperor and the authorities during the sociopolitical tempest of 1848 can be seen from an open letter he addressed to the Jews of Moravia. In it he pleaded with his coreligionists to be discreet, patient, and quiet. He adjured them not to show any discontent and to restrain the members of their families, particularly the youth, from any overt or covert act that might be construed to be disloyalty.[65] The assertion that Hirsch's memorandum secured Jewish emancipation in Austria is quite exaggerated.[66] The new emperor, whose government had just suppressed a widespread uprising and who was still occupied with its aftermath, particularly in Hungary, could ill afford to antagonize his loyal subjects needlessly. The vast masses of subservient Jews hardly constituted a threat to his regime, and a magnanimous promise of equality was a cheap price to pay under the circumstances.

Certain political considerations, not Hirsch's eloquent and compassionate pleas, induced the emperor to grant the Jews civil and political rights. If eloquence and efforts *had* played a role, which is doubtful, the credit should go to the influential Jews of Austria, some of whose names have been mentioned. Undoubtedly, Mann-heimer's passionate speeches, highly patriotic in tone and humanitarian in spirit, delivered in the halls of the parliament and in the streets of Vienna, had a far greater impact than the words of the new chief rabbi of a rural non-Germanic province. Hirsch's addressing the emperor at Olmütz must not be considered a major historic event. As the titular religious head of Moravian Jewry, he was expected to convey the good wishes and salutations as well as the loyalty of the Jews of the province to the new emperor. The fact that the new rabbi, unlike his predecessors, spoke flawless German may have pleased Francis Joseph, who wanted German to be the dominant language of his multilingual empire.

It should be pointed out that Hirsch grew apprehensive about the newly won freedom and equality for his flock. Jews, freed from the traveling and domicile restrictions, took advantage of the new opportunities to move to different localities. As a result, many Jewish communities dwindled and could no longer maintain themselves. Since it was no longer obligatory to belong to a particular community, many Jews grew indifferent, and adherence became a matter of choice. Similarly, with the abolition of special Jewish taxes, many Jews failed to pay for the upkeep of the Jewish community.

It is noteworthy that all this happened rapidly and that the effects were noticed by Hirsch at once. He appealed to the Jews to continue their contributions to the Jewish community voluntarily as they had been compelled to do by force before.[67]

Internal Difficulties

The difficulties Hirsch experienced in Moravia as a result of the political storm in the Habsburg Empire pale in significance in comparison with those he encountered as chief rabbi. Moravia, though nominally and politically part of central European Austria, was socially, economically, and culturally closer to eastern Europe, and its Jewish inhabitants were religiously and culturally nearer to the Polish Jews, whom Hirsch had always abhorred, than to German Jews. Yiddish was their current language and served as the language of instruction in the *hadarim* and *yeshivot*. From early childhood the pupils were drilled in the study of the Talmud, which was deepened and broadened by the *pilpul* dialectic in adolescence. Even the study of Bible and Aggadah was looked down on as a symptom of Enlightenment.

The Moravian Jews, like their coreligionists in nearby Bohemia, were strongly opposed to the Haskalah, and their rabbis and communal leaders watched vigilantly for any manifestation thereof. Joseph II's *Toleranzpatent* was viewed by many Jews as an evil decree to be circumvented in every possible way. The influence of Rabbi Ezekiel Landau, who had condemned Mendelssohn and Wessely, was still strong, and in many circles his views remained unchallenged. The extreme efforts of Herz Homberg, with the assistance of the government, to secularize and assimilate the Jews

met with great resistance by the Jewish population. Despite all
efforts to integrate the Jews of Moravia and neighboring Bohemia,
they clung steadfastly and tenaciously to their traditionalist beliefs
and way of life.

Still, Haskalah views infiltrated into some segments of the Jewish population, particularly the young and well-to-do. They spread
slowly and surreptitiously, but the ranks of the Maskilim gradually
increased. Moreover, the Frankist heresy found some adherents
and sympathizers in this bastion of traditionalism. The fact that
Jacob Frank had spent some time in Moravia could not be ignored,
since his influence had survived him in this region. The fissures
opened by the Enlightenment, Frankism, and a host of other general and local factors paved the road for the spread of the Reform
movement. The proximity to Germany and the fact that the
younger acculturated and semiacculturated Jews were conversant
with German facilitated the dissemination of the Reform ideology
emanating from Germany in the German language.

All these rumblings for progress and Reform notwithstanding,
the vast majority of Moravian Jews in the 1840s remained traditionalist both in outlook and in practice. Many of the communal
leaders, however, advocated a change in the rabbinic leadership.
To forestall an antitraditionalist revolt, avert a schism between the
Orthodox and the liberals, and prevent the disintegration of that
community, they recommended a chief rabbi who in addition to
his talmudic knowledge and piety would be sufficiently modern,
cultured, and eloquent to impress the potential defectors from
traditional Judaism as well as the authorities and the non-Jewish
population with whom the Jews came in contact. This problem
emerged with the demise in 1842 of Rabbi Naḥum Treibitsch,
chief rabbi of Moravia and Austrian Silesia. For five years the
communal leaders could not reach a decision, since the opposition
to a modern chief rabbi, even though he was circumspectly pious,
was exceedingly strong. While many conceded rationally a need
for a modern German-speaking rabbi, some could not become
psychologically reconciled to this new image. For the more conservative elements in Moravia it was difficult to accede that the
sacred office of its chief religious leader should bow to the exigencies of the Zeitgeist. Nikolsburg was the seat of many illustrious
traditionalist rabbis, including Yom Tov Lipmann Heller and Mor-

decai Benet. It was in this city that Rabbi Shmuel Shmelke Horowitz, leading disciple of Rabbi Dov Baer of Mesritsch, had expounded the teachings of Hasidism, and many laymen were still
well versed in Talmud and rabbinic literature.[68]

By 1847, the decision was finally reached to elect Hirsch to this
post. Apparently by this time it became known that he had associated himself wholeheartedly with the traditionalists against
the Reformers. His traditionalist affirmation most likely pacified
the conservatives, while the progressives were impressed by his
florid German style. It seems that at this period Hirsch did not yet
alarm the Reform camp, since his installation was greeted and
praised by Isaac Noah Mannheimer, the leading Reform preacher
of Vienna. Indeed, it is possible to argue that Mannheimer's greet-
ing, aside from being a tactful gesture, celebrated Hirsch's election as a significant dent in this bastion of ultratraditionalism.

It is significant that Hirsch accepted this post, since, as it turned
out, it was one of the gravest errors in his life. As already mentioned, Hirsch had been very cautious about presenting himself as
a candidate for an old, well-established traditionalist post. In Oldenburg, he had declined such suggestions by Graetz regarding
Posen and Wollstein, opting for a smaller and less lucrative community in northern Germany. Had the position of Moravia been
offered to him then, it is most likely that he would have rejected
it. However, a number of new elements provoked his new attitude. First was his dissatisfaction with his role as rabbi in the
apathetic and eroding small Jewish communities of northwestern
Germany. It has already been pointed out that he had hoped to
become chief rabbi of London and leave the newly assumed position in East Friesland. The radicalization of the Reform movement
during the forties may have also impelled him to enter the larger
arena and participate in the battle instead of being a mere specta-
tor or follower. Moravia, a most prestigious post, may have offered
him just such an opportunity.

It is unknown whether Hirsch still had reservations and anxie-
ties about his scholastic shortcomings similar to those he had had
in Oldenburg. If he did, he apparently believed that he could
counterbalance them with his positive qualifications. By this time,
he had more than a decade and a half of experience in the rabbinate. He had published the *Neunzehn Briefe*, *Horeb*, and many

pamphlets which had evoked a great deal of interest and comment in Jewish communities at large. He was an eloquent speaker, his German was perfect, and his general knowledge was more than ample to impress the provincial Jews of Moravia, particularly their rabbis, whose German was corrupt and laced with Yiddishisms. It is also possible that Hirsch, who had continued to pore over the Talmud, now had less trepidation about his deficiencies in this area than previously.

It seems, however, that Hirsch miscalculated. Neither his background nor his mentality qualified him for the leadership of a community of that nature. In the area of Talmud and rabbinics, not only the local rabbis under his jurisdiction but even the laymen towered high above him. The latter, who had devoted their entire lives to the acquisition of the intricacies of rabbinic literature, were master dialecticians in this field. Hirsch's expositions of the Talmud appeared simplistic to them and abecedarian. To avoid embarrassment, Hirsch discontinued the traditional halakhic discourses that had been held by his predecessors.[69] As customary, these discourses were followed by a discussion in which the scholarly audience participated. Many of the theses proposed by the chief rabbi were challenged, arguments were advanced, and authorities quoted. It was the task of the chief rabbi to defend his views and disprove those of his challengers. In the past, these discourses had been the high points of the season, anticipated by everyone, including the unlearned, as great intellectual sporting events to be subjects of discussion long after they were over. For Hirsch, such events were traumatic and to be avoided at all cost. Not only did he abhor this type of *pilpul* dialectic, but he was inadequate to match, let alone surpass, the knowledge of many of his listeners. Such discourses would have meant his absolute defeat and humiliation in front of his flock. The rabbis and lay scholars who were aware of his shortcomings eagerly anticipated such contests, but Hirsch robbed them of their inevitable victory. Though disappointed, the rabbis and scholars attained some measure of triumph. The very fact that Hirsch had to discontinue these discourses was sufficient proof of his inadequacy in Jewish scholarship.

Hirsch instead attempted to stress subjects in which he considered himself knowledgeable, such as the exposition of the Pentateuch and Psalms. But these subjects, despite their importance, were not then viewed among scholarly Jews as deserving the attention of the scholar unless they served as a springboard for rabbinic dialectics. Ordinarily, they were taught to young children or pursued by the untutored and underprivileged who were unable to rise to a higher intellectual level. Thus, when Hirsch began to expound upon them in his ornate German from the standpoint of his speculative etymology and philosophy, he was ridiculed and derided. His new system of study sparked many witticisms and humorous remarks throughout the province. In this context, one of the *dayyanim* caustically remarked: "Vor Zeiten hat man Gemore gelernt und Thillim gesagt, jetzt sagt man Gemore und lernt Thillim."[70] ("Heretofore they used to study Talmud and recite psalms; presently, however, they recite Talmud and study psalms"). Such a frivolous attitude exhibited by the local rabbis and scholars toward the chief rabbi could not have engendered a deep respect for him from the rest of the community.

Not all the difficulties Hirsch encountered came from his scholastic shortcomings; many of them evolved from his attitude and personality. Accustomed to the small and apathetic communities of northwestern Germany, where his responsibility had been primarily toward the ruler of the province, Hirsch continued to assert his authority over those under his jurisdiction. He expected that he would be the sole arbiter in all religious, educational, and communal matters, and that the local rabbis and religious functionaries would unequivocally abide by his decisions.[71]

Much to his chagrin, Moravia was not Oldenburg or East Friesland. The rabbis here were scholars, and even the laymen were highly opinionated and committed Jews. Even those who were willing to recognize Hirsch as the titular chief rabbi refused to accede to him in practice, since in their eyes he was grossly inferior. His demands for recognition and respect were countered with resentment, lack of cooperation, and, most devastating of all, derision. At times, they tried to embarrass him by posing certain questions he could not answer or whose humor he could not fathom. As mentioned, they called him a *siddur lamdan*, a "prayer book scholar." Some rabbis adamantly refused to show him even the most elementary courtesies. Thus, when Rabbi Solomon Quetsch of Leipnick, nominally under Hirsch's jurisdiction, came to Nikolsburg, he refused to even pay Hirsch the customary courtesy call, thus showing his utter contempt for the new *Landes-rabbiner.*[72]

Hirsch not only antagonized the rabbis but the other Jews in the community as well. He showed an utter lack of sensitivity for the feelings of the people to whom he had to minister. His arrogance, his disdain for eastern European Jews and their mode of life, coupled with his *erleuchtet religiös* background, hardly endeared him to them. The causes may not have been major from a technical, halakhic standpoint, but they constituted a source of irritation to many tradition-oriented and custom-observing Jews. Thus, they resented his manner of dress, which suggested a Reformist image, and objected to his performing weddings in the synagogue, considered by many rabbis to be a Christian custom adopted by the Reformers. Among those opposing the practice were the highly influential rabbis Moses Sofer and Moses Schick. Hirsch ignored these objections in the very heart of the pietistic Moravian Jewry. At a time when women were permitted in the synagogue only in the women's section, he let the bride's mother accompany her daughter within the synagogue proper. His address to the bride and groom at the marriage ceremony was objected to as an unwarranted innovation.[73]

It was not easy for an acculturated German Jew to live up to the high standards of piety and modesty set by the Moravian Jews, but for a chief rabbi such accommodations should have been a small sacrifice indeed. But Hirsch apparently refused to make it. He continued to offend them by promenading with his wife through the streets of Nikolsburg, a thing inconceivable of pious Jews, particularly rabbis. Many of the elderly people still remembered that when the former chief rabbi, Mordecai Benet, appeared in the street, all women would vanish from sight. It was therefore hard for these people to accept the fact that Hirsch, who appeared to them not much different from a Reform rabbi, should occupy the seat of the saintly Rabbi Benet.[74]

These constant irritations mounted until resentment against Hirsch could no longer be restrained and occasionally surfaced, becoming exceedingly vocal. One Yom Kippur eve when Hirsch disregarded custom by addressing the congregation not before but after Kol Nidre, he was publicly and loudly rebuked by one of the leading elders of the community. Apparently, this man could no longer endure Hirsch's highhanded disregard for the hallowed customs of Moravian Jewry and he protested most vigorously. The embarrassed and irritated Hirsch left the synagogue right then and there, and although the protestor was penalized he won the sympathy of many.[75]

This and similar incidents convinced Hirsch that his acceptance of this rabbinic post had been a most unfortunate decision. While by the standards of Oldenburg and East Friesland he may have been considered an Orthodox rabbi, he found the criteria in Moravia quite different. Had Hirsch been more flexible and less arrogant he might have had some success here, but apparently he was not. It is noteworthy that the liberal Mannheimer, in more worldly Vienna, had sufficient insight to realize that radical reforms feasible in Germany had to be modified in accordance with the social, religious, and cultural requirements of the Viennese Jews. The traditionalist Hirsch was apparently unwilling or unable to make any such allowances.

From a literary standpoint, the Moravian period was for Hirsch absolutely barren. The unsettled situation apparently gave him neither the time nor the peace of mind to think and write. It seemed the longer he was away from Oldenburg the less he wrote. He had concentrated all his efforts on becoming a leading rabbi and communal leader, and in this respect he had failed. Indeed, he had attempted to organize a union of Jewish communities or *Landessynagoge*.[76] His difficulties in gaining respect and cooperation in his day-to-day dealings nullified all his endeavors, including this one.

After four years of frustration, Hirsch decided to leave his post, which carried the glorified title *Oberlandesrabbiner von Mähren und Schlesien* but whose actual significance was far more prosaic and modest. According to the definition as formulated by the authorities, its bearer was supposed to pray diligently, preach, and watch over the school and community ("im fleissigen Beten, Predigen, Bewachen der Schule und der Gemeinde").[77] Apparently some members of the community tried to influence Hirsch to stay and may have offered some financial inducements, but Hirsch knew that these well-intentioned people did not represent the sentiments of the vast majority, and unable to cope with his intractable opponents or endure the unhospitable climate about him, he declined to alter his decision.[78] Judging by the fact that his next post was small and bestowed no prestige, honors, or titles, it becomes apparent that Hirsch's departure from Moravia was virtually a rout.

Frankfurt am Main

The extent of Hirsch's anguish in Moravia can best be appreciated by his willingness to exchange the highly prestigious office and title of *Landesrabbiner,* to which he had been accustomed for more than two decades, for the humble post of rabbi of a small group of dissidents in Frankfurt am Main. There must have been, however, an additional factor that induced him to accept such an insignificant position after having served as chief rabbi in three important Jewish communities and having gained a measure of distinction and recognition. It seems that at forty-three Hirsch reached the conclusion that an *erleuchtet religiös* outlook toward Judaism could not be implemented in an already-existing, struc- tured community. He realized from his own experiences that an existing community has an old, established pattern which is ori- ented either to the right or to the left. To accept a post in another structured community would only entangle him in problems simi- lar to those he had departed. He would thus be forced into the uncomfortable dilemma of either accommodating his viewpoint and mode of life to the exigencies of the structure, or of shattering the structure by defying it and imposing his will and outlook upon it. Both horns of the dilemma were unpalatable as well as unrealiz- able.

As evidenced by his traumatic experience in Moravia, Hirsch was aware that he was not constituted of the flexible fiber required for compromise and accommodation. To defy the established pat- tern of any given community meant to court displeasure, resent- ment, and even open disobedience. The only possible solution was to form his own community, which he could then structure and mold to his own image. Needless to say, such a venture for a man of forty-three with a wife, five sons, and five daughters was hazard- ous;[79] it was also his last chance to achieve fulfillment. Unable to evolve an acceptable theoretical Weltanschauung for Judaism in the context of the exigencies of his time, he hoped to at least present a model in practice. It is possible that had he not been compelled by the agonizing circumstances to flee Moravia, his marked caution, prudence, and circumspection might have inclined him to follow the line of least resistance and forgo such a risk. However, forced to look for a new post and fearful of encountering similar difficulties, he apparently opted for the chance to form a community that would be in consonance with his views. This opportunity presented itself when he was offered the religious leadership of the Israelitische Religionsgesellschaft in Frankfurt am Main in 1851.

To understand the significance of this organization, a brief excursus into the Frankfurt Jewish community would be helpful. This was one of the oldest, most populous, and most important Jewish communities in Germany, whose known history goes back to the twelfth century and nondocumented history to centuries before. As all Jewish communities, Frankfurt am Main was solidly Orthodox, and many of its rabbis were renowned for their piety and scholarship—among them Rabbi Meir Schiff (known as the Maharam Schiff), Rabbi Aaron Samuel Kaidanover, Rabbi Isaiah Horowitz or the Shelah, Rabbi Jacob Joshua Falk, and Rabbi Pinḥas Horowitz.

Though serving the community at different times, the task of these rabbis remained essentially the same and their occupation was primarily the study of Torah. Rabbi Pinḥas Horowitz, however, already witnessed the first cracks in this heretofore impregnable fortress of tradition. Much to his chagrin, he noticed that some members of his community were attracted to the vernal Haskalah movement, subscribing and reading the *Biur* and the *Ha-Meassef.* His authority and denunciations did little to stem their interest, much less eradicate it.

It is noteworthy that this centuries-old, tradition-bound community became one of the strongholds of the Reform movement in the nineteenth century and served as the terrain for one of the fiercest clashes fought between the traditionalists and Reformers. The trend toward Reform had modest beginnings in Frankfurt. In 1804, a small Jewish school, which became known as the Philanthropin, was opened for poor children with a total enrollment of two orphans. Headed by such dedicated headmasters as Siegmund Geisenheimer and Michael Hess, it became one of the most formidable educational institutions and the model for others of its kind throughout Germany. The headmasters and some of its influential teachers such as Joseph Johlson and Michael Creizenach, were imbued with the spirit of Reform, and their zeal in the dissemination of its ideas was all-consuming. They did not confine themselves to the teaching of Judaic and secular subjects, but also instituted a special chapel, the *Andachtssaal* (devotion hall), for services. The sermons were preached in German, special services were conducted, and confirmations were held, along with similar Reform innovations. Officially, the Philanthropin was only a school for children and not a communal synagogue. In practice, however, it was attended by many adults who were attracted to its subtle innovations. As a result, this school became the focal point for Reform in Frankfurt, and its influence spread beyond its nominal confines.

The Jewish community, *(Gemeinde)* as such remained as heretofore under the religious direction of an Orthodox rabbi, although many members of the community were no longer Orthodox.

Gradually, however, the number of the un-Orthodox accelerated sharply. Many of these were either former students or parents or friends who had come under the influence of the Philanthropin; others had attended German Gymnasia or been tutored in secular subjects. These Reform-oriented Jews began to demand changes and innovations which shocked the traditionalists, particularly the communal rabbi, Solomon Abraham Trier, a former delegate to the Napoleonic Sanhedrin. Since the law promulgated by the Senate left all religious matters to the Jewish community, disallowing any interference from the outside, including the state, the demands for the modernization of Jewish religious life was considered an exclusively Jewish affair. The advocates of Reform now felt entitled to certain concessions, among which was the request for a German-speaking rabbi.

Far more vociferous and more militant was the already-mentioned Verein der Reformfreunde, a group of laymen headed by M. A. Stern of Göttingen, who were impatient with the progress of the Reform rabbis, whom they accused of being reticent, accommodational, and expediential. According to them, even the liberal rabbis lacked the strength of their conviction to pursue vigorously and uncompromisingly the struggle for reforming Judaism. The members of this group demanded the open abolition of the ceremonial, dietary, and ritual laws, including circumcision, the repudiation of the Talmud as an authoritative corpus juris and of its views as having obligatory power, and denial of the belief in the coming of the Messiah.

These radical demands were decried not only in traditionalist circles but also among the liberals; even leading Reform rabbis such as Geiger, Holdheim, and David Einhorn opposed them. Indeed, some of these objectors were more concerned with the bad timing of the demands than with their content, fearing that such extreme demands might discredit the entire Reform movement and alienate many of its sympathizers. Among the many traditionalist protestors were Hirsch, Ettlinger, and the octogenarian Rabbi Trier of Frankfurt. The debate over the requirement of circumcision as a sine qua non in Judaism was most heated and acrimonious, extending beyond the limits of the Jewish community and reaching out to the Senate for a decision on this issue. Despite his age, Trier was in the forefront of this battle, and he enlisted the support of many leading European rabbis and scholars, among them Zunz, Samuel David Luzzatto, and Solomon Yehudah Rapoport. The opinion of Hirsch, then in East Friesland, was vigorously sharp and unequivocal, declaring the members of the Verein der Reformfreunde as apostates who deserved to be recognized and treated as such.[80]

Although the latter were a minority in the *Gemeinde* and their views were considered extreme, their audacious stand and public assertions, along with the fact that they had many overt and covert sympathizers, filled the traditionalists with grave apprehension. The latter could not fail to realize that their own religious influence was waning, and the Reformers' domination of the *Gemeinde* was simply a matter of time.

The well-justified fear of the traditionalists, however, became a reality sooner than they had anticipated. In view of the fact that Trier was advanced in age, the *Gemeinde* elected Leopold Stein as his associate. Stein was one of the most outspoken opponents of the Verein der Reformfreunde and was known for his polemics

with the spokesman of that group, Stern. It is possible that this fact
was a consideration in his candidacy. As an opponent of the Reform extremists, the leaders of the *Gemeinde* expected that he
would be accepted by the traditionalists and by Trier. As a modern, German-speaking rabbi, Stein would also please the growing
number of liberals in the community. It now seems that the community's leadership miscalculated by misjudging the reaction of
the traditionalists, and even more so by underestimating the courage and stamina of Trier. Notwithstanding his opposition to the
Verein der Reformfreunde, Stein was known to have been a Reform rabbi in Burgkunstadt, Bavaria; and while his views were
moderate, he was a Reformer nevertheless. Trier saw in Stein's
election not only an affront to himself, but a virtual attack on and
usurpation of the Frankfurt rabbinate, with its glorious tradition
of famous Orthodox rabbis. Unable to dissuade the leadership
from their course, Trier resigned in protest at the age of eighty-
seven; Stein thus became the rabbi of Frankfurt.

Trier's resignation and Stein's installation had a shattering effect
upon the traditionalists of that city. Unlike the Reformers, who
pressed vigorously ahead, the traditionalists were disorganized
and confused. As long as the rabbi of the *Gemeinde* had been an
Orthodox rabbi, they had tolerated the steady encroachment of
the liberals; now when this self-deceptive façade was gone, they
had no course of action. Since the election of a rabbi was an
internal Jewish affair, they could not expect government intervention, nor did state law permit secession from the general Jewish
community and the establishment of a separate one.

Tension in the community mounted and tempers rose high. The
Reform synods which followed (one of them meeting in Frankfurt)
and the revolutionary fever that gripped Europe in 1848 only
exacerbated the feelings of the traditionalists and deepened their
anxiety. Nevertheless, in 1849 a small group of traditionalists decided to act and petitioned the Senate to permit them the establishment of a special communal organization. The Senate, while
disallowing the formation of a separate community, granted them
the right to organize a religious association which became known
as the Israelitische Religionsgesellschaft.[81]

Not many joined the newly formed association. It was an audacious step which implied a kernel of secession, and the close ties

formed by many Frankfurt Jews through generations did not permit such a radical venture. Many traditionalists were therefore in
a quandary as to which was a more exorbitant price to pay—to
preserve Jewish tradition by sacrificing ethnic and communal soli-
darity, or vice versa? Thus in 1850 the Israelitische Religionsgesellschaft had only about sixty members, increasing to approximately one hundred by the following year.

The vast majority of the members of the new association, while
opposed to Reform, was not ultraconservative. They, too, wanted
a modern, cultured, German-speaking rabbi whose eloquence
would attract the youth, but whose views would conform to the
basic tenets of Jewish tradition. This is best illustrated by the fact
that the first choice for rabbi of the Israelitische Religionsgesellschaft was Michael Sachs,[82] whose views were moderate and scholarly and whose actions were those of a middle-of-the-roader. As
rabbi in Berlin, Sachs had attracted many followers of Holdheim
and combatted the latter's radicalism. Sachs, however, was not an
Orthodox rabbi in the sense that Trier or any of the previous
rabbis of Frankfurt were. That Sachs should have caught the imagination of the members of the Israelitische Religionsgesellschaft
tells a great deal about their own views and leanings. It was only
after Sachs had declined the offer that Hirsch was invited to serve
as rabbi of the association, a post which he gladly accepted in
1851.[83]

This traditional but at the same time progressive outlook of the
majority of the association did not displease Hirsch. For the first
time he dealt with Jews who like him were *erleuchtet religiös,*
committed to tradition and yet open-minded to the exigencies of
the time. They were of the same milieu and spoke the same language. Unlike the Jews of Moravia, many of whom had an eastern
European mentality, his new congregants were German Jews
whose roots were sunk deep in German soil and culture and whose
mode of life did not differ from his own. He was not compelled to
make frivolous concessions in order to appease potential rivals or
frustrated contenders. Nor was he in mortal terror of being humi-
liated by boastful talmudic scholars bent on trapping him with
their casuistry. The fact that this group was small and unstructured
was a great asset for him. The unifying factor of the association was
rather a negative one—their opposition to Reform. However, they

had not developed a crystallized positive ideology by which to live and one they could present and propagate. It was this vacuum that Hirsch hoped to fill.

But Frankfurt of the 1850s was not Oldenburg of two decades earlier. Confronted with organized Reform institutions and militant elements, Hirsch had to devote his time to practical matters rather than to theory, to action rather than to abstract philosophies. However, Hirsch demonstrated his ability to rise to the new challenges.

Already at Oldenburg Hirsch had evinced great interest in the modernization of Jewish education and the role it was destined to play in the changing times. In Frankfurt, he realized that education could also be employed most effectively as a vehicle for the dissemination of new ideas. The success achieved by the Reformers in Frankfurt was in considerable measure due to their educational institution, the Philanthropin. Hirsch therefore viewed education as the highest priority on the list of the Israelitische Religionsgesellschaft and advocated the immediate establishment of a modern traditionalist school, notwithstanding the fact that the religious services were held in humble quarters rented in a private house. He immediately began to organize the school on the basis of *Torah im derekh eretz*, the harmonization of Jewish and secular disciplines. The school, known as Unterrichtsanstalt der Israelitischen Religionsgesellschaft, was opened on April 1, 1853.[84]

Not every member of the association was happy with Hirsch's venture. Some disagreed with his priorities and wished to see the construction of a synagogue before a school; others disagreed with his new, modernistic approach to Jewish education. Nevertheless, these differences were not crucial and did not impede Hirsch's action. The association was too young and ideologically amorphous, and those who differed did not do so as outright adversaries. However, Hirsch encountered opposition from the Reform elements who sensed that Hirsch intended to beat them at their own game. The first sign of sensitivity in this respect was displayed by Michael Hess, headmaster of the Philanthropin, who attacked Hirsch's educational project in an anonymous article in the *Frankfurter Journal*. Hirsch immediately responded in an article published in the *Frankfurter Intelligenzblatt*.[85] Perceptively, Hirsch pointed out that Hess's criticism had arisen not because Hirsch's school was insufficiently modern, but rather because it was *too* modern. Had the new school been less mindful of secular subjects than religious ones, Hess would not have been overly exercised since it would not have constituted competition for the Philanthropin. It was the modernity of Hirsch's school that provoked the attack. The polemics between Hirsch and Hess gave the new school as well as its parent organization the necessary publicity. The fact that a leading liberal attacked Hirsch's school made this institution less objectionable to the ultra-Orthodox members of the association. On the other hand, Hirsch's masterful replies, reflecting his understanding of modern culture and humanism, made it more acceptable to the more acculturated elements in the community.

Hirsch's efforts seemed to succeed. A grant from the Rothschilds enabled the Israelitische Religionsgesellschaft to erect their own synagogue, thus presenting a threat to the general *Gemeinde*. This apprehension was soon voiced by the latter's rabbi, Leopold Stein, who published a pamphlet denouncing the Israelitische Religionsgesellschaft as a most reactionary association wishing to turn back the clock of progress and revert to the Middle Ages. Stein's attack on the association, like Hess's criticism of its school, only sharpened Hirsch's wit and emboldened his aggressive polemics. In reply, Hirsch issued in 1854 a pamphlet entitled *Die Religion im Bunde mit dem Fortschritt* (*S* 3:489–530—Religion allied with progress), and significantly signed it "v. einem Schwarzen" ("from a reactionary"). In it, he showed himself a master polemicist whose biting sarcasm was as charming as it was devastating. It was not only a defense of the association he was heading, but an attack on the ideology of the Reform movement in general. Thus, Hirsch's position vis-à-vis the *Gemeinde* as well as the Reform movement became sharply drawn, and the seeds of the eventual schism were planted.

Literary Activity and Polemics

Hirsch's first years at Frankfurt were marked by undaunted determination, unrelenting effort, and great courage to transform the Israelitische Religionsgesellschaft from a humble local association into a strong, affluent, and influential organization of national importance. Within a relatively short time after his arrival, he proved himself to be not only a gifted orator capable of inspiring an audience of divergent opinions, but also a talented organizer able to attract many new members, some of whom were substantially well-to-do.

To augment his ranks, Hirsch displayed a remarkably flexible and pragmatic approach to the religious qualification of membership. He distinguished between one's conduct in private life and that in the organized Jewish community. The fact that one was not observant, even to the extent of flagrantly violating the dietary laws and desecrating the Sabbath, did not bar him ipso facto from being a member of the traditionalist Israelitische Religionsgesellschaft. Only the uncircumcised and those who had not married in accordance with Jewish law were excluded from membership; the other transgressors could even be elected to the governing board of the association.[86] Hirsch thus transferred the emphasis of the time-hallowed criterion of traditional Judaism—observance of the Law—from the individual to the community. Neither the individual's views nor his personal conduct decided his religious status, only his willingness to belong to a community which, as a community, was committed to the standards of traditional Judaism. His dual standard was not only novel but revolutionary, since it went far beyond tolerance of the transgressors in the hope that they would eventually repent and fully accept the yoke of Torah and *mitzvot*. Hirsch's act was tantamount to an endorsement of an incongruous but common concept in his day—the *Schinkenorthodoxie*, ham-eating Orthodoxy. It is hardly conceivable that rabbis of a previous age, or even of that time in eastern Europe, would have concurred with Hirsch's elastic definition of Jewishness. While halakhically a nonobservant Jew does not cease being Jewish or a part of Jewry, he was never accorded the status Hirsch now tacitly bestowed on him—the ability to violate Jewish law and simultaneously belong to or even hold office in the traditionalist bastion of the Israelitische Religionsgesellschaft. Moreover, by implication if not by intent, Hirsch did exactly what his opponents, the Reformers, had done—localize Judaism within the synagogue.

The view that the Torah had become a community matter rather than an individual one was expressed subsequently in his commentary: "Not to individuals, but to the Jewish community as a whole has God entrusted His Torah as a heritage, for only the community lives on forever and only the community has means for everything" (*CD* 33:4).

The extent to which religious idealism, pragmatic considerations, and efforts to attract the wealthy nonobservant Jews who had a romantic attachment for the authentic traditional synagogue were factors in Hirsch's ideological differentiation using these dual standards is difficult to determine. It is at least doubtful whether lacking the financial assistance of these nonobservant traditionalists he would have been able to accomplish in a short time what he had set out to do.

Unlike Moravia, where he had been distrusted and hampered in all his ventures, in Frankfurt Hirsch enjoyed free rein. The traditionalists were a disorganized minority having only one thing in common—their dislike for the *Gemeinde*. They were grateful to Hirsch, who within a few years had transformed their small group into a wealthy, prestigious organization, and he, therefore, had greater authority than traditionalist rabbis in other communities. Hirsch could therefore ignore or override any objections raised against his activities. Nor did he have to be concerned about the opinion of other traditionalist rabbis in Germany. By this time, the type of rabbi who had lived exclusively within the "four cubits of the Halakhah" had disappeared, to be replaced by rabbis who felt the impact of the Zeitgeist and were grappling with it to the best of their ability. Among the outstanding traditionalist rabbis of that period were Hirsch's former teacher Jacob Ettlinger, Seligmann Baer Bamberger of Würzburg, and Esriel Hildesheimer of Eisenstadt. Although all were distinguished talmudic scholars, particularly Ettlinger, each also possessed a good secular education; Hildesheimer had even been graduated from the University of Halle. Regardless of whether they approved of Hirsch's specific activities, they could not condemn him, particularly when he was so essentially engaged in fighting their common adversary—Reform. Moreover, Hirsch was at this time considered as popular and influential as they. As a result, he did not fear censure or even the disapproval of his colleagues. He felt free and independent to pursue his own course regardless of whether it met with the expectations of other traditionalists, rabbi or layman.

In the light of the prevailing circumstances, Hirsch did not hesitate to make his synagogue service aesthetically attractive to rival the Reform temple in decorum and dignity. Unlike in other traditionalist synagogues, the congregants recited their prayers quietly, without gesticulations, responding aloud only at the appropriate intervals. He also eliminated the elaborate cantorial chants that many found so disagreeable, and instituted a male choir instead, although some ultratraditionalists found this objectionable. His sermon was always given in perfect, highly polished, cultured German.[87] Thus, Hirsch's synagogue, while remaining strictly within the boundaries of the Halakhah, was a pleasingly modern house of worship, a source of pride to the members affiliated with it.

One of Hirsch's major achievements was the school he founded shortly after his arrival in Frankfurt. After encountering initial difficulties from within his congregation and from without by those who objected to a model institution in which religious and secular studies would be pursued on an equal basis and with the same seriousness, he soon overcame the early hesitancy on the part of some enlightened-religious parents who were reluctant to send their gifted children to such an experimental school; slightly over a decade later, the enrollment totaled some 259 students, 103 of them girls. The fact that Hirsch viewed the education of girls as being no less important than that of boys was as revolutionary as the coequality of secular and religious subjects in the school curriculum, perhaps more so. Even more revolutionary was the fact that he permitted coeducation of boys and girls in the first three grades. Only Hirsch's assertiveness and a period of anarchy and confusion within the traditionalist ranks in Germany could have made such an event possible without causing alarm.

Having succeeded in completing his dual-curriculum elementary school, Hirsch proceeded to establish a secondary school based on the same principle and with a similar program. This school too became widely popular and was subsequently recognized by the government authorities. By the year 1885, three years before his death, Hirsch was pleased to note that the enrollment in his elementary and secondary schools had reached five hundred students, surpassing that of the rival Philanthropin.[88]

Hirsch was not content to merely make an imprint on his own

community; he aspired to be recognized throughout Germany. In order to carry his message beyond the confines of Frankfurt, he embarked on a new project—a monthly publication which would eventually become the clarion of the traditionalists. The Jewish press in Germany had steadily increased in importance throughout the nineteenth century, reflecting each shade of opinion.[89] The Reform movement was represented by the *Allgemeine Zeitung des Judentums* under the editorship of Ludwig Philippson, and the Conservative or Historical school, associated with Zachariah Frankel, was represented first by the *Zeitschrift für die religiösen Interessen des Judentums* and, beginning in 1851, by the *Monatsschrift für Geschichte und Wissenschaft des Judentums*, with Frankel as editor.

The traditionalists had an organ, too: *Der treue Zionswächter*, which appeared in 1845 at the initiative of Ettlinger and under the editorship of Samuel Enoch. This German-language publication also had a Hebrew supplement, *Shomer Tziyon ha-Ne'eman*. After a decade, these two papers ceased publication, and thus Hirsch's new monthly replaced his former teacher's publication, which had been discontinued in 1856.[90]

The name of Hirsch's monthly was *Jeschurun*, after the Hebrew name of the Israelitische Religionsgesellschaft. According to its subtitle, it was designed for the furtherance of the Jewish spirit and Jewish living in the home, community, and school.[91] For sixteen years Hirsch edited this monthly, which enjoyed a wide circulation in Germany. The *Jeschurun* differed considerably from *Der treue Zionswächter*, for the latter was limited in scope, with little appeal to a wider audience. *Jeschurun*, on the other hand, served as a vehicle for views and opinions on a great variety of subjects which were of great concern to German Jews. Many articles appearing in its columns dealt with theology, philosophy, politics, biblical exegesis, education, law, current events, reviews, and even belles lettres. Hirsch himself was not only an editor, but also contributed many important articles, essays, and studies. The polemics with the nontraditionalist segments of Jewry and their leaders and some intramural conflicts with differing traditionalists occupied an important and intriguing place in the issues of *Jeschurun*.

Of particular interest and significance were Hirsch's polemics against the mentors of the Jüdisch-theologisches Seminar at Breslau expounded in the pages of *Jeschurun*. This seminary, which had opened in 1854, was headed by Zachariah Frankel and aimed at a middle-of-the-road policy equidistant from the traditionalists and Reformers, whose doctrinal positions had become rigid and unyielding. Rejecting the arbitrary and radical changes introduced by the Reformers, the mentors of the seminary also disapproved of the concept of the immutability of religious forms and the unconditional retention of rites discarded in the historic evolutionary process. They indicated that Judaism as a living organism contained both static and dynamic elements. While the former remained constant, the latter were modified in consonance with themselves and the transformations inherent in time and space. The conservatives also objected to the confessionalization of Judaism advocated, paradoxically, by both extremes, the traditionalists and the Reformers. Rooted in the study of Jewish history, the conservatives showed a greater appreciation for Jewish positive historical and cultural values and, most emphatically, for the concept of Jewish nationhood.[92]

Hirsch, who only a decade ago had aspired to bridge the extremes in Jewry, had abandoned the conciliatory endeavors of his younger years at Oldenburg. He was therefore suspicious of the trend that was about to emerge from the Breslau seminary and asked Frankel to be specific about his aims, methods, and intended curriculum at the seminary. Frankel was apparently offended by this abrasive demand and saw it as an inquisitorial challenge tantamount to asking for a declaration of faith, and consequently he ignored it. Hirsch was deeply stung by Frankel's silence, which he seemingly interpreted as a personal affront, implying that he did not merit an answer. To Hirsch's further chagrin, among the members of the faculty of the Jüdisch-theologisches Seminar was the son of his own former teacher, *Ḥakham* Isaac Bernays, Jacob, and his own former student Graetz.

Hirsch's opportunity to discredit the mentors of the Breslau seminary was not long in coming, and his first target was Graetz. The latter, who had spent three years in Hirsch's home at Oldenburg, had remained loyal to him even after his departure. This is evident from the fact that Graetz dedicated his doctoral dissertation, *Gnostizismus und Judentum*, to Hirsch.[93] He had also visited

Hirsch with his wife, Marie, at Nikolsburg, soon after their marriage. Hirsch, however, could not excuse Graetz for joining the faculty of the seminary at Breslau, and perhaps the fact that Graetz had once been his student made the offense even less pardonable. As a result, when Graetz had published the fourth volume of his *Geschichte der Juden von den ältesten Zeiten bis zur Gegenwart*,[94] Hirsch published a scathing review in *Jeschurun* in several installments.[95] In the review, entitled *"Geschichte der Juden* von Dr. H. Graetz," Hirsch criticized Graetz's work as superficial and replete with fantasy.[96]

Not long thereafter, Hirsch found occasion to direct his attack against the founder and president of the Jüdisch-theologisches Seminar, Zachariah Frankel. In 1859, Frankel published his work *Darkhei ha-Mishnah, ha-Tosefta, Mekhilta, Sifra va-Sifri*, which engendered a heated controversy among scholars and theologians. In this pioneering study, Frankel traced the development of the Oral Law from Ezra in the fifth century B. C. E. to Judah the Prince at the end of the second century C. E., thus embracing a period of seven hundred years. During this period, a huge body of laws had come into existence, some of which may have been derived from the biblical text by a special methodology employed by such men as Hillel, Rabbi Ishmael, Rabbi Yosé ha-Galili, and others. Some of these laws were enacted in accordance with the exigencies of the time, while a few were considered to be *halakhah le-Mosheh mi-Sinai*, a law of Moses from Sinai.

Frankel endeavored to remain true to the objective criteria of scholarship while remaining within the boundaries of Jewish tradition. Accordingly, his attitude toward the Written Law was that it must not be tampered with. The Oral Law, however, must be conceived as interpretations by the Rabbis in conformity with the spirit, rather than with the letter, of the Written Law. Thus, the rabbinic interpretation of the biblical *lex talionis* to signify pecuniary compensation may have been a departure from its literal meaning, but not from the essential meaning.

These views expressed by a rabbi who demonstratively left the Reform synod at Frankfurt, protesting its antitraditionalist stand, appeared dangerous. Granted that his attitude toward the Bible was that of *noli me tangere* and hence laudable, his views on the Oral Law caused apprehension, particularly at a time when the latter was in greater danger than the Bible. The traditionalists objected to Frankel's ambiguity concerning the divine origin of the Halakhah and the hermeneutical rules and methodology or *midot* employed by the Rabbis for the interpretation of the Bible. Most disturbing to them was Frankel's view that the laws categorized as *halakhah le-Mosheh mi-Sinai* should not be considered literally but metaphorically, signifying ancient laws whose origin was unknown but which had been commonly accepted as if given to Moses on Sinai. Indeed, Frankel echoed an opinion already expressed by such unquestionable traditionalist authorities as Samson of Sens[97] and Asher ben Yeḥiel.[98]

Notwithstanding Frankel's arguments and the traditionalist opinions he cited, his *Darkhei ha-Mishnah* became the target of criticism. The traditionalists, above all Hirsch, saw this work as insidious to the point of heresy. A condemnatory review was written in Hebrew by Gottlieb Fischer from Hungary, which Hirsch translated into German and published in *Jeschurun*[99] with additional critical notes, *"Anmerkung der Redaktion zu dem Artikel von Gottlieb Fischer."*[100] Hirsch's criticism of Frankel evoked a sharp rebuke from the latter's supporters, who resented the attack on their master.[101] Hirsch was thus placed in the position of being not only an implacable foe of Reform, but also the adversary of Conservative Judaism.

This position apparently caused Hirsch no anxiety. He now had a following of his own and was determined to pursue the course he had undertaken. He paid no heed to the Reform leadership in his own city and not only avoided Leopold Stein, but also his former friend Abraham Geiger when the latter was appointed rabbi in Frankfurt in 1863.[102] Nor did he treat Geiger's successor, Nehemiah Brüll, any differently after Geiger assumed the rabbinic post at Berlin in 1870.

Hirsch continued his communal and literary work, publishing his translation of and commentary on the Pentateuch during the years 1867–78 and, four years later, his translation of and commentary on the Psalms.[103] His commentaries grew out of his lectures on these subjects held over a period of many years. According to his preface to the Pentateuch commentary, he had availed himself of the notes taken by his listeners and submitted them for publication with only some minor revisions.

His commentary, like most of his writings, was in German. In this respect he departed from the centuries-old custom of rabbis writing their commentaries and exegeses in Hebrew. Not only was Hebrew employed in exegetical works by medieval scholars, but the exegetes of Hirsch's time did likewise. Thus, Jacob Zvi Mecklenburg's biblical commentary *Ha-Ktav ve-ha-Kabbalah* (1839) and Meir Loeb Malbim's *Ha-Torah ve-ha-Mitzvah* (1844) were both written in Hebrew. Moreover, even Mendelssohn, who had translated the Bible into German, used the Hebrew alphabet for transliteration, and the *Biur* commentary was exclusively in Hebrew. It seems that in this respect, Hirsch tacitly agreed with the Reformers that notwithstanding one's reverence for Hebrew, it was German which his contemporaries spoke, read, and understood best. An important factor in this choice may have been that, as noted, Hirsch did not write this commentary per se, but merely compiled the notes taken by his listeners. Those notes were written in German based on his lectures delivered in that language, and he published them as they were.

Nevertheless, it must not be overlooked that Hirsch's attitude toward German was not the same as that of the other traditionalists of his time who were conversant in that language. To the latter, it was a language they knew and employed, but nevertheless a non-Jewish language.[104] Hirsch, on the other hand, had a deep emotional feeling for German and a strong attachment to German culture. None of the contemporary traditionalists could wax as ecstatic over Schiller as did Hirsch at the celebration of the poet's centenary, nor would any of them admonish their listeners that by hedonistic pursuits one betrays not only Judaism but also the ideals of that great German poet (*S* 6:351).

Hirsch kept up his literary activity till his very last years, completing his translation and commentary on the Hebrew prayer book, which was published seven years after his death.

Not only was Hirsch attached to the German language and culture, but his interests revolved almost exclusively about the furtherance of traditional Judaism in Germany. In this respect, he was even more insular than some Reform rabbis. Hirsch, so sensitive to any theological or communal problems within Germany, displayed unusual calm during the stormy Damascus and Mortara affairs in his younger days, and remained equally unruffled by the

Tisza Eszlar case during his later years. Even in the campaign to help Russian Jewry during the pogroms he played a minor role. Hirsch similarly avoided any involvement with organizations such as the Alliance Israélite Universelle, whose aim was to defend Jewish rights and liberties wherever endangered.

Although Hirsch, unlike the Reformers, did not theoretically replace Jerusalem with Frankfurt, his practical efforts on behalf of the Holy Land were insignificant. In contradistinction to the leading traditionalist rabbis, who were enthusiastic in their endeavors to assist the *yishuv* in the Holy Land—Zvi Hirsch Kalischer, Ettlinger, Bamberger, and Hildesheimer—Hirsch remained conspicuously aloof and noncommittal. As early as in the *Neunzehn Briefe*, written during his Oldenburg period, he asserted that "the former independent state life of Israel was not even then the essence or purpose of our national existence, was only a means of fulfilling our spiritual mission. Land and soil were never Israel's bond of union but only the common task of the Torah" (*NL* 161).

When approached during his stay at Nikolsburg to head the fund for the support of the Jewish community in the Holy Land, he declined the offer under the pretext of lack of time and stated the need to explore the situation on the spot before entertaining such a commitment.[105] Even the faint assistance he did render was merely of a philanthropic nature,[106] and with the exception of the economic crisis of 1866, his *Jeschurun* devoted little space to news from the Holy Land and was generally cool to Jewish national aspirations.[107]

The emerging Jewish nationalist movement whose precursors, Zvi Hirsch Kalischer and Moses Hess, came from Germany, did not penetrate Hirsch's German insularism to which, like his Reform opponents, he remained unconditionally true as a typical German rabbi.

The Secession—A Modern Excommunication

For over two decades Hirsch diligently applied himself to building and developing the Israelitische Religionsgesellschaft, which served most of the religious, educational, and social needs of its members. This success, however, increased the frustration of some members of the association, who, although self-sufficient, were legally compelled to belong to the general *Gemeinde* and continue their contribution, *Gemeindebeitrag,* toward its maintenance. This arrangement followed the law which dictated an obligatory association, *Zwangsangehörigkeit,* with one's confessional community and prohibited anyone or any group within a given confessional community from seceding from it. As a result, the Frankfurt *Gemeinde* served in actuality as a supercommunity or umbrella organization for all of Frankfurt Jewry, the members of the Religionsgesellschaft included.

While this arrangement may have irritated some of the latter group, few would have advocated secession from the general Jewish community. Frankfurt was not the only city in Germany where traditionalist Jews had maintained similar religious enclaves but remained within the framework of the *Gemeinde.* The law prohibiting secession was not the only block against separatism. Many Jews felt that ideological differences notwithstanding, they had more things in common than things which divided them. Secession would have broken up families and destroyed precious links which had been forged through generations—as in fact it subsequently did. The well-founded fear existed that by permitting separation, many Jews would break away altogether without affiliating themselves with any Jewish communal group. Thus, the pulverization of Jewish communal life in Germany, already shattered and fragile, would be total and beyond any possible reconstruction. Moreover, with the fragmentation of the Jewish community and the elimination of the obligatory contributions, the most vital religious, educational, social, and charitable services would have to be suspended, since no group would be sufficiently solvent to maintain them. The more farsighted Jews realized that secession would enfeeble the political, social, and economic status of German Jewry in the face of the prevailing hostility toward their ascending role in public life. The sentimental attachment to a community by people whose ancestors had built it over a period of generations and served in some capacity of leadership could not be minimized.

To what extent Hirsch shared the views of his congregants on the issue of possible secession in the first two decades of his ministry in Frankfurt is unknown. Being an outsider, he did not share their sentiments for the general *Gemeinde* and frequently ignored local customs.[108] He was, however, irked by the fact that although the Religionsgesellschaft was larger and richer than many Jewish communities in Germany, it was not recognized as an independent community and that he, a former *Landesrabbiner* in three important posts, was not even accorded the title of rabbi of Frankfurt. The fact that despite his success in organizing a strong community and his popularity reaching far beyond the limits of Frankfurt he remained merely a rabbi of a local organization with no official status apparently deeply wounded his pride.

Hirsch's opportunity for action in this respect coincided with the Kulturkampf which began soon after the unification of Germany and the ascension of Bismarck as its chancellor. Wishing to break the power of the Catholic Church, which was considered unpatriotic and whose numbers were decried as ultramontanes, Bismarck with the active assistance of Adalbert Falk, minister of ecclesiastical and educational affairs, promulgated the "May Laws." Among these was the Law of Secession, *Austrittsgesetz*, which permitted any Protestant or Catholic to leave his church while remaining within his former confession. Bismarck, as well as many of the liberals who supported him, had expected to enable many Catholics to defect from the Church, which they may have thought excessively rigid, dogmatic, or ultramontanic, and to establish independent churches, thus enfeebling the highly centralized power of the Catholic Church. Similarly, they wished to nullify or at least avert the influence of the papacy on German politics. The reactionary encyclical *Quanta Cura* and the appended *Syllabus Errorum Nostri Temporis* issued by Pius IX in 1864, and the newly announced doctrine of infallibility ex cathedra by the Vatican in 1870, increased the apprehension of Bismarck and his liberal supporters regarding the Church. It also gave them hope that many liberal or nationalistic Catholics—*Altkatholiken* and *Reformkatholiken*—unable to accept these papal views would take advantage of the May Laws and opt for separate ecclesiastical organizations. Since the Jews constituted no danger to the regime, they were not entitled to the newly granted right of *Austritt*, secession.

The majority of German Jewry were satisfied with the fact that the *Austrittsgesetz* did not apply to them since it would have endangered the existence of the already weakened Jewish communities. Permitting further subdivisions and the right of individuals to leave existing communities would only have accelerated the already rampant assimilation and defection. Only Jews of the caliber of Edward Lasker and Moritz Warburg, whose liberalism was their most overriding consideration, objected to this so-called community oppression *(Parochialzwang),* obligatory association *(Zwangsangehörigkeit),* or oppression of conscience *(Gewissenszwang),* as many termed this law, and considered it discriminatory—a *Spezialjudengesetz.*

Hirsch, who had been frustrated for many years by the inferior role he had to play in Frankfurt, decided to exploit this seemingly discriminatory law for the independence of the Israelitische Religionsgesellschaft. He espoused Lasker's cause and, in the name of freedom of religious conscience, prevailed upon the latter to exert pressure to make the Law of Secession apply to the Jews as well. To the government, this concession was inconsequential since it did not feel itself menaced by the Jewish community. The liberals, on the other hand, easily accepted the argument—eloquently presented by Lasker—that the denial of the right to secede was discriminatory, particularly since some Jews favored this right. The fact that it could adversely affect the existing Jewish communities and accelerate the process of assimilation only made it more attractive to them. Thus, paradoxically, Hirsch allied himself with liberal German Protestants, freethinkers, and liberal nonreligious Jews in the defense of traditional Judaism. In July 1876, the German parliament ruled that the *Austrittsgesetz* was also applicable to the Jews, thereby enabling Hirsch to secede from the Frankfurter *Gemeinde.*

The *Austrittgesetz,* advocated by Lasker with Hirsch's blessings, was vigorously opposed by the leaders and spokesmen of the Jewish communities. Ludwig Philippson[109] and the jurist Hermann Makower[110] endeavored to convince the government to continue to uphold the *Parochialzwang,* compulsory community affiliation.[111] Hirsch reacted sharply to their efforts in a lengthy article "Das Princip der Gewissensfreiheit und die Schrift des Herrn Rechtsanwalts und Notars Makower über die Gemeinde-Verhältnisse der Juden in Preussen" (*S* 4:254–94), directed particularly against Makower's recently published *Die Gemeindeverhältnisse der Juden in Preussen.* But in spite of all the efforts of the opponents of secession, the *Austrittsgesetz* was affirmed by the parliament.

For Hirsch, this year constituted a year of wonder, and he hailed it as a most spectacular event, purportedly marking the liberation of the traditionalists from the yoke of the Reformers.[112] However, few German Jews, traditionalists included, shared Hirsch's elation; most of them viewed secession as rather a pyrrhic victory. This is best illustrated by the fact that the overwhelming majority of the members of Hirsch's own Israelitische Religionsgesellschaft refused to withdraw from the *Gemeinde,* and the few who went along with him did so reluctantly and under duress. According to one of Hirsch's most ardent admirers, "only 85 members, a small minority which included the teachers and employees of the Religionsgesellschaft, participated in the *Austritt.* Strangely enough, some of them hesitated to admit to the judge that their own conscience—and not only the demands of their spiritual leader—had caused them to take the step. The majority of the members preferred to remain voluntarily in the Reform community."[113] It seems patent that only those whose very livelihood depended on Hirsch felt constrained to accede to his demand. They may have been joined by a few newcomers to Frankfurt who had neither interest in nor concern for the welfare of the existing Jewish community.[114] Thus, the predominant majority, at least 75 percent of Hirsch's congregants, opted for the status quo ante—to maintain their independent religious and educational services while simultaneously continuing their affiliation with the *Gemeinde.* This arrangement implied neither satisfaction with this institution nor an endorsement of the policies pursued by its leaders. In fact, many traditionalists within and without the Israelitische Religionsgesellschaft were displeased and angered by the course of action taken by these leaders. Not infrequently they deplored and criticized the leaders of the *Gemeinde* for their arrogance, high-handedness, and lack of consideration for the tax-paying traditionalist minority. All their grievances notwithstanding, most traditionalists were reluctant to sever their connections and destroy the *Gemeinde,* which was the only officially recognized Jewish representative body vis-à-vis the government and the non-Jewish community. Many of Hirsch's members were scions of old Frankfurter Jewish

families with deep roots in the community. Some of their ancestors had been its founders, builders, and contributors, whose
names were inscribed in its annals and whose record was a source
of pride for their descendants. To many Frankfurt Jews, secession
signified separation from relatives, friends, and business associates.

Many intelligent and perceptive Jews viewed Hirsch's crusade
for secession with genuine apprehension. Cognizant of the political realities of the time, they knew that behind the liberal,
progressive rhetoric of religious or conscientious considerations,
confessionelles Bedenken, lay the Bismarckian stratagem to break
the cohesive power of the Roman Catholic Church in Germany.
They were aware that the Law of Secession was intentionally
promulgated to strengthen political authoritarianism rather than
to facilitate religious liberty. For the Jews to advocate secession
meant to lend support to the Kulturkampf and to incur the displeasure of a large segment of the non-Jewish population. Furthermore, many Jews feared that the Law of Secession, if applied to
the Jews, would have most deleterious consequences. Unlike the
Catholics, who numbered in the millions, who constituted a
majority in many German states, and who were supported by
neighboring Catholic countries and by the papacy, the Jews were
an insignificant, disliked, and at best tolerated minority. Thus if
the Law of Secession signified a challenge to the well-disciplined,
highly organized, and hierarchically directed Catholics, to the
disorganized and polarized Jews it meant disaster.

In retrospect, after an intervening century, it is difficult to understand what prompted Hirsch to undertake this course of action.
Neither the religious nor the political situation warranted it at the
time. By the end of the 1860s and the beginning of the '70s, the
Reform movement had lost the élan and éclat it had in the '40s.
Its outstanding dramatis personae, who were most active, vocal,
aggressive, challenging, and belligerent at the synods of 1844–46,
had since aged, mellowed, retired, or died. The younger Reformers were more reticent, less zealous, and rarely provocative. Unlike their optimistic liberal and revolutionary predecessors of two
decades before, they reflected the spirit of their age, which was
marked by conservatism. The two Reform synods, which had convened in Leipzig in 1869 and in Augsburg in 1871, reflected this
subdued mood. These synods had been poorly attended, and al-

though held two years apart the declining number of delegates attending the second synod—thirty as against sixty congregants represented two years earlier—was adequate testimony that Reform's crest of success was long past.[115] The demeanor of the delegates and the tone of their deliberations hardly indicated any militancy or insidious design against the traditionalists. They avoided major controversial theological issues and except for the question of the halakhically required ritual for the dissolution of a levirate dependency, *halitzah,* they occupied themselves with matters of liturgy, education, solemnization at weddings during the *sefirah* period, the celebration of Hanukkah, and similar items. Most questions concerning the Sabbath and intermarriage were either tabled or the resolutions regarding these concerns were phrased in ambiguous platitudes. In some areas, such as circumcision, the delegates displayed greater respect for tradition than had heretofore been customary in Reform circles and conferences.

By the time Hirsch made secession the cause célèbre of German Jewry, the vast majority of Jews had already eschewed all theological shibboleths and quibbling regarding ritualistic and ceremonial matters. Three theological trends had evolved—the traditionalist, Reform, and Conservative. Each of these factions had its own rabbinical seminary: the Reform Hochschule für die Wissenschaft des Judentums in Berlin, the traditionalist Rabbinerseminar für das orthodoxe Judentum in Berlin, and the Conservative Jüdisch theologisches Seminar in Breslau. These three groups carried on a lively polemic through their respective organs: the *Allgemeine Zeitung des Judentums, Israelitische Wochenschrift,* and *Israelit.* Each group had its followers and even devotees; to most nonobservant Jews, however, the differences were irrelevant. To them the battle over the primacy of the *Shulhan Arukh* was a quixotic exercise. Compelled by law to belong to the Jewish community of their respective domicile, many of these apathetic Jews grudgingly paid their communal taxes during their lifetime and were buried in its cemetery after their death.

In view of this climate, it is difficult to perceive any apparent urgency that might have precipitated Hirsch's demand for secession. Paradoxically, it seemed to best serve the nonobservant Jews, facilitating their flight from Judaism altogether. If secession appears hardly justifiable on religious grounds, it is even less defensible on political grounds. It is enigmatic that Hirsch should have embarked on a course to fracture the Jewish community in Germany while all the ominous political changes there dictated unity. Bismarck's victories, which transformed an unwieldy conglomerate of weak, vying German kingdoms, dukedoms, principalities, and free cities into a unified powerful militaristic Reich, was fraught with premonitory significance for the Jews. Paralleling the military triumphs, a new anti-Semitic wave was cresting that threatened to inundate the entire country. Notwithstanding the fact that Jews were no less patriotic than their non-Jewish compatriots, their loyalty was impugned nevertheless. The new anti-Semitism was multifaceted, at times consisting of many contradictory components. Political, social, and economic factors combined with long-festering prejudices of a religious and racial nature to create a most virulent wave of hatred toward the Jews. This was exacerbated by the enormous financial debacle, the *"grosse Krach,"* in 1873, for which Jewish capitalists and speculators were blamed.[116]

Hirsch could not have been unaware of the anti-Semitic propaganda waged in the press, particularly in the influential conservative *Kreuzzeitung* and the Catholic *Germania.* Anti-Semitic works such as August Rohling's *Der Talmudjude,* which repeated the old libels of Eisenmenger, Constantin Franz's *National-liberalismus und die Judenherrschaft,* charging Jewish domination of the liberal movement, Otto Glogau's *Der Börsen- und Gründungsschwindel in Berlin,* alleging the Jews' responsibility in manipulation of the stock market—to mention but a few—were widely circulated and avidly read. This propaganda accelerated steadily and was subsequently taken up by such celebrated academicians as Heinrich von Treitschke.

All kinds of conjectures for Hirsch's heedlessness is possible, ranging from the assumption that he really believed that secession was the only means of saving traditional Judaism to the suggestion that he was moved by personal ambition and perhaps by vendetta. Regardless of theory, the fact remains that Hirsch pressed relentlessly to implement the schism in his own congregation and to overcome all opposition. Contrary to his expectations, a Kulturkampf broke out among the traditionalists, dividing them into *Austrittler* (secessionists) and *Kompromissler* (antisecessionists).

Attempts were made to heal the breach before it widened, but Hirsch rejected all concessions offered by the *Gemeinde* and barred any possible rapprochement. To forestall any such eventuality, he issued a rabbinic injunction, or *issur*, on belonging to the *Gemeinde*. This injunction was in fact a virtual *ḥerem*, excommunication—*issur* being merely a euphemism, since *ḥerem* was repugnant to most German Jews.

In his relentless drive for secession, Hirsch apparently overestimated the extent of his influence and the mood of the other traditionalist leaders of his time. He was dismayed that his injunction met with no more success than had his previous call for withdrawal. Despite his campaign against the *Gemeinde* and his ban on affiliation with it, few showed any concern for his admonitions. His shock was even greater when one of most respected leading traditionalist rabbis in Germany, Seligmann Baer Bamberger, known as the Würzburg Rav, dismissed Hirsch's *issur*, declaring it to be lacking any valid halakhic foundation. Having made secession the touchstone of traditional Judaism and having staked his authority and reputation on the *issur*, Hirsch was infuriated by Bamberger's statement. In an open letter Hirsch challenged Bamberger's opinion (*S* 4:316–43). A heated polemic ensued between these two traditionalist leaders in which Bamberger expressed his views in a scholarly, dispassionate manner while Hirsch's tone and style, though admittedly appealing, were argumentative and bellicose. It was evident that Hirsch was not interested in halakhic clarification but insisted on unqualified support for his course of action. When Bamberger asserted his independent judgment and refused to go along, Hirsch turned his wrath against him in his sermons and writings. Carried away by his zeal and anger, he charged Bamberger with supporting idolatry, thus representing the antisecessionist position. The extent of Hirsch's vindictiveness may be gauged from the fact that when Bamberger died in 1879, mourned by all the traditionalist Jews in Germany, Hirsch did not attend the funeral.

To sever the final connecting link between his followers and the members of the *Gemeinde*, Hirsch now demanded a separate cemetery, thus extending his *ḥerem* to the dead as well. To the dismay of his audiences, he declared that it was preferable to be interred in the Christian cemetery in Sachsenhausen under the cross than in the burial ground of the Jewish *Gemeinde*.

To Hirsch, secession became a virtual obsession eclipsing reason, propriety, and prudence. He was far more anxious to discredit the *Gemeinde* as nontraditionalist than to keep his congregation traditionalist, so that the contrast between should be apparent. Ironically, this puritanical effort did not extend to his own membership, which included nonobservant Jews. His obsession led him, paradoxically, to obstruct the efforts of the *Gemeinde* to provide for the religious needs of its traditionalist members. This became glaringly evident when the *Gemeinde* began looking for a traditionalist rabbi to take charge of the traditionalist synagogue and all other religious aspects of the community. Hirsch and his followers intimidated all candidates for this post, and only the young Rabbi Marcus Horvitz, a strong opponent of secession, dared accept it, thus incurring the hostility of the secessionists.

As expected, Hirsch's action was emulated by malcontents in other communities in Germany such as Berlin, Karlsruhe, Darmstadt, Wiesbaden, Giessen, Cologne, Bingen, and Strassburg. By and large, most communities were spared the agony of the schism. Weakened by the internal struggle, the German Jewish community at large confronted a far more formidable enemy in the 1880s —full-blown anti-Semitism orchestrated by Adolf Stöcker, Wilhelm Marr, Heinrich von Treitschke, Bernhard Förster, Max Liebermann von Sonnenberg, Ernst Henrici, de Lagarde, and a legion of others.[117] Outside Germany, the situation was even worse. The Jews in the Austro-Hungarian Empire were frightened by the the Tisza Eszlar blood libel, and in Russia pogroms assumed staggering proportions.

How these events registered on Hirsch is difficult to gauge. He was now advanced in age. His wife had passed away after fifty years of marriage. The battle for secession had undoubtedly left some scars, and to be considered a bête noire when he thought his case was just was not a pleasant experience. Except for some interest in the fate of Russian Jewry,[118] Hirsch continued to occupy himself with the cause he had espoused—strengthening traditional Judaism. Only two years before his death, in 1886, he

organized the Freie Vereinigung für die Interessen des ortho-
doxen Judentums, a union designed to assist and strengthen the
struggling traditionalist communities. However, he was too old to
assume its leadership and to give it the direction it required. Two
years later, the last day of the calendar year 1888 was Hirsch's final
day on earth.

Part Two
A NEW APPROACH

4

The Maimonidean Mantle

Similarities and Allusions

The most influential mentors of the Maskilim were Moses Maimonides and Moses Mendelssohn. Their respective works, particularly Maimonides's *Guide of the Perplexed*, were to these Maskilim second only to the Bible.[1] So great was their admiration for these two mentors that some even adopted their names. Thus, the well-known critical exponent of Kant, Solomon of Nieswiecz, chose Maimon as his surname in honor of Maimonides. Likewise, as already mentioned, Hirsch's uncle changed his surname to Mendelssohn out of admiration for the Dessau philosopher. Hebrew poets and versifiers such as Adam ha-Cohen, A. B. Gottlober, and Samuel Aaron Romanelli, among others, linked these two Moseses to Moses the Lawgiver,[2] thereby emphasizing that only these three represented authentic Judaism in its pristine form. This adulation of Maimonides and Mendelssohn prompted a series of new editions, translations, and popularizations of their works and biographical sketches in the eighteenth and nineteenth centuries. These works were read avidly and surreptitiously by the Maskilim and would-be Maskilim.

The *Guide of the Perplexed* was the first philosophic book to which Mendelssohn was introduced by Israel of Zamość,[3] and one of Mendelssohn's early literary endeavors was a commentary on Maimonides's *Milot ha-Higgayon*, a treatise on logic. Likewise,

Maimon's earliest contribution to philosophy was his commentary *Givat ha-Moreh* on the *Guide.* Another popular commentary on the *Guide of the Perplexed* was published by the Maskil Isaac Halevi Satanov. In order to reach a wider audience, Menahem Lefin retranslated the *Guide* from its difficult medieval Hebrew translation by Samuel ibn Tibbon into the more familiar mishnaic Hebrew.

The influence of these two philosophers was far greater on the writers of the Haskalah and post-Haskalah eras. It is evident everywhere, particularly in the works of Nahman Krochmal and Isaac Dov Levinson. Even in eastern Europe, where every glimmer of Haskalah was harshly suppressed and Maimonides's philosophic works were barred in the *yeshivot,* young Orthodox students pored over the *Guide* in secrecy, seeking guidance in their perplexities.[4]

As already indicated, the reasons for the interest in the works of Maimonides and Mendelssohn were many. The interest in Maimonides, in addition, was motivated by a psychological element—the desperate need for a guide. This yearning for an intellectual master of Maimonides's stature continued into the period of the National Renaissance[5] and lingers in many circles to this day.

Hirsch, whose Maskilic background has already been extensively discussed, shared this admiration for Maimonides and Mendelssohn. He praised Maimonides as "the great authority on the Talmud" (*NL* 191), "the great systematic orderer" (*NL* 183), "an observant Jew" (*NL* 191) who preserved "Judaism to our time" (*NL* 181). Similarly, Hirsch appreciated Mendelssohn's "brilliant respect-inspiring personality" (*NL* 189), integrity, and commitment to Judaism. All this respect and tribute notwithstanding, Hirsch was not blind to their shortcomings or to the deficiencies of their respective works. Maimonides's rationale for Judaism in general and for its *mitzvot* in particular was dated, while Mendelssohn failed to provide a rationale altogether.

Mendelssohn's concept of revealed laws was correct, but a new rationale for their observance had to be formulated for the Jews of Hirsch's era, just as Maimonides had evolved a rationale befitting his times. Such a task required a new Maimonides who could produce a new *Guide* to validate Judaism in general in the terms of nineteenth-century thought and a new *Mishneh Torah* to state the *mitzvot* as well as to interpret them in an idiom that would be meaningful and relevant to the times. Unfortunately, no such intellectual giant stepped forward. Mendelssohn never wanted to do it; others may have entertained such ambitions but were discouraged by the enormous difficulties of such a task. Hirsch, though young and not so erudite, reached out for Maimonides's mantle.

That Hirsch nurtured a secret ambition to become a modern Maimonides is evident from the nomenclature of his writings in Oldenburg. The titles and content of his early works bear a remarkable resemblance to those of Maimonides, which can hardly be considered coincidental. The Hebrew title of Hirsch's *Neunzehn Briefe über Judentum von Ben Usiel* (1836—translated as *The Nineteen Letters of Ben Uziel*)—*Igrot Tzafon* (Letters to the North)—parallels Maimonides's *Iggeret Teman* (Letter to the South). It suggests that Ben Uziel—Hirsch's pen name—hoped to resolve the religious dilemma for the Jews of the North, a euphemism for Germany in Haskalah literature, just as Ben Maimon—Maimonides—had helped to solve the religious problem of the Jews of the South approximately seven centuries earlier.

Hirsch's *Horeb* (1837), which aimed at being a *"vade mecum* to be consulted in various situations when problems of religious law arise,"[6] did not differ essentially in content and purpose from Maimonides's *Mishneh Torah.* Each was a code of Jewish law whose compilation was motivated by the exigencies of the time. Maimonides wrote his work in an era during which "disasters continually follow one another."[7] Hirsch published his *Horeb* "because the time seemed to demand something of the kind."[8] Hirsch, while asserting that his intention was not to ask "why these commandments devolve upon us,"[9] opened the *Horeb* with a section entitled *"Torot,"* which deals with fundamental matters of creed, just as Maimonides began the first section of his *Mishneh Torah.* Likewise, Hirsch prefaced each section of the *Horeb* with biblical verses, which can only be interpreted as a conscious imitation of Maimonides, who introduced each section of the *Mishneh Torah* with a biblical verse—something uncommon in other Jewish codices.

Hirsch's designation of his legal guide as *Horeb* and not *Sinai*—

the more popular name for the site of the revelation—also seems to suggest his conscious desire to emulate Maimonides. The latter called his code *Mishneh Torah*, a term used for the Book of Deuteronomy. Following in this vein, Hirsch seems deliberately to have chosen *Horeb*—the Deuteronomic term for Sinai—for his own code of Law.[10] Apparently he envisioned that it would play the same role as Maimonides's *Mishneh Torah*. Although the two works are not comparable, Hirsch is obviously attempting, in all his deliberately suggestive concealments and *jeux de mots*, to assume Maimonides's mantle.

This aspiration is singularly evident in his intention to write a new *Guide of the Perplexed*, to be entitled *Moriah*. In a letter written in 1835, when he was twenty-seven, to the registrar general of the Deutsch-Israelitische Gemeinde of Hamburg, Hirsch stated that he was contemplating a philosophic work that would present "the theoretical foundations of the Bible's teaching on God, the universe, man, and Israel."[11] A plan of such scope, encompassing the foundations of Judaism, paralleled Maimonides's effort in the *Moreh Nevukhim*. The expressed view that "Hirsch chose *Moriah* as the title of his work because it was the scene of the intended sacrifice of Isaac,"[12] seems unlikely. *Moriah*, symbolizing metarational faith, is hardly a fitting title for a book dealing with the rational philosophical aspects of Judaism. It is more likely that Hirsch's choice was dictated by the remarkable phonetic and derivative resemblances between *Moriah* and Maimonides's *Moreh*. To Hirsch, as to the Rabbis of the Talmud, *Moriah*, like *Moreh*, signified teaching.[13] Thus, in sound, significance and purpose, *Moriah* was deliberately analogous to Maimonides's *Moreh*.

Besides the resemblance in the titles, there is also a similarity in the setting of these works. Both authors attributed the genesis of their respective books to queries posed to them by young students. Maimonides said that the problems presented to him by his student Joseph ibn Aknin prompted him to write the *Moreh Nevukhim*. Hirsch, at the outset of the *Neunzehn Briefe*, which seems to be an outline of his intended *Moriah*, named his young student-colleague Benjamin as the motivating spirit of the book. Both Joseph and Benjamin were young men who combined a religious background with a secular education. Joseph had a thirst for knowledge, a fondness for speculative pursuits, and a love for poetry and mathematics;[14] Benjamin too was familiar with many aspects of the culture of his time (*NL* 5). Neither represented the extremes of the Jewish community. They were, in Hirsch's term, *erleuchtet religiös*, and as such were compelled to maintain a paradoxical intellectual position. Hirsch's Benjamin, like Maimonides's Joseph, was a "religious man who has been trained to believe in the truth of our holy Law, who conscientiously fulfills his moral and religious duties, and at the same time has been successful in his philosophical studies."[15] However, it was this success in both spheres, this duality of culture, which made him "lost in perplexity and anxiety."[16]

In both works, *Moreh* and *Moriah*, some time elapsed between the questions and the answers, since either master or student had to depart. In the case of Maimonides, it was Joseph: "By the will of God we parted, and you went your way."[17] In the case of Hirsch, it was the master who was hurried by an impatient coachman (*NL* 3). Perspective and depth were attained during these interruptions of the dialogues; Maimonides's answers became more profound and Benjamin's questions more articulate. In his letter to Joseph, Maimonides maintained that "our discussions aroused in me a resolution which had long been dormant. Your absence has prompted me to compose this treatise."[18] In Benjamin's letter to Naphtali, however, it was the student who claimed that the discussions with his master prior to their separation induced him to articulate his questions:

You have, therefore, made me distrustful, my dear Naphtali, of the opinions I have hitherto held, but you have not refuted them nor given me better ones in their stead. I, therefore, take advantage of your kind permission, and repeat to you in writing a number of my charges, not for the purpose of defending my present mode of life, but in the sincere desire of information and guidance. (*NL* 3)

These variations, however, are not major and may be part of Hirsch's literary game of hide-and-seek. It may not, therefore, be farfetched to suggest that this practice of transparent concealment in which he delighted—as already indicated in the case of his nomenclature and pseudonyms—induced him to call his interlocutor Benjamin as a biblical allusion to the brother of Joseph.

Hirsch's modern Benjamin was an intellectually perplexed brother of Maimonides's medieval Joseph ibn Aknin. Consideration should also be given to both authors' determination to express their respective views regardless of other people's approbation or disapprobation. Maimonides categorically stated: "When I find the road narrow, and can see no other way of teaching a well-established truth except by pleasing one intelligent man and displeasing ten thousand fools—I prefer to address myself to the one man and to take no notice whatever of the condemnation of the multitude."[19] Hirsch likewise asserted:

Thousands may forsake the cause of life and light, thousands may tear themselves away from the lot and the name of Israel, whose mode of life they have long since rejected—the cause of truth counts not the number of adherents. If only one remains—one Jew with the book of the law in his hand, with Israel's law in his heart, Israel's light in his spirit—that one suffices. (*NL* 208)

Criticism of Maimonides

Hirsch's desire and conscious effort to pattern his works after those of Maimonides must not, however, be construed as his endorsement of the latter's philosophy. He accused Maimonides of having adulterated the purity of the Jewish religion by permeating it with Greco-Arabic elements and thus evolving a syncretic philosophy which only added to the confusion of an already-perplexed generation (*NL* 181).

However, paradoxical and enigmatic Hirsch's as ambivalent attitude to Maimonides may appear, it is quite understandable. Hirsch seems to have approved of Maimonides's intentions and efforts but disagreed with his views and the substance of his thought. He agreed with Maimonides that Judaism had to be explicated philosophically, but he found the latter's explication unacceptable. Maimonides was therefore to Hirsch a model in approach but not in the execution of his concepts. Hirsch aimed at embarking on the same course that Maimonides had taken centuries before, that of constructing a philosophy of Judaism compatible with the exigencies of the times; but he hoped to build it on a different and more authentic foundation, one in harmony with the nineteenth, rather than the twelfth, century. Before dwelling on the difference in the explication of Judaism as conceived by Maimonides and Hirsch, we must set the nature of Hirsch's criticism in its proper perspective. At first glance, Hirsch's criticism of Maimonides's Greco-Arabic mentality seems to echo the opinions and sentiments of the many medieval and the few nineteenth-century anti-Maimonideans and anti-Hellenics. Opponents of Maimonides in the Middle Ages objected to his admiration of Greek thought, his rationalism, his rationalization of the commandments, and his code, *Mishneh Torah,* which they feared might supplant the Talmud. Maimonides's opponents in the nineteenth century were disturbed by the resurgence of Greek values in western Europe, which struck them as menacing to the existing religious and ethical values, particularly those of Judaism.

However, none of these anti-Maimonidean strictures are to be found in Hirsch. Unlike the anti-Hellenics, Hirsch highly valued the great contributions of Greek civilization. To him, Judaism and Hellenism were not irreconcilable foes, but two harmonious manifestations of civilization. As an admirer of Schiller, Hirsch was greatly appreciative of the aesthetic qualities of Greek culture so eloquently praised and extolled by this distinguished German poet.[20]

Educated in German schools and attuned to German culture, Hirsch could not escape the universal veneration of Greece that permeated German art and literature and captivated German intellectual circles. So strong was this influence that it was aptly called "the tyranny of Greece over Germany."[21] Hirsch shared in the enchantment with Greece kindled by Winckelmann, Lessing, Herder, Hölderlin, Goethe, Schiller, and Hegel.[22] No traditional Jew cognizant of the historic clash between Hellenism and Judaism in the Maccabean era could have exclaimed, as Hirsch did: "We do not have to fear Greek idealism but Roman materialism" (*S* 2:47).

It is therefore inconceivable that Hirsch should have objected to Maimonides's predilection for Greek thought, since, unlike past or contemporary anti-Maimonideans, Hirsch entertained no such fears. He wrote about Hellenism in the most glowing terms. The Hellenic spirit, Hirsch asserted,

stimulates the mind and spirit to develop through joy in knowledge and through pleasure in everything that is noble; provides
them with symmetry of harmony and beauty to overcome brutish
outbursts of passion. It teaches man self-respect, self-confidence
and autonomy, and expects him to ennoble himself by controlling
himself and by doing away with all that is evil and vulgar and
would disturb the harmony of beauty and decency in character
and disposition, in word and deed. The Hellenic spirit makes man
civilized, gentle, joyful, and free. (S 2:28)[23]

This panegyric is a fragment of an essay entitled "Der Hellenis-
mus und das Judentum" (S 2:24–40) written, ironically, on the
occasion of Hanukkah, the festival commemorating the victory of
Judaism over Hellenism.[24] To Hirsch, the spirit of Greece symbolized Western culture, which was not antagonistic but complementary to Judaism. The combination of cultures would eventually
transform and elevate mankind, Hirsch contended. He associated
Judaism with the biblical Shem, and Westernism with Japheth, the
children of Noah: "Both were sent to cover the animal nakedness
of mankind; called up to elevate man to be *human* and *divine"*
(S 2:26). In his commentary on Genesis, written about thirty years
after the *Neunzehn Briefe,* Hirsch continued to maintain the importance of the common role of Judaism and Western culture in
the universal education of mankind (*CG* 9:18–29):

Right to the present day it is only these two races, the descendants
of Japheth and Shem, the Greeks and the Jews, who have become
the real educators and teachers of humanity. For all the spiritual
treasures which the world has acquired, these two have to be
thanked, and everything, which, even today, works at the culture
and education of mankind, connects up with that which Japheth
and Shem brought to the world. The spiritual gifts of the Romans,
too, was only a gift of the Hellenes. Japheth has ennobled the
world esthetically. Shem has enlightened it spiritually and morally. Hellenism and Judaism have become the great active forces
in the educational work of mankind, and the rest of the world
has been merely the passive material on which they worked.
(*CG* 9:27)

Nor was Hirsch displeased with Maimonides's intellectual approach to Judaism. Hirsch insisted upon the understanding of Judaism and its commandments (*NL* 14). The subtitle of the *Horeb*
states that the volume is intended "*. . . für Jissroels denkende
Jünglinge und Jungfrauen"*—for thinking Jewish young men and

women. The adjective *denkende,* thinking, can hardly be considered anti-intellectual. Nor did Hirsch object to Maimonides's endeavor to rationalize the commandments, for he surpassed Maimonides in this respect. "We must," Hirsch insisted, "follow also the same method in studying the *mitzvot* when they assign a purpose for any particular object, or ordain some symbolic practice. There, we must strive to discover analytically the connection of the purpose with this particular object; here, the natural method of practically expressing such an idea in consideration of its reason and connection" (*NL* 15). To those who based their objection to his rationalization of the commandments on the Talmud, Hirsch replied: "The injunction not to *darshinan ta'ama di-kera,*[25] which was often held up to me, has no other than the very proper meaning that we should not attach any importance in practical decision to the conjectural reason of a *mitzvah,* because it is only conjecture" (*NL* 185). He alluded to Nachmanides's rationalization of *sha'atnez* and *kilayim,* although these have been considered irrational commandments.[26]

Hirsch's criticism of Maimonides is primarily attributable to the radical change in the philosophic outlook that had taken place in the intervening centuries. In the twelfth century, when Aristotle reigned supreme, the validation of Judaism in Aristotelian terms was sufficient. In the nineteenth century such harmonization was no longer acceptable. The validation of Judaism had to exist within its own context and its own inner criteria. Maimonides's very endeavor to reconcile two dissimilar outlooks, explicating one in the terms of the other, was doomed to failure, since it negated the concept of self-contained, distinct organismic entities, a notion current since the days of Herder. Accordingly, the most distinguishing characteristic of each organismic entity—social, religious, or cultural—was its intrinsic nature and uniqueness. As such, it could only be understood by its own inner criteria. Its functions related exclusively to its own unique inner structure, which is dissimilar to all others, notwithstanding outward similarities. Therefore, to interpret Judaism, which is distinct and self-containing, by a philosophy external to it was not only impossible, but counterproductive and self-defeating.

Hirsch, therefore, considered Maimonides's efforts futile despite his good intentions. He failed "because he sought to reconcile Judaism with the difficulties which confronted it from *without* instead of developing it creatively from *within*. . . . He entered into Judaism from *without*, bringing with him opinions of whose truth he had convinced himself from extraneous sources" (*NL* 181–82).

Among the inherent differences between Judaism and Aristotelianism is their respective attitudes toward knowledge and deeds as ends and means. To Judaism, *knowledge* is only a *means*, while the *deed* is the end; in Aristotelianism, the opposite is true. By interpreting Judaism in Aristotelian terms, Maimonides relegated the *mitzvot*, which are deeds, to serve as means to a greater end—knowledge—an untenable view in traditional Judaism. Stated Hirsch:

Self-perfecting through the knowledge of truth was the highest aim, the practical he deemed subordinate. For [Maimonides] knowledge of God was the end, not the means; hence he devoted his intellectual powers to speculations upon the essence of Deity, and sought to bind Judaism to the results of his speculative investigations as to postulates of science or faith. (*NL* 182)

This brought about a distorted notion of the value and purpose of the commandments. In their role as a means rather than ends, they could be discarded if and when the end—knowledge—could be attained without them. Thus, instead of searching from *within* the structure of Judaism and inquiring in the light of its organismic totality the reason for any given deed, "people set up their standpoints *outside* of Judaism, and sought to draw it over to them; they conceived a priori opinions as to what the *mitzvot* might be without disturbing themselves as to the real appearance of the *mitzvot* in all their parts" (*NL* 184). The validity of normative Judaism, the most crucial problem in the nineteenth century, was impaired by Maimonides's attitude. The entire juridical-ceremonial regimen of Judaism became merely a by-product of the abstract truth which it embodied; because it was extrinsic it was even expendable:

The *mitzvot* became for [Maimonides] merely ladders, necessary only to conduct to knowledge or to protect against error, this latter often only the temporary and limited error of polytheism. *Mishpatim* became only rules of prudence, *Mitzvot* as well, *Ḥukkim* rules of health, teaching right feeling, defending against the transitory errors of the time; *Edot,* ordinances, designed to promote philosophical or other concepts. (*NL* 182–83)

Little wonder that the Reformers and liberals of the nineteenth century, who wished to legitimize their antinomianism, claimed the discipleship of Maimonides. Geiger undoubtedly expressed the sentiments of many when he stated: "Maimonides was the teacher of the whole Middle Ages and every enlightened mind that arose later drew eagerly from him and gladly acknowledged himself his pupil."[27]

The consequence of this attitude was unbridled antinomianism. The men who believed themselves the possessors of the knowledge which the commandments were designed to inculcate, thought themselves absolved both from the fulfillment of the commandment—intended only as a guide—and from the study of the science of the commandment, which had lost for them all intellectual significance.

Criticism of Mendelssohn

Maimonides was not the only Jewish philosopher criticized by Hirsch for failing to validate the normative aspect of Judaism. Mendelssohn, too, in spite of his insistence on the obligatory character of the Law, was taken to task. Unlike Maimonides, Mendelssohn was closer to Hirsch's age, and he should have therefore realized that the time demanded the evolvement of a philosophy of Judaism from *within,* rather than from *without.*

Indeed, Hirsch, despite his respect for Mendelssohn, was aware of his shortcomings:

This commanding individual, who had not drawn his mental development from Judaism, who was great chiefly in philosophical disciplines, in metaphysics and esthetics; who treated the Bible only philologically and esthetically, . . . did not build up Judaism as a science from itself [*das Judentum als Wissenschaft nicht aus sich selber erbauend*], but merely defended it against political stupidity and pietistic Christian audacity. (*NL* 189)

Hirsch thus realized, as did many others of that era, that Mendelssohn was not a philosopher of Judaism but a philosopher of Jewish origin.

Mendelssohn's main purpose was to point out to an intolerant non-Jewish society that a Jew could be a person of culture and a loyal citizen of the state. He "showed the world and his brethren that it was possible to be a strictly religious Jew and yet [*und doch*] to shine distinguished as the German Plato" (*NL* 189).

Hirsch was disturbed by this *"und doch,"* because it implied that normative Judaism was an impediment to the Jews that only an exceptional person could overcome. It seemed to be an admission that the juridical-ceremonial aspect of Judaism was neither relevant nor significant for modern man—"and yet" the Jew was bound by it. By failing to relate the *mitzvot* to the new reality and life, Mendelssohn merely accentuated the tension between the domains of *Mensch* and Jew. In the absence of an adequate rationale, the precepts which he considered obligatory could no longer be performed by the modern Jew since they appeared puerile.

It was precisely this normative aspect of Judaism, glossed over by Mendelssohn, that Hirsch thought should be subjected to thorough investigation. The precepts and rites had to be examined and analyzed in the light of the original sources which would reveal their true essence and meaning. Such a scientific analysis would disclose their significance and relevance for modern times, as well as their compatibility with modern culture. It would show that the Jew could be a person of culture as well as a loyal citizen —not despite his faithfulness to Judaism, but because of it.

Hirsch termed such a projected study a development of science, *Aufbau einer Wissenschaft,*[28] a phrase that was more than stylistic. Since the term *Wissenschaft* harks back to Fichte's *Wissenschaftslehre* and subsequently became associated with that of Hegel, its philosophic connotation was closer to the concept of "systematic knowledge" than to its present accepted usage which is largely reserved for the natural sciences. Its applicability to Judaism dates back to 1819, when the term *Wissenschaft des Judentums* was employed in the circle of the Jewish Hegelians (discussed earlier), known as the Verein für Cultur und Wissenschaft des Judentums, who attempted a systematic study of literary productions reflecting the Jewish spirit. It was in this sense that the term *Wissenschaft* was employed by Leopold Zunz, Immanuel Wolf, and other members of the Culturverein.[29] Hirsch employed this term seventeen years after it had been coined and introduced by Edward Gans,[30] and similarly called his initial endeavor *Weg zum Aufbau des Judentums als Wissenschaft*.[31]

Hirsch realized that it would be exceedingly difficult to undertake this task after the rebellion against normative Judaism was in full force. The battle between the Jewish partisans was raging; neither side was amenable to reason or moderation. Had such an effort been undertaken in Mendelssohn's time, at the first glimmer of the Enlightenment and prior to the outbreak of the antinomian revolt, the state of Judaism might have been in a more enviable position. "In Mendelssohn's days," Hirsch contended, "when the new movement of the spirit had begun but the Jewish life was yet untouched, then it would have been possible to construct *the science of Judaism* and to bring to the strong formal life the light and warmth of the spirit, and our condition would be different now" (*NL* 217–18).

Irretrievable as that era was when Judaism could have been reconstructed with ease, Hirsch believed that there was still a chance to do so. A diligent and assiduous study had to be undertaken to discern what was intrinsic and what extrinsic to Judaism, "so that many who still observe may comprehend what they observe; that many who reject may hesitate and examine that which they reject; that many a hand now raised, perhaps in honest zeal, to tear down or build up something new, be held back" (*NL* 218). Hirsch thus advocated a new and thorough investigation of Judaism and a fundamental analysis of its sources and essential luster, which would be rediscovered under the dust of the ages.

He felt that first and foremost normative Judaism must be updated, reinterpreted, and made relevant. He rejected the prevailing viewpoints concerning the *mitzvot*. They were neither a means to an end, as Maimonides thought, nor defunct vestiges of ancient Jewish state laws, as maintained by Spinoza, nor obsolete, as maintained by the exponents of Reform. They must not, however, be accepted because of any mystical nature ascribed to them, as some pietists insisted. Being of divine origin, the *mitzvot* were meaningful and significant, reasonable and rational, relevant to life's needs, provided they were comprehended in their true spirit.

Hirsch attributed the rise of antinomian tendencies among many of his Jewish contemporaries to a lack of understanding of the spirit of Jewish law, due to the long period of exile and the sufferings and persecutions endured by the Jews in the Diaspora. These abnormal conditions adversely affected the profound and creative study of the Law, so that its true indigenous spirit was obscured and consequently misunderstood. This despiritualization of the laws destroyed their content, leaving only their external ramifications. It made them seem out of tune with life and antagonistic to reason: "The excessive pressure of centuries in its accumulated weight had finally only permitted the rescue of the externals of the Law, but that the spirit had no longer found room" (*NL* 99). The long exile with its many vicissitudes had transformed the religious-juridical system of the Jewish laws into a mere lifeless "mummy."

Hirsch maintained that "the literary sources of Judaism, in which the spirit was contained, being misunderstood and misinterpreted, themselves aided in corporealizing and disguising the spirit" (*NL* 100). He not only opposed the antinomians who rejected the Law, he also criticized those who upheld it irrationally. He complained about the obscurantist and neomystical currents affecting Jewish law:

A perverted intellect comprehended the institutions which were designed and ordained for the internal and external purification and betterment of man as mechanical, dynamic, or magical formulas for the upbuilding of higher worlds and that thus the observances meant for the education of the spirit to a nobler life were but too frequently degraded into mere amuletic or talismanic performances. (*NL* 100)

Hirsch considered that these irrational tendencies, which had developed as a result of the abnormal conditions of Jewish life in exile, had made Jewish law appear antiquated, obsolete, and moribund. A new approach had to be found which would reveal the rationality, cogency, and applicability of the Jewish law, regardless of historical tides and socioeconomic changes. To accomplish this, it was necessary for Hirsch to discover the true *esprit des lois* of Judaism that would make it comprehensible to his contemporaries of the post-Emancipation era.

Challenge and Response

It was a formidable task, since neither side was receptive to reason or moderation. A new way, suggested by a fledgling rabbi lacking distinction or reputation, could not hope to gain approbation. Hirsch's nonpartisan independence could not have endeared him to either faction. As he stated:

> In an age when the contrasts stand so sharply over against each other, and when truth is on neither side, in such an age the man who belongs to no party, who has only the cause in his heart and serves it alone, cannot, unless he be a divine master who comprehends the divine truth in its purity and has the power to show it so brilliant in its divine radiance that all spirits, subdued, acknowledge its divinity and do it homage, such a one cannot, I repeat, expect approval or agreement on any side. (*NL* 212–13)

Indeed, Hirsch had misgivings about his chances for success. He was, however, skeptical neither about the righteousness of his cause nor about the truth in his evolving outlook. He was concerned with the impression his exposition of Judaism would make upon those who enjoyed a far greater reputation than he did by virtue of their seniority, scholarship, and distinction. He admitted that "modest diffidence has restrained me so long from undertaking a task which must long since have spoken within me" (*NL* 212). He was concerned that his "attempts would arouse but a pitying smile and be forgotten" (*NL* 212). As a young man full of dreams, ideals, and ambitions, he was not insensitive to derision and to the possible rejection of his ideological presentation:

> If the attempt should fail, would not those who would like to erase from the book of life the cause for which I live, would they not make use of my unsuccessful attempts as a means of strangling the dearly beloved cause? How they would gloat over my failure and say, "See there, some new attempts to rehabilitate Judaism—entire failures!" (*NL* 214–15)

In spite of these misgivings, he responded to the challenge. Heretofore, he had always "thought more than spoken, spoken more than written" (*NL* 215), but now he determined to state his views in writing: "I knew too well both my own limitations and the character of the age, to be led astray by such roseate hopes. But I consider it the duty of everyone, in a time of such solemn import, and in behalf of a cause which is to us the holiest and most sacred, to make known his opinions openly and honestly" (*NL* 210–11). Three factors seem to have impelled Hirsch to overcome his initial hesitations and fears of rejection and ridicule: his urgent sense of duty to save the younger generation; his firm belief in the truth of his outlook; and his sense of mission to propagate his views. Hirsch expressed the duty and urgency to save the Jewish youth in a most vivid manner:

There is the question of duty. I see a child enveloped in flames; the bystanders are timidly inactive, or seek only to save the building. I see the child, I rush in; need I ask first my neighbor whether he, too, sees the child; have I the right to consider whether, in my hasty rush, I may not knock some neighbor bloody; may I even ask whether, in my haste to save the child, I am not hindering the task of saving the building or producing a draught, which may start the fire to fresh activity? But suppose you see the child too late, and before you reach it the building falls with hiss and crash upon its poor head? Even if it should bury me, too, in its ruins, I would have but done my duty. (*NL* 216–17)

This transparent parable not only indicates Hirsch's all-consuming sense of duty, but also reveals his sense of priority. To save the younger generation from defecting from Judaism was more important than "saving the building," the traditional structural pattern. It similarly reflects his displeasure and impatience with the Orthodox elements who were either "timidly inactive" or more concerned with the external structure of Judaism than with its inner spirit. Indeed, he realized that the building was in flames and in imminent danger of collapse. But, important as it was, it was only a means and not an end. The child must be saved. Hirsch did not minimize the dangers or the possibility of failure. He even wondered if his efforts might not create new problems, "producing a draft which might impel the fire to fresh activity," or cause others chagrin and harm, perhaps "knock some neighbor bloody." But when a child is engulfed in flames, such considerations are inconsequential.

As a result, Hirsch's works of the Oldenburg period were addressed to the Jewish youth. In his *Neunzehn Briefe* he corresponded with a young man, Benjamin, who was perplexed and confused by the Zeitgeist. His *Naftulei Naphtali: Erste Mitteilungen aus Naphtalis Briefwechsel* (1838), dealt with Peretz, a youth who, as his name signifies in Hebrew, had *broken* with his ancestral faith and joined the pyromaniacs of his generation in burning the temple of Judaism.

Hirsch expressed conviction in the correctness of his ideas in an almost mystical manner. He told of an "inner voice" that prompted him to affirm his views and continue his efforts,

which, though I listen and examine my inmost thoughts a thousand times, speaks ever to me the same words, saying: "There is some truth in your views, some of that truth which, you think, must ultimately struggle forth into the light of victory; the way upon which you have begun to walk is perhaps only a by-path, but it leads in the right direction, and if one abler than you should begin to pursue it, the cause of truth would surely prevail." (*NL* 213)

The phrase "if one abler than you" should not be taken seriously. Hirsch believed that he was the one chosen and consecrated by Providence to save Judaism.

In *Naftulei Naphtali,* Hirsch described his consecration in an apocalyptic style. Having portrayed the conflagration of the temple kindled by Peretz and his comrades, in which they themselves were consumed, Hirsch contrasted it with a scene of salvation and bliss; he beheld the sages, mentors, prophets, and rabbis of all generations, and leading this august group was Moses, whose face shone with celestial glory:

And behold, Moses our teacher approached me and said: "How could you hesitate, my son, as you saw the struggle of delusion against truth, of man against God! Human arrogance and lack of insight had removed Heaven from Earth, had called *my* work that which was in reality the work of God, and had described the loyal Messengers of the Divine word deceivers and imposters. And you could hesitate inactively even for a moment!"[32]

While this vision may be partially attributable to the poetic and literary style of the time and the homiletic embellishments of a young preacher, it nevertheless reveals a certain psychological frame of mind. It is strikingly similar to the consecration visions of the great prophets, particularly Isaiah. However, the fact that Hirsch was called by Moses and not by God, as had been the prophets, is understandable. Claiming consecration by God might have been considered blasphemous in Orthodox circles and ridiculous in liberal ones. In the presence of the great prophets, elders, sages, and rabbis, Hirsch was merely commissioned to be the mentor of modern Jewry and the custodian of Judaism.

Hirsch's sense of mission and his high goal are similarly reflected in the pseudonym he selected for his first work, *Neunzehn Briefe über Judentum,* published in 1836 in Altona under the nom de plume Ben Uziel. The *Neunzehn Briefe* was merely a prospectus for two volumes to follow, and Hirsch apparently preferred to have his real name appear on the major work. Indeed, when one of these promised volumes, *Horeb,* appeared the following year, it bore Hirsch's name. Possibly Hirsch needed the anonymity of a pen name to gauge the impression that would be created by the book which he expected to herald a new course in Judaism.

Regardless of motive, it is interesting to consider the reason for the specific pseudonym Ben Uziel, since this was neither etymologically nor phonetically related to Hirsch's name or to the names of his parents. Hirsch, who delighted in hermeneutics and speculative etymology, had undoubtedly given considerable thought to the selection of a nom de plume for a work designed to mark a turning point in Judaism. Connecting the Hebrew title of the *Neunzehn Briefe, Igrot Tzafon,* with the pseudonym, we obtain the reading *Igrot Tzafon Ben Uziel,* which is a close approximation of the name of the Levitic prince Elizaphan ben Uziel mentioned in the Book of Numbers.[33]

An analysis of the biblical, aggadic, and exegetical references to Elizaphan ben Uziel will clarify Hirsch's predilection for this pen name. Elizaphan was Moses' cousin, the son of his youngest uncle, Uziel. Although there were older men who aspired to leadership, Moses appointed Elizaphan as prince of the most noble Levitic order, the Kehathites. The latter were entrusted with the most sacred vessels of the tabernacle—among them the holy ark, the candelabrum, and the altars—which they carried on their shoulders.[34] The other Levitic orders, the Gershonites[35] and the Merarites,[36] were assigned to transport the external appurtenances of the tabernacle—the tapestry, boards, bolts, pillars, and sockets—on wagons and carts. Moses' selection of Elizaphan ben Uziel was bitterly contested by the other Levites who were older, wealthier, and better known. According to the Aggadah, Moses' appointment of Elizaphan ben Uziel caused the great mutiny of Koraḥ. Paraphrasing the Aggadah, Rashi—on the basis of midrashic sources—described Koraḥ's argument:

My father and his brothers were four in number as it is said: "and the sons of Kohath were Amram and Izhar and Hebron and Uziel." As to Amram, the eldest, his two sons have themselves assumed high dignity, one as King and the other as High Priest; who is entitled to receive the second? Is it not I who am the son of Izhar, who was the second to Amram amongst the brothers? And yet he has appointed as prince the son of [Amram's] brother who was the youngest of all of them.[37]

Koraḥ, however, erred. Moses' selection of Elizaphan ben Uziel was neither dictated by personal consideration nor was it an arbitrary decision. Elizaphan ben Uziel's appointment to the most elevated post was done *al pi ha-dibbur*,[38] in accordance with divine command. It was God who had advised Moses to entrust the young son of Uziel with the most sacred symbols of Judaism as well as with the holy ark which contained His word. Ominous as Koraḥ's revolt was, considering his formidable strength, he failed in his contest against the young Elizaphan ben Uziel. Not only was the rebel doomed, but his children—according to the Aggadah— continue to proclaim that Moses was right.[39]

Familiar with the biblical text and the aggadic and exegetic embellishments, Hirsch must have been so impressed with the image of Elizaphan ben Uziel that he identified with him. Like Elizaphan, Hirsch was young and unknown, but nevertheless felt that he too had been chosen by Moses to become prince of the most sacred order. He was certain that his leadership would be contested by many who were older, more prominent, and more erudite. But all their protests and revolts against his leadership would fail, since he too, like Elizaphan ben Uziel, had been appointed by Moses *al pi ha-dibbur*, in accordance with divine command. Indeed, there would be other Levites—rabbis, scholars, and community leaders—who would carry the tabernacle of Judaism. They, however, would carry its externalities on wagons and carts, whereas he and his followers would carry its innermost sacred objects—the ark, candelabrum, and altars—on their very shoulders. It would be he and his adherents who would rebuild the tabernacle of Judaism from its collapse in the intellectual wilderness of nineteenth-century Germany.

That Hirsch anticipated strong resistance and a difficult battle in the ensuing years is evident from the name, Naphtali, he assumed for himself as the interlocutor in the dialogue with his skeptical friend Benjamin in the *Neunzehn Briefe* and *Naftulei Naphtali*. The most obvious reason for this pseudonym seems to be Jacob's comparison of Naphtali to a "deer," which is the German equivalent of "Hirsch." He may, however, also have been attracted to this name because it means "wrestling." This is borne out by the Hebrew title *Naftulei Naphtali*, signifying his own struggles or wrestlings. It was an apparent reference to the biblical verse *naftulei Elohim niftalti im aḥoti gam yakholti*,[40] which he translated as "a sacred wrestling match did I wrestle with my sister and I have been able to do it." It undoubtedly implied that the battle he set out to wage with his sister was not for personal aggrandizement or glory, but one dictated by God. Here again, an overwhelming sense of mission is evident. Hirsch's comment upon this verse in Genesis is of interest, too: "A sacred *wrestling competition* did I wage with my sister, not a match that struggles for something low or common, of which one would be ashamed, but for a sacred end did I compete against my sister, to do my part, too, for the spiritual building up of our house" (*CG* 30:8).

The fact that his pseudonym[41] and the title *Naftulei Naphtali* refer to the aforementioned biblical phrase may also indicate that while the theological and ideological divergencies between Hirsch and the leaders of Reform had begun to widen, he still considered them members of the same family. Although he was compelled to struggle, it was a family fight, fought with the best intentions and compassion "for the spiritual building of *our* house."

The young men of Hirsch's generation who commanded his anxious concern were of two types: redeemable and irredeemable. The latter were typified in *Naftulei Naphtali* by Peretz, whose name signifies "breaker," "rebel," and "destroyer of the temple of Judaism." By burning the temple he destroyed himself and was consumed in the fire he had kindled: "It devoured the torch bearers themselves. As I gazed into the gruesome night, I saw the last flicker of Peretz's torch going up in smoke."[42] Peretz died a spiritual death and apparently could no longer be rescued. However, not all young men were, like Peretz, beyond redemption. Most of them were perplexed and confused, in need of guidance and direction. They were typified by a second young man, the intellectual brother of Joseph ibn Aknin, Benjamin, to whom Hirsch addressed his *Nineteen Letters.* The young men and women whom Hirsch hoped to save were of Benjamin's caliber. In the eyes of the pessimists all young Jews were lost to Judaism; to Hirsch, most of them were redeemable.

Unlike the timid traditionalists, Hirsch did not fear change. Indeed, to him the new era would

be different; our time leads necessarily to such a change. Do not think our time so dark and hopeless, friend; it is only nervous and uncertain, as a woman in childbirth. But better the anxiety which prevails in the house of a woman about to give birth than the freedom from anxiety, but also from joy and hope, in the house of the barren one. This time of labor may outlast our lives and the lives of our children and grandchildren, but our later posterity will rejoice in the child that has struggled out into light and life and its name will be—*sich selbst begreifendes Judentum*— self-comprehending Judaism." (*NL* 201–2)

5

An Outline of the New Guide

A Rudimentary Sketch

From a letter addressed by Hirsch to his cousin Zevi Hirsch May, it is evident that in the early part of 1835 his book *Horeb* was nearing completion.[1] Unable to publish it in rural Oldenburg, he requested the assistance of May, who lived in the larger city of Hamburg. May must have been a man of influence, for he occupied the position of registrar general of the Deutsch-Israelitische Gemeinde in that city. Nevertheless, publication was not easy, for the author was unknown and the subject of the book did not augur any substantial profits. Despite May's endeavors, no publisher seemed eager to undertake the financial risk. To facilitate matters, Hirsch sent his cousin an incomplete manuscript of the *Horeb*. It consisted of the first five sections, of which the last was "a little still unfinished."[2]

Although Hirsch pressed for the publication of the *Horeb*, it was not his first work. The *Horeb*, an exposition of the normative aspect of Judaism, was preceded by *Moriah*,[3] which was devoted to its philosophic aspect. Together, *Moriah* and *Horeb* were to constitute a comprehensive presentation of theoretical and practical Judaism, similar to the *Moreh Nevukhim* and the *Mishneh Torah*. Hirsch stated his intention clearly in the letter to May:

This book bearing the title *Horeb* represents an independent work; and only after the eventual appearance of the book called

144

Moriah will the *Horeb* form its second part. Hence, the double title. The first part of *Moriah* is intended, God willing, to present the theoretical foundation of the Bible's teachings on God, the universe, man and Israel, whereas this second part, *Horeb*, tries to describe Israel's duties in practical life.[4]

That *Moriah* should have preceded *Horeb* was consonant with Hirsch's outlook during that era. Hailing, as he described it, from an *erleuchtet religiös* background and aspiring to a "self-comprehending Judaism" (*NL* 202), he was aware that "the noble life can only be erected upon ideas inwardly recognized as true" (*NL* 202). Normativism without such intellectual recognition was futile. It is therefore understandable that Hirsch's original intention was to publish *Moriah*, the philosophic part, before the normative part, *Horeb*. Circumstances, however, compelled him to act contrary to his inclination and he published his work on the practical aspect of Judaism first.

As the *Landesrabbiner* of Oldenburg, Hirsch was also supervisor of the religious education of the Jewish children of the grand duchy. He was "in charge of a few hundred young souls,"[5] whom he had to provide with religious instruction. The teachers in the small scattered communities of the duchy were for the most part ignorant of Judaism. We may assume that Hirsch did not employ any eastern European *melamdim*, whom he scorned and whose language he considered corrupt. As a result, he had to rely on local talent or native-born German Jews whose knowledge of Judaism was scanty: "I cannot ask [knowledge of Judaism] of the teachers, because they themselves do not know what Judaism really means, and one cannot even blame them for their ignorance. Moreover, there is no textbook available which I could give them for guidance."[6] Hirsch was therefore compelled to relegate theoretical work to the background and to prepare the *Horeb* to serve as educational material for the uninformed teachers in his schools.

Hirsch was chagrined that he had to yield to expediency and publish the *Horeb* before *Moriah:* "To publish these essays first and now is in reality contrary to my original plan."[7] Nevertheless, he recognized the paramount need to publish the *Horeb*, a work geared not to science but to life, so that Jewish teachers could first gain for themselves a true picture of Judaism: "They must first become Jews themselves before they can successfully make Jews of others."[8]

Again and again Hirsch felt it necessary to apologize for publishing the *Horeb* before *Moriah*. At the conclusion of the *Neunzehn Briefe* he dwelt at length on this agonizing necessity:

If Heaven will vouchsafe me health and understanding, I shall endeavor to declare in a first part the views on Judaism concerning God, the world, man, Israel, the Torah; in a second part to expound the *mitzvot*, as far as it is incumbent upon us, deprived of our national soil, to fulfill them. . . .

This second part I intend—God willing—to publish first. To be sure you are right, in your description of the plan, that the knowledge of the general should precede that of the particular, and such is, indeed, the plan of my work. Nevertheless, I shall publish the particular first. I know well that I will thereby rouse up more opponents, for people are readier to acknowledge principles before they have obtained a full view of the consequences to which they logically lead. Still I cannot do otherwise. (*NL* 219–20)

In his prospectus to the public, Hirsch even found a rationale for postponing the publication of *Moriah*, which he had not mentioned in his personal letter to May. Thus, he argued that it would be beneficial for his readers to familiarize themselves with the *Horeb* first in order to be able to appreciate *Moriah* later:

If the first part appeared first, people would look upon that which I say of Israel as a mere dream picture [*Traumbild*], a creation of the enthusiastic fancy, nowhere existing in reality. (*NL* 221)

This reason was, as he himself admitted, illogical, working against the acceptance of the work itself.

A rudimentary outline of *Moriah* must have been in existence before the publication of the *Horeb*. This is evident from the fact that the first edition of the *Horeb*, published in 1837 in Altona, bears the dual title *Moriah* and *Horeb*. Had *Moriah* been merely an idea at that time, Hirsch probably would not have permitted it to appear on the title page. We may assume that since an outline of *Moriah* was completed, or at least nearing completion, the author did not hesitate to print both titles. He undoubtedly hoped to soon develop that outline of *Moriah* into a published book on the philosophy of Judaism. The very fact that *Moriah* and *Horeb* were actually one work, the sequence of which was reversed by circumstances, dictated the mentioning of both titles. It was probably designed to herald the expected appearance of *Moriah,* as well as to forestall any anticipated criticism for publishing a book on traditional practice without any adequate rationale.

That an outline of *Moriah* was actually in existence at the time the *Horeb* was published is substantiated in a footnote to the *Horeb* 's first chapter, which states: "The Torah up to the Revelation on Sinai, to the development of which the first part of *Moriah* is principally devoted, and of which letters III–IX of the *Neunzehn Briefe über Judentum* contain a sketch."[9] It is clear from this footnote that the *Horeb* began where *Moriah* ended. The latter dealt with the philosophical and theological ramifications up to the moment of revelation; the former concerned itself with the details of revelation.

It should be pointed out, however, that the assumption of the existence of an outline of *Moriah* does not necessarily imply that this work had been fully evolved at that time. It is worthwhile to remember that Hirsch was only twenty-seven years old when he informed his cousin about his work. The completion of a comprehensive modern philosophy of Judaism required time and erudition. As will be seen, both *Moriah* and *Horeb* were intended merely as outlines to be developed and elaborated at a later, more tranquil time by a more mature Hirsch. Regrettably, *Moriah* never appeared. Hirsch's first philosophic work, meant to become the modern *Moreh Nevukhim* and "intended to present a general conception of the essence of Jewish nationhood,"[10] was not published. Nevertheless, although *Moriah* never saw light, its content in sketchy outline form did reach us due to some peculiarly fortuitous circumstances. A publisher in Altona suggested that Hirsch summarize his views and ideas in a small brochure, the publication of which would not be too expensive. Based upon the success or failure of this summary, the publisher expected to decide whether the actual, more extensive work merited publication and the financial investment this would involve. Hirsch seized upon this offer and in the following year, 1836, published the *Neunzehn Briefe über Judentum,* which contained an outline of his fundamental outlook and the basic ideas he intended to express in his magnum opus.

An examination of the *Neunzehn Briefe* shows that only a small portion—letters 10–14—serves as an outline of the *Horeb.* The first nine letters, however, deal with the philosophical and theological foundations of Judaism; most of them constituting a summary of *Moriah,* which was already in existence in an initial draft awaiting further revision. Although it is unfortunate that *Moriah* never saw print, we may consider as partial consolation the fact that its basic ideas are presented in sketchy form in the first half of the *Neunzehn Briefe.* Although far from complete, they enable us to reconstruct Hirsch's "theoretical foundation of the Bible's teachings on God, the universe, man and Israel,"[11] which he evolved at the time. The above-mentioned footnote is partial proof that the content of *Moriah* was outlined in letters 3–9 of the *Neunzehn Briefe.*

Cognizant of the fact that his outline had to impress not only the publisher but also the Jewish community of Germany, Hirsch made his *Neunzehn Briefe* more than a mere, conventional summary; it is an independent work calculated to evoke its own response from readers. Nevertheless, the first half of the *Neunzehn Briefe* can also be read as an outline of *Moriah,* enabling us to discern the ideas and views he hoped to elaborate extensively at a future date. Subsequent analysis of the *Neunzehn Briefe* should therefore be also considered as an analysis of the nonexistent *Moriah,* allowing, of course, for the limitations imposed by the brevity of a rudimentary sketch. Although the references will be to the *Neunzehn Briefe (Nineteen Letters)* it must always be remembered that they reflect the concepts of *Moriah.*

A New Approach

The *Neunzehn Briefe über Judentum* published by the twenty-eight-year-old Samson Raphael Hirsch in 1836 surpassed the expectations of not only the publisher, but also the author. The *Briefe* stirred up a great deal of comment and had a sensational effect upon the Jewish public.[12] Although German Jewish intellectuality of that time was not conducive to an exposition of traditional Judaism, Hirsch's *Neunzehn Briefe* revived just such an interest. Some of the intelligentsia, who had previously abandoned the Talmud as a body of lore which "perverts the mind and leads it astray into subtleties and the minutiae of petty distinctions" (*NL* 5), returned to it with renewed determination. They began "to pierce to its depth, acquire a philosophical knowledge thereof and . . . publicly demonstrate its truth and utility."[13] Hirsch's *Briefe* captivated young men of intellect and scholarly attainment such as Heinrich Graetz, who found in the work "a view of Judaism . . . never before heard or suspected."[14] Graetz devoured every word,[15] and, as already indicated, asked Hirsch, the author of the "Divine Epistle," for the opportunity to become his disciple.[16]

A superficial and uncritical reading of the *Briefe* fails to disclose the fresh view that seemed to have startled many men of Hirsch's generation. Aside from the novelty of form, namely, the attempt to defend traditional Judaism and the meticulous observance of the law in highly polished poetic German—there seems to be nothing new here. Hirsch's insistence on the absolute authority and divinity of the Torah and his assertion that the Jews must "go back to the ancient fountains of Judaism, Bible and Talmud, . . . to obtain the concept of life out of Judaism and to comprehend Judaism as the law of life, . . . to learn and to teach, to keep and to do" (*NL* 203) could have come from any traditionalist writer. Nor was there anything new in his symbolical interpretation of the commandments, only sketchily alluded to in the *Briefe*. Ever since Philo, and even prior to him, the precepts of the Torah had been subject to exegetical, allegorical, and hermeneutical elaborations. The talmudic, midrashic, rabbinic, and cabalistic literature is replete with similar explanations. The speculative etymology[17] subsequently developed and interpreted by Hirsch could hardly have had a determining influence upon scholars versed in their contemporary lexicography, philology, and comparative linguistics. For, although speculative etymology was in vogue in some circles during Hirsch's time, it was not taken seriously by scholars.

Still, the *Neunzehn Briefe* must have contained something unusual in its approach to traditional Judaism which fascinated Graetz,[18] "electrified" Kaufmann Kohler,[19] and compelled Abraham Geiger to publish a lengthy comprehensive review in the *Wissenschaftliche Zeitschrift für jüdische Theologie.*[20] Something fresh and different in the *Briefe's* exposition of Judaism was not only sensed by the readers at that time, but was stressed by Hirsch himself. He maintained that he had entertained those new ideas "for a long time as my dearest treasure" (*NL* 210). There was, however, great hesitancy on his part as to the advisability of their publication; he was gravely concerned over whether his new approach would be "acknowledged by all as truth or that I may deem it with certainty the pure gold of truth" (*NL* 210).

Hirsch also seems to suggest that the views he expounded in the *Neunzehn Briefe* were not yet fully developed. While he realized that their implications might have far-reaching effects, all he presented that was promising were the rudiments of a new approach to Judaism. However, this approach still had to be carefully explained, elaborated, and applied:

If I should only succeed in demonstrating that the matter has not been thoroughly investigated in all its aspects, that there is, perhaps, a way by means of which one could reach entirely different results than those hitherto attained, a view in the light of which everything would present an appearance quite different from that hitherto customary and usual; . . . my reward would even then be greater than I have dared to hope. (*NL* 211–12)

It is clear that in 1836 Hirsch had only a glimmering of a new approach, or a bare outline of a new method "concerning Israel and Israel's duties—or rather concerning the duties alone, for my thoughts on Israel are still only a project of my mind" (*NL* 212). Despite his "modest diffidence," Hirsch obeyed the call of his inner voice which told him to proceed with his project (*NL* 213).

In the *Neunzehn Briefe*, Hirsch speaks of "one dear friend" assisting him "a little in the smaller, easier, and clearer part," and "only one star" guiding him "somewhat in the beginning" (*NL* 214). This may mean that he was introduced to this new approach, which had not previously been applied to Judaism, by a person whom he considered a friend of some scholastic attainment. Hirsch saw in this new approach great possibilities for the reconstruction and reinterpretation of the basic views of Judaism, the details of which were "evolved almost alone out of my inner consciousness" (*NL* 214).

Hirsch realized that the reconstruction of Judaism in the light of the new ideas he had acquired would be immensely difficult. It would not be easy to fit the enormous, cumulative mass of Jewish religious experience, literature, tradition, and ritual into a neatly constructed philosophic system. Such conformity was bound to produce hazardous strictures resulting in the discomfiture of Jews or the inefficacy of Judaism. Hirsch admits that he met "at every step thorns and refuse [that] had to be removed, and I, with my limited powers, was called upon alone to take issue with the entire past and the entire present" (*NL* 214).

The task was gigantic and fearful, for the reconstruction of Judaism in the new light was fraught with the danger of numerous defects and the acceptance of "a thousand errors as truths" (*NL* 214). Hirsch was afraid that if he failed to reinterpret it, the opponents and critics of traditional Judaism would have an opportunity to gloat, and the abortive results of Hirsch's effort might be devastating. Nevertheless, he remained determined to present his exposition, even if not fully analyzed or developed, because, as he says, he had "climbed *alone* to a height from which a *new view* displays itself to me. . . . I only wish to give what I have *until now* been able to gather together, *not as a perfect work*, but truly as essays" (*NL* 216). Hirsch repeats this last statement and underscores it in his preface to the *Letters:*

I did not attempt in the sketches to map out for you an accurate design of the entire ground-plan superstructure but only a general *outline* of the edifice of Judaism. I have only led you through one majestic nave of the edifice, from which you can form a partial conception of the imposing whole.[21]

Indeed, Hirsch knew that

the natural way would have been to have labored first only for the scientific evolvement, and whatever would have demonstrated in the battle of minds its truth and tenability would have been afterwards quietly transferred into the practice of life. That would have been the quieter, the surer, the pleasanter way. (*NL* 217)

The exigencies of life and the demands of time, however, required that he not delay. He therefore decided to state his new views, and "later it would devolve upon the *men of science* to establish in *science* and as *science* the principles which he had actively defended in life" (*NL* 218). And so he published his *Letters*, which were merely an outline of a system according to which either he or the "men of science" who would come after him, or

both together, would establish and reinterpret Judaism in consonance with the principles he had laid down.

An Organismic Comprehension

Considering the *Briefe* primarily as a rudimentary outline of a
new approach according to which Hirsch had "scientifically" attempted the reconstruction and reinterpretation of traditional
Judaism, the question arises as to the nature of this approach.
As noted, Hirsch does not claim originality for his method; he
was assisted by "one dear friend" and guided by "only one star"
(*NL* 214), who was directly responsible for having introduced
Hirsch to this new approach. Who this was is difficult to ascertain.[22] However, the approach itself as employed by Hirsch, as
well as some of its underlying philosophical principles, seems to
bear a striking similarity to the basic ideas and methods of Hegel.
Hegel died only five years before the publication of the *Briefe*,
in which Hirsch endeavors to probe traditional Judaism and justify
its existence, continuity, applicability, and objectiveness in modern times, and Hegel's views had reached the peak of popularity
not only among non-Jews but in Jewish circles as well.[23]

The Hegelian influence becomes evident in Hirsch's attempts to
explain the difference between his approach and those of other
exponents of Judaism. As already indicated, Hirsch takes issue with
Maimonides because the latter "sought to reconcile Judaism with
the difficulties which confronted it from *without* instead of developing it creatively from *within*" (*NL* 181). Maimonides did not
view each precept in the light of the totality of the Torah; instead,
he tried to interpret it arbitrarily in the light of a priori concepts
from the *outside*. Similarly, Hirsch disapproves of Mendelssohn,
who "did not build up Judaism as a *science from itself*" (*NL* 189).
Hirsch insists that Judaism must be organically comprehended—
"sich selbst begreifendes Judentum." No outside criterion or clev-
erly constructed hypothesis can be applied to Judaism; it must be
comprehended from within—"aus sich selbst heraus."

Hirsch's differentiation between the negative investigation of
Judaism from without and the positive one from within was akin
to Hegel's distinction between comprehension of a thing *für uns*

and *für sich*. In order to appreciate a point of view fully, one cannot merely observe it externally, since the view as it appears to us—*für uns*— from the outside is meaningless. Only when we establish an intellectual sympathy by endeavoring to discover its intrinsic meaning—*für sich*— do we grasp its vital experience and inner nature. By placing ourselves in the middle of the unfolding reality it is possible, according to Hegel, to discover its *inner spirit*, its inherent laws of growth, and its significance. Likewise, Hirsch maintains that any changes in Judaism effected from the outside will be of no avail, since "the spirit, the *inner* harmonious life-principle, is lacking, and that you cannot supply through polishing the *outside* frame" (*NL* 196–97). It is therefore imperative "to find the indwelling spirit" (*NL* 194) in the various laws. We have to go back to the original "sources of Judaism, to Bible, Talmud, and Midrash" (*NL* 197) and "to know Judaism *out of itself*, to learn from its utterances its *science* of life" (*NL* 197). Hirsch thus suggests that

the doctrine of God, world, man, Israel, and Torah should be drawn from the Bible, and should become an *idea*, or *system of ideas*, fully comprehended. In this spirit, Talmud should be studied; in the Halakhah only further elucidation and amplification of ideas already known from the Bible should be sought for; in the Aggadah only figuratively disguised manifestations of the same spirit. (*NL* 198)

Hirsch's idea, apparently following the theory of Johann Gottfried Herder[24] and August Boeckh,[25] was that the literature of a people reveals its fundamental characteristics, a view also accepted by Leopold Zunz, who applied it in his studies of Jewish history and literature.[26]

Hirsch thought the basic spirit of Judaism was a potential in the Bible which became actualized in subsequent rabbinic literature; this idea is analogous to Hegel's concept of the actualization of the spirit in the history of the world: "World history is the exhibition of spirit striving to attain knowledge of its own nature. As the germ bears in itself the whole nature of the tree, the taste and shape of its fruit, so also the first traces of the spirit virtually contain the whole of history."[27] In characteristic Hegelian fashion Hirsch asserts, "one spirit lives in all, from the construction of the Holy

Tongue to the construction of the universe and the plan of life, one spirit, the spirit of the All-One" (*NL* 199).

The inner spirit of Judaism, like the Hegelian *Geist*— or perhaps identical with it—cannot and should not be arrested: "Time, if left unhindered, will wash away what it itself has brought into existence, and room will always remain for the higher edifice which yet awaits us" (*NL* 206). As is evident from this quotation, Hirsch not only accepted the Hegelian concept of the continuously unfolding spirit during the march of time, but also subscribed to Hegel's idea of the progress of time being synonymous with evolution toward ethical perfection. "The time-process," for Hegel, "is from the less to the more perfect, both in an ethical and in a logical sense. Indeed, these two senses are, for him, not really distinguishable, for logical perfection consists in being a closely knit whole, without ragged edges, without independent parts."[28]

The Individualistic-Eudaemonistic Challenge to Judaism If we accept the premise that the *Neunzehn Briefe* were written under the impact of Hegel, the significance of the letters' presentation, as well as the order in which they were written, assumes new meaning. Rereading the *Briefe*, we sense the intellectual tensions of the perplexed Jewish youth of Hirsch's era. Benjamin is a Jew typical of the nineteenth century—confused by its impact, remaining intellectually suspended between traditional Judaism and the spirit of the age. He vacillates between both, finding them incompatible and irreconcilable. His arguments are of the same nature as those of Rousseau, Basedow, Pestalozzi, Froebel, Goethe, Fichte, and Schlegel, who emphasized and overemphasized the significance of the individual. Accordingly, the paramount aim in life is the attainment of the harmonious development of the individual's abilities and potentialities. Religion, like any other cultural manifestation, should therefore enable the individual to achieve happiness and perfection and must avoid restrictive or coercive means.

This highly individualistic, anthropocentric, eudaemonistic concept, with its natural corollary of excessive subjectivism, was bound to come into sharp conflict with a religion like Judaism, which stresses law and duty, uniformity, and objectivism. The individualistic-subjective view of man as self-centered, independent, and unrelated to his surroundings is antithetical to the normative view of Judaism, which implies the curtailment of the individual's unrestricted rights and pleasures. Consequently, subjective freedom clashes with the objective legality imposed by traditional Judaism.

Benjamin, in the individualistic manner of an enlightened man, considers it his right to make his own decisions on questions concerning Judaism, on the validity of the Torah, on the observance or the abrogation of the *mitzvot*, as well as on the general status and obligations of the Jew: "Every religion, *I believe*, should bring man nearer to his ultimate end. This end, what else can it be than the attainment of *happiness* and *perfection* [*Glückseligkeit und Vollkommenheit*]?" (*NL* 3). To him, Judaism obviously does not measure up to this standard, since "the Law itself interdicts all enjoyments, is a hindrance to all the pleasures of life" (*NL* 4). Nor does the Torah seem justified to him when measured by the *external* standards of Virgil, Tasso, and Shakespeare, or by the philosophical systems of Leibniz and Kant.[29]

Historical Objectivism versus Individual Subjectivism   In the second letter, Hirsch begins to present his own point of view designed to refute the contentions of individual subjectivism. In that letter he postulates the Hegelian concept of objectivism. This view denies the right of the individual to set himself up as the sole criterion of what is right or wrong. He also questions the eudaemonistic teleology of life extolled by the romantics: "I could ask: Is it so sure that *happiness* and *perfection* form the goal and object of man's being? I could ask upon what basis you found this opinion?" (*NL* 11). If man becomes the measure of all things, then civilization and morality remain without standards and without values. True morality, in the Hegelian sense, exists when the individual identifies his own good with the universal good. Hirsch shows the absurdity of individualism. As someone else has said: "Pure individualism would mean social dissolution."[30] Reason, Hirsch held, is not man's subjective view but constitutes an objective reality which in turn reveals and unfolds itself progressively in history:

True speculation does not consist, as many would-be thinkers suppose, in closing the eye and the ear to the world round about us and in constructing out of our own inner ego a world to suit ourselves; true speculation takes nature, man, and history as facts, as the true basis of knowledge, and seeks in them instruction and wisdom; to these, Judaism adds the Torah, as genuine a reality as heaven or earth. (*NL* 147)

The individual cannot determine the validity of ideas, practices, or institutions, because he must first understand the *whole*.

In the second letter, Hirsch delays the development of his concept of objectivism versus subjectivism: "Let us put aside for a while the standard of measurement, and let us try to know that which we desire to measure—Judaism, in its history and teachings" (*NL* 12). He then commences to introduce Hegel's historical method as it might be applied to the investigation of Judaism.

An institution or civilization must be understood "aus sich selbst heraus"—out of itself. In order to comprehend Judaism one must understand it in its historic context, "for Judaism is a *historical phenomenon*, and for its origin, its first entrance into *history*, and for a long subsequent time, the Torah is the only monument" (*NL* 13). The Torah is thus the *historical* record of the Jewish people, and if we study it assiduously, if we gain a larger historical perspective, the inner spirit that permeates Judaism will become evident. Only when we go back to the original sources of the Jewish religion will the intelligibility of its inner laws become apparent. Hirsch, therefore, suggests rereading these sources in this new Hegelian light: "Let us read as though we had never read them; as though we had never heard of them. Let us arouse in our soul the life questions, 'What is the world in me, and around me, to me? What am I; what should I be to it? What am I; what should I be as *Man-Israel* [*Mensch-Jissroel*]?' " (*NL* 16).

The Hegelian Metaphysical Doctrine   In the third letter, the influence of the Hegelian philosophy becomes even more pronounced. Here, Hirsch seems to employ the Hegelian metaphysical doctrine, according to which

the character of any portion of the universe is so profoundly affected by its relations to the other parts and to the whole, that no true statement can be made about any part except to assign its place in the whole. Since its place in the whole depends upon all other parts, a true statement about its place in the whole will at the same time assign the place of every other part in the whole.[31]

Applying this doctrine to the comprehension of the task of the Jew, Hirsch maintains that we must, in like manner, relate this task to a larger whole. The Jew is a part of Israel, but in order to understand Israel, which "is a historical phenomenon among other manifestations of the world's records" (*NL* 17), we must understand history. The question of history, however, is contingent upon the problem of man in general: "But man is not isolated, he is a creature amidst the other creatures, affected by and affecting them, therefore we must next ask what is the world?" (*NL* 17–18). Thus, Hirsch widens the circle to include the entire cosmos in order to determine the role and significance of one of its constituent parts, the Jew. This difficult and complicated procedure was essential to Hirsch, since in the Hegelian philosophy "there is no truth except the whole truth, and similarly nothing is quite real except the whole, for any part, when isolated, is changed in character by being isolated, therefore no longer appears quite what it truly is."[32]

The conglomeration of all the phenomena in the cosmos does not necessarily imply meaning unless they are comprehended through the spirit that permeates them. Without the spirit, they constitute mere *disjecta membra* and consequently are unintelligible. Hirsch, too, asserts that the task of the Jew can be ascertained only by determining his relation to the rational whole to which he belongs—the cosmos—and comprehended only through God, "as a work of art is only then perfectly understood when we have an insight into the plans of the master" (*NL* 18). The Torah, being in rabbinic tradition the divine plan of the cosmos, is the best source to lead us "through the concept of Israel and Israel's duties to the knowledge of God, the world, the missions of mankind and history" (*NL* 18).

The method of the Torah seems to be identical with the metaphysical doctrine of Hegel. The aim of the Torah is primarily to teach the Jew his obligations and role in the world. It does not begin with that exposition, however, but rather with the larger perspective, the creation of the cosmos. Only when the significance of the whole—the universe—is imparted to us and then narrowed gradually down to the part—the people of Israel and the individual Jew—will the task of the Jew become self-evident.

Therefore, to understand man, Hirsch asserts, we must understand creation or the multifarious manifestations of God in nature and history: "God reveals Himself only in His works" (*NL* 18). The unfolding of the Hegelian *Geist* and Hirschian God takes place in the dual areas of nature and history: "The Idea develops both in space and in time. The Idea developing in space is nature, the Idea subsequently—or rather consequently, for it is all a *logical* process—developing in time, is spirit. The latter, the development of the Idea in time, or of spirit, is history."[33] Nature thus can serve as a guide to discover the task of man. For, to Hirsch and Hegel, nature is neither inert nor a mere mechanism; it is a rational exhibition of the *Geist,* or the *logos.* Nature is "petrified intelligence,"[34] or the externalization of the spirit. "Nature is in itself rational, and knowledge has to apprehend the reason actually present in it."[35]

According to Hirsch, when we analyze nature it is possible to observe its constitutive and regulative principles, which themselves manifest rationality. Behind the constant mutations "of originating and passing away, of blooming and withering, of life and death, eternally struggling from ceasing, fading, and death, to ever new existence, bloom, and life" (*NL* 19), we perceive the existence of law, in unconditional obedience "to which a stone falls or a seed of corn grows into a plant," and "the force and the law in accordance with which the planets move in their orbits or the intellect expands" (*NL* 21). Nature, Hirsch felt, also reveals a remarkable interdependence of its constituent parts: "None is by or for itself, but all things exist in continual reciprocal activity—the one for All; the All for One" (*NL* 29).

Though nature consists of numerous antithetical forces "separated and distinguished by peculiar construction and different purposes" (*NL* 22), they are nevertheless reconciled by God, whom Hirsch calls by a term that has a peculiar Hegelian dialectic ring: "Harmonizer of Contrasts [*Vermittler aller Gegensätze*]" (NL 22). These antithetical forces are held together by love, "love which bears and is born is the type of creation. *Love* is the message which all things proclaim" (*NL* 30). Hirsch seems to have applied to the realm of nature the force of love, which Hegel considered as the foundation of social union and its controlling organizing principle on the self-conscious level. Hirsch's anthropomorphic concept of love in the organic world may have evolved because, in his philosophy, God takes the place of the Hegelian *Geist* and His spirit is immanent in nature: "Not only all *was* through Him, all *is* through Him. His blessing is every bloom and blossom; His blessing every germ and every fruit; His blessing the mother's offspring; His blessing the babe pressed to the loving breast" (*NL* 22–23). The fact that God's spirit is immanent in all creation accounts for the existence of love in the organic world since, as Hegel said, "the spirit finds itself bound to another and in this tie feels the assurance of its own existence."

The Teleological Aspect and Dualistic Nature of Man   In the fourth letter, Hirsch takes up the position of man "in this God-filled world" (*NL* 31). Although man belongs to the realm of mind and the world to the realm of nature, there is no radical difference between them. For Hirsch, as well as Hegel, there is a dominant principle of unity underlying both spheres in spite of their seeming differences: "In spite of all their apparent conflicts, the kingdoms of nature and of spirit are essentially one."[36] Consequently, the rationality manifest in the sphere of mind is also present, although not as apparent, in the sphere of nature. The only distinguishing characteristic is consciousness, not reason. While nature carries out its rational functions dutifully, without awareness, mind is cognizant of its purpose. Man, who is partly nature and partly mind, serves as a bridge linking the organic world and the realm of consciousness. Man connects the sphere of nature, in which reason is externalized, with the sphere of the mind.

But the complete consciousness of man, his full awareness of his moral freedom and his cognizance of his duty and role in the universe, is only potential. It is incumbent upon him to actualize this inherent potential and gain the true perspective of totality. Man's potential, however, does not display itself automatically at the dawn of his life. At that stage, man's mind is only subjective and close to the state of nature: "The individual in the state of nature is governed by blind instinct, by brutal passions and by that egoism which characterizes animal life."[37]

Since one aspect of man's constitutional duality is his kinship with nature, he should, according to Hirsch, act in a manner similar to that of other natural phenomena:

Since all things, the smallest and the greatest, are God's chosen messengers, to work, each in its place, and with its measure of power, according to the law of the Most High, taking only that it may give again, should man alone be excluded from this circle of blessed activity? . . . The world and all which is therein serves God; is it conceivable that man alone should only serve himself? (*NL* 32)

For Hirsch, that which distinguishes man from the vast variety of natural phenomena is the image of God he carries in his consciousness (*NL* 32). Man's consciousness must be elevated from its subjective state and subordinated to the objective mind of the Torah. Man must not act in accordance with his unenlightened, subjective desires and follow his egotistical inclinations. He should submit his subjective mind to the objective one, which regulates his desires, disciplines them through law, and harmonizes them with the will of God. The Torah, to Hirsch, like the law of the state to Hegel, represents a higher reason than the limited subjective reason of the individual. Thus, when man acts in accordance with the law of the Torah, he is not hampered by it but gains true freedom, since freedom in Hegelian philosophy is achieved when the individual consciously identifies his power *within* with the power *without.* To the Hegelians,

In knowing the external world, and identifying himself with the ethical substance, [man] comes gradually to the fulfillment of the command *gnoti sauton*— first to know and therewith to be himself—to feel his calling to be that of a co-worker in the realization of the divine purpose "to which the whole creation moves."[38]

Hirsch likewise maintains that when man subordinates his subjective will to the higher will of the Torah and limits his subjective freedom in accordance with its demands, he attains true knowledge and true freedom: " 'Knowledge and freedom,' these words indicate at once the sublime mission and the lofty privilege of man" (*NL* 33). Consciously recognizing his role in the universe, man ceases to demand the possessions of the world as his exclusive property. On gaining the proper perspective, he freely limits himself and recognizes the rights of others. His subjective mind emerges from its natural state, and he becomes aware that all the possessions with which he has been endowed,

spirit, body, human beings, wealth, every ability and every power, they are means of activity; *le-avdah u-le-shamrah,* to promote and preserve the world they were given—love and righteousness. Not thine is the earth, but thou belongest to the earth, to respect it as divine soil and deem every one of its creatures a creature of God, thy fellow being. (*NL* 32–33)

The law evident in the realm of nature, whether in the inorganic, chemical, or organic spheres, is also applicable to the sphere of mind, and hence to man: "The law to which all powers submit unconsciously and involuntarily, to it shalt thou also subordinate thyself, but consciously and of thy own free will" (*NL* 33). Whereas all the forces of nature carry out their task without awareness of their duty—"their capacity is hidden from themselves and covered are their countenances, so that they cannot see the reason of their mission" (*NL* 33–34)—man who is endowed with mind also has the ability partially to understand his obligation. Hirsch phrases this thought poetically, saying that man's "countenance is half uncovered, thy capacity is half revealed, thou canst comprehend thyself as creature of God" (*NL* 34). Man gradually lifts himself up from the state of nature into the state of spirit. His role in the universe is neither that of a god nor of a slave, "but as brother, as co-working brother, occupying, however, the rank of first-born among his brother beings, because of the peculiar nature and extent of his service" (*NL* 44).

It should be noted that Hirsch emphasizes the teleological principle, which is the dominant characteristic of all phenomena in the world. His teleology resembles that of Hegel, who distinguished between external, finite teleology, in which the means and the ends are completely distinct objects, and "inner-design" teleology, which is "a relation of means and ends where each exists solely in and for the other, where the one could not exist without the other and where, in the last analysis, the one is identical with the other."[39] In the realm of nature, which is devoid of consciousness, the "inner-design" teleology is inherent. On the human level, consciousness seems to sever this true teleology and separate the object from the notion. Only man's understanding of his task tends to coalesce the object with the notion and reestablish in man the "inner design" existing unconsciously in nature.

The Subordination of the Subjective Mind to the Absolute Mind
Hirsch points out in the fifth letter the dangers menacing the human mind when it is permitted to pursue its subjective course

unrestrained. Man, being a transition between the realm of nature and the realm of spirit, can be easily carried away by his blind instincts and passions: "Through his animal portion, his body with its desires, he is threatened with sensual lust" (*NL* 46). In order to emerge from the state of nature into the state of spirit, man must yield to the Absolute Mind—God:

Man should subordinate himself to his creator, for him highest wisdom consists in *obeying the will of God as the will of his God.* But to be willing to fulfill the behests of that will only when or because they appear also to us right and wise and good, could that be called obedience to God? Would not that rather be obedience to oneself? (*NL* 47–48)

This statement indicates a position similar to that of Hegel, who maintained that man's true freedom is attained only by unconditional obedience: "Obligatory duty can appear as a limitation only to undetermined subjectivity or abstract freedom, and to the desires of the natural will, or to that moral will which determines its indeterminate good through its own caprice."[40] Hegel believed it is only when the individual responds to the demands of the "environing ethos" that ethicality becomes second nature to him. Similarly, Hirsch says,

the law, which lays down reverence, love and faithfulness as the three foundation-stones, does not cripple the heart, but that, *when comprehended and assimilated to the mind,* its fulfillment becomes a new *power, a life from within,* not a mere barren and external dwarf of existence, stimulating all the faculties to a freer development and a more intense use. (*NL* 149)

In the Hegelian dialectic, the subjective mind submits to the molding influences of the objective mind, which is society or the state. According to Hirsch, the subjective mind has to subordinate itself directly to the Absolute Mind, which is God, or to His manifest will, the Torah. This exposition of the conscious mission of the objective mind should not be considered a serious departure from the Hegelian philosophy; the different interpretation is due to the social difference between the two interpreters. The German Hegel, living in a German-Christian state, saw in the latter the objectification of the spirit, for it endeavored to put into law the socio-

ethical ideas in which he believed. To Hirsch, the Jew, the German-Christian state did not present the fulfillment of Jewish ideals
and values. He therefore could not see in that state the epitome
of spirit. Not infrequently were the laws of that objective mind—
the German-Christian state—detrimental to Judaism. Insistence
that the subjective mind of the Jew be subordinate to the objective
mind—in this case the German-Christian state—would have implied the destruction of Judaism. Consequently, Hirsch deviates
pragmatically from this particular Hegelian view and makes the
subjective mind of the Jew directly subject to the Absolute Mind
—God and Torah:

The path to pleasure is made difficult to discourage the development of the animal side of [man's] being and to render less arrogant his pride; that the real man in him be led upwards to God,
through realization of the limitations of his power, and that something else must be his task and his greatness than that which can
be thus easily conferred upon him, or taken from him. (*NL* 49)

To Hirsch, the Torah is the expression of the will of the Absolute
Mind. Its principles are neither arbitrary nor restrictive. Their
legal aspect appears limiting only to the subjective, self-centered
individual who does not realize that his freedom does not express
itself in his carnal appetites but in the full acceptance of morality.
By adhering to the Torah, the Jew gains his absolute freedom.
Only when the supposed legality of the Torah is transformed into
ethicality, when the *nomos* becomes *ethos*— or in Hegelian terminology, when the objective mind becomes a subject—is the Jew
truly free. To paraphrase a Hegelian statement, Torah is to Hirsch
"the legality of the heart, the law which is identified with the will
of the individual."[41] The seeming difficulties that the Jew encounters in the fulfillment of his Jewish duties do not affect the objective existence of the Law, nor are they a valid excuse for its abrogation:

If our view of life is earnest and serious; if we comprehend Judaism
as the charge with which we are entrusted, and which we are to
bear through time and tribulation; if we realize that it is our
life-code of duty, can the difficulty, the burdensomeness of an
obligation dispense us from its fulfillment? Should it not rather
make the duty of fulfillment more solemn and urgent? (*NL* 151)

Once man abandons the will of the Absolute Mind and reverts to the dictates of his own subjective mind, he loses sight of the will of God. His failure to comprehend the "whole" transforms all phenomena of the universe into an irrational maze of contradictory "parts" struggling with one another. Hirsch states it thus:

As soon as man ceases to look upon himself as the empowered guardian and administrator of the earth-world, as soon as he endeavors to carry out, not the will of God, but his own will, and ceases to be a servant of God; he sees no longer in the strength-endowed beings around him the servitors of Deity, but independent forces which seek possession, lust, and power; he has no eye any more for the law of the All-One whom they all serve, and the world divides itself for him into as many gods as he sees forces in operation. (*NL* 51)

According to Hegel's *Phenomenology*, "jedes Moment, weil es Moment des Wesens ist, muss dazu gelangen, als Wesen sich darzustellen." The exaggerated sense of importance that each part has when it does not relate itself to the whole is evident in every aspect of human endeavor. In such circumstances, there is always an element of danger that the subjective mind will magnify the particular and ascribe to it the attributes and qualities of the whole. "The human mind is incurably 'idolatrous,'" Hegel maintained, "because it moves in concentric circles. It worships at this shrine or that shrine the particular gods that attract and excite it."[42]

The Culmination of the Dialectic Spiral   In the sixth letter, Hirsch gives a Hegelian interpretation to the biblical narrative of the generation of the Tower of Babel: because those people rebelled against God and did not surrender their subjective minds to the Absolute One, they lost their theocentric comprehension of the world as a whole, and the world disintegrated into a multitude of anthropocentric parts, each vying with one another and struggling for supremacy and its own deification. Man, deluded by his partial and fragmentary vision, became incorrigibly idolatrous— that is, he magnified a part to the status of the whole. God, however, although He did not wish to destroy the world, was, in a Lessingian manner, determined to educate humanity by the dialectical march of the *Geist* through history: "When one race has gone through all the stages of the sinful illusions which weaken and corrupt mankind, and is enervated, exhausted, and unfit for the divine purpose, it shall yield its place to a stronger and hardier race, which shall begin a fresher, purer life" (*NL* 54).

Hirsch followed the Hegelian view of the role of nations in the unfolding of the spirit of history, a view that he unknowingly shared with another Jewish thinker, Naḥman Krochmal.[43] Hegel maintained that according to the principle of historical development, "in every age, there is some one nation which is charged with the mission of carrying the world through the stage of the dialectic that it has reached."[44] Hirsch similarly states that "from this time on, nation after nation enters into the arena of history; each presents some new power, some new capacity of the human intellect, and uses these faculties in battle with nature and with each other" (*NL* 55). Indeed, these nations crave eternity, but "a higher hand" dashes their attainment to the ground. When a nation has reached its zenith, it collapses and "forsakes the sphere of its activity for similar attempts on the part of the succeeding generations" (*NL* 56).

In Hirsch's philosophy, as in Hegel's, there is a definite historic reason and purpose for the emergence and decline of nations and for their place in the divine blueprint:

All nations that were or are anywhere upon the surface of the earth, whether in the east or the west, the north or the south, each with its life and disappearance from the stage of history, with its successes and failures, with its virtues and its vices, its wisdom and its folly, its rise and its fall, in a word, with whatsoever it leaves to posterity as the sum total of the results and products of its existence. All of these efforts and actions are bricks contributed to the edifice of human history; all tend to the carrying out of the plan of the one, same God. (*NL* 143)

Each nation makes its own contributions to the sum total of history and presents a certain aspect of the spirit as revealed in history:

The same result is attained by the art of the Greeks when morally pure and devoted to the refinement of the mind, and of their science, when sharpening the intellect to the better apprehension of truth; even the sword of the Roman and the peaceful commerce of the European have united nations in brotherhood for the working out of the same ideals. (*NL* 144)

Here again, we must emphasize the differences between Hegel and Hirsch. In the former, this dialectic spiral terminates in the Prussian state, which he glorified.[45] For Hirsch, this dialectic spiral culminates in the "End of Days" of the messianic era. Furthermore, Hegel, who posited the objective mind as an intermediate stage between the subjective and the absolute, could see in the triumph of the state the victory of the *Geist*. Hirsch, who had to eliminate the intermediate phase and subordinate the subjective mind to the all-encompassing Absolute Mind, was compelled to terminate the dialectic spiral by the unconditional surrender of the nations to God and the recognition of the only reality (the whole) and the illusion (the parts). The historical dialectic process will be fulfilled only, Hirsch states,

after mankind, which had, in strange delusion, placed all creatures, and even man himself, upon the throne of the Most High, has learned, in the destruction of human ambitions, the nothingness of these puny rivals of Deity, and lifts its eye, unobscured by superstitious veil, to the All-One. (*NL* 56)

The Historical and Metahistorical Aspects of Israel   In the seventh, eighth, and ninth letters, Hirsch attempts to explain the position of the Jewish people. As has already been pointed out, Hirsch's views on this subject were not yet fully developed at that time: "My thoughts on Israel are still only a project of my mind" (*NL* 212). One of the primary difficulties in Hirsch's explanation is the uniqueness of the role of the people of Israel, which seems to defy Hegel's dialectical approach to the history of other nations. The latter are destroyed in the historical process, but the Jewish people, though "a historical phenomenon" (*NL* 17), seem to defy this historical imperative.

Hirsch thus encountered the same difficulty as Krochmal, who tried to save the Jewish people philosophically from the irrevocable doom entailed in the historical process. It is remarkable that Hirsch independently employed an idea similar to Krochmal's,[46] that of making the Jewish people directly subject to the Absolute

Spirit, *ha-ruḥani ha-muḥlat*. Whereas each of the other nations had "to learn to know God and itself from its manifold vicissitudes" (*NL* 66) inherent in historical development, the Jewish people were *"externally* subordinate to the nations armed with proud reliance on self, but fortified by *direct* reliance on God" (*NL* 67). The historical aspect of the Jewish people, was therefore only an outward manifestation. Intrinsically, the Jewish people were dependent on the Absolute Spirit, or God, and consequently were immune to the inherent destructiveness which is a necessary corollary of the unfolding of the *Geist*.

The inner contradiction existing between the external aspect of Israel, which is historical and hence perishable, and its internal aspect, which is spiritual and hence eternal, is obvious. Small wonder that Hirsch's grandson, Isaac Breuer, who carried on Hirsch's thought, emphasized the *metahistorical* aspect of the people of Israel.[47] Breuer reached the logical conclusion of Hirsch's philosophy and therefore resolved the inner contradiction by removing the Jewish people entirely from the realm of history and placing them exclusively in the realm of spirit.

It is not difficult to account for Hirsch's promulgation of the inner contradiction between the external, historical aspect and the internal, spiritual one. Had Israel been completely spiritual, no coexistence with the outer non-Jewish state in the post-Emancipation period would have been possible. Spiritual Israel under such circumstances would have become extraterrestrial. For Hirsch, who welcomed the Emancipation and certainly could not oppose it in his generation, it was necessary to show that the Jews are capable of external adjustment to their historical time and environment: "How beautiful it would be if Israel, obeying the word of its prophet, should *attach itself closely to every state* which has accepted its children in citizenship, and should seek to promote the welfare and the peace thereof!" (*NL* 85). Perhaps it is not too farfetched to suggest that the peculiar term *Man-Israel* or *Mensch-Jissroel*, frequently employed by Hirsch, may reflect this dual concept. *Man* implies the common external aspect historically uniting the Jew with the rest of mankind, while *Israel* is the internal aspect which has a spiritual metahistorical quality distinguishing the Jew from the rest of mankind. The Jew is a combination of these two components.

This seemingly new term *Man-Israel* represents an old concept. It harks back to Mendelssohn, who divided man into a confessional and extraconfessional being. The confessional aspect of man remains forever separate and distinct from the extraconfessional, which serves as the common denominator for all mankind. In this domain, man, regardless of his confessional loyalties or commitments, appears solely as *Mensch*. He is therefore able to coexist with others who share this aspect with him. It is this aspect, Mendelssohn maintained, which entitles the Jew to emancipation. The confessional aspect of the Jew is internal; the extraconfessional, external. Hence, the Jew can meet the requisites of the modern state which is only concerned with externalities, as Mendelssohn indicated in *Jerusalem*. Hirsch in his *Mensch-Jissroel* merely echoes Mendelssohn's fundamental idea; and, like him, Hirsch considered emancipation possible and desirable.

Emancipation to both Hirsch and Mendelssohn meant symbiosis, not synthesis. The Jew will retain his confessional distinctiveness, "dwelling in freedom in the midst of the nations" (*NL* 163). His distinctiveness, however, will be beneficial to all the citizens of the state. Like Mendelssohn, Hirsch endeavors to show how unobtrusive the Jews will be in the state, and the great benefits to be derived from their *still und ruhig Leben* by the state. Every Jew will be "a respected and influential exemplar priest of righteousness and love" (*NL* 163). As if to further reassure the non-Jews that their Jewish compatriots will not influence their religious beliefs, Hirsch emphasizes that these "priests" will not disseminate Judaism, guaranteeing them that proselytism is prohibited. They will merely spread "pure humanity" (*NL* 163).

Hirsch regretted that the non-Jews in the Middle Ages missed such a great opportunity to admit into their midst a group as docile and noninterfering as the Jews:

How impressive, how sublime it would have been, if, in the midst of a race that adored only power, possessions, and enjoyment, and that was oft blinded by superstitious imaginings, there had lived quietly and publicly human beings of a different sort, who beheld in material possessions only the means of practicing justice and love towards all; whose minds, pervaded with the wisdom and truth of the law, maintained simple, straightforward views, and emphasized them for themselves and others in expressive, vivid deed-symbols. (*NL* 163–64)

While hoping for emancipation and blessing it (*NL* 165–66), Hirsch does not make it a sine qua non for the existence and survival of the Jewish people: "Emancipation, like our *external state* altogether, is a matter, religiously speaking, of secondary consideration. We may indeed take part in accelerating its coming,[48] but in itself it makes us neither greater nor smaller" (*NL* 169). Hirsch leaves a margin of safety here: should emancipation fail, the survival of the Jewish people would thereby not be jeopardized. The failure of emancipation would signify only a change in the external conditions of the Jewish people; the essential and spiritual core of Israel's existence would remain unaffected.

The Jewish people, according to Hirsch, are unique, since they do not need a state for the objectification of the Law, but "the Torah, the fulfillment of the divine will, was to be its soil and country and aim; its national existence, therefore, was neither dependent upon, nor conditioned by, transitory things, but eternal as the spirit, the soul and the word of the Eternal One" (*NL* 76).

Despite the eternality of the Jewish people and despite Judaism's metaphysical existence, Hirsch apparently succeeds in differentiating some dialectical process in its history. He distinguishes the phase of the national existence of the Jewish Commonwealth, which appears analogous to the thesis, and the phase of the Diaspora, which is analogous to the antithesis. This dialectic process may derive from the fact that Hirsch, unlike Breuer, has not completely transformed Israel into a metahistorical nation. Since externally it was historical, it could not escape some of the destructive effects involved in the historical process. But in Hegelian thought, "destruction means the annulling of external existence, not the destruction of what is essential."[49] The destruction of the external Jewish state did not affect its essential spirit. Indeed, "through the annihilation of Israel's state-life its mission did not cease, for that had been intended only as a means to an end. On the contrary, this destruction itself was part of its fate" (*NL* 79–80). This last remark by Hirsch again confirms the Hegelian point of view, in which the antithesis is just as much a part of the dialectic process as the thesis.

Is there a synthesis in Hirsch's thought? As already pointed out, Hirsch's synthesis is the messianic era, when the physical thesis of the state and the spiritual antithesis of exile will be merged into a spiritual state. At that time "the great day shall arrive when the Almighty shall see fit, in His inscrutable wisdom, to unite again His scattered servants in one land, and the Torah shall be the guiding principle of a state, an exemplar of the meaning of divine revelation and the mission of humanity" (*NL* 162). But this historical process has a logic of its own, and the *Geist* cannot be hurried. It must advance and progress along its own lines: "Actively to accelerate its coming is sin, and is prohibited to us" (*NL* 162).

Different Roads to the Same Goal   The distinction Hirsch makes between the course of history for the Jews and for the non-Jewish nations is as old as Judaism; however, his rationale for this difference was grounded in modern thought. There existed two views concerning the concealed operations of Providence in the history of mankind. Lessing, veering away from the nonhistorical Weltanschauung of the Aufklärung, suggested that Providence educates mankind through the dynamics of historic phenomena. Their will uninhibited, the nations learn by trial and error, making their course through history long and tortuous. Despite many difficulties, however, they progress and eventually attain their aim.

Mendelssohn, true to the Leibnizian outlook, which conceived everything in logical rather than historical terms, rejected Lessing's notion. He thought that his friend "was misled by I don't know what scholar of history."[50] To Mendelssohn, truth is eternal and cannot be subject to the fluctuations of history. That an idea could be true at one stage of history and erroneous at another only indicates its contingency. And temporal truth is no truth at all. As a result, Mendelssohn rejected Lessing's hypothesis, which subsequently became popular among the Reform theologians.

Hirsch, who was slightly more receptive to the idea of history than was Mendelssohn, seems to offer a compromise: Providence operates in history in dual fashion. In the history of nations, it follows the trial-and-error course. In Lessingian fashion, Providence educates nations gradually and in accordance with their development. Consequently, their religious notions change frequently; what is true at one stage may later prove erroneous. They have the right to affect these changes and to act accordingly. Not so the Jews. With them, Providence operates according to eternal verities; they are guided from above. The trials and errors, so confusing and agonizing to other nations, are ipso facto eliminated. However, so as not to deprive them completely of the free will which such guidance might imply, the Jews have an external aspect, which belongs to history and thus is uncontrolled. It follows that since the Jewish course is that of eternal verities, their truths, unlike those of the other nations, are not subject to change. Their truths were not conceived by them at a given moment in history, but revealed to them from outside its flux. Subsequent eras, no matter how enlightened, cannot invalidate the verities once received, since they are eternal and hence immutable.

Thus, Hirsch incorporates the seemingly irreconcilable views of both Lessing and Mendelssohn by applying the former to the history of all nations and the latter to the Jewish people. In addition, Hirsch's distinction between non-Jewish nations and the Jews may echo the Hegelian difference between nature and spirit. Both constitute different aspects of the same reality; nevertheless, it is nature that has to be elevated to the level of the spirit. It is within the domain of nature that subjectivity is possible, hence error cannot be excluded. Not so in the domain of the spirit. The non-Jewish nations are analogous to Hegel's nature. Error is inherent as is subjectivity, but all is eventually resolved by a gradual unfolding progress. The Jews, being more akin to Hegel's domain of the spirit, remain constant, and therefore their religious ideas are not subject to change. The goal of both Jews and non-Jews, however, is the same, although the roads to its attainment are different.

Other Aspects of Agreement   In the tenth through the fourteenth letters, Hirsch suggests his rudimentary classification of the precepts of the Torah. He divides these precepts into six categories and presents merely their *Titel- und Begriffsnennung*—the nomenclature of terms—which he promises to elucidate.

The fifteenth, sixteenth, and seventeenth letters are somewhat argumentative and exhortative in tone, taking issue with the critics of traditional Judaism of Hirsch's time. Hirsch here restates his fundamental views concerning the relationship of God, world, man, Israel, and Torah. He negates the idea of a "world without an active God or of a God without a world that serves Him" (*NL* 137). This view is similar to Hegel's that a "godless world and a worldless God are both alike abstractions."[51] This concept of the world is thus a teleological one, man included. Israel's unique position is justified, in addition to the traditional view, by the idea of mission, a favorite doctrine in the circles of the Reform movement, and by the Hegelian concept that the state of exile "is a part of the scheme of its God-revealing existence" (*NL* 138). The exilic state is the antithetical manifestation of the national thesis, the state. The Torah, as has been noted, is neither restrictive nor inhibitive. It does not interdict or suppress any normal legitimate desire, but merely makes "the lower cravings subordinated to higher law and limited by the Creator's wisdom for His infinitely wise purposes" (*NL* 138–39). If this statement is translated into Hegelian terms, it implies the subordination of the subjective mind to the absolute one.

In addition to the Hegelian philosophical concepts, there is in the *Neunzehn Briefe* a variety of views and ideas on the philosophy of religion in which the remarkable similarities to Hegel can hardly be accidental. The following views on religion will show the points of agreement between Hegel and Hirsch. Both objected to subjective speculation on religious fundamentals by the individual. The individual must become absorbed in his religion as it has evolved historically.[52] Hegel opposed, on the one hand, rationalism in religion, which "makes the concept of God empty and finite,"[53] and on the other, the rigid literalness of orthodoxy, which "clings to the literal expression of dogmas."[54] Similarly, Hirsch decries rational speculation in the sphere of religion, considering it "baseless reasoning, transcending the legitimate bounds of our intellectual capacity, however brilliantly put together and glitteringly logical it may appear to be" (*NL* 147). Thus, any speculation overreaching the inherent limitations of man's intellect is futile and counterproductive. At the same time, Hirsch opposes the abdication of reason within the limits of the possible and attainable. He consequently deplores the orthopraxis of the eastern European Jews who performed the *mitzvot* mechanically, disregarding their inner spirit and deeper meaning and transforming them into anachronisms. They made the Torah "a dull and prosaic dialectic [which] had reduced to merest mummies laws full to overflowing of life and spirit" (*NL* 99). Like Mendelssohn,[55] Hirsch rejects the concepts of dogmatism in the Jewish religion: "Judaism enjoins six hundred and thirteen duties but knows no dogmas" (*NL* 146).

Just as Hirsch excludes excessive rationalism and sterile dogmatism in religion, he also rejects its emotionality. Like Hegel, he objects to the vague, diffused emotionalism and irrationalism extolled by Schleiermacher and his followers: "Feeling alone cannot justify itself; its worth rests on its content and its object. Feeling cannot decide, for man has it in common with the brutes."[56] This negation of the emotive aspect of religion explains why Hirsch, like Hegel, objects to the emotive concept of prayer advocated by many romantic religionists. Although prayer is frequently charged with emotion and sentimentalism, its aim is "the purification, enlightenment, and uplifting of our inner selves to the recognition of the Most High and our duties toward Him in truth; not mere stirring up of emotions, swiftly vanishing devotion, empty sentimentalism, and unreasoning tears, but the cleansing of thought and heart" (*NL* 129–30).

Although Hirsch was fundamentally a theologian and Hegel primarily a philosopher, their basic views on religion agreed not only in approach but in intrinsic meaning. Thus, Hegel considered religion to differ from philosophy in form alone. In religion the philosopher's ultimate conceptual relationships "are regarded as historical events and are conceived in figurative form."[57] For Hirsch too, some precepts and rites were pictorial forms symbolizing concepts, doctrines, historic events of a national or universal significance. We must bear in mind, however, that one of the categories in Hirsch's doctrinal system, *edot*, embraces precepts and rites which have primarily a symbolic character: "These symbolic acts and seasons all give expression to ideas without splitting them into words as speech must" (*NL* 122). Note that for Hirsch, religious symbols are in this instance analogous to philosophical ideas. There is, however, one important difference: for Hirsch the symbol has an intrinsic value and must not be discarded, although the person may comprehend the ideas behind it; its religious concept must be concretized into a religious act and the act is no less important than the concept it represents. In theory, Hegel appears more consistent, maintaining that since the religious symbol is merely external to the idea it embodies, there is no harm in its abandonment.[58] However, it is not difficult to understand why Hirsch, whose aim was the upholding of normative Judaism, had to insist upon its absolute validity and the essential importance of performing it.

Considering the strong influence of Hegel upon Hirsch's formative thought, one is almost tempted to identify Hirsch's profound interest in exegetical research and the construction of a specific Jewish symbolism as a corollary to his Hegelian thought. Thus, Hegel believed that "the religious ideas of bygone times can only retain their value if we are able to discover that in one way or another they express our own experiences and our own thought."[59] Hirsch attempted to reinforce not only religious ideas of bygone days but also religious practices of antiquity by validating them in terms plausible to men of modern times. He used hallowed exegetical and symbolical methods to substantiate the *mitzvot* in all their ramifications and in the light of contemporary philosophy. Although the use of exegetical and symbolical methods was not new to Judaism, Hegel's sanction may have been decisive for Hirsch, who developed extensive exegetical and symbolical elaborations of his own.[60]

Hegel and Hirsch agreed upon the equal coexistence of religion and philosophy; both contain the truth. Religion reveals to mankind what philosophers had to evolve during subsequent centuries and millennia. Hirsch's distinction between the truth theophanically revealed to Israel and the truth eventually to be recognized by the rest of mankind after a long, arduous, and tortuous process of trial and error may have had its origin in analogous Hegelian thought.

Hegelian Parallelisms

That the Hegelian outlook should have appealed strongly to Hirsch is not difficult to understand. Hegel's traditionalist views seemed to coincide remarkably with Hirsch's. Hirsch, whose avowed aim was the validation of traditional Judaism and its defense against the various neologistic attempts to reform it by radical and revolutionary means, found an excellent ally in Hegel. The latter's aims were similar, particularly in the realm of law and social institutions, whose foundations had been undermined by the insidious currents of the new age. To counteract these destructive forces, Hegel "assumed the task of justifying in the name of rational Idealism the doctrines and institutions which were menaced by the new spirit of science and popular government."[61] It was this very traditionalism in religion[62] and conservatism toward social change, for which Karl Marx castigated Hegel, that made Hegel preeminently acceptable to Hirsch. Hirsch deserves credit for applying Hegelian philosophical categories that were used by many Protestant theologians to strengthen the tottering foundations of Protestantism to defend traditional Judaism. Apparently, Hirsch accepted many Hegelian views and ideas de facto and applied them to Judaism without extending de jure recognition to their author.

The Hegelian concept of law, or right, closely approximates Hirsch's concept of law, which he frequently employed in lieu of the Torah. This substitution was undoubtedly designed to underscore the legal aspect of Judaism and the obligatory character of its commandments. Both Hirsch and Hegel used *law* as an all-inclusive term whose ramifications are much broader than its conventional connotation. For Hirsch, the law "opens a field for the broadest investigation and profoundest research into the essence and relations of all things to each other; it rouses us to the endeavor to understand the world, man, human history, and God's plan operating therein" (*NL* 146). Much in the same vein can be said of *law* and *right* as defined by Hegel in his *Rechtsphilosophie:* "In speaking of Right in this book, we mean not merely what is generally understood by the word, namely, civil law, but also morality, ethical life, and world history; these belong just as much to our topic, because the concept brings thoughts together into a free system" (*PR* 233). The criticism Marx leveled at Hegel's *Rechtsphilosophie,* that it was teleological in nature,[63] certainly did not render it objectionable to Hirsch, for whom the Law (Torah) had definite teleological implications. It constituted a mighty engine "for propelling mankind to the final goal of all human education" (*NL* 86).

Hirsch's opposition to subjectivism within the domain of Jewish law and his rejection of ethical laissez-faire, whereby "everyone must be permitted to be his own judge of what constitutes happiness for him" (NL 11), is paralleled by Hegel's vehement rejection of the romantics and subjectivists, who wished to base law upon each man's feelings and sentiments. Hegel even reprimanded Kant,[64] who "expressly stated that 'truth itself cannot be known,' that that only is true which each individual allows to rise out of his heart, emotion, and inspiration about ethical institutions" (PR 5). Hegel acrimoniously criticized those who maintained that law should "come from below, from the people itself" (PR 6). To Hegel, it was "the quintessence of shallow thinking to base philosophic science not on the development of thought and the concept but on immediate sense-perception and the play of fancy" (PR 6). He regarded it as synonymous with epicureanism, which evaluated conduct by the criteria of feeling and impulse, and truth by sensory standards, thus making law and ethics a matter of the "subjective accident of opinion and caprice" (PR 6).

By the same token, Hegel rejected the views of Schleiermacher and his followers who, in the name of piety, exalted subjective feelings and personal convictions above the objective standards of law. True religion, Hegel maintained,

sheds the form of this emotional region so soon as it leaves the inner life, enters upon the daylight of the Idea's development and revealed riches, and brings with it, out of its inner worship of God, reverence for law and for an absolute truth exalted above the subjective form of feeling. (PR 6)

Hegel decried the devastating results of these subjectivistic-individualistic theories:

The result of this levelling process is that concepts of what is true, the laws of ethics, likewise become nothing more than opinions and subjective convictions. The maxims of the worst of criminals, since they too are convictions, are put on the same level of value as those laws; and at the same time any object, however sorry, however accidental, any material however insipid, is put on the same level of value as what constitutes the interest of all thinking men and the bonds of the ethical world. (PR 9)

Hirsch echoes this severe criticism of subjectivism, which elevated the opinions of the criminal to the same axiological level as that of the divine law embodied in the Torah. Hirsch challenges the hedonistic, subjectivistic point of view:

I could ask, is it so sure that happiness and perfection form the goal and the object of man's being? I could ask upon what basis you found this opinion, or what could you answer to the careless pleasure-seeker or criminal, who thinks the excitement and sensual lust of the moment a greater happiness than all temporal or eternal blessings? (*NL* 11)

There is a remarkable parallel between Hirsch's criticism of the exponents of Reform and Hegel's criticism of the romantics, ethical subjectivists, and abstract idealists, whose position, outside the pale of Judaism, was strikingly analogous to the Reformers' view: that the legal aspect of Judaism was more detrimental to the survival and development of Jewish religion than its aspect of supernaturalism.[65]

Hegel distinguished between the laws of nature and the laws of the land: "The laws of nature simply are what they are and are valid as they are; they are not liable to encroachment, though in certain cases man may transgress them. To know the law of nature, we must learn to know nature, since its laws are rigid and it is only our ideas about them that can be false" (*PR* 224). The laws of the land, however, having originated from man, are not absolute: "In nature the highest truth is that there is a law; in the law of the land, the thing is not valid simply because it exists; on the contrary, everyone demands that it shall comply with his private criterion" (*PR* 224).

Hirsch also draws a distinction between two laws, the laws of nature and the laws of the Torah:

In nature all phenomena stand before us as indisputable facts, and we can only endeavor *a posteriori* to ascertain the law of each and the connections of all. . . . We must, therefore, acquire all possible knowledge concerning the object of our investigation, and know it, if possible, in its totality. If, however, all efforts should fail in disclosing the inner law and connection of phenomena revealed to us as fact in nature, the facts remain, nevertheless, undeniable, and cannot be reasoned away. (*NL* 194–95)

However, while Hegel could see the difference between the inviolability of natural laws and the possibility of passing judgment on the positive laws of the land, Hirsch insists on the complete identification of the laws of the Torah with the laws of nature. The former, being divine, therefore belong in the same category as the laws of nature, where any element of arbitrariness is a priori excluded.

Hegel clearly stated his opposition to the type of historical relativism which was a natural corollary of the view propounded by Savigny and his followers:

To generalize, by this means the relative is put in place of the absolute and the external appearance in place of the true nature of the thing. When those who try to justify things on historical grounds confound an origin in external circumstances with one in the concept, they unconsciously achieve the very opposite of what they intend. Once the origination of an institution has been shown to be wholly to the purpose and necessary in the circumstances of the time, the demands of history have been fulfilled. But if this is supposed to pass for a general justification of the thing itself, it turns out to be the opposite, because, since those circumstances are no longer present, the institution so far from being justified has by their disappearance lost its meaning and its right. (*PR* 17)

Hegel's opposition to the exponents of the historical school of jurists, who obscured "the difference between the historical and the philosophical study of law" (*PR* 17), is analogous to Hirsch's opposition to the leaders of Reform, who substituted the historical approach to Judaism for the conceptual one. The consequences of confusing historical development of law with its conceptual development were as dangerous to the institutions which Hegel was interested in preserving as they were to the legal and ritual systems of Judaism which Hirsch wished to perpetuate.

Hirsch and the Ideas of the Culturverein

The attempt to reinterpret Judaism along Hegelian lines was not altogether new, nor did it originate with Hirsch. The popularity and influence of Hegel's philosophy at the beginning of the nineteenth century transcended social and political thought, and extended to the domain of religion. It was only natural that in an intellectually confused time some groping Jews should endeavor to anchor the tottering foundations of Judaism to the moorings of a generally accepted religious philosophy that claimed to be scientific, objective, and all-encompassing.

Such an attempt, as previously mentioned, was made seventeen years prior to Hirsch's publication of the *Neunzehn Briefe* by the young Jewish intellectuals of the Verein für Cultur und Wissenschaft des Judentums. The members of the Culturverein, as we have seen, wanted to rehabilitate Judaism to dignity and rationality by applying some aspects of Hegelian methodology in a reinterpretation of their religion. Therefore, it is significant that despite the colossal ideological differences between the Culturverein members and Hirsch, the future champion of neo-Orthodoxy, there is a remarkable similarity in their methodological approach to Judaism. Some ideas contained in the programmatic outline of the Culturverein by Immanuel Wolf (Wohlwill)[66] antedated similar views subsequently expounded by Hirsch in his *Neunzehn Briefe*. Aside from the term *Wissenschaft*, which applies to both the inquiry and the study of Judaism, Wolf also insisted that Judaism had to be treated as a whole and not studied in fragments. A scientific study of Judaism—*Wissenschaft des Judentums*—could accomplish its task only if it endeavored to comprehend Judaism in all its ramifications. Just as Hirsch required that Judaism be organically comprehended, "aus sich selbst heraus," in accordance with the inner spirit that permeated its original literary sources (*NL* 197–98), the members of the Culturverein maintained that "Judaism as a whole, based on *its own inner principle* and embodied, on the one hand, in a *comprehensive literature*, and, on the other, in the life of a large number of human beings, both can and needs to be treated scientifically."[67]

Both considered their respective methods of investigation of Judaism as new and previously untried. Wolf asserted:

Hitherto, however, [Judaism] has never been described scientifically and comprehensively from a wholly independent standpoint. . . . The content of this special science is the systematic unfolding and representation of its object in its *whole* sweep, for *its own sake*, and not for any ulterior purpose.[68]

Similarly, Hirsch inveighs against the great variety of methods employed before him (*NL* 13) and calls upon Benjamin to forget

all annoyance which the reading of these writings [that is, the original sources of the Jewish religion] caused you in your youth; forget all the prejudices which you may have imbibed from different sources against these writings. Let us read as though we had never read them; as though we had never heard of them. (*NL* 16)

In the light of this new approach, Hirsch hoped "these writings" would assume a new significance for Jewish youth.

Hirsch's methodological approach and that advocated by the exponents of the Culturverein were strikingly similar. Both proposed that (1) the science of Judaism encompass Judaism in its entirety; (2) it proceed systematically to trace the individual parts to the basic principle of the whole; and (3) it set out to treat its subject "in and for itself, for its own sake, not for a special purpose, or with a definite intention."[69] The spokesman for these Jewish Hegelians of the Culturverein employed a terminology concerning Judaism that was nearly identical with that subsequently used by Hirsch. Accordingly, Judaism was conceived of as a particular, autonomous whole whose concept, in and for itself, was "to develop in accordance with its inner reasonableness *(Vernünftigkeit)* present in its truth."

There can be no doubt about Hirsch's familiarity with the program of the Culturverein. Any sensitive, young, concerned Jew eager to revitalize Judaism would not have overlooked or ignored their endeavors. Despite their youth, the members of the Culturverein gained prominence by their rare intellectual brilliance, impressing even those who did not subscribe to their views. The fact that they attempted to employ Hegelian philosophy for the reinterpretation of Judaism at a time when Hegel's popularity was at its height only added to their general prestige.

We may further assume that Hirsch's familiarity with the views of the Culturverein members came not only from reading their writings, but from direct contact. Although the Central Verein guided by Gans was located in Berlin, there were also chapters outside the Prussian capital. One of these was in Hamburg, known as the Hamburg und Altonaer Special Verein. Among its members were men of great prominence and wealth as well as leaders of the Hamburg Temple, Drs. Kley and Salomon. The differences and disagreements that existed between the Special Verein in Hamburg and the Central Verein in Berlin were of an organizational rather than an ideological nature.[70]

Wohlwill, who had lived in Hamburg for fifteen years, wrote the ideological platform of the Culturverein, *Über den Begriff einer Wissenschaft des Judentums*, and occupied the position of teacher of the *Freischule* in Hamburg.[71] An excellent pedagogue and eloquent preacher,[72] he must have impressed many young men in Hamburg, including Hirsch. Heine, who was closely associated with the Culturverein, also visited Hamburg frequently,[73] and while it is doubtful whether he made any effort to expound his views on Judaism or Hegelianism there, his mere presence enhanced the importance of the Culturverein.

That there was an affinity between certain Hegelian ideas and Judaism was not apparent to the members of the Culturverein only. The entire cultural climate was saturated with Hegel's views. They infiltrated the minds of ordinary men through the sermons delivered by preachers with Hegelian leanings. This practice was not merely confined to Christian homiletics; many Reform rabbis avidly imitated the Protestant preachers.[74] Thus, a reinterpretation in Hegelian terms of Jewish values and ideas became widely popular among German Jews in the early part of the nineteenth century. It is therefore possible that Hirsch absorbed these views early in life before he was formally introduced to the works of Hegel. It is just as likely that some of these seminal Hegelian ideas converging upon him from pseudo-Hegelian sources furnished him with the rudiments of his subsequent Weltanschauung. The extent of the influence of these sources as compared to the influence of Hegel's original works may never be known.

The similarity in concept and in methodological approach between Hirsch and the spokesmen of the Culturverein is readily understood, since both were strongly influenced by Hegelian thought. Nevertheless, it raises the query whether Hirsch consciously imitated them, was unconsciously influenced by them, or even directly borrowed from them. This intriguing question cannot be resolved on the basis of his writings. Hirsch admits indebtedness neither to Hegel nor to the Jewish Hegelians.

Hirsch's reluctance to name any direct or indirect influence is not difficult to understand. In time, he became the exponent of traditional Judaism and the father of the Orthodox separatist movement in Germany; he certainly could not confess to a philosophical or methodological affinity with men like Heine, Gans, or even Zunz. The first two embraced Christianity,[75] the last lost his

faith in the future of Judaism and in the possibility of Jewish survival.[76] Basically, Hirsch could ill afford to admit his indebtedness
to Hegel. Aside from the fact that it did not behoove the spokesman of Orthodoxy to give credit to a non-Jew for his exposition of
Judaism, the Christian element in Hegel's philosophy would have
been objectionable. As Marx observed, the heart of the Hegelian
philosophy is "the speculative expression of the Christian-Ger-
manic dogma."[77]

Although Hirsch subscribed to many of Hegel's views, he was
undoubtedly aware that Hegel considered Christianity the highest
expression of religion. Hegel's reconciliation of the Oriental concept of God with the Greek concept of man, bringing about the
synthesis of the God-man, left Judaism, at its best, merely an inferior forerunner of Christianity.[78] Hegel's uncomplimentary
views on Judaism were well known, and an acknowledgment by
Hirsch of Hegelian influence would have been detrimental to the
acceptance and popularity of his exposition of Judaism in Jewish
circles in general, and in traditional circles in particular.

Aside from these specific considerations, Hirsch could not afford
to credit any outside influence, since it was he who had criticized
Maimonides for having "entered into Judaism from *without*,
bringing with him opinions of whose truth he had convinced himself from extraneous sources" (*NL* 182). An open confession by
Hirsch that he too had applied a foreign, extraneous yardstick to
Judaism, particularly a Christian yardstick, would have made his
exposition of Judaism a mockery in the eyes of the modernists and
anathema to the traditionalists.

Despite the fact that Hirsch never attributed any of his thoughts
to Hegel or to the Jewish Hegelians of the Culturverein, the implications of those influences are present. It was, perhaps, the
trained eye and ear of the highly gifted Graetz, who was an anti-
Hegelian as well as an opponent of the leaders of the Culturverein,
which may have detected a hint of Hegelian dialectic in Hirsch's
personal conversations. Although the reason for the alienation
between Hirsch and Graetz is not fully documented, it is a fact
that the latter's boundless admiration and devotion cooled
strangely after the two had been such intimate friends. There is
good reason to suspect that the overtones of Hegelian dialectic
which the sensitive Graetz may have perceived in his studies and

conversations with Hirsch added to this disenchantment.[79]

Another interesting question must likewise remain unanswered, namely, how could Hirsch, the exponent of traditional Judaism and a person of high religious and moral integrity, honestly and sincerely accept the views and methods of the outspokenly Christian Hegel? Perhaps it was the consciousness of his duty to reconstruct and save Judaism from utter collapse that impelled Hirsch to overlook such considerations.

Part Three
THE RATIONALIZATION
OF THE
COMMANDMENTS

6
The Quest for a Rationale

Compendium and Primer

Moriah was something Hirsch wanted to do, *Horeb,* something he had to do. The need for a new philosophy of Judaism could not compare with the urgent need for strengthening and fortifying the Jewish socioreligious, normative system which was in imminent danger of collapse. Indeed, it was much easier to write a manual of Jewish practice than to evolve a new philosophy. The *Horeb* could be composed sooner than *Moriah;* whereas there was sufficient material available for the former, the latter almost had to be created from nothing. Aside from this pragmatic consideration, however, there were certain factors that made early publication of the *Horeb* an absolute necessity.

The decline of Jewish learning in Germany had alienated the vast majority of the Jews from the sources of Jewish knowledge which heretofore had been accessible to all. By the end of the eighteenth century, not many laymen were conversant with the Talmud and rabbinic literature.[1] The *Shulḥan Arukh,* universally acknowledged as the final Jewish code, was of little value to the vast majority of German Jews in Hirsch's time. This sixteenth-century compendium by Joseph Caro with emendations by Moses Isserles had been originally designed to simplify the complexity of the Law and to facilitate its comprehension for the layman. Paradoxically, by virtue of the commentaries and supercommentaries

187

appended to it, the *Shulḥan Arukh* became a stupifyingly intricate work in itself, accessible only to scholars and rabbis. Attempts were made in the eighteenth and nineteenth centuries at partial or more comprehensive abridgments and simplifications of the *Shulḥan Arukh*, which had become complicated by excessive exegesis. These digests were meant to guide the average person in his daily religious, social, and ethical conduct. Among the most popular codes of the nineteenth century were the *Ḥayye Adam* by Abraham Danzig and the *Shulḥan Arukh* by Shneor Zalman, mentor and founder of the *ḤaBaD* wing of the Hasidic movement.[2]

Whether Hirsch was familiar with these digests is unknown. The fact that in preparation for the *Horeb* he limited himself "almost exclusively to the *Shulḥan Arukh* with the *Ba'er Hetev*"[3] may indicate the contrary, although not conclusively so. However, even if he was familiar with the aforementioned digests, Hirsch quite likely felt that they did not meet the needs of his contemporaries. Their authors, writing for laymen of eastern Europe, composed them in Hebrew and in a distinctive rabbinic idiom. They took for granted a substantial knowledge of talmudic and even posttalmudic sources on the part of their readers. However, what was considered a minimum of scholarship in eastern Europe was more than a maximum in nineteenth-century Germany. Aside from the rabbis and a small number of scholarly individuals, Hebrew was not commonly understood, the rabbinic idiom even less so. The ordinary German traditionalist Jew required a simple digest of the *Shulḥan Arukh* in German to serve him as a manual.

The need for a concise, informative compendium of Jewish law was particularly keen in the domain of Jewish education. The general decline of Jewish scholarship in Germany made knowledgeable teachers of Jewish subjects a rarity. The vacuum left by the unpopular Polish *melamdim* could not be filled by German-born Jewish educators. Seminaries for the training of teachers were still in the embryonic stage of development. The low esteem in which the teacher of Jewish religion was held and the meager salary he received made Jewish education hardly a lucrative profession to attract young German Jews.[4]

The need for Jewish teachers was even greater in the smaller communities. While in the larger cities a few men with some mediocre knowledge of Judaism could have been induced to teach, scarcely any were available in the small communities. To ameliorate this situation, rabbis had to train men whose knowledge of the fundamentals of Judaism was nonexistent to enable them, in turn, to teach young pupils. In his letter to May, Hirsch stated that he wrote the *Horeb* for teachers who had no knowledge of Judaism themselves.[5] He also added, significantly, that "there is no textbook available which I could give them for guidance."[6]

Hirsch's last statement requires some qualification. Actually, there had never been so many manuals available for Jewish religious instruction as in the first three decades of the nineteenth century. According to Zunz, between the years 1799 and 1832 fifty such works had appeared.[7] It was not, however, the dearth of textbooks which impelled Hirsch to write the *Horeb*, but rather the content they provided and the form in which they presented it. The manuals of Judaism to which Zunz referred were catechisms, many of which were designed primarily for the preparation of children for confirmation, a ceremony then gaining popularity among liberal Jews.[8] With the development of the Reform movement accelerating, the confirmation ceremony and the catechisms became widespread. Both were taken over from Christianity, and both were justified on educational and even religious grounds.[9]

The avidity with which Jews pursued secular education made the catechism a necessity. Burdened by an intensive program of general subjects, the pupils had hardly any time left for Jewish learning. They could not afford to devote as much time as Jewish children once had to Hebrew, Bible, exegesis, Talmud, and codes. All the essential knowledge of Judaism had to be condensed into a compact manual. In the absence of such a digest, the Christian catechism seemed an appropriate model. As a result, there was an ever-increasing production of such manuals of the Jewish faith.[10] In 1807, a textbook for Judaism actually bearing the title *Katechismus* by M. H. Bock was published.[11] This Christian genre and nomenclature were agreeable to many German-born Jews and even to Maskilim hailing from Poland who composed such catechisms. Noted among them were the Hebrew philologist and writer Judah Loeb Ben-Ze'ev[12] and the Hebrew poet and editor of the *Ha-Meassef,* Shalom ha-Cohen.[13]

Although the avowed purpose of these catechisms was to introduce young children to the Jewish religion, many of them were permeated with a distinct antinomian and antitalmudic spirit. Writes one observer: "The evaluation of the Talmud itself, in the literature of the catechisms and manuals, varies from lack of enthusiasm, through damnation with faint praise, to hostile rejection."[14] Even Ben-Ze'ev, who included many of the commandments and observances in his catechism, stressed only those of biblical origin and avoided even the talmudic terminology.[15] Needless to say, the exponents and leaders of Reform were even more outspoken and radical in their catechisms. Thus, the manuals for religious instruction by Eduard Kley,[16] Solomon Herxheimer,[17] and Isaac Ascher Francolm,[18] which antedated the *Horeb*, exhibited a hostile attitude toward the Talmud.[19]

The schematic form of many catechisms followed the Decalogue. However, even this seemingly Jewish aspect was not original, since it was Luther who had first made the Ten Commandments the foundation for his instruction. Another favorite form was the thirteen articles of faith formulated by Maimonides, although the affirmative phrasing of some, particularly that of the messianic hope, was toned down.

In later years, when Hirsch had abandoned all hope of uniting the divergent groups in Jewry, he spoke out unequivocally against all forms of catechisms and manuals for the teaching of Judaism. He asserted that "der Juden-Katechismus ist sein Kalender,"[20] the calendar is the Jew's catechism. Hirsch felt that knowledge of the Decalogue does not make one a Jew, and he pointed to the ancient custom of daily reciting the Ten Commandments in the Temple in Jerusalem, which had been forbidden by the sages when it became obvious to them that some people deliberately or erroneously accepted the Decalogue as the alpha and omega of Judaism.[21] Hirsch saw in this renewed emphasis on the Ten Commandments a similar and perhaps even greater danger to Judaism.[22]

Hirsch likewise rejected the stress on the Maimonidean thirteen articles of faith. Although important, they could not replace the extensive study of the Torah. Moreover, the affirmation of these articles without the study of Torah was a contradiction in terms, since they included the belief that the Torah could never be altered or replaced. The substitution of catechisms for Torah study made this affirmation appear senseless.[23]

In 1836–37, when Hirsch published the *Neunzehn Briefe* and *Horeb*, he was not yet militantly outspoken against such reforms. As previously pointed out, he wished to bridge the chasm dividing the traditionalists from the liberals and did not then polemicize against these manuals, preferring to offer an alternative. Indeed, most of the Orthodox rabbis objected to these textbooks as they did to the confirmation ceremony.[24] At the time, however, Hirsch considered such nonconstructive opposition barren and ineffective. Instead of the catechisms, which constituted a diluted and even distorted presentation of Judaism, he introduced the *Horeb*, which was designed to encompass "the whole content and range of the divine commandments and regulations so that we know what in actual life we must do or avoid."[25] This implied not merely ethical precepts having some deistic, humanistic, or moral value, but all the commandments of both oral and written transmission.[26] No distinction was to be made between precepts of biblical and rabbinic origin, because both were integral parts of Judaism. The rabbis of the Talmud and the posttalmudic era did not invent new laws. In their regulations they merely "discharged their God-imposed duty of guarding the Law and protecting its observance."[27]

That such a concise compendium of Jewish law was urgently needed can be seen from the fact that in absence of a better religious primer, Rabbi Mordecai Benet of Nikolsburg endorsed Herz Homberg's *Bnei Zion: Ein religiöses-moralisches Lehrbuch für die Jugend israelitischer Nation* (1808),[28] even though the latter was one of the leading mentors and propagators of the Haskalah.[29] An alternative had to be offered to the Judaically deficient, deleterious catechisms employed by teachers and pupils. The *Horeb* was intended as such an alternative.

Meaning and Relevance

Although the *Horeb* was to serve as a teachers' manual and a concise religious compendium for the average German Jew, it would be erroneous to assume that this was its entire purpose. Even a cursory reading of the *Horeb* discloses that Hirsch intended it to be more than a vernacular digest of the *Shulḥan*

Arukh or an improved version of the current religious primers. The classical Jewish codifiers avoided in their works any rationalization of the precepts. Even Maimonides, who devoted a considerable portion of the *Moreh Nevukhim* to this subject, refrained from it in his *Mishneh Torah*. Not so Hirsch. He set two objectives for himself in the *Horeb*, one normative, one philosophic. The first aimed to familiarize the reader or would-be teacher with the wide range of commandments and prohibitions; the second was intended to analyze and reflect upon the commandments, to gain some insight into their meaning and significance. The strict, normative aspect of the *Horeb* Hirsch termed *shema'ata*, traditional law, the philosophic aspect, *aggadata*, homiletical interpretation. Both these aspects were considered important, although not equally so.

In view of the antinomian current in Hirsch's time, to have presented merely another legalistic treatise or compendium of perfunctory observances and rituals would have been absurd. Since he was aware of the potentially explosive antinomian mood of his generation, Hirsch wished to provide a rationale for the commandments. He hoped to validate them on an acceptable basis in face of the widespread rebellion against them. Notwithstanding his declaration that the divine commandments did not need to be defended before the court of human reason,[30] it was exactly this that he hoped to do.

This quest for a plausible and relevant explanation of the commandments places Hirsch within the school of Jewish thinkers who considered such a rationale possible. In the Talmud, there are two conflicting opinions on whether such a quest is possible or even desirable.[31] Some maintained that the real value of the commandments was their heteronomous character, which gave them categorical importance precisely because men could not comprehend them. By implementing commandments that are validated by his own reason, man does not obey God, but himself.

The medieval Jewish philosophers were inclined toward rationalization of the commandments, although they differed in their rationales. Even Saadia, who maintained that certain commandments were essentially commandments of obedience, did not consider them arbitrary or devoid of any rationality. While these commandments fundamentally imply man's submissiveness to

God, "nevertheless one cannot help noting, upon deeper reflection, that they have some partial uses as well as certain slight justification from the point of view of reason."[32] To Maimonides, the very notion that some commandments may be irrational and others nonrational was repugnant. An ardent rationalist, he could not conceive that only man's commandments must conform with reason, whereas those of God should not. Such a view was not only preposterous, but made God inferior to man: "According to [this] theory, . . . man is more perfect than his creator. For what man says or does has a certain object, while the actions of God are different; He commands us to do what is of no use to us, and forbids us to do what is harmless."[33] This notion was undoubtedly echoed by many of Hirsch's contemporaries, as it was by many of Maimonides's. To counter it, Hirsch, like Maimonides, had to demonstrate that "every one of the six hundred and thirteen precepts serves to inculcate some truth, to remove some erroneous opinion, to establish proper relations in society, to diminish evil, to train in good manners or to warn against bad habits."[34]

A rationale encompassing all the commandments was not readily available. In this respect, Hirsch was confronted with the same problem Maimonides had encountered centuries before. Both were eager to evolve a rationale for the commandments, both espoused a general philosophy current in their time. Neither, however, was able to ground the desired rationale for the commandments in the matrix of the philosophy he affirmed. In this respect, Hegelianism proved no more advantageous for Hirsch than had Aristotelianism for Maimonides. Neither philosophy could explicate or rationalize the multifarious precepts and observances enjoined by the Jewish religion, since they had no precepts analogous to the normative regimen of Judaism. As a result, both Maimonides and Hirsch presented many reasons rather than one reason for the commandments. Hirsch, whose rationale was far more extensive than Maimonides's, was also more eclectic.

It is possible that in 1837, the year the *Horeb* appeared, Hirsch entertained a hope eventually to publish a more comprehensive work providing the aforementioned rationale. The *Horeb* may have been a precursor of a more profound and encompassing magnum opus of Jewish law, just as the *Neunzehn Briefe* was to have been followed by *Moriah*, a work Hirsch hoped would deal with the philosophy of Judaism. This may account for the subtitle of the *Horeb: Versuche über Jissroels Pflichten in der Zerstreuung* (Essays on Israel's duties in the dispersion). The term *Versuche* connotes not only essays but also attempts, efforts, and experiments, which indicate an aspiration eventually to revise, alter, expand, and improve such a philosophy. Mindful of the fact that the *Horeb* did not represent his last view on this subject, Hirsch called the attention of the reader to the incompleteness of his work. "It is only *Versuche* which I venture to offer, not a complete treatise."[35] That Hirsch entertained hopes to publish a work qualitatively, and perhaps also quantitatively, superior to the *Horeb* can also be seen from his promise to enlarge upon this theme. He speaks of "special treatises in which, please God, I shall examine the whole again with references to the sources, and in which I hope to be able, to the best of my ability, to correct mistakes and inaccuracies from which these chapters will certainly not be free."[36]

Fortunately, the availability of the *shema'ata* material coupled with the urgency to publish a manual for teachers of the Jewish religion favored immediate publication of the *Horeb*. Had Hirsch delayed it until he could evolve a more comprehensive rationale for the commandments, the *Horeb* might have shared the fate of *Moriah*.

Shema'ata and Aggadata

The two aspects of the *Horeb*, *shema'ata*, law, and *aggadata*, homiletics, though integral constituents of the work, do not enjoy equal status. The relationship of *aggadata* to *shema'ata* is that of hypothesis to data, the former being conjectural, the latter determined. *Shema'ata*, as divine, is independent of the speculative rationalizations of the *aggadata*. The latter, as a product of human thought, is contingent upon *shema'ata* and is only meaningful when it takes all details and ramifications into consideration. However, even then the *aggadata* is postulatory at best. Should a given *aggadata* prove inadequate, its repudiation would affect neither the authority, nor the mandatory claim, nor the rationality of the *shema'ata*. Having been divinely ordained, it is, ipso facto, rational. God, the source of reason, could not have dictated irrational commandments or instituted arbitrary laws. The failure of an *aggadata* to explain a *shema'ata* merely attests to man's intellectual limitation but does not impute irrationality to the commandments.

Hirsch's distinction between *shema'ata* and *aggadata* echoes Maimonides's view concerning the obligatoriness of the Law and man's right to meditate and reflect upon it. In his *Mishneh Torah*, Maimonides stated: "Although the statutes in the Law are divine edicts, as we have explained at the close of *Laws Concerning Sacrilege*, yet it is proper to ponder over them and to give a reason for them, so far as we are able to give them a reason."[37] Notwithstanding such permission, man must comply with the Law even if he fails to comprehend it: "It is fitting for man to meditate upon the laws of the holy Torah and to comprehend their full meaning to the extent of his ability. Nevertheless, a law for which he finds no reason and understands no cause should not be trivial in his eyes."[38] It is noteworthy that his rationalism and intellectualism notwithstanding, Maimonides added admonishingly: "Let him not break through to rise up against the Lord lest the Lord break forth upon him."[39]

Maimonides's approach to the commandments was maintained by Mendelssohn. Although man's vision is limited and his comprehension circumscribed, he is allowed to inquire and "form conjectures and to draw conclusions from their results, as long as he remains mindful of the fact that he may do nothing but form conjectures."[40] Thus Hirsch, who had criticized Maimonides and Mendelssohn, followed in their footsteps.

The conjectural and nonmandatory quality of the *aggadata* gave Hirsch free rein to suggest hypothetical interpretations of the commandments. It enabled him to exercise freely his creative imagination and his intellectual, homiletical, and moral propensities. His reflections and speculations on the commandments frequently exceed that of Philo, the allegorists, and aggadists. He borrowed many ideas from the Talmud, Midrash, Jewish medieval philosophy, and modern philosophy, including Hegel. While Hegelianism could not serve as a matrix for all commandments, it seemed appropriate for the strict juridical norms Hirsch classifies as *mishpatim*. In the absence of any authoritative sources, he does not hesitate to suggest his own. Thus, he buttresses the *shema'ata*, the legalistic part, with more or less imaginative *aggadata*, homiletical explanations.[41]

It should be pointed out that Hirsch's term *aggadata* is not synonymous with the term *aggadah* frequently used in talmudic, midrashic, and later rabbinic literature. The latter is extravagant and hyperbolic in tone and content, to the discomfiture of many Jewish philosophers,[42] while Hirsch's *aggadata* is a homiletical, speculative rationalization and intellectualization of the *mitzvot*.

Anchorage in Symbolism

In his endeavor to rationalize and intellectualize the commandments, Hirsch espoused symbolism and allegory. While the *mitzvot* have to be observed as prescribed in the Written and Oral Law, they have a deeper meaning than their external appearance suggests. They constitute a concrete vehicle of profound ideas of which man must constantly be reminded since they tend to escape him in their abstract form. The idea of an underlying significance hidden in the commandments and Scripture was not new; it was as old as biblical exegesis and was employed with great skill and insight, although independently, by the talmudic Rabbis and by Philo.[43] The former developed an extensive hermeneutics as seen in the midrashic literature. The latter, in his effort to intepret the Bible in philosophic terms acceptable to the intellectuals of his time, evolved the allegorical method which became an integral part of biblical exegesis.

Nor was Hirsch's method of interpretation novel in its application. The Greeks employed it before Philo in the interpretation of their ancient myths and the poetry of Homer and Hesiod.[44] Both the myths and poetry were endowed with philosophic meaning superimposed upon the literary, although not supplanting it. Similarly, Philo, while he suggested that the laws of the Torah have a deeper, inner philosophic meaning, did not imply that they should not be observed in their external form:[45] "They were all to be observed in their literal meaning and were not to be explained away as allegories. But their supposed literal meaning was not really what the letter of the law meant."[46]

This dual approach to the interpretation of the Scriptures in general and the commandments in particular became very popular in Christianity. It was used by Paul and taken up by the leading Church Fathers such as Clement of Alexandria, Origen, Jerome, and Augustine, to mention but a few.[47] This method was carried on in the Middle Ages, notably by the mystics Hugo of Saint Victor and Peter Lombard.[48] However, they were not the only ones engaged in this endeavor since many allegorists "vied with one another in discovering new meaning in visible things."[49] In medieval Judaism, too, the mystics were predominantly attracted to allegory and symbolism: "The whole world is to the Cabbalist such a *corpus symbolicum*. . . . In particular the religious acts commanded by the Torah, the *mitzvot,* are to the Cabbalist symbols in which a deeper and hidden sphere of reality becomes transparent."[50]

That Hirsch should have resorted to allegory and symbolism in the nineteenth century is astounding, since he eschewed any semblance of mysticism and theosophical schematism, which he terms "magical mechanism" (*NL* 187). Nor was his era favorably predisposed to this genre of rationalization, which it considered sophistry at best. If at all times "the attitude of mankind toward symbolism exhibits an unstable mixture of attraction and repulsion,"[51] Hirsch's era was more inclined toward repulsion. The men of the nineteenth century were too sophisticated to accept the earlier unsubstantiated, subjectivistic views on symbolism, yet not perceptive enough to discover its depth of meaning as did those of the subsequent century. The condescending view held by many in the nineteenth century, "to regard symbols as temporary concessions to our ignorance,"[52] is disappearing even in empirical and analytical circles in the twentieth century as scholars are again attracted to symbolism as an unexplored dimension of culture that offers many possibilities and challenges.[53] The evocative power of the symbol surpasses any rational or logical expression, since it appeals directly to deep levels of human consciousness and experience: "It is a language which has different logic from the conventional one we speak in the daytime, a logic in which not time and space are the ruling categories but intensity and association."[54]

The early nineteenth-century scholars and intellectuals lacked insight into the value of symbolism, and they no longer accepted

the *sensus allegoricus* of the medieval philosophers. Symbolism to
them had an opprobrious connotation and was the province of the
mystic "pushing out from harbor to the vast stormy sea of the
divine."[55] It was thus relegated together with its corollary, mythology, to the limbo of the esoteric and occult. The romantics at
best "strove to replace the allegorical view of myth by a purely
tautegorical interpretation."[56] Nevertheless, the perennial "al-
legoresis" continued to fascinate some scholars. Georg Creuzer[57]
and Johann von Görres[58] looked on myth as an "allegorical symbolic language concealing a secret meaning, a purely ideal content
which can be glimpsed behind its image."[59]

Whether Hirsch was familiar with these studies on symbolism is
unknown. He may have known about Creuzer's view from Hegel's
works,[60] particularly since the former had engendered a great
deal of controversy.[61] Hirsch's theory of the symbolic significance
of the commandments, however, came from more indigenous
sources. It had its roots in Mendelssohn's *Jerusalem*, with which he
was unquestionably more familiar. The ceremonial law in Judaism,
according to Mendelssohn, is "a living kind of script"[62] evoking an
emotive response and stimulating contemplation. Its function is to
preserve the eternal verities of religion and to remind man, who
may easily be misled and confused, of his task in life. Many people
in antiquity attempted to represent these verities by images, and
in the course of time the demarcation between the real truth and
the image representing it vanished. Unable to distinguish the form
from the content, men welded them indissolubly together, thus
giving rise to idolatry. Nor did writing prove a proper medium for
the preservation of the eternal verities of religion. Notwithstanding the fact that literacy has benefited mankind, advanced culture,
and revolutionized civilization, it still possesses inherent shortcomings. Prior to the era of literacy, "theory was more intimately
connected with practice, contemplation more closely associated
with action."[63] Writing per se could not transmit the full meaning
of these verities, since by its very nature it reduces them to dead
letters.

Judaism overcame the shortcomings of both approaches by endeavoring to find the best modus operandi in the human context.
This the mentors of Judaism found in the symbolic nature of the
mitzvot. According to Mendelssohn, "images and hieroglyphics

lead to superstition and idolatry, while alphabetic script makes man too speculative."⁶⁴ The *mitzvot*, however, seemed to be the best "link between thought and action, between theory and practice."⁶⁵ In this sense, Mendelssohn's idea of the symbolic quality of the *mitzvot* was similar to Kant's concept of symbolism. According to the latter, a symbol is "a perception or presentation which represents a conception neither conventionally as a mere sign, nor directly, but indirectly though appropriately through a similarity between the rules which govern our reflection in the 'symbol' and the thing or idea symbolized."⁶⁶

Impelled by the need to find a rationale for certain commandments which could not be justified on their own, Hirsch was compelled to resort to allegory and symbolism. Although like his contemporaries he was disinclined to mysticism, he found in symbolism an anchor for many of the commandments. The fact that Mendelssohn, whom he admired, considered such a rationale cogent and prudent mitigated his disinclination considerably.

Criteria of Validation

Hirsch was fully aware that the Philonic methodology of allegory and symbolism was hardly consonant with the tenor of his generation. To the Jews of nineteenth-century Germany, this method, originated by the Cyrenaic philosopher Euhemerus, lacked the appeal it had had for their first-century coreligionists of Alexandria whom Philo had wanted to impress. Philo's contemporaries had been fascinated by it; Hirsch's viewed it as deception at its worst, as self-deception at best.⁶⁷

Actually, the very need to consider the *mitzvot* as symbols was a tacit admission that they had no value of their own. It was the idea they symbolized that justified their observance, while they themselves could hardly claim any significance.⁶⁸ Had Hirsch been a cabalist, he could have transformed the *mitzvot* into sacraments having a raison d'être of their own. Each *mitzvah* as such would have become "an event of cosmic importance, an act which had a bearing upon the dynamics of the universe."⁶⁹ However, Hirsch was no cabalist.⁷⁰ He feared mysticism no less than Reform. Tenuous as symbolism was, he wished to maintain it. Cognizant that in an environment of critical thought its credibility was vulnerable, Hirsch published in *Jeschurun* during the years 1857–61 an extensive study entitled "Grundlinien einer jüdischen Symbolik" (A basic outline of Jewish symbolism).[71] That Hirsch considered it necessary to elaborate on this subject twenty years after the publication of the *Horeb* is illustrative of his concern about the credibility, or rather the incredibility, of symbolism. His sensitivity may have been heightened by the discussions of the nature of the *mitzvot*, during the conferences and synods of Reform rabbis in 1844–46.[72]

In his outline, Hirsch dwells on the superiority of symbols over language. He elaborates on a view he had succinctly expressed in the *Neunzehn Briefe:* "These symbolic acts and seasons all give expression to ideas, without splitting them up into words as speech must. They come to mind each a unit, like thought itself, and like the resolve which they should beget; they present themselves with all the force of a single undivided and indivisible appeal to the soul" (*NL* 122–23). To counteract criticism, Hirsch suggests treating symbolism as a science— *Wissenschaft*. It must be critically scrutinized and evaluated to eliminate any semblance of ingenious fabrication, artificiality, or ambiguity. Hirsch thus sets forth several criteria by which to examine, analyze, and judge symbols. Among these are:

1. *Intention.* No manifestation, action, law, or rite may be considered to be of symbolic quality unless it can be unequivocally ascertained that it is intended to denote, communicate, or impart an idea. A flower does not signify love unless it is given by a lover to his beloved. Thus, by intention the ordinary flower is endowed with a symbolic quality of love and thereby has the power to evoke this sentiment. It is intention that transforms an insignificant flower into a message of importance.

2. *Context.* Since the object designated is not inherently but only metaphorically symbolic, it must be examined and evaluated in the context of its surroundings, time, conditions, and situation. No symbol can be considered as such in isolation without leading to ambiguities and a multiplicity of unsubstantiated interpretations. Only a flower proffered in the context of an amorous situation may indicate love. In the absence of such

contextual ramification, it may be meaningless and worthless. 3. *Relationship.* The symbol serves as a communicating medium between the communicator and the receiver of the communication. To comprehend its message it is necessary to know as much as possible about the nature of the sender and receiver of the symbolic communication and their relationship. 4. *Reminder.* The symbol can serve only as a reminder of ideas already known; it cannot be a revealer of new ideas never before presented. The symbol may, however, present known ideas in a new context, requiring the receiver's meditation and search for their meaning and implication (*S* 3:217–27).

Thus, Hirsch hoped to endow symbolism with an aura of intellectual and even scientific respectability. He wanted to convince his contemporaries that the eternal ideas of Judaism could only be preserved in the symbolic *mitzvot* which are superior, more impressive, and of longer duration than the most discursive expositions. Fundamentally, however, he was hoping, like all who resorted to symbolism before him, "to preserve the vitality of religious experience in a traditional, conservative milieu."[73] Apprehensive as he may have been of introducing symbolism as a rationale of the commandments to a highly incredulous and skeptical generation, Hirsch nevertheless hoped that its advantages would outweigh its disadvantages: "The richness of meaning that [symbols] seem to emanate lends new life to tradition which is always in danger of freezing into dead forms."[74] It was this revitalization of the formal *mitzvot* which was Hirsch's greatest concern, and for their sake he dared to advocate the old Philonic methodology of allegory and symbolism.

Major Reasons for Minor Details

In his endeavor to rationalize the commandments, Hirsch enjoys the distinction of having attempted to interpret not only their essential aspects but their minutiae as well. He gives considerable attention to explaining each detail, no matter how seemingly insignificant. He endows these supposedly trivial details with importance and profound meaning as if the fate of not only the Jewish people but of all mankind depended on their observance. In this respect, Hirsch differed from most previous interpreters of the commandments, who were satisfied to find a cogent reason for a *mitzvah* as a whole, rather than endeavor to explicate its ramifications.[75] Illustrative of this approach is Maimonides's view that the numerous details and minutiae prescribed for a *mitzvah* are gratuitous and inconsequential except as tests of obedience. Commenting on this subject in his *Guide of the Perplexed*, Maimonides stated: "I will now tell you what intelligent persons should believe in this respect; namely, that each commandment has necessarily a cause, as far as its general character is concerned, and serves a certain object; but as regards its details we hold that it has no ulterior object."[76]

Hirsch could not accept Maimonides's view, since Hirsch's concern was not only with the antinomians who rejected the laws, but with the Reformers who accepted some of them in principle but objected to their detailed ramifications. For example, the Reformers accepted the prohibition of work on the Sabbath; however, they differed sharply as to the meaning of work and its ramifications. The more conservative Reformers affirmed the commandment of circumcision, but denied the detailed rituals and observances traditionally connected with it.

It was, therefore, the details that needed the most rigorous defense. Moreover, the very admission of the inconsequentiality of the details and minutiae endangered the observance of the commandments altogether, since the relationship of the details to the commandments was the same as that of the commandments to the ideas they represented. If the commandments could be kept without their details, the ideas could be maintained without the commandments. Furthermore, in cases where the ideas themselves were no longer relevant, they could be abandoned altogether. Thus, the commandments concerning sacrifices or the prohibition against seething a kid in its mother's milk, which according to Maimonides were designed to counteract heathen practices, would no longer be valid. To concede the irrelevance of minor ritualistic details might have set in motion a chain of reasoning that would have abrogated most of the commandments. The enlightened Jew of the nineteenth century, like the rationalist in any age, would thus be confirmed in his ineluctable conclusion that "the Halakhah either had no significance at all, or one that was calculated to diminish rather than to enhance its prestige in his eyes."[77]

To counteract such a possibility, Hirsch was compelled to defend not only the commandments themselves but all the details and minutiae surrounding them. Thus, paradoxically, at a time when the validity and obligatoriness of the most salient commandments were coming under attack, their details had to be defended just as courageously. As in time of war, the disregard of the smallest crack in the wall could doom the most formidable fortress. Consequently, the more volatile a rite and the weaker its observance, the more strongly Hirsch defended it; the more precarious a ritual detail and the more endangered its continuity by abuse or disuse, the more complex was Hirsch's rationale urging its performance.

As a result, Hirsch's rationalizations and elaborations are inversely proportional to the magnitude and importance of a given aspect of a *mitzvah*. He dwells more extensively on the concomitant rites of circumcision than on its very performance. Similarly, the more abstruse the rite and the more unintelligible its observance, the more complex and weighty is Hirsch's explanation. At times, some of his interpretations resemble an intricate filigree of ideas, thoughts, and speculations precariously balanced on the point of a needle. The complexity of his rationale mounted steadily in proportion to the radicalization of the Reform movement. Thus, the explanations of the commandments and their details were more abundant and more elaborate in his later writings than in his *Horeb*.

Since the Reform challenge grew more aggressive and vociferous after 1837, the year the *Horeb* was published, Hirsch's defensive and apologetic interpretations grew appropriately more involved. In his commentary on the Pentateuch and other writings, he encrusted minor practices and trivial details with elaborate and subtle dialectics, endowing them with almost cosmic significance. Frequently in his later works he superimposed upon a simple reason, given in the *Horeb*, a cumbersome interpretation for a given observance. Apparently in the course of time he realized that such observances had become enfeebled since 1837 and were in need of additional rationalization in order to legitimize and fortify them. Since this was the fate of many such observances, Hirsch's elaborations grew in proportion.

The Value of the Commandments to Non-Jews

Among the other distinctive characteristics of Hirsch's interpretation of the commandments is his ascription of their value to non-Jews. As a rule, Jewish scholars viewed the commandments as an exclusively Jewish matter and of no concern to non-Jews. Their exclusivity for Jews emanated from the covenantal relationship established between God and Israel at Sinai. In absence of such a covenant, non-Jews were not enjoined to abide by the numerous commandments, except the seven Noaḥide laws, which are of a universal nature. In essence, Jewish scholars agreed with the statement of Rabbi Hananiah ben Akashia: "The Holy One, blessed be He, was minded to grant merit to Israel; therefore hath He multiplied for them the Law and commandments."[78] If any disagreement existed, it concerned the benefits that would accrue to the Jews from the observance of the commandments. A variety of theories were propounded as to the nature of these possible benefits—eschatological, eudaemonistic, educative, prophylactic, to mention only a few.[79]

To counter the possible accusation of God's partiality to the Jews, early rabbinic sources suggested that the Torah had been offered to all the nations. Only when the latter rejected the offer was it given to Israel.[80] Since the Jews voluntarily or through coercion[81] accepted the Torah, they are obligated to carry out the commandments and entitled to the concomitant advantages. The non-Jews, on the other hand, have neither the obligation nor the benefits. This view was commonly accepted and at the end of the eighteenth century was echoed by Mendelssohn. In clarifying the obligatoriness and nonobligatoriness of the commandments, Mendelssohn reiterated the old rabbinic principle that "anyone not born into the Law need not bind himself to the Law, but that anyone born into the Law must live and die in accordance with it."[82]

As already stated, Mendelssohn's reaffirmation of the traditional view of the commandments evoked little enthusiasm among his coreligionists. Unlike Rabbi Hananiah ben Akashia, who saw in the multiplicity of the commandments a "grant of merit to Israel" and a most precious gift, Mendelssohn presented it as a gratuitous, burdensome obligation. All men can attain happiness and salvation without the commandments, but only the Jews are subject to its rigorous, oppressive yoke.

To correct this notion, Hirsch suggested the view that the commandments have universal significance. Although the obligation of their performance devolves exclusively upon the Jews, their intrinsic values and benefits are significant for non-Jews as well. Indeed, the commandments are for the Jews primarily educative in nature. They constitute instrumentalities conducive to correct thinking, balanced feeling, and ethical conduct. In addition, they serve as preservers of great verities which were originally given to mankind at the dawn of history. In the course of time, these were abandoned and might have been completely forgotten had these verities not been preserved in the form of commandments entailing a variety of prescriptions, prohibitions, and numerous such details. Thus, by performing these *mitzvot* the Jews are preserving the verities applicable to all mankind. Many commandments contain a universal message which the Jews keep alive by their meticulous observance of them.

The Sabbath, as will subsequently be pointed out, is a case in point. Originally, its concept was communicated to all mankind; only upon its abandonment was it given to the Israelites. However, to prevent such an eventuality, the pure concept of the Sabbath was safeguarded by a host of minutiae, symbols, and prohibitions that were enjoined upon the Jews alone. Thus, the Jews by their observance of the commandments are actually performing a great task for humanity. The practice of the *mitzvot* is not a meaningless burden but a great universal service. The Jews are thus the custodians of the eternal verities that will eventually become the heritage of all mankind. Indeed, the observance of the commandments limits and restricts the Jews and deprives them of comforts enjoyed by others. Such sacrifices, however, are imperative for the Jews and are not an exorbitant price to pay to assure the happiness and salvation of humanity: "Is there any truer greatness for men than to be the bearers of revealed instruction concerning God and the duty of man, and to show by example and life that there are higher things than wealth and pleasure, than science and culture, to which these should be but subordinate means of fulfillment?" (*NL* 141).

Thus, Hirsch endowed the commandments with universal significance for Jews and non-Jews alike. The observant Jews are depicted as wearing the wreaths of heroes and the halos of idealists for enduring hardships and suffering privations in the cause of mankind's salvation. Furthermore, the social tensions between Jews and non-Jews engendered by the dietary laws and marital restrictions were now cast in a different light. These laws were not enacted out of hostility to strangers, but out of love and consideration. It was in the interest of the non-Jews that the Jews keep themselves apart. Should the Jews relinquish their separateness and become amalgamated with the other nations, the commandments containing the eternal verities and values would also be abandoned. This would constitute an irretrievable loss for mankind as a whole and must therefore be prevented by every means:

Does not this law erect a wall of separation between its adherents and the rest of mankind? It does, I admit, but had it not done so, Israel would long since have lost all consciousness of its mission, would long since have ceased to be itself. Do you not perceive what struggles the preservation of the true Israel spirit in our midst requires, despite this separation? How, then, could the holy flame have been kept burning in our breasts had there been no distinctive laws and ordinances to remind us that we are consecrated to a sacred duty, a divine mission? (*NL* 141–42)

Systematization and Classification

The systematization of the commandments has always presented a most formidable problem to Jewish codifiers and compilers of the laws. To arrange and reduce the *mitzvot*, of which there are traditionally six hundred thirteen,[83] into a logical system is no easy task. The most insuperable difficulty is their heterogeneity, not their multiplicity. Embracing a vast variety of subjects, they seemed to defy any conceivable attempt methodically to categorize them in a coordinated, comprehensive system. As a result, Jewish codifiers pursued many courses in their attempt to classify the commandments. Of the various systems evolved, the following are the most notable:

1. *Pentateuchical order.* Some codifiers related the Oral Law to the Written Law and thus arranged the commandments in the same sequential order as they appear in the Pentateuch.
2. *Talmudical order.* Certain codifiers organized the commandments in the consecutive order of the tractates of the Talmud.
3. *Topical order.* This most logical system, and probably the oldest, was employed by Judah the Prince at the end of the second century in the compilation of the Mishnah. It was subsequently espoused by the most influential codifiers: Maimonides in his *Mishneh Torah,* Ya'acov ben Asher in his *Turim,* and Joseph Caro in his *Shulḥan Arukh.*[84]

The pentateuchical and talmudical systems present a sequential enumeration rather than a logical classification. Compilers followed the ready-made pattern found either in the Pentateuch or in the Talmud. As a result, only a few readers could marshal the numerous commandments strung together by sequences, which themselves were in need of classification. However, the topical order aimed at solving this difficulty was no easy road for the codifiers either. They found no well-established pattern or well-trodden path to follow. Judah the Prince's early endeavor in this direction was only partly successful. Frequently, the inclusion of certain laws in a particular division of the Mishnah appears puzzling: "Groups of heterogeneous rules, sometimes strung together by the slenderest thread of association of ideas, occur so constantly as to become one of the Mishnah's characteristic features."[85] To structure the commandments in precise topical categories required enormous erudition, temerity, and ingenuity; and even with such qualifications no absolute success was assured. Small wonder that from all the codes arranged in the topical order, only two gained universal popularity—the *Mishneh Torah* of Maimonides and the *Turim* of Ya'acov ben Asher. However, even in these codes the reader is occasionally mystified by given commandments inexplicably subsumed under unrelated topics. Apparently, despite all their efforts, even the greatest codifiers were compelled to stretch and hyperbolize their logical ramifications to include commandments in categories for which no adequate classification could be found.

   Notwithstanding the fact that the systematization of the *Mishneh Torah* is superior to that of the *Turim,* it was the latter that gained in popularity and became the model for subsequent codes and legal digests, the most famous of which was the *Shulḥan Arukh* of Joseph Caro. The reasons for this paradoxical preference were many, one of which may have been the practical character of the *Turim*. Unlike Maimonides, who included in his juridical magnum opus all the commandments regardless of whether they were current or in abeyance, Ya'acov ben Asher limited himself only to those that were still in force. Indeed, Maimonides's catholic approach may have been prompted by his desire to summarize the entire Oral Law and to make his *Mishneh Torah*, as it literally signifies, a work only secondary in importance to the Torah. It is also possible that he entertained the idea of providing a constitution for the future Jewish state.[86] Subsequent scholars, however, were more modest and less ambitious in their aspirations; and therefore the more limited and judicious system of Ya'acov ben Asher seemed to them more adequate in answering the exigencies of the time.

Hirsch's classification of the *Horeb* is topical. Like most subsequent compilers of the law, he too follows the practical course of Ya'acov ben Asher rather than the academic and encyclopedic one taken by Maimonides. The *Horeb* is limited, with very few exceptions, to laws that were applicable in the Diaspora in his era. Fundamentally, he is guided by the principle that "everything unconnected with actual practice must be dispensed with."[87] However, the topics of the classification as well as their inner order and content, as will be subsequently pointed out, are closer to those of Maimonides's *Mishneh Torah*.

Hirsch having chosen the minimum course of Ya'acov ben Asher rather than the maximum pursued by Maimonides, the number of divisions he imposes has to be less than that of the *Mishneh Torah*. Hirsch does not, however, follow the divisions of the *Turim*. The former, embracing all the commandments, consists of fourteen divisions, the latter of four; Hirsch's *Horeb* contains six divisions. Since the subject matter in the *Horeb* is less than that in the *Turim*, the reason for augmenting the number of the divisions of the *Horeb* is puzzling. It is possible that since his limited subject matter did not warrant fourteen divisions analogous to the *Mishneh Torah*, Hirsch selected six, corresponding to the oldest division of the Oral Law, the Mishnah.

The nomenclature of these six divisions of the *Horeb* are: *"Torot"* (doctrines), *"Edot"* (symbolic observances), *"Mishpatim"* (judgments), *"Ḥukkim"* (statutes), *"Mitzvot"* (commandments), and *"Avodah"* (divine service). Except for *avodah*, which as will be shown necessitated a special division, the titles of all the divisions are mentioned in the Book of Psalms:

The law [*torah*] of the Lord is perfect, restoring the soul;
The testimony [*edot*] of the Lord is sure, making wise the
  simple.
The precepts of the Lord are right, rejoicing the heart;
The commandment [*mitzvah*] of the Lord is pure,
  enlightening the eyes.
The fear [*yir'ah*] of the Lord is clean, enduring for ever.
The ordinances [*mishpatim*] of the Lord are true, they are
  righteous altogether.[88]

In his commentary on the Psalms (*CP* 19:10), Hirsch states that the expression *yir'ah* denotes *ḥukkim*. In his works he preferred the better-known term *ḥukkim* to *yir'ah*.

Although the *Horeb* was designed as a compendium for German Jewry to guide them in the observance of the commandments, Hirsch deliberately deletes certain customs that might have evoked a negative reaction from non-Jews or might have discredited his work among liberal Jews. To avoid misunderstanding by non-Jews, he omits, as already pointed out, the recitation of Kol Nidre on the eve of Yom Kippur. It is possible that for similar reasons he does not mention the custom of releasing from vows, *(hatarat nedarim)* or the practice of a transaction permit *(heter iska)* whereby a Jew was permitted to charge interest by a legal fiction that made the lender a partner of the borrower. By the omission of *tashlikh, kapparot, ḥibbut aravah*, and similar customs, Hirsch follows the path of many *erleuchtet religiös* elements in the Jewish community that took exception to them.

However, it is inexplicable and enigmatic that Hirsch should omit such fundamental customs as selling of the *ḥametz* to a non-Jew and the laws of *niddah* and *mikvah*. Though he dwells extensively on marriage, divorce, and procreation (*H* 523–47), Hirsch does not discuss the most essential religious problems involving menstrual impurity and the process of purification. Paradoxically, Hirsch mentions the purification of vessels by immersion (*H* 465) and the washing of the hands (H 464), but not the most important laws of *niddah* with its numerous ramifications. To assume that he inadvertently overlooked such cardinal laws is hardly conceivable. To suggest that he considered them lightly is absurd.[89]

In conclusion, it should be noted that the commandments that Hirsch classifies in six divisions which will be discussed in the remainder of this work embody the following three concepts:

1. *Justice*—that is, consideration for every being as a creature of God, for all possessions as arrangements willed by God, of all governments and systems as ordained by God, and fulfillment of all duties toward them incumbent upon us.

2. *Love*—that is, kindly acceptance of all beings as children of God, as brethren; promotion of their welfare, and the endeavor to bring them to the goal set for them by God, without motive or benefit, but simply to fulfill the divine will and command.

3. *Education*—that is, the training of oneself and others to such work by taking to heart these truths as life principles, by holding them fast and preserving them for oneself and others, and by endeavoring to regain them whenever the influences of worldly life have torn them from our possession (*NL* 105–6).

7

"Torot": Fundamental Principles

"Torot" and the "Sefer ha-Madda"

The first of the six divisions in the *Horeb*, as noted, is entitled *"Torot,"* instructions and doctrines. In the *Neunzehn Briefe,* Hirsch had defined this as a division dealing with "the historically revealed ideas concerning God, the world, the mission of humanity and of Israel not as mere doctrines of faith or science, but as principles to be acknowledged by mind and heart, and realized in life" (*NL* 103–4).

This division consists of twenty chapters written, as is the rest of the book, in an ornate, hortatory, grandiloquent style. Most of Hirsch's themes in *"Torot"* are analogous to those of Maimonides's *"Sefer ha-Madda."* The latter was indeed more extensive, consisting of five subdivisions comprising forty-six chapters. However, seventeen of the twenty chapters of Hirsch's *"Torot"* have their corresponding topics in *"Sefer ha-Madda."*

The views expressed in the *"Torot"* are a delineation of Hirsch's philosophy which he expected to develop in the never-published *Moriah.* In this respect, Hirsch follows Maimonides, whose *"Sefer ha-Madda"* was a brief introduction to the *Mishneh Torah.* In it, Maimonides stated succinctly and in a popular manner his fundamental philosophic concepts of Judaism, which he subsequently elaborated in technical terms in the *Moreh Nevukhim.* Hirsch likewise intended to set forth in the *"Torot"* simplified philosophic ideas for the unsophisticated laymen as a prelude to his code of Jewish laws and observances.

The formal thematic similarity between the *"Torot"* and *"Sefer ha-Madda"* does not imply philosophical or ideological agreement. Notwithstanding external resemblance and terminological parallelism, there exist significant differences between the two, attributable in part to the dissimilarities inherent in the philosophic matrices of their authors' respective outlooks. Thus, the first chapters in *"Sefer ha-Madda"* and in the *"Torot"* commence with the idea of God, an idea fundamental to any theistic outlook or system. A careful analysis of the treatment of this idea in both works, however, discloses a vast internal ideational divergence despite the external thematic similarity.

Existence and Faith

Before comparing the various aspects of Hirsch's *"Torot"* and Maimonides's *"Sefer ha-Madda,"* it is imperative to analyze Hirsch's view on the fundamentals of Judaism, which he omits in *Horeb*, having expected to expound them in *Moriah*. In the absence of *Moriah* and in view of the paucity of the *"Torot"* it is necessary to analyze Hirsch's views on these fundamentals in his later works, admitting that some of them may have altered with time.

The two pivotal concepts of Judaism among Jewish philosophers and moralists are *metziut ha-Shem*, God's existence, and *emunah*, faith. The Jewish medieval rationalists presented a complexity of ingeniously elaborated proofs to demonstrate the logical necessity for God's existence, and the Jewish moralists formulated articles of faith. Hirsch, however, seems to have ignored all the vast literature on this subject and unqualifiedly accepted the views of Mendelssohn in this respect.

To Mendelssohn, God's existence, dominion, and providence needed no proof: "The Supreme Being has revealed them to all rational creatures through concepts and events inscribed on their souls with a script that is legible and intelligible at all times and in all places."[1] He quotes Psalm 19, which states that nature itself proclaims God's existence and attests to a divine creator. Mendelssohn's affirmation of God's existence emanated more from the

Cartesian-Newtonian world view than from the psalmist he quoted. The newly discovered laws of nature pointed to a supreme intelligence, which prompted the deists to look for God in nature rather than in the Bible.

Although Hirsch, unlike Mendelssohn, was strongly opposed to deism, he nevertheless accepted Mendelssohn's view that God's existence needs neither logical nor empirical demonstration. In his early work, *Horeb*, Hirsch does not dwell on the issue of God's existence. Apparently, he considered it so self-evident that it needed no elaboration. In his later commentary on the Psalms he seems to echo Mendelssohn's view on this subject: "The revelation at Sinai was not essential for the recognition of the fact that there must be someone who is the omnipresent creator, regulator, and ruler of the world. The realization that there must be a God could come to anyone who thoughtfully contemplates nature, and the heavens in particular" (*CP* 19:1).

Entranced by the great scientific discoveries, Hirsch like Mendelssohn sees in each advancement of science a new affirmation of God's infinite intelligence: "This evidence of the presence of God in nature, and of His sovereignty through nature, can be readily understood if one contemplates one particular heavenly body, that is, the sun" (*CP* 1:5). For Hirsch, science was not the foe of religion but its most trusted ally, and therefore, he maintains, an unbelieving scientist would constitute a contradiction. A scientist's denial of God's existence would be tantamount to a denial of the very scientific approach he is affirming: his quest for the laws of nature. If nature is devoid of an intelligent creator, it would be futile for him to search for intelligent laws governing it. Hirsch therefore points to the incongruity of an unbelieving natural scientist whose very discoveries reveal the divine imprint: "The naturalist who denies God discloses a trace of the very God he denies, with every law, with every force, with every purpose he works out of any form or shape he investigates" (*CG* 2:2).

Since God's existence is self-evident, faith seems unnecessary. Furthermore, the very term *faith* has an irrational connotation and was objectionable in the Age of Reason. According to Mendelssohn, the greatest merit of Judaism lies in the fact that it never demanded that its adherents believe, only act. Defending his loyalty to Judaism, Mendelssohn pointed to the fact that unlike Christianity, Judaism never constrained man to profess dogmas that he could not intellectually accept but addressed itself to his will only: "You are not commanded to believe, for faith accepts no commands; it accepts only what comes to it by reasoned conviction."[2]

As a result, Mendelssohn translated the Hebrew term *emunah* not in the customary way, faith, but *"trust,* confidence or firm reliance on pledge and promise."[3] Thus he rendered the expression *emunah* in the following biblical verses as *trust* and not faith: "Abraham trusted [*he'emin*] in the Lord and He counted it to him for righteousness."[4] "And Israel saw . . . and trusted [*va-ya'aminu*] the Lord and Moses His servant."[5]

Echoing Mendelssohn, although not mentioning him, Hirsch states:

Emunah is not belief. . . . In making religion into a belief, and then making the cardinal point of religion believing in the truth of theses quite untenable to intelligence, religion has been banned from everyday life and made into a catechism of words of belief which will be demanded as a passport for entry into the next world. (*CG* 15:6)

That Hirsch followed Mendelssohn's reinterpretation of the term *emunah* can be seen from the fact that in his translation of the Pentateuch he renders *emunah* in the aforementioned biblical verses as trust instead of faith: "Abraham *placed his whole confidence* [*he'emin*] in God and this He reckoned unto him for righteousness." "Israel saw . . . and *trusted* [*va-ya'aminu*] God and Moses His servant."

It may seem strange that Hirsch is more consistent in substituting trust for faith than Mendelssohn, for in his translation of the Pentateuch the latter had retained the traditional equivalent *Glaube,* faith, for *emunah,* which Hirsch does not.[6]

Hirsch's insistence upon attenuating the importance of faith in Judaism, where it had always occupied a preeminent position, may have been motivated by the rise of Romanticism and the popularity of Schleiermacher's theology. The latter made faith, feeling, and the sense of dependency the cornerstones of religion,[7] and the impact of his ideas was strongly felt in the liberal and reform circles of German Jewry.[8] This resulted in a subjectivization of religion and a dissolution of religious norms, further undermining the already weakened structure of traditional Judaism. Hirsch's dictum, *La loi und nicht la foi ist das Stichwort des Judentums*—Judaism's motto is law and not faith (*S* 2:422)—may have been intended to counteract the influence of Schleiermacher's theology, which denigrated law and elevated faith as the most sublime aspect of religion.

God-Ideas

Personalism While most of the crude ancient and medieval concepts of divinity no longer constituted a problem for Hirsch, some of the concepts current in his generation caused him great chagrin. In time he became increasingly aware of their danger and the need to deal with them in his commentary on the Pentateuch. Paradoxically, the gates of the metaphysical realm, which Kant seemed to have shut forever, were reopened by his heirs, Fichte, Schelling, Hegel, and Schleiermacher, who transmuted his transcendental philosophy into a variety of metaphysical systems. In the early part of the nineteenth century Germany witnessed a remarkable efflorescence of theologies in which old and new metaphysical notions commingled or existed side by side. Some outlooks, like Spinozistic pantheism, were recast and reformulated in a spiritual, aesthetic, and dialectic terminology. Regardless of the differences in outlook and approach, the patent tendency of those metaphysical systems and complex theologies was to depersonalize God and transform Him into a glorified abstraction. Whether God was thought to be synonomous with nature, a force pervading the universe, an ineffable, immutable, and impassive substance, He was not the personal ethical God of the Bible, who is involved in the world and stands in a dialogical relationship with man. The metaphysical God of the nineteenth-century philosophers and theologians was a sublime concept but irrelevant to man.

Indeed, the Jewish philosophers from Philo on made every possible endeavor to depersonalize God; they rationalized any anthropomorphic allusions to Him in the Bible and explicated figuratively. Nevertheless, the Jewish rationalists somehow retained the aspect of divine personalism in the ethiconormative domain. Intellectual strictures notwithstanding, the very same philosophers who deprived God of all the personalistic attributes in the sphere of man's cognition retained them in the sphere of man's action. The very same Maimonides who so radically negated the divine attributes in his *Guide of the Perplexed,* posited in his *Mishneh Torah* laws that only a personalistic divine lawgiver could decree.

Such inconsistency was not true of the German philosophers and theologians of the nineteenth century. As a result, normative Judaism seemed most threatened by this trend of abstraction and depersonalization of the God-idea. If Christianity could somehow be reconciled with such a notion, normative Judaism, whose God is involved in a personalistic covenantal relationship with the Jewish people and addresses Himself in personalistic imperatives to man, could not.

The extent of Hirsch's fear of abstraction and the depersonalization of the God-idea can be seen from the fact that he considered it worse than anthropomorphism, a concept rejected by most Jewish scholars. To the Jewish rationalists anthropomorphism was worse than idolatry. According to Maimonides: "By the belief in the corporeality or anything connected with corporeality you would provoke God to jealousy and wrath, kindle His fire and anger, become His foe, His enemy, and His adversary in a higher degree than by the worship of idols."[9]

After centuries during which the affirmation of incorporeality and the negation of anthropomorphism became an integral part of the Jewish credo, Hirsch dared to defy this consensus and side with Abraham ibn Daud, an old opponent of Maimonides, who considered anthropomorphism admissible[10]:

The danger of getting some corporeal conception of God is not nearly so great as that of volatilizing Him to a vague, obscure, metaphysical idea. It is much more important to be convinced of the personality of God, and of His intimate relations to every man on earth, than to speculate on the transcendental conceptions of infinity, incorporeality, etc., which have almost as little to do with the morality of our lives as algebraic ciphers. (*CG* 8:21)

This quotation reveals that Hirsch's seeming endorsement of anthropomorphism is only intended to convey the danger of abstraction and depersonalization of the Divine.[11] The new notions were so deleterious, in his opinion, that the crude archaic concept of anthropomorphism was to be preferred. Hirsch could offer such a preference knowing that in the nineteenth century it would not be taken seriously.

Immanentism Another metaphysical notion that disturbed Hirsch was divine immanentism. Denying explicitly or implicitly the Jewish concept of transcendental personalism, according to which God stands over and against the world as separate and distinct, immanentism obliterated this distinction to the point of merger and identity. God was no longer the creator and ruler of the world, which was external to Him, but He was immanent in it as a pulsating cosmic force. The world was the terrain in which God actualized His potentialities through the ever-unfolding process of nature and in man through the manifest dynamics of history.

The immanentist view not only negated the traditionalist Jewish God-idea of transcendental personalism, but also questioned the rationalistic concept of the Enlightenment, which viewed God and the world as an eternal duality never to be bridged.

For Hirsch, immanentism, even more than depersonalization, dissolved God into nothingness, made the world—heretofore contingent upon the intelligent will of a creator—self-subsistent and autonomous, and emancipated man from any heteronomous morality; in a word, immanentism was a euphemism for atheism. Expressing his opposition to this concept, Hirsch points to the biblical text in Genesis which deliberately

expresses the complete objectivity of the creation toward the creator, the world to God, and thereby opposes all those erroneous thoughts that make the master-worker become absorbed by His work, God by the world, that teach the doctrine of immanence of God in the world, and draw God down to a world-god, to the soul of the material world, to a force of nature that beyond the world and without the world has no existence. (*CG* 1:4)

Hirsch argues for the recognition of the complete otherness of God, who, though near, concerned, and attentive, is nevertheless transcendental and distinct. Unlike the mystics, who yearned for a *unio mystica*, for the utter disintegration of the human personality, to be absorbed by God, or for the Divine to pervade man's being, Hirsch emphasizes nearness yet otherness—God and man, like God and the world, retaining their respective distinctiveness.

In this vein Hirsch interprets the Hebrew term for divine presence, *shekhinah*. According to him, it derives from the word *shakhen*, neighbor, thus signifying that "the Divine is the *shakhen* [neighbor] of man, and man of the Divine, but neither [has] become completely absorbed by the other. . . . While Judaism does teach us the most intimate nearness of God to man, it wants to keep us to the clearest, most comprehensible, we would say sober, way of contemplating it" (*CG* 9:27).

Volition and Dynamism   As is evident from his writings, Hirsch was not only averse to the immanentist and monistic theologies, which removed any disjunction between God, world, and man, but equally rejected the naturalistic mechanistic theologies of the Enlightenment, modified vestiges of which were still current in his time. The latter, like Judaism, presupposed a distinct separation between God and the world and between God and man; unlike Judaism, however, the Enlightenment theologies denied any continuous relationship between God and His creation. The personalistic God-idea of traditional Judaism had two concomitant notions: conscious volition and dynamic action, a continuous process that did not cease with creation. In the naturalistic-mechanistic theologies of the Enlightenment, particularly deism, God was a retired watchmaker who, once He set the world in motion in accordance with His established, permanent, perfect and eternally fixed laws, took no further part in it.

To Hirsch, an inactive God was no God, since His existence was irrelevant. A God uninvolved in the world and a God unconcerned for man's conduct and salvation could be at best an intellectual principle but never a living God. He therefore repudiated such a notion because "not only the coming into existence of things but also their continuance in existence is directly dependent on the free will of God and on His satisfaction" (*CG* 1:4).

The immutability of the natural laws does not signify God's withdrawal from the world or lack of interest in the welfare of man; on the contrary, the world's stability is predicated upon the will of God, who at any given moment is free to alter the heretofore seemingly unalterable laws. Like the classical medieval Jewish philosophers, particularly Halevi[12] and Maimonides,[13] Hirsch distinguishes between the two distinct divine appellations: *Elohim* and the Tetragrammaton. The former denotes God as He manifests Himself in the unchangeable laws of nature, whereas the latter betokens God as revealed in His free dynamic operations in the history of man, principally in the history of Israel: "As *Elohim*, God has created heaven and earth and fixed its development on law and order; as [the Tetragrammaton] He interferes with this development and alters and regulates it every second in accordance with its purpose, the education of mankind" (*CG* 2:4).

For this reason Hirsch rejected Mendelssohn's rendering of the Tetragrammaton as *Der Ewige*, the Eternal. Without mentioning Mendelssohn, Hirsch states: " 'Eternal' is a metaphysical, transcendental conception which has scarcely any practical application to anything else, certainly not to our own lives and existence." The Tetragrammaton, however, wishes to convey that

God is not some eternal "Ancient One of Days" who, having created the world, now reposes in the depth of His eternal existence. He is . . . the living, ever-ruling God, from whom not only the whole past originated but who also grants every coming moment in accordance with the educational requirements of mankind. (*CG* 2:4)

If man were merely a part of nature, governed absolutely by its laws and developing accordingly, the divine aspect symbolized by *Elohim* would suffice. Since man is endowed with free will, which enables him to defy nature and rise above its deterministic constrictive laws, the Tetragrammaton was added to emphasize the free interaction of God and man independent of nature:

With man the name [the Tetragrammaton] was added to *Elohim*, and so there are two factors that rule the further development of the world: (a) the ordinary laws of nature, which God had already set in the original creation and (b) the guidance and modification, which the same God gives every moment to this development with reference to, and in consideration of, the behavior of mankind. (*CG* 2:4)

Antideterminism   The voluntaristic aspect of the Jewish personalistic God-idea presupposed absolute divine freedom in the process as well as the matter of creation. The preexistence of matter coexisting with God was not only incompatible with monotheism but seemed to restrict God's freedom in the creation of the world in accordance with His absolute free will. Notwithstanding the numerous arguments marshaled by many Jewish and non-Jewish scholars about the eternity of the world, as opposed to *creatio ex nihilo*, the overriding consideration in favor of the latter hypothesis was the notion of divine freedom. Were it not for this consideration many Jewish philosophers could have accepted the idea of a *materia prima*, for, as Maimonides points out, the Bible is inconclusive on this point.[14]

For Hirsch, *creatio ex nihilo* was an accepted doctrine, no longer debatable. Like most of the Jewish traditional exegetes, he translates the first verb in the opening verse in Genesis, *bara*, as "bringing something into reality that hitherto had only existed inwardly, in the mind. It is creating something purely out of one's mind and will and out of nothing else" (*CG* 1:1).

Creatio ex nihilo had no metaphysical or cosmological significance for Hirsch, since the Bible neither reveals the secrets of God nor discloses the mysteries of the universe. It had, however, a theological and ethical value. Theologically, it seemed to negate the deterministic philosophies, some of which emanated from the Cartesian-Newtonian logical-mathematical-mechanistic outlook on the world and from the rediscovery of Spinoza and the fascination with his Weltanschauung:

Everything, all material, all forms, everything existing, has sprung from the completely free, all-mighty creative will of God. Still, today the creator rules completely freely over the material and form of all creatures, over the forces that work in matter, over the laws that govern that working, and over the resulting forms, for it is His free, almighty will that created the matter, that embodied the forces which work within it, and it is His law which governs the result. (*CG* 1:1)

Not having any *materia prima* to contend with or to constrain Him, God was absolutely free to create the world according to His will. Unhindered by the inherent imperfections of a preexisting primeval matter, God was free to select deliberately the best matter out of which to create the world. Affirming the traditional Jewish view that God is benevolent, omnipotent, and omniscient, Hirsch reached the ineluctable conclusion that the world created by God is not the best possible of all worlds, as Leibniz stated, but the actual best: "With all its seeming evils, it corresponds to the plans of wisdom of its creator, who could have created it otherwise if such had been more in accordance with His will" (*CG* 1:1).

The seeming imperfections in the world are therefore not a result of determinism, whether inherent in an imperfect primordial substance or in the rigid impersonal laws of nature, but constitute a part of God's design.

Ethically, *creatio ex nihilo* has profound implications for man, whose free will is unrestricted. Neither the external world nor his own nature have any inherent elements capable of impeding his God-given potential of attaining the highest perfection. His nature, as well as the nature of the world in which he operates, was created by the will of a free God to be conducive to the attainment of such perfection.

Cognition and Action

Maimonides, as an avowed rationalist, considered man's intellectual cognition of God as the most important principle of Judaism. Affirming the existence of God on the basis of Aristotelian metaphysics, Maimonides considered this acknowledgment by man to be the most important axiom upon which the normative and ethical superstructure of Judaism rests. The opening sentence of *"Sefer ha-Madda,"* which is the philosophical prolegomenon to the *Mishneh Torah,* stated: "The basic principle of all principles and the pillar of all sciences is *to know (leida)* that there is a First Being who brought every existing thing into being."[15]

This cognition of divine existence predicated on the rational arguments formulated by Aristotle, Avicenna, and others will, according to Maimonides, inevitably induce man to execute God's will. Once man comprehends that "the sphere is always revolving and that it is impossible for it to revolve without something making it revolve,"[16] he will rationally conclude the existence of a prime mover, a *causa causarum.* It is this intellectual cognition which is referred to in the first verse of the Decalogue, "I am the Lord thy God."

A confirmed rationalist, Maimonides was convinced that this intellectual cognition would impel man, a rational being, to rational action. As a result, this cognition would not remain abstractly confined within the boundaries of the intellect but would move man to relate himself instantaneously to God:

> When a person *contemplates* His great wondrous works and creatures and from them obtains a glimpse of His wisdom which is incomparable and infinite, he will straightway love Him, praise Him, glorify Him and long with an exceeding longing to *know* His great name.[17]

Thus, for Maimonides the rational comprehension of a concept is sufficient to motivate man ethically, elevate him religiously, and activate him socially. Knowledge as such therefore constitutes the cornerstone of Judaism and is a fundamental requirement for the Jew: "Knowledge endows man with the bliss of this immediate communion with God, and gives rise to the emotion of the love of God, and to the happiness of the communion. The *eudaemonia* of knowledge becomes transformed into the bliss of communion with God."[18]

This hyperbolical view of intellectual cognition enabled Maimonides to proceed immediately from the affirmation of this metaphysical-theological principle to his monumental ethical-normative code. Reason is strong enough to motivate man to act in accordance with the will of God; no other inducements are necessary. The precepts stated in the *Mishneh Torah* are the logical corollaries devolving upon man from his basic rational affirmation of God's existence. Once this ontological principle has been acknowledged by man's intellect, the acceptance and performance of the laws and rituals present no problem. The precepts merely instruct man how to relate to God, whom he already affirmed and wished to emulate.

Hirsch also begins his *"Torot"* with the concept of *Gottheit*, divinity. Unlike Maimonides, Hirsch was not impressed by the efficacy of man's abstract intellectual cognition of divinity. Although he respected man's intellect, he shared neither Maimonides's panrationalism nor his conviction that theoretical knowledge alone is adequate to motivate man to instantaneous rational, ethical, and religious conduct. Many reasons contributed to Hirsch's attitude.

The nineteenth century was less in awe of reason than had been the twelfth. Man's behavior in the intervening seven centuries had failed to vindicate the overconfidence of the rationalists in this highly admired but volatile faculty. Living in the afterglow of deism and the Enlightenment, Hirsch was aware of the disparity between theoretical knowledge and ethical behavior, intellectual cognition and moral conduct. Above all, he realized the lack of correlation between the rational affirmation of divine existence and the acceptance of religious normativism. None of the Reform theologians and few of the radical intellectuals in the nineteenth century were atheists; yet their ontological cognition, contrary to Maimonides's expectation, did not motivate them to religious normativism. The abyss between thought and action, between cognition and implementation, and particularly between the affirmation of God and performance of *mitzvot* was less easy to bridge in Hirsch's era than in Maimonides's.

Philosophically, Hirsch agreed with Hegel that man's consciousness, his cognition in a state of nature, unless influenced and molded by the objective mind, is dangerously subjective. It is therefore devoid of any ethical implications inherent in the objective cognition attained only on a higher level, which is in a state of spirit. Hirsch may have been aware of Kant's distinction between theoretical and practical reason, and of the latter's insistence on the overriding importance of practical reason in the moral sphere.[19] In consonance with the philosophic climate of his time, Hirsch de-emphasized Maimonides's view that intellectual cognition is the "basic principle of all principles and the pillar of all sciences." Important as it may be, "knowledge alone is not enough" (*H* 1). Hirsch followed the mainstream of Hegelian thought, as is clear from the *Neunzehn Briefe*, and subordinated man's subjective mind to the Absolute Mind or God as the cornerstone of Judaism. It is therefore insufficient for man merely to conceive of divine existence intellectually and then, on the basis of this cognition, to fulfill God's will as stated in the Torah. Man must, according to Hirsch, do the reverse: his primary task is to conform his subjective will to the objective will of God, thus achieving liberation by elevating himself above his subjectivity. Man must not "fulfill the behests of that will only when or because they appear also to us right and wise and good" (*NL* 47), for this implies subjectivity; under such circumstances man is not submitting to God but, actually, to himself. By setting himself up as a judge who decides what he should or should not do, man subordinates the Absolute Will to his subjective one, for it is now his own will that critically determines whether the will of God should or should not be obeyed. Only when man by his inherent prerogative of free will surrenders his subjective will, which is grounded in nature, to the overriding dictates of the Absolute does he rise to the true state of man. By "obeying the will of God as the will of *his* God" (*NL* 47) man attains true freedom and knowledge.

Therefore, Hirsch, in contrast to Maimonides, emphasizes as the first and most fundamental principle of Judaism not man's intellectual cognition of God, but man's submission to His will. Man's knowledge of God is secondary to the paramount concept of unqualified acceptance of God's sovereignty. Consequently, in his preface to the *Horeb*, Hirsch stresses this concept and the obligations that emanate from it: "So long as you do not receive God into your heart as *your* God, and embrace Him with *your* whole being as *your* God, so long as this concept is a mere denizen of your brain, so long will this sovereign idea be without influence on your actual life" (*H* 2). It is evident that Hirsch did not believe that man's rational, ontological cognition would by itself move him to action. Knowledge alone is sterile and reason barren, unless man recognizes God's existence as having personal significance for him and committing him to active involvement.

Relating his fundamental principle, in a manner similar to Maimonides, to the first verse of the Decalogue, Hirsch interprets it as an imperative directed, not to man's intellect, but to his volition. God did not proclaim His metaphysical existence in the words "I am the Lord" but manifested His juridical claim on man. It is this claim, implying man's obligation to God, that is expressed in the relational pronoun phrase "*thy* God." It is this pronoun that the Decalogue emphasizes, indicating a personal and covenantal relationship that demands compliance of will and fulfillment of obligation. Hirsch further elaborates this view in his commentary on the Bible. He summarily dismisses all the speculations and problems which agitated medieval and modern theologians concerning the message of revelation: "Not the fact that there is a God, also not that there is only one God, but that this one, unique true God, is to be *my* God" (*CE* 20:2). The essence of Judaism's revelation is not man's cognition of God, but his fealty to Him: "Not the knowledge of the existence of God but the acknowledgment of God as *my* God" (*CE* 20:2) constitutes the basis of Jewish life.

By shifting the essence of Judaism from cognition to action, Hirsch departed from Maimonides's position, but seems to have adopted Mendelssohn's viewpoint. It is significant to note that despite the fact that the Mendelssohnian Weltanschauung and its Leibnizian-Wolffian substructure were discarded in the nineteenth century, some of Mendelssohn's ideas continued to exert an influence. Hirsch, who was conditioned in the Haskalah milieu, clung to many of Mendelssohn's ideas. According to Mendelssohn, "all commandments of the divine law are addressed to man's will, to his capacity to act."[20] While this normative concept of revelation was unacceptable to the liberals and the Reform theologians of the era, Hirsch did not find it objectionable. On the contrary, Mendelssohn's view that revelation was normative rather than cognitive made it less problematic epistemologically. It thus avoided the disapprobation of the Kantians, whose views were espoused by many Jews. By de-emphasizing the importance of man's intellectual cognition of God, Hirsch not only conformed to the Mendelssohnian tradition but avoided the epistemological problem of reaching out into the realm of the noumena. Thus, he skillfully circumvented the "dark ocean without shores or beacons" which Kant had closed to navigation for man's intellect.

Einheit *and* Yiḥud

Liberated from the multitude of metaphysical questions which had fettered generations of Jewish and non-Jewish theologians, Hirsch was able to dispense with many of the questions Maimonides had to deal with in his *Mishneh Torah.* Questions of corporeality, eternity, attributes, and others of a similar nature were as irrelevant to Hirsch as they were archaic to his times. The only subject which seems to have a metaphysical quality in his discussion in the *Horeb* is that of the unity of God. However, a comparison between Hirsch's idea of *Einheit* and Maimonides's idea of *yiḥud* discloses that, aside from a similarity in nomenclature, they have little in common. Maimonides, living in the Middle Ages, endeavored to disprove any possible assumption, notion, or allegation of dualism, trinitarianism, or polytheism. Though he did not elaborate on the concept of oneness in the *Mishneh Torah* to the extent that he did in the *Guide of the Perplexed*, he considered it important to emphasize the metaphysical absurdity of polytheism: "If there were plural deities, these would be physical bodies; because entities that can be enumerated and are equal in their essence are only distinguishable from each other by the accidents that happen to physical bodies."[21] Such a discussion was no longer tenable in the post-Enlightenment nineteenth century, which was not menaced by a resurgence of polytheism.

Hirsch's chapter on *Einheit* has a terminological but not a substantive similarity to Maimonides's *yiḥud*. His aim was not to prove God's indivisibility; this was not only superfluous in his era but, having a noumenal implication, was beyond the range of man's comprehension. Hirsch's definition of unity is thus not metaphysical, but ethical, not designed to prove the oneness of God but to teach man that there is an intelligent constant behind the bewildering phantasmagoria of the antithetical phenomenological permutations in nature, history, and man himself. Hirsch wanted to convey the concept of cosmic unity, which he had already introduced in the *Neunzehn Briefe.* Man, unaware of this unity, may view these changeable and at times contradictory manifestations as disjointed and unrelated phenomena. Such a view would not be merely metaphysically unsound, but also socially and ethically pernicious, since it could lead him to wrong conclusions, to egocentricity, self-deification, unbridled hedonism, and similar immoral and antisocial tendencies. Hirsch, therefore, emphasizes the anthropological implications of *Einheit:*

Just as the world, with all its variety, history with all its change has its origin in the one source, is guided by one hand, serves One Being and strives upwards towards this One; so must you recognize and feel your life with all its changes to issue from one source to be guided by one hand, to follow towards one goal. (*H* 7)

Thus, while Maimonides proceeded from a series of rational and logical categories to prove the metaphysical unity of God, to Hirsch the latter needed neither verification nor substantiation. On the contrary, on the basis of this a priori affirmed *Einheit*, man must organize and direct his own life that it "may be a unity just as your God is one" (*H* 7).

The Ethicization of Theological Terminology

From the concepts of divine sovereignty and unity Hirsch passes to the concept of idolatry, omitting many topics discussed by Maimonides in his *"Sefer ha-Madda"* between the opening paragraphs of *"Hilkhot Yesodei ha-Torah"* and *"Hilkhot Avodat Kokhavim."*[22] This continuity is not necessarily due to its sequential place in the Decalogue, but stems from the fact that Hirsch saw a substantive interrelatedness between the concepts of sovereignty, unity, and idolatry. In the fifth of the *Neunzehn Briefe* he had maintained that man's failure to surrender his subjective mind to the Absolute Mind and his miscomprehension of the cosmic "whole" has pernicious social and ethical consequences. Losing sight of meaningful totality, man is confounded by the myriad senseless, independent, and unrelated fragments struggling for their transitory egocentric goals (*NL* 51). With the disappearance of the concept of unity from the cosmos, each entity, man included, strives to attain its own goals. There is no longer any responsibility toward other entities or other men. In a chaotic universe there is no reason for man to act harmoniously or morally. As a result, "he will break out into all kinds of excesses, and abandon himself to arrogance and dissoluteness" (*H* 12).

Idolatry is, therefore, not an intellectual error, as Maimonides had maintained, but a moral one. Its danger lies not in man's fallacious cognition of the Divinity, but in the deleterious effect upon his character and conduct. Hirsch therefore considers idolatry in Hegelian terms, as signifying man's defiance by preventing his uncontrolled natural will to be disciplined by the Absolute Mind—in Hirsch's view, God. This defiance by man is tantamount to idolatry. It destroys man and society and causes him to sink "to a lower level" (*H* 12).

Two offenses lead to idolatry, *minut* and *zenut*—heresy and immorality. The first connotes excessive rationalism, the second unrestrained hedonism. These two terms are mentioned in the *Mishneh Torah*[23] and are based upon the rabbinic interpretation of the biblical verse "so that you do not follow your heart and eyes in your lustful urge."[24] The heart and the eyes were considered by the Talmud as the two agents of transgression, leading respectively to moral depravity and social disintegration.[25]

These two factors were responsible for most defections from traditional Judaism in the nineteenth century. Hirsch therefore elaborates upon these transgressions in the fourth chapter of his *Horeb* without adding anything substantive. Again, he de-emphasizes the importance of mere intellectual cognition attained by reason yet failing to motivate the correlative obligatoriness on the part of man. It is possible for man to discover the existence of the primary force behind all phenomena, which is God. It will not, however, be the personal God posited by the Torah (*H* 14). By retracing the steps in the chain of causality, it is possible for man to arrive rationally at the Aristotelian-Maimonidean prime mover. This deduction, rational as it may be, is nevertheless devoid of any ethical or social significance. It is merely a logical abstraction. Being impersonal and nonmandatory, it remains inconsequential. This distinction between the God of reason and God of Torah harks back to Halevi's contrast between the God of Aristotle and the God of Abraham.[26] Echoing Kant, Hirsch asserts the limitation of reason, which is operative in the phenomenological sphere but incapable of transcending it: "Your understanding is competent only to investigate the created world; for that purpose it was given to you" (*H* 18). The noumenal sphere, having no practical value for man's life and well-being, is closed to him. Man must therefore avoid the application of human standards, values, and criteria, operative in the domain of phenomena, to God, whose very concept is that of a noumenon. It is incongruous "to measure the creator with the yardstick of the creature" (*H* 18). Even the Torah, which is divine, does not disclose anything about this metarational domain. Any speculation about that domain leads to mysticism. Even a search of the Torah for some supernatural esoteric clues must not be pursued, since the Torah does not disclose what is unattainable by man (*H* 18).

Though hedonism may appear antipodal to rationalism, it is just as pernicious. In the latter, man surrenders to his subjective mind; in hedonism, he yields to his subjective will. In both cases, man loses his perspective of cosmic organic unity. Man no longer senses any obligation in his relationship with God or the surrounding world, but considers himself the measure of all things. This erroneous outlook results in a distorted axiology. Good signifies personal gratification, evil any impediment to its attainment. Thus, ethical relativism, situational morality impelled by untrammeled selfishness, becomes the motivating force in the world.

External Circumstances and Internal Free Will

The concept of free will was very important to Hirsch, not only as a traditional Jew, but also as a modern man to whom the dignity and freedom of the individual were the highest values. He therefore emphasizes this concept, despite the fact that he accepted the heteronomic or theonomic norms of traditional Judaism. Despite Kant's objections, Hirsch viewed man's autonomy as unstable and dangerous. Only by man's voluntary acceptance of the theonomic laws is true autonomy possible. Hirsch therefore stresses that Judaism does not address itself to man in an imperative, mandatory manner, but in an educative, suggestive manner, leaving the option to man: " 'Should' not 'must'; for whether you will really fulfill it depends entirely on yourself" (*H* 23).

Nothing in the nature of man or in the nature of the world can deprive man of his freedom and his ability to act in accordance with the will of God. As mentioned, man's physical nature and the material substance of the universe were so constituted by a free God as to make man's absolute moral freedom and perfection possible. Hirsch therefore repudiated the Christian doctrine of original sin, which considers man inherently sinful and only redeemable by an external supernatural power. He states clearly the Jewish position vis-à-vis Christianity:

Mankind is in no manner whatsoever placed under a ban for his first disobedience. . . . Every human child still comes from the hand of God as pure as Adam did; every child is still born to mankind pure as an angel. This is one of the cardinal points of Jewish life and of the essential Jewish nature. . . . The dogma of original sin, . . . upon which a whole structure has been built, [is one] against which, if against anything, the whole being of a Jew has to raise the most emphatic protest. (*CG* 3:19)

Hirsch seems completely unconcerned about the circumstantial factors which might affect man's acceptance or rejection of the divine will through inhibition and determinism. He describes man's environment as completely circumscribed and determined a priori with total disregard of its impact on man's freedom. Man is born at a given time and place, endowed with certain abilities and shortcomings. In his formative years, his outlook is influenced by parents, teachers, friends, and circumstances over which he has no control. It is they that shape him, not vice versa (*H* 23). The question thus arises whether all these influences do not actually determine man's response, or at least condition his possible reactions. Hirsch apparently considered man's freedom of will as transcending all external factors that are conducive or inhibitive to man's ethical and religious conduct. Guided by the Torah, which is God's manifest will, man is able to overcome any adverse circumstantial and environmental impediments: "Perform what you have recognized to be your duty at any moment, and do not be led astray by circumstances" (*H* 27). It is thus in action where man's true autonomy lies. In the final analysis, it is the individual himself who decides, and this moral decision, like the categorical imperative of Kant, must not be contingent, conditioned, or motivated by anything or anybody. Regardless of all circumstances, favorable or otherwise, man's will and action remain totally unconstrained.

Man's destiny is therefore free, undetermined by fate, conditions, or external phenomena. Anyone believing otherwise is violating the biblical injunction against divination and soothsaying.[27] Again, Hirsch refers to the same biblical verses that Maimonides did in *"Sefer ha-Madda,"*[28] but with a different connotation. Both quote the verse "You must be wholehearted with the Lord your God"[29] and refer to the commandments prohibiting superstitious heathen practices. To Maimonides they had merely a juridical significance, but to Hirsch they have a philosophic implication: any outlook which seems to deprive man of his free will "is an abomination to the Lord who calls upon you to act like free human beings" (*H* 29). Just as the Jew in antiquity could not allow astrology or witchcraft to interfere with his ethical duties, so the modern Jew must not permit present-day ideologies of determinism to interfere with his religious and moral task.

Evident in all his works is Hirsch's preoccupation with man's free will, a concept to which a great part of the commandments of Judaism seem to address themselves. This is shown most strongly by Hirsch's views on death and the seemingly esoteric laws of defilement by contact with a human corpse. He dismisses the hygienic hypothesis advanced by some scholars, the notion that these laws were promulgated in order to prevent infectious diseases caused by noxious effluvia and harmful exhalations from a disintegrating body. Their purpose is to impress man with the most fundamental ethical idea of "freedom of will in moral matters" (*CN* 19:22).

Nothing is as overwhelming to man or as pernicious to his moral concepts as death. Death seems to underscore man's frailty and to emphasize his utter helplessness in the face of the inexorable laws of nature. All the eloquent dissertations about man's alleged freedom appear to be a myth, and man, like animals and plants, must submit to the unyielding law of nature—death. No elaboration is needed to prove the deleterious effect of this view on morality, which presupposes man's ability to act freely contrary to his own nature or the forces of nature that surround him.

To counteract this erroneous notion, Judaism, unlike other religions, decrees death to be *tum'ah*, defilement. The physical contamination it connotes symbolizes the more important ideational contamination that results from the physical. The laws governing *tum'ah* address themselves to man symbolically: "Be not depressed, let not the fact of the death of physical life rob you of, or make you have doubts about, the consciousness of the freedom of your moral spiritual life, the freedom of your God-like spiritual self, which does not come under the force and power of death" (*CL* 5:13).

The stringent laws of defilement upon contacting a human

corpse or the carrion of a mammal, whose anatomical structure resembles that of a man, were designed to alert man to the distinction between his unfree body and his free spirit. The dead body is not man, and the natural laws to which it succumbs do not affect his free spirit and did not affect his spirit or his moral decisions when they were joined together in life. During his life it is the body, now a source of uncleanness, that is governed, controlled, elevated, and even sanctified by the spirit: "Man can master, rule and use even his sensuous body with all its innate forces, urges, and powers with God-like free self-decision, within the limits of, and for the accomplishments of, the duties set by laws of morality" (*CL* 11:47).

To further emphasize the concept of man's superior power of free will, Hirsch offers a most convoluted and highly complex explanation for the rite of purification of one's defilement after coming in contact with a human corpse—the red heifer (*CN* 19:21–22). This enigmatic law, which the Talmud and the greatest Jewish philosophers declared irrational, metarational and inexplicable, Hirsch endeavors to explain in order to vindicate his most important premise—man's unconditional and unrestricted free will.

Revelation or Génie

Hirsch's chapter on revelation, which contains elements mentioned in the last four chapters of *"Hilkhot Yesodei ha-Torah,"* deals with (1) revelation on Sinai, (2) prophecy, (3) the attestation of a true prophet, and (4) false prophets. Concerning the Sinaitic revelation, Hirsch merely states the factualness of this historic phenomenon, publicly manifested and experienced by the senses of "two and a half million souls" (*CE* 19:4). He thus reiterates the argument presented centuries ago by Saadia and Halevi and in modern times by Mendelssohn.

In *"Sefer ha-Madda"* Maimonides stressed the sense-experience aspect of this historic manifestation.[30] Similarly, Hirsch considered the collective phenomenon perceived at Sinai as conclusive evidence of the truth of revelation: "Face to face, God spoke the words of life to the whole people of Israel. It is this fact, free from all possibility of deception, which guarantees the Torah as unchangeable for all generations, for all times" (*H* 34).

In his biblical commentary, written many years after the *Horeb*, Hirsch rejected the new sophisticated reinterpretation of the concept of revelation given by the nontraditionalists. According to the latter, it was the innate *génie* of the Jewish people that produced the Torah. Revelation was an inverted process. Instead of coming from God, it came from the people of Israel. Hirsch was unalterably opposed to such a view. The Torah, he argues, "did not come out of the people but to the people" (*CE* 19:10–13). Similarly, he emphasizes that God's messages to Moses came not from "within Moses" but from without (*CL* 1:1). The view current in liberal circles which transformed traditional revelation into romantic inspiration is contradicted by historical facts. Had the Torah been a product of the Jewish genius and an indigenous creation, the ancient Israelites would not have militated against it. Replying indirectly to the biblical critics and radicals, Hirsch states that it is impossible to employ the same historical and sociological criteria to Judaism as to other religions and cultures. The latter are of human origin and consequently subject to change with the advancement of time. As man progresses, his views continue to develop; hence his ideas concerning art, morals, and various aspects of knowledge are accordingly transformed. Judaism, however, did not emanate from the people. On the contrary, it is divine, hence immutable, although evoking rebellion then as it does now: "Right from the beginning, the law of God found itself in opposition to the people in whose midst it was to find entrance" (*CE* 19:10–13).

This argument does not exist in the *Horeb*. Here, Hirsch is primarily concerned with the unqualified permanency of normativism which cannot be abrogated in the future by any man, no matter how great, influential, or convincing. Even the prophets, who were divine messengers long after revelation, could not alter the norms set forth forever at that historic moment. Hirsch repeats Mendelssohn's argument that the normative aspect of Judaism can only be revoked by God Himself: "Since the Torah declares itself to be closed for all time, it follows that only a like occurrence, equally direct and with an equal number of eyewitnesses, can add so much as a single word to the Torah or take one away or declare one repealed" (*H* 34).

In this last statement, Hirsch merely paraphrases Mendelssohn's words in *Jerusalem* that the Torah might be modified "only if and when it pleases the supreme Lawgiver to let us recognize His will —to make it known to us just as openly, publicly, and beyond any possibility of doubt and uncertainty, as He did when He gave us the law itself."[31]

Hirsch's allusion to his contemporary antinomian "prophets" is thus implicit in pointing to the fact that even the ancient prophets, so frequently invoked by the Reform theologians, called for "the observance of the law" (*H* 35) and not for its abrogation. Nor did the prophets of old, in contrast the "new," institute new laws and practices as did the Reform innovators: "They were not to be law-giving prophets, for the Law, both Written and Oral, was closed with Moses" (*H* 35).

Hirsch's anxiety over the antinomian tendencies and the increasing antagonism to the Oral Law that was spreading in ever-widening circles of German Jewry may account for his ascribing far greater importance to the Oral Law than to the Written Law. While in the traditionalist Jewish view both laws have equal standing, both being divine in origin, the Written Law was nevertheless considered the basis of the Oral Law; the concepts and the precepts of the latter were deduced from its text.

To the liberals and Reformers of the nineteenth century the Oral Law was neither divine nor did it equal the status of the Written Law. Although they may have doubted the latter's divinity and revelational character, they still treated it with respect. Not so the Oral Law. Here, historical and scientific research, intellectual difficulties, socioeconomic considerations, and practical reasons militated against it. As a result, even those inclined to accord to it some cultural-historical value denied its coequal status with the Written Law and rejected its mandatory quality.

The inferior status of the Oral Law could only lead to its total abandonment, threatening Judaism with a new manifestation of Karaitism or a Jewish brand of Lutheranism. Moreover, Judaism without the Oral Law would be barely distinguishable from Protestant Christianity, thus removing the last impediment to conversion.

Apprehensive of these potential dangers, Hirsch's contemporary exegetes, Jacob Zvi Mecklenburg and Meir Loeb Malbim, made every possible endeavor to prove in their commentaries that the Oral Law is implied in the text of the Written Law, thus restoring the traditional belief in their coequality.

Hirsch, wishing similarly to counteract these radical tendencies, expresses an even more extreme view: not only is the Oral Law equal to the Written Law but it is in a sense superior, being quantitatively more extensive and qualitatively richer and more profound. In this strange Copernican revolutionary view, the Written Law is merely "an aid to memory and reference when doubts arise" (*CE* 21:2). The relationship of the Written Law to the Oral Law is analogous to the meager fragmentary notes taken at a lecture, which only aid in recalling the subjects discussed but never go beyond those limits.

For the student who has heard the whole lecture, short notes are quite sufficient to bring back afresh to his mind at any time the whole subject of the lecture. For him a word, an added mark of interrogation or exclamation, a dot, the underlining of a word, etc., etc., are often quite sufficient to recall to his mind the whole series of thoughts, a remark, etc. For those who have not heard the lecture from the master, such notes would be completely useless. (*CE* 21:2)

Thus fear for the survival of the Oral Law prompted Hirsch to reduce the nonthreatened Written Law to sketchy jottings.[32]

Fear and Love

The chapter on revelation is followed by two chapters devoted respectively to the fear of God and the love of God. In the *Mishneh Torah*, these sentiments are considered a natural outcome of man's cognition of God: "When a person *contemplates* His great and wondrous works and creatures and from them obtains a glimpse of His wisdom which is incomparable and infinite, he will *straightway love* Him. . . . And when he ponders these matters, he will *recoil affrighted*."[33]

To Hirsch, intellectual cognition does not necessarily motivate man's actions or emotions. Both love and fear of God came only from man's recognition of his obligations and commitment to the Torah: "The fear of God consists in laying to heart all that Scripture has so far taught you about the greatness of God" (*H* 38). Similarly, "to love God means nothing until you begin to love His Torah" (*H* 49). For this reason, Hirsch unlike Maimonides, does not put love and fear after the chapter dealing with the concept of divinity, but after the chapter dealing with the revelation.

To Hirsch, love does not imply an irresistible blind passion, but man's conscious surrender of his natural subjective will to the objective will of God. The biblical command to love God "with all your heart"[34] signifies the transformation of man's animalistic aspect into a human one. It requires not the destruction of man's instinct, but its elevation and ennoblement, so that he may consider good and honorable only such things which God so considers and avoid those which God wishes him to avoid (*H* 54).

The Educative and Redemptive Qualities of Evil

Chapters 10 and 11 of the *Horeb* are interrelated in content. Chapter 10 deals with the idea of trust in God, chapter 11 with training through suffering. Both constitute a theodicy and a vindication of divine goodness, notwithstanding the evil that persists in the world. This problem is not found in the *Mishneh Torah*. It is possible that Maimonides, having posited the ideas of love and fear of God, considered trust superfluous. A God that cannot be trusted cannot be loved. Moreover, evil per se did not exist for Maimonides and God did not have to be absolved of its occurrence. It was inherent either in the imperfection of matter or in man's deficiency of wisdom. In either case, it was merely a negative manifestation, a deficiency rather than a creation of God.

To Hirsch, living in the nineteenth century, evil could no longer be explained as inherent in the nature of matter, as nonexistent, or as a deficiency of the human intellect. Evil is real and therefore disturbing. Many Jews may have been influenced by the writings of Voltaire, for whom the question of evil was real and not one to be glossed over with Leibnizian theodicies. Throughout Voltaire's works, the tremors of the Lisbon earthquake with all its ethical and theological implications were still vibrating. It is therefore understandable that *"Torot,"* dealing with the fundamentals of

Jewish faith, should consider evil as an agitating problem of paramount importance.

Hirsch considered evil a real and meaningful part of the divine cosmic plan. It is not necessarily antithetical to the concept of divine goodness, but rather a corollary of divine justice and universal purpose which cannot always be comprehended by man. If evil exists—and Hirsch did not dispute its existence—it has a purpose. Trust in God—which demands that man transcend his experience and reason, both of which are merely fragmentary and unable to perceive the cosmic "whole"—is therefore paramount, particularly in moments when everything in man's limited experience militates against it. Moreover, because man lives in a fraction of universal time, he is unable to comprehend his present predicament in the context of eternity. Therefore, man must consider that if God tolerates violence and suffering, there must of necessity be a reason—undoubtedly an important purpose in God's cosmic plan—for their existence (*H* 70). But the man who acknowledges the sovereignty of God, His infinite wisdom and justice, has no right to judge God's acts, however irrational, irredeemable, irritating, or frustrating they may appear, on the basis of his own limited criteria, since what seems to him "to be injustice is the product of the highest justice" (*H* 71).

To the vexing problem of the suffering of the righteous and the well-being of the wicked, one of the most agonizing problems in theistic philosophy, Hirsch offers a simple solution. He differentiates between transitory and permanent values, between rewards of an enduring nature and those of an evanescent nature. In this vein, he translates in a significant and novel manner the biblical verse "But [He] instantly [*el panav*] requites with destruction those who reject Him—never slow with those who reject Him, but requiting them instantly."[35] The expression *el panav* he renders "in dem Kreis seiner Wünsche" ("in the sphere of his desires"). Thus God rewards the wicked, whose only desires are external and transitory, with fleeting material acquisitions for the few good deeds they perform. However, he deprives them of eternal glories, which are reserved for the righteous, whose "sphere of desires" consists of eternals (*H* 71).

Apparently no single theory was adequate to explain the existence of evil; Hirsch therefore offers a variety of explanations.

Accordingly, evil, even death, may serve as a positive factor for the betterment of mankind as a whole, "inasmuch as the incurably bad dies out and the future moves on slowly more and more toward the good" (*CD* 7:10) until perfection is attained. At times, evil has a purgative quality leading man to eventual happiness (*H* 71). It may serve an educational purpose by testing and even strengthening man's character. Suffering may restore man's perspective, revealing to him his utter dependency on God. Hirsch also suggests that not everything that appears evil is evil. Occasionally, it may be a product of man's exaggerated subjectivity and lack of understanding. When overwhelmed by problems, man in his shortsightedness is prone to exaggerate the dimensions of evil; this robs him of any hope for the future (*H* 72). Man, however, must elevate himself above the limitations of his present circumstances and gain a broader perspective on the totality of his life and destiny in order to clarify his present difficulties. In this, Hirsch echoes Maimonides, who considered man's propensity to see evil a result of his subjectivity, limitation, and egocentricity:

For an ignorant man believes that the whole universe exists only for him; as if nothing else required consideration. If, therefore, anything happens to him contrary to his expectation, he at once concludes that the whole universe is evil. If, however, he would take into consideration the whole universe, form an idea of it, and comprehend what small portion he is of the universe, he will find the truth.[36]

Hirsch, whose respect for the dignity of the individual was far greater than was Maimonides's, does not ask man to see himself as an infinitesimal part of the universe whose suffering is inconsequential. The fact that his own suffering may have some meaning for the greater cosmos was of little comfort and an unacceptable rationale in the climate of the emerging individualism of the nineteenth century. Hirsch therefore asks man to consider an evil occurrence within the perspective of the totality of his own existence. Man must judge an event not within its circumscribed time, but in light of the totality of his entire life, which may eventually reveal its beneficial significance (*H* 72).[37]

The last nine chapters of the *"Torot"* have their analogous counterparts in *"Hilkhot De'ot"* of *"Sefer ha-Madda."* They constitute sermonettes on subjects concerning moral behavior. Specifically, they deal with pride and humility, covetousness, self-sanctification, hatred, love, compassion, resentment, listening to evil, and judging one's neighbor. Hirsch's presentation of these ethical themes is edifying, without contributing anything substantially novel.

8
"Edot": Temporal Symbolic Observances

"Edot" and "Zemanim"

The second division of the *Horeb* is entitled *"Edot: Denkmäler für Jissroels Leben begründende Wahrheiten,"* symbolic observances representing truths which form the basis of Israel's life. It embraces a host of precepts and observances designed to impress certain fundamental religious ideas on the individual as well as on the Jewish community. In the *Neunzehn Briefe* Hirsch had defined the *edot* as "symbolic observances, monuments or testimonies to truths essential to the concept of the mission of man and of Israel. These testimonies are symbolic words or actions which bear a lesson for the individual Jew, collective Israel, or mankind in general" (*NL* 104).

Although most of the subjects dealt with in the *"Edot"* section have their counterparts in the *"Zemanim"* division of the *Mishneh Torah*, the *"Edot"* is more comprehensive and includes precepts not found in the latter. The reason for this is simple. The fact that the *Horeb* has only six divisions, whereas the *Mishneh Torah* has fourteen, made it imperative for Hirsch to compress into one division subjects which Maimonides included in a more specialized classification. The very title of the section, *"Edot"*— testimonies—indicates a broader and more embracing category than the limited term *"Zemanim,"* signifying seasons. It therefore enabled Hirsch to include in *"Edot"* the precepts of *bekhor* (first-born), *gid ha-nasheh* (thigh vein), *ḥadash* (new produce of the field), *orlah* (fruit of trees of the first three years), *ḥallah* (priests' share of the dough), and counting of the *omer*, treated by Maimonides in the respective sections of the *Mishneh Torah:* "Sacrifices," "Holiness," "Seeds," and *"Avodah."* Similarly, Hirsch includes in *"Edot"* the precepts of circumcision, phylacteries, *tzitzit*, and *mezuzah* discussed by Maimonides in the section *"Ahavah."* Maimonides was thus limited by the narrow term *"Zemanim"* to precepts pertaining to seasons, festivals, and the *mitzvot* related to them. However, Hirsch was free to subsume under the broad term *"Edot"* a variety of precepts which were testimonies and symbols not necessarily contingent upon time. The section concludes with the laws of mourning. Apparently, it was the element of time regulating mourning which induced Hirsch to include it here. The suggestion that mourning constitutes a personal event and therefore earns its inclusion in *"Edot"* seems somewhat farfetched.[1] It should be noted that these laws were also poorly classified by Maimonides, who for some obscure reason placed them in *"Shoftim."*[2]

The *edot*, providing man with symbols of a temporal or spatial nature, serves an educational and psychological function. Since cognition alone is barren and there exists a gulf between *knowing* the right and *doing* the right, man needs the *edot* as media of motivation for proper action. It is therefore insufficient to impress the mind with the ideas of the *torot* without also impelling the heart with the evocative means of the *edot*, which require repetition and emphasis so that they may become part of man's response translated into action: "A truth, in order to produce results, must be impressed upon the mind and heart repeatedly and emphatically. This is the essential concept of the *edot*. The symbols are chiefly those of actions, of practices which serve as signs of an idea" (*NL* 118).

The need of impressing "the mind and heart repeatedly and emphatically" is the reason that the very same idea has to be presented in so many different precepts. Similarly, it is the reason the *mitzvot* have to be constantly performed with almost monotonous regularity, although the ideas they represent are known. The *edot* were designed not only to impress man intellectually, but to activate his entire being. Such a task necessitates a constant, life-long educational process. All minutiae are important; nothing is trivial or dispensable. Isolated, these minutiae seem meaningless and even ridiculous; related to one another as an integral part of a larger whole, they constitute a part of an action language:

The greatest and the least of them, even the never-enough-to-be-ridiculed prohibition of the use of an egg laid on Sabbath or holiday, symbolically teach a lesson, and the strict attention paid to so-called trifles is not more worthy of ridicule and not less sensible than your care to use a clear and intelligible language or a legible and neat handwriting. (*NL* 123)

The Sabbath

Exertion or Production   The first precept of the *"Edot"* is the Sabbath. Similarly, this is the first commandment in Maimonides's *"Zemanim."* Faithful to his general approach in the *Mishneh Torah*, Maimonides avoided any rationalization in the case of the Sabbath, and explained the complexity of the laws governing the Sabbath without discussing its ideational basis. In the *Guide of the Perplexed*, however, he offered two reasons for the observance of the Sabbath.

In chapter 31 of book 2 Maimonides stated:

Thus God commanded us to abstain from work on the Sabbath, and to rest, for two purposes; namely, (1) That we might confirm the true theory, that of the creation, which at once and clearly leads to the theory of the existence of God. (2) That we might remember how kind God has been in freeing us from the burden of the Egyptians. The Sabbath is therefore a double blessing: it gives us correct notions, and also promotes the well-being of our bodies.[3]

In the third Book of the *Guide*, chapter 43, Maimonides briefly summarized the purpose of the Sabbath, reiterating the same two reasons:

The object of Sabbath is obvious, and requires no explanation. The rest it affords to man is known; one seventh of the life of every man, whether small or great, passes thus in comfort and in rest from trouble and exertion. This the Sabbath effects in addition to perpetuation and confirmation of the grand doctrine of the creation.[4]

This dual rationale for the observance of the Sabbath, undoubt-edly cogent and meaningful in Maimonides's time, was far from satisfactory in Hirsch's. Maimonides's first reason was the affirma-tion of the principle of *creatio ex nihilo*, a problem that had agi-tated philosophers and religionists in the Middle Ages and im-pelled Maimonides to deviate from Aristotle. With the decline of metaphysical and cosmological speculations, by the nineteenth century this medieval preoccupation seemed overrated and ir-relevant. Maimonides's second reason, that of comfort and "rest from trouble and exertion," although greatly appealing, was the very rationale which seemed to militate against the thirty-nine categories of "work" from which one must abstain on the Sabbath as defined and elaborated in the *Mishneh Torah*. With the para-mount metaphysical principle ignored and only the personal rea-son of man's comfort left, few men in the nineteenth century could echo Maimonides's statement:

It is perhaps clear why the laws concerning Sabbath are so severe, that their transgression is visited with death by stoning, and that the greatest of the prophets put a person to death for breaking the Sabbath.[5]

Thus was revived the old controversy of whether man was created for the sake of the Sabbath or vice versa. By Maimonides's reason-ing that the aim of the Sabbath is to assure man comfort and rest; the Sabbath seems to have been created for the sake of man. Consequently, any activity on the Sabbath which enhances man's comfort and promotes his well-being should be permitted. The numerous restrictions and prohibitions enumerated by Maimon-ides and present in all rabbinic codices seem baseless since these interdictions had nothing to do with actual work or exertion. They interfere with man's comfort rather than assuring it. The problem of the Sabbath remains one of the most difficult and perplexing problems for the modern Jew. Little wonder that when the Re-form synod convened in Breslau in 1846, nine years after the publication of the *Horeb*, the Sabbath was one of the most crucial issues under debate.

Hirsch therefore resorted to a different rationale from the one offered by Maimonides. Hirsch linked the Sabbath with man's most essential attribute, his free will. Distinguishing him from the rest of creation, freedom entails grave dangers to man, since rooted in nature he may misuse his freedom. Instead of consciously subjecting it to the ethicizing influence of the Absolute Mind, he may pursue his own subjective will, thus losing sight of the universal *telos* and cosmic plan. He will become egocentric, assuming that everything has to please him and to conform to his interests. As a result, he will render himself incapable of administering the world, a task designed for him by God. He will become a dissonant element in the scheme of nature, which is devoid of free will but which unknowingly and involuntarily acts in conformity with the Absolute Will, carrying out its tasks according to a preconceived divine plan. Man, by abusing his prerogative of freedom, may possibly even impede the development of the cosmic plan, hindering the progressive process and the teleological *eschaton* for which the entire world, including himself, was created.

Had God deprived man of his freedom or limited it, it would have destroyed man's essence. God, therefore, did not curtail man's freedom, but instituted the Sabbath as a testimony and reminder of man's role in the world within the context of the cosmos. The Sabbath, symbolizing the cessation of the physical creation of the world by God and the beginning of man's rule over it, thus "became the symbol of man's appointment by God; symbol of God's rule and man's destiny" (*H* 139). To prevent man from transcending his rights of dominion in the world, God commanded him to observe the great variety of laws and prohibitions associated with the Sabbath. Although deplored and criticized by many, they were designed to show man that he was not the absolute ruler of the world but an administrator of the world in accordance with the God's will. However, man has no right over the world when he wishes to exploit it for his own selfish purposes.

To emphasize this idea, man must desist from any work on this commemorative day: "On each Sabbath day, the world, so to speak, is restored to God, and thus man proclaims, both to himself and to his surroundings, that he enjoys only a borrowed authority" (*H* 141). Hirsch had stated this view in the *Neunzehn Briefe* with unusual clarity:

The day upon which the newly created world first lay extended in its completeness before man that he might possess and rule over it, this day was to be to him an eternal monument of the great truth that all around him was the possession of God, the Creator, and that God it was who had conferred upon him the power and the right to rule it, in order that he should not grow overweening in his dominion and should administer his trust as the property of God and in accordance with His supreme will. In order to retain this idea ever fresh and vivid, he should refrain on this day from exercising his human sway over the things of earth, should not place his hand upon any object for the purpose of human dominion, that is, to employ it for any human end; he must, as it were, return the borrowed world to its divine owner in order to realize that it is but lent to him. (*NL* 124)

According to Hirsch, abstention from work is not due to the cognitive affirmation of the metaphysical concept of *creatio ex nihilo*, nor is it practiced for the sake of man's comfort and leisure. Abstention from work objectifies the ethical idea that man's dominion of the world and his claims to its benefits are tenuous and conditional. Only when man attunes his subjective will to the will of the Absolute may he continue to administer the world; but when he transgresses against the will of God, he automatically forfeits his right to dominion.

Since man's dominion over the world is expressed by fashioning and transforming, he must therefore refrain from such acts on the Sabbath. By refraining from purposeful creativity, man ipso facto acknowledges God's sovereignty and mastery of the world (*H* 142). Affirming this educational-psychological purpose of the Sabbath, Hirsch no longer had to rationalize every prohibition and restriction, since they were all designed to proscribe any manifestation of creativity.

To emphasize his opposition to Maimonides and to contemporary Reform theologians who castigated the traditionalists for having transformed the day of delight into a day of anguish, Hirsch states that abstention from work does not mean mere physical rest or even leisure for spiritual contemplation (*H* 150).

Avoiding polemics, Hirsch formulates a definition of *melakhah*, work in the talmudic sense, as *melekhet mahshevet*, purposeful work. *Melakhah* signifies "the execution of an intelligent purpose by the practical skill of man, or, more generally, production, creation, transforming an object for human purposes" (*H* 144). Frequently, the prohibition against writing two letters on the Sabbath was pointed out as illustrative of the casuistic reasoning and excessive ritualism of traditional Judaism. Indeed, writing two letters is not considered exertion, but in light of Hirsch's definition it is considered *melakhah*. The Reform theologians conceded that exertion was a desecration of the Sabbath, but to Hirsch any activity, however taxing, which does not involve a constructive exercise of man's intelligence does not fall within the purview of *melakhah*. On the other hand, any transformation, however small and insignificant, but engendered for man's purpose is considered halakhically *melakhah* and constitutes a desecration of the Sabbath (*H* 144). This restraint of tone and avoidance of controversy is characteristic of the *Neunzehn Briefe* and *Horeb*. In his commentary on the Pentateuch written in his more militant period, Hirsch quite sharply denounced those who defined *melakhah* as "hard physical work" (*CE* 20:10) and permitted activities which were not physically strenuous.

Hirsch's view that the Sabbath symbolizes man's returning the world to God seems to echo a similar interpretation of the sabbatical year. Accordingly, the latter was instituted to remind man that God and not man is the master and owner of the world.[6] Since the sabbatical year is also termed Sabbath,[7] Hirsch apparently applies the concept of the latter to the weekly Sabbath. In his commentary on Leviticus Hirsch alludes to this conceptual similarity. The weekly Sabbath represents man's "acknowledgment of God as creator and master of the world" (*CL* 25:2). The sabbatical year, coming once every seven years, constitutes man's "acknowledgment of God as the owner and master of the land" (*CL* 25:2).

A Social Rationale   As expected, Hirsch enumerates the thirty-nine activities prohibited on the Sabbath. This list includes *hotz-a'ah*, carrying an article from a private domain to a public one or vice versa. Since this activity presents no manifestation of man's intelligent purposeful creativity, its prohibition could hardly be rationalized by his definition of *melakhah*. It was merely, in his words, "a change of relationship in space" (*H* 147). In his subsequent works, Hirsch offered a more plausible rationale for the interdiction of carrying. In his essay *"Der jüdische Sabbath,"*[8] he suggested a social reason: by abstaining from the thirty-eight forms of productive activity, man proclaims God's sovereignty over nature; by refraining from the thirty-ninth form, carrying from public to private domain or vice versa, man symbolically manifests that God is not only the master over nature, but that He governs man's history and social order as well (*S* 1:202–5).

This rationale borders on mysticism, an area Hirsch carefully avoids. The alleged assumption that the prohibition of carrying from a private to a public domain concretizes and affirms man's acknowledgment of God's sovereignty of the social order (*S* 1:203) requires a great effort of imagination to comprehend. While we may sympathize with Hirsch's attempt to find an admissible explanation for the restriction of carrying on the Sabbath, his interpretation is hardly convincing. Assuming that the intent of this prohibition is symbolically to safeguard the respective freedoms of the individual and the community by preventing either from infringing or encroaching upon the rights of the other (*S* 1:203), the Karaitic Sabbath would make an ideal representation.

Hirsch's explanation is not only astounding, but completely out of tune with the traditional spirit of the Sabbath. According to his contention that man has to place his social life under the divine law, the natural conclusion would be the complete isolation of the individual on the Sabbath. Man would have to sever all relationships and associations on that day. This would indeed render it more extreme than the Karaitic Sabbath, but would conform to the principle of noninterference between community and individual which Hirsch enunciates as "Die Einzelfreiheit nicht die Gesamtordnung störe, das Band der Gesamtheit nicht die Einzelfreiheit vernichte" (*S* 1:203).

Despite the weakness of his rationale, Hirsch continued to espouse it. In his commentary on the Pentateuch published many years later, he still asserted that while all *melakhot* interdicted on the Sabbath are designed to impress man with God's rule in nature, *hotza'ah*, carrying from domain to domain, is impregnated with the idea that God rules history and society (*CE* 35:2). Furthermore, Hirsch failed to explain why the Torah had to institute thirty-eight prohibitions to show God's mastery over nature and only one weak interdiction[9] to manifest His dominion over history. The fact that Hirsch believed that the God's kingdom on earth would not be realized until man acknowledged both aspects of the Sabbath, the natural and the social (*CE* 35:2), should have made him wonder why more rules were not formulated to stress the social aspect.

Abstention—A Positive Act Hirsch's overemphasis of the idea of abstention, while understandable on socioeconomic and historical grounds, transforms the Sabbath into a negative institution. Despite his rhetoric about the beauty and glory of the Sabbath, it is impossible to escape the conclusion that he felt its highest virtue lay in negation. It is not what man does on the Sabbath that makes it sacred but what he abstains from doing; it is not the positive Sabbath service, with its lofty sermon and emotional prayer, which constitutes the convenantal sign—*ein Erkennungsmittel*—between God and Israel, but the negative abstention from work, *Werkenthaltung* (S 1:201).

Hirsch objected to the manner in which the Reformers hallowed the Sabbath by mere externalities. However, he does not suggest anything positive in its place. Instead, he sees the Sabbath as representing man's self-abnegation and self-sacrifice designed to accentuate the lordship of God. Consciously and willingly, man curtails his own freedom, suppresses his will and retreats from creation and history, demonstrating by such inaction his absolute vassalage to God (S 1:201). Again and again, Hirsch reiterates the all-important concept of abstinence on the Sabbath. Only by *issur melakhah*, abstinence from work on the Sabbath, is God glorified, the Sabbath sanctified, and Israel consecrated for its mission in the world (S 1:201). The child who abstains from catching a butterfly or from plucking a flower on this sacred day contributes more to the adoration of God than the most eloquent preachers and poets (S 1:201). Thus, the Sabbath is neither a day of joy and delight nor even one of spiritual elevation, but a twenty-four-hour sacrifice whereby man restrains himself and his creative will by doing nothing.[10]

Hirsch's overemphasis of the negative aspect of the Sabbath—abstention rather than rest and delight—was a result of the prevailing conditions of his time. Since many Jews had entered the mainstream of German economy, the Sabbath laws became increasingly more onerous to observe. The Reform theologians advocated changing the character of the Sabbath by making it similar to the Christian Sunday. To prevent such an eventuality, Hirsch was compelled to emphasize the abstention that distinguishes the Jewish Sabbath from the Christian Sunday, rather than the rest and delight which they have in common.

Remembrance and Observance   One of Hirsch's basic assumptions was that the Sabbath is a universal institution. Soon after man was created—and with his creation the universe was complete—the Sabbath was ordained. It was given to man as "an eternal monument of the great truth that all around him was the possession of God" (*NL* 124). Provided as a check to man's unbridled will, the Sabbath had to be instituted at the dawn of history. Hirsch alludes to the universality of the Sabbath in a cryptic passage in *Horeb* stating that the men of ancient Babel rejected the notion of the Sabbath of creation, thus courting disaster. Consequently, the Sabbath was transferred to the people of Israel, through whom God educates mankind (*H* 140).

This statement is left unexplained by Hirsch, since at the time it was written, he still intended to publish *Moriah*. He apparently developed, or hoped to develop, its implication in that work, which was to be devoted to the philosophical aspect of Judaism. In the absence of *Moriah* it is nevertheless possible to reconstruct the meaning of this passage from views Hirsch subsequently incorporated into his commentary on the Pentateuch. Commenting on the commandment in the Decalogue "Remember the sabbath day and to keep it holy,"[11] Hirsch argues that the institution of the Sabbath existed prior to the Sinaitic revelation, since the Decalogue refers to it as a well-known concept. There was apparently a need to remind the Israelites not to forget the already-existing Sabbath—as the other peoples had in ancient times—and thus the commandment did not proclaim a new or previously unknown idea or institution (*CE* 20:8).

Hirsch thus assumed that the Sabbath was given to all humanity prior to revelation. However, this view contradicts the Talmud, according to which non-Jews are interdicted from observing the Sabbath.[12] The seven universal commandments of the sons of Noah do not include the observance of the Sabbath.[13] Some consider Hirsch's assumption to be based on the distinction between "the so-called universal Sabbath, *Shabbat bereshit,* and the Jewish Sabbath."[14] The former was given to all mankind, whereas the latter was limited to the people of Israel. However, the term *Shabbat bereshit* does not refer to any specific era in history, nor does it imply a universal day of rest. The weekly Sabbath, as such, is designed in the Talmud as *Shabbat bereshit* to distinguish it from the festivals which, on occasion, are also called Sabbath.[15]

Hirsch's assumption of a universal Sabbath given to all mankind is part of a larger assumption, namely, that primordial men, prior to their transgressions, had knowledge of the entire Torah. The idea of the Sabbath was therefore not unique. However, Hirsch distinguishes between remembrance and observance, *zakhor* and *shamor*. He was undoubtedly aware of the absolution of non-Jews from observing the Sabbath. Furthermore, since man's cognition of universal verities does not include ritual observances, the Sabbath, with its ritualistic regimen, could not have been a universal verity accessible to all mankind. Hirsch maintains therefore that man originally had merely cognitively and intellectually to remember the Sabbath, *zakhor*. Subsequently, when mankind failed to live up to God's expectations, the Sabbath was given to Israel in the form of observances, *shamor* (*CE* 20:8).

The Jews are commanded to observe the Sabbath in concrete forms that it might not suffer the fate of the primeval Sabbath, which was only an idea. By observing the Sabbath with all its intricate laws, the Jews actually preserve one of the most sublime ideas for the sake of all mankind. Here Hirsch refers to a statement in the *Pesikta*,[16] the meaning of which is unclear. It should be noted, however, that the distinction between remembrance and observance was already made by Rabbi Solomon Ephraim of Lęczyca,[17] whose commentary was very popular and could not have escaped Hirsch's attention.

Hirsch also had a more practical reason for making the distinction between remembrance and observance. At the time he wrote his commentary on the Pentateuch, the liberals and the Reform theologians were rebelling against the concept of observance. At the Breslau synod, Samuel Holdheim eloquently argued that the sanctification of the Sabbath, not its observance, is important in the rabbinic sense. Hirsch was therefore anxious to point out that the Reform attitude was a reversal of an effort that had already failed at the dawn of civilization. Primordial man had also *remembered* the Sabbath but did not *observe* it. According to tradition, the simultaneous utterance on Sinai of *shamor* and *zakhor* "is the most emphatic protest against the misconceived attempt to relegate the Jewish Sabbath solely and entirely to a 'spiritual commemoration,' applying solely to the mind, to the *zekhirah*, and rob it of its essential component, the *shemirah*" (*CE* 20:8).

The ancient generations of the antediluvian and Tower of Babel eras had also rebelled against God. By yielding to their subjective will, they transcended the will of God as symbolized by the Sabbath and brought destruction upon humanity. God therefore endeavored to establish the Sabbath on a more solid foundation by concretizing its sublime ideas in a variety of observances. These strictures were imposed on the people of Israel only, but their ennobling results were to have a beneficial influence upon all mankind. Hirsch therefore maintains that the Jew who violates the Sabbath in the belief that he is thereby breaking down the barrier separating Jews from non-Jews is actually performing a disservice to non-Jews. Desecrating the Sabbath by working and by relegating it to a mere intellectual concept, he endangers its very existence. It might once again be forgotten as it once had been at the dawn of history and serve to unleash disastrous consequences. On the other hand, the seemingly negative self-abnegation and sacrifices the Sabbath entails for the observant Jew, will eventually bring salvation to all mankind. The Jews are therefore duty bound to endure all these difficulties and hardships for themselves and for the greater destiny of humanity (*CE* 20:8).

Festivals and Fast Days

The second subject in the *"Edot"* deals with the prohibition of work and eating on the Day of Atonement and the prohibition of work on Rosh Hashanah. According to Hirsch, Yom Kippur is essentially like the Sabbath, except that in addition to abstention from work the former is also marked by privation of bodily pleasures, a privation strictly forbidden on the Sabbath. By the two forms of negation as expressed in privation of pleasure and abstention from work, man manifests the natural consequences which should have resulted from his disobedience of God. By his insubordination to the will of God and by misusing the powers with which he was endowed, man forfeits his rights to fashion anything in the world in accordance with his will along with the right to his very existence. Man's recognition of sinfulness and his forfeiture to the world is concretized by abstention from work, his loss of the right to live by avoidance of gratification.

Yom Kippur does not require any self-inflicted pain, torment, or castigation. Such acts would negate the concept of atonement which they are meant to evoke in man, and may even vitiate the fundamental purpose of Yom Kippur by implying that self-castigation in itself atones for sins, deviations, and wrongs (*H* 157). Hirsch therefore emphasizes that renunciation of gratification, known as the five *yinuyim*, is neither intended for the mortification of man nor for the propitiation of God. *Yinuy nefesh* per se is not an atonement but "an acknowledgment that by our misdeeds in the enjoyments of life we have forfeited the right to a continuance of our life, just as *issur melakhah* is the acknowledgment that by wicked actions we have lost the right to act" (*CL* 23:29).

After Yom Kippur, Hirsch discusses the four festivals: Passover, Shavuoth, Succoth and Shemini Atzereth. These holidays are stations in time for man's spiritual examination and consecration (*H* 159). There is an intrinsic distinction between the nature of the High Holidays and the other festivals. The intent of the former, which is repentance for previous wrongs, relates to the past, whereas the purpose of the other festivals, relates to the future.

Consistent with Hirsch's designation of nature and history as the two terrains of divine operation and manifestation, the festivals have a dual aspect—natural and historical. The festivals embody the idea of God revealing Himself in both domains, nature and history, and the relatedness of these domains is expressed by their concurrence in time. Each festival simultaneously marks an event in nature and an event in history in which God has made Himself manifest (*H* 164).

The connection of the major festivals with nature is self-evident, since they occur at the changing seasons of the year. Even the High Holidays—where this relationship is not explicitly stated in the Bible—nonetheless occur during the seasonal change at the beginning of autumn (*H* 166).[18] The historic significance of the major festivals revolves around the events beginning with the Exodus from Egypt, the revelation on Sinai, and the wanderings in the desert. They were intended to impress the Jews with God's special relationship to their forefathers. The festivals celebrated in the spring commemorate Israel's physical or national foundation.

Passover represents its physical aspect, and Shavuoth its spiritual one. Shavuoth "gave spiritual completion to that which had begun physically in Egypt" (*H* 165). The festivals celebrated in autumn stress preservation rather than foundation and serve a similar purpose. Shemini Atzereth signifies the spiritual completion of Succoth. Succoth commemorates Israel's physical survival in the desert, and Shemini Atzereth its spiritual one. Thus, the four festivals share the profound educational aim of instilling the sense of divine dominion and Providence in mankind.

The Bifurcation of Nature and History Hirsch's stress on the dual aspect of the holidays, the natural and the historical, serves an additional purpose. To him, God's election of Israel does not imply the rejection of other nations. Both Israel and the rest of mankind are advancing to the eventual *eschaton* of history. However, as indicated in the *Neunzehn Briefe*, their paths toward it are not the same. The festivals are time symbols in the life of man; although observed only by Jews, they are directed not only to Israel but to all humanity. Hirsch considered the divine message to be bifurcated: the festivals' natural aspect applies to all mankind, whereas their historical aspect is directed to Israel alone. Hirsch's fundamental distinction is that mankind in general is part of nature, with all the implications this term connotes, but that Israel is part of history. Nature and history are not antithetical but complementary; similarly, the God who reveals Himself to Israel in history reveals Himself to the rest of humanity in nature. The verities conceived by Israel through reflection on its historic experience are perceived by the rest of mankind through contemplation of nature.

The universal message of the major festivals to mankind is evident in the natural manifestations at the time of their occurrence. Passover signifies God's rule in nature and the history of nations (*H* 169); Shavuoth—"God summons everything in nature and humanity to its task, educates mankind to its mission" (*H* 169); Succoth—"God is the sustainer of nature and mankind, master and distributor of all means of life" (*H* 169); Shemini Atzereth—"God rejuvenates again and again the forces of development" (*H* 169).

The particular national message directed to Israel is noted in the historical significance of these same holidays. Passover signifies that "the one God is Israel's creator and savior—Israel is God's property, God's servant" (*H* 169); Shavuoth—"The one God is Israel's lawgiver. Israel's only task: To bear and fulfill the Divine Law" (*H* 169); Succoth—"God sustains and preserves the people of Israel" (*H* 169); Shemini Atzereth—"[God] keeps His spirit eternally alive in Israel: the Torah is protected in Israel by God, and men of spirit are aroused within Israel by God" (*H* 169).

Hirsch points out that there are some festivals which are marked by the absence of any special symbols, whereas others are replete with them. The former includes Shavuoth and Shemini Atzereth, which have an exclusive spiritual significance. The absence of symbols indicates their sublimity and spirituality, the very essence upon which Israel's existence depends (*H* 182). The other holidays are marked by special symbols or distinctive prohibitions. Thus, the Sabbath and the Day of Atonement, as previously discussed, are singled out by abstention from work, the latter by avoidance of gratification in addition. Rosh Hashanah, Passover, and Succoth have a variety of distinctive symbols to which Hirsch ascribes great educational value.

The most important symbol of Rosh Hashanah is the shofar, whose basic sounds are *teki'ah, teruah,* and again *teki'ah.* The first and last are long notes, the middle one a series of broken notes: "The initial *teki'ah* signifies introspection and a rising above ourselves; the *teruah* a purification of ourselves; and the final *teki'ah* a determination to follow a more righteous future" (*H* 229). Furthermore, the three sounds were designed to evoke in man the three fundamental concepts concerning God, namely, lordship, judgeship, and fatherhood. The simplicity of the shofar, which may be taken from any clean animal except the bull,[19] indicates that man must rid himself of all pretense and artificiality and appear before God in his most natural and unaffected manner, similar to the natural and unaffected sound of the shofar.

The significance of Passover is essentially theological. It marks the Exodus from Egypt, which constitutes a divine revelation as well as divine creation of history. Its manifestation in history is analogous to the act of creation in nature. The deliverance of the Israelites from Egypt must therefore not be conceived in historical, sociological, or economic terms, but viewed as "another divine imperative: 'Let there be' in the history of mankind" (*H* 197). The acceptance of the concept that God singled out the people of Israel for redemption implies the existence of a special relationship. Such a relationship demands a continuous awareness and special obligations on the part of the Jews. To impress this idea, Passover is observed by certain symbolic "testimonies" possessing negative and positive qualities. The first category includes the prohibition of *ḥametz*, which represents the bread of free men, whereas the unleavened bread, *matzah*, constituted the bread of the Egyptian slaves. The Israelites ate unleavened bread until they were miraculously delivered from Egypt by divine intervention. They themselves had no means of obtaining *ḥametz*. Thus, by removing *ḥametz* from our possession and abstaining from its use or enjoyment, we attest to the divine aspect of the Exodus independent of human factors. The Israelites did not prepare any food for that moment; the deliverance was exclusively a divine act (*H* 199). By eliminating the *ḥametz* prior to the commencement of the Passover, we symbolically declare that "our freedom, and with it our whole vocation as Israelites, [exist] entirely by the grace of God" (*H* 200).

The very same idea which is expressed negatively by the abstention from *ḥametz* is embodied in a positive manner by the commandment to eat *matzah*. Consumption of *matzah* in a spirit of gladness further emphasizes not only that the Jew recognizes the fact of the divine aspect of the Exodus, but that he consciously, willingly, and resolutely accepts the obligations emanating from that extraordinary manifestation (*H* 205). Since the concepts conveyed by Passover are of great importance, they must be transmitted to the younger generation upon whom the future and continuity of the Jewish people depends. This educational task is accomplished during the Seder by reading, interpreting, and expounding upon the Haggadah (*H* 208).

The festival of Succoth is also replete with symbolism. Its fundamental concept is that God is the sustainer of life. Man should not feel secure in his wealth nor despair in his poverty but trust in God who sustained the Israelites in booths in the wilderness. The *succah*, or booth, has not only a personal message to the individual, but collective messages to him as a Jew and as a man. The first message—to the Jew—is that the *succah* represents the long history of martyrdom and suffering in exile. Were it not for God's protection, the Jewish people could not have endured those critical centuries of oppression, degradation, and misery.

Hirsch was mindful that the Jews of his own era enjoyed a more advantageous position than those living in previous ones. Some in the post-Emancipation era did not consider the frail, feeble, and temporary *succah* to be representative of their new era of existence in western Europe, which offered them a sense of security and permanence unparalleled in postexilic history. To this younger generation Hirsch directed his statements that emancipation and equality are only new divine tests. He had given Emancipation a qualified blessing in the *Neunzehn Briefe:*

I bless it, if Israel does not regard emancipation as the goal of its task, but only as a new condition of its mission, and as a new trial, much severer than the trial of oppression; but I should grieve if Israel understood itself so little, and had so little comprehension of its own spirit that it would welcome emancipation as the end of the *Galuth,* and the highest goal of its historic mission. (*NL* 167)

Hirsch forcefully emphasizes this idea in *Horeb* in his discussion of the rejection of symbolic representation of the *succah* in practice and in concept. To Hirsch's contemporaries, all of normative Judaism represented intellectual segregation, ethnic isolation, and a cultural barrier to social interrelationships between Jews and non-Jews. Eager to escape these restrictive boundaries, they rejected the concept of the figurative *succah.* Hirsch considers that their rejection negated all of Jewish history; there was no need for Israel to suffer two thousand years of separation just so that at last it would be completely submerged and forgotten. There is need for some aspect of separateness even in the post-Emancipation era, to "keep aloof from the madness of the moment" (*H* 220).

However, the *succah* does not merely point to Jewish separatism but also to a universal ideal. It has a message for the Jew as a man, as a citizen of the world (*H* 221). Alluding to Zechariah's prophecy that eventually all nations will celebrate Succoth, Hirsch considers this festival to symbolize the future of all mankind's brotherhood (*H* 221).

In addition to the *succah,* the festival is celebrated by four plant species—the *ethrog,* palm branch, myrtle, and willow, which represent the various aspects of nature designed for man's benefit.

The myrtle's natural aroma represents those elements in nature which benefit man directly without his improvement upon their quality. Many are the manifestations of nature which need neither transformation nor modification to sustain man's life in the world. Air, light, beauty, and pleasing scents are some of the things given directly by God. The palm branch, or *lulav*, represents elements in nature which man must modify in order to use—a combination of the natural and artificial, which necessitates a joint effort between man and nature to produce the final product. Most of man's food falls into this category. The willow represents elements in nature which must be completely altered by man since they cannot be used in raw form. Man must therefore exercise his skill, intelligence, and power to make them useful and beneficial. The *ethrog* combines the qualities of the myrtle and palm branch; it represents those natural elements which can either benefit man directly or be modified by him.

These four species are symbols of thanksgiving on the festival of Succoth. They evoke in man a sense of gratitude to God for giving him all four kinds of material in nature to promote his welfare, enhance his life, and sustain him in the world. According to Hirsch, the two main symbols of Succoth were designed to convey a lesson about worldly possessions. Man has to effect a balance between rejection and acceptance of mundane goods. On the one hand, the frail *succah* teaches him not to overestimate the value of material possessions but to recognize God as the only source of sustenance; on the other hand, the four species teach him that these possessions are important, but that he must attenuate their importance in the context of the entire scheme of things. Their value must be determined as a means by which God assists man to attain lofty spiritual aims in this world: "The *succah* prevents us from becoming too earthly, the *lulav*[20] reminds us not to soar too high above the earthly" (*H* 223).

Concealed Providence   The two minor festivals, Hanukkah and Purim, are treated by Hirsch after the sections dealing with the fast days. Both festivals represent the concealed and indirect action of divine Providence. They commemorate events in which God did not intervene in history openly, as at the time of the deliverance from Egypt.

Nevertheless these events can be explicated neither in historical terms nor in sociopolitical categories. Unlike the major festivals, Hanukkah and Purim were instituted during the Second Jewish Commonwealth, an era of relative independence and numerous difficulties. According to Hirsch, these festivals were intended to prepare the Jews for the long duration of their subsequent exilic existence. Of all the commemorative festivals of those troubled days, only Hanukkah and Purim were instituted for observance by posterity. These two minor festivals were to signify to the Jews that God, though invisible, watches over them even in exile. His redemptive acts may not be apparent, but they exist nonetheless (H 245).

Hanukkah commemorates the attack upon the spirit of Israel manifested in the persecution of the Jews under Antiochus, which thus foreshadowed the series of similar events during their subsequent exile. The miracle of the cruse of pure oil whose contents lasted for eight days was intended to convey to all generations the message of spiritual renewal: a single cruse of pure oil can light up the entire world and save it from contamination (H 246). Although Israel may be downtrodden, its spirit will once again kindle the light of the world.

If Hanukkah marks the concerted assault on the Jewish spirit, Purim signifies the attack on the Jew's physical existence. This event was likewise premonitory of similar ones in the future. Bereft of human assistance, the Jews of Persia turned to their God, who in hidden fashion rescued them from their enemies. Should such crises recur, God will once more save His people when they turn to Him again.

The two minor festivals, like the major ones, possess both physical and spiritual aspects. Purim is analogous to Succoth, and Hanukkah to Shemini Atzereth. If Succoth represents the notion of Israel's physical preservation by God, Purim betokens the same, with special emphasis on His protection in exile. If Shemini Atzereth signifies Israel's spiritual preservation, Hanukkah merely stresses the applicability of this idea in exile (H 249). In his commentary on Leviticus, Hirsch connects Purim with Passover, and Hanukkah with Shemini Atzereth, on the basis of their affinity to the lunar month: "Purim is the Passover of the Galuth and, like it, falls on the fourteenth day of the lunar month. Hanukkah is the

Shemini Atzereth of the *Galuth*" and like it takes place at the time of the declining moon (*CL* 23:7–8).

The Fast Days   The fast days, like the festivals, are testimonies of important milestones in the past whose message holds a lesson for the future. If the festivals teach the Jews to revere God for their salvation, the fast days impart to them the lessons they should have derived from misfortunes brought about by their own ethical and religious misconduct. The sufferings they have experienced are not a result of either blind fate or historic determinism, but a paternal reproval for bad behavior, particularly for pleasure seeking and self-seeking—modes of life deleterious to Israel's spiritual well-being (*H* 234).

Historic events are neither isolated nor self-contained. Their impact as well as their message, when properly understood, have great value for the future. Man must learn not only from his successes but from his failures as well: "Generations rise and fall so that those who follow may well learn from the glow of their sunrise as well as from that of their sunset" (*H* 234). Therefore, five commemorative fast days were ordained, three of which were related to the sins committed during the time of national independence, and two to the sins at the time of the exile. The fasts of the tenth of Teveth, the seventeenth of Tammuz, and the ninth of Av, belong to the first category; the fast of Gedaliah and the fast of Esther belong to the second.

The fasts of the first category are designed to recall that the destruction of the Temple and the ensuing exile were caused by Israel's sins; neither punishment, however, was motivated by a sense of divine vindictiveness but rather as a means of education. The destruction of their possessions, loss of their independence, and dispersion were historical events meant to impress the people with their utter dependence upon God alone. Only by living in accordance with His dictates as stipulated in the Torah is their existence assured (*H* 236).

Although the fast days commemorate historic experiences constituting chastisement of the Jewish people, they also contain a universal object lesson: the destruction of the moral order causes the destruction of the physical order, whether national or individual. However, God's chastisement has redemptive as well as educative and admonitory qualities. The end of Jewish statehood and the dispersion of the Jews constituted a gift to all mankind in that the Jews became the messengers of ethical monotheism in the world. Thus, they were given a new opportunity to carry out their mission under different circumstances (*H* 236). Hirsch echoes the mission theory persistently advocated by Reform theologians and exalted by them as the raison d'être of Judaism, and like them he sees in the dispersion of the Jews an act of Providence calculated to spread this mission among the nations.

The fasts of Gedaliah and Esther seem especially relevant politically to the problems confronting the Jews of Hirsch's era. The fast of Gedaliah, which commemorates the abortive revolt against the Babylonian conquerors, contains a significant admonition to the Jews of the future. The assassination of Gedaliah was considered a sin not only against the conquering power, but also against God, since it was God who caused the Babylonians to destroy Jerusalem and exile its inhabitants; and a revolt against their authority was an insidious rebellion against the divine scheme. Gedaliah, who was appointed governor of Judah by the conquerors, was not a collaborator but a man who understood the deeper religious implications of the unfolding historic events. The invaders were instruments in the hands of God, and therefore it was Gedaliah's duty, as it was the duty of all the Jews, to cooperate with the Babylonians, painful and distasteful as it might have been.

In describing Gedaliah's attitude, Hirsch seems to portray the Jew's attitude to the princes, rulers, and kings in the pre-Emancipation period when docility and surrender was the accepted policy (*H* 237). To Hirsch, Gedaliah was the ideal Jewish leader who could by his meekness and obsequiousness appease the wrath of the non-Jewish tyrants who oppressed his people. He rendered, in Mendelssohnian fashion, his homage to both God and Caesar.[21] The fact that many years later Hirsch would speak out in behalf of equality and citizenship for the Jews does not render his religious-political philosophy any less quietistic. At this early period in his development, he considered Jewish submissiveness to the Nebuchadnezzars of all time—including his own—not only politically expedient but also religiously mandatory and laudable. He unequivocally states that the message of the fast of Gedaliah warns us against actively engaging in breaking the chains of the oppressors or lifting the yoke of oppression (*H* 237). Hirsch's views coincided with those of German Jewry in general and of Oldenburg Jewry in particular. Again and again, Hirsch elaborates upon Jeremiah's advice to the exiles to "seek the welfare of the city,"[22] to submit to rulers of even the most oppressive kingdoms: "Give yourselves up entirely to Him and show this surrender in loyal attachment to your protecting ruler and realm and in resigned obedience even to your oppressors" (*H* 237).

If the fast of Gedaliah represents an admonition to the Jews to retain their loyalty to Judaism even under adverse circumstances, the fast of Esther symbolizes a warning to Jews to maintain their faith under more auspicious conditions. The benevolent reign of Ahasuerus was meant to test Israel's commitment to God under liberty. Hirsch seems to consider that era similar to the one in which he lived. Like many of his contemporaries, the Jews in the ancient Persian provinces defected from their religion. The faith that they had displayed in times of oppression disappeared under freedom. Hirsch felt that the Persian Jews endeavored to assimilate themselves with their non-Jewish environment out of a sense of gratitude to the liberal spirit that prevailed in the land, or because some wished to become amalgamated with the rest of the population, just as Hirsch's contemporaries did (*H* 238). The results of the efforts of the Jews of Persia were disastrous for them.

In contrast to this prevalent and erroneous attitude, Mordecai, the hero of Purim, demonstrated his courage and firmness in his faith. He exemplified loyalty both to God and to the king without compromising either, and this attitude won him the recognition of all. It was the integrity of this "eternal example in Israel's *Galuth*" (*H* 238) which saved the king, the kingdom, and the Persian Jewish community. The fast of Esther commemorates the error of those Jews who attempt to curry national favor by violating their obligation to God. Its lesson is clear: Jews must retain their faith in God and loyalty to His Torah under a liberal ruler as well as in a hostile environment. No matter how attractive the liberal climate may be, Jews must not surrender their religion in exchange for political, social, and economic gains. Such an act would only mean spiritual suicide (*H* 238).

Encounter with God in Freedom

Rosh Hodesh constitutes the last of the testimonies of time in the division of *"Edot."* In a lengthy dissertation, Hirsch elaborates on the significance of Rosh Hodesh as the measurement of time. Without such measurement, time would be one continuous, monotonous flux, deprived of any commemorative milestones through which events of the past are transmitted to the future and reexperienced by posterity. Man is commanded to measure and calculate his time by the two most significant celestial bodies in the solar system which influence his planet and thereby his life—the sun and the moon: "The sun not only rules the earth but is beneficial to other planets as it is to the earth, so the moon really belongs to the earth; and the earth and the moon together form this terrestrial world which is stirred to life by the sun" (*H* 252). As a result, both the sun and the moon are to be considered in the measurement of time. The Jewish calendar is, therefore, a combination of the solar and lunar years. Each renewal of the moon signifies a moment for man's introspection, critical self-examination, and consecration (*H* 259).

It is in his commentary on the Pentateuch that Hirsch elaborates on the concept of Rosh Hodesh as one of the most important symbols of the Jewish faith (*CE* 12:2). The fact that this commandment was given on the eve of the Exodus from Egypt was indicative of its paramount importance. Hirsch, therefore, suggests that this precept, given to the Israelites on the threshold of their national birth, contains a fundamental idea designed to demonstrate the difference between Judaism and paganism. The heathen Weltanschauung knew no renewal. It is absolutely closed and ironclad. *Creatio ex nihilo* exists in neither the cosmological nor the moral domain. It is deterministic in all respects. Consequently, the pagan outlook could not conceive of a free will able to change the order of the universe or the ethical conduct of man: "Everything swims down the stream of blind unalterable necessity, all freedom is but an illusion, anything new is only that which existed in the old" (*CE* 12:2). For this reason, the commandment concerning the new moon was given in Egypt, the land which to Hirsch represented the epitome of the pagan concept of immutability. The reemergence of the crescent moon was to symbolize to the new nation, the actuality of *ḥiddush*, renewal. It concretized the possibility of rebirth in all spheres, in nature as well as in morality.

In discussing the importance of Rosh Hodesh, Hirsch suggests that it signifies man's encounter with God. Rosh Hodesh, like the festivals, is called *moed*, a term meaning meeting, conjunction, or encounter. To heighten this idea of man's encounter with God, it was not sufficient formerly to celebrate Rosh Hodesh by mere astronomical calculations; it had to be observed by witnesses and its sanctification pronounced by a court which represented the Jewish community and was therefore empowered to give it official sanction. Thus, the observance of Rosh Hodesh was established by both the natural appearance of the new moon and the proclamation of the representatives of the Jewish community. It is a conjunction of a natural phenomenon and man's free will symbolizing God's encounter with man.

Were Rosh Hodesh merely a relic of an ancient rite of nature worship, the sanctification of the court would have been meaningless, since the sanctity of the day would have been determined exclusively by the natural manifestation. Moreover, according to the Talmud, the court was empowered under certain circumstances to intercalate the calendar. The judges thus had the right to declare Rosh Hodesh on the day following its natural occurrence. Similarly, if the judges erred in their calculation, even intentionally, their proclamation of Rosh Hodesh was to be considered valid, and the festivals calculated on the basis of this erroneous proclamation were to be observed in accordance with the judicial pronouncement. All this suggests to Hirsch that the natural revolution of the moon was not the deciding factor of Rosh Hodesh, but rather the free will of the community as expressed by its representatives: "This is striking evidence that it is not the actual procedure up above, but the consecrating declaration of the representatives of Israel that is the decisive factor on which the beginning of the month depends" (*CE* 12:2).

The right of the court deliberately to alter time which is strictly regulated by natural law clearly demonstrates man's overriding freedom. Man, by his free will, can rise above nature and successfully defy those of its laws which might compel him to act immorally:

Were the beginnings of our months, and consequently, the dates of the *moadim* to be fixed exactly by the astronomical phases of the planets, so that, for example, the phase of the moon automatically made Rosh Hodesh and the *moadim*, then we and our God too, would appear to be bound by the blind and unalterable laws of nature, and our *moed* of the New Moon above all, would give an impetus to the idolatry of a cult of nature. But that is exactly what it should not be. (*CE* 12:2)

Since Rosh Hodesh was determined in antiquity by the court's proclamation and not by strict mathematical calculations, Hirsch considered the present calendar a regression. According to him, the so-called sanctification of Rosh Hodesh, based on the observance of witnesses in antiquity, was not due to any deficiency in astronomical knowledge, but was practiced to demonstrate to the people the power of free will and the fact that man's encounter with God has to be voluntary on both sides. The appearance of the crescent signifies God's readiness to meet man. Man, on his part, has to agree voluntarily to meet God:

It is not to be the master ordering the attendance of his servants, it is to be God who wishes His people to come to Him. He accordingly specifies the time about which this "coming to Him" is to take place, but leaves the fixing of the exact day to His people so that this "coming together" shall be a mutual arrangement. (*CE* 12:2)

Although necessity demanded the fixation of the calendar according to unalterable rules, the idea of freedom in the encounter between man and God was symbolically preserved. This symbol was manifested in the exilic observance of supernumerary festivals, *yom tov sheni shel galuyot*. Notwithstanding the fact that the calendar has been fixed, the supernumerary holidays are still to be observed: "For these second days had their origin in those better times when we still had a national center and still had our national representatives for whose decision all outlying communities had to look and wait before they could fix the date of their festivals" (*CE* 12–2). It was this uncertainty and expectation of the court's decision that impressed Jews with the idea of the voluntary encounter with God.

Having developed this rationale, Hirsch counters the Reformers' view that Rosh Hodesh and the Jewish festivals were of primitive origin. Moreover, he presents a novel justification for the observance of the supernumerary holidays, which many Reform rabbis rejected as relics from the precalendaric days when the festivals had been based upon the testimony of witnesses who observed the new moon. According to Hirsch, the observance of the second days of the festivals contains a profound philosophical and theological message: "It is therefore, a profound truth that for Israel in *Galuth*, it is only the second day of *Yomtov* that ensures the first day its sacred Jewish character" (*CE* 12:2).

9
"Edot": Nontemporal Symbolic Observances

Circumcision

Act and Idea Having completed his interpretation of the series of testimonies of time, Hirsch goes on in *"Edot"* to discuss a number of nontemporal laws, connotative and emblematic in nature. Four of the latter belong to a definite ideational unit: circumcision, *tefillin, tzitzit,* and *mezuzah.* These are signs on the body, head and arm, garments, and home (*CN* 15:41). The most important is circumcision. Its importance is underscored by the fact that it antedated revelation. It had been commanded to Abraham as a sign marking the covenantal relationship between God and the patriarch's descendants.

Circumcision objectifies moral perfection. It signifies man's control of his unbridled sexual passions, their sublimation and sanctification for the sublime purpose for which he was created. In His command to Abraham concerning circumcision, God spoke of perfection, *tamim.* To Hirsch, this implies wholesomeness of body and spirit. Unlike the dualistic view that polarizes man's nature into a sacred spirit and a sinful body, Judaism aspires to a psychosomatic harmony. Man must not only elevate his spirit, but sanctify his body as well (*H* 262).

In order for man to maintain the purity and sanctity of his body, he must control and limit his sexual passion. Circumcision in infancy therefore signifies man's obligation to "stifle animal desires at their onset, stifle them at their birth" (*H* 263). In this respect, Hirsch differs with Maimonides, who viewed circumcision as a surgical device designed "to limit sexual intercourse, and to weaken the organ of generation as far as possible, and thus cause man to be moderate."[1] Hirsch avoids any medical speculation on this subject, perhaps because changes in medical science in the nineteenth century rendered Maimonides's theory about the effect of circumcision on sexual potency rather dubious. Hirsch prefered to view circumcision as a symbol rather than as a contravention of man's ethical behavior by surgical means. Furthermore, such physical tamperings with man's natural desires would imply interference with his free will. By deliberately weakening man's powers and instincts, we deprive him of his freedom to be moral or immoral. Man thus becomes dehumanized, since if it were God's will to limit man's passions, He would not have implanted them in him. Man would not only be acting contrary to his nature out of lack of freedom, his moral conduct would be artificially induced and hence ethically insignificant if not reprehensible.

In addition, Maimonides's view implies that the uncircumcised man, or man as God created him, is biologically predisposed to unethical behavior, an assumption inconceivable to Hirsch, since it would make natural man thoroughly immoral. Ethicality would be contingent upon a physical operation rather than a moral will. Hirsch believed that man as created with all his physical and mental faculties has the power and ability to be moral and the freedom to be immoral (*CG* 1:27). Circumcision is merely a symbol signifying "the bond of God with Israel to rebuild a purer mankind" (*CG* 1:27), not a necessary condition for ethical behavior. However, it is an important symbol, since the desecration of the body by dissolute behavior disturbs the natural equilibrium of the body and spirit and encourages the dominance of the animalistic potential within man. Thus, instead of the spirit ennobling the body, the body would brutalize the spirit (*H* 265).

In the *Horeb*, Hirsch does not elaborate on the meaning of the various laws connected with the rite of circumcision. There is no doubt, however, that he already perceived some of their symbolism, which he subsequently expounded. Thus, he mentions that this ritual must be performed during daytime, since it "lifts man out of his animal pursuits into a humanism pure, effective, and creative" (*H* 268). It must take place on the eighth day in order to indicate that "its aim is not some physical goal or some sure means of body-building" (*H* 268), but "a meaningful symbol of the mission of the man and Israelite" (*H* 268). These vague symbols were fully developed later in Hirsch's voluminous writings, particularly in his essay "Grundlinien einer jüdischen Symbolik" (*S* 3:211–477) and his commentary on the Pentateuch.

In later years Hirsch's tendency was to complicate and convolute his *ta'amei ha-mitzvot*, but his subsequent embellishments on the rite of circumcision were motivated by important social and religious factors which were not compelling at the time he wrote the *Horeb*. As we have mentioned, in 1842 a number of radical laymen in Frankfurt organized themselves into a Verein der Reformfreunde, which advocated the abrogation of many laws and practices still officially current in liberal circles. In the following year, they audaciously called for the abandonment of circumcision. This declaration was revolutionary even to many Reformers and caused considerable bitterness in Jewish communities inside and outside Germany.

When the Orthodox rabbi of Frankfurt, Solomon Abraham Trier, solicited the assistance of other leading rabbis and the city senate in order to refute the view of the Verein der Reformfreunde, the controversy grew even more acrimonious. Twenty-eight of the forty-one responses[2] received from traditionalist and Reform rabbis defended circumcision as most fundamental to Judaism.[3] Among those rabbis was Samson Raphael Hirsch; his view of the Verein was severe and condemnatory.

Despite the strong sentiment of the leading rabbis and scholars in favor of circumcision, the Verein had many sympathizers.[4] In a letter to Zunz, Geiger referred to the rite of circumcision as "a barbaric gory rite which fills the infant's father with fear and subjects the new mother to harmful emotional strain."[5] Although Geiger considered the declaration of the Verein unfortunate, he did not contest its view on the subject. Geiger's objection was directed rather to the poor tactics employed by its leaders: "Instead of choosing a more circumspect approach to the masses and refraining from moving by such leaps and bounds, they elected to attack the rite of circumcision which was still considered the very nerve fiber of Judaism."[6] This question continued to agitate the Reform rabbinic conferences at Brunswick in 1844, at Frankfurt am Main in 1845, at Breslau in 1846, at Leipzig in 1869, and at Augsburg in 1871. Besides the ideological and social opposition to circumcision, many parents considered it dangerous medically. Cases were cited in which circumcision was the alleged cause of infant mortality.

Because of the ever-spreading sentiment against circumcision, Hirsch continued to strengthen his rationale for this fundamental commandment. Twenty years after the appearance of the *Horeb*, he published a highly sophisticated interpretation of circumcision in his "Grundlinien einer jüdischen Symbolik" in which he endeavored to validate the *act* of circumcision, not just the idea it represented. Hirsch rejected the efforts of the antinomians to consider circumcision in the Deuteronomic sense—"Cut away [circumcise], therefore, the thickening [foreskin] about your heart and stiffen your necks no more"[7]—since this view, under the guise of sublimity and ethics, discarded a commandment fundamental to Judaism. To those who emphasized the importance of the holiness of the spirit rather than the sanctity of the body, Hirsch points out that it is the actual physical act of circumcision that determines conversion to Judaism and not some vague consecration of the spirit;[8] he further points out that the idea alone, no matter how sublime, can never replace the deed itself (*CG* 17:10).

Limitation and Freedom   Far more difficult than the defense of circumcision proper was the justification of the procedure and the various concomitant laws regulating this commandment. The Halakhah requires the performance of *periah*, the splitting of the membrane and uncovering the corona at circumcision. Circumcision has to be performed during the day and not at night; and it is imperative that it take place on the eighth day after the child's birth.

As radicalized as many segments of German Jewry were becoming, they generally still permitted circumcision of their sons due to family or social pressures. Often, however, they did not perform it on the stipulated day or at the correct time, or omitted the rite of *periah* altogether. Since these laws were absolute halakhic requirements and an integral part of circumcision, Hirsch felt compelled to offer some plausible explanation of them to people who were not even convinced of the need for circumcision as such. Only in the light of these circumstances, brought about by the revolt against traditional Judaism, can Hirsch's rationalizations be appreciated. Many of his explanations seem shallow and preposterous, for they were intellectual improvisations dictated by necessity.

Thus, in the case of *periah*, Hirsch suggests a philosophic reason why it is inextricably connected with circumcision and why the law states that *mal ve-lo para ke'ilu lo mal*, circumcision without *periah* is not considered circumcision at all. Actually, circumcision and *periah* are contradictory acts. The former signifies cutting and limiting; the latter, exposing and liberating. The very term *periah* means the loosening of all restraint and compulsion (*S* 3:287). The union of these seemingly contradictory acts that are performed simultaneously and contingent upon one another conveys an important idea. While circumcision signifies limitation of man's unbridled passion, *periah* signifies freedom within the confines of the law. Circumcision thus prohibits uncontrolled promiscuity, but *periah* indicates that within the limitations of the law man's act of propagation becomes pure and holy, even divinely mandatory (*S* 3:287).

Nocturnal and Diurnal Religion   Concerning the requirement that circumcision be performed during the day and not at night, Hirsch offers a sophisticated theory in which he distinguishes between two types of religion: nocturnal and diurnal. In nocturnal religion, man's relationship to God is determined by fear; robbed of his personality and freedom, at night man is transformed into a frightened, helpless animal who surrenders to God not out of recognition of God's greatness but out of a sense of his own impotence. In the nocturnal setting of religion man's relation to God is that of frightened surrender and tragic dependence.

Hirsch is critical of this nocturnal type of religion. Although he does not mention any specific religious system by name, it is clear that this criticism is directed at Schleiermacher's followers and at those Jews who were enchanted by a religion of feeling rather than by a religon of norms, by a sense of helpless submission rather than by independence. A religion rooted in *Abhängigkeitsgefühl*, a sense of dependency, best represented by the symbol of darkness and night, dehumanizes man by continuously accentuating his frailty and impotence. To find God, man must completely negate his entire being: "Sie lässt den Menschen da Gott finden, wo er sich verliert" (*S* 3:292); man reaches out to God, overwhelmed by the terror of His all-engulfing might. For this reason, many of the mystery religions preferred darkness and night.

The opposite of nocturnal religion is diurnal religion, which aims to elevate man through freedom and independence. It endows him with dignity by expecting not his abject surrender to God but rather his willing acceptance of God's sovereignty. Diurnal religion stresses openness and clarity, consciousness and freedom. Man confronts God not in fear but in freedom, not in the darkness of the night but in the bright light of day (*S* 3:293–94).

To Hirsch, Judaism is synonymous with diurnal religion; it is the actual embodiment of it. For this reason, he suggests that circumcision, which marks man's entrance into Judaism, should be performed during daytime in order to show man that this religion represents daylight and freedom, not submissiveness brought about by an overwhelming fear. Furthermore, since the very act of circumcision might be misinterpreted as a sanguinary act of self-mutilation to appease an invisible supernatural power, and thus seem to be a rite of nocturnal religion signifying the surrender of a part of man's body to some cruel demonic deity for the sake of appeasement (*S* 3:300), Hirsch stresses that daytime circumcision is designed to demonstrate that this precept was not so dictated. Nor does it emanate from any feeling of dejection and fear compelling man to self-mutilation. This commandment addresses itself to a free man in broad daylight, asking him to voluntarily and freely curtail his animalistic passions, channel his instincts and sensuality, and consecrate them for noble, constructive, and moral purposes.

Nature and History   The reason for circumcision being performed on the eighth day is even more complicated. To justify this requirement, Hirsch resorts to the mystical symbolism of numerology, in which the number seven represents completion and perfection of phenomena related to the domain of nature. The creation of the universe was completed in seven days: even though the actual creation of the physical world lasted six days, the seventh day does not stand apart from the process of creation but is an integral part of it (*S* 3:305). The Sabbath belongs to the domain of nature by completing it and sanctifying it, but it does not transcend it. It differs from the other days only in the moral and educational function it has for mankind (*CG* 2:2; *CL* 12:3).

In addition to the domain of nature is the domain of history, which begins where nature leaves off (*CG* 2:2). For this reason, a new symbolic number was introduced—eight, signifying a new creation of a higher supranatural order, Israel (*S* 3:310–11). Israel, whose very existence negates all natural phenomena and contradicts the developmental processes of other nations, points to a different domain. If the Sabbath marks the outer limits of the domain of nature, Israel constitutes the beginning of the domain of history, which will culminate in the establishment of the divine kingdom on earth (*S* 3:310–11).

It should be pointed out that what Hirsch calls history is more accurately metahistory, since history also has its laws of natural development and all the nations of the world are subject to these laws. Israel, however, is not governed by these laws and frequently defies them. In the *Neunzehn Briefe*, Hirsch had placed the essence of Israel outside the domain of history and therefore not subject to its fluctuations: "While mankind, educated by experience, was to learn to know God and itself from its manifold vicissitudes, the final goal of this experience was to be made surer and speedier of attainment by a special ordainment" (*NL* 66). This makes it abundantly clear that to Hirsch the number eight does not symbolize the ordinary concept of history current in the writings of that era, but rather a special *Heilgeschichte* or metahistory.

In order to concretize this concept, it was ordained that circumcision take place on the eighth day. It was supposed to indicate that although natural man is completed on the seventh day, the Jew begins where man ends; he participates in all aspects of natural man, but he also transcends him. The insistence that circumcision be performed on the eighth day is therefore of utmost significance, since it emphasizes the Jew's special task to transcend the determined sphere of nature; only in the free-will sphere of history can he carry out his distinctive mission (*S* 3:312–14).

It should be pointed out that Hirsch does not mention the rite of *metzitzah*, draining of the blood by suction, which is mentioned in the Talmud,[9] in the *Mishneh Torah*,[10] and by all codifiers. Hirsch could not have overlooked this rite inadvertently, because *metzitzah* was one of the disturbing issues in the nineteenth-century Jewish community and caused great concern among Orthodox rabbis and laymen. This rite, which in the talmudic era was performed by mouth for prophylactic reasons, was allegedly responsible for infant disease and mortality, for infants were often infected by a sick *mohel* performing oral suction. As a result, some rabbis subsequently advocated the elimination of oral suction, while others were reluctant to dispense with it, although the halakhic reason for oral *metzitzah* was tenuous. It is therefore strange that in discussing the details of circumcision such a hotly debated issue should have been overlooked by Hirsch. It is possible that Hirsch may have been reluctant to become involved in this emotional debate, preferring to avoid ideological or halakhic entanglements at that time. By mentioning *metzitzah*, he would have been compelled to take a stand.

How sensitive the issue of *metzitzah* was can be seen from the acrimonious controversy that raged over the very rite of circumcision. In 1837, an epidemic attributed to oral *metzitzah* broke out in Vienna, causing many children's deaths.[11] Fearful of the danger of the possibility that parents would stop circumcising their children altogether, Rabbi Moses Sofer permitted the draining of blood with cotton instead of oral suction.[12] But despite the latter's authority and the respect accorded him by the great rabbis, there was strong objection to the elimination of oral *metzitzah*. Among those speaking out against it was Hirsch's former teacher, Jacob Ettlinger.[13] Many years later, in 1886, Hirsch, who had become extremely conservative in his views, sided with Ettlinger.[14] However, shortly before his death Hirsch approved of suction through a hygienic glass tube that had been invented in 1887.[15] This innovation met with opposition, too, but many leading German rabbis besides Hirsch, including Hildesheimer and Stern of Hamburg, endorsed it, as did the great rabbi of Kovno, Isaac Elḥanan Spector.[16]

Gid ha-Nasheh

The law of circumcision is followed by the prohibition of *gid ha-nasheh*, sinew of the thigh vein. Hirsch considered this prohibition to be of singular importance since it chronologically preceded all other dietary laws. According to tradition, these laws had originated in the Sinaitic legislation, but the prohibition of the sinew of the thigh vein had begun with Jacob. Furthermore, it possesses commemorative significance, recalling Jacob's mysterious encounter with a supernatural being.[17] It also has great importance because, as a result of this encounter, the patriarch's name was changed to Israel, the subsequent name of the Jewish people. Hirsch, therefore, considered this law to have sufficient historical significance to be included in the category of *edot*, rather than with the dietary laws.

In his commentary, Hirsch points out that the prohibition of the sinew of the thigh vein constitutes one of the four *edot* mentioned in the Book of Genesis. The others are Sabbath, circumcision, and —not a law—the sign of the rainbow. He divides these four symbols into two universals of importance for all mankind and two particulars relevant only to the Jewish people. The particulars are actually the counterparts of the universals: the Sabbath points to the spiritual and ethical task of mankind; circumcision points to the spiritual and ethical role of the Jewish people; the sign of the rainbow evokes in mankind the universal historic experience of the deluge; and the law of the sinew of the thigh vein evokes in Jews the specific historical experience of Jacob's struggle. The victory of the patriarch in his battle with the supernatural wrestler in the darkness of night symbolizes the spiritual victory of the Jewish people, who like their ancestors are physically weak but spiritually powerful. Similarly, the transformation of Jacob's name to Israel represents the position and mission of his descendants, outwardly *ekev*, a lowly heel, inwardly *sar*, a prince (*H* 269).

Like many Jewish homilists and preachers, Hirsch also interprets Jacob's struggle as a battle between the Jews and their adversaries. This battle was viewed in light of the biblical narrative as lasting until the dawn of the modern era. To Hirsch, its essence is not that Jacob survived or that he was victorious; such a victory might prove a pyrrhic one if the Jews assimilated after the long historic battle. It is the singularity and religious identity for which the Jews fought that must be preserved. Eventually, the nations of the world will recognize that by guarding their separate existences, the Jews have actually guarded the great spiritual values of all mankind (*CG* 32:27).

The prohibition of the sinew of the thigh vein has great importance for the special historic consciousness of the Jewish people. However, Israel's historic experience has also worked a salutary effect upon mankind in general. The sufferings the Jews have borne were not only intended for their own eventual happiness but for all mankind's. In their long struggle throughout history, the Jews have preserved the great spiritual and ethical ideals that sustain humanity. Hirsch intimates that the portentous battle between Jacob and the supernatural figure symbolizing Esau did not terminate with enmity. Such a view might have implied that the centuries-long struggle between Christians and Jews would remain unresolved because Judaism represents an irreconcilable barrier. Hirsch describes the anti-Jewish persecutions as a grave error on the part of the Christians, but deemed them a struggle which would end in friendship when the Christians finally acknowledged that the Jewish battle for religious identity and singularity has also been beneficial to mankind.

Tefillin

Subsequent chapters deal with commandments which have obvious symbolic characteristics: *tefillin, tzitzit,* and *mezuzah.* Actually, these three precepts should have followed the chapter dealing with the laws of circumcision since they shared a recognition of the sanctity of man's personal unit: body, mind, emotions, dress, and home (*CN* 15:41). Hirsch's placement of the discussion of the law concerning the sinew of the thigh vein between circumcision and the other three symbols is illogical, and the only reason for its inclusion after the chapter on circumcision is, as already indicated, its chronological order in biblical history. Both precepts antedate the Sinaitic legislation and were commanded to Abraham and Jacob, respectively.

Resuming his interpretation of the visible ritualistic symbols,

Hirsch begins with *tefillin*. The four biblical portions encased in the *tefillin* contain the basic ideas of Judaism and stress the Jew's mission of implementing these ideas in life. But ideas must be externalized by a concrete symbol. Therefore, it is not sufficient to entertain such ideas in abstraction; the *tefillin* must be worn: "Putting on *tefillin* therefore means really accoutering oneself in the service of God" (*H* 271).

Echoing the traditional interpretation, Hirsch ascribes the ennobling influences of the *tefillin* upon the intellect, the will, and the action of man as related to the head, heart, and arm upon which and near which they are worn. The fact that the four portions in the *tefillah* of the head are placed in separate compartments, and the one in the *tefillah* on the arm in a single compartment, signifies that the various ideas conceived separately by the intellect must be coordinated in one concentrated action (*H* 272). Significantly, Hirsch sees an important message in the law requiring the placement of the *tefillah shel yad* on the arm, prior to donning the *tefillah shel rosh* on the head. In Hirsch's view, this is to indicate the paramount importance of action over contemplation. Aware of the prevailing tendency of many in his generation to prefer religious contemplation over action and the knowledge of Judaism over its practice, Hirsch sees a contradiction of this attitude in the law on the *tefillin*. Unless knowledge is translated into action, it becomes barren and futile (*H* 274). Thus, Hirsch advocates that commitment to Judaism should take priority over philosophic contemplation of it. This view is cardinal in Hirsch's outlook as discussed in the beginning of the section called *"Torot."* In contrast to Maimonides and the Neo-Maimonideans in his generation, who stressed thought and knowledge, Hirsch emphasizes will and action.

In the course of time, Hirsch compounded the symbolism of the *tefillin* in his essay "Grundlinien einer jüdischen Symbolik" (*S* 3:348–69) and in his commentary on the Pentateuch. He attaches importance not only to the content of the *tefillin*, but to their external form as well. The latter is known as *bayit*, house or home. Hirsch suggests that the term *bayit* be taken literally. It signifies man's task to build a "house" permeated with the ideas derived from the Exodus and revelation, the portions of which are contained in the *tefillin*. This task must be accomplished by man's free will and with his intention. This is symbolized by the square shape of the *tefillin*, signifying a geometric design deliberately fashioned by man. The *tittura*, or base of the *tefillin*, indicates the relevance of these ideas to the world and to mundane matters. The house for the Torah must have a *tittura*, a solid "base," on earth, since the Torah is related to life and relevant to it (*CD* 6:8). The *ma'abarta*, the hollow rim by which the *tefillin* are attached to man's body, signifies that the Torah has to become an integral part of man and permeate his entire being (*CD* 6:8).

Drifting on a wide sea of symbolism, Hirsch, much like the mystics he deplored, ascribes meaning to every detail of the *tefillin*. At times, he multiplies symbols and grafts one upon another. Thus, the *tefillin* come to resemble the Ark of the Covenant in miniature (*CD* 6:8), the *kesher*, or knot, joining the concepts of the Exodus and Torah (*CD* 6:8). From the *kesher* on the back of the head "they stream down on the right to the seat of our earthly sensuous organs and on the left to the seat of our higher moral wishes" (*CD* 6:8). Needless to say, Hirsch elaborates on the letter *shin* and the four-headed *shin* which are embossed on the *tefillin* (*CD* 6:8).

Hirsch wished to demonstrate the significance of every detail of each precept. However, the further he strays from the simplicity and the genuineness which marked his interpretation of the commandments in the *Horeb*, the less credible his rationale comes to appear.

Tzitzit

The precept of *tzitzit*, like other symbolic commandments, constitutes a means by which to direct man's attention "from the visible to the invisible" (*H* 277). Attached to one's garment, the *tzitzit* are designed to recall the traditional biblical reason that caused primordial man to be clothed when his animalistic instincts sent him astray. Having been denuded morally, man experienced an overwhelming sense of humiliation and sinfulness. At that moment, God clothed the first man in order to conceal his animal aspect and to guard him against the possibility of being brutalized by it. The garment became the symbol distinguishing man from beast. Man ordinarily tends to forget this fact, and therefore Judaism enjoined the *tzitzit* on his garments as a visible reminder to conduct himself as a man spiritually and morally, and not to revert to the animalistic behavior of his first ancestor. Since man is inherently dualistic—belonging to the realms of both nature and spirit —he must guard himself against descending completely into nature. The *tzitzit* on the garment externalize this danger for him by recalling the primeval fall that first necessitated the wearing of garments. Furthermore, they remind man, who lives within the limitations imposed by time, space, and reason, "that those things which are invisible and past and which exist beyond the ken of what is visible and present also have reality" (*H* 281). This is not an invitation to metaphysical or mystical speculation; it is merely an acknowledgment that an invisible realm exists which man, while affirming it, cannot penetrate.

Since the *tzitzit* serve as "a protective reminder in our intercourse with the vulgar mundane world" (*H* 283), they ought to be worn only during the daytime when man is actively engaged in the world. At night, when man retires from his involvement with mundane affairs and is not subject to its provocations and challenges, there is no need to wear *tzitzit*.

As noted, *tzitzit* are associated with man's ethical behavior. They symbolically guide man in the path of morality and shield him from possible deviations. While in the ancient and medieval worlds such ethical guidance and assistance were welcomed, in the post-Kantian era they were viewed as immoral. The commandment to wear *tzitzit* as a means of overcoming immorality seemed to imply that man's decision for moral behavior is not freely determined. Such morality is heteronomous. Regardless of results, it robs man of his moral autonomy and free will. Only acts performed out of man's own inner commitment and free of any external mandates or prophylactic media constitute true morality.

Hirsch answers this challenge by pointing out that *tzitzit* are merely a lesson, not a command. There is no law requiring the wearing of *tzitzit* unless a garment has four corners. This gives man absolute freedom, since he may elect to wear clothes of a different shape. Man's morality is therefore unconstrained and absolutely autonomous. Indeed, he may avail himself of this precept and "grasp the staff which stands by him in the battle" (*H* 285) against sensuality, or abandon the *tzitzit* precept altogether (*H* 285).

In his essay on Jewish symbolism and in his commentary on Numbers, Hirsch shows that the very grammatical construction of the commandment indicates freedom of choice rather than strict compliance. The verb employed in this connection is *ve-asu*[18] and not *ve-ya'asu*. The former denotes freedom, the latter, command. Hirsch therefore translates the words *ve-asu lakhem tzitzit* in a manner indicating voluntary acceptance: "das Sie ihretwillen Schaumal machen," say it to them *so that they make* fringes (*CN* 15:38). In his interpretation, he adds: "Explain to them, bring all the preceding and all the consequences that are attached to it so home to them that they will gladly make 'fringes' on their garments as I bid you" (*CN* 15:-38).

The precept of the *tzitzit* discarded by the liberals and Reformers of the time assumes in Hirsch's interpretation a new significance of great universal and moral dimensions. In his later works, however, the interpretation becomes overladen with excessive symbolic connotations. In the eight threads of the *tzitzit*, Hirsch sees the numerological significance already mentioned in the discussion dealing with circumcision. It represents a new, higher creation transcending the world of creation to which the numbers six and seven are assigned. The number eight in *tzitzit* signifies that man must subordinate all his powers and energy to the idea symbolized in the numerological concept of "eight" (*CN* 15:41). The fact that the *tzitzit* have to be coiled and tied into knots implies voluntary subordination to moral control as symbolized by clothing (*CN* 15:41). The fact that the free-hanging part of the fringes constitutes two-thirds of the *tzitzit* and the bound part only one-third signifies that notwithstanding the alleged rigors of Judaism, it contains more freedom than restriction (*CN* 15:41). Judaism does not negate freedom, it merely channels and directs it for the benefit of man as an individual, and for mankind at large. The blue thread of the *tzitzit* indicates that the confines of man's perception and understanding limiting him from entering the domain of the supernatural (*CN* 15:41).

Mezuzah

The last of the fourfold ideational units is *mezuzah*, which signifies the dedication of man's home to the divine ideals and the commitment of its inhabitants to God's service (*H* 289). Hirsch does not contribute anything new to this accepted view. Hirsch leaves *mezuzah*, unlike the other three precepts, unencumbered with symbolic and homiletical explanations. The reason for this simplicity seems to be the inoffensive character of *mezuzah* and the lack of difficulty in using it; all a person has to do is to affix it to the doorpost of his house. Since it does not interfere with man's private or public life, the commandment was generally obeyed. Only those who were militantly antagonistic to Judaism rejected it. Since apparently there was no danger of Jews discarding this precept, Hirsch felt no need to rationalize it excessively.

Bekhor, Ḥadash, Orlah, *and* Ḥallah

Among the *edot* Hirsch includes four precepts which were originally connected with the Temple: *bekhor*, or the law of the firstborn, *ḥadash*, *orlah*, and *ḥallah*. Although most of the laws relating to the Temple and the priesthood are no longer operative, these four remained mandatory in modified form in the Diaspora. Hirsch therefore endeavored to find a cogent rationale for their continued applicability in modern times.

The law of the first-born is related in the Bible to the deliverance from Egyptian bondage. Like Passover and the *tefillin*, it was designed to remind the Jew of the religious and ethical implications of that extraordinary event. The law of the first-born embraces three categories of sanctification: human, cattle, and asses. The first represents man's children, the second movable property for his personal use, the third property which serves him as implements (*H* 296). In his commentary on Exodus, Hirsch considered these three categories to represent family, food, and possessions respectively—all belonging to God (*CE* 13:13).

The sanctity of the first-born further emphasizes man's tenuous rights to his possessions in this world by demonstrating that his children and his property are merely a sacred charge entrusted to him by God. Only by His grace can man enjoy his children and property. Man's children are actually God's children, and he is therefore obliged to treat the latter in accordance with the wishes of God and not impose upon them his will or mastery. He must educate them to become *Mensch-Jissroel* bring them up in the ideals of Judaism, and not merely prepare them for success in their social and economic endeavors.

Similarly, the sanctity of the firstlings of cattle signifies that man must view his possessions as given to him by God. Man therefore has to employ them not in accordance with his own whims and caprices but as "something holy entrusted to you only for the fulfillment of the will of the Giver" (*H* 296).

Hirsch offers two explanations of why only the first child should be considered holy and not all children. The first reason is that the first-born serves as a symbol of the entire family. Through his dedication, the entire family is conscious of its divine mission in life (*CE* 13:12). Hirsch suggests yet another view for which there is no basis in the Halakhah, namely, that not only the first-born but *all* offspring are considered holy: "In *bekhor* it is not just the first that becomes holy; by the consecration of the first-born the mother's womb becomes sanctified to God, together with everything that it bears henceforth" (*CE* 34:19).

Like *bekhor*, the laws concerning *hadash, orlah,* and *hallah* are still operative at the present time. As late as the seventeenth century the question of *hadash* stirred a great controversy among leading rabbinic authorities.[19] The prohibition of *orlah* applies only to definite *orlah* fruit. Due to its very nature, *orlah* never presented a problem, since unripe fruit is hardly edible. The most commonly observed of these four precepts is *hallah*.

These laws are interpreted by Hirsch as reminders to man that the earth and its abundance belong to God. Their lesson is directed to all mankind. All men must acknowledge God as the exclusive owner of all possessions, and therefore man must not use them or abuse them, contrary to His will. When the Jewish people had a land of its own, the laws emphasizing this idea were numerous. They included, among others, laws governing first fruits and tithes of various form.

For the most commonly observed precept, *hallah*, Hirsch gives three reasons: (1) it signifies that man's daily bread is granted to him by the grace of God; (2) "it keeps fresh in our minds and in our hopes the idea of a nation manifest among nations" (*H* 307); and (3) it links every Jewish home in an invisible spiritual bond with the people of Israel (*H* 307).

Thus, Hirsch endows all the aforementioned precepts with an ever-present religious-ethical rationale. They ought to be observed not as relics from a remote past, but as symbols of the sacred glory of the Temple in Jerusalem. These precepts have universal significance and consequently transcend time and space. They are not limited to the time of national sovereignty nor to the spatial boundaries of the land of Israel. These precepts teach man, and particularly the Jew, the important lesson of humility. In the flush of success and achievement, man tends to forget that it is by the grace of God that he has attained prosperity and instead believes that he has gained his position and possessions all on his own. Such an erroneous outlook augurs disastrous consequences for him, especially in his social relationships; it hardens his heart and leaves him indifferent to the needs of those less fortunate than he.

Mourning

Strangely, the *"Edot"* is concluded with the laws concerning mourning. As already pointed out, the classification of these laws is problematic even in the *Mishneh Torah.* Unlike the other laws, Hirsch does not introduce these by quoting biblical passages. Hirsch felt the need to explain the reason for including these laws in this section: "We include them in the section *'Edot'* because they also teach us how, by symbolic observances, to commemorate what is primarily a private occurrence and the emotions which it engenders" (*H* 310).

Grief constricts a man's horizon and renders him too weak to cope with the problems of life (*H* 309). Neither an excess of grief nor the stifling of this emotion is desirable. Both extremes are dangerous. For this reason, Judaism distinguishes three periods of mourning: *aninut, avelut,* and *nivvul.*

The first represents the initial shock and grief following the loss of a close member of the family. The Torah does not propose restraining the emotions of the mourner at this moment; excepting the high priest, it permits the mourner to give full vent to his feelings at a time when no reason could master it. Nor is the *onen*, or mourner—so termed immediately after the death of a very close member of the family—restricted by any of the customary laws (*H* 313). To allow the mourner an absolute catharsis, the Rabbis exempted him from all religious obligations so that he might devote himself exclusively to the last rites of the departed.

The second period of mourning is that of *avelut*. During the seven days of mourning, it is the duty of the bereaved to meditate and try "to understand the meaning of what has happened" (*H* 314). The third period of mourning, *nivvul*, lasts until the thirtieth day following death. With the termination of the seven days of mourning, the bereaved's reason slowly and gradually reemerges as he regains his spiritual and psychological equilibrium. However, he is not considered to have sufficiently recovered to care for his outward appearance—hence *nivvul*, meaning the neglect of personal appearance, which continues for thirty days (*H* 315).

Hirsch does not elaborate on the laws of mourning since these laws were apparently being observed at that time and he saw no special need for their rationalization, as is evident regarding the prayer of Kaddish, of which he merely makes mention (*H* 32). The fact that Kaddish was being meticulously observed, perhaps for social or psychological reasons, freed Hirsch of lending it symbolism and elaboration.

10
"Mishpatim":
Laws of Justice toward Man

From Maimonides to Hegel

The third division of the *Horeb* bears the title *"Mishpatim"*—
judgments. It is defined by its subtitle as "Aussprüche der Gerechtigkeit gegen Menschen," declarations of justice toward human
beings. In the *Neunzehn Briefe, "Mishpatim"* is listed as the second division, immediately following *"Torot."* It consists of twelve
chapters dealing with man's legal and moral obligations toward his
fellow man and his possessions.

Unlike the preceding division, *"Edot,"* which deals with laws of
a religious and symbolic nature in need of rationalization, the laws
of *"Mishpatim"* present no such problem. They are primarily
legal and ethical norms of a universal nature. Justice is indivisible
and cannot, therefore, address itself to the Jew differently from
man in general: "Every man, as man, is born for justice" (*H* 329).
The Jew's task is not to live by different standards of justice from
the rest of mankind. He merely has to implement these universal
principles with great care and circumspection, since as a Jew he
is "doubly called upon to fulfill the image of justice" (*H* 329).

Justice is another manifestation of order. The former applies to
the social domain, the latter to the natural domain. Both constitute
part of the "universal activity of the just taking and the just giving." (*H* 323). In the realm of nature, order prevails when "each
creature discharges its task in proportion to its strength, taking

284

from its fellow creatures only what God has allotted to it for its development, and for its part faithfully giving of its own to the best of its ability" (*H* 323). Similarly, in the social realm, justice will prevail when man will "allow to each all that God has allotted to him, to give to each all things in your control to which God has allotted him a claim" (*H* 321).

The difference between order in nature and justice in society is consciousness, which is inherent in the latter and absent in the former. Nature acts unconsciously in accordance with divinely preconceived and preordained laws from which it cannot deviate. These deterministic laws, manifested by natural phenomena, are actually the embodiment of divine laws of justice. In the social sphere, deterministic laws are inoperative, since they would have deprived man of his free will. Were the principle of order discernible in nature to govern society, society's harmony would be assured at the expense of man's freedom. The advantage of order would be offset by the dehumanization of man. Deprived of free will, man is no different from the rest of nature. Thus, a predetermined social order would make justice superfluous. The order of nature could thus be extended to society, amalgamating both domains without any distinctiveness.

It is the unique endowment of free will in man that necessitates a new manifestation of order in the form of justice. Free of any possible restrictions and compulsions, man has the ability to create order or disorder in the social domain, a choice inconceivable in the domain of nature. True, such freedom is replete with dangers. However, to a generation brought up in the afterglow of Kant and Hegel, danger emanating from autonomy was preferable to harmony grounded in heteronomy.[1] Unless man is able to act badly, he has no free will, and thus his deeds, even when formally just, cannot be considered moral.[2] According to Hirsch, man was created for justice since he alone in all creation is capable of being unjust (*H* 324). Only man, in contrast to all other phenomena of nature, is able to act against to the will of God. Man alone was given the ability to deny the rest of creation, his fellow men, and even God (*H* 324). However, it is this quality with all its concomitant dangers that distinguishes man from his natural surroundings and elevates his acts to the level of conscious ethicality. God granted man absolute autonomy to act not from inner compulsion or outer motivation, but from his own free will, undetermined and unrestrained (*H* 324).

Although man is free to act justly or unjustly, morally or immorally, he possesses an insight and a capacity for ethical discernment. He is endowed with an awareness of the fundamental principles of truth and right, an inherent sense of the divine cosmic order (*H* 324). Here Hirsch seems to echo Kant's view of the categorical imperative which is not empirical but an a priori cognition.[3] This awareness, however, neither constrains man's will nor limits his freedom to act contrary to it.

It ought to be pointed out that this Kantian view, which Hirsch emphasizes in the *"Mishpatim,"* transcends the laws of this division. Hirsch employed it on many occasions and applied it not only to laws of *derekh eretz* in the legal sense, but in its broader extrajuridical Jewish connotation of Torah.

It has been pointed out that in the previous two divisions of the *Horeb* Hirsch follows, with some minor modifications, the schematic pattern of Maimonides's *Mishneh Torah*. The *"Torot"* discloses a strong resemblance to *"Sefer ha-Madda,"* and the *"Edot"* shows a predominant influence of *"Zemanim."* In the third division of the *Horeb*, *"Mishpatim,"* such an analogy seems impossible. In *"Mishpatim"* Hirsch displays an unusual sense of selectivity, and out of the numerous laws in the four books of Maimonides's *Mishneh Torah*—*"Nezikin," "Kinyan," "Mishpatim,"* and *"Shoftim"*—Hirsch merely deals with a few, adding some laws that Maimonides treats in *"Sefer ha-Madda."* All this seems to indicate that in this division Hirsch does not follow Maimonides's schema.

Upon analyzing Hirsch's interpretations of the laws classified under *"Mishpatim"* in *Horeb* and in his commentary on the Pentateuch, we notice a remarkable similarity between many of these interpretations and many elements in Hegel's *Rechtsphilosophie* (*Philosophy of Right*), particularly those Hegel called "abstract rights." Strongly influenced by Hegel, Hirsch considered the latter's philosophy of law the acme of perfection and its juridical concepts fundamental and ideal. The laws of Judaism, being divine in origin and perfect, ought consequently to be permeated with this philosophy and its concepts; it was therefore natural for Hirsch to scrutinize these laws closely and to probe them for underlying Hegelian principles. Thus, the laws of Judaism, particularly those of the *mishpatim* category, would be considered not as contradictory to reason and life, but rational and reasonable, essential to the welfare of man and to the attainment of the highest social order and perfect justice.

Hegel's *Philosophy of Right* was published in 1821, sixteen years prior to the publication of the *Horeb*. Its impact at that time was immense. Furthermore, the *Philosophy of Right* constitutes the most intelligible of Hegel's works, and so Hirsch could easily employ its rationale for the laws he categorized as *mishpatim*. Comparing the latter to the first part of Hegel's *Rechtsphiloso-phie*, entitled "Abstract Rights," we are struck by their similarity in the external order and internal content. It becomes apparent that in this section Hirsch follows Hegel and not Maimonides, as he does in the previous section. Apparently in the *"Torot"* and *"Edot,"* which are of a specific religious nature, he is forced to follow Maimonides; *mishpatim*, however, are of a univeral nature, and in the division of that name he chooses to turn to Hegel. It is possible that by proving the conceptual identity of *mishpatim* and Hegel's *Rechtsphilosophie*, Hirsch thought to validate by implication the other precepts of Judaism for which there was no such analogy.

The Cognitive-Volitional Basis of Right

Right, according to Hegel, has its foundation in the *mind*[4]— specifically, in the acting aspect of the mind, namely, the *will*, rather than the cognitive aspect (*PR* 21–22). To Hegel, will and mind do not represent two disjointed categories, distinct and independent of one another, but are two different manifestations of the same essence: "The will is a special way of thinking, namely, it is thought translating itself into reality and becoming practice."[5]

This relationship between mind and will and their fundamental unity was axiomatic to Hirsch, an exponent of traditional Judaism. *Law*, a term he employs interchangeably with *Torah*, emanates directly from God, who is Absolute Mind. The Law is the "Will of God" (*CG* 2:16),[6] which was embodied in the Torah and communicated to man through revelation. Since a dichotomy between the cognitive and volitional aspects of the Divine is inconceivable, as it would imply anthropomorphism and corporeality, the absolute unity and identity of will and mind are foregone conclusions. To Hirsch, therefore, as to Hegel, the basis of right is mind. God, who is Absolute Mind, expressed His will in the Torah-Law, which is the embodiment of right. Thus, the essential and fundamental unity between mind and will and their ultimate manifestation in right seem to both Hirsch and Hegel to be inseparable.

However, this unity in the realm of the absolute does not yet exist on the level of man. The latter's will, prior to its actualization, does not correspond to the "will of God." Man's will, unless subordinated to the will of God, is, owing to its own subjectivity, indistinct. The generic essence of right as willed by God is implicit only in man. In order that the subjective will of man be correlative to the absolute "will of God," man has to actualize his potentialities in conformity with the divine will and in accordance with it make them explicit, externalized, and objectified.

The correlation by Hirsch of the subjective will of man with the absolute will of God, and its gradual objectification in the external world by Hegel, are inextricably bound up with the concept of *freedom*. Both Hegel and Hirsch emphasize that the essential element of the will, as well as its very substance, is freedom: "Without freedom will is an empty word; freedom becomes actual only as will, as subject. But a will which resolves on nothing is not an actual will."[7]

This concept of freedom of will is the foundation of Hegel's theory of jurisprudence. In the sphere of abstract rights, Hegel considers the will as gradually emerging from its inwardness and subjectivity. To attain its full objectification in the external world, the will must not encounter any restriction; it should unfold in an unimpeded and unqualified manner (*PR* 30). According to Hegel, the relationship of freedom to will is not that of an accidental attribute ascribed to a self-sufficient essence:

Freedom . . . is just as fundamental a character of the will as weight is of bodies. If we say: matter is "heavy," we might mean that this predicate is only contingent; but it is nothing of the kind, for nothing in matter is without weight. Matter is rather weight itself. Heaviness constitutes the body and is the body. The same is the case with freedom and the will, since the free entity is the will. Will without freedom is an empty word, while freedom is actual only as will, as subject. (*PR* 226)

Having identified freedom with will, Hegel insisted that the attainment of freedom is the will's only aim. Thus, he arrived at a definition that has a tautological ring: "the free will which wills the free will" (*PR* 32). It is the free will striving to achieve freedom that realizes itself in right, for the system of right is the province of actualized freedom:[8] "An existent of any sort embodying the free will, this is what right is. Right therefore is by definition freedom as Idea" (*PR* 33).

Hegel succinctly expressed the relationship between mind, will, right, and freedom in the following statement:

The basis of right is, in general, mind; its precise place and point of origin is the will. The will is free, so that freedom is both the substance of right and its goal, while the system of right is the realm of freedom made actual, the world of mind brought forth out of itself, like a second nature. (*PR* 20)

The concept of free will as a sine qua non of right is fundamental in Hirsch, whether in its theological aspect governing the relationship between man and God or in its juridical aspect regulating relations between man and man. In fact, man's will on the level of immediacy is subjective, aspiring eventually to correlate to the will of God. This ultimate objectification of his will constitutes the aim of man. We endeavor to achieve it by "subordinating the dictates of our senses to the expressed will of God, a condition which is inseparable from, and forms a part of, the morally high station and calling of man" (*CG* 2:16). Yet it is this very subordination of the subjective will of man and his acceptance of the divine will which presupposes man's absolute freedom of will. Man's free will must be unconditional and totally unqualified; in order to assert its absolute freedom, it must possess even the ability and the possibility to disobey and act contrary to the will of God, behavior that is viewed theologically as sin. "Moral freedom, freedom of will, that fundamental palladium of the greatness of man, is itself unthinkable without the ability to sin" (*CG* 2:16).

The idea of free will is an integral part of Jewish religious thought, and its doctrinal preeminence in medieval Jewish philosophy needs no elaboration. However, Hirsch's frequent stress on the idea of freedom, not only in its theological ramifications but also in connection with its juridical aspects, suggests its relationship to the idealistic school of philosophy of his time. By emphasizing the importance of man's free will and wishing to underscore its absolute, unqualified, and unrestricted nature, Hirsch asserts that it is second only to the will of God: "Next to the *ne plus ultra,* the highest conceivable height, the one free-willed God, Jewish conception places, *as second, the pure free-willed man"* (*CG* 3:19).

Man's free will is not only linked with God's free will but emanates from it. Man's freedom has its roots in the absolute freedom of God: "If there is no free God, if complete and absolute freedom of will does not exist in God, how can man have obtained moral freedom of will, and how then can there be talk of right and wrong?" (*CL* 24:21). With this unlimited freedom, man has the ability to actualize it in the domain of right. Thus, man's will, of its own accord, will freely extricate itself from its sensual and subjective confines and identify itself with the will of God as embodied in the Law of the Torah: "The law to which all powers submit unconsciously and involuntarily, to it shalt thou also subordinate thyself, but *consciously* and of *thy own free will"* (*NL* 33).

The fact that God singled out man from all other creatures to bestow upon him this unusual gift of free will has theological and ethical as well as juridical implications. This divine endowment is unalterably related to the concept of right through unconditional freedom: "Man, however, you alone are created for justice" (*H* 324). God intentionally and deliberately liberated man from the deterministic laws that govern the universe and regulate the involuntary behavior of the nonhuman species (*NL* 33). This unique status of man, whom God has freed from the inexorable laws of right inherent in the entire cosmic structure, was given to man so that he might defy those laws and act contrary to them. Any limitation upon man's freedom would have invalidated the concept of right and justice. Hirsch is quite emphatic on this point: "He who denies moral free will must keep his mouth closed on the subject of justice" (*CL* 24:21). Being unqualifiedly free, man has the ability to attain justice freely: "For God, by giving you a will, detached you from His compulsive law—so that you may of your own free will do justice to God and every creature" (*H* 324).

The first place where man's will can assert itself in its pursuit of the right is the domain Hegel called the sphere of abstract or formal rights. The laws belonging to this category were previously known as *jus naturale*.[9] They express rights which are self-evident and which accrue to a person as a person, autonomous in his universal, undifferentiated form and irrespective of any other considerations. The domain of abstract rights is the first stage in the progressive dialectical process of the realization of the concept of right, which should eventually become consummated in the Idea.

Hirsch's section *"Mishpatim"* is quite analogous to Hegel's abstract rights. It, too, is concerned with natural laws self-evident and comprehensible to everyone. The laws subsumed under this classification form the "general conception of right, of what man owes to his fellow man" (*CL* 18:4).

In the *Neunzehn Briefe*, Hirsch had defined these laws as "statements of justice toward creatures similar and equal to yourself, by reason of this resemblance and equality, that is, of justice toward human beings" (*NL* 104). Despite the fact that they are reasonable and natural, they had to be included in the Torah, for these "laws of social right, on which alone the whole human social happiness can truly flourish and blossom, the Rights of Man, as God sees them, require study from the revealed Word of God no less than the *Ḥukkim*" (*CL* 18:4). Although these laws are natural, God's legislation in this sociojuridical domain was necessary since man-made laws are by their very nature imperfect and arbitrary. Any law of human origin is bound to have been motivated by certain utilitarian reasons. Only divine law can be completely objective without

giving advantage to one at the cost of the other; in every case they are fair to everyone, ensure harmoniously a suitable position to everyone, and demand that everybody does his share, all in accordance with his rights as a human being and with his condition in life. God's right is nothing else but the practical application of truth. (*CL* 18:4)

Hirsch's distinction between divine and human laws seems to echo Hegel's differentiation between "absolute" and "positive" laws. The former are objective, whereas the latter "are something posited, something originated by men" (*PR* 224), and hence subject to arbitrary determination. However, Hirsch disagrees with Hegel on man's ability to discover the objective right without assistance.

While Hegel maintained that "exact thinking" about the right is possible through diligent effort and scientific human apprehension (*PR* 225), Hirsch insists upon divine legislation.

The abstract laws, which in Hegelian philosophy accrue to a person per se divested of all possible contingencies except that of being a person, are likewise defined by Hirsch as *mishpatim*. The latter are composed of

God's pronouncements concerning those things which each man has a right—merely because God has created him a man—to demand of you, that is, to which he has a claim because he is a man.
. . . Man has a right, first, to everything which God has allotted to him by virtue of his very existence, such as life, health, mental and spiritual powers, liberty, honor, peace, happiness, etc.; secondly, to everything which he has acquired in accordance with his mastery over earthly goods which God has accorded to him. (*H* 328)

It is clear that Hirsch follows Hegel's fundamental concept of right, which is the manifestation of the free will asserting itself in the first stage of abstract rights. Since in Hegelian *Rechtsphiloso-phie* the concept of free will in relation to the concept of right is inextricably connected with the idea of personality, it is necessary to analyze Hegel's and Hirsch's views on this subject.

The Interdependence of Personality and Right

Freedom of will, so highly valued in Hegel's philosophy, is centered in *personality*. It is the latter's self-reference, to the exclusion of everything outside itself, that distinguishes it as a unit. Personality is "the abstract will consciously self-contained" (*PR* 235). This reference to consciousness transcends mere phenomenological consciousness,[10] implying a higher degree, that of self-consciousness: "A person, then, is a subject aware of this subjectivity" (*PR* 235).

Free will having thus been restricted to personality, the problem of right arises. This involves the manifestation of one's free will and its assertion vis-à-vis other personalities possessing the identical free will. A plurality of equal free wills or personalities must in some way encroach upon one another or limit one another in some way: "Personality essentially involves the capacity for rights and constitutes the concept and basis—itself abstract—of the system of abstract and therefore formal right" (*PR* 37).

Thus, Hegel arrived at his fundamental distinction between *person* and *thing*. Since the infinitude of the human personality makes it an absolute end, it follows that one person can never be treated by another person as a means. The basic axiom of right with regard to persons is therefore expressed in the following injunction: "Be a person and respect others as persons" (*PR* 37). The concept of "thing," however, is the exact antithesis. While a person has no right over another person, who like him is "a unit of freedom aware of its sheer independence" (*PR* 235), he does have rights over things. The latter are defined, not substantively, but as "that whose determinate character lies in its pure external-ity" (*PR* 40). The idea of "things" is quite broad; it is not neces-sarily limited to inert matter but also embraces sentient beings which, despite their consciousness, lack self-consciousness, self-limitation, and self-determination and are therefore considered finite. Consequently, Hegel viewed an animal as a thing. Indeed, "animals are in possession of themselves; their soul is in possession of their body. But they have no right to their life, because they do not will it" (*PR* 237).

The concept of personality and its interdependence with right, strongly underscored by Hegel, is similarly stressed by Hirsch. In different forms, Hirsch frequently repeats the Hegelian precept "Be a person and respect others as persons":

The first requisite is justice. Respect every being around thee and all that is in thee as the creation of thy God. . . . Honor every human being as thy equal, regard him in his essence, that is to say, in his invisible personality, in his bodily envelope and in his life. (*NL* 109)

The essence of human personality for Hirsch is the human soul, which, as part of divinity, is absolutely free. In defining personal-ity, Hirsch states: " 'Person' is naught but a being who, in all moral matters, can decide for himself. Personality is really only the incor-poration of moral freedom of will in an individual" (*CL* 24:21). The respect that must be accorded man extends to his soul-personality. Hirsch is quite explicit about this, asserting that justice with re-spect to man does not mean being just to any of his limbs, for the latter are merely his property; it is concerned with the invisible God-like soul: "The essence of man, being like unto God, is invisible, the personality or the soul, for which the body with all its members and forces is but a tool" (H 331).

From the fact that man's soul is part of God it follows that his personality, which is synonymous with the soul, is also part of the divine personality. Since personality and rights are inextricably united, and since man's personality merely reflects that of God, the basic concept of right must of necessity be primarily connected with God's personality, which therefore serves as the cornerstone of the rights of man:

This fundamental conception of all justice, this indispensable condition for all rights of Man, is simply a conception of the Personality of God. Remove the Personality of God from the world and you have banished "justice" from the world. For justice is a demand that can only be really demanded by the free. (CL 24:21)

Hirsch transformed Hegel's legal concept of personality as the foundation of rights into a theological-juridical concept. It is the personality of God, whose freedom is absolute, that makes possible a free personality in man possessing the ability to decide between right and wrong: "Just as the idea of right and wrong, and its necessary corollary of moral freedom, are unthinkable without a completely free God, in the same way the fact of God being a 'personal God' is an indispensable conception for the idea of human personality" (CL 24:21).

Hirsch continues to develop the notion that if a personal God whose freedom is absolute and transcendental, did not exist, man could have no freedom at all and would be merely a product of the material world with all its materialistic concomitants, and thus be reduced to the status of things, devoid of personality:

If there is altogether no personal world creator outside the world who has endowed man, His noblest earthly creation, with spirit of His spirit, set him in His world and said to him "be free, have the power to make your own decisions," if there is only this material world and man is naught but a product of this material world, then man, too, is only one of the other "things" of the world, is no longer a personality. (CL 24:21).

Consequently, the difference between man and all other species (classified as things) would be merely quantitative and not qualitative. Man would be "only a more complicated animal. But, of a specific difference of kind, of a specifically higher dignity of man, human personality, there can be no question" (*CL* 24:21).

In typical Hegelian fashion, Hirsch draws a sharp line between the concepts of "person" and "thing." A person must be considered an absolute end in himself; he can never be employed as a means. A thing, however, can and ought to be used by a *person* as a means: "All creatures about you were given to you by God for your use. . . . But man must never and can never become the vehicle for another man's actions, because man is not a body but divine *spirit* to which God has given a body as a *tool*" (*H* 330). A person has the right to master, use, transform, and even destroy a thing for his own need and satisfaction: "God gave the creatures on earth to man for him to transform, to use as the *means* for his purpose, since—as it were—He had created them for the service of man" (*H* 330).

Like Hegel, Hirsch places animals in the category of "things." In discussing a certain law concerning crimes committed against man and animals, Hirsch says that "if we sum up the laws given here on the rights of life and property, they, too, all seem to have their point in this maxim of law differentiating between animal and man. It hangs on the difference between *nefesh adam* and *nefesh behemah; nefesh adam* is a *person, nefesh behemah* is a *thing*" (*CL* 24:21). It is on the basis of this Hegelian distinction that Hirsch attempts to rationalize the difference in the biblical treatment of crime against a man and crime against an animal.

The Ontological Hypostatization of Property

From the concept of the free personality and its relationship to unfree things, Hegel tried to deduce the right of the individual to possess property. This theory of property based on the concept of personality originated in rudimentary form with Kant. It was subsequently transformed by Fichte, and reached its ultimate level of sophistication in Hegel:[11] "To be free one must have a sphere of self-assertion in the external world. One's private property provides such an opportunity."[12] The free will of personality, divested of all particularizing contingencies, manifests itself in the sphere of abstract rights by the mode of appropriation of things. By impressing one's personal will upon an object and making the latter a part of one's own being, the will, which is the constitutive element of the person, asserts itself and attains fulfillment. The appropriation of property by the will is therefore essential to freedom. Being absolutely free, the will asserts its right over the thing which lacks the quality of freedom. Hegel thus emphasized that "a person has as his substantive end the right of putting his will into any and every thing and thereby making it his, because it has no such end in itself and derives its destiny and soul from his will. This is the absolute right of appropriation which man has over all 'things' " (PR 41).

In the "Additions" appended to the Philosophy of Right, Hegel elaborated more extensively and presented more lucidly this concept of the appropriation of property and its relation to the concept of freedom:

"To appropriate" means at bottom only to manifest the preeminence of my will over the thing and to prove that it is not absolute, is not an end in itself. This is made manifest when I endow the thing with some purpose not directly its own. When the living thing becomes my property, I give to it a soul other than the one it had before, I give to it my soul. (PR 236)

This communication of "soul" to "things" by the will of personality constitutes the rationale of private property, since the latter has no raison d'être unless the will of personality appropriates it.

The analytical process by which Hegel deduced property from the concept of free will can be summarized thus:

The free will comes into existence as the pure will to freedom. This is "the idea of right" and is identical with freedom as such. But it is only the idea of right and of freedom. The materialization of this idea begins when the emancipated individual asserts his will as a freedom to appropriate.[13]

In Hirsch, the relationship between free personality and the right to property is similar to that posited by Hegel. God, who is absolute free will, has given man the right to appropriate things:

"Human concourse shall be ruled not by the visible or by force, but by the *invisible,* by *ideas* and *right,* the action of the human spirit authorized by God" (*H* 335). Since God has endowed us with personality and freedom, He has also given us the right to property (*CE* 20:2). There is a distinct connection between freedom and property. A slave who is deprived of his freedom is not entitled to property. The right of the Israelites to own property, therefore, began only after their redemption from the Egyptian bondage. When God restored Egyptian slaves to the status of human beings, He gave them the right to own property (*CE* 22:24).[14]

Man's right to possess property and to exercise it fully without any interference is inalienable, and constitutes an integral part of his very essence in the same way that his body must not be violated or harmed: "Just as God gave a body to the human spirit as a tool for his human activities, and the body must be respected for the spirit within it; so He gave him the earth with all that is on it and that belongs to it so that he may freely acquire it and dispose of it according to his destiny" (*H* 334). Hirsch sees the foundation of man's right to property in the biblical expression *ve-khivshuha,*[15] "subdue it": "*Kivshuha* is property; the mastering, appropriating and transforming the earth and its products for human purposes. . . . This makes the acquisition of property itself into a moral duty" (*CG* 1:28).

To Hirsch, the verb *kavash* implies man's dominating will impressing itself forcibly upon a "thing," which thereby acquires his stamp. Hence, he defines *kavash* as "forcibly trodden down so that it cannot arise, to completely force or change and reform something in its innermost nature. This calling to impress *his* stamp on a thing to change it completely to *his* 'thing' man is given only over lifeless nature" (*CG* 1:26).

Man's right to appropriation and mastery over things has an unmistakable Hegelian ring in Hirsch's exegetical elaboration of the biblical expression *va-yirdu,* that man shall "have dominion over the fish of the sea and the birds of heaven and over animals and over the whole earth and over all creeping things that creep on the earth" (*CG* 1:26). In Hirsch's view, the term *va-yirdu* implies man's obligation "to exercise his mastery over living creatures, and on the earth itself, to bring some of them *out* of their *free independence* under his hand for the fulfillment of his human calling" (*CG* 1:26). This definition, as well as its repetition—that the term *u-redu*, "ye shall have dominion," signifies "bringing something out of its free independence into your power, making it subservient to you" (*CG* 1:26)—has its corollary in Hegel's statement that appropriation means primarily "the pre-eminence of my will over the thing and to prove that it is not absolute, is not an end in itself" (*PR* 236).

However, there seems to be a certain reservation on Hirsch's part concerning the extent of man's rights in the appropriation of property. While to Hegel, man's free will on the level of immediacy in the domain of abstract rights seemed to be boundless, Hirsch considers man's mastery over things, particularly over living beings, as contingent. It is not natural man who has the right to master things, which also are a part of nature, but spiritual man, who has elevated himself to the state of God's image. For Hirsch as for Hegel it is spirit that has right over natural things, but nonspiritual things lack such rights. Man, being dualistic, belonging simultaneously to the realm of mind and the realm of nature, is obliged to actualize his spiritual potential, the *tzelem Elohim*. Hirsch therefore contends that if man approaches the realm of things as the representative of God, then "the whole world bows willingly to pure God-serving man. But if man misuses his position, if he does not approach the world as *adam*, as the representative of God, but in his own power of mastery, then even animals do not willingly bow their neck to him" (*CG* 1:26). This dialectical exegesis is apparently tied to Hirsch's theological concept that man's personality and free will emanate directly from the free personality of God, and consequently man's rights of mastery depend on the extent to which his will corresponds to God's will. Although Hirsch does not state it explicitly, his distinction bears a certain similarity to the Roman differentiation between *dominium*, rule over things by the individual, and *imperium*, rule over all individuals by the prince. God, therefore, exercises *imperium* over man, but man has *dominium* over things. However, man's *dominium* over things depends on his complete obedience to, and compliance, with the *imperium* of God.

Hirsch shares Hegel's view on the importance of property. The latter "removed the institution of property from any contingent connection and has hypostatized it as an ontological relation."[16]

While Hirsch may not have gone as far as Hegel in his ontological hypostatization of property, it is nevertheless impossible to ignore his almost metaphysical reverence for it and the importance he attached to private ownership. Although he seems merely to restate the laws and regulations concerning the inviolability of personal property as set down in the Talmud and rabbinic codes, his frequent stress on its importance and its deserved respect makes it unmistakably clear that Hirsch's attitude toward private ownership went beyond mere rabbinic legality. It seems rather to have reflected a then-current Hegelian outlook, or a socioeconomic interest, or both.

To Hirsch, the sanctity of private property was only secondary to the sanctity of human life:

Just as it is God's command that thou shalt not kill or injure, that thou shalt respect the body for the Divine spirit within it, so also is it God's command that thou shalt not steal nor rob. You must respect all human property even though it may be under your control, because of the human spirit which owns it and because of the Divine order by virtue of which it is his; for property is but an artificial extension of the body. (*H* 335)

In his commentary on Deuteronomy, Hirsch further emphasizes the intrinsic connection between the value of life and property and their central position in Jewish law:

Life and property are the two principle valuables which are placed under the protection of the laws of God administered by the state, and their inviolable sanctity in the land of God's Torah proclaimed immediately that land is taken in possession, with, we would say topographic and thereby permanent duration. The cities of refuge distributed to be available throughout the land proclaimed the sanctity of human life, the borders of the holdings being fixed forever proclaimed the sanctity of property. (*CD* 19:14)

In an apologetic endeavor to explain why the Bible permits a person to be sold into slavery for theft but not for any other crime, Hirsch rationalizes this severe punishment by stating that although man's freedom and dignity are paramount, when he offends the metaphysical idea of property he stands to be deprived of even these elementary rights, because theft shows that most direct contempt of the idea of the rights of property, and is exercised just at the time when the owner entrusts his property to the sense of honesty and respect for the Law of his fellow men. Man's whole position in human society begins with the idea of personal possessions, and men prove their right to civilized social life by their respect for the idea of personal possessions. We can understand that it is just in the case of theft only, that the whole personality of the thief is used for the repayment of the theft. (CE 21:6)

Hegel's almost metaphysical reverence for property can be readily understood, for "the Philosophy of Right is the philosophy of middle-class society come to full self-consciousness."[17] Whether this is also true of Hirsch, who was a product of the middle class and served the middle class, or whether he was merely unconsciously following Hegel, is not easy to determine. The fact remains that Hirsch constantly emphasizes the great importance of property:[18]

The property of a person is fundamentally only an extension of his own body; and just as any man with intelligence is responsible for the actions of his own body, so when he takes possession of any unreasoning property, he becomes its guardian and is responsible for any damage it may do, as we have already learned with regard to inanimate property. (CE 21:35)

The view that a person's property—*Menscheneigentum*— contains man's spirit—*Menschengeist*— is also expressed in the *Horeb:*

Property is but an artificial extension of the body. If you steal or rob you sin not against matter but against the invisible human spirit which hovers over it. . . . It is not material how large or how small is the object which you may steal, filch or withhold, no matter how long and from whom you do so. However minute the object, whoever the victim, as long as it is a human being, you commit treason against the human spirit. (H 335, 337)

These passages seem to suggest that man somehow communicates his soul to his property, and consequently the property becomes part of him. In injuring it, we also harm man's soul which resides therein. By the same token, when a man's property causes damage to someone else, it is as if the owner had caused the damage, for it is the owner as the controlling intelligence who is as responsible for watching over the live and lifeless possessions in his own actions (CE 21:35).

The following passage from *Horeb* concisely and succinctly summarizes Hirsch's concept of property and man's right and relationship to it, and his responsibility for it:

Man, in taking possession of the unreasoning world, becomes guardian of unreasoning property and is responsible for the forces inherent in it, just as he is responsible for the forces of his own body; for property is nothing but the artificially extended body and body and property together are the realm and sphere of action of the soul—i.e., of the human personality which rules them and becomes effective through them and in them. Thus is the person responsible for all the material things under his dominion and in his use. (*H* 360)

Modes of Acquisition and Alienation

According to Hegel, the relationship between the will and property is expressed by three types of connection: *(a)* taking possession; *(b)* use of the thing; *(c)* alienation of property. The act of taking possession is designed to concretize the will of personality in relation to the thing, which is devoid of a will of its own. The will of personality cannot, therefore, remain inward and subjective but must be externalized and fully objectified. This externalization must be expressed by some definite assertive act, as occupation, formation, or designation: "We take possession of a thing *(a)* by directly grasping it physically, *(b)* by forming it, and *(c)* by merely marking it as ours" (*PR* 46). The positive act of taking possession also serves to signify that this particular thing was appropriated by a definite, single will to the exclusion of all other wills.[19] Since a given property constitutes the objectification of the will of a person, it follows that disregard for a person's property ought to be considered disrespect for his personality. The most elementary mode of acquisition is direct physical possession. This form, being physical in its manifestation, is of necessity limited.

The second mode of property right is expressed in the *use* of the thing. This prerogative is inherent in the relationship between person and thing. Since the latter does not belong to itself, it can only serve as a means for the former, but has no claim against him: "The relation of use to property is that of accident to substance, outer to inner, force to its manifestation."[20] Hegel, however, recognized that on certain occasions it is possible to separate the use of property from its proprietorship. This separation must of necessity be only temporary. This is personified in a usufructuary possessor whose use of the thing may be completely separated from its nominal owner, or in a mortgagor-mortgagee relationship regarding the use and revenue of an estate similar in relationship to the full ownership and use of property.

Alienation constitutes the third form of connection between will and property.[21] It results directly from the basic concept of acquisition, for just as a person has the right to infuse an object with his will, making it a part of his personality, so he has the right to relinquish it as a *res nullius.* He may also abandon his will with regard to a certain thing, thus creating a volitional vacuum and enabling another will to replace and supersede his own. Hegel, however, believed that man has no right to relinquish his own life; hence, suicide is considered unjustifiable.

The need for modes of acquisition of property was not unfamiliar to Hirsch. They must have seemed to him analogous to similar requirements fixed by the Talmud. The latter provides certain modes of occupation depending on the type of property to be acquired. Thus, the Talmud enumerates such modes of acquisition as the act of delivery *(mesirah),* the act of drawing *(meshikhah),* the act of lifting up *(hagbahah),* and the act of usucaption *(ḥazakah).*[22] In *Horeb,* Hirsch restates the talmudic laws of acquisition in the following manner:

An article passes from its free and ownerless state into man's ownership and becomes part of his personality by real and physical seizure by that personality, (1) by taking it up, the literal *kana (hagbahah);* (2) by drawing it from its original location toward oneself *(meshikhah);* (3) by bringing it within the orbit and the sphere of influence of his artificially extended personality, such as in his house, courtyard, etc. *(ḥatzero);* or finally by open manifestation of his dominion over it—e.g., by productive transformation of it, etc. *(ḥazakah). (H 346)*

According to Hirsch, man was commanded by "the original owner of the world" (*CL* 25:14) to exercise his dominion over the property therein *(ve-khivshuha).* Though apparently Hirsch merely elaborates on the meaning and implication of this biblical term, in doing so he approximates Hegel's concept of property and modes of acquisition. Thus, he maintains that *ve-khivshuha* signifies God's command to man to possess property, to

> master it, i.e., to make it his own by exercising his power over it. So that what a man takes to himself out of the wild, i.e., from a virgin tract that has not yet been appropriated by any other, with the expressed or implied intention to make it his own, that, by the expressed consent of the Original Owner, becomes *"his."* It must be respected and treated as such, and without his consent cannot be transferred into the possession of anybody else. So that for ownerless goods the exercise of force, *kevishah*, just "taking them into possession," *meshikhah*, or *hagbahah*, constitutes a right, they become one's property. (*CL* 25:14)

It is noteworthy that although God gave man the right of possession, it is ineffective by itself; man must exercise the proper modes of acquisition and concretize his free will and exclusive dominion over the property he wishes to possess in an external demonstrative act.

That these external modes are an absolute necessity in the acquisition of property was axiomatic to Hirsch, partly because of the Hegelian influence, but primarily due to his knowledge of the Talmud. He emphasizes that

> all this must be the manifestation of his presumed or actual will of acquisition; for it is only through man's manifest act of designation that the free and ownerless object becomes man's property. But once it has thus been seized by man's *personality*— i.e., has become his property—it must be respected as such by all other human beings; and only through the proprietor's free determination can it either return to its ownerless state or pass on to another person. (*H* 346)

Although Hirsch accepted the physical forms of acquisition prescribed in talmudic law, he seems to have been inclined to regard them as ordained for man in the realm of nature rather than given to man in the realm of law. In nature

> there are no owners and so no personal relations involved, and there alone, force, actual seizing an object is a source of right to it. But here, where goods have already passed into possession, they become part and parcel of their possessor, and not even complementarily is actual "grabbing" to be even an additional title to ownership. Between man and man, rights, and rights, alone, are

to be the source of ownership. Once the right to an object has been acquired, it passes automatically, wherever it happens to be, into the legal possession of the new owner.[23] (*CL* 25:14)

Hirsch saw this idea embodied in the opinion of Rabbi Yohanan, who maintained that according to biblical law the transfer of movable goods *(metaltelin)* is completed with the payment of money without any physical possession. The rabbinic requirement that transfer be accompanied by the act of drawing *(meshikhah)* was dictated by the malpractice and dishonesty which prevailed in commercial dealings. Since men chose to put themselves outside the biblical law that entitled them to ownership on the basis of right rather than on basis of possession, it was necessary for the Rabbis to revert, in transactions involving movables, to modes of acquisition originally applicable in the realm of nature.[24]

Wherever such precautionary measures are not necessary, acquisition may take place in a more symbolic manner. This is especially true in transfers of real estate, which unlike portable property is fixed and easily recovered. Title to real estate, therefore, is acquired not by actual physical possession but by the payment of money, by a document, "which is naught but the expression of the transference of rights incorporated in writing, [but which] is at the same time considered as a transference of the object itself."[25] This type of property can also be acquired by *hazakah,* which is a symbolic act of possession, such as closing in, fencing off, or opening up a recognizable part thereof.[26] Another symbolic mode of acquisition is *halifin,* or *kinyan sudar,* applicable both to land and to movable property (*CL* 25:14; *H* 346). These symbolic modes of acquisition are intrinsically analogous to Hegel's "marking," which has a universal quality.

The modes of acquisition described by Hegel exhibit a gradual process leading from the particular to the universal. The actual grasping of the object to be possessed is by its very nature limited. The use of property is more universal than physical grasping, but less so than marking. The more symbolic the mode of acquisition, the greater is its application:

These modes of taking possession involve the advance from the category of singularity to that of universality. It is only of a single thing that we can take possession physically, while marking a thing as mine is taking possession of it in idea. In the latter case I have an idea of the thing and mean that the thing as a whole is mine, not simply the part which I can take into my possession physically. (*PR* 238)

The notion that symbolic acquisition is preferable to physical acquisition was also held by Hirsch: "Any act of taking it [an object] into one's possession can in no wise and never have the meaning of concretely actually bringing it into one's power, so that, like movable goods, exercising one's power over it could be reckoned as a source of rights to it" (*CL* 25:14). This seems also to be the underlying reason for Hirsch's argument that from the standpoint of biblical law, movable property may be acquired by money, and immovable property—according to the Rabbis—by money, document, or *ḥazakah*. Moreover, *ḥalifin*, being the most symbolic act of all forms of acquisition, applies to both land and to portable goods.

While in Hegel's theory symbolic acquisition implies "taking possession" of the thing as such in a universal way, the use of it implies a still more universal relation to the thing, since when it is used, the thing in its particularity is not recognized but is negated by the user (*PR* 239). Thus, marking a land by fencing, while a proper symbolic acquisition, does not change the character of the land, whereas the use of it, as by planting, transforms it (*PR* 239). Hirsch sometimes employs the term *ḥazakah*, too. Although we previously noted that *ḥazakah* is regarded merely as a symbolic mode of acquisition, Hirsch sometimes defines it, in line with Hegel, as the actual use of the thing. Thus, in *Horeb*, Hirsch describes *ḥazakah* as "productive transformation of property" (*H* 346).

Hegel's view that the complete use of property implies unqualified ownership thereof, although use may be divorced from proprietorship for a temporary period, seems to have had a bearing on Hirsch's notions on the Sabbath, and particularly on the juridical-theological implication of the sabbatical and jubilee years. God is the master and proprietor of the world; His relation to it is that of *dominium directum*. He gave the world to man for his use; man's relation to it is that of *dominium utile*. On the seventh day, however, man must cease his use and mastery of the world, thereby acknowledging its true proprietor, God:

The recognition of God as the master of the world which He created, which Sabbath ensures, the stepping back of man's mastery of the world in face of this recognition, the laying of himself and his creative powers at the feet of God, is the necessary condition for solving the problem of how to bring about the ultimate happiness of humanity. (*CE* 20:11)

The sabbatical year also represents the concept that God is the real proprietor of the land, and that man has only the temporary use of it for six years, at which time it reverts to its original owner (*CL* 25:1-13). Were man to retain mastery over his property indefinitely, it would imply that God's proprietorship is meaningless and void. Man, who is only entitled to its use, would actually usurp the rights of God, the real owner of the world.

Hirsch may have found Hegel's concept of alienation, which gives a person the right to withdraw his will from an object, to be analogous to the talmudic concept of *hefker*. Man may renounce his rights completely thus return the property to its original ownerless state, or he may relinquish his rights in favor of another will. No sooner is the will of the first owner removed than the will of the second replaces it:

Just as he freely acquired it, so can he dispose of it freely. Only if he gives up his right to it—either in general terms, so that it reverts to the earth *(hefker)*, or in favor of a stated person by gift, sale, loan, etc. *(netinah, halva'ah, mekhirah)*— can it be acquired again, in the first case by any, and in the second by the stated, human being.[27] (*H* 334)

We have already noted that Hegel denied man the right to relinquish his own life: "The comprehensive sum of external activity, i.e., life, is not external to personality as that which itself is immediate and a *this*. The surrender or the sacrifice of life is not the existence of *this* personality, but the very opposite. There is therefore no unqualified right to sacrifice one's life" (*PR* 57). The denial of the right of suicide is emphasized in the Bible. Hirsch therefore distinguishes between man's right to kill an animal, which is a thing, and the prohibition against killing oneself:

The animal's body, and blood, and soul are yours, are at your disposal, but your blood which belongs to your soul is mine, is not yours. That, *edrosh*, that I demand as my property, that is there at my disposal, and I demand an account for every drop of it. . . . When God declares *edrosh* concerning blood consigned to human souls, He claims the right to human blood as His possession and denies the right of disposal of our own blood. It primarily forbids suicide. (*CG* 9:5)

Just as Hegel included a small section on contracts in the "Abstract Rights," so Hirsch devotes a small part of *"Mishpatim"* to "justice in transfer of property and in services." Neither Hegel nor Hirsch deals with this problem extensively.

Negation of Universal Right and Its Rectification

The last part of Hegel's "Abstract Rights" deals with the idea of wrong. Wrong arises from disharmony between the universal will and the particular will. It is "an opposition between the principle of rightness and the particular will as that in which right becomes particularized" (*PR* 64). Wrong is therefore a negative phenomenon expressing a will that is only seemingly real, a will whose unreality is revealed when it is judged by the universal standards of right.

Wrong may appear under three different manifestations: *(a)* unpremeditated or nonmalicious wrong, when the deed committed is wrong but the perpetrator of the act is unaware of its unlawfulness; *(b) fraud,* when the wrongdoer is cognizant of his violation of the right but deliberately attempts to conceal it and alleges that he is acting in conformity with the law; and *(c) crime,* when right is openly and flagrantly violated. In the case of nonmalicious, unpremeditated wrong, right as a universal is not infringed upon. Although an act of injustice has been done, the perpetrator considers his act to be in accordance with the principle of right which he sincerely affirms and wishes to uphold. His own subjective interest may obscure his vision of right, but since he has not rejected right as a universal, his act does not require punishment. Fraud and crime, however, where right as such has been willfully transgressed, must be vindicated by punishment in order to be proved a necessary reality. By penalizing the criminal, the universal will annuls the particular will, which is wrongly externalizing itself and destroying its own conception.

The similarities between Hirsch and Hegel regarding the concept of wrong are not difficult to trace. In the case of nonmalicious wrong, there is no need to search for Hirsch's view, since a universal has not been actually violated and both parties engaged in the litigation recognize the validity of right: "Each of the parties wills the right and what is supposed to result to each is the right alone. The wrong of each consists simply in his holding that what he wants is right" (*PR* 245). In this context Hirsch avers: "An assertive oath, at which the one who makes it honestly believes his statement to be true, even if afterwards it is proved to be false, is far removed from any idea of a sinful false oath, and is considered a pure *oness*" (*CL* 5:4). This statement makes it clear that a wrong, in this case an untrue assertive oath committed nonmaliciously— that is, without any wish to infringe universal right—is not liable to punishment.

However, where fraud is present the situation is different, for "at this second level of wrongdoing, the particular will is respected, but universal rightness is not" (*PR* 245). Consequently, this infringement calls for punishment, since the principle of law must be rectified. In *Horeb*, Hirsch dwells at length on the various manifestations of fraud, including falsehood, lying, flattery, and hypocrisy. In this case, the offender "instead of truthfully expressing in words what he has experienced to be real, communicates a false image of it to his brother; who accepts it and bases his behavior on it" (*H* 370). From the ethical point of view, this offense is more wicked than theft, for the latter violates the law, whereas the former completely destroys the foundation and principle of justice upon which the law is based: "The liar steals the first condition of that justice, namely, truth, and gives falsehood in exchange, thus giving birth to injustice; the liar is even more dangerous than the thief. The thief takes only the means of life as such, while the liar takes those of a just life, producing in turn, injustice—and misery" (*H* 370).

The need of punishment for the infringement of the principle of right in the case of fraud is echoed in Hirsch's interpretation of the Law concerning the fraudulent trustee. If the latter swears falsely that the article entrusted to him has been stolen, he is liable to double restitution. The reason for this penalty is that the fraudulent trustee

has been guilty of showing the greatest disdain of the basic principle of general respect for the Law (to atone for which the fine is imposed) inasmuch as he has declared on oath his *pretended upkeeping of this principle* at a time when he himself has committed the greatest crime against the right of property. In *to'en ta'anat gannav* he has misused the principle of respect for the Law, to mock the Law, similarly to a thief, whose theft only becomes possible through the trust with which the owner left his property to the protection of this general respect for the Law. (*CE* 22:8)

In Hegel's definition, therefore, the fraudulent trustee is cognizant of the principle of right that he is violating, but nevertheless takes unfair advantage of the person who sincerely believes and has faith in the principle of right, and on this basis had entrusted to him the article for safekeeping. By pretending that he too subscribes to this principle, the fraudulent trustee deliberately violates it, although he feigns to be acting in conformity with it. It is therefore logical that in the case of fraud, the law must punish the wrongdoer, not only by depriving him of his advantage gained illegally, but by imposing a fine upon him. The latter thus annuls the infraction by the wrongdoer of the principle of right.

This view is echoed by Hirsch when he explains why goods stolen from a thief are not subject to double restitution. Hirsch argues that "one who has obtained possession of an article by mocking at, and disregarding the principle of, the protective power of the general recognition of the rights of property, such a person cannot place that article under the protection of that principle" (*CE* 22:8). The principle of right which the thief deliberately and maliciously exploits cannot protect him against another, similar offender. Only when the principle of right has been vindicated and the wrong fully rectified is the wrongdoer entitled to the protection of the Law. Hirsch emphasizes that the fundamental principle of the Bible is that "everybody has a right to anything, only as long as he respects a similar right in his fellow man" (*CE* 21:25).

According to Hegel, punishment for a crime committed is inherent in the act of the criminal. The fact that the latter has employed force to destroy the principle of right results in his own self-destruction. Since crime openly negates the universal will, it demands punishment, which is the negation of the negation. In civil cases, this negation appears as compensation or restitution; with acts of violence, force possibly may have to be employed to annul the negativism established by a self-contradictory will wrongly manifested.

Similarly, Hirsch upholds the inherent connection between crime and punishment: "By shedding the blood of his brother-man, his own blood has lost its justification, he himself has forfeited the right to go on living" (*CN* 35:33). Like Hegel, Hirsch insists that the relation of punishment to crime is that of negation to negation. Thus, by punishing the criminal, right is restored, and the nullity of the crime becomes manifest:

Nakam—connected with *kum*—is the raising up of Right, Justice which is downtrodden lying on the ground, also used referring to persons. Not the stricken one who cannot be brought back to life, but the stricken principle of Right is to be avenged, to be re-erected. (*CG* 4:15)

Hegel's influence on Hirsch is further evident in the implication that punishment held for them both. According to Hegel, punishment must not be regarded as a deterrent or as a means to reform the criminal. Punishment is an act of justice; consequently, it is not a means to an end but an end in itself. Punishment may indeed have utilitarian concomitants, but these are incidental, not primary or essential. To consider punishment as anything other than an act unqualifiedly demanded by justice—such as deterrent, educational, or reformative—is to place man in the category of an animal whose obedience comes out of fear, not reason. Hirsch identifies himself with this Hegelian position when he asserts: "Behind the judicial punishment ordained by the Torah, there is neither the idea of deterrence nor of retaliation" (*CG* 9:6). Deterrence is neither the prime objective of nor the motive for punishment: "To the intelligent, all punishments are *kapparah*, atonement" (*CG* 9:6).

Hirsch was naturally aware that the Bible tied in punishment with the notion of deterrence. Thus, in the cases of a seducer to idolatry (*CD* 13:7–12), plotting witnesses (*CD* 19:15–21), a judge who defies the ruling of the supreme court (*CD* 17:12–13), and a disobedient son (*CD* 21:18–21), the Bible seems to emphasize that the death penalty should be carried out in public so that "all Israel shall hear and fear." However, Hirsch maintains "the fact that the publicity or the publication of the carrying out of the death sentence is demanded only for these four cases proves that otherwise, in general, deterrence is *not* the motive for punishments" (*CG* 9:6).

Although Hegel insisted on retribution as the only way to eliminate and nullify crime, he unconditionally objected to any manifestation of revenge. Punishment must never contain any element of the particular will, since this would actually be a form of legitimized revenge. While Hegel admitted that requital cannot be made to equal the crime, murder must be punished by death: "The reason is that since life is the full compass of a man's existence, the punishment here cannot simply consist in a 'value' for none is great enough, but can consist only in taking a second life" (*PR* 247). However, even when the life of the murderer must be taken, there should be no thought of revenge. Hegel therefore insisted that punishment should be meted out, not as *crimina privata*, but as *crimina publica* (*PR* 73). In the former, a residue of revenge is unavoidable, rendering the punishment defective.

Hirsch agrees with Hegel that murder must be punished by the death penalty: "By shedding the blood of his brother-man, his own blood has lost its justification, he himself has forfeited the right to go on living" (*CN* 35:33). It is the very act of the murderer that justifies his execution. The criminal who takes a person's life "feels the same blade drawn against him that he used against his fellow man" (*CE* 20:13). However, Hirsch also insists that while capital punishment is justified and even mandatory, it must be free of any element of revenge, since the latter is not an act of justice designed to nullify the crime, but constitutes a new wrong:

All attempts to look on the death penalty as taking revenge on the criminal, as a deterrent, or even only as a repayment, are opposed. If any of these were the case it [the Bible] would indubitably have had to say *ve-lakahta*, that the forfeited life has to be taken from the murderer. *Ve-natata* makes us look on the punishment as "restitution" making good again the damage done by the murder, whether to justice, to the Law, to the idea of the value and dignity of a human life, or to all of these, which overlap each other. The community has to *give up* the life of the criminal to these ideas, which have been destroyed by the crime.[28] (*CE* 21:23)

The severity of the punishment in cases of murder is connected with the concept of personality. Murder is a direct attack on personality, which, for Hirsch—as for Hegel—constitutes the cornerstone of all law: "Murder is to be looked upon as a scornful denial of the *tzelem-elohim* nature of a human being. So that murdering anybody is an attack on the godly nature of the whole of the human race, and in particular that of the circle to which the victim belonged" (*CE* 21:20). It is for this very reason, Hirsch maintains, that the Bible commands the execution of an animal that has killed a man. The execution of the animal is not motivated by a primitive desire for vengeance, nor is it intended to prevent a similar incident or to punish the owner for not having curbed his property. The fundamental reason for this penalty is to secure the importance and preeminence of the human personality, "to keep the God-like dignity of the earthly life of a human being vividly conscious in the human mind" (*CE* 21:28).

Hirsch sees the principle of human personality as underlying the biblical precept that kidnapping is punishable by death. Robbing a person of his freedom, which is, as already noted, an integral part of his will, is regarded as "social murder" to be punished equally with murder (*CE* 21:16).

Eclectic Reinterpretation

Hirsch's treatment of the section *"Mishpatim"* is illustrative of his mode of reasoning. Unable to apply Hegelian concepts to the entire range of Judaism, he endeavors to apply them wherever possible. To Hirsch, the laws under this classification seemed to correspond to Hegel's abstract laws. Notwithstanding the fact that the former lack the dialectical progression of the latter, they seem to possess many analogous aspects. Applying the rationale ascribed in his commentary on the Pentateuch to the laws classified in the *Neunzehn Briefe* and in the *Horeb* under *"Mishpatim,"* we realize that although the strict, systematic, dialectical pattern of Hegel's *Rechtsphilosophie* is lacking, many of the Hegelian concepts, explanations, and rationalizations are present.

To recapitulate, we have seen that Hirsch interprets certain Jewish laws as having a distinct Hegelian connotation. One is the unusual emphasis on the importance of free will in its relationship to right. Although Jewish law insists upon awareness *(da'at),* sometimes even contrary to will,[29] Hirsch consistently stresses the element of will in both its theological and juridical senses. His concept of personality and his almost reverential metaphysical attitude toward property can be explained only in the light of the central position they occupy in Hegel's philosophy of right. As a religious mentor, Hirsch could not be as aloof as Hegel in stripping the *mishpatim,* which also constitute a part of divine legislation, of any element of ethicality. Hegel could afford to treat morality as a separate entity in a separate section of his *Rechtsphilosophie,* a thought that was perhaps repugnant and even sacrilegious to Hirsch when applied to Torah. Hirsch therefore seeks to ethicize many of the Hegelian views and to endow them with ethical-religious meaning in place of their socioeconomic implications as set down by Hegel. Hirsch elevates the institution of private property—which plays an important role in Hegel's philosophy—to a theological plane, whereas in Hegel it is devoid of any such connotation:

No universal order has entered Hegel's deduction, nothing that bestows the sanction of a universal right upon individual appropriation. No God has been invoked to ordain and justify it, nor have men's needs been cited as responsible for producing it.[30]

Hirsch's modes of acquisition and alienation of property also show traces of Hegelian reasoning behind the rabbinic terminology that he employs to discuss them.

Hegel classified wrong in the category of abstract right, where the element of morality does not enter into consideration: *"The Philosophy of Right* does not place wrong in any moral category but introduces it under the head of 'Abstract Right.' Wrong is a necessary element in the relationship of individual owners to one another."[31] While Hirsch's similar classification of wrong under the head of *"Mishpatim"* is not of crucial significance, particularly since he did not keep law and morality strictly apart, the concepts subsumed under wrong, such as fraud, murder, punishment, and revenge, seem to indicate Hegel's influence.

The treatment of the laws in *"Mishpatim"* clearly shows that Hirsch pragmatically employs Hegelian views and concepts where he thinks them applicable. It is extremely significant that Hirsch is able to transvaluate the materialistic understructure into a religious one, thus underpinning the shaky biblical-talmudic-juridical superstructure:

At its roots the *Philosophy of Right* is materialist in approach. Hegel exposes in paragraph after paragraph the social and economic under-structure of his philosophic concepts.[32]

For his part, Hirsch employs all his ingenuity, knowledge, and homiletical skill to transform portions of this philosophy of right into a rationale supporting the validity and the eternity of a juridical system considered by his opponents archaic, if not actually defunct.

11

"Hukkim": Laws of Justice toward Animate and Inanimate Objects

Relating to the Nonrational

The fourth division of the *Horeb* is entitled *"Ḥukkim."* According to its subtitle, it consists of "laws of righteousness toward those beings which are subordinate to man: toward earth, plant, animal, toward one's own body, mind, spirit, and word." Similarly, it is defined in the *Neunzehn Briefe* as "statements of justice toward subordinate creatures by reason of the obedience due to God; that is, justice toward earth, plants, and animals, or, if they have become assimilated with your personality, toward your own body and soul" (*NL* 104).

The difference between the laws of the *"Mishpatim"* and those of the *"Ḥukkim"* is the difference between man's relation to man and man's relation to nature. The laws of the *"Mishpatim"* division, regulating the relationships between man and man, operate in the social sphere, where empathy is possible: "Your duties towards humanity are more intelligible to you simply because you have only to think of yourself, your own views and feelings, in order to recognize and sympathize with the demands and needs of your fellow man" (*NL* 111). The laws of the *"Ḥukkim"* division regulate the relationships between man and nature, of which he has no understanding. It is, therefore, quite possible for man to abuse nature, since he does not encounter the opposition of a conscious will. Unrestricted by a higher protective law, man may

315

destroy the world which he ought to cultivate.

Since in his relationship with nature man is unable to guide himself by empathy, he must be guided by laws of the *"Ḥukkim"* which were instituted by God in full comprehension of nature. These laws do not emanate from "the concept of identical personality" (*NL* 110) but flow from the "fundamental notion of equal subordination to God, who defends all which is lower in order and subject to you against your caprice and the ebullitions of unregulated will" (*NL* 110–11).

The *ḥukkim* are neither arbitrary nor irrational laws, although some of them may seem so due to man's limited knowledge of the realm of nature. Had man a more profound understanding, many of the *ḥukkim* would seem reasonable to him: "Could you put yourself as thoroughly in the place of other beings, could you even understand the conditions of the union and the combined activity of your own body and soul, you would find it as easy to comprehend *ḥukkim* as *mishpatim"* (*NL* 111).

Nature is a great intelligent order created in accordance with a remarkable design in which each aspect of nature has its place, function, and destiny. Nothing in nature is superfluous or so self-contained that it has no benevolent effect on the rest, and together all represent a universal harmony: "One glorious chain of love, of giving and receiving, unites all creatures; none is by or for itself, but all things exist in continual reciprocal activity—the one for the all; the all for the one" (*NL* 29).

The teleological Weltanschauungen of Kant and Hegel contributed immeasurably to such a harmonious view of nature, which is rooted in ancient and medieval theistic concepts. Kant in particular emphasized the unconscious *telos* inherent in every aspect of nature, which he termed "purposiveness without purpose."[1] Although the optimism regarding the harmony of nature was subsequently shattered in the eighteenth and nineteenth centuries by Darwin, to Hirsch that divine harmony was still reigning.

The transition from *mishpatim* to *ḥukkim* had always presented a problem to Jewish philosophers and theologians. Unlike the *ḥukkim*, the *mishpatim* are rational and therefore in no need of divine confirmation; but the *ḥukkim* remained problematic. Many of them were irrational or at best nonrational. Their divine origin made them mandatory, but never explicable. Saadia's characterization of the *ḥukkim* as "commandments of obedience" in contradistinction to "commandments of reason" did nothing to clarify their relevance. Like the Fayyumite philosopher, Mendelssohn centuries later strongly emphasized the need for compliance with the commandments without doing anything to make them any more reasonable or relevant.

In the post-Mendelssohnian era, the position of these "commandments of obedience" became untenable, since conforming to laws for which no explanation could be offered seemed an insult to human reason, dignity, and freedom. Therefore, Hirsch makes every possible effort to mitigate the irrationality of the *ḥukkim* by pointing to the absence of any demarcation in the Bible in its enumeration of *ḥukkim* and *mishpatim*. The consecutive order of these laws in the Book of Leviticus, in which both categories of law commingle, indicates an underlying relationship between them: "They must act mutually toward forming one another and be mutually complementary to each other" (*CL* 19:18).

To underscore the importance of the metarational *ḥukkim*, Hirsch points out that the very first law God addressed to man belonged to this category. The prohibition not to eat of the fruit of the tree of knowledge was a *ḥok*, since no reason for it was ever given. Moreover, that first law contained all the characteristics that modern Jews are critical of: it was a negative commandment, irrational, of a dietary nature, and, as mentioned, it was, to Eve and her children, an oral law.

With this prohibition the education of man for his moral, high, godly calling begins. It is the beginning of the history of mankind, and shows all following generations the path they are to tread. It is a *prohibition*, and it is not a so-called "reasonable prohibition," no *mitzvah sikhlit*, but rather one which all human means of judgment speak against; taste, sight, appeal to imagination and mind are all in favor of eating the fruit. Of oneself one would never have come to forbid it, and even after the prohibition no other reason for it could possibly have been found than the absolute will of God; accordingly it is a *ḥok* in *optima forma*. Furthermore, it is a dietary law, and it reached the one to whom it applied only by way of tradition, oral communication. . . . At every demand of God's laws of morality every one of us still stands, like the first human pair, before the tree of this knowledge and has to decide whether he will follow the voice of his bodily sensuality, his own judgment and sense, and the wisdom of instinctive animal life, or, conscious of his higher calling, the voice of his God. (*CG* 2:16)

The difference between *mishpatim* and *ḥukkim* lies not in their intrinsic rationality or irrationality, but in our ability to empathize. *Mishpatim*, as already pointed out, deal with man's relations to man, and *ḥukkim* with man's relations to nonhumans, which makes *ḥukkim* no less rational. Only when man elevates himself to a total view of the cosmic order will the *ḥukkim*—which seem so irrational from his limited vantage point—assume their true rational significance. Since such cosmic comprehension is rare, man has to forfeit understanding and simply abide by these seemingly enigmatic laws: "From the summit of these lofty demands, the Torah now makes us look into the sphere of the whole organic world lying deep beneath us, to show us that [the] world too, is a world of God's laws" (*CL* 19:19).

Use and Abuse

The starting point for the *"Ḥukkim"* division is the prohibition against wanton destructiveness. Hirsch's main thesis sounds like an introduction to a modern book on ecology. If we assume that there is order, design, and purpose in nature, then the needless felling of a tree is contrary to the original divine plan. Although man is endowed with claims upon nature, he is obliged to use it responsibly, for the improvement of man or for nature. For this reason, nature was given to man "to till it and tend it."[2] This implies a privilege and an obligation. By employing the bounties of nature properly, "nature itself finds its appointed purpose promoted" (*CG* 2:15). Man must therefore be sure not to abuse nature or capriciously waste its resources since their constructive utilization means fulfilling the purpose for which they were created, thus actualizing the original intent that brought them into existence: "By his work on it [the earth], man raises its purely physical nature into playing a part in the sphere of the moral purposes of the world" (*CG* 2:5).

Heedless destruction implies man's arrogance in proclaiming himself the absolute master of the world. By such acts he displays contempt for nature and disregard for God, who created it. Hirsch therefore takes the prohibition against destroying trees in a time of siege[3] as the fundamental law of all *ḥukkim*, accepting it in its widest connotation and most far-reaching ramifications. It "is the first law which is opposed to your presumption against things: Regard things as God's property and use them with a sense of responsibility for wise human purposes" (*H* 401).

This law against wanton destruction therefore constitutes the underlying principle upon which man must relate himself to the realm of nature or "things" of which he has no experiential knowledge. He has to use nature judiciously, intelligently, and in accordance with the laws of the Torah, because those laws, seemingly incomprehensible to man, are based on the infinite profound understanding of nature possessed only by its divine creator.

Destructiveness is not only caused by excessive use but by extreme denial as well; through his avarice, man withholds the bounties of nature that God granted him to share with others. The miser who denies his possessions to society is acting contrary to the divine understanding of the purpose of wealth. Through the denial of his possessions, he indicates that he rather than God is the master of the mundane riches. Furthermore, he shows that possessions are an end in themselves, rather than a means to a greater moral and spiritual goal.

The Great Le-Mino Law

There is yet another form of destruction—the tampering with the order of creation. The pre-Darwinian teleological view that nature, despite its dissimilar manifestations and enigmatic phenomena, constitutes a harmonious whole was affirmed by many, including Kant. According to Kant, "the teleological view of an organism is not only that as a whole it is adapted to a purpose or end, but that every organ is also adapted to a purpose or end which is an element in the total purpose or end."[4] Furthermore, Kant maintained that reason "in considering living beings must necessarily accept the principle that no organ, no faculty, no impulse, indeed nothing whatsoever, is either superfluous or disproportionate to its use, but that everything is exactly adapted to its purpose [*Bestimmung*] in life."[5]

Kant's view of nature, shared by his contemporaries and by many in the first part of the nineteenth century, was not "arbitrary or irrational but an essentially rational and necessary product."[6] Although we may not know *das Ding an sich* —the thing itself— of the natural manifestations, we have sufficient data to assume it. Such a view is conducive to the prohibition of man's tampering with the species of nature. Assuming that each of them has a definite *Bestimmung* toward whose fulfillment it is moving, man had no right to change its course. Since man's knowledge of nature is limited exclusively to its phenomena—and even that is not fully comprehensible to him—he must avoid mixing the species of creation—deliberately intermingling them by copulation of diverse animals or grafting of trees of different kinds—since the transformations may have disastrous consequences which man cannot foresee. Hirsch maintains that the Torah understands the noumenal aspect of nature, and that this prohibits the intermingling of species: "You should not interfere with the natural order which you find fixed by God in His world for its ultimate good" (*H* 402).

Man's conformity to the *ḥukkim* is not an abdication of reason: "Even if we were possessed of all human knowledge, we should still know only the external appearance of things" (*H* 402). Nevertheless, Hirsch endeavors "as far as we are able to do so with our limited powers to gain some insight into the laws which ask us to respect the divine order of the universe" (*H* 402). Hirsch's effort to rationalize these nonrational laws and to penetrate their impenetrable meaning came about in response to the enormous challenges posed to these laws by his contemporaries. The *ḥukkim* had always been the most controversial category of the Jewish normative system; the Rabbis described them as laws with which Satan and the Gentiles taunt the Jews, demanding: "What is this command and what reason is there for it?" For this reason, the Torah termed these laws *ḥukkim*, implying that they are a divine enactment that no man may question.[7]

However, what may have satisfied Satan and the Gentiles failed to satisfy the Jews of the nineteenth century. The latter, living in an era when freedom and reason were valued as the most priceless possessions of man, could not abide by any enactments which negated these advantages. The conjectural view that the *ḥukkim* may possess a noumenal significance was insufficient to validate them to these Jews and could hardly be accepted as imperative. Moreover, the noumenal domain posited by Kant was hermetically closed to man, who could not penetrate it with his reason, while at the same time it made no claim upon him. The *hukkim*, however, did make such demands and hence they could not be easily justified on the basis of the Kantian epistemological dichotomy.

Aside from the philosophical considerations, it must not be overlooked that many of the *hukkim* interfered with the ordinary life of the Jew. They regulated his diet, apparel, and conjugal relationships, to mention but a few significant areas. In this fashion, the Jew was constantly brought into conflict with the *hukkim*, and their violation became in many circles the rule rather than the exception. Hirsch therefore proposes a rationale for the *hukkim* which had heretofore been avoided and even forbidden. Employing the highly respected inductive method, he arrives at the hypothesis underlying the *hukkim* —which he calls the great law of species, *das grosse le-mino-Gesetz*. Accordingly, "every creature first transforms all that it absorbs from creation into suitable food for itself, enlarging itself, and then uses the surplus of its corresponding powers to generate a being similar to itself" (*H* 408). This view, as previously indicated, coincides with the teleological concept of nature commonly held in the pre-Darwinian era. With the modesty of a scientist and the piety of a traditionalist Hirsch then concludes that even should his hypothesis prove incorrect, the mandatory character of the *hukkim* remains inviolable: "Even if we stand far from the truth with these thoughts, it is not these or other human thoughts which form the basis of our obligation" (*H* 410).

On the basis of this *le-mino-Gesetz*, Hirsch explains five *hukkim:* copulation of diverse animals, grafting of diverse trees, yoking together of diverse animals, wearing of *sha'atnez*, and mixing of milk and meat.

Of these five, the first two seem most obviously to conform to the *le-mino* principle. The fact that this prohibition also extends to the sowing of mixed seeds "only effects a mental acknowledgment of the great world lawgiver, who reveals Himself in the law of species which is so wonderfully kept even in the world of vegetable life" (*CD* 22:9).

No apparent changes in nature take place in the yoking of diverse animals. The law prohibiting it is not evidently intended as a means of preserving the species. This is probably why Hirsch offered a subsequent explanation for this law in his commentary on Deuteronomy. Since yoking diverse animals does not produce a negative effect on their nature, the prohibition against it serves as rather a moral symbol for the Jew, reminding him of the distinctive role he has been assigned in the history of humanity. The le-mino law appoints different tasks to different species on different levels. Just as these differences are concretized by setting different animals apart, so the Jew has to contemplate his mission amid the rest of mankind (CD 22:10).

The above laws, although in need of interpretation, are primarily academic. There were few Jews whose daily lives could clash with these religious laws. The socioeconomic reality of the then-current Jewish existence made these laws irrelevant; farming was no longer a Jewish occupation, and so laws concerning crossbreeding, grafting, and yoking had no practical significance. However, the prohibition against sha'atnez, the wearing of garments whose fabric is combined wool and linen, presented a practical problem. Hirsch's dialectic waxes in proportion to the difficulty of obtaining observance of this law. According to his explanation in the Horeb, the prohibition of sha'atnez is rooted in the primeval days of Cain and Abel, who represent two distinct cultures in the early stages of human development, the agricultural and the pastoral. In the former, man "clings to his possessions and develops external technical skill" (H 409); in the latter, he has "more freedom of movement [and] can devote more attention to his inner development" (H 409). Man therefore should not clothe himself in a garment which is constituted of a fabric symbolic of the combination of these two distinct trends.[8]

The weakness of this argument apparently compelled Hirsch years later to suggest another explanation that is similar to the one concerning the yoking of two different kinds of animal. Like the latter, sha'atnez apparel is not an interference with nature, but its prohibition a reminder to the Jew to safeguard his spiritual and ethical distinctiveness (CL 19:19). That such a reminder should be limited to wool and linen suggests to Hirsch a rationale reminiscent of the Jewish medieval concept of the four elements of creation: inert, vegetative, sentient, rational, or spiritual. Linen represents the vegetative element and wool, the sentient one—

elements present in both animals and man. The vegetative element consists of nutrition and reproduction, and the sentient element consists of perception and movement. However, an animal's
higher endowments are used only to gratify its lower vegetative
nature: "Perception, feeling and motion are used entirely in the
service of the vegetative purposes, the urge for food and reproduction" (*CL* 19:19).

Man possesses both these elements, vegetative and sentient, but
in addition, he is endowed with a spirit. Vulnerable as man is,
there is always the danger that like the animal he might subordinate his higher qualities to the gratification of the lower. That is
the reason the Torah commands man not to wear any fabric in
which wool and linen are interwoven, just as he is commanded to
keep his spiritual aspect separate from his animalistic nature. Each
and every element in man ought to be confined to its proper
function. Moreover, it is the lower aspect which should serve the
higher, not vice versa: "Not downwards toward vegetative sensuality, upwards toward the pinnacle of mankind, to the understanding and God-like free-willed mind of man, is the animal element
in him to ennoble itself in accomplishing purposes which are holy
to God" (*CL* 19:19).

The last of the five *le-mino ḥukkim* enumerated by Hirsch is the
law prohibiting the mixing of milk and meat. This was the most
controversial law of all, since it created numerous problems in
daily life, within the household and outside it. It also constituted
an intellectual problem which could not be easily explained away
on the basis of separation of species. Milk and meat both come
from the same animal and each are separately permissible, but
together they are most strictly forbidden. Even when boiled together and given as a gift to a non-Jew they represent a transgression.

Hirsch's explanation of this law in the *Horeb* is brief. Meat and
milk, despite their apparent relatedness, are contrasts, "the former belonging to the animal self and the latter separated for the
preservation of the species" (*H* 409). However, in the course of
time Hirsch apparently realized that a more adequate rationale
was called for, and in his commentary he offers an explanation
analogous to the one he gives for *sha'atnez:* milk, like linen, represents the vegetative element, and meat, like wool, the sentient

element. In higher animals "these two joint systems, the animal and the vegetable, appear in two separate parts. The diaphragm separates the body of the animal into a vegetable realm of alimentation and reproduction and a purely animal realm of movement and thought" (CE 23:19). The animal, however, knows no such distinction and is entirely dominated by its vegetative aspect: "The animal is nothing more than a moving and living plant" (CE 23:19). Its entire existence revolves around food and sex.

To prevent man from becoming degraded to the animal level, he is commanded to avoid the "animal and animal vegetable in intimate intermixture" (CE 23:19). The prohibition of milk and meat concretizes the admonition that "thought and action are not to fall under the domination of alimentation and sexual life" (CE 23:19). The separation of milk and meat is a reminder to man that although his organism is constituted of vegetative and sentient elements, they are meant to serve his spirit: "Their function is no longer to mutually intermix and serve each other but both to subordinate themselves to the *human* and to let themselves be penetrated and led by the spiritual-moral human creature" (CE 23:19).

Consideration and Respect

Some of the laws which Hirsch subsumes under "*Ḥukkim*" are not alien to man's reason or feeling. Laws against maltreatment of animals are neither irrational nor hard to justify, but since these laws concern man's relationship to nonhumans, Hirsch includes some of them in this division:[9] the laws of sparing the mother bird,[10] assisting an animal in distress,[11] not killing an animal and its offspring on the same day,[12] and not muzzling an animal while treading out the corn.[13]

Some of these laws of compassion have other reasons besides prevention of cruelty to animals. Sparing the mother bird is intended to teach man to respect all creatures while they are preforming the functions for which they were created. The Torah forbids the appropriation of the mother bird "at the moment of its service to its species" (H 412). Hirsch echoes Maimonides's view about the feeling of animals. Maimonides stated that killing an animal with its offspring on the same day is prohibited so that people should be restrained and prevented from killing the two together in such a manner that the young is slain in the sight of the mother; for the pain of animals under such circumstances is very great. There is no difference in this case between the pain of man and the pain of other living beings, since the love and tenderness of the mother for her young ones is not produced by reasoning but by imagination, and this faculty exists not only in man but in most living things.[14]

Hirsch applies this view to the need for kindness toward animals in general: "Man so easily forgets that injured animal muscle twitches like human muscle, that the maltreated nerves of an animal sicken like human nerves, that the animal being is just as sensitive to cuts, blows, and beating as man" (*H* 415). Furthermore, Hirsch points to the specific moral and educational value of these laws for man. They were designed to ennoble his feeling and make him sensitive to the plight of every creature. Disregard for the suffering of nonhuman creatures may result in insensitivity to the agony of human beings: "The boy who, in crude joy, finds delight in the convulsions of an injured beetle or the anxiety of a suffering animal will soon also be dumb toward human pain" (*H* 416).[15]

Consideration extends not only to sentient animals but also to the corpse of man. Although the essence of man is his divine spirit, his body must also be accorded the proper respect. During man's lifetime, his soul and body constitute an indivisible unit, but after the soul has departed, the body must be returned to the earth "so that it might serve a new life formation in the household of creation" (*H* 419). Burial serves a dual purpose by returning the body's natural elements to nature after the soul no longer needs them. Thus, burial is a fulfillment "toward the elemental world in its demands upon the human body" (*H* 420) while it also protects the dignity of man by preventing the disintegration and decomposition of the mortal frame (*CD* 21:23).

Respect for life and nature includes respect for man's own life and health. Man is neither the sole master of the world surrounding him nor the owner of his self. His body, life, health, energy, ability, and talents were given to him by God. Man therefore has no right to determine whether he wishes to continue or discontinue his existence. Only God who grants life has the right to take it. Man has no such right. Suicide is therefore tantamount to murder. It also constitutes a flagrant interference with the divine plan:

everything in nature was created to play a part in the cosmic design; by terminating his own life, man goes against the will of God.

Hirsch considers suicide not merely a sin in the theological sense but a social offense as well. It is an escape from responsibility which in itself is a crime against the circle of human beings with whom the potential suicide is related, associated, or involved. Even when circumstances seem to have conspired against man, he has no right to surrender to the temptation that suicide offers but instead must transform his life into a blessing. Not only suicide, but any form of deprivation which might endanger man's health, is forbidden. Both body and spirit were created by God and must be preserved by man (*H* 429). For this reason, asceticism, extolled in other religions, is undesirable and even sinful in Judaism.

Since man must respect his body, the Torah prohibits self-mutilation and disfigurement (*CL* 19:28; *CD* 14:1–2). Such practices, common in antiquity as forms of mourning, are strongly condemned in Judaism. Allowances are made for the expression of grief and sorrow over the loss of a relative, but excessive mourning is prohibited. Excessive mourning in the form of self-mutilation signifies boundless despair and an implicit denial of divine reason and purpose in both life and death. It seems to indicate that death terminates not only man's physical existence but also his spiritual life, rendering all existence futile. Judaism, however, views death as a transition from one form of existence to another: "Death leads out of life to life, out of being here to being there; here as there, a realm of the one God, of life and love" (*CL* 19:28).

Once man affirms this view, he will not resort to self-destructive practices: "However dear and valuable, however important the existence of somebody else may be to us, our own importance and our own worth may never end with the end of his existence, may never even be allowed to lessen" (*CL* 19:28).

External Distinctiveness and Spiritual Superiority

To impress man with the sanctity of his body, certain rules are set forth with regard to his outward appearance. Thus, the Torah forbids trimming of the hair of the temples or rounding the corners of the head.[16] Similarly, it is forbidden to shave with a razor.[17] All these enactments remind the Jew "that his body belongs to God and that he is duty bound to keep it holy" (*H* 432).

These restrictions, particularly that of shaving with a razor, were widely violated in the nineteenth century, and Hirsch fortified these laws with a more sophisticated rationale than the one he offers in *Horeb*. In his commentary on Leviticus he suggests that the Torah "forbids the removal of the externally visible division between the frontal part of the head and the rear part of it, coinciding with the cerebrum and the cerebellum respectively" (*CL* 19:27). The cerebellum controls muscle coordination common to man and animal; the cerebrum is the largest, most complex part of the brain controlling the higher, distinctively human functions such as thinking, memory, perception, consciousness, and voluntary acts.

The cerebrum is symbolic of man since it is the part where all his psychological and intellectual activities are integrated. The division between the cerebellum and the cerebrum is outwardly marked by the hair of the temple, and Hirsch suggests that the Torah intends that man shall not obliterate the visible distinction between these two parts of the brain, which remind him of "the existence of these two specifically different elements in man's nature, and of the higher dignity of the intellectual moral spiritual factor to which the animal factor has to subordinate itself and be kept in the background" (*CL* 19:27).

The prohibition against shaving also has a physiopsychological basis. The two most important bones of the human face are the maxilla and the mandibula. In mastication, common to animal and man, the mandibula is the most active, while the maxilla and the rest of man's upper face, which "pertain primarily to the spiritual intellectual activities of the mind" (*CL* 19:27), are passive. In adult males, the mandibula is covered with hair, leaving "only the purely intellectual human face exposed to view" (*CL* 19:27). By preserving the beard, man demonstrates that his preeminence lies in the human aspect represented by the hair-free maxilla. The mandibula, which represents his animalistic aspect, ought to remain covered.

The fact that Jewish tradition does not insist upon the wearing of a beard but merely prohibits shaving it with a razor, Hirsch explains, is sufficient to remind man of his spiritual superiority. The avoidance of a razor serves "as a reminder not to destroy this hair which veils the 'sensual part' of man's countenance and to take to heart the lesson it preaches, not to trifle away his manly calling" (*CL* 19:27). The requirement of distinguishing between the intellectual and the sensual parts of man's face is made only of the male, "who is more inclined of sexual depravity than the female" (*CL* 19:27). No similar demand is made of women, "thanks to the innate modesty of their nature" (*CL* 19:27).

A Spiritual Eugenic Hypothesis

The laws against immorality and promiscuity are part of the *"Ḥukkim"* division. God implanted the desire for procreation in men and women, and they have no right to abuse this profound drive but must channel it toward the sacred purpose for which it was given: "Every union of the sexes which is not done for this purpose is a misuse of the given powers, is a degradation of man to the level of the animal" (*H* 436), and thus contributes to the decline of civilization.

The Torah insists upon absolute morality and modesty. Men must not wear women's clothes or women men's, so that the boundaries of modesty can be strictly preserved (*H* 433). Hirsch attributes the puzzlement over the Torah's numerous consanguine restrictions to man's limited knowledge. He makes no attempt to rationalize them on the basis of health or of mental and social hygiene: "If it is difficult to understand the reasons for the laws of God in general, it is doubly difficult to understand the reason for these [particular] laws, which deal with the mystery of life and death. We know so little about the beginning and end of our life" (*H* 441).

In his commentary on the Bible, Hirsch attempts to offer a rationale based on a eugenic hypothesis: "To obtain nobler and higher species of plants and animals, human gardeners and breeders do not leave the planting of seeds for the production of the desired objects to chance and do not allow any and every kind of seed to mix, or to be planted in any and every condition or time" (*CL* 18:6). This view, Hirsch suggests, may be the underlying reason for the even stricter limitations imposed in the chain of gradation. The higher the station, the more stringent the marital restrictions. For this reason, the laws governing the conjugal relations of priests, and especially of the high priest, are the severest of all.

In his commentary on Leviticus, Hirsch proposes another reason for the prohibition of consanguine marriages. According to this view, the Torah considers marriage as the beginning of a union from which will issue a multiplicity of new relationships. Since consanguinity implies the preexistence of relationships other than sex, a union of close relatives will not contribute anything to spiritual enhancement: "The less there is in existence before marriage any bond of attachment of family love, the more that strongest form of attachment starts with marriage, the more does the sexual side of marriage become a basic factor in the whole moral sphere of happy married life full of love in every phase" (*CL* 18:6). In consanguine marriage where love already existed, the addition of the sex dimension would tend to degrade the previous relationships rather than ennoble them: "A mother cannot become a wife without ceasing to be a mother, a sister cannot be a wife without ceasing to be a sister" (*CL* 18:6).

Marriage between two dissimilar individuals is preferable since it is better that husband and wife complement each other. In consanguine marriages, the chances are that husband and wife may have the same virtues and the same faults: "The union would only strengthen and intensify the characteristics in both directions, good and bad, but they would not complement each other" (*CG* 2:24). But despite all these explanations and rationalizations, Hirsch admits even in his more elaborate commentary that the true reason for these restrictions eludes man's understanding:

The reasons for His laws on the choice of mates surely lies deep in the very source of human nature, unfathomable to man himself, and are certainly only clear and apparent to the One who can see the result already when it is just beginning to form, and who has woven, and weaves, that most mysterious combination, the union of heavenly spirit and earthly body. (*CL* 18:6)

Psychosomatic Interaction

As already indicated in the discussion of the law prohibiting the mixing of milk and meat, the entire regimen of the dietary laws was challenged in Hirsch's generation. Even those who conceded that Judaism is an ethical religion failed to realize the connection between morality and diet. A credible rationale for these laws was imperative but unavailable. Medical science had not yet discovered any harm in the consumption of nonkosher foods, or any benefits to man's health in abstention from them, which precluded Hirsch's using any medical or hygienic rationale in his interpretation of the dietary laws: "It is not our bodily health, but our spiritual and moral purity and capability, our *kedushah,* our being ready, our becoming ready, our remaining ready for everything which is godly and pure, which is the expressed object of the lawgiver of these laws" (*CE* 22:30).

The purpose of the dietary laws is therefore strictly ethical-religious. Their aim is to transform man's body into the proper instrument of his divine spirit, since in Judaism the importance of the body cannot be overestimated. The complex regimen keeps it in a state of purity and holiness as the vehicle of the human soul and the medium of communication of man's spirit with the outer world (*H* 454).

Great care must be taken, therefore, that this instrument remains sensitive and responsive to serving the spirit. Anything which might negatively affect the human body and deprive it of its fundamental function "to be an intermediary between the soul of man and the world outside" (*H* 454) is forbidden. The observance of the dietary laws does not make a man holy; however, it makes him more receptive to the ennobling influences of the spirit: "One has not achieved holiness simply by observing the dietary laws, but one can then achieve it more easily" (*CL* 11:47).

Although Hirsch does not claim any medical advantages for the dietary laws, he insists that they embody an invisible moral and spiritual relationship. Like many medieval scholars,[18] he links nutrition with man's mental, spiritual, and ethical aspects. Some foods exert a benevolent or malevolent influence on man's outlook and behavior. Man therefore is obliged to consume foods which will keep his body in a state of readiness and responsiveness to the exigencies of the spirit: "Not our bodily health, but the spiritual and moral health of our souls is to be ensured by the observation of these laws, which protect our sensuousness from animallike unrestrained passion, and our spiritual and moral powers of will from becoming dull and irresponsive to higher and nobler conceptions" (*CL* 11:47).

Modern materialistic scientists, who believe that the body exerts a strong influence on man's mind, should not find the Jewish dietary laws incomprehensible:

If the material part of our bodies is able to exercise so great an influence on our minds and will that the modern lies of materialism can have the narrowminded presumption to relegate even spirit and will to mere attributes of the material, and to make all their activities purely the product of material forces, . . . how understandable is the care which only allows this "instrument" of the spirit, which is constantly being renewed, to be rebuilt each time only with such materials as will keep it in a condition of readiness and responsiveness for the service of the spirit, and make it easier for the spirit to master and use the instrument for the higher purpose of its mission. (*CL* 11:47)

Hirsch was undoubtedly aware that in his age nobody could prove the influence of nutrition on ethics. He therefore admonishes his readers not to surrender to critics who insist upon empirical evidence. Even if man never empirically discovers a relationship between given nutrients or chemical substances and mental or psychological makeup, he is still obligated to obey these laws: "Even if experience were never to teach you how instincts can be aroused or controlled by bodily gratification, how mental clarity can thus be improved or killed" (*H* 448), the dietary laws remain mandatory for the Jew because God ordained them.

Hirsch's shift from a psychosomatic theory to theonomic authority is partially due to his basic attitude that compliance with God's laws is mandatory even in the event that his theories and hypotheses about them prove erroneous. God's knowledge, even more than His authority, is implicit in Hirsch's reliance on divine law. Despite all advances in the realm of science, man still remains an outsider to nature, unable to penetrate it. Because of this "lack of insight into the essential nature of things" (*H* 454), man must rely on the law of God as expressed in the Torah. It is God who prohibits or permits consumption of foods, because He knows their negative or positive effects on man's nature, disposition, and ethical behavior.

Despite disclaiming any definite reasons, Hirsch in his usual manner suggests some explanations about the negative influence of some forbidden foods on the nature of man. In accordance with his basic assumption that the Torah's strictures were designed to eliminate "the exciting or depressing effect of certain foodstuffs on one's temperament and feelings" (*CE* 23:19), Hirsch suggests that the best of all foods are vegetables. They are of a passive substance and do not tend to arouse any aggressive or animalistic tendencies in man. Similarly, the most herbivorous of animals have no deleterious effects on man. These animals possess a plantlike nature. They "show little vivacity, little passion, temperate instincts and little powerful animal activity" (*H* 454). The two characteristics of the "clean" animals—cud-chewing and cloven hooves—testify to their docile nature. Chewing the cud shows that "these animals spend a great deal of time in the absorption of food, which may be termed the vegetative activity of animals" (*H* 454). Cloven hooves show that they were designed for standing and not "for being used as weapons or tools" (*H* 454).

Some foods may contain certain "dulling substances which deaden the finer qualities of man" (*H* 454). To this category belong many "unclean" fish, worms, and forbidden animals. The reason that even the meat of kosher animals must be drained of blood is due to the role of blood as a factor in maintaining life:

The animal body is only allowed to be used for food when the blood is no longer under the control of the soul; the tissues of animal body can become tissues of the human body for it is something entirely passive, inert, but the animal soul can never become, is never to become, the human soul. (*CG* 9:4)

At times it is difficult to tell whether Hirsch considered a given forbidden food as merely a symbol, or as actually injurious to man's ethical well-being. In this case, however, it seems that Hirsch believed that each part of the animal's anatomy is converted by man's ingestion into the corresponding human part. Thus, he explains why animal fat and blood were sanctioned and even preferred in sacrifices, but forbidden as food:

Symbolically, i.e., in an animal offering, animal blood can be used to represent the human being, the human ego, and animal *ḥelev* can express human aims. But concretely, the animal ego may never become the human ego, and the animal aims are never to become human aims. (*CL* 3:17)

Similarly, Hirsch explains why only kosher animals have to be ritually slaughtered. This requirement is due to the fact that the latter's "bodies and life-activity approach in external similarity to that of the bodily life of human beings" (*CD* 12:21). Ritual slaughtering, *sheḥitah*, is necessary in such instances because

when the tissue of their nerves and muscles is converted into human nerves and human muscles, by this conversion they leave the realm where they are bound by physical necessity and enter the realm where all bodily material matter is subjugated to free-willed moral mastery. (*CD* 12:21)

However, a nonkosher animal is completely alien to the physiological and biological makeup of man. It is organically "in such contrast to the personality envisaged by the Jewish Torah that it is absolutely excluded from being absorbed in any way in the bodies of such personalities" (*CD* 12:21).

Hirsch explains the need for *sheḥitah* as the preparation of the animal for human purposes. This act demonstrates that the animal is now to become "subservient to the free-willed self-determination of the human being" (*CD* 12:21) and is no longer to follow "the laws of physical necessity" (*CD* 12:21). However, this law does not apply to fish and locust, which have absolutely nothing in common with man's organism (*CD* 12:21). Fish and locust, however, are not antithetical to man's organism, as are the nonkosher animals.

Somewhat more sophisticated is Hirsch's stated reason for the prohibition of *nevelah*, meat from an animal which has not been slaughtered in accordance with laws of *sheḥitah*. In his commentary on Deuteronomy, Hirsch maintains that a Jew must not ingest the "unfree nature of the animal world which falls back to the world of elements" (*CD* 14:21). The Jew has to constantly remember that his task is to elevate the vegetative and animalistic elements within him to the level of the spirit, and not vice versa. *Neveleh* represents a reversion from a higher to a lower level and hence is forbidden.

Similarly, meat from a *trefah* animal is prohibited since it, like the *nevelah,* is no longer a source of nourishment for man but belongs to the domain of nature. Sick and moribund, it belongs to the elements and must be returned to them:

> A *trefah* animal is one which is already taken over to be nourishment for another sphere. As such it belongs to the *sadeh,* as physical and chemical nourishment for nature, and is forbidden as nourishment for human beings who belong to a holy morally free calling. (*CE* 22:30)

All these explanations notwithstanding, Hirsch completes this section on dietary laws by once again noting that his views are merely conjectural, while the laws remain mandatory. Just as one can theorize about natural phenomena to his heart's content yet in the final analysis it is theory which has to conform to the natural manifestations and not vice versa, similarly one may speculate about the laws of the Torah but even should such a theory or theories fail to explain these laws adequately, the Torah remains in force and it is the theory that has to be revised (*H* 454).

Between Man and Animal

As already noted, many of the dietary laws seek to accentuate the distinction between man and animal. At all times man must remember his divine spiritual superiority and live up to it. Since man is close to the animal realm and can easily be overwhelmed by the animalistic elements within him, the Torah promulgates additional laws to prevent such an eventuality.

Man's sense of shame and modesty serves as a powerful deterrent against the rise of the animal instincts in man, but this inborn safeguard has to be cultivated. Every function man performs, even of the most elemental nature, must be done in a manner befitting human dignity. Man must dress himself in a way that distinguishes his spiritual nature from the animal, so that "all naked animality of human beings and everything that reminds one of it, is kept in the background, in your appearance, in your acts and speech, in your thoughts and feelings" (*CD* 23:15).

Gratification of man's physical needs brings him closest to animalism, so it is at those times that the danger of sinking to the level of the animal is most acute. Thus, while eating is a necessity for both man and animal, it is the manner of eating that distinguishes them. Judaism endows each meal, no matter how humble, with the aspect of holiness. Man should partake of food as if it were a sacrificial meal, he a priest, and the table an altar. The goal of consuming food is not merely to still one's animalistic appetite, but to sustain life for the service of God. Hirsch admonishes men not to "kill their humanity in the service of their stomach" (*H* 466).

Similarly, man's functions have to be selective, dignified, and human at all times. Jewish law tries to hallow even the most elementary physical functions which are common to all mammals, including man. It is this distinctive sanctification that makes man a human being (*H* 462). Thus, the mouth must be kept clean not only by the intake of food from without but by the speech that emanates from within. Man must guard himself against profanity and obscenity. It is speech that distinguishes man from his animal kingdom; man must therefore be exceptionally careful not to desecrate this God-given power by degrading it to the level of the brute. The sanctity of speech is evident in the laws regulating vows and in similar utterances by man: "To break your word in the case of a vow is self-desecration, and in the case of an oath is also a desecration of the divine name" (*H* 471).

Hirsch explains why he includes the laws concerning vows, free dedication, and binding oaths in the division *"Ḥukkim."* Besides the fact that vows may assist man in restraining his unbridled will, they also can be easily violated by the very same man who made them. It is therefore God who insists that we carry out our promises and vows, even when they only concern the one who made them:

There is no law which more rightly belongs to this class than the one in which God, as the representative of our word against ourselves, demands worthy regard for our word, regard for ourselves in our word, even when the right of another is not concerned. (*H* 467)

Hirsch concludes the *"Ḥukkim"* division with a discussion of the halakhic categories and criteria applicable in many of these laws. The demarcation line between the permissible and prohibited is not always clear. At times, decisions of such a nature have to be arrived at on the basis of majority rule, presumption, and probability.

The Torah does not demand the impossible of man. Recognizing man's limitations, God did not insist on absolute certainty and detailed precision in the observance of His precepts. At times, a judicious approximation will suffice when only such an approximation is possible by man (*H* 476). God asks of man only what is humanly possible, but man is obliged to strive honestly and sincerely for this God-granted possibility.

12
"Mitzvot": Commandments of Love

Imitatio Dei

The fifth division of the *Horeb*, *"Mitzvot,"* consists of twenty-six chapters. The laws of this division are defined in the *Neunzehn Briefe* as "precepts of love toward all beings without distinction, purely because of the bidding of God and in consideration of our duty as men and Israelites" (*NL* 104).

The distinction between the laws designated *mitzvot* and those of the preceding two divisions, *"Mishpatim"* and *"Ḥukkim,"* is qualitative. Those in the latter two "show you how to avoid sinking below the level of the rest of creation, how to submit yourself of your own free will to those requirements which the rest obey under compulsion, but *"Mitzvot"* shows you how through love translated into action you can raise yourself above the level of creation to God" (*H* 480). Thus, the laws of *"Mishpatim"* and *"Ḥukkim"* aim to make man conform to the will of God and the harmony of nature. Since due to his instability, man is apt to abuse his freedom to his own detriment and to that of the rest of the world, the *mishpatim* and *ḥukkim* endeavor to check his undesirable inclinations and impulses toward regression to the animal level.

However, in abiding by the laws of *mishpatim* and *ḥukkim,* man does not prove his superiority over the rest of creation but is merely aligned with it, by aligning his will with that of God. Man achieves real distinctiveness by implementing the laws within the *mitzvot* category. These laws go beyond the formal relationships of justice to man, as do *mishpatim*, or to nature, as do *ḥukkim*. The *mitzvot* laws are of a different nature, reaching out to a level beyond the realm of any natural or animal creature. They require the complexity of the human mind and heart, a display of intellect and sensitivity which is the exclusive characteristic of man.

From the schematic point of view, the laws included in this division constitute a conglomeration of ethical, communal, and domestic laws that are unrelated to one another. They may be considered as miscellaneous, since the internal schematic grouping of the laws of this division shows no order; religious, social, civic laws and a great variety of others crisscross each other without any design or apparent purpose. Some of these laws might have been placed in divisions other than *"Mitzvot."* Thus, the prohibition of vengeance should have been placed in the *"Torot,"* where the concept of *netirah*, resentment, is discussed; the law of writing a *Sefer Torah* rightfully belongs to the *"Avodah"* division.

This lack of order seems to indicate that Hirsch was either pressured or overanxious to complete his work and therefore did not organize it properly. Unlike the previous divisions, there is no particular effort on his part to rationalize the laws of the *"Mitzvot"* division. Since they are primarily of an ethical, humane, and civic nature, they consequently were never contested in the socio-cultural milieu of the predominantly law-abiding and morally conditioned German Jewry. Hirsch's twenty-six chapters of the *"Mitzvot"* division are basically edifying sermonettes on noncontroversial, ethical-religious subjects.

The first precept of the *"Mitzvot"* division is to endeavor to attain sublimity. Of all creatures, only man is endowed with the spirit of God and he therefore has to aspire to actualize the divine potential he possesses. He can never attain divinity, but having a model of divine perfection, he ought to try to approximate it as closely as possible. The essence of God is beyond man's comprehension, but God's activity, and hence His scale of values, are apparent. Man, created in the image of God, should therefore aspire to live and act in accordance with these values. Man's first task is *imitatio Dei*. Hirsch alludes to the rabbinic interpretation of the biblical verse "Follow none but the Lord your God."[1] According to the Talmud, following the Lord implies the imitation and emulation of such divine qualities and attributes as love, mercy, kindness, faithfulness, and forgiveness.[2] The quality of mercy, Hirsch emphasizes, must be predicated on justice: "The way to love leads only through justice" (*H* 484). Without justice, love is meaningless.

The emphasis on the precedence of justice before love may reflect the spirit of the age. Many of Hirsch's contemporaries had little objection to the laws of the *"Mitzvot"* division, but objected to some in the *"Mishpatim"* and to most in the *"Hukkim"* sections. Since love was considered to be at a higher level than justice, a view to which Hirsch also subscribed, many liberals were ready to begin there. To counter such an antinomian attitude, Hirsch insists: "Let no man boast that he is fulfilling *mitzvot* who tramples on *mishpat* and *hok"* (*H* 484).

Man as a Source of Blessings

To become a source of happiness and blessings for others, man must first perfect himself. A morally imperfect person cannot bring happiness to others. The perfection of oneself is a long and arduous process. It necessitates continuous cultivation and careful preparation.

The first step in man's road to self-perfection is to respect his parents. The latter are the source of transmission of knowledge, culture, mores, ethical values, as well as religion. Respect for one's parents transcends mere sentiment; it must be concretized in deeds. Reflecting the mood of an authoritarian, patriarchal society, Hirsch demands unconditional obedience and unqualified conformity with the wishes of parents: "You must be clay in their hands, plastic and flexible, you must have no will of your own in opposition to them" (*H* 486). Only when the demands of the parents contradict the laws of the Torah should parents be disregarded. Parents, on the other hand, have a sacred obligation to bring up their children to be mentally and physically fit and, as a special duty, in the spirit of the Torah. They must not, however, overindulge or pamper the child: "Protect him as far as it lies in human power from sickness and deformity, but beware of making the body so soft that it will not be able to stand up against the storms of life" (H 550).

Parents must be living examples of morality, purity, and religion. They have to watch over the child's environment and guard him from possible negative influences. Special care and vigilance must be exercised during the period of adolescence, when young men and women are tormented by rising passions and drives. At this age, they must be treated with special consideration and sympathy. It is most important that the home and school complement each other, particularly with regard to morality and conduct.

Respect and consideration should be shown to the elderly and wise, and to men of notable accomplishment. The Jew's main occupation is the study of Torah. He is not born to be merely a businessman, a craftsman, or a professional, but to fulfill the tasks of Israel (H 491). This he can attain only through the assiduous study of the Torah, which must occupy a position of preeminence in his life and must not be considered merely another branch of knowledge:

We are altogether always to bear in mind the specific higher level of our knowledge which differs from all other scientific knowledge through its divine origin and not place it on the same level as other sciences, as if it, too, rested on the basis of human knowledge. (CD 6:7)

However, Hirsch is careful to point out that the Jew's reverence for the Torah does not preclude seeking knowledge of other disciplines, which is presupposed and desirable. But the Jew has to place secular studies in their proper perspective (CL 18:5).

Hirsch denies the allegation that the Torah is a divisive factor in the relationship between the Jew and the rest of mankind. Such criticism was voiced by many, and Hirsch echoes their complaints in the Neunzehn Briefe. His young friend Benjamin blames the Torah for the Jews' peculiar status in the world: "The Law is chiefly at fault for all this: by enjoining isolation in life, and thereby arousing suspicion and hostility" (NL 4).

Hirsch rejects this allegation: "The Torah does not segregate you from your fellow creatures; rather does it bring you into relationship with every one of them and teaches you what you ought to be to each and what each should be to you" (*H* 494). Moreover, it is incorrect to assume that the Torah rejects general culture and the attainments of science. On the contrary, "the more enlightenment you gain on these subjects, the clearer will be your insight into the Torah" (*H* 494). For this reason, and contrary to the general practice in Jewish traditionalist circles, Hirsch advocates a Torah education for women (*H* 494). Aware of the objections to such an innovation, Hirsch later differentiated in his commentary between the academic aspect of Torah, which is not necessary for women, and the practical aspect, which is essential (*CD* 11:19).

Obedience to the Torah requires unqualified obedience to its exponents. Coming as it did at a time when disrespect for and disregard of religious authorities were widespread, Hirsch's emphasis is readily understood. Significantly, he absolves the children of the rebels against the authority of traditional Judaism because the children never received the proper instruction (*H* 509). Hirsch's view with regard to the alienated descendants of liberal and antinomian Jews is analogous to that of Maimonides concerning the treatment of the latter-day Karaites.[3]

To further enhance one's religious and moral outlook, one should select an environment conducive to a spiritual atmosphere and associate with people whose Weltanschauung, demeanor, and general conduct is in accordance with the spirit of the Torah (*H* 496–99). Nor should one's chosen occupation cause any religious or moral conflicts (*H* 524). Of course, no man is perfect at all times, and many may occasionally transgress. But such failures should not destroy man's personality, for the gates of repentance are always open. Along with confession, charity, and contrition, the road to God is unimpeded for man (*H* 513).

In this respect, Hirsch adds nothing besides paraphrasing Maimonides's words in the *Mishneh Torah* concerning repentance. In his commentary, Hirsch remarks that confession in Judaism bears no similarity to that in Catholicism, nor does it signify man's disclosing his sins to God. God being omniscient, such disclosure is superfluous. Confession rather is man admitting to himself that he has failed religiously and morally. Such an admission is therefore the first step to true and meaningful repentance.[4]

Status of the Jewish Woman

Hirsch was exceedingly sensitive to the status of the woman in Judaism. The Reformers frequently alleged that Judaism's Oriental origin reduced the Jewish woman to the role of a mere passive onlooker in Jewish life and religion. At the conference of Reform rabbis at Breslau in 1846 and at subsequent synods, the religious status of women occupied an important part of the agenda.

Hirsch was aware of the explosive nature of this issue. In a special essay entitled "Das jüdische Weib" (The Jewish wife— S 4:160–208), he tries to show the important position the woman occupies in traditional Judaism. He accuses the Reformers of deliberate distortions in order to win over the allegedly disfranchised Jewish women to the liberating Reform movement (S 4:161). To the sarcastic observation that in traditional Judaism the Jew buys his wife, Hirsch retorts that the Jew considers his wife the most precious and holiest possession (S 4:177).[5]

Homiletically and pseudoetymologically, Hirsch attempts to prove woman's equality with man. The concept *man* signifies the combination of both sexes (S 4:162).[6] In his commentary on Genesis, Hirsch maintains that "the name *ishah* [woman], accordingly, does not designate the dependence of woman on man, but rather the equality, the two belonging together, the division of the one human calling between the two sexes" (*CG* 2:23).

In answer to the charge that divorce in Judaism is basically a husband's prerogative, Hirsch offers a very weak explanation: since the woman occupies an exalted place in Jewish life, no abuse of this right is to be feared. Judaism "could quietly leave the decision for divorce primarily to the heart of the husband" (*CD* 24:1). Hirsch's oversimplification in this instance is baffling, since as a rabbi he was undoubtedly aware of the many problems arising even among traditionalists when the wife wanted a divorce and her husband was neither chivalrous nor accommodating enough to grant it. Nor is Hirsch more explicit in the case of *ḥalitzah*, the rite of dissolving a levirated dependency, which was frequently the cause of great chagrin in Jewish families. The wife of the deceased man who left no children was at the mercy of her brother-in-law, who often took unfair advantage of the helpless widow. Hirsch rejects the contention that *ḥalitzah* is archaic and obsolete and affirms it as an act of nobility. It is "an act of publicly clearing any suspicion of lack of fraternal love, and expresses the deepest feelings of love and readiness for brotherly actions in which the attachment of Jewish families has its root" (*CD* 25:7). On other questions of marriage, Hirsch criticizes the prevalent practice of breaking an engagement upon failure of the bride's parents to provide a dowry as a religiously offensive and morally degrading act (*H* 528).

Closely related to the subject of marriage is intermarriage, a thorny problem for Hirsch but even more so for the liberal theologians and the exponents of Reform. The priority of this question is indicated by the fact that it was third on the agenda of the twelve questions submitted by Napoleon on July 29, 1806, to the Sanhedrin he convened in Paris. The members of the Sanhedrin, meeting in an atmosphere of fear and intimidation, phrased their reply in an ambiguous, negative manner. Accordingly, a marriage contracted between a Jew and non-Jew is not forbidden, but neither can it be solemnized religiously. Thus, contrary to the implicit wishes of Napoleon, the Sanhedrin did not legitimize intermarriage. Thirty-eight years later, in 1844, the question came up at the Reform synod at Brunswick. Despite the liberal spirit permeating the deliberations, the move to weaken this prohibition encountered strong objections. Some felt that the prevailing hostility between Jews and non-Jews makes intermarriage undesirable. But this problem continued to plague the Jews during the nineteenth century.

To Hirsch, anti-Semitism was not the reason for the prohibition against intermarriage. Such a reason might have implied that under more favorable circumstances and a more conducive social climate, intermarriage would be legitimate. However, the prohibition is unconditional and aims at preserving the transmission of Judaism to offspring, and such ethical-religious transmission necessitates that both parents be unqualifiedly committed to Judaism (*H* 500).

With the ascendancy of liberalism, Hirsch beheld great danger to the future spiritual integrity of the Jews. The closer the socioeconomic ties with non-Jews are, the greater is the need for religious fences to maintain Jewish singularity. Thus, the reason for laws prohibiting non-Jewish foods is not that they are "looked upon as unclean, which would be both ridiculous and absurd" (H 503), but merely to preserve the Jewish spirit. The more friendly, the more considerate, the other people become to the Jews, the greater becomes the importance of these laws (H 503).

Attitude toward Non-Jews

The laws of the "Mitzvot" division seek to make the Jew a paragon of justice, morality, and love. By leading an exemplary life, he sanctifies the name of God; by doing the reverse, he profanes it. Any misconduct by a Jew causes hillul ha-Shem, a desecration of Judaism. The Jew, therefore, must make every effort to help his fellow man, to aid the poor, to visit the sick, to comfort the bereaved, and generally to promote the welfare of others. Even a foe's animal must be helped when it is in distress. Thus, the underprivileged must be restored to a meaningful, dignified position in life. True tzedakah implies helping the poor to be self-sufficient and self-sustaining. The very term tzedakah connotes justice. This signifies that the wealth possessed by the rich is not exclusively theirs; they are merely custodians of it for the poor, and must therefore share justly with them (H 571).

Loyalty and obedience to the government has to be unconditional, and its laws and orders conformed to without question. The fact that the authorities are hostile or oppressive does not excuse noncompliance with their demands: "Even should they deny your right to be a human being and to develop a lawful human life upon the soil which bore you, you should not neglect your duty" (H 609).

Hirsch denies the contention that Jews are a nation and hence cannot be considered loyal citizens. Jews are an am, signifying a Gesellschaft, a religious society but not goy, a separate nation. The prayers offered for the restoration of Zion merely have a religious connotation devoid of any nationalistic concomitants: "Not in order to shine as a nation among nations do we raise our prayers and hopes for a reunion in our land, but in order to find a soil for the better fulfillment of our spiritual vocation" (H 608). Thus, the difference between Hirsch and the Reformers with regard to Jewish nationalism was minimal.

The relations between Jews and non-Jews deserve to be motivated by the same noble sentiments as those between coreligionists. The sad memories of persecution and hostilities should be erased and committed to oblivion: "Learn to forget the centuries of oppression and misery, of the inhuman scorn and the inhuman degradation which folly and lack of understanding brought upon you in your wandering in the *Galuth* and remember gratefully the good that you found everywhere—and still find" (*H* 587). Hirsch thus echoes the sentiments of the liberals of his age for a rapprochement with the non-Jews and the elimination of prejudice between heretofore alien and hostile groups. Many of his contemporaries who shared this sentiment felt constrained at times by certain references to non-Jews in the Bible and rabbinic literature, which seemed discriminatory and prejudicial.

Among the laws offensive to the liberals was the biblical prohibition against taking or giving interest on a loan.[7] Such a prohibition refers only to Jews, whereas interest may be collected from or given to non-Jews. The anti-Semites exploited this seemingly discriminatory law fully. The fact that many non-Jews often owed money to Jews made this an inflammatory issue—significant enough so that the last two of the twelve questions posed by Napoleon before the Sanhedrin at Paris dealt with it. Irked by this differentiation, some liberals discounted it completely while others attempted to apologize for or rationalize it.

Hirsch was neither perturbed by this law nor apologetic for it. Apparently, the advent of capitalism made the prohibition against interest rather disadvantageous to the Jews, since the prohibition against taking or giving interest to fellow Jews restricted their ability to obtain loans. It thus limited them in the free competitive economy of the nineteenth century instead of working to their advantage, as it probably had done in an ancient agricultural society. It was therefore unnecessary to apologize to the non-Jews for a law which curtailed the Jews only, and was detrimental to their economic welfare.

However, a need existed to explain this law to the Jews who felt hampered by it in a capitalistic society. Hirsch considers the prohibition against interest as a special law directed to the Jewish people because of their singular status and religious mission. Charging interest on loans as such is neither an illegal nor an unethical practice: "The Torah in no wise looks on interest on loans as something that is morally wrong. Otherwise it would not forbid with equal solemnity the paying of interest as it does the taking of it, nor would it restrict the prohibition to Jews only" (*CL* 25:36).

Since charging interest is neither illegal nor immoral, Hirsch places this prohibition in the division *"Mitzvot"* rather than *"Mishpatim"* or *"Ḥukkim."* Its aim is not unlike that of the Sabbath, the sabbatical year, and the jubilee year, which address themselves exclusively to the Jews (*CD* 23:20). Like the latter three, the prohibition against interest emphasizes God's dominion over man's possessions. While the laws of the sabbatical and jubilee years revolve around agriculture, concretely symbolizing divine mastery over man's immovable possessions, the prohibition on interest emphasizes God's sovereignty over movable ones (*CE* 22:24). Although this law causes hardships to Jews in the modern economic system, such a sacrifice is incumbent upon them (*CL* 25:36).

Despite the legitimacy of interest, Hirsch maintains that the Torah perceived a social evil in it. He was undoubtedly familiar with the strident voices raised in his time against the evils of capitalism. Banking had become a formidable force in western Europe, and interest-bearing loans were a vital factor in banking operations. Hirsch therefore suggests that the Torah wished to limit this evil by eliminating the motivation of interest. In phrases which sound almost socialistic, the conservative Hirsch explains the social evils caused by interest and the attempt of the Torah to mitigate them:

This law takes away the worst effect of the power of money, that potent factor in causing social inequality. It breaks the too great power of capital. If this prohibition is strictly kept, all capital is in itself dead and unproductive and can only be of use by wedding it to labor. It raises labor to the primary and essential factor of social well-being. Capital is forced to recognize the equality of labor. The rich man must either bring his otherwise dead capital to production by his own powers of work, or must associate himself with the power of labor of the poor man, share profit and loss with him, and in his own interests further the interests of labor. Every crisis of labor becomes to an even higher degree a crisis of capital, and capital can never make profit from the ruin of labor. The possibility of that shocking contrast, where the wretchedness of the laboring class is rampant right next to the most luxurious opulence, has the ground cut away under its feet by this law. (*CE* 22:24)

After reading this interpretation it seems strange that such a prohibition should not have been extended beyond the interrelationship of Jews. The evils brought about by capitalism could not be eliminated by restricting interest between Jews and permitting it from non-Jews. Furthermore, according to this view, the law against interest should have been considered unethical and perhaps even illegal altogether. However, Hirsch did not take these corollary assumptions into consideration, since his main concern was to rationalize the biblical law concerning interest, a law which seemed discriminatory.

13
"Mitzvot": Education

Interest in Education

Although Hirsch devotes only one chapter of the *"Mitzvot"* division to the subject of education, it was most central to his Weltanschauung. His philosophy of Jewish education was inextricably related to his own *erleuchtet religiös* family and educational background and to the heightened interest in general education in Germany during the era of the Haskalah. The very principle of *Torah im derekh eretz*, upon which his educational philosophy was founded, was first enunciated by Wessely, the leading mentor of the Haskalah, who exerted great influence on Hirsch's grandfather and uncle, and possibly on Hirsch himself. In his day, Wessely was severely castigated for advocating *Torah im derekh eretz*, a combination of religious and general education, but when this idea was subsequently echoed by Hirsch, many people greeted it enthusiastically. In the course of time, this talmudic dictum became so exclusively associated with Hirsch that its true originator, Wessely, was almost completely forgotten. *Torah im derekh eretz*, the slogan of the Haskalah, became the watchword of modern enlightened traditionalists, whose predecessors had bitterly and uncompromisingly fought the very same idea.

Hirsch's own education was a combination of *Torah im derekh eretz*. His parents gave him a general education buttressed by religious studies, which Hirsch apparently appreciated sufficiently

348

to wish to foster it, with considerable modifications, among his contemporaries.

The post-Napoleonic era in which Hirsch lived constituted an additional important factor in his educational outlook. It was an age of great intellectual ferment, vigor, and originality in the field of educational theory and practice in western and central Europe, particularly in Germany. Never before had there been such "great diversity of educational development in different parts of Europe, corresponding to the diversity of national conditions produced by the Napoleonic wars."[1] The humiliating debacle of the Prussian armies at Jena in 1806 had a sobering and salutary effect on German education, since the leading German intellectuals, defeated in battle and deprived of political power and military glory, began to concentrate their efforts on education, the only province not controlled by the occupying French authorities.

During the winter of 1807–1808, Johann Gottlieb Fichte delivered his fervently patriotic *Reden an die deutschen Nation.*[2] He challenged the German people to use their educational system in order "to produce a generation which shall be capable of choosing great aims and sacrificing itself for them."[3] A host of educators, some as practical and able as Wilhelm von Humboldt, soon set out to reorganize German schools. Educational philosophic theory was advanced by men like Friedrich Herbart[4] and Friedrich Froebel. Their profound interest was shared by the great philosophers of the age, particularly Hegel, who served as a private tutor for eight years and subsequently for another eight years as the rector of the new Gymnasium at Nuremberg.[5] Like Fichte, Hegel felt that the political situation in Germany required a reorientation in educational theory and practice.

This general preoccupation with educational thought and experimentation was hardly paralleled in Jewish education in Germany at that time. The extreme Orthodox elements viewed any attempt at modernization with misgivings and suspicion; they associated modern education with apostasy.[6] The non-Orthodox were primarily interested in general education and at best paid only lip service to Jewish education.[7] Even the exponents and founders of Jewish scientific research, who evinced an interest in the deepening of the philosophy of Judaism, were not in favor of similar efforts with regard to Jewish educational thought: "[Leopold] Zunz and other leaders were opposed in general to the teaching of religion. They not only wanted religious instruction to be left to the home but they were more interested in Jewish culture than *cultus,* or Jewish ritual."[8] This lack of interest in Jewish education was even characteristic in Jewish educational circles. Speaking about the Philanthropin[9] in Frankfurt am Main,[10] Heinrich Graetz observed that "the managers and teachers of the school and the members of the lodge[11] favored a radicalism repugnant to Judaism."[12] Little wonder that at a time when general education was on the ascendancy in Germany, Jewish education dwindled steadily, among the non-Orthodox elements reaching its lowest ebb,[13] while the type fostered by the Orthodox was rigid and barren.

A New Philosophic Orientation

This general interest in philosophy of education seems to have affected Hirsch, who early in his career set out to reeducate the Jews of his generation by introducing them to the sources of Judaism. Hirsch shared the high regard in which education was held by the great theorists and mentors of the nineteenth century. His boundless faith in education, its historic mission, and its decisiveness in the phylogeny of man is consonant with the value ascribed to it by the exponents of idealism.[14] In the typical spirit of post-Napoleonic Germany, Hirsch emphasized that neither by diplomacy nor by military strategy but by education is the fate of nations decided.[15] Firmly believing in the power of education to transform man individually and in groups, Hirsch was anxious to employ it as an instrument for revitalizing Judaism in the post-Emancipation period. He therefore pleaded for "schools for Jews" (*NL* 199) and urged they be established even prior to the erection of houses of worship.

Hirsch was afraid that the radical changes brought about by the Emancipation would prove detrimental to the cause of Judaism. The perpetuating and preserving factors of Judaism in the ghetto-habit and upbringing had weakened. In the freedom of the modern world, Judaism had to display dynamism of the spirit (*S* 1:276) "which, independent of emancipation or non-emancipation, strives to fulfill the Israel-mission" (*NL* 166). The danger existed that the Jews would forget their ideals and consider Emancipation merely as "a means of securing a greater degree of comfort in life and greater opportunities for the acquisition of wealth and enjoyments" (*NL* 167).

Hirsch felt the new age demanded an ideological and philosophical reorientation as well as a new approach to Jewish education. The conflicting factions vying for supremacy over Jewish education could not help the Jew solve his transformed political, cultural, and socioeconomic problems:

The one party has inherited uncomprehended Judaism as a mechanical habit, *mitzvat anashim melumadah,* without its spirit; they bear it in their hands as a sacred relic, as a revered mummy, and fear to rouse its spirit. The others are partly filled with noble enthusiasm for the welfare of the Jews, but look upon Judaism as a lifeless framework, as something which should be laid in the grave of a long since dead and buried past. (*NL* 196)

For the Jew to survive in the post-Emancipation period, he must revise his attitude to the world *within* him and to the world *around* him (*NL* 16). The newly evolved spiritual and philosophic climate and radically changed socioeconomic conditions dictated the Jew's reeducation. Emancipation was not a boon for the Jews alone, but a new phase in the unfolding of the divine plan for all humanity. For the Jews, it also constituted "a new trial, much severer than the trial of oppression" (*NL* 167).

To meet this test, Hirsch urges Jewish youth to reeducate themselves for life in accordance with the ideal of Man-Israel *(Mensch-Jissroel),* which, as previously indicated, signified a symbiosis of two different elements. The modern Jew has to maintain a delicate equilibrium between the domains which Mendelssohn had termed *Mensch*—or worldly—and *Jew*—or religious. The combined term *Man-Israel* signifies an individual who is a man in all respects of Occidental culture and an Israelite in his religious convictions and practice. Hirsch believed that this combination signifies a symbiosis: Israel and man may complement one another externally and functionally rather than negate one another, as they had during the period of medieval oppression.

Prior to the Emancipation of the Jews, during their ghetto period, the Jewish people could live merely as Israel. They were segregated and thereby isolated from the main course of history. But once ejected from the rigid corporate social structure of the Middle Ages into a free, individualistic, and competitive society, the Jew in the post-Emancipation period was forced to live as man, which implied his full participation in the natural and historical process common to the rest of humanity. As envisioned by Hirsch, the main difficulty for the Jew in the new era would be the extraordinary tension under which he would have to live, since while living and acting as man, he would still have to retain the quality of Israel with all the duties and obligations this involved. Political, economic, and cultural integration would have to be maintained with social and religious separation. Only as Man-Israel, symbiotically constituted, would the Jew be able to survive the opposing forces in his life.[16] He would thus have to function on two levels and exhibit two different, at times even contradictory attitudes, being simultaneously alike and different, near and remote, friendly and aloof. By this difficult and exemplary conduct, the Jew would become a mighty educative force "for propelling mankind to the final goal of all human education. More quietly, but more forcefully and profoundly would it effect mankind than even our tragical record of sorrows" (*NL* 86).

Man-Israel would not be spontaneously generated but would have to educate himself in order to acquire the dual qualities and duties required in both domains: "The language of the Bible and the language of the land should be [his]; in both [he] should be taught to think" (*NL* 199). This dual education should not be limited to linguistics, but must embrace everything pertinent to every Jew as man and as Israel. They must study nature and history —which constitute all men's common ground—as well as the precepts of the Torah—which are the singular and exclusive domain of Israel:

Their eye should be open to recognize the world around them as God's world and themselves in God's world as His servants. Their ear should be open to perceive in history the narrative of education of all men for this service. The wise precepts of Torah and Talmud should be made clear to them as designed to spiritualize their lives for such sublime service to God. (*NL* 199–200)

Hirsch calls upon educators and Jewish parents alike to evolve a well-balanced education for young Jews which would enable them as adults to function in the modern world as Man-Israel.

Primary and Ancillary Aims

In order to transform the post-Emancipation Jew into a Man-Israel, Hirsch had aspired while still in his twenties to establish an educational system in which the humanities, sciences, and Judaic subjects would be taught together. Many years later, he succeeded in establishing such a school in Frankfurt am Main[17] "in which the elements of religious living and of general social education should be cultivated and furthered with equal amount of care."[18] Hirsch was not surprised when this school was attacked by both Orthodox and progressive elements, although for diametrically opposed reasons.[19] Even in 1836, when his educational project had been a mere vision, he had anticipated vehement opposition and pleaded for patience, forbearance, and sympathetic understanding—especially from parents. He asked them to let their children prepare themselves in the new school for a new task in life imposed upon them by Providence, and to live as Man-Israel:

> While this training was going on and until Israel's houses were built up of such sons and daughters, the parents should be implored and entreated not to destroy the work of the school, not to crush or choke with icy and unsympathetic mood the tender shoots of Jewish sentiment in the breasts of their children. (*NL* 200–201)

Hirsch's educational system was founded on the principle of *Torah im derekh eretz,* which according to him implied a combination of religious knowledge and general culture.[20] Hirsch's objective was in harmony with his philosophic outlook. In order for the Jew to be educated to become Man-Israel, he must be imbued with the spirit of both Torah and *derekh eretz.* The latter, comprising the natural and social sciences, was designed for the Jew's aspect of man, the former for his spiritual aspect of Israel.

Despite the clarity with which Hirsch emphasized his principle and its avowed purpose, it was frequently misinterpreted. The misunderstanding was primarily over the relationship between the dual aspects of the principle; Hirsch was accused or commended by both the right and the left for nursing hidden designs to vitiate the coequality of the two spheres. On the left, it was alleged that Hirsch intended *derekh eretz* as a camouflage for Torah, which would constitute the essential core of the curriculum to the detriment of general education (*S* 2:450–51). His critics on the right thought that the term *Torah* was introduced to allay the fears of the Orthodox elements over the *derekh eretz* aspect,[21] and therefore they viewed Hirsch's efforts with anxiety and distrust (*S* 2:451).

So acrimonious became the controversy over this simple talmudic dictum that neither Hirsch's death nor the collapse of his school system terminated it. Isaac Breuer, who admired Hirsch but was disillusioned with Western civilization, tried to diminish the significance of *derekh eretz* in Hirsch's doctrine, saying that Hirsch had never considered *derekh eretz* equal in importance to Torah: "Hirsch's fight was not for balance and not for reconcilement, nor for synthesis and certainly not for parallel power, but for domination—for the true and absolute domination of the divine precept over the new tendencies. The divine precept can countenance no collateral rule and certainly no toleration."[22] On the other hand, Hirsch was castigated for having employed Torah merely as a subterfuge for propagating Occidental culture, thereby deliberately luring Orthodox Jews into the camp of their adversaries. This charge was leveled by Gershom Scholem, whose own outlook was not Orthodox, who accused Hirsch of having promoted a *grauenhafte Akkommodationstheologie*—a gruesome theology of accommodation—which demoralized the Jewish substance of the *gesetzestreue Judentum* (Torah-true Jewry) in Germany. The latter "had to pay dearly for that ambiguous *Torah im derekh eretz.*"[23] Scholem charged that Hirsch's educational dualistic principle contained diabolical potentialities which would explode in the course of time:

It was one of those formulas, whose hidden life reveals itself only too late, namely, when its dialectics have turned against its advocates. It was a conception designed in that comfortless world of progress, to facilitate for the pious of the old world adaptation to something most strange to them. This function it has fulfilled only too thoroughly. It became a vehicle of a kind of assimilation whose demonic triumphs in the Orthodox camp would require a Jewish Balzac to describe them in their full extent. The watchword that was intended in a changed world to strengthen the Jewish backbone of the pious, has done more than anything else to break it.[24]

According to Breuer, Torah was primary and *derekh eretz* ancillary, while according to Scholem, Hirsch intended the reverse. The basis of this controversy appears to have been the incorrect assumption that the equality in form did not really imply equality in content. Hirsch's own view on this debatable dictum may be found in the numerous references to Jewish education in his extensive writings and addresses. They prove conclusively that he believed in unqualified coequality and parity of Torah and *derekh eretz*. Hirsch declares: "Our institute devotes the same care and attention to general educational subjects as to the specifically Jewish and in fact, it is one of its declared principles that both should be put on the same footing" (*S* 2:450).[25] Thus, the great importance Hirsch attached to secular studies was neither the result of expediency nor a concession to the times; it was an integral part of his Weltanschauung. Hirsch clearly asserts that his aim is to pay no less attention and devote no less care to subjects of general education than to the specifically Jewish ones (*S* 2:466). The values of Judaism are divine, hence eternal. They cannot, therefore, conflict with any discipline or set of values true and essential to the welfare and progress of man. Thus, by retaining its own identity, Judaism will contribute immeasurably to the intellectual and ethical development of man.

The entire controversy concerning which aspect in Hirsch's educational theory ought to be considered primary and which ancillary is, indeed, baseless. It reflects a state of mind produced by subsequent events which negated the progressive climate of opinion prevalent in the idealistic and hopeful age in which Hirsch lived.

The Monistic Matrix of Coequality

The status of coequality accorded to Torah and *derekh eretz* in Hirsch's educational theory is primarily attributable to the monistic concept which underlies his philosophic outlook. The monistic view, which has had its exponents throughout the history of philosophy, reasserted itself in the nineteenth century, particularly in the philosophy of Hegel. In antiquity, monism was advocated by Parmenides of the Eleatic school and subsequently by the Neoplatonists. During the Renaissance, it was upheld by Giordano Bruno and Jacob Boehme.

In the nineteenth century, Hegel rejected the Kantian epistemological dichotomy and attempted to establish the monistic Idea, devoid of any particular determinative quality, as the basis of his entire system. The seemingly irreconcilable dualism of matter and thought was resolved into monism by Hegel by deducing matter from thought.[26] Thus the Idea becomes the only absolute reality from which all manifestations are evolved. Nature, though unqualifiedly real, does not exist independently of the Idea: "Since the Idea posits itself as the absolute unity of the pure Notion and its reality, and consequently assumes the form of immediate being, it is as the totality of this form, nature."[27] Omitting the various difficulties relating to the actual transition from the Idea to nature in Hegelian thought,[28] we can observe that nature was considered by Hegel to be "the resolve of the pure Idea to determine itself as external Idea."[29] For the world is "pervaded and characterized by externality, a world in which everything is external to everything else."[30] The glaring contrasts between nature and Idea as to their aspects of irrationality and rationality, contingency and necessity, are not problems of dualism since, according to the Hegelian dialectic, any two antithetical terms are also identical. Thus, underneath all apparent opposites there exists a fundamental unity. Nature, though it constitutes the antithesis of the Idea, is actually the very same Idea in its aspect of self-estrangement and otherness.

This Hegelian concept of fundamental unity underlying the entire universe was carried into the field of education by Friedrich Froebel,[31] an older contemporary of Hirsch. Froebel saw the all-encompassing monistic principle permeating the entire universe: "In all things there lives and reigns an eternal law."[32] Anyone endowed with a clear and penetrating vision can behold "the inner in the outer and through the outer, and sees the outer proceeding with logical necessity from the essence of the inner—this law has been and is enounced with equal clearness and distinctness in nature—the external, in the spirit—the internal, and in life which unites the two."[33] Despite all the seeming differences, there is in the universe a fundamental unity that the discerning eye can and ought to detect: "All things have come from the Divine Unity, from God. And have their origin in the Divine Unity, in God alone. God is the sole source of all things. In all things there lives and reigns the Divine Unity, God."[34] Nature and spirit are merely different manifestations of God, the former being the outer aspect and the latter, the inner one. Froebel, like Hegel, postulated that a fundamental unity underlies the antithetical forces which become reconciled dialectically in a synthesis.[35] The law of opposites has its complement, the law of connection; and these two contrary laws are united in the synthesized form of the Froebelian triune pattern of a higher unity.[36]

Due to this interrelatedness between the antithetical and the identical, the opposites and the connection, the unity and the diversity, the complete comprehension of one is impossible without a thorough knowledge of the other. The knowledge of God, who is the ultimate absolute Unity, is unattainable without the knowledge of the diverse manifestations of the world, which are subject to the law of polarity or opposites.[37]

Hirsch, who was strongly influenced by Hegel, must have drawn implications for his theory of education from Hegelian philosophy. Although Hegel himself never wrote a treatise on education,[38] his influence on philosophies of education, particularly those of Friedrich Froebel and Johann Karl Friedrich Rosenkranz,[39] was considerable. Since in Hegel's view the entire universe in all its multiplicity and complexity forms one single unified whole and is explicable only when viewed as such, a thorough knowledge of nature and man is essential for the comprehension of reality. Like Hegel, who considered nature an integral part of reality through which God manifests Himself,[40] Hirsch, too, could not relegate the knowledge of nature to an inferior status. Nature has as much to teach man about his obligations and his role in the universe as does the Torah. Nature, moreover, as part of the divine manifestation, certainly could neither negate nor contradict Judaism, which is another aspect of God's manifestation. The exclusion of *derekh eretz*, the elimination of the natural and social sciences from the curriculum designed for Man-Israel, would detract from the true knowledge of the ways of God that is so vital and essential for the salvation of man. True knowledge, regardless of its origin, is therefore in accordance with the spirit of Judaism and something to be avidly pursued, not so much for the sake of knowledge but as a religious duty. Consequently, the study of the natural and social sciences deserves a place within the curriculum of the Jewish school. As Hirsch expresses it: "It is the Jewish view that truth, like God its source, is one and indivisible, and therefore the knowledge of it can be only one and indivisible" (S 2:454).

The concept that one can learn how to come closer to God through the teleological comprehension of nature had already been emphasized by Hirsch in his *Neunzehn Briefe*. Sketchily, he points out how through the observation of natural phenomena man may become conscious of God and cognizant of his own role in the scheme of creation:

He, in His infinite wisdom, ordained this *mutual interdependence* in order that each individual being might contribute with its measure of force, whether much or little, to the preservation of the All. . . . Thus water, having penetrated the earth, is collected in cloud and sea; light having pierced the earthy crust and brought forth plants, children of light and heat is concentrated again into sun, moon and stars; the germ, the offspring of earth, is taken from the earth and given to the crown of ripened fruit. (*NL* 29)

The knowledge of nature and the behavior of its phenomena have a religious and moral message for man. Conversely, the lack of such knowledge implies the heedlessness of man to God's lessons through nature.

Since exclusion of *derekh eretz* is detrimental to Judaism, Hirsch bemoans the fact that excessive persecutions and merciless oppression had deprived Israel

of every broad and natural view of the world and of life and the Talmud had yielded about all the practical results for life of which it was capable. [Thus] every mind that felt the desire of independent activity was obliged to forsake the paths of study and research in general open to the human intellect and to take its recourse to dialectic subtleties and hairsplittings. (*NL* 186)[41]

Judaism, pursuing an exclusive one-sided education of Torah, was destined to disintegration and to becoming a "stationary mechanism" (*NL* 187). It had created "extra-mundane dream worlds"

(*NL* 187) and was eventually transformed into a "magical mechanism, a means of influencing or resisting theosophic worlds and anti-worlds" (*NL* 187). According to Hirsch, true Judaism considers the estrangement of the Jew from general culture as unfortunate, since the fundamental aim of the Torah is to promote knowledge and improve the moral and intellectual standards of mankind. Judaism "is perhaps the only religion which does not say, *extra me nulla salus*, which gladly welcomes every advance in enlightenment and virtue wherever and through whatever medium it may be produced" (*S* 2:454). Reconciling Torah and *derekh eretz* as two complementary aspects of the same divine reality would have immeasurably beneficial consequences. Far from contradicting Judaism, the natural sciences would enhance it. Having learned that the world from the smallest submicroscopic particle to the largest galaxy is governed by law, students would learn that man's behavior and thought must also be governed by law, the law of the Torah, and that God is the author of that Law. Through the study of nature, men will gain new insight into the sacred Scriptures.[42] They will admire the striking similarity of Job's description of nature to that of Newton (*S* 2:461). The psalms of David will have a new ring, demonstrating the constancy and consistency of both the natural and moral laws.

Hirsch was anxious to find qualified teachers who could intellectually and psychologically combine within themselves the harmonious principle of Torah and *derekh eretz*. They would be

teachers with a Jewish education, men whose own intellectual and spiritual education has matured in a harmonization of its Jewish and secular components, who have absorbed with equal thoroughness and earnestness both Jewish learning and secular learning; men whose roots are in Judaism, mind and heart, but who have learned to appreciate Judaism from the standpoint of secular philosophy and secular philosophy from the point of view of Judaism. (*S* 1:279)

Nominative and Substantive Quality

Because of the monistic spirit which permeates Hirsch's educational theory, the constituent parts of his dual curriculum could only nominally be referred to as religious or secular. Their division is neither intrinsic nor substantive. The ethical-religious spirit, like the omnipresent divine spirit, permeates all subjects, regardless of their nominal nonreligious nomenclature. According to Hirsch, the entire school atmosphere should be pervaded by that ethical-religious spirit which is its only raison d'être. An educational institution solely dedicated to stimulating intellectual growth is destructive of ethical values (S 1:286–87). Such a school could only promote an animalistically competitive spirit and deify utilitarianism, thus destroying man's sense of moral obligation, cooperativeness, and sense of higher purpose.

Hirsch objects to the so-called "religious instruction" or "systematic religious instruction" popular in the nontraditional circles of his day (S 1:266). He criticizes this reduction of religion to a mere "subject" among a host of others. He objects to the idea of a Jewish catechism, patterned along similar Christian abridgments, from which the fundamentals of Judaism were to be taught (S 1:273). Religious education should introduce the pupil to the main sources of Judaism so that he can become religiously self-sustaining. Fragmentary religious instruction compels the student to remain a perpetual spiritual infant and prevents him from direct access to the words of God. (S 1:275).

True Jewish religious education must be comprehensive and all-inclusive, as well as independent from other, so-called nonreligious subjects. As a result of holding this view, which maintains the pertinence of religion, and particularly of Jewish religion, to all aspects of nature, history, and daily life, Hirsch makes no attempt to balance the secular and religious parts of the curriculum. Thus, *Horeb*'s outline of subjects to be taught in his contemplated school system includes Hebrew, German, Bible, natural and social sciences *(Natur- und Menschen-Kenntnisse)*, history, practical ethics *(Lebensweisheit)*, writing, and arithmetic (H 553).

A careful analysis will reveal that out of all the above-mentioned subjects, only Bible could be properly called a religious subject. The status of the Hebrew language as a religious subject in Hirsch's educational system is less certain. Although Hebrew serves as a key to the great religious heritage of Judaism, Hirsch rather emphasizes its importance as a universal educational means, waxing eloquent over its excellent pedagogical values.[43]

Hirsch's particular enchantment with the Hebrew language was not merely due to the fact that he attributes to it a mystical qual-ity,[44] and it certainly was not due to his alleged extreme religious nationalism,[45] a view which cannot be substantiated. On the con-trary, in advocating the Hebrew language as a school subject, Hirsch is emphatic in underscoring its universal and cosmopolitan aspect and its importance for general education. It serves as a valuable instrument in the development of logical thinking and comprehension, as well as awakening sensitivity to nuances and shades of meaning in fields unrelated to Hebrew (*S* 2:440). Hirsch's adulation of Hebrew is akin to that of the Maskilim, who wor-shipped it not as an expression of nationalism but as "the cultural work of Jewish historical identity."[46] Like them, Hirsch admires the clarity and the brevity of the Hebrew language, the etymology of which is not a mere ingenious approximation, but the most articulate philosophy on man and nature reflected in words (*S* 2:440–41).

The greatest value of Hebrew in education lies not in its reli-gious or strictly linguistic aspect, but rather in its worldwide hu-manism and role as a transfer of learning value. The study of Hebrew and the accumulation of an extensive vocabulary by stu-dents will prove useful for the cultivation of their powers of thought and general cultural improvement (*S* 2:444). Hirsch's predilection for Hebrew was, like that of the Maskilim, humanistic rather than nationalistic. It is noteworthy that in Hirsch's educa-tional system Hebrew had to be taught in accordance with its standard grammatical rules. In his school he avoided the homilet-ic-hermeneutic and pseudoetymological conjecture of his *Laut-verwandtschaft*, the sound associations he so frequently employs in his writings.[47] Hirsch's belief in Hebrew's ability to improve logical reasoning and thought was similarly evinced by Hegel in regard to the European classical languages.[48] The positive attrib-utes that Hegel had ascribed to Greek and Latin, Hirsch applies to Hebrew. Therefore, Hebrew in Hirsch's outline, although seemingly a religious subject, cannot actually be categorized as such.

The subject denoted by Hirsch as "practical ethics" can hardly be classified as an exclusively religious or Judaic subject. Although the principles of this study had to be derived from the Written and Oral Law, *Mishneh Torah, Shulḥan Arukh* (*H* 553), and other

Jewish religious sources, the essence of it did not differ appreciably from the character education emphasized by all great educators of the time: "The intellectualism of Herbartian, the voluntarism of Froebelian education aim alike at the goal of character."[49]

This seeming overbalance of secular subjects did not disturb Hirsch, since the nominal character of the subject matter does not affect its intrinsic substance. It is the inner spirit that determines the religious quality of any given subject. Even the Bible loses its religious quality when studied as a subject of philological interest, antiquarian research, or as aesthetics and literature (NL 13). It is, therefore, the spirit with which one approaches any subject that determines its corresponding quality, not the subject matter per se. Hence the seeming imbalance between the subjects nominally classified as Torah and derekh eretz in Hirsch's curriculum.

Reconciliation with Newtonian Science

Hirsch's affirmation of the principle of coequality of religious and general education poses the problem of the reconciliation of specific subjects, notably science and religion. It seems strange that Hirsch, who vigorously defended Jewish tradition against the negative influences which endangered its position in the modern world, should court such danger from the scientific outlook which had undermined all biblical religions, Judaism included. However, most of the tensions between the scientific and religious outlook in modern times were caused by the post-Darwinian concept of nature which toppled the great eighteenth-century triad—nature, reason, and utility—and replaced it with the idea of evolution. It was evolution that revolutionized the traditional religious beliefs which seemed only recently to have come to terms with Newtonian science.

Hirsch was already fifty-one by the time Darwin's Origin of Species appeared in 1859, and sixty-three when The Descent of Man was published in 1871; thus Darwin's shattering impact on philosophy and religion had hardly any effect on Hirsch, whose outlook on religion and nature was already solidly molded into the Cartesian-Newtonian world view, which does not necessarily negate biblical concepts: "Newton had believed that God made the solar system and its laws at a single moment in time; it was a machine, but a machine created by God with a definite purpose in mind."[50] The Hegelian philosophy which influenced Hirsch in his formative years was also pre-Darwinian in nature. Although Hegel's thought encompasses the concept of evolution, it is dialectical and logical rather than naturalistic and temporal.[51]

Unaffected by Darwinism, Hirsch's cosmological view as outlined in the *Neunzehn Briefe* and elaborated in his other works remained fundamentally mechanistic. His admiration of the laws of nature is akin to Newton's, for whom this "supremely elegant structure of the solar system cannot have arisen except by the device and power of an intelligent being."[52] The laws of the natural sciences in the Newtonian outlook serve as a potent ally rather than an antagonist of religion: "It is precisely this law of nature itself which is the most vital and living revelation of God, and the fact that it appears to us eternal and unchanging is the unambiguous testimony to the miracle of His omnipotence" (*S* 1:18–19).[53]

Unmindful of the theory of evolution, Hirsch emphasizes the biblical view of the uniqueness, permanence, and stratification of species where no variation has taken place since Genesis. This concept, which Hirsch considered "das grosse le-mino-Gesetz" (*CG* 1:11),[54] is strikingly similar to the Aristotelian *genera* and the doctrine of *nullae speciae novae*, which fit well into the Newtonian order. In typical pre-Darwinian fashion, Hirsch sees each species as endowed with a particular ethical-religious *telos*: "Behold now separately each created thing, from the blade of grass to the vast sun-ball, each with its special purpose and each specially adapted in its form and matter for that purpose; the same Almighty wisdom formed and designed each for its special purpose" (*NL* 20–21). Eliminating the religious aspect of inherent purposefulness from Hirsch's view yields something not unlike Hegel's *Naturphilosophie*, where all reality "is a system of strata or grades, higher or lower."[55]

This classic notion of immutable species, which reigned supreme prior to the appearance of *The Origin of Species*, cemented relations between the then-prevailing science and the similar biblical concept; it also substantiated the traditionalists' teleological outlook. This compatibility of pre-Darwinian science with religion was pointed out by John Dewey:

The design argument thus operated in two directions. Purposefulness accounted for the intelligibility of nature and the possibility
of science, while the absolute or cosmic character of this purposefulness gave sanction and worth to the moral and religious endeavors of man. Science was underpinned and morals authorized by
one and the same principle, and their mutual agreement was
eternally guaranteed.[56]

The inclusion of man within the scope of the cosmic process of
evolution, the denial of first and final causes in the universe, and
the introduction of the principle of natural selection—to list only
a few of the implications of Darwinism dangerous to religion—
were unknown to Hirsch before his declining years and consequently did not disturb him when they began to emerge later.
Pre-Darwinian science was "safe" from a religious standpoint,
since it did not threaten man's ethical preeminence or reduce him
to animality, a state subject to nonteleological changes contingent
on blind forces. Hirsch agreed with Hegel's preevolutionistic concept of man, according to which "man is, on the one hand, an
integral part of nature. He is an animal. He is an external material
existence subject to the dominion of natural laws. He is on the
other hand, a spiritual being, a living embodiment of reason and
of eternal mind."[57] This philosophic-scientific concept of man and
nature is so easily harmonized with Judaism that Hirsch could
recommend the study of natural history, physics, geography, psy-
chology, and anthropology as an integral part of his curriculum
without hesitation (*H* 53).

Copernican Heliocentrism and the Emerging Cosmogonies

The conclusion that Hirsch's affirmation of Torah and *derekh
eretz* applies only in the context of Newtonian, pre-Darwinian
science calls for further clarification. While Newton's views did
not contradict or negate the general outlook of the Bible—Hirsch
could even find in the Book of Job notions subsequently expounded in Newton's *Principia* (*S* 2:461)—particular divergencies
did exist, the most noteworthy being the problem of whether the
universe is heliocentric or geocentric. It was Newton who cor-
roborated and developed the heliocentric hypothesis propounded

by Copernicus in the latter's *De Revolutionibus Orbium Coeles-tium* (1543). The agitation that this theory caused among theologians who affirmed the literal scriptural geocentric point of view needs no elaboration. It is, therefore, interesting to see how Hirsch, who still accepted the theophanic nature of the Bible, meets this challenge.

Unlike numerous Christian theologians, who despite all evidence clung tenaciously to the Ptolemaic outlook, Hirsch courageously accepted the Copernican one, which had become universally adopted by his era. Candidly, Hirsch asserts that the Bible does not describe the universe in scientific terms but in metaphorical ones, addressing itself to man in the *Sprache der Menschen*, the language of man, which is neither objective nor precise. Even scientists' everyday speech reflects unscientific, metaphorical notions. No doubt, Copernicus, Kepler, and other astronomers of note in their ordinary conversations spoke about the sun rising and setting, even though in their scientific writings they maintained that it is the earth that revolves around the sun, not the sun around the earth. Similarly, no modern scientific theory about the solar system can be based upon biblical phrases. To evolve a dogma from the biblical passage in which Joshua allegedly halted the sun in Gibeon and the moon in the valley of Ajalon is futile and preposterous. Speaking in the language of man, the Bible describes natural phenomena as they register on man's sensory apparatus, not as they can scientifically be demonstrated to operate. It is therefore impossible to decide between a heliocentric and a geocentric theory of the universe on the basis of biblical descriptions, narratives, phrases, or allusions (*S* 1:291–92).

Commenting on the psalmist's description of the sun, a description with an unmistakably geocentric quality,[58] Hirsch reiterates his theory about the metaphorical style of the Bible. Accordingly, the psalmist spoke the speech of men to men:[59] "It is not the aim of the Holy Scriptures to teach us astronomy, cosmogony or physics, but only to guide man to the fulfillment of his life's task within the framework of the constellation of his existence" (*CP* 19:7). This last statement of Hirsch's sounds like the maxim expressed by Cardinal Baronius, quoted by Galileo, "that the intention of the Holy Ghost is to teach us not how the heavens go but how to go to heaven."[60]

Although Hirsch indicates that the Bible is indefinite and non-

commital so far as the Ptolemaic-Copernican controversy is concerned, there can be no doubt with whose views Hirsch identified.
In the *Neunzehn Briefe* he characteristically translates the Hebrew word *eretz*, "earth," as "swift runner" on the basis of his
Lautverwandtschaft etymology, deriving it from the Hebrew root
rutz, "run" (*NL* 19). Hirsch hints homiletically that the Bible
employs a term which suggests the earth "running" or revolving
around the sun.

Similarly, Hirsch suggests that the Hebrew term *shamayim*
does not mean "heaven," but generally the "whole extraterritorial
world which surrounds the earth in space" (*CG* 1:8). This definition clearly indicates that the solid firmament of the Ptolemaic
universe had collapsed and heaven lost its concrete meaning in
endless space. The concept of infinity which was contributed by
Giordano Bruno to the emerging Newtonian world view seems to
have necessitated a new interpretation of the old Hebrew noun
shamayim. Only when viewed in the light of Newtonian science
can we appreciate Hirsch's philological manipulations to divest
this Hebrew word of any definite, directional, spatial qualities.
Shamayim thus becomes a relative term signifying outer space or
the entire extraterrestrial domain: "For every point in the universe, the whole of the rest of space with all its bodies, would be
shamayim" (*CG* 1:1).

Hirsch was fully aware that the Cartesian-Newtonian world-
machine has no room for the miracles narrated in the Bible. The
universe is strictly governed by laws, and no measure of interference with these eternal rules can be brooked. Hirsch therefore
suggests that the biblical miracles did not affect the entire cosmos
since they were merely local occurrences of "national experience"
designated to impart certain moral ideas to the people of Israel
(*S* 1:292–93). This interpretation of miracles is unsatisfactory to
both the fundamentalist theologian and the Newtonian scientist.
The localization and reduction of miracles to a mere national
experience for didactic purposes unquestionably minimizes their
cosmic importance and universal splendor, especially to a fundamentalist. To the Newtonian scientist for whom nature means
cosmic order and regularity, these "experiences," even when national in scope, geographically circumscribed, and educational in
purpose, constitute violations of the laws of nature and are consequently inadmissible.[61]

Indeed, not all of pre-Darwinian science could "safely" be reconciled with the Bible and Jewish tradition. Laplace's nebular hypothesis, Hutton and Smith's doctrine of uniformitarianism, and Lyell's principles of geology, were bound to conflict with the Mosaic cosmogony. We may assume that these theories were not yet considered a part of generally accepted science. Hirsch may also not have felt their impact strongly enough to attempt an interpretation or an explanation of an individual theory or hypothesis; or his scientific background and knowledge may not have been very deep. His brief attendance at the University of Bonn hardly rendered him conversant with all the scientific theories and speculations of his time or aware of all their possible implications.

The Applicability of Empirical Methodology to Judaism

We may conclude that the coequality of Torah and *derekh eretz* as affirmed by Hirsch was due neither to expediency nor to accommodation. It was sincere and genuine, although prompted by the new era ushered in by the Emancipation. Living not so much in a pre-Darwinian as in a post-Newtonian age, Hirsch could not foresee the fundamental conflicts between science and religion which resulted from the wide acceptance of Darwin's theory of evolution.[62] By making certain adjustments in Jewish traditional beliefs, he was convinced that he was not weakening the position of Judaism but rather underpinning it with modern science. So impressed was he by the scientific approach that he even suggests applying the empirical methodology employed in the natural sciences to the Torah:

Two revelations are open before us, nature and *Torah*. In nature all phenomena stand before us as indisputable facts and we can only endeavor *a posteriori* to ascertain the law of each and the connection of all. Abstract demonstration of the truth, or, rather, the probability of theoretic explanations of the facts of nature is an unnatural proceeding. The right method is to verify our assumptions by the known facts, and the highest attainable degree of certainty is to say, "The facts agree with our assumption"—that is, all observed phenomena can be explained according to our theory. A singly contradictory phenomenon will make our theory untenable. We must, therefore, acquire all the possible knowledge concerning the object of our investigation and know it, if possible, in its totality. If, however, all efforts should fail in disclosing the inner law and connection of phenomena revealed to us as facts in nature, the facts remain, nevertheless, undeniable, and cannot be reasoned away. The same principles must be applied to the investigation of the Torah. (*NL* 194–95)

Hirsch was fully convinced that Torah and *derekh eretz,* particularly the natural sciences, complement one another and when studied properly would develop the true Man-Israel.

According to Hirsch, man is confronted by both an ontological and a religious-ethical problem. The ontological problem can be solved by man's contemplation of a descriptive study of nature and history and his comprehension of the scientific laws governing them. However, this knowledge will remain informative rather than instructive and not enlighten man with regard to his relationship to nature, man, or God. Being intellectual rather than ethical, such knowledge will remain unrelated and barren. It is not the Torah's purpose to supply information which can be obtained from the social and natural sciences.

The divine law revealed on Sinai aims at relating man to his fellow man, to nature, to God and to himself, thus harmonizing man's will with the will of God. Recognition of man's moral harmony with nature ushers in true equilibrium. Such an inner balance is the very essence of what is implied by Hirsch in his seeming duality of Man-Israel.

14
"Avodah": Divine Service

"Avodah" and "Ahavah"

The sixth and last division of the *Horeb* is entitled *"Avodah,"* divine service. In the Talmud, this term connotes the sacrificial worship in the Temple in Jerusalem; however, it is also applied to prayer. The *Sifrei* had already interpreted *avodah* to signify prayer. Commenting on the biblical verse ". . . serving Him [*u-le-avdo*] with all your heart,"[1] the *Sifrei* noted that a service of the heart—*avodah sh-ba-lev*—refers to prayer[2] because a sacrificial service takes place on the altar. Although Maimonides alluded to the aforementioned Deuteronomic verse at the beginning of the laws concerning prayer, he did not designate the division of the *Mishneh Torah* dealing with synagogue service and prayers as *"Avodah"* but as *"Ahavah."* He used the term *avodah* in its original connotation of Temple service and thus applied it to the eighth division of the *Mishneh Torah,* devoted to this subject.

Hirsch, who like Maimonides makes reference to the Deuteronomic verse as interpreted by the *Sifrei,* designates the division in *Horeb* dealing with synagogue and prayer service *"Avodah."* It is possible that since Hirsch, unlike Maimonides, does not deal with the Temple cult, which was no longer in existence, he could therefore apply the term *avodah* to a subject currently in force. This application was particularly justified not only because of the statement "just as the service of the altar is called *Avodah* so is

369

prayer called *Avodah*,"[3] but also because prayer was viewed as substitute for sacrifice, and the synagogue a miniature Temple.[4]

It is possible to suggest that the German term *Gottesdienst*, by which religious services were known in Germany, constituted a factor in Hirsch's designation. The Hebrew equivalent of this German term is *avodat ha-Shem*, which for the sake of brevity or to avoid using the word for God—*ha-Shem*—in vain was termed merely *avodah*. That this may be so seems evident from the fact that the preceding five divisions of the *Horeb* bear Hebrew titles with no equivalent German translations. There are German subtitles explaining in general the subjects subsumed under the Hebrew titles, but the only division that has a German equivalent without any lengthy subtitle to explain it is *"Avodah."* Hirsch apparently felt that the German equivalent, *Gottesdienst*, was adequate and needed no further elaboration or elucidation.

It is noteworthy that before and after Hirsch's publication of the *Horeb* the Reformers frequently called their prayer books *Seder ha-Avodah*.[5] This does not imply that Hirsch imitated the Reformers, but may imply that a term used by the Reformers, even a term associated with the controversial prayer book of the Hamburg Temple, was not objectionable to Hirsch on that account. Years later when Hirsch published his own prayer book, he was more circumspect in his nomenclature. His *siddur*, written at a time when the lines between him and the Reformers were sharply drawn, does not include the term *avodah* but is entitled *Siddur Tefillot Yisrael: Israels Gebet übersetzt und erläutert.*[6]

By and large, Hirsch follows the schema of Maimonides's *"Sefer Ahavah"* in the *"Avodah"* division of the *Horeb* except for the laws of circumcision, *tefillin*, *tzitzit*, and *mezuzah*, which because of their symbolic significance he places in the *"Edot"* division. At the end of the *"Avodah"* division, Hirsch deals with laws of reverence for the Temple of Jerusalem, regarding idol worship, picture making, sanctity of priests, sacrifices outside the Temple mount, and idolatrous representations. These laws are not included in the *"Sefer Ahavah"* but are found in other divisions of the *Mishneh Torah*, such as *"Sefer ha-Madda"* and *"Sefer Avodah."*

The reasons for including these laws in the *"Avodah"* division of the *Horeb* are not clear. Hirsch undoubtedly encountered the same difficulties in his efforts to classify the precepts as Maimonides and other codifiers and systematizers. Frequently, as pointed out, the latter found that certain laws and rules defy the neatly divided lines of categorization.[7]

Synagogue-oriented Judaism

Although prayer is "the central phenomenon of religion, the very hearthstone of all piety"[8] and the synagogue is viewed as a miniature Temple, it is strange that Hirsch should devote an entire division—one sixth of his exposition of the doctrinal system of Judaism—to prayer and synagogue. Valuable as these subjects may be, they cannot compare in halakhic importance to other Jewish institutions to which Hirsch is quantitatively less generous. The overemphasis on prayer is particularly enigmatic in that some of the foremost halakhic authorities did not consider standardized, regular daily prayer as biblically mandatory but as rabbinically ordained.[9]

Hirsch's *"Avodah"* division comprises twenty-one chapters, exceeding the number of chapters in each of the *"Torot," "Mishpatim,"* and *"Hukkim"* divisions, which deal with the relationship of man to God, to his fellow man, and to the world, respectively. Indeed, the *"Edot"* exceeds *"Avodah"* by two chapters and *"Mitzvot"* by five. However, considering the numerous laws regarding them, it is clear that synagogue and prayer are, at the least from the quantitative point of view, the subjects Hirsch wished to stress most. His elaboration of this aspect is even more puzzling, however, in that neither the synagogue nor prayer needed any rationale to justify them. Unlike other precepts, their importance was not challenged by any group, either on the right or the left. Nor was Hirsch's detailed outline and description of the prayers necessary. All traditional prayer books, which contained the order of the services, were available in every home. Hirsch's effort in this respect seems gratuitously elaborate.

No less puzzling is the very distinct categorization of *"Avodah"* as a separate division. Its laws could logically be subsumed under *"Mitzvot,"* where they rightfully belong. Assuming that Hirsch wanted the *Horeb* to consist of six divisions, analogous to those of the *Mishnah*, it is still enigmatic why he devoted the sixth division to the subjects of prayer and synagogue worship, which were universally accepted.[10] When these questions are considered in the context of Hirsch's times, his concern with the laws classified under *"Avodah"* appears justifiable. The centrifugal socioeconomic forces operating in the German Jewish community at that time compelled Judaism to confine itself primarily if not exclusively to the domain of the synagogue. The Jewish religion, which had permeated all aspects of life, was gradually forced to limit itself to the precincts of the house of worship and frequently terminated its activities and influence at that threshold. With the advent of Reform and the spread of its philosophy, Judaism, like Protestantism, became a locale-oriented religion limited in space, nature, and scope. Many decades after writing the *Horeb*, when Hirsch realized the implications of this excessive preoccupation with the synagogue worship and prayer, he indignantly protested against it.[11] So revolted was Hirsch by this synagogue-oriented attitude that in an essay entitled "Das Zion der Zukunft und die heutige Reform"[12] he asserts that perhaps the best cure for Judaism might be the closing of all synagogues for one hundred years. Such a radical move might have a sobering effect on the Jews and redirect their efforts from the means to the end, from the tangential to the essential.[13]

However, at the time of the composition of the *Horeb* in Oldenburg, these deleterious effects may not have been apparent, and Hirsch, who wished to attract and unite the conservatives and liberals in the community, may have considered stress on synagogue worship and prayer as beneficial. "These sanctuaries," he asserts, "are the indispensable condition of Israel's existence" (*H* 706). They constitute sources of spiritual replenishment (*H* 705) the values of which are inestimable for the enhancement of Judaism. This elaboration of *avodah* to an entire division was tantamount to accepting the prevailing view in liberal circles that synagogue worship was central in Jewish life. Recognizing the important role the synagogue was to play in Judaism, Hirsch was as eager as the Reformers to eliminate many inelegant practices widespread in the traditional synagogues.[14] Along with the liberals, he was chagrined over unaesthetic practices which detracted from the solemnity of the synagogue and rendered the service less inspiring. He, too, was irked by the "excessive flourishes" of some cantors who conducted the services "in a manner undignified and thoughtless" (*H* 689). Hirsch recapitulates many laws and rules from the Talmud and codes concerning proper conduct in the house of worship. At first glance, it seems that he merely restates these in his own idiom, but a closer look discloses a distinctive, contemporaneous concern on the part of the author.

Hirsch's preoccupation with synagogue decorum is singularly evident in the *Synagogenordnungen* which he promulgated in the *Israelitische Religionsgesellschaft* in Frankfurt am Main in 1874.[15] Such formulated sets of rules concerning the order and decorum of the synagogue were the hallmark of the Reform temples. Many of the *Synagogenordnungen* were politically motivated, designed primarily to legitimize, sanction, or enforce liturgical innovations or deletions or other synagogue reforms. Frequently, these rules were established with the assistance of, or even actively initiated by, the government, whose interests they may have served.[16]

Despite the possible connection of such arrangements with Reform Hirsch did not hesitate to introduce such a *Synagogenordnung* in his separatist community in Frankfurt am Main. Although that community became the symbol of militant Orthodoxy deploring any Reform practices, Hirsch's concern for order and dignity in the synagogue was the overriding factor.[17] It is possible that his desire to enhance the prestige of the synagogue played an important role in his decision to permit a choir and to excise Kol Nidre. The former might have served as an attraction; the latter might have eliminated an irritant. Considering the overall importance of the synagogue, such concessions may not have seemed exorbitant to Hirsch.

Although Hirsch accepted the centrality of the synagogue and prayer, he did not share the liberals' view that these constituted the alpha and omega of Judaism. To him, they were only the omega, and consequently he places them at the end of the *Horeb*. Even in Oldenburg, when his outlook was still liberal-oriented, Judaism transcended the confines of the synagogue; and unlike the liberals and Reformers, whose chief preoccupation was with *Gottesdienst*, Hirsch considered synagogue worship only one aspect of the vast context of Judaism. He distinguished between *avodah* in the narrow sense of synagogue worship and *avodah* in the broader sense of divine worship. *Avodah* in the narrow sense does not make the Jew into an *eved ha-Shem*, a servant of God. To become *homo Judaicus*—in Hirsch's terminology, a *Mensch-Jissroel*—one must fulfill all commandments of the Torah.

The term *avodah* in the broader aspect is all-encompassing and full of ramifications. Its limited aspect, after all, evolved from other sources:

> If we take to heart the truths which the *Torot* teach us, absorbing them in spirit and mind, if we demonstrate and make them eternal for us and for others through the *Edot*, if we implement them joyfully in word and deed, in righteousness and love, as the *Mishpatim* and *Ḥukkim* and *Mitzvot* teach us: then we are *avdei ha-Shem*, real servants of God. (*H* 616)

The view that *avodah*, though important, must not assume priority over the other commandments may have induced Hirsch to depart from Maimonides's order in the *Mishneh Torah*. The latter placed the *"Sefer Ahavah,"* part of which deals with synagogue worship and prayer, immediately after the *"Sefer ha-Madda."* Hirsch leaves *"Avodah"* for the end of the *Horeb*. It is inconceivable that Hirsch did this to counter the overimportance assigned to it by the exponents of the Reform ideology.[18]

Restructuring of the Prayer Book

Hirsch's detailed elaboration of the order of the prayers—listing their component selections, explaining the significance of each and its relationship to the entire structure of the service—must also be viewed in the light of the era and its problems.

True, it may be suggested that in the section on prayer, as in many other sections of the *Horeb*, Hirsch merely follows Maimonides, who also presented an outline of the prayers in *Mishneh Torah*.[19] However, in Hirsch's time such an outline was superfluous, while Maimonides's summary[20] was a necessity as a "compromise between some universally acceptable rituals and the chaotic variety of local observances."[21] Maimonides had aimed at unifying and standardizing the diversity of prayers in a form acceptable to all Jewish communities. Moreover, the fact that there were no printed prayer books at that time made such an outline imperative to prevent changes.

In Hirsch's time, however, these problems no longer existed. The text of the prayer book *(siddur)*, except for minor variations between the Ashkenazic and Sephardic rituals, was well established;[22] the ritual of the services was fully consolidated; printed prayer books were common in every home. The *siddur* was the most popular book next to the Bible in every Jewish household, and from point of view of use it even surpassed the Bible.[23]

Hirsch's detailed outline of the prayers must have therefore been motivated by a far more cogent reason than mere imitation of Maimonides. The reverential attitude to the *siddur,* whose content and form were considered sacrosanct at the end of the eighteenth century, was subject to considerable Reformist inroads during the early part of the nineteenth century. At first, these changes were modest, but within a relatively short period they reached a point that evoked concern. The first move in this direction was David Friedländer's translation of the traditional prayer book into German in 1786.[24] This translation intended no reforms either in form or content. The fact that the German translation was printed in Hebrew characters is sufficient indication that the Jews had not yet mastered German well enough to read it in either roman or gothic letters. Apparently, Friedländer, like his mentor and friend Mendelssohn, aimed at educating his coreligionists in the German language. He therefore applied the same method to the *siddur* that Mendelssohn did to the Bible. This was a precursor of Reform, since the *siddur* had never before been translated into the vernacular. Although there is no prohibition against praying in other languages, it was nevertheless an established custom to pray in Hebrew, even by those who did not understand the language.

Thirty years after Friedländer's translation of the traditional *siddur,* a new prayer book appeared in Berlin entitled *Gebete am Sabbath-Morgen und an den beiden Neujahrs-Tagen.* Probably restricted to the initial Reform services conducted under the aegis of Israel Jacobson in Berlin, and still falling within the boundaries of the Halakhah,[25] it nevertheless contained several departures and some minor deletions from the traditional *siddur.*[26] Some of the traditional prayers were recited in German instead of Hebrew. Whether halakhically justifiable or not, these changes were sufficient to disturb the traditionalists in the Jewish community. The real storm over the emerging trend to reform the *siddur* broke out over the publication of the prayer book bearing the significant title *Die deutsche Synagogue* (1817–18) by Eduard Kley and Carl Siegfried Günsburg.[27] The adjective *deutsche* seemed to underscore its distinction from the universally accepted Jewish prayer book,[28] and the traditionalists sensed that unless this trend was checked it would destroy the unity of Judaism and of the Jewish people. It presented the dangerous potential that each country or community would have a different order of prayers.[29]

The fact that many variations, deletions, and innovations were motivated by political or aesthetic considerations made them no less dangerous, since they bore extensive social and theological implications. A disregard for tradition itself was at stake. In addition to substituting German for Hebrew, the Reformers also abolished the silent recitation of the *amidah*, substituted the *kedushah* of *musaf* for that of the *shaharit* service,[30] and arbitrarily interchanged texts from the Sephardic and Ashkenazic rites for no apparent reason. Some prayers were abridged and certain verses deleted.

The polemics that erupted between the proponents and opponents of the new prayer book bore all the characteristics of the *Kampfsliteratur* commonly employed in religious disputes.[31] Amid the fervor of this vituperative debate, in which the leading rabbis of the time participated, the new prayer book of the Hamburg Temple appeared in 1819.[32] It was edited by two scholarly laymen, Meyer Israel Bresselau and Seckel Isaak Frankel. While this prayer book did not initiate the controversy, it certainly exacerbated it, being far more radical than the previous prayer books. The fact that it proceeded from left to right, like a German book, was not halakhically objectionable, but for the traditional Jew brought up on the centuries-old *siddur* it was psychologically irritating. It contained no explicit abolition of the daily prayer services, but the very designation *für den Sabbath und Festtage des ganzen Jahres* implied that the Sabbath and festivals were the only days when services need take place. That this prayer book confined itself to these days and that the Hamburg Temple was only open at those times made the abolition of daily prayer services an inescapable conclusion.

The Meaning of Prayer

At the time of this acrimonious controversy, Hirsch was only eleven years old, and it is unknown to what extent it affected him. However, even if he was too young to comprehend it fully, the animosity and controversy it engendered in his native city and among all German Jewry for many years could not have failed to register upon him. Since his parents belonged to the *erleuchtet religiös* segment of the community, they were less vindictive but no less opposed to the new prayer book. The opposition to it was not limited to the extreme Orthodox only. Hirsch's uncle Moses, although a Maskil, reacted sharply against the Hamburg prayer book.[33]

Since the prayer book and the order of prayers were such important issues, it would be natural to expect that Hirsch should allude to them in the *"Avodah"* division. However, he treats these controversial subjects as if they had never been a matter of dispute. This should not be interpreted as indifference, since it was a calculated attempt to avoid any involvement that might be interpreted as partisan. Wishing to steer a neutral course during a bellicose era, Hirsch tried during his stay in Oldenburg to eschew any polemics. His calm tone and detached treatment of the subjects in the *"Avodah"* division are illustrative of this overriding desire to refrain from such involvement.

However it would be erroneous to assume that Hirsch was in fact neutral. It was just that he saw no need to add another piece of ineffective *Kampfsliteratur* to the already raging cacophony. Instead, Hirsch resorts to the expository method to interpret the meaning of the traditional *siddur*. Rather than criticize the new prayer books and dispute every abridgment, deletion, and substitution, he dwells on the structural cohesiveness of each order of prayers. He points out their relevance and underscores their organic interrelationship. Without resorting to a critique of the new Reform prayer books, he stresses the positive aspects of the traditional *siddur*.

Unlike a hymnal, the *siddur* cannot be changed at random; nor is it a desultory liturgical anthology from which selections can be arbitrarily excised. The overall structure of the *siddur* as well as its component prayers were arranged methodically by the early mentors of Judaism—the Men of the Great Assembly—with great care and deep insight: "They, and the sages following them, in a similar spirit, handed to Israel the inexhaustible source of its elevation to God, in the form of *tefillot,* in which Israel of today still raises itself up to God and gains the sanctification of its life" (*H* 626). Thus, any tampering with the standard *siddur* might destroy the delicately woven fabric of prayer that had so ingeniously and masterfully been elaborated by the great ancient authorities who grasped life in its most important aspects (*H* 626). By invoking the authorship and thus the authority of the Men of the Great Assembly, Hirsch precludes changes by his contemporaries who, being centuries removed from the time of the original composition of the traditional prayers, were unable to grasp their significance. Excision or alteration of one prayer, might cause irreparable damage to the conceptual continuum of Jewish prayer as such.

There is nothing original in Hirsch's view; similar opinions are replete in the volume *Eleh Divrei ha-Berit,* written by the leading rabbis of the time. Hirsch's contribution was his unargumentative tone and uncombative approach. Such a positive expository method explains Hirsch's in extenso description of all prayers, which at first glance seems superfluous. In view of the challenges to the traditional *siddur,* it was imperative for Hirsch to enumerate all prayers and to indicate the importance of each. Thus, without debating with the advocates of the new prayer books, he clearly states his position in this matter.

Man-Oriented Prayer

Beneath the expository calm of Hirsch's outlook in the *"Avodah"* division there are definite views and, at times, even a veiled polemic with the Reform endeavors. Hirsch introduces the division with a relatively lengthy essay on the meaning of prayer, viewing it, as did many of his contemporaries, not as God-oriented but rather as man-oriented. The aim of prayer is neither metaphysical nor eudaemonistic. Prayer does not intend to influence God or to induce Him to deflect His will for the sake of man. Its purpose is to prepare man psychologically and philosophically for the ethical-religious tasks he has to perform, for the problems he has to encounter, and for the battles in which he is engaged.

The Hebrew term *tefillah* clearly defines the Jewish concept of prayer. The verb "to pray" in Hebrew is always expressed in the reflexive form, *le-hitpalel*, which originally meant "to deliver an opinion about oneself, to judge oneself" (*H* 618).[34] As such, it differs from any of its equivalents in other languages. Neither the German *Gebet* nor the English *prayer* corresponds to the Hebrew *tefillah:* "In prayer the Jew becomes his own judge" (*CG* 9:7). Thus, prayer is neither mere supplication nor a mere spiritual experience, but rather a moment of serious soul-searching and critical self-examination when man judges himself, shedding all pretense and deception. Praying, Hirsch maintains, denotes man's endeavor to attain the proper perspective on himself vis-à-vis God and world (*H* 618).

In a similar manner, Hirsch defines the nature of the *"Avodah"* division in the *Neunzehn Briefe* to be, not God-oriented, but directed toward man. Its goal is "exaltation and sanctification of the inner powers by word-or-deed symbols to the end that our conception of our task be rendered clearer, and we be better fitted to fulfill our mission on earth" (*NL* 105). Thus, prayer does not attempt to influence God in any way or to solicit from Him any special favors for man. It is directed to man's thoughts so that he might contemplate his position in the world and redirect his actions in accordance with the larger perspectives which such meditation will disclose to him. Meditation in prayer is not an end in itself. Its consummation is not in passivity or in a subjective psychological religious experience; rather, its function must express itself dynamically, either in action, as in Temple worship, or in verbal articulation, as in prayer (*H* 616). As such, prayer, like *avodah* in general, serves fundamentally an educational purpose, as do all other aspects of Judaism. Hirsch gives no intimation as to the impression of prayer on God, nor any allusion to the talmudic view that God longs for the prayers of the righteous.[35] Again and again, Hirsch stresses prayer's educational value for man: "The fruit of prayer is the purification of thoughts and emotions" (*H* 688). By meditating and contemplating on "the most important thoughts contained in the prayers, our inner self becomes purified" (*H* 688). The liturgy transmitted through generations was designed to "improve our intellectual and emotional life and thus educate all generations of Israel to the zenith of our religious national existence" (*H* 688).

Hirsch's constant and consistent emphasis on the man-oriented educational significance of prayer is related to the view then prevalent in intellectual circles highly critical of God-oriented prayer. It was considered "an absurd and presumptuous delusion to try by the insistent opportunity of prayer whether God might not be deflected from the plan of His wisdom to provide some momentary advantage for us"[36] Kant spoke out against any form of worship aimed at influencing or pleasing God: "Every initiatory step in the realm of religion, which we do not take in a purely moral manner but rather have recourse to as *in itself* a means of making us well-pleasing to God and thus, through Him, of satisfying all our wishes, is a fetish-faith."[37] Prayer in this sense was particularly objectionable to Kant, since it implies that man "tries to work upon God."[38] It is "a superstitious illusion—a fetish-making; for it is no more than a *stated wish* directed to a Being who needs no such information regarding the inner disposition of the wisher."[39] God-oriented prayer is even blasphemous and offensive to the true spirit of religion. Kant again: "Prayer appears to be a presumptuous act and an act of distrust in God's knowledge of what is good for us. Continuous, unremitting prayer may be construed as an attempt to coerce God by constant begging into granting our desires."[40]

Although the early advocates of reformation of the prayer book were partly motivated by expediency, they too may have been aware of the criticism of God-oriented prayer, particularly that of Kant, whom they highly regarded. The very attempts to modernize the prayers to conform with the aesthetic, linguistic, and ideational requirements of the times indicate that their aim was to please man rather than God. The introduction of choirs and instrumental music, although in direct violation of the Sabbath, point in this direction. There is an emphasis on the psychological effects of prayer on the worshipper. Terms like *Andacht* (devotion), *Erbauung* (edification), *Erhebung* (elevation), *Begeisterung* (enthusiasm), *Erweckung* (awakening), and *Veredlung* (ennoblement) became current in the sermons and literature of the Reform movement. All these terms are inherently man-oriented and clearly demonstrate that what was sought in worship in general, and prayer in particular, was to influence man rather than God. The early Reformers also spoke of ethical and educational values inherent in the modernized liturgy. Friedländer in his preface to *Gebete der Juden auf das ganze Jahr* (1786) mentioned both the psychological and ethical-educational values of prayer: "Prayer will teach the rich man to put his advantage to noble use, and will soothe the turmoil in the mind of unhappy man."[41] Significantly, he also considered prayer as self-examination which in turn leads man "to a renewed resolve to keep God's commandments."[42]

Hirsch, who defended the traditional prayer book, tacitly accepted the prevalent view of man-oriented prayer, which—although emphasized by the Reformers—did not originate with them but was part of the general intellectual climate and familiar in Judaism. Maimonides, explaining the commandment to pray and cry to God in time of distress, "to sound short blasts on the trumpets,"[43] did not interpret this as God-oriented but rather as man-oriented: "We are told to offer up prayers to God, in order to establish firmly the true principle that God takes notice of our ways, that He can make them successful if we worship Him, or disastrous if we disobey Him, that [success and failure] are not the result of chance or accident."[44]

The notion that prayer was designed to establish firmly the principle of divine watchfulness and concern is only relevant with regard to man. Hirsch accepted this man-oriented concept of prayer which was in accord with his times and rejected any mystical implications. Kant had also distinguished between objective and subjective prayer. While he deplored the former as unnecessary to an omniscient God, Kant considered the latter "necessary for our own sakes, and not in order that God, who is the object and direction of our prayer, be made cognizant of something and be moved to grant it."[45] For the aim of man-oriented—or as Kant termed it, subjective—prayer

can only be to induce in us a moral disposition; its purpose can never be pragmatic, seeking the satisfaction of our wants. It should fan into flame the cinders of morality in the inner recesses of our heart; it is a means of devotion, which in turn is a practice, the object of which is to impress the knowledge of God upon our hearts with a view to action.[46]

Prayer as Education

The Men of the Great Assembly, who conceived prayer as self-appraisal, self-criticism, and education, formulated and structured it in a unique manner to fulfill its proper function. They designated three times during the day when man has to retreat from the turbulence of life and meditate upon his course of action in the world surrounding him. These times are morning, afternoon, and evening, for which the services of *shaḥarit, minḥah* and *ma'ariv* were correspondingly instituted.

The *shaḥarit* service, which takes place before man embarks upon his daily mundane occupation, aims at teaching him the "sanctification of the inner self for the worthy use of the day" (*H* 628). In the afternoon, when man is ordinarily involved in his work, he has to stop for the *minḥah* service, which is intended for his dedication in active life (*H* 643), while *ma'ariv* is for the dedication of the night (*H* 646).

To convey these concepts, a properly elaborated liturgy had to be constructed, since no haphazardly innovated or imitated hymnology or litany could serve this complex educational purpose. The early mentors of Judaism introduced several categories of liturgy, each having a specific aim. These include *tefillah,* which connotes self-judgment, and *tehillah,* contemplation of God, universe, mankind, and Israel (*H* 620). These two categories were primarily designed to refashion one's outlook on life (*H* 620). In addition to those teaching man the aspect of right reflection, two other categories were added, *bakashah* and *teḥinah,* which properly focus on man's strivings for his future (*H* 621). Hirsch defines the difference between these latter two—"the former referring more to possessions, the latter more to yourself" (*H* 621). These are followed by more categories, *todah, viddui,* and *berakhah,* expressing the themes of gratitude, confession, and blessing, respectively (*H* 622–23).

The last category was somewhat puzzling to many of Hirsch's contemporaries, since it seemed either blasphemous or ridiculous for man to bless God. Ordinarily, the bestowal of a blessing implies that the granter is more powerful than the receiver, who needs something he is unable to attain on his own. Applied to the relation between man and God, this connotation is theologically untenable. For this reason, Hirsch suggests that the concept of *berakhah,* or blessing, frequently found in the prayer book has a special significance in the sense of man pronouncing a *berakhah* for God. In this respect, it does not mean man granting something to God that He does not possess, or God being in need of man's benediction; what it connotes rather is man's resolution to execute God's will in word and in deed. *Berakhah* signifies "either to further by deed the purpose set by God for free development, which is the good that He wishes, namely, to resolve to fulfill His will; or to declare to Him the furtherance in word, namely, to fulfill His will" (*H* 623). Years later, in commenting in his *siddur* on the meaning of "Blessed art Thou," Hirsch writes that it signifies "I pledge myself to fulfill your will."[47] Similarly, referring to the opening verse of the *amidah*, which also begins with the word *barukh*, blessed, he observes that it "is our pledge of obedience."[48]

The authors of the traditional *siddur* carefully designed the liturgical categories and their order in the structure of worship to produce a wholesome, intellectually balanced comprehension in man. For this reason, *tehillah* and *tefillah*, designed for reflection and meditation, precede *bakashah* and *teḥinah*, which are more concerned with man's desires and strivings. For only when man becomes cognizant of the multiple dimensions of God, universe, nature, history, and the mission of Israel can he properly formulate his personal desires.

Hirsch's presentation of the traditional liturgy in which every selection and the order of the selections are so methodically worked out that nothing may be changed implies a criticism of the Reformers. Without openly challenging the Reform prayer books (particularly that of the Hamburg Temple), Hirsch insinuated that only ignorance of the meaning, purpose, and methods of Jewish prayer could have prompted the authors of those prayer books to such innovations.[49] Hirsch apparently hoped that once the authentic ideas concerning Jewish worship and prayer as expounded in the *Horeb* became known, the traditional *siddur* would be restored to its historic role in Judaism.

Prayer and Sacrifices

In his presentation of prayer, Hirsch ties in its origin with the ancient sacrificial rites practiced in the Temple of Jerusalem. The latter harked back to the classical act of faith demonstrated by Abraham, who volunteered to sacrifice his son to God. Although God did not permit Abraham to execute this act, the readiness to do so demonstrated by the patriarch came to symbolize the pinnacle of faith. The *akedah*, as this episode is termed, became central in Judaism, and the ram substituted for Isaac served as the prototype of the subsequent sacrificial worship in the Temple on Mount Moriah. The animal sacrifices offered on this altar evoked the concept of the *akedah*, signifying man's duty to dedicate himself unqualifiedly to God. Abraham's "descendants would symbolically perform that which he had wished to execute in actuality" (*H* 624).

In the Temple, divine service expressed itself in dual form—in the symbolic act of the sacrifices and the verbal articulation of prayer: "The word was not missing in the act of sacrifice" (*H* 624). The external service of the symbolic rites was paralleled and abetted by the internal service of prayer. These two aspects of divine worship, *avodah* in the cultic sense and *avodah she-ba-lev* in the devotional sense, complemented one another. The destruction of the first Temple abruptly ended the cultic-symbolic mode of worship and left the devotional one unrelated and unobjectified.

Upon return from the Babylonian exile, the Men of the Great Assembly attempted to formulate and standardize the devotional aspect of the *avodah she-ba-lev* current in the Second Jewish Commonwealth. Moreover, they had undertaken "to transfer into the direct word the symbolic action of the sacrifice" (*H* 626). The mentors of Judaism, who lived at a time when the full meaning of the symbolism of the sacrifices was known, infused its ideas and concepts into the prayers they had instituted. The *amidah* in particular is a prayer containing the spirit, symbolism, and allusions which in their time were embodied in the sacrificial rites. This relationship was not a new concept. Commenting on the verse "we will render for bullocks the offering of our lips,"[50] the Talmud states that "the offering of our lips," or prayer, is as acceptable to God as the offerings of bullocks.[51]

The Talmud cites two reasons for the three daily services. According to Rabbi Joshua ben Levi, the *shaḥarit* service corresponds to the *tamid* sacrifice of the morning, and the *minḥah* service to the *tamid* sacrifice of the afternoon.[52] According to Rabbi Yose ben Hanina, the daily services antedate the Temple worship and were ordained by the patriarchs.[53] Although these two divergent opinions are harmonized in the Talmud,[54] Maimonides quotes only the view of Rabbi Joshua ben Levi, who linked the prayer services with the order of the sacrifices in the Temple.[55] Hirsch, predominantly following Maimonides, also connects the services with the *tamid* sacrifices (*H* 624).

However, according to Rabbi Joshua ben Levi the connection between sacrifices and prayer services refers only to the correspondence in time. During the hours prescribed for the *tamid* offerings of the morning and afternoon, *shaharit* and *minhah*, respectively, ought to be recited. There is no intimation that the devotional services correspond in content or in essence to the original sacrificial services.[56] To Hirsch, on the other hand, the correspondence between the sacrifices and devotional services signifies an identity of essence. In a note in his *"Avodah"* division of the *Horeb*, Hirsch indicates that such a relationship exists, but he gives no detailed exposition of the correspondence (*H* 702). In his commentary on Numbers, Hirsch states this analogy of essence and considers the *"Tamid-* vows translated into words in *shaharit* and *minhah"* (*CN* 28:2).

Many years later, in an essay entitled "Die Schemone Esre" (*S* 4:209–38), Hirsch worked out a complicated analogy between the symbolic ritual of the *tamid* sacrifice and that of the *amidah*. The latter is "verbal transfer" of the former. "Die Schemone Esre ist nichts als eine Wortübertragung der Thamid-Opferhandlung" (*S* 4:211). Hirsch considered it inconceivable that the relationship of the *amidah* to the *tamid* is only of a correspondence in time. The Men of the Great Assembly would not have been content with that unless it also implied a parallel in content.[57]

On the basis of this premise, Hirsch in this essay compares the three constitutive sections of the *amidah* with the three constitutive rites of the performances of the *tamid*. The *amidah* consists of three opening benedictions or praises, thirteen intermediate petitions,[58] and three concluding blessings or thanksgivings. Similarly, the *tamid* consisted of three fundamental rites: *zerikah*, sprinkling of the blood, *haktarah*, burning of the sacrificial portions, and *minhah* and *nesakhim*, the meal offering and libations. This broad comparative outline is followed by a more detailed one, in which Hirsch points out how every benediction in each of the three sections of the *amidah* has a correspondence with the component acts of each of the three rites of the *tamid*. Thus, the three benedictions of the first section of the *amidah*—*avot, gevurot,* and *kedushah*[59]—are analogous to the three acts of the first rite of the *tamid*—*kabalah, holakhah,* and *zerikah.*[60]

For the intermediate benedictions, Hirsch elaborates a complex analogy with the *tamid* ritual. According to the Talmud, the *tamid* was dissected into various parts and handed to the priests, who followed each other in a procession to offer the parts on the altar.[61] Hirsch endeavors in a most abstruse manner to show the symbolism of each anatomical organ of the sacrificial animal and how it in turn is reflected in the thirteen blessings of petition. Needless to say, both the symbolism and its alleged relationship to the intermediate section of the *amidah* are less than convincing. Finally, the three closing benedictions of thanksgiving, *avodah, hoda'ah,* and *shalom,* correspond to the final stages of the *tamid* sacrifice. Of these three, only *hoda'ah* was a symbolic rite; *avodah* and *shalom* were expressed in prayer even at the time of the Temple worship,[62] recited by the priests at the conclusion of the sacrificial service. Thus, the latter two prayers were incorporated in the *amidah,* the only difference being that whereas in antiquity they were recited only by the priests, subsequently they have been recited by everyone.

This convoluted effort to establish an ideational concordance between prayer and sacrifice necessitates an explanation. Nothing in rabbinic literature demanded such an interpretation. Indeed, the term *keneged* in Rabbi Joshua ben Levi's statement *tefillot keneged temidim tiknum*[63] can be interpreted "in lieu." Such an interpretation might have given rise to the idea that since prayer was instituted in place of the *tamid,* it had to contain all the symbolism and concepts of that sacrifice. There is, however, no evidence that this was the compelling reason.

Hirsch's essay on the *amidah* clearly indicates that he knew of the correct meaning of the term *keneged* as signifying correspondence in time. However, he was determined to go beyond this meaning and to interpret it in a far more intricate manner.[64] He seems to insist on identity of essence rather than on mere correspondence in time (*S* 4:211). Nor can we attribute this forced reinterpretation to Maimonides, whose influence in the composition of the *Horeb* is otherwise so pronounced. Maimonides was disinclined to base new ideas on the ancient Temple cult, since to him, this was a divine concession to the ancient Israelites who lived in a pagan world where cult and sacrifices were the only modes of worship. Had they been deprived of such means, they would not have been able to worship at all: "It was in accordance with the wisdom and plan of God, as displayed in the whole creation, that He did not command us to give up and to discontinue all these manners of service, for to obey such a commandment it would have been contrary to the nature of man, who generally cleaves to that to which he is used."[65] The reason for Hirsch's unusual eagerness to relate prayer to the ancient sacrifice must be sought in the historic issues of his time.

The Reformers' tendency was to obliterate any allusion to the former Temple service and to eliminate any prayer calling for its restoration. Although the most radical changes in this respect took place many years after the appearance of the *Horeb*, initial attempts in this direction had already been undertaken. The Hamburg prayer book of 1819 had omitted references in the *musaf* to the hope for the restoration of the ancient Temple service.

This recision itself was not only contrary to Halakhah, but threatened the entire structure of Jewish tradition. The same premise underlying the abandonment of the hope that the once-central sacrificial cult would be reconstituted and the belief that it had been forever replaced by a new mode of worship might be applied to other aspects of the Jewish religion. If one form of Judaism can be transformed by virtue of external historic circumstances into a different one, so can the other ancient religious rites be changed by the flux of history. An admission of the obsolescence of the Temple mode of worship and the possibility of substitution would have opened the floodgates to reforms, abrogations, and innovations in all areas of Judaism.

It was therefore important to Hirsch to emphasize that prayer had never replaced sacrifices but had been designed only to accompany them. Moreover, the continually recited *amidah* is virtually impregnated with the concepts and symbolism of the sacrifices, and for Hirsch this was tantamount to the assertion that the hope for the restoration of sacrifices in the future was not abandoned but still continued to operate conceptually in our daily prayers. Indeed, in the *Horeb,* seeking to avoid controversy, he never states this view openly. However, in his essay on the *amidah,* written at the time when the confrontation between him and the Reformers was an established fact, he denounces the latter's presumption that the sacrifices had been replaced by prayer.[66] Thus, Hirsch paradoxically became the defender of sacrifices in the nineteenth century, whereas centuries earlier Maimonides had disapproved of them.

Hirsch indicates that the universality of the psychological motivation for a sacrificial cult accounts for its prevalence. Sacrifices have been common to all people since the dawn of civilization. They "are as old as mankind and so must be the natural expression of our pure human feelings and thoughts" (*CG* 4:3–6). Hirsch dismisses Maimonides's contention that sacrifices were merely a concession to the ancient Israelites living in a polytheistic culture in which this mode of worship was universal. He points to the first offering of Cain and Abel during the earliest stage of human history, which did not come as a heteronomous command or as a lesson from the environment; rather it was a spontaneous, voluntary act resulting from an inner psychological necessity: "No idolatry existed as yet, so that the opinion that offerings are only to be explained as a concession to polytheism is at once shown to be untrue. Offerings are older than polytheism" (*CG* 4:3–6).

Sacrifices in early history and in the subsequent Jewish state were not merely ritualistic performances but acts saturated with deep emotion. The prophets who decried sacrifice referred only to those which were devoid of any ethical-religious experience; they favored sincere sacrificial offerings. The rejections of the offerings of Cain, Nadab, and Abihu illustrate that the inner sentiment was the decisive factor, not the formal sacrifice (*CL* 10:1). Only when man's sincerity, faith, loyalty, repentance, or commitment were reflected in the sacrifice was it favorably received by God. Thus, the *akedah,*[67] though unconsummated, remained a hallmark in the history of Judaism and in the life of the Jewish people since it was undertaken in the spirit of sincerity and absolute commitment.

The relationship between prayer and the *tamid* sacrifices also emphasizes the importance of daily prayer. Just as the *tamid* sacrifices had to be offered daily, so the prayers analogous to them have to be recited daily—a practice directly opposed to that of the Hamburg Temple, which had abandoned daily services. Only when prayers are offered daily is it logical to add a *musaf* service on Sabbath. This additional service to the daily *shaḥarit* underscores the importance of the Sabbath and festivals, or as Hirsch puts it: "This was in addition to the continual offering—the *tamid* — which expressed the daily concept" (*H* 652).

Hirsch was familiar with the polemics against the Hamburg Temple which instituted two services, *shaḥarit* and *musaf* on the Sabbath, and none during the week, and in this respect he echoes the opinion of Rabbi Moses Sofer, who pointed to the incongruity of abandoning the daily service which corresponds to *tamid* and instituting a *musaf* service on the Sabbath. The latter is only meaningful and logical when it serves as an addition to the ordinary, everyday service.[68]

Subjects of Contention

Hebrew or Vernacular   The question of what language should be used for prayer is only casually mentioned in rabbinic codes. However, Hirsch devotes an entire chapter in the *"Avodah"* division to it (*H* 688). This emphasis was necessitated by the Reform efforts to reduce Hebrew in the synagogue service and eventually eliminate it. Such efforts were particularly evident in the Hamburg Reform prayer book. Some of the exponents of Reform delighted in the Talmud's statement that the importance of the comprehension of prayer is primary to the sanctity of the language in which it is recited.[69] This reference to talmudic sanction was used as propaganda in the Reform campaign to denationalize the Jewish religion, an effort harking back to the dawn of the Emancipation. The urge to purge the Jewish service of distinctive national elements and particularistic references had already been expressed by David Friedländer in 1812,[70] reflecting the direction in which Reformers were moving.

Such a trend would have eventually eliminated Hebrew altogether. Without resorting to any debate, Hirsch accepted the Reformers' argument that the Talmud permits prayer in the vernacular. However, he differentiates between individual prayer and congregational prayer. An individual who for some valid reason does not know Hebrew may pray in the vernacular, but no such permission can be granted a congregation. The prayers composed by the Men of the Great Assembly were "the expression of Israel's collective religious-national thoughts" (*H* 688). They must therefore be authentically preserved in form, content, and spirit; these elements which are inextricably bound together cannot be separated without irreparable damage. The contention that the content and spirit of prayers may be preserved in translation is misleading, since no translation, no matter how accurate, can reproduce the original idiom. As a result of the delicate distinctions in semantics, "certain thoughts may be introduced that are strange not only to the Hebrew language but to the whole spirit of Judaism" (*H* 688). Sensing the Reformers' assimilationist objective, Hirsch also maintains that Hebrew serves as a strong deterrent to ethnic and religious disintegration and amalgamation (*H* 688).

Hirsch counters the demand pressed by the opponents of Hebrew that the people pray in the language they speak with the following argument: although at the time the traditional prayers were composed most of the people spoke Aramaic, still the Men of the Great Assembly composed them in Hebrew, a language then no longer spoken or even understood. This is illustrated by the fact that the reading of the Torah had to be followed by an Aramaic translation or *targum*. The Men of the Great Assembly believed that there was something essential in the Hebrew language which made it the exclusive medium of prayer. They did not yield to the transitory expediencies of their age, since as men of vision "they wished to set standards towards which Israel should be educated in the future" (*H* 688). Hirsch's veiled implication is that the spokesmen of Reform, unlike the Men of the Great Assembly, were rooted in the present, lacked insight and vision, and consequently resorted to expedience in substituting the vernacular for Hebrew. Finally, Hirsch argues that the elimination of Hebrew would endanger "the continuity of the national institution of the *Avodah*" (*H* 688). It was the Hebrew language that had united the Jews throughout history and continued to unite the Jews of the Diaspora. By abandoning the language of the Bible, the entire Jewish religious heritage would be severely impaired (*H* 688).

Once again the arguments presented by Hirsch are similar to those of the polemical literature of the time. Hirsch's contribution in this case, as in the case of prayer in general, is his calm exposition—a subsurface but resonant dialogue with the Reformers. Some of his arguments merely paraphrase those published in the anti-Reform volume *Eleh Divrei ha-Berit.* Thus, Hirsch reiterates the views of Rabbi Moses Sofer's responsum in the aforementioned volume, without directly referring to him. Sofer had stated that the frequently quoted mishnah permitting prayer in the vernacular only applies to an individual on a chance occurrence and prohibits it on a sustained basis in a congregational service. Hirsch's reference to the composition of the prayers in Hebrew at the time when the vast majority of the people needed a translator for the reading of the Torah was also stated in Sofer's responsum. Sofer also stressed the care with which the Men of the Great Assembly had composed these prayers in Hebrew. Every word and letter of the prayers was voted upon and impregnated with certain ideas *(kavanot)* which are simply not transferrable into another language.

Hirsch's love for Hebrew may perhaps be attributable to the Haskalah spirit, whose residue still lingered in his family. Despite the fact that he spoke and wrote German almost exclusively, he held Hebrew in high esteem.[71] Hirsch praises Hebrew in the most glowing terms and underscores its importance in general education and culture. In an essay[72] as well as in his commentary on the Pentateuch (*CG* 9:7), he endeavors to show the profundity of Hebrew etymology and morphology, a unique quality unequaled by any other language.

Hirsch's concern over the status of Hebrew in the synagogue service was apparently justified. A fierce debate over the language issue broke out, eight years after publication of the *Horeb,* at the conference of the Reform rabbis at Frankfurt am Main in 1845. The moderate and erudite Zachariah Frankel left this conference in protest over the radicals' decision to leave the amount of Hebrew in the service to the discretion of each congregation and rabbi. In his passionate plea for the retention of Hebrew, Frankel employed the same semantic argument advanced by Hirsch: there is an emotional and evocative element in every language which develops in a given cultural milieu and which becomes interwoven with its fabric. To the Jew, the German term *Gott* can never convey the same emotional and psychological feeling or the theological and philosophical meaning of the seemingly equiva- lent Hebrew term, *Adonai*.[73] Thus Hirsch and Frankel, who were ideologically so far apart,[74] both favored Hebrew in the service, although not always for the same reasons.

The Piyyutim   Fear of tampering with the text of the traditional prayer book may account for Hirsch's retention of the *piyyutim* in the service. This vast medieval liturgical genre consisting of hymns, admonitions, lamentations, and doxologies had been op- posed by leading rabbinic authorities since the Gaonic era. Many of the Gaonim saw in the *piyyutim* unauthorized accretions which threatened to adulterate the purity of prayer. Halakhic objections were also raised against their recitation since they constituted interruptions in the schema of the ordained prayers.[75]

Maimonides was offended by the *piyyutim* on philosophical grounds. He considered the *paitanim*, the medieval liturgical po- ets, foolish and grandiloquent,

extravagant in praise, fluent and prolix in the prayers they com- pose, and in the hymns they make in the desire to approach the creator. They describe God in attributes which would be an offense if applied to a human being; for those persons have no knowledge of these great and important principles, which are not accessible to the ordinary intelligence of man.[76]

Maimonides maintained that the *piyyutim* sounded either blas- phemous or ludicrous: "Such authors write things which partly are real heresy, partly contain such folly and absurdity that they natu- rally cause those who hear them to laugh, but also to feel grieved at the thought that such things can be uttered in reference to God."[77]

In view of such authoritative opposition to the *piyyutim*, it was reasonable to assume that they would be the first to be excised from the Reform congregational services. Aaron Chorin, a Reform protagonist, cited the opinions of Maimonides, David Kimhi, and Abraham ibn Ezra advocating the excision of the *piyyutim*,[78] a suggestion which was implemented in many Reform congrega- tions,[79] some even including a special clause in the *Synagogenord- nungen* explicitly forbidding their recitation.[80]

Displeasure with the *piyyutim* was also prevalent in non-Reform circles, particularly those inclined toward the Haskalah.[81] Hirsch's great uncle Loeb Frankfurter and his uncle Moses Mendelssohn of Hamburg were unalterably opposed to the *piyyutim*, not for theological or legalistic but for aesthetic and linguistic reasons: they considered the *piyyutim* grammatically and morphologically corrupt, distortions of the beauty, purity, and logicality of the Hebrew language.[82] Despite this historical and contemporary opposition, Hirsch considered the retention of the *piyyutim* so important that, according to Graetz, he refused to eliminate even the most abstruse and incomprehensible *piyyut.*[83]

Graetz, who unlike Hirsch was moved by emotion rather than reason, failed to realize the consequences of eliminating some seemingly grotesque-sounding Kalirian poem. To the simple and unlearned Jews of Germany, the distinction between Eleazer ha-Kalir's obfuscating *piyyut Atz Kotzetz,*[84] recited on Purim, and the biblical *Shema* might have been indistinguishable. Thus what Graetz failed to consider was that the elimination of the unimportant *piyyut* might have eventually brought about the abolition of the mandatory *Shema.*

Hirsch felt the *piyyutim* were forms of interpretation of the Torah, a task which was performed prior to the *paitanim* by the sages and the interpreters whose ideas had been incorporated by the *paitanim* in their compositions. Their cryptic expressions had once been understood by all, since the knowledge of the Torah was widespread. The most delicate allusion sparked an association of ideas in the minds of the worshippers. The fact that these allusions no longer evoked any concepts did not mean that the *piyyutim* ought to be discarded. It was deplorable that "that which was formerly the common possession of the whole community of Jacob has fled into the sphere of a limited class of scholars" (*H* 671). Hirsch asserts that the incomprehensibility of the *piyyutim* is due neither to their involved style nor to the fact that they were composed in Hebrew; the paucity of Jewish knowledge is responsible for this state of affairs: "They would have been alien to our generation even if they had spoken to it in its mother tongue" (*H* 671). Although they are supplementary to the service, they cannot be discarded, unless the existing generation can rise to the religious and scholastic level of the *paitanim* who composed them.

In this, Hirsch seems to paraphrase the talmudic view that no court may invalidate the decision of another court unless it surpasses it in numbers and wisdom.[85]

Instead of abrogating the medieval *piyyutim*, Hirsch advocates deepening the Jewish education of the younger generation. To the critics, perhaps even those in his own *erleuchtet religiös* circle and family, who considered the *piyyutim* aesthetically wanting, Hirsch responds that the *piyyutim* compensate for their form with their content, which synoptically condenses and summarizes ideas from the Bible, Talmud, Midrash, Halakhah, and Aggadah: "They had to be short, allusive, and yet faithful to the language of the writings from which they were drawn, even at the cost of elegance" (*H* 671). In passing, Hirsch touches on the problem of composing new prayers and hymns, a trend growing in popularity among Reform congregations: "Could a *paitan* compose today?" (*H* 671). Again without any polemics he refutes the Reformers by countering that while no such prohibition existed, there also was no person living who could match his knowledge with that of the original *paitanim*.

Had Hirsch accepted the view that the *piyyutim* should be rejected because they were no longer understood, he would have felt compelled by logic to dispense with Hebrew altogether, since it too was no longer commonly understood. In both cases, Hirsch advocated raising the knowledge of the people to the level of the liturgy, *piyyutim* included, instead of watering down the liturgy to the level of the people's prevalent degree of education.

A Sacerdotal Vestige   Another subject encompassed in the indirect dialogue with the Reformers was the status of the priesthood, *kohanim,* and particularly of the benediction pronounced by them during the service. The Reformers' urge to sever all ties between modern Judaism and the Temple cult and to obliterate any reference to its restoration made the special status of the *kohanim* a painful sacerdotal vestige. According to Halakhah, the biblical and rabbinic laws governing ritual purity and marriage of the Aaronides remain in force; and although the Temple is no longer in existence and sacrifices are not offered, every descendant of the former priesthood is obliged to keep himself in a state of holiness. The *kohen* is not permitted to come in contact with the dead, with the exception of his close relatives, or to marry a divorcee. Of his former functions, he retains the exclusive right to pronounce the priestly benediction during the congregational services, to redeem the first-born, the honor to be called up first to the Torah, and to recite grace after meals.

Whatever difficulties presented by these laws—specifically those of purity and marriage—to the *kohanim* as individuals, the Reformers considered the very existence of a distinctive priestly group a source of embarrassment. It suggested to them the priestly castes of antiquity which claimed an inherent charisma or supernatural power. It seemed a remnant of religious hierarchy, a concept irreconcilable with the modern temper. As in other cases, the implementation of reforms in this respect lagged considerably behind the ideological changes, even though the sentiment against a hereditary priesthood observing distinctive sacerdotal laws and theoretically aspiring to serve in the reestablished Temple in Jerusalem had long since been expressed. It was not until 1845 that the radical Reform congregation of Berlin decided upon the transfer of the priestly benediction from the *kohanim* to the preacher.[86]

As in other matters of dispute, Hirsch sets out in the *Horeb* to elucidate the vexing problem of the significance of *kohanim* in modern times. Originally, Judaism had no priesthood, and man's relationship to God was simple and direct. The first-born in each family represented its individual members and had the right to offer sacrifices in the ancient manner of worship, on many altars rather than in a centralized temple (*H* 715).

After the Israelites, including those first-born, worshipped the golden calf in the desert, the priestly functions were handed over to the Levitic tribe, whose members had remained faithful to God. Their status among the Jewish people was analogous to that of the Jews toward the rest of mankind. Just as after the rebellion of man at the dawn of history God had been compelled to make Israel the custodian of man's religious-ethical values, so after the revolt of the people of Israel, God had to entrust the Aaronides with this stewardship over the Jewish people. However, the Aaronides possessed no special powers but merely served as the representatives of the people, and sacrificial worship was centralized in the Temple of Jerusalem to the exclusion of all other heretofore permissible altars: "Thus the *kohen*, like the Temple sanctuary and its sacrifices, is a symbol representing an idea, but not the representative of God upon earth" (*H* 717). The *kohen*, therefore, is neither a person, a theurgist, a shaman, nor a divine plenipotentiary endowed with special powers; he is merely a symbol. To enhance this symbol, the *kohen* must be perfect in every respect. He must observe the ritual laws of purity; his family background must be wholesome, whether from the point of view of heredity or the marital union he himself contracts, and he must be physically without blemish, "just as everything that symbolically expresses an idea in its perfection must also be perfect externally" (*H* 717).

To dispel any association with the notion of an ancient cultic, pagan priesthood, Hirsch insists that the priests must always be "conscious of the fact that their priesthood is not due to any special qualities of their own" (*CL* 21:1). As a symbol of religious and moral perfection, the *kohen* therefore has an important modern function because the modern Jew, like modern man in general, is no less in need of a symbol of perfection than had been man in antiquity. The *kohen*'s symbolic mission did not become obsolete with the ending of the Temple mode of worship. Contrary to the Reformers' contention, "the *kohen* has even today to observe the prohibition against defiling himself in respect of the dead and to take heed of the special laws relating to his marriage" (*H* 719).

The priestly benediction must not be misinterpreted to mean that the *kohen* has special powers to grant blessings or to withhold them: "It is not the authority to bless the children of Israel that is here conferred to the Aaronides, but a duty which is given them to perform. The blessing of the priests does not flow from their well-wishing, their benevolence but is part and parcel of their service to the sanctuary" (*CN* 6:23). As Hirsch had already indicated, a blessing signifies the affirmation of the community as a whole. The priestly benediction also implies a communal declaration through its representatives, the *kohanim*, that the blessings it expects to receive will come from God alone: "It is not the *kohen*, who blesses or who has the power to bless; it is God that blesses" (*H* 684).

Again and again Hirsch emphasizes that all the rules concerning the priestly benediction were designed "to remove the erroneous idea that the *kohen* himself is the possessor and granter of the blessing" (*H* 685). Hirsch suggests that the prohibition against watching the *kohanim* pronounce that benediction is to indicate that they are merely an instrument, that it is God who bestows the blessing (*H* 685): "The priests do not bless Israel, their words have no power of conferring blessing, their mission is only . . . to lay the name of God impressively on Israel" (*CN* 6:27).[87]

In his reaction against the Reformers, Hirsch seems inflexibly conservative with regard to the synagogue ritual. That he should have exhibited such a stand in Oldenburg, when his attitude to the advocates of Reform had not yet hardened, shows that he recognized that it was in the realm of synagogue service that a concrete community effort must be made. The violation of the other commandments did not represent an effort to change Judaism in its last collective center. However, reforming the synagogue service and the structure of prayers constituted a concerted, widespread effort to violate the last bastion of organized Judaism in the Diaspora. His *erleuchtet religiös* spirit notwithstanding, Hirsch could not accept this assault on Judaism. Apparently the shadow of the Hamburg Temple that had touched his childhood followed him even into the calm and serene atmosphere of Oldenburg.

Epilogue

Hirsch's aspiration to become the Maimonides of the modern
era was never realized. *Moriah*, his intended new *Guide of the
Perplexed*, never appeared, and his *Horeb* was never developed
into a new *Mishneh Torah*. The promise he so solemnly made in
Oldenburg—to evolve a comprehensive philosophy of Judaism
and a consummate rationale for all its laws, rites, and rituals—
remained unfulfilled.

Although Hirsch never explained the reasons for abandoning his
projects, they are self-evident when viewed in retrospect. It is
clear that the air of confidence that permeates the *Neunzehn
Briefe* and *Horeb* in reinterpreting Judaism and rationalizing its
entire juridical-ceremonial aspect in a manner surpassing Maimonides must be attributed to Hirsch's youthful exuberance and enthusiasm. Impelled by the urgency of events and the need for a
modern Maimonides, he may have overestimated his ability, or
underestimated the task—or both. The desirable was mistaken for
the possible, and the vision judged a reality. Kindled by the ideas
of Hegelianism, Hirsch saw in them unlimited possibilities for the
reinterpretation of Judaism. Hegel's philosophy seemed to Hirsch
an excellent matrix for Jewish law. On the basis of Hegelian juridical theory, the rules and regulations of Bible and Talmud could
now be explained as denoting universal concepts and principles of
thought of unqualified rationality, and hence valid and mandatory
for all times. The Law which had been criticized in antinomian

398

circles as petty and provincial could now be justified on a universal conceptual basis, and the complaint that "the broad principles of universal morality are narrowed down into anxious scrupulosity about insignificant trifles" (*NL* 5) could be shown up as erroneous.

However, as Hirsch matured intellectually he must have realized that his youthful pledge, given in all sincerity, could not be easily fulfilled. His grandiose aspirations to equal and even surpass Maimonides foundered; the serious promise to his contemporaries, proclaimed so confidently and eloquently at the age of twenty-eight, had to be silently abandoned.

The philosophic work *Moriah*, which Hirsch contemplated publishing and in which he hoped "to present the theoretical foundation of the Bible's teachings on God, the universe, man and Israel,"[1] never saw light. Students of Hirsch's writings are puzzled that this basic work, envisioned at the outset of his career, was never written. They admit that "it is difficult to find a convincing reason why *Moriah* did not appear, especially when one considers that there were forty years of productive literary activity in front of Hirsch, who was a very prolific writer."[2]

The suggestion that the ideas which were to be set forth in *Moriah* were subsequently incorporated into the numerous articles published in *Jeschurun*[3] is not convincing. Nor is there any more validity to the view that Hirsch did not carry out his original plan because he "came to the conclusion that his contemplated work might be construed as admitting the existence of a so-called Jewish theology, to which he was strongly opposed."[4]

Nothing would have delighted Hirsch more than to have been able to present a philosophy sufficiently comprehensive, scientifically valid, and rationally cogent to defend the principles of tradition and combat the neological theologies of his opponents. Much to his chagrin, he realized his inability to accomplish this noble but formidable task. The hopes entertained at twenty-seven and the promises made at twenty-eight had to be abandoned by an older and wiser Hirsch. The realization that he was not a Maimonides and that his *Moriah* would never be another *Moreh* compelled him to give up the project altogether. While he continued to explain and rationalize isolated laws, he became convinced that he could not present a comprehensive philosophy that would elucidate and interpret the fundamentals of Judaism to the satisfaction of the modern Jew, which was what *Moriah* purported to do. One may suspect that his subsequent aversion to Jewish theology was due not to the fact that he considered it unnecessary and unwarranted, but to his inability to formulate and evolve one of his own.

Unable to work out a systematic interpretation substantiating the early hypothesis of his "Jewish doctrinal system," Hirsch had to reconcile himself to literary works of a smaller scale. He wrote articles and essays, engaged in polemics, preached sermons, and participated intensely and extensively in the communal activities devolving upon him as rabbi of a great embattled community and as leader of the Jewish Orthodox separatist movement in Germany.

Hirsch's only literary undertaking of great magnitude during his mature period was his commentary on the Pentateuch and the Book of Psalms. Into these works he incorporated many of his ideas and views on Judaism and elaborated on the reasons for many *mitzvot* without, however, the need to provide an overall systematic explanation and rationalization of all of Judaism's ramifications. In a running commentary, Hirsch could employ certain eclectic philosophic ideas which seemed applicable, including some Hegelian views, while glossing over those which did not. In a commentary, unlike a systematic work, dialectical order is not imperative.

The intellectual maturity that came with age may have prevented Hirsch from bringing to fruition the ambitious aspirations of his youth. However, speculation about these factors is only that. The quest for Hegelian concepts was admirable; if they could have been found in Jewish law, he would have won the field against his opponents. In the *Neunzehn Briefe* he sets for himself very high and rigorous standards by which he promises to validate his hypothesis:

At every point we put to ourselves the questions "What have I heard here?" "What is the underlying concept of this statement?" "What is its purpose?" "What is the object of this symbolic act?" "What is its natural meaning under the given conditions and purpose?" (*NL* 101–2)

A lifetime would not have sufficed to answer all these questions with relation to the multitude of laws, rules, regulations, rites, rituals, and ceremonies; to find an adequate rationale that would encompass all of them as a unit was apparently beyond any one man's comprehension and ability. Hirsch may have realized that while many aspects of Judaism can be expounded in Hegelian terms, others might not be that easily reconciled. He was undoubtedly confronted with the same problem that all synthesizers and rationalists have faced since the days of Philo. In his contemplative moments, he may even have sympathized and commiserated with Maimonides, whom he had so sternly castigated in his youth for his unsuccessful synthesis, and may even have appreciated Mendelssohn's reticence for not having attempted to compose a successful one. We may hazard the guess that the general disenchantment with Hegel that Hirsch experienced by the time he reached intellectual maturity was an added factor in abandoning a comprehensive philosophy of Judaism. Hegel, who had been extolled and praised, was no longer the idol of the generation: "By the middle of the nineteenth century, the influence of Hegelianism was almost dead."[5] Thus, the foundation upon which Hirsch had intended to build his philosophy and rationale of Judaism collapsed.[6]

Just as an aggregate of social, political, and economic factors favored the acceptance of Hegelian philosophy during the age of Restoration, so did the subsequent changes in the sociopolitical climate cause its decline:[7] "The orthodox Hegelian tradition was considerably modified by the later neo-Hegelians. In addition, many powerful and able writers completely broke with Hegel's metaphysical background."[8] The fascination Hegel's ideas had presented in the realms of philosophy, religion, and art waned. The area in which his influence was still felt was that of political thought. However, even here his views had undergone a radical transformation and were considerably modified.[9]

The radicalization of the Reform movement might have been one of the reasons compelling Hirsch to abandon *Moriah.* If in the 1830s some rapprochement between the *erleuchtet religiös* and the advocates of Reform still seemed a possibility, the 1840s dispelled such illusions. The decade following the publication of the *Neunzehn Briefe* saw the ascendancy of the militant Reformers whose views, no matter how moderate, could never be reconciled with traditional Judaism. The Geiger-Tiktin controversy was transformed from a local dispute over a rabbinic post into a theological cause célèbre with widespread implications. It further widened the chasm that already divided the two warring factions of Jewry.[10] The heated controversy which had seemed to subside over the Hamburg Temple and its prayer book was rekindled by a new edition of the Reform prayer book appearing in 1841. It stirred the glowing embers of the controversy to a new conflagration.[11]

The conferences of the Reform rabbis which were convened in the years 1844–46 at Brunswick, Frankfurt, and Breslau manifested most glaringly the incredible distance the Reformers had traversed and the colossal divergencies between themselves and the traditionalists. They revealed that the Reformers were not interested in reinterpreting Judaism, but in revolutionizing it. The most fundamental tenets of the Jewish religion—Sabbath, circumcision, the messianic hope, to mention but a few—were challenged and considered expendable. Hirsch's intended philosophic work could not bridge such a hiatus. Thus, the entire raison d'être for writing *Moriah* had vanished. The Orthodox did not need it, the Reformers did not want it. The hope that Hirsch had entertained in Oldenburg of offering a new philosophic modus vivendi to the contending factions of Jewry disappeared into thin air. The Benjamins for whom *Moriah* was to be written became Peretzes, for whom no philosophy of traditional Judaism was needed. The latter held off any attempt at reconciliation with the torch of "critical reason"[12] and with it marched "to storm the Bastille of the Talmud."[13] In this radicalization process, it seems that the small moderate group of *erleuchtet religiös* Jews to which Hirsch belonged disappeared altogether, although reluctantly. They were compelled to move either to the right or to the left, since the middle no longer existed.

Thus, the intellectual difficulties encountered in the reinterpretation of Judaism along Hegelian lines, coupled with the radicalization of the Reform movement, affected Hirsch's Weltanschauung and his course of action. The aspiring moderate philosopher became a zealous preacher, the anxious guide of the perplexed became a defender of the faith, and the avid pursuer of unity became the champion of separation.

NOTES
BIBLIOGRAPHY
INDEX

Notes

PART ONE
HIRSCH IN THE
CONTEXT OF HIS AGE

1. The Intellectual Temper

1. Bernard Drachman, "Samson Raphael Hirsch: A Biographical Sketch," preface to Samson Raphael Hirsch, *Igrot Tzafon: The Nineteen Letters of Ben Uziel*, trans. Bernard Drachman (New York, 1942), pp. xiii–xiv; Mordekhai Breuer, "Prakim Mitokh Biographiah," in *Ha-Rav Shimshon Raphael Hirsch: Mishnato ve-Shitato*, ed. Jonah Immanuel (Jerusalem, 1962), p. 12.
2. Gershom G. Scholem, *Major Trends in Jewish Mysticism* (New York, 1946), p. 304; Nathan Rotenstreich, *Ha-Mahshavah ha-Yehudit be-Et ha-Hadashah* (Tel Aviv, 1945), 1: 122–27.
3. Julius Guttmann, *Philosophies of Judaism*, trans. David W. Silverman (Philadelphia, 1964), pp. 18–29; Salo Wittmayer Baron, *A Social and Religious History of the Jews* (Philadelphia, 1958), 1:199–207; Harry Austryn Wolfson, *Philo: Foundations of Religious Philosophy in Judaism, Christianity, and Islam* (Cambridge, Mass., 1962).
4. Guttmann, *Philosophies of Judaism*, pp. 47–285; Baron, *History of the Jews*, 8:55–137.
5. Milton Steinberg, *The Making of the Modern Jew* (New York, 1948), p. 178.
6. David Philipson, *The Reform Movement in Judaism*, rev. ed. (New York, 1967), pp. 9–38.
7. Heinrich Graetz, *History of the Jews* (Philadelphia, 1945), 5:566–73.
8. Yoseph Klausner, *Historiah shel ha-Sifrut ha-Ivrit ha-Hadashah* (Jerusalem, 1952), 1:98–102.
9. Concerning the differences between Maimonides and Mendelssohn,

see Hans Joachim Schoeps, *Geschichte der jüdischen Religions-philosophie in der Neuzeit* (Berlin, 1935), 1:34–36. Just as there was no substance to the claim that Mendelssohn was a modern Maimonides, so there was nothing to substantiate Heine's view that he was a Jewish Luther who had overthrown the Talmud as Luther overthrew the papacy. Nor is it true that Mendelssohn rejected Jewish tradition by making the Bible the exclusive source of Judaism—Heinrich Heine, *Religion and Philosophy in Germany*, trans. John Snodgrass (Boston, 1959, p. 94). That this is fallacious hardly needs elaboration. Mendelssohn never rejected the Talmud or the rabbinic tradition. His *Jerusalem* is replete with quotations from the Talmud, which are accorded equal authority with the Bible. Neither in his conduct nor in his writings did he manifest anything contrary to the prevailing traditional views expounded by the Rabbis. The fact that both Luther and Mendelssohn translated the Bible into German is an insufficient basis on which to posit their ideational identification. Suffice it to say that whereas Luther never asked papal approval for his translation, Mendelssohn eagerly sought rabbinic endorsement. Similarly erroneous was Heine's claim that Mendelsohn "was a reformer of the German Israelites, his co-religionists; he destroyed the authority of the Talmud; he founded pure Mosaism"—ibid. The groundlessness of this claim was already recognized by Holdheim—see Samuel Holdheim, *Geschichte der Entwickelung und Entstehung der jüdischen Reformgemeinde in Berlin* (Berlin, 1857), p. 120; see also Philipson, *The Reform Movement*, p. 8, and Julian Morgenstern, *As a Mighty Stream: The Story of Reform Judaism* (Philadelphia, 1949), p. 173.

10. Avot 2: 21.
11. Avot 1:3.
12. Moses Mendelssohn, *Jerusalem*, trans. Alfred Jospe (New York, 1969), p. 61.
13. This emasculation of Judaism's most essential aspect, revelation, was sincerely bemoaned by many Jews in the post-Mendelssohnian era. Steinheim, born three years after Mendelssohn's death, criticized the latter's limitation and minimization of revelation. He states: "Mendelssohn took away from the old definition of religion the first part, namely, cognition, as a *modus cognoscendi et colendi Deum.* He left it only the second part, namely, the mode of worship. With this he cut through its essential vital nerve, thus preparing for the conversion of immediate successors which he himself had resisted despite all of Lavater's importuning. Mendelssohn had misunderstood, platitudinized, and misinterpreted the holy concept of revelation, thus opening the gate to the shallow rationalism of the day"—S.L. Steinheim, *Vom Bleibenden und Vergänglichen im Judentum* (Berlin, 1935), p. 22, trans. and quoted by W. Gunther Plaut in *The Rise of Reform Judaism* (New York, 1963), p. 129. This criticism of Mendelssohn's denigration of revelation, which seemed to strike at the very foundation of Judaism, continued into the twentieth century. It was reiterated by Hermann Cohen, who saw in Mendelssohn's view an absolute contradiction of the outlook that had pre-

vailed throughout Jewish history—Cohen, *Religion der Vernunft aus den Quellen des Judentums* (Leipzig, 1919), p. 421.

14. Hans Joachim Schoeps, *The Jewish-Christian Argument*, trans. David E. Green (New York, 1963), p. 101.

15. Noah H. Rosenbloom, "Mendelssohn's Redefinition of Judaism: Tension and Solution," *Judaism* 21 (1972): 477–89.

16. The Wolffians, like the English rational supernaturalists, accepted both rational or natural theology, with its tenets of God, virtue, and immortality, and the Christian revelation. To Wolff, revelation and reason constituted two sources of knowledge, different but not necessarily contradictory. Nothing, therefore, in either Mendelssohn's experience or his philosophic outlook warranted a reinterpretation or reformation of the historical religions, including Judaism. Just as it was possible for some Christian Wolffians to preserve the doctrines of orthodoxy unchanged, so was it possible for him to be a deist though he held to the Mosaic law—John Herman Randall, Jr., *The Career of Philosophy* (New York, 1965), 2:89–90.

17. The following statement by Mendelssohn indicates his sadness over the collapse of the Leibnizian-Wolffian outlook: "Ich freue mich, in Deutschland einen Philosophen zu finden, der sich nicht schämt, Wolffianer zu sein. Den Schriften dieses Weltweisen habe ich meine erste Bildung zur Philosophie zu verdanken; daher ich eine Art von Vorliebe für ihn jederzeit behalte, und mir ein Vergnügen machen werde, alles zu retten, was aus seiner Feder geflossen ist"—Mendelssohn, *Gesammelte Schriften* (Leipzig, 1844), 5:631–32. Actually, however, Wolffianism continued to linger in Germany for many years. Heine wrote in 1833: "The traces of this deluge are visible even down to our own day, and here and there on our most sterile academic summits may still be found old fossils of the Wolffian School"—Heine, *Religion and Philosophy*, p. 84.

18. Immanuel Kant, *Sämtliche Werke*, ed. Rosenkranz and Schubert (Leipzig, 1838–42), 11:1.

19. Nathan Rotenstreich, *The Recurring Pattern* (New York, 1964), pp. 23–47.

20. H. J. Paton, *The Categorical Imperative* (New York, 1967), pp. 58–77.

21. In support of his denial of Judaism's ethical-religious element, Kant offers several arguments: (1) The nature of the commands of Judaism are those of a political organization, and its stipulated coercive laws relate to external acts. This externalism and unethicality is applicable even to the Decalogue, which seems to be ethical in form but is devoid of ethical content because its commandments are directed to external acts and observances. (2) The rewards and punishments for complying with or violating these laws are of a mundane, material nature. Furthermore, they extend to posterity, which is not responsible for acts committed by its forebears, making such punishment, or even reward, repugnant from an ethical point of view. The absence of any reference in the Bible to the hereafter, which was considered by Jewish rationalists as a positive quality of Judaism since it avoided metaphysics, became now a negative quality. Ac-

cording to Kant, Judaism, because of its political nature, deliberately avoided such references, thus reflecting its nonreligious character, since no religion can ignore the belief in a future life. He does not exclude the possibility that the Jews as individuals entertained a belief in a life after death, but the Jewish commonwealth as such had merely political ambitions. Consequently, the rewards and punishments set forth by the Jewish religion had to be confined to man's terrestrial existence only. (3) Judaism is not a universal religion but an ethnic confession. The very concept of a God-chosen people implies an exclusiveness and even an enmity toward people of different persuasions, thus incurring the hatred of all.

The last reference, which seems to endow anti-Semitism with a historical, theological, and psychological justification, was supposed to emphasize not only the nonethicality of Judaism but also its immorality. The fact that the Jews were the first monotheistic people was minimized by Kant. Kant even commends the polytheism of the nations of antiquity and condemns the monotheism of the Jews. In a polytheism which venerates many deities subordinated to one God, ethics is still possible, whereas in Judaism, God is an absolutist monarch demanding unqualified obedience. A God whose exclusive concern is unqualified compliance with His rituals and formal statutes is less divine in an ethical sense than the moral deities of polytheism. According to Kant, not only is Judaism an unethical religion, but its God is an unethical God—Kant, *Die Religion innerhalb der Grenzen der blossen Vernunft* (Leipzig, 1793), pp. 134–37; Sidney Ayinn, "Kant on Judaism," *Jewish Quarterly Review* [Philadelphia, hereafter cited as *JQR*] 59 (July 1968):9–23.

22. Rotenstreich, *Ha-Maḥshavah*, 2:7–113.
23. Guttmann, *Philosophies of Judaism*, pp. 304–49.
24. This distinction of first and second generation of Reformers was made by David Philipson in *The Reform Movement in Judaism*. Among the first generation were Israel Jacobson and David Friedländer; the second generation included men of the caliber of Abraham Geiger and Samuel Holdheim, among many others.
25. See *Igrot Shadal* (Przemyśl-Cracow, 1882–1899), 8:1134.
26. Rotenstreich, *The Recurring Pattern*, p. 41.
27. Samuel Holdheim, "Reformbestrebung und Emancipation," appendix to *Das Ceremonialgesetz im Messiasreich* (Schwerin, 1845), p. 123; Philipson, *The Reform Movement*, p. 42.
28. Philipson, *The Reform Movement*, pp. 39–50.
29. Holdheim, "Reformbestrebung," p. 50.
30. See Abraham Geiger, *Das Judentum und seine Geschichte* (Breslau, 1865), 1:145–46.
31. Schleiermacher defined *revelation* as "every original and new communication of the universe to man. . . . Every intuition and every original feeling proceeds from revelation. As revelation lies beyond consciousness, demonstration is not possible, yet we are not merely to assume it generally, but each one knows best himself what is repeated and learned elsewhere, and what is original and new. If nothing original has yet been generated in you, when it does come

it will be a revelation for you also"—Friedrich Schleiermacher, *On Religion: Speeches to Its Cultured Despisers,* trans. John Oman (New York, 1958), p. 89.

32. Ibid., p. 36.
33. Heine, *Religion and Philosophy,* p. 78.
34. The *génie,* which frequently occurs in Herder's writings, particularly of the Sturm und Drang period, is somehow akin to the *daimon* of Socrates. It entered the stream of thought of the eighteenth century through Shaftesbury. Regardless of its original meaning and the transformation of its application, it gained in popularity and in usage. "The deification or semi-deification of the artist under the rubric *Genie* reflects the 'breaking through' or *Durchbruch,* as the Germans call it, of the theory of spontaneous feeling to which the 'individualistic' monads of Leibnitz and the theory of imagination popularized by Addison merely added further elements"—F. McEchran, *The Life and Philosophy of Johann Gottfried Herder* (Oxford, 1939), p. 30.
35. Geiger, *Das Judentum,* pp. 27–28.
36. Ibid.
37. Ibid.
38. Isaiah Berlin, "Herder and the Enlightenment," in *Aspects of the Eighteenth Century,* ed. Earl R. Wasserman (Baltimore, 1965), p. 75.
39. Judah Halevi, *The Kuzari,* trans. Hartwig Hirschfeld (New York, 1964), p. 207.
40. Mendelssohn, *Jerusalem,* pp. 67–68. In spite of his admiration for Lessing and his long friendship with him, Mendelssohn sharply disagreed with his friend in this respect. He considered Lessing's theory imaginative but lacking factual foundation. Mankind, Mendelssohn argued, cannot be viewed as a macroorganism resembling an individual man of larger dimensions. A man's intellectual progress and rational maturity may parallel his chronological advancement. Mankind, however, as a collective, has never shown that its progress is related to its chronology. It has always constituted a diversity of cultural and intellectual manifestations. Its cultural standards are frequently more closely related to geography than to time. At any given era there are people in some localities who are infantile intellectually while highly advanced in other areas. Furthermore, the history of humanity abounds in examples wherein chronologically later stages in history were marked not by progression but by regression. Many examples exist in which an enlightened era was succeeded by a dark age, and in which one step forward was followed by several steps backward. Considering the objective data of history, Mendelssohn could not accept Lessing's view of progressive revelation and the constant educational advancement of humanity. He disagreed with Lessing, who conceived of "mankind not as a collectivity but as an individual whom Providence, as it were, has sent to school here on earth in order to raise him from childhood to manhood"—*Jerusalem,* p. 67. Similarly, he considered it absurd to attribute this to a preconceived design by God: "At least, this is by no means an established fact, nor is it a logically necessary assumption

that has to be made to prove the providence of God"—ibid., pp. 67–68.

It is noteworthy that Lessing himself considered his view on revelation as merely hypothetical. This is evident in the motto that he employed for *die Erziehung des Menschengeschlechtes,* taken from Augustine, which reads: "Haec omnia inde esse in quibusdam vera, unde in quibusdam falsa sunt" ("All this is therefore in some respects true, as in some respects false"). Lessing, it is apparent, was not concerned with historical facts. His aim was the liberalization of the Christian theology of his time, which was petrified in its doctrinal mold. It was undoubtedly this implicit aim which made his views, historically insupportable and factually untenable, appealing to the exponents of the Reform movement in Judaism.

41. Randall, *The Career of Philosophy,* 2:89.
42. Holdheim, "Reformbestrebung," p. 50. For a translation, see page 18.
43. Sidney Hook, *From Hegel to Marx* (New York, 1958), p. 17.
44. G. W. F. Hegel, *Science of Logic,* trans. Johnston and Struthers (New York, 1929), 1:60.
45. Richard R. Niebuhr, *Schleiermacher on Christ and Religion* (New York, 1964), p. 179. Hook, *From Hegel to Marx,* pp. 232–33.
46. Hook, *From Hegel to Marx,* p. 114.
47. Frederick Copleston, *A History of Philosophy* (Garden City, N.Y., 1965), 7:197.
48. Walter Kaufmann, *Hegel: A Reinterpretation* (Garden City, N.Y., 1966), p. 15.
49. Ibid., p. 13.
50. Richard Kroner, introduction to G. W. F. Hegel, "On Christianity," in *Early Theological Writings,* trans. T. M. Knox, (New York, 1961), p. 8.
51. Ibid., p. 8.
52. Hegel's familiarity with Mendelssohn's works began very early. He read Mendelssohn's *Phaedon* before Plato's, and the former's concept of Socrates had a lasting effect on him—Kaufmann, *Hegel,* p. 10; Rotenstreich, *The Recurring Pattern,* p. 53. Hegel inherited from Kant not only his philosophic outlook on Judaism but also his prejudicial attitude toward the Jews. Hegel's negative attitude toward Jews and Judaism must not be attributed exclusively to Kant, however; there were many sources for this influence. Nevertheless, the fact that these views were maintained by such a celebrated philosopher as Kant enhanced immeasurably their influence and credibility. As a result, it is difficult to distinguish in Hegel, as in Kant, between the sociopsychological aversion to Jews and the philosophical-theological deprecation of Judaism. Despite the lack of documentary evidence, there is little doubt that the gestation of Hegel's outlook on Judaism originated in his psychologically negative attitude toward the Jews. Like Kant and other Christian illuminati of the era, Hegel did not rise above the prejudices of his generation. Consequently, his early writings, despite their insight, are replete with superficial, prejudicial oversimplifications and emo-

tional fulminations clad in sophisticated philosophic terminology. So deep-seated was his antagonism to the Jews that neither their sufferings nor their endurance evoked in Hegel any sympathy or understanding. "The great tragedy of the Jewish people is no Greek tragedy; it can rouse neither terror nor pity, for both of these arise only out of the fate which follows from the inevitable slip of a beautiful character; it can arouse horror alone"—Hegel, "On Christianity," in *Early Theological Writings*, p. 204. This unmitigated hostility toward the Jews was readily transferred to Judaism and was obvious in spite of Hegel's intellectual scope. In Hegel's early period, this aversion to Judaism remained constant, regardless of his attitude toward Christianity. At the time that he displayed anti-Christian sentiments and a strong fascination with Hellenism, Hegel considered Judaism anti-Hellenic. When he subsequently became reconciled with Christianity he maintained that Judaism negated the moral beauty inherent in the former. This emotive, irrational attitude was revealed when he compared Judaism with Hellenism. Hegel contrasted the "ugliness" of Judaism with the beauty of Greece. He castigated the Jews for secluding themselves and for their submission to a demanding, jealous God. Unlike the Greeks, whose spirit was marked by union and love of nature, the spirit of the Jews was that of discord and hostility to nature—Kroner, introduction, pp. 9–10.

53. Emil Fackenheim, "Samuel Hirsch and Hegel," in *Studies in Nineteenth Century Jewish Intellectual History* (Cambridge, Mass., 1968), pp. 175–76.

54. Rotenstreich, *The Recurring Pattern*, p. 67.

55. Guttmann, *Philosophies of Judaism*, p. 307.

56. Fackenheim, "Samuel Hirsch and Hegel," p. 201.

57. The Culturverein was severely criticized by Gershom Scholem in *Luaḥ ha-Aretz* (Tel Aviv, 1944).

58. Alexander Altmann, "Theology in Twentieth Century German Jewry," *Leo Baeck Institute Year Book* [hereafter cited as *LBYB*] 1 (London, 1956): 193.

59. Luitpold Wallach, *Liberty and Letters* (London, 1959), p. 12.

60. Ibid., p. 13.

61. All quotations from here until the end of the chapter are from Immanuel Wolf [Immanuel Wohlwill], "On the Concept of a Science of Judaism," trans. Lionel E. Kochan, *LBYB*, 2 (London, 1957): 194–204.

2. The Enlightenment Tradition

1. Simon Dubnov, *Divrei Yemei Am Olam* (Tel Aviv, 1958), 8:129; M. Grunwald, *Hamburgs deutsche Juden bis zur Auflösung der Dreigemeinden, 1811* (Hamburg, 1904), pp. 20, 24. Azriel Shoḥet, *Im Hilufei Tekufot* (Jerusalem, 1960), p. 18; Salo Wittmayer Baron, *The Jewish Community* (Philadelphia, 1945), 2:23, 3:107.

2. Hermann Kellenbenz, *Sephardim an der unteren Elbe* (Wiesbaden, 1958), pp. 452–62.

3. Cecil Roth, *A History of the Marranos* (New York, 1966), p. 229.
4. Graetz, *History*, 4:693.
5. Ibid., pp. 56–65; Dubnov, *Divrei*, 6:225–29, 248–49; Ephraim Shemueli, *Bein Emunah li-Kefirah* (Tel Aviv, 1962), pp. 63–160.
6. Roth, *History of the Marranos*, passim.
7. Scholem, *Jewish Mysticism*, p. 299.
8. Glueckel of Hameln, *The Life of Glueckel of Hameln*, trans. Beth Zion Abrahams (London, 1962), pp. 20–21.
9. Gershom G. Scholem, *Shabbetai Tzevi* (Tel Aviv, 1967), 2:454.
10. Jacob Sasportas, *Tzizit Novel Tzevi*, ed. Yeshayah Tishbi (Jerusalem, 1954), pp. 132–33.
11. Scholem, *Shabbetai Tzevi*, p. 469.
12. Ibid., p. 468.
13. Ibid., pp. 468–92, 545–46. Sasportas's *Tzizit Novel Tzevi* constitutes a classic document of the opposition to Sabbateanism. Modern scholars do not consider Sasportas quite as brave and courageous as he gives the impression of being in his book. Strong arguments have been advanced to show that the author revised it substantially to give the impression that he dared to dissent and resist the current of credulousness and heresy which inundated Jewry.
14. Tishbi, introduction to Sasportas, *Tzizit Novel Tzevi*.
15. Scholem, *Shabbetai Tzevi*, pp. 640–41.
16. Ibid., pp. 671–76.
17. Jacob Katz, *Bein Yehudim le-Goyim* (Jerusalem, 1960), pp. 166–67; Shohet, *Im Hilufei Tekufot*, pp. 220–35.
18. Concerning Eibeschütz's leanings toward Sabbateanism, see M. A. Perlmutter, *Rabbi Yehonatan Eibeschütz ve-Yahaso el ha-Shabtaut* (Jerusalem, 1946); see also Mortimer Cohen, *Jacob Emden: Man of Controversy* (Philadelphia, 1937).
19. About the attitude of the Metz Jewish community toward the Emden-Eibeschütz controversy, see Arthur Hertzberg, *The French Enlightenment and the Jews* (New York, 1968), pp. 209–12.
20. Raphael Mahler, *Divrei Yemei Yisrael: Dorot Aharonim* (Merhavyah, 1954), 2:46–47; Shohet, *Im Hilufei Tekufot*, pp. 89–122.
21. Among the important literary contributors to the *Ha-Meassef* were the Hamburgians Abraham Ben David Meldola, Shalom ha-Cohen, and Hirsch's uncle Moses.
22. Only married men, Eibeschütz maintained, could be the recipients of this distinction. That this was merely a pretext was already pointed out by Hirsch's uncle Moses, who attested that on another occasion Eibeschütz had no such compunction. The fact that even after Mendelssohn's marriage the title *haver* was not granted him is a further indication that matrimony was hardly an issue in this consideration—Moses Mendelssohn of Hamburg [Moses Frankfurter], *Penei Tevel* [hereafter cited as *PT*] (Amsterdam, 1872), p. 231.
23. Shohet, *Im Hilufei Tekufot*, pp. 249–50.
24. *Ha-Meassef* (1785): 170–86; *Bikurei ha-Ittim* (Vienna, 1823), 4:237–38.
25. Peretz Sandler, *Ha-Beur la-Torah shel Mosheh Mendelssohn ve-Si'ato* (Jerusalem, 1940), pp. 17, 194–218.

26. The subscription of the Danish king was planned by Mendelssohn to silence any opposition to the *Biur.* See Klausner, *Historiah,* 1:70.
27. According to Gershom G. Scholem, there was a definite relationship between Sabbateanism in the seventeenth century and the Reform movement in the nineteenth century: "Around 1850, a consciousness of this link between Sabbatainism and reform was still alive in some quarters. . . . Prossnitz and Hamburg, both in the eighteenth century centers of Sabbatian propaganda and the scene of bitter struggles between the orthodox and the heretics or their sympathizers, were among the chief strongholds of the reform movement in the beginning of the nineteenth century"—Scholem, *Jewish Mysticism,* p. 304.
28. "Sie wissen, wie bereits in früher Jugend diese Gegenstände meine Seele beschäftigt; wie von erleuchtet religiösen Eltern erzogen"— Samson Raphael Hirsch, *Igrot Tzafon: Neunzehn Briefe über Judentum von Ben Usiel* [hereafter cited as *NB*] (Altona, 1836), p. 5.
29. Jonathan Eibeschütz, *Ya'arot Devash* (Karlsruhe, 1782), 2:44–45.
30. Jacob Emden, *Megillat Sefer,* ed. Kahana (Warsaw, 1897), pp. 97–98. About the enlightenment of the Jews in the pre-Mendelssohn era and particularly concerning the attitude of Eibeschütz and Emden to secular education, see Shohet, *Im Hilufei Tekufot,* pp. 198–241.
31. Naphtali Herz Wessely, *Divrei Shalom ve-Emet* (Berlin, 1782). About the relationship of Wessely's views to those of Mendelssohn, see Yehezkiel Kaufmann, *Golah ve-Nekhar* (Tel Aviv, 1930), 2:30–39.
32. Wessely, *Divrei,* chapter 8.
33. Shohet, *Im Hilufei Tekufot,* pp. 254–55; Isaac Barzilay-Eisenstein, "The Ideology of the Berlin Haskalah," *Proceedings of the American Academy for Jewish Research* 25:1–37.
34. Graetz, *History,* 5:506.
35. Hans Kohn, *The Mind of Germany* (New York, 1965), pp. 69–75; Koppel S. Pinson, *Modern Germany* (New York, 1966), pp. 32–33.
36. Hirsch's uncle Moses was one of the most outspoken opponents of the French and openly rejoiced at the conquest of Hamburg by the Russian forces. When the French army subsequently recaptured Hamburg, Moses was compelled to flee the city—*PT,* pp. 3–22. Also, one of the Maskilim and subsequent founders of the Hamburg Temple, Isaak Seckel Frankel (1765–1835), wrote a long poem in Hebrew: *Hevlei Haemonia ve-Kinatel,* in which he described the suffering endured by the inhabitants of Hamburg during the French occupation. The poem is permeated with a sense of hostility toward Napoleon and his invading forces. "Haemonia" is the poetic name for Hamburg. See Barukh Mevorakh, *Napoleon u-Tekufato* (Jerusalem, 1968), pp. 159–69.
37. "Ein verständig närrischer Mann mit vieler Gutmütigkeit und bon mots, . . . un brave homme avec beaucoup de bonhomie"—Heinrich Graetz, *Tagebuch,* 2:131, quoted in *Monatsschrift für Geschichte und Wissenschaft des Judentums* [Breslau—hereafter cited as *MGWJ*] 63:354. This diary has not been published and is at the National Library of the Hebrew University in Jerusalem—ms var. 263 (1, 2). Excerpts of it were published by M. Brann in *MGWJ*

(1918–1919), in three articles entitled "Aus H. Graetzens Lehr- und Wanderjahren," 62:231–65, 63:34–47, 343–63. See also Philipp Bloch, *Heinrich Graetz: Ein Lebens- und Zeitbild* (Posen, 1904), Eng. trans. Heinrich Graetz, a memoir, in Heinrich Graetz, *History of the Jews*, vol. 6, (Philadelphia, 1945); Reuven Michael, "Yomano shel Graetz," *Kiryat Sefer* 37 (Jerusalem, 1962): 523–31; Zvi Graetz, *Darkhei ha-Historiah ha-Yehudit*, ed. Shmuel Ettinger (Jerusalem, 1969), pp. 243–75; Reuven Michael, "The Unknown Graetz—From His Diaries and Letters," *LBYB* 13 (London, 1968): 34–56.

38. Graetz, *Tagebuch*, 2:132. *MGWJ* 63:359.
39. "Glaubte ich dann einen solchen Versuch glücklich gelöst zu haben und war es mir am Abend, wenn dass Geschäft ruhte, vergönnt, meinem Vater, dessen zweite Seele *Tenakh* war und der den hellsten Blick und die zarteste Empfindung für die Wahrheiten und Schönheiten der heiligen Schriften hatte, meine jugendlichen Versuche vorzutragen und aus seinem Munde Beifall und Tadel, Belehrung und Förderung zu erhalten—wer war dann glücklicher und seliger als ich!"—Samson Raphael Hirsch, in *Gesammelte Schriften* [hereafter cited as *S*], ed. N. Hirsch (Frankfurt, 1908–1912), 1:324.
40. Isaac Heinemann, "Samson Raphael Hirsch: The Formative Years of the Leader of Modern Orthodoxy," *Historia Judaica* [New York— hereafter cited as *HJ*] 13 (1951):30; idem, "Meḥkarim al R. Shimshon Raphael Hirsch," *Sinai* (Jerusalem) 24 (1949):251. The pictures of Hirsch's parents and his uncle Moses Mendelsohn of Hamburg appear in *Israelit*, S. R. Hirsch anniversary issue (Frankfurt am Main, 1908).
41. Shoḥet, *Im Ḥilufei Tekufot*, pp. 55, 56, 58, 138, 160, 232.
42. Eduard Duckesz, "Zur Genealogie," *Jahrbuch der jüdisch-literarischen Gesellschaft* [Frankfurt am Main—hereafter cited as *JJLG*] 17 (1926): 104.
43. Ibid., p. 124.
44. Ibid., pp. 130–32.
45. Ibid.
46. Glueckel of Hameln, *Life*, p. 16.
47. Ibid., p. 17.
48. Ibid., p. 16.
49. Duckesz in "Zur Genealogie," pp. 103–32, lists the names of Hirsch's paternal and maternal ancestors on the basis of documents, monuments, and *pinkasim* extant at the time. Except for a few members of the family, the references to most are sketchy, vague, and platitudinous. There are the customary traditional references extolling the goodness, kindness, piety, and charitableness of the deceased. Some, however, are referred to as *parnesim*, a term indicating leaders and officers of the Jewish community.
50. Ibid., pp. 107–8.
51. Ibid., p. 115.
52. *PT*, pp. 4, 286.
53. Ibid., p. 286.
54. ואדוני אבי זצ"ל העיד עליו את אשר למד בחברתו כל יום ויום שעור גמרא ופוסקים על יד הרב המפורסם ר' צבי הירש זצ"ל (פני תבל עמ' 229).... כאשר הייתי בברלין הייתי חבר לרמ"ד, גם למדנו שעור פו"ת על יד הגאב"ד דקהילה

ובכל שבת התפללתי השכמה בבית רמ"ד ואחר כלות התפילה כמה פעמים
יובילני בחדר לימודו לעשות אתו קידוש ולברות אתו פת שחרית. ‹פני תבל
עמ' 234›.

Rabbi Hirschel Lewin was at first sympathetic to the Maskilim. Later, when the latter became more radical in their views and acts, he opposed them strongly—Simon Bernfeld, *Dor Tahapukhot* (Warsaw, 1897), 1:33–34, 79–80, 104–5; Eliezer Landshuth, *Toledot Anshei ha-Shem u-Pe'ulatam* (Berlin, 1884), pp. 85–86. Rabbi Lewin's own son Saul, a brilliant scholar, allegedly became a radical Maskil. His anonymous but venomous satires and criticism of traditional Judaism and Jewish customs provoked the Orthodox and may have caused his father's change of attitude—Bernfeld, *Dor Tahapukhot*, 1:91, 2:68–77. Frankfurter's association with Mendelssohn seems to have lasted a long time. From an episode related by his son Moses it would appear that Frankfurter visited Mendelssohn at the time when the former was at least thirty-seven years old. According to Moses, his father was in Mendelssohn's house one time when the philosopher Solomon Maimon paid him an unexpected visit. Maimon handed Mendelssohn a manuscript dealing with a philosophic interpretation of some cabalistic aspect. The only work of this nature by Maimon was his unpublished work *Ḥeshek Shelomo,* now in the Bodleian Library, Oxford, which he completed in 1778. Since Maimon did not arrive at Berlin before 1779, it would indicate that Frankfurter, born in 1742, was still visiting Mendelssohn at the age of thirty-seven. See *PT,* p. 248; Abraham Geiger, "Zu Salomon Maimons Entwickelungsgeschichte," *Jüdische Zeitschrift für Wissenschaft und Leben* 4 (Breslau, 1866): 189–99.

55. Duckesz, "Zur Genealogie," p. 122. While approving Wessely's works, Frankfurter objected to the works of the later more radical Maskilim—ibid., p. 120.
56. Mordekhai Eliav, *Ha-Ḥinukh ha-Yehudi be-Germaniah bi-Yemei ha-Haskalah ve-ha-Emantzipatziah* (Jerusalem, 1960), pp. 159–61.
57. *Ha-Meassef* (Dessau, 1810): 22–25.
58. Eliav, *Ha-Ḥinukh,* loc. cit.
59. *PT,* p. 227.
60. Published in Altona in 1815 and reprinted in Vilna in 1888 with a commentary, *Moda le-Binah,* by Wolf Heidenheim. Hirsch knew Loeb Frankfurter and was familiar with his work *Ha-Rekhasim le-Bikah* (*CG* 4:10; *CL* 11:24), which he received from Frankfurter. Years later Hirsch was accused of having taken ideas from it without crediting the author. Hirsch's refutation appeared in *Jeschurun* 14 (Frankfurt am Main, 1868): 113–33, under the title "Die Distellese des Herrn Kirchheim." Referring to Loeb Frankfurter and his work, Hirsch stated: "Die Schrift *Ha-Rekhasim le-Bikah* besitze ich selber und habe sie zufällig aus den Händen des Verf. selbst, der zufällig mein Grossonkel war, und was das Citat betrifft, zu welchem ich auf so weiten Umwegen gekommen sein soll, so habe ich diese Erklärung eben so zufällig aus seinem eignen Munde"—ibid., p. 133.
61. Leopold Zunz, *Die gottesdienstlichen Vorträge der Juden historisch entwickelt* (Frankfurt am Main, 1892), chapter 21.

62. *PT*, pp. 98–100.
63. Breuer, "Prakim Mitokh Biographiah," p. 11.
64. *PT*, p. 230.
65. Ibid., p. 239.
66. Moses wrote for the *Ha-Meassef, Jedidja, Allgemeine Zeitung des Judentums,* Fürst's *Orient,* and many others—Grunwald, *Hamburgs deutsche Juden,* pp. 65–66.
67. The Hebrew title of the book was *Metziat ha-Aretz ha-Hadashah.* He also wrote *Shoshan Edut,* aggadic elucidations of the Pentateuch (Stuttgart, 1840–1842). In the introduction to his translation of Campe's book (1807) and in *Penei Tevel,* published posthumously in 1872, Moses acknowledged his father's influence and his intellectual indebtedness to his father.
68. Like the radical Maskilim, Moses depicted the obscurantist rabbi as the embodiment of all evil. Sarcastically he named him Arsela, after the man who, according to the Talmud (Yoma 66a), led the scapegoat to its doom *(azazel)* on the Day of Atonement. To Moses, the Maskil, unenlightened rabbis like Arsela led the Jews to a similar fate. Most devastating was his criticism of Arsela's talmudic discourses, which revealed the rabbi's ignorance. His *pilpul*istic dialectic distorted the logic of the Talmud, and his mysticism marred the beauty of Judaism. Among the four negative elements supporting Arsela in the Orthodox community, he included Samuel Horowitz, rabbi of Nikolsburg, disciple of the maggid of Mesritch and brother of Pinhas Horowitz, rabbi of Frankfurt am Main. Whether this criticism was directed against Rabbi Horowitz as an individual or against the Hasidic movement as whole cannot be answered with certainty. However, from the tone and style, it appears that like other Maskilim, Moses held the entire Hasidic movement in contempt—*PT*, pp. 196–207.
69. *Judaism Eternal: Selected Essays from the Writings of S. R. Hirsch* [hereafter cited as *JE*], trans. and annotated and with an introduction by I. Grunfeld (London, 1956), 1:xxiii.
70. Ibid.
71. Eliav, *Ha-Hinukh,* p. 159.
72. Ibid., pp. 155–57.
73. Ibid., pp. 209–12.
74. Ibid., pp. 169–71, 311–47.
75. *NB*, p. 1.
76. Like the Maskilim, Hirsch put as much emphasis on the knowledge of Hebrew as on German—Hirsch, *Igrot Tzafon, The Nineteen Letters of Ben Uziel* [hereafter cited as *NL*—as distinguished from references to the German edition, *NB*, for *Neunzehn Briefe*], trans. Bernard Drachman (New York, 1942), p. 199. Similarly, he admired the beauty and the logic of the Hebrew language—*NL*, p. 14. Nor did his attitude toward Yiddish differ from those of the Maskilim. In an essay "Aus der Mappe eines wandernden Juden," he bemoaned the fact that neither the Torah nor ethics were taught in the Orthodox synagogue in the culturally appealing *Nationalsprache,* German, thus having deplorable consequences for the more affluent and educated Jews: "Warum musste ich selbst das Wort der *Tokhahah,*

Mussar, und Torah in gebildeter, ansprechender Nationalsprache vermissen, ja als unstatthaft verurteilen hören, und so schmerzlich eben die Folgen jenes Mangels an gründlichem jüdischen Wissen erkennen, die ich überhaupt im Mittelstand so bedauerlich gewahrte"—*S,* 1:448.

That the influence of the Haskalah spirit which Hirsch absorbed in his family remained with him is also evident in the respect he accorded its leading exponents. Though by the time he reached maturity the Haskalah in Germany was merely a faint memory, Hirsch continued to share his grandfather's and uncle's admiration for Mendelssohn. In his first published work, Hirsch referred to Mendelssohn, already anathema in Orthodox circles, as "a brilliant, respect-inspiring personality." Similarly, Hirsch shared his grandfather's and uncle's respect for Wessely, although the latter was severely denounced by the leading Orthodox rabbis. Hirsch's respect for Wessely can be seen from the fact that, even in later years when Hirsch had already become the leader of the militant Orthodox, he did not hesitate to quote Wessely in his own commentary on the Bible—Hirsch, *The Pentateuch Translated and Explained by Samson Raphael Hirsch,* trans. Isaac Levy (London, 1958–62)—*CL* 13:4, 20:23, 25:1; also in his commentary on *Pirkei Avot* 1:1. [In references to this work, Hirsch's commentary is denoted by *C* and the book of the Pentateuch by its first letter, and the numbers following denote the chapter and verse in question. Thus, this reference is to Hirsch's commentary on Leviticus 13:4, 20:23, and 25:1.] Although Hirsch seldom credited his sources, in this case he had no misgivings in citing the leading Maskil in Germany. Apparently, in the eyes of Hirsch, as in the eyes of his grandfather, Wessely's works were beyond reproach. The extent of Hirsch's admiration for Wessely can be seen from the testimony of his uncle Moses that Hirsch was in possession of Wessely's unpublished manuscripts—*PT,* p. 211. Regrettably, these manuscripts were lost. They might have revealed a greater influence of Wessely on Hirsch in areas other than educational theory designated as *Torah im derekh eretz.* According to Moses there were among them a supercommentary on Nachmanides's commentary on the Bible, the last part of Wessley's *Gan Naul,* and a dialogue between a rabbi and his disciple—ibid.

77. Graetz, *Tagebuch,* 5:577.
78. The fact that an enlightened rabbi, no matter how pious and observant, was to sit in the place formerly occupied by Raphael Cohen, who battled any manifestation of Enlightenment, was very distasteful to the Orthodox. A traditionalist rabbi with a university education was a *contradictio in adjecto* to men familiar with the views expressed, only a few decades earlier, by Jacob Emden of nearby Altona, who had strong reservations about anyone studying medicine at a university, although such knowledge could save lives— *Mishpat Sofrim* (Altona, 1865), p. 71; *She'elat Ya'avetz* (Altona, 1839), p. 41; *PT,* p. 243. A rabbi with an academic education was disapproved of not only in 1821—nineteen years later it still constituted one of the major challenges leveled by Rabbi Solomon Tiktin against Abraham Geiger over the latter's candidacy for the rab-

binic post of Breslau. In 1840 Tiktin declared that "anyone who had attended a university was *ipso facto* disqualified to be a rabbi. . . ." As late as 1870 Esriel Hildesheimer was attacked by his orthodox friends because he would not limit rabbinic training to the realm of halakhah"—Ismar Elbogen, *A Century of Jewish Life* (Philadelphia, 1945), p. 574. That Bernays, who attended the University of Würzburg when Geiger was only a little boy and Hildesheimer had not yet been born, should become the traditionalist rabbi of Hamburg must have caused the Orthodox elements in the city much chagrin and consternation—E. Duckesz, "Zur Biographie des Chacham Isaak Bernays," *JJLG* 5 (Frankfurt am Main, 1907):304.

79. That this was a most important consideration can be seen from the fact that the Hamburg Jewish community asked the opinion of non-Jewish scholars concerning their future rabbi. One of them was Professor von Kalbe, a Christian theologian from the University of Munich, where Bernays had studied one semester. The fact that a recommendation of a Christian theologian carried weight in the appointment of a traditionalist rabbi of Hamburg mirrors the transformation of attitudes as well as the desperate crisis in which traditionalist Jewry found itself. While von Kalbe's recommendation was highly complimentary to Bernays, it was somewhat condescending regarding the cultural level of Jews in general. Such an attitude about Jews from a non-Jewish academician was not unique. In his recommendation von Kalbe wrote that he had never met among Jews anyone as cultured and as educated as Bernays: "Zwar bin ich christlicher Theologe nur, indessen, wer mich kennt, weiss auch, dass dessfalls auch über die Theologie der Juden zu urtheilen weiss. Nicht genug aber mit dieser seiner jüdischen Gelehrsamkeit, sondern er verbindet damit auch eine tiefe Kentnniss in der Welt und Menschengeschichte und Politik, überhaupt, in einem solchen Grade, wie ich ihn selten bei christlichen Gelehrten—nie aber bei einem Juden angetroffen habe. Ich möchte daher mit der Behauptung nicht irren, dass vielleicht das Judenthum—wenigstens meines Wissens—nie einen Mann hatte, der die Zeitverhältnisse unter allen und jeden Umständen, erforschend und erkennend, das Judenthum selbst durch alle Ereignisse vollkommen durchzuführen im Stande wäre, ohne irgend an Verfassung und locale Institutionen zu verstossen, als dies Bernays zu bewirken vermögend wäre"—Duckesz, "Bernays," p. 300.

80. *PT*, pp. 51–53.

81. Isaac Heinemann, "Ha-Yaḥas she-bein S. R. Hirsch le-Yitzḥak Bernays Rabbo," *Zion* 16 (Jerusalem, 1941): 56–61.

82. In 1838 Wessely's son Solomon published posthumously a fragment of his father's manuscript on Genesis, entitled *Ollelot Naftali*. Bernays warmly endorsed this endeavor. This fact is significant because Bernays's predecessor, Raphael Cohen, had condemned Wessely's work most severely—Duckesz, "Bernays," p. 307. Subsequently, Isaac Samuel Reggio published a few more fragments of the same work. Finally, it was printed by the *Mekitzei Nirdamim* association in Lyck in 1868 under the title *Imrei Shefer*.

83. Eliav, *Ha-Ḥinukh,* pp. 232–33.
84. J. Goldschmidt, *Geschichte der Talmud Torah Realschule in Hamburg* (Hamburg, 1905), p. 52.
85. Hans Bach, " 'Der Bibelsche Orient' und sein Verfasser," *Zeitschrift für Geschichte der Juden in Deutschland* (1937), pp. 14–45.
86. Heinemann, "Ha-Yahas," pp. 48–49.
87. Alexander Altmann, "The New Style of Preaching in Nineteenth Century German Jewry," in *Studies in Nineteenth Century Jewish Intellectual History* (Cambridge, Mass., 1968), pp. 77–78.
88. After listening to one of Bernays's sermon, Heine wrote that it was superior to those of the Reformers Kley, Salomon, and the Auerbachs, but that none of the laymen had understood it—*Heinrich Heine Briefe,* no. 62 (Mainz, 1948), pp. 71–72. Graetz considered Bernays more profound than Mendelssohn—*History,* 5:574.
89. The only Ashkenazi rabbi to assume the title of *ḥakham* was Zvi Ashkenazi, the father of Jacob Emden. The reason for Bernays's preference for the Sephardic title *ḥakham* rather than the Ashkenazic title rabbi has never been satisfactorily explained. The assumption that Bernays may have wished to court the small but prestigious and influential Spanish-Portuguese community of Hamburg cannot be substantiated. That Bernays may have objected to the title rabbi because it was illegitimately appropriated by the Reformers is likewise improbable. Indeed, the Orthodox rabbis considered the Reformers to be usurpers of this traditional, hallowed title and denied them the right to it. The Orthodox rabbis, however, never relinquished this title on account of the Reform leaders bearing it, or changed it for a different one. The most likely suggestion is that Bernays assumed the title of *ḥakham* because it connoted wisdom and knowledge. He apparently wished to convey the idea that, unlike the Orthodox rabbis who preceded him, he was a *ḥakham*—a man of wisdom and culture. Thus he may have hoped to win back many members of the Jewish community who joined the Reform Temple because they found the Orthodox synagogue unattractive and the Orthodox rabbis uncultured.
    All his efforts notwithstanding, Bernays's achievements in Hamburg were less than spectacular. As a moderate caught between two extremes, he pleased neither. Even the small group of the *erleuchtet religiös* became disenchanted with him. Hirsch's uncle, who sang Bernays's praises upon the latter's arrival, later felt disappointed by his reticence and extreme caution. Though displeased, Moses did not break with Bernays, however. He realized the limitations within which Bernays worked and the difficulties he encountered. He attributed the rabbi's premature death to the rancor and strife which made life intolerable—*PT,* p. 54.
90. Breuer, "Prakim Mitokh Biographiah," p. 12; Heinemann, "The Formative Years," p. 30.
91. *JE,* 1:xxv.
92. Heinemann, "The Formative Years," pp. 30–31.
93. Heinemann, "Ha-Yahas," pp. 44–90.
94. Ibid.

95. Bernays was alleged to be the anonymous author of the *Bibelsche Orient*, which he strongly denied. Hirsch was disinclined to believe this allegation. He also disclaimed the contention that his commentary on the Pentateuch was influenced by Bernays: "Der sel. Bernays, dem Hr. Kirchheim ohne Weiteres den bibl. Orient zuschreibt, hat sich nie als Verfasser dieser Schrift bekannt, und Jeder, der demselben persönlich näher gestanden, oder ihn auch nur aus seiner langjährigen Wirksamkeit kennen zu lernen Gelegenheit gehabt, deren Geist und Gesinnung noch in allem zu Tage liegt, was das gegenwärtige Geschlecht seiner Gemeinde in Torah und *Yirah* hegt und pflegt, muss die ihm supponirte Autorschaft des biblischen Orient in hohem Grade für unwahrscheinlich, fast für unmöglich halten. War er der Verfasser dieser Schrift, so war diese Verirrung für ihn schon ein völlig überwundener Standpunkt, als er den Kreis meiner Vaterstadt betrat. Uebrigens steht mein Commentar auch mit dem, was ich aus dem belehrenden und geistweckenden Umgang mit Bernays zu schöpfen so glücklich war, in keiner näheren Beziehung als der allgemeinen Anregung und des verleuchtenden Strebens die Hallen der Torah mit dem Durst nach Erkenntniss zu betreten. Was ich Weises oder Thörichtes auf diesem Wege gefunden und in meine Arbeit niederzulegen gewagt, habe ich, wo ich keinen Urheber citire, vor Gott und Welt allein zu vertreten"— *Jeschurun* 14 (1868):133.

96. See *CG* 4:26, *CN* 20:8, *CP* [commentary in Hirsch, *The Psalms Translated and Explained by Samson Raphael Hirsch*, trans. Gertrude Hirschler (New York, 1960)], 16:1.

97. *Israelit*, S. R. Hirsch anniversary issue, p. 8.

98. Heinemann, "Ha-Yaḥas," p. 45.

99. Ibid., p. 47.

100. Ibid., pp. 51–56.

101. Ibid., pp. 56–61.

102. Ibid., pp. 62–69.

103. Noam Chomsky, *Cartesian Linguistics* (New York, 1966); Ernst Cassirer, *The Philosophy of Symbolic Forms*, trans. Ralph Manheim, 3 vols. (New Haven, 1965–66); J. G. Herder, *Abhandlung über den Ursprung der Sprache;* idem, *Ideen zur Philosophie der Geschichte der Menschheit* (1784–1791); Wilhelm von Humboldt, *Ideen zu einem Versuch die Grenzen der Wirksamkeit des Staats zu bestimmen* (1792); idem, *Über die Verschiedenheit des menschlichen Sprachbaues* (1836); Georg Creuzer, *Symbolik und Mythologie der alten Völker* (1810–1823); Johann von Görres, *Mythengeschichte der asiatischen Welt* (1810).

104. Eliav, *Ha-Ḥinukh*, pp. 150–51.

105. S. Bamberger, *Geschichte der Rabbiner der Stadt und des Bezirkes Würzburg* (Wandsbeck, 1905), p. 87. Bing was one of the few rabbis in Germany concerned with the young prospective German rabbis who devoted most of their time to academic university studies and only a fraction of it to Jewish studies.

106. Jacob Ettlinger, *Binyan Tziyon* (Altona, 1868), responsum 86.

107. Max Heller, "Samson Raphael Hirsch," *CCAR Yearbook* [hereafter cited as *CCARYB*] 18 (Cincinnati, 1908): 195–96.

108. Ibid.
109. "He sat at the feet of Rabbi Ettlinger for but one year. Whence, then, did he derive his prominence in Torah, in Talmud, and codes?"—Breuer, "Prakim Mitokh Biographiah," p. 12. According to some Hirschians, Rabbi Abraham Samuel Benjamin Sofer, author of the *Ketav Sofer,* allegedly remarked after meeting Hirsch that luckily Hirsch "considered us more learned than himself. If he realized what a scholar he is, we could have no peace from him"—ibid., p. 13, P. Fischer, "Samson Raphael Hirsch in Ungarn," *Israelit* anniversary issue, p. 45. One has to be utterly unimaginative to consider this comment other than in jest. It reflects Sofer's sense of humor rather than Hirsch's scholarship.
110. Ibid., p. 14.
111. Heinemann, "The Formative Years," p. 33.
112. Breuer, "Prakim Mitokh Biographiah," p. 14.
113. H. D. Schmidt, "Chief Rabbi Nathan Marcus Adler," *LBYB* 7 (New York, 1962): 292–94.
114. Zwi Asaria, "Samson Raphael Hirsch's Wirken im Lande Niedersachsen," *Udim: Zeitschrift der Rabbinerkonferenz in der Bundesrepublik Deutschland* (Frankfurt am Main, 1970), 1: 2–3.
115. Ibid., p. 3.
116. Ibid.
117. Breuer, "Prakim Mitokh Biographiah," p. 14.
118. Heinemann, "Meḥkarim al R. Shimshon Raphael Hirsch," p. 268.
119. Breuer, "Prakim Mitokh Biographiah," p. 15.
120. M. Friedländer, "The Late Chief Rabbi Dr. N. M. Adler," *JQR* (Philadelphia), 1890, p. 373; Asaria, "Hirsch's Wirken."
121. Friedländer, "Adler."
122. Hirsch was appointed by the government without the participation of the Jewish communities of Oldenburg—Heinemann, "The Formative Years," p. 30; Asaria, "Hirsch's Wirken."
123. Schmidt, "Adler," p. 292.
124. *Jeschurun* 1 (1914):73ff.
125. Heinemann, "The Formative Years," p. 34; Altmann, "The New Style of Preaching," pp. 65–116.
126. Schmidt, "Adler," pp. 292–93; Heinemann, "The Formative Years," pp. 33–38.

3. Rabbinic Profile

1. Brann, "Aus Graetzens Jahren," *MGWJ* 63 (1919):348n.
2. Breuer, "Prakim Mitokh Biographiah," p. 15.
3. Graetz, *Tagebuch* 2:76, quoted in Brann, "Aus Graetzens Jahren," *MGWJ* 62:247.
4. Heinemann, "The Formative Years," pp. 46–47; Kurt Wilhelm, "The Jewish Community in the Post-Emancipation Period" *LBYB* 2 (London, 1957):64.
5. Max Wiener, *Abraham Geiger and Liberal Judaism,* trans. Ernst J. Schlochauer (Philadelphia, 1962), pp. 28–31.
6. Mendelssohn, *Jerusalem,* p. 110.

7. It is noteworthy that a similar admonition was issued by the city council of Hamburg in 1602: "Even if magistrates were godless, tyrannical, and avaricious, subjects ought not to rebel and disobey but should accept it as the Lord's punishment which the subjects deserved for their sins"—quoted in Hajo Holborn, *A History of Modern Germany* (New York, 1967), 2:30.

8. Heinemann, "The Formative Years," p. 34.

9. Zunz, *Gottesdienstlichen Vorträge*, p. 491.

10. *MGWJ*, 1920, p. 144.

11. Mordekhai, Yoma 726, quotes Paltoi Gaon, who supported it. Among the Gaonim objecting to Kol Nidre were Natronai and Hai.

12. Philipson, *The Reform Movement*, p. 35. Neither the Reform prayer book of Berlin of 1817 nor the Hamburg Temple ones published in 1819 and 1841 contain Kol Nidre.

13. *Protokolle der ersten Rabbinerversammlung zu Braunschweig vom 12 bis zum 19 Juni, 1844* (Braunschweig, 1844), pp. 33–42.

14. The objection to these customs was not made only by the Reformers but also by many enlightened traditionalists. Graetz tells of his anguish before the Day of Atonement brought about by the custom of *kapparot*. Although at the time he was very religious, he could not accept this *"törichten und närrischen"* custom. Apprehensive that his parents might compel him to perform it, he ran away from home. Graetz refers to *kapparot* contemptuously as a Polish custom: "Il est de de coutume parmi les Juifs polonais de tourner un coq en sacrifice autour de la tête"—*Tagebuch*, 1:115, quoted in Brann, "Aus Graetzens Jahren," *MGWJ* 62:256. It should be noted that, although Hirsch included *tashlikh* and *kapparot* in his *siddur*, which he published many years later and under different circumstances, he did not translate these selections into German. *Ḥibbut aravah* or the beating of the willow on Hoshanah Rabbah was considered offensive in many liberal synagogues. Such practice was explicitly forbidden in various *Synagogenordnungen*—Jakob J. Petuchowski, *Prayerbook Reform in Europe* (New York, 1968), pp. 114–18.

15. According to Immanuel Jakobowitz, there is a family tradition that Hirsch abolished the recitation of Kol Nidre not in Oldenburg but later, in Emden, due to certain dishonest practices by some members of the community—see Petuchowski, *Prayerbook Reform*, pp. 337, 391 n. 10. Others, however, maintain that this episode took place in Oldenburg—Joseph Aub, *Die Eingangsfeier des Versöhnungstages* (Mainz, 1863); Wilhelm, "The Jewish Community"; Leo Trepp, *Die Landesgemeinde der Juden in Oldenburg, 1827–1938* (Oldenburg, 1965); Heinemann, "The Formative Years," pp. 42–45. Petuchowski is inclined to accept both traditions, namely, that Hirsch abolished Kol Nidre in Oldenburg as well as Emden—*Prayerbook Reform*, pp. 337–38.

16. Heinemann, "The Formative Years," p. 44.

17. *MGWJ* 63:352–53; see Hirsch's eloquent address on the occasion of the Schiller centenary on November 9, 1859, at Frankfurt am Main —*S*, 6:308–21.

18. "Ich wusste aber, dass eine Reform, d.h. Auslassungen einiger mit

dem Ganzen verflochtener Gesetze, das ganze Gesetz aufheben würden"—*Tagebuch*, 1:91, quoted in Brann, "Aus Graetzens Jahren," *MGWJ* 62:250.

19. Ibid., 1:117, in *MGWJ* 62:257.
20. Quoted and translated by Bloch, *Heinrich Graetz*, pp. 12–13.
21. *Tagebuch*, 1:142, in *MGWJ* 62:258–59.
22. "Jede Zeile mir ein rettender Engel gierig verschlang, und welche das Eis des starren schrecklichen Skepticismus von meinem Herzen schmeltzte und meine Gefühle und Gesinnungen in rein und echt jüdische verwandelte"—*MGWJ* 62:258.
23. Pessaḥim 112b.
24. "Sie haben sich im Feuer des Gefühles ein Ideal vom Verfasser der Briefe entworfen, das weit über die Wirklichkeit ragt. Reduzieren Sie daher dieses Bild auf die Hälfte, ja auf das Viertel Ihres Ideals, und prüfen Sie sich, ob Sie auch dann noch zu ihm sich hingezogen fühlen; erwarten Sie keinen schon vollendeten Meister, sondern einen selbst noch in Forschen begriffenen Mann"—*MGWJ* 62:261.
25. *Tagebuch*, 2:55, in *MGWJ* 63:46.
26. Wessely, *Divrei*, pp. 3–32.
27. At Bonn Hirsch had studied the satires of Juvenal and experimental physics—Raphael Breuer, *Unter seinem Banner* (Frankfurt, 1908), p. 213. This may indicate that Hirsch was not a full-time student at the university but may have merely taken a few courses. In his *Neunzehn Briefe* he claimed to know Virgil, Tasso, and Shakespeare —*NL*, p. 5.
28. "Wir lasen gemeinsam H. Heine's *Salon*, der voller Blasphemien und *Minut*, unter anderem auch Lästerung des heiligen göttlichen Nahmens, des *Shem ha-Meforash—Tagebuch*, 2:58, in *MGWJ* 63:47.
29. *Tagebuch*, 2:76, in *MGWJ* 63:347.
30. *Tagebuch*, 2:66ff., in *MGWJ* 63:348.
31. *Tagebuch*, 2:57, in *MGWJ* 63:47.
32. *MGWJ* 63:352–53.
33. Ibid., p. 356.
34. *Tagebuch*, 2:158, in *MGWJ* 63:360.
35. *MGWJ* 63:356–57.
36. *MGWJ* 62:259.
37. אלי, קטנתי מכל החסדים אשר עשית את עבדך כי בער וריק בי אין תוחלת יצאתי מעירי לפני ארבע שנים ועתה אסיר תקוה אני לעלות במעלות החכמה לבא אל איש אשר תכונות נפשו כמלאך אלוקים צבאות. (*MGWJ* 62:265)

38. ה' א' איכה בראת את האדם! גם אם יתהלך במו אש, אם ברחים יעבוד בפרך כחמור, עוד ישאג אם ינסו להוציא אותו מכור הברזל! הוא פה ללעג ולחרפה. יושבי אלדענבורג בל יכירו אותו, בל ישמעו לקולו באשר ידרוש להם מידי שבת ואשר יהגה בה יומם ולילה כלמדן פולני בלי לדעת את צאת ואת מבוא העם! ועוד זאת בכל סביביו היהודים עוברים על תורתו, גם בניו גם בני ביתו יחטאו וילמדו ממנו והוא כחרש לא ישמע. (*MGWJ* 63:360)

39. "Er berührte Geschichte, aber nur allgemein, weil er das Detail nicht kennt"—*MGWJ* 63:356.
40. *Tagebuch*, 2:93–94, in *MGWJ* 63:348–49.

41. *Tagebuch,* 2:152–58, in *MGWJ* 63:357–62.

42. "Da kalkuliert er nun kleinlich, wieviel das Mehl, Fleisch, Huhn und Gänse dort und hier differieren—alles *schemuos* eines Kleingeist-krämers, das echte prosaische Philistertum. Und dieser soll dem Judentum auf die Beine helfen, Dieser soll eine geist-und lebens-volle Gestaltung hervorrufen!"—*Tagebuch,* 2:158, in *MGWJ* 63:360.

43. See *MGWJ* 63:348n.

44. Ibid., p. 362.

45. Holborn, *History of Modern Germany,* 3:27–28.

46. Asaria, "Hirsch's Wirken," pp. 6–8.

47. Ibid., pp. 8–9.

48. Ibid., p. 12.

49. Ibid., pp. 11–12.

50. Ibid., p. 6.

51. Ibid.

52. Ibid.

53. Ibid. Levi Herzfeld was a pioneer in Jewish economic history. He published *Handelsgeschichte der Juden des Altertums* (Brunswick, 1894) and other works that were praised by the great German his-torian Theodor Mommsen. See also Salo W. Baron, *History and Jewish Historians* (Philadelphia, 1964), pp. 322–43.

54. Ibid., pp. 8–9.

55. Ibid., pp. 12–18.

56. W. Ayerst, *The Jews in the Nineteenth Century* (London, 1848), p. 347.

57. Published in Altona, 1844.

58. Published in Schwerin, 1843.

59. "Sie werden den Juden, der bereit ist Alles, Alles, nur nicht seine Religion dem Staate zu opfern, eben um dieser Religiösität wegen als willkommenes Glied ihrers Verbandes begrüssen. Sie wissen es, und ihr hohes Rechtsgefühl wird es selbst auf dem einfachen Boden des staatsrechtlichen Princips nicht vergessen lassen, dass ja der Jude seine Religion sich nicht gewählt, sich also nicht selbst und freiwillig in eine Lage versetzt hat, in welcher ihm nach der beste-henden Staatsordnung manche Leistungen moralisch unmöglich sind, die andere Staatsangehörige unbehindert leisten; sondern, dass er mit ihr geboren sei, und dieselbe Geburt, die ihn zum Staate verpflichte, ihn auch mit dem Bande des Judenthums umschlinge; dass daher der Staat, als moralische Person, diese moralische Unmög-lichkeit mindestens ebenso zu achten und dem Träger nicht ent-gelten zu lassen haben dürfte, wie er irgend eine physische Unmög-lichkeit achtet und dem Träger nicht entgelten lässt"—*Zweite Mitteilungen aus einem Briefwechsel über die neueste jüdische Literatur* (Altona, 1844), p. 34.

60. "Sobald aber ein Staat die Autonomie der Juden aufgehoben und die ausschliessliche Gerichtsbarkeit als eine Regalie betrachtet, sobald wird vermöge *dina de-malkhuta* es dem Juden religiöse Pflicht, sich in privatrechtlichen Angelegenheiten der Gerichtsbarkeit des Staates zu unterwerfen, wie dieser Unterschied bereits im Rosh, Gittin 81:10, begründet ist und dies ja auch der Verf. in NR II erkannt hatte—ibid., p. 49.

61. Graetz, *History,* 5:523.
62. *JE,* 1:xl.
63. Ibid.
64. Published in Nikolsburg, March 20, 1848.
65. The full letter was published in the S. R. Hirsch anniversary issue of the *Israelit,* p. 26. Hirsch wrote the letter on March 23, 1848.
66. *JE,* 1:xxix.
67. Adolf Frankl-Grün, *Geschichte der Juden in Kremsier* (Frankfurt am Main, 1899), 2:128–31.
68. David Feuchtwang, "Samson Raphael Hirsch als Oberlandesrabbiner von Mähren," *Israelit,* S. R. Hirsch anniversary issue, pp. 19–25.
69. Frankl-Grün, *Juden in Kremsier,* 2:17.
70. Quoted in Feuchtwang, "Hirsch"; see also Ignaz Maybaum, "Dubnow's Assessment of the Reform Movement of German Jewry," in *Simon Dubnow: The Man and His Work* (Paris, 1963), pp. 109–10.
71. Feuchtwang, "Hirsch."
72. Yekutiel Yehudah Greenwald, *Le-Toldot ha-Reformatzion ha-Datit be-Germaniah uve-Ungariah* (Columbus, Ohio, 1948), pp. 55–58.
73. Ibid.
74. Ibid.
75. Ibid.
76. Hirsch preferred the term *Synagoge* to that of *Gemeinde* ("community"), because the former had merely a confessional connotation whereas the latter's was sociopolitical—Frankl-Grün, *Juden in Kremsier,* 2:14.
77. Feuchtwang, "Hirsch," p. 25; Frankl-Grün *Juden in Kremsier,* 2:20.
78. Greenwald, *Le-Toldot ha-Reformatzion,* pp. 57–58. Hirsch had entertained plans for building a school and a rabbinic seminary, but in view of the prevailing circumstances had to abandon them.
79. Hirsch's five sons all became prominent: Mendel became the principal of Hirsch's secondary school, Naphtali was a lawyer and edited Hirsch's *Gesammelte Schriften,* Marcus was a physician, and Julius and Isaac were businessmen; Isaac also became the editor of the new series of the *Jeschurun,* continuing his father's literary project. Hirsch's daughters were Sarah, Julie, Therese, Jenny, and Sophie. Sophie married Salomon Breuer from Hungary, who succeeded his father-in-law as rabbi of the *Israelitische Religionsgesellschaft* in Frankfurt am Main.
80. Solomon Abraham Trier, ed., *Rabbinische Gutachten über die Beschneidung* (Frankfurt am Main, 1844).
81. Emanuel Schwarzschild, *Die Gründung der israelitischen Religionsgesellschaft zu Frankfurt am Main und ihre Weiterentwicklung bis zum Jahre 1876,* Frankfurt am Main, 1876.
82. Hermann Schwab, *The History of Orthodox Jewry in Germany, 1830–1945* (London, 1950), p. 40; Breuer, "Prakim Mitokh Biographiah," p. 27.
83. Schwab, ibid.; Breuer, ibid.
84. Mendel Hirsch, *Samson Raphael Hirsch und die israelitische Religionsgesellschaft zu Frankfurt am Main* (Mainz, 1897).

85. Samson Raphael Hirsch, "Das rabbinische Judentum und die sociale Bildung: Ein erstes und letztes Wort zur Verständigung," *Frankfurter Intelligenzblatt* (Frankfurt am Main, 1853), no. 8; idem, "Das rabbinische Judentum und der Herr Hess," *Frankfurter Intelligenzblatt* (1853), no. 22.
86. Heinemann, *Ta'amei ha-Mitzvot be-Sifrut Yisrael* (Jerusalem, 1956), 2:194. According to Mordekhai Breuer, persons not observing the dietary laws or desecrating the Sabbath in public could vote but not be elected to the governing board—"Prakim Mitokh Biographiah," pp. 30–31.
87. Heinemann, *Ta'amei ha-Mitzvot*, 2:146–47.
88. Eliav, *Ha-Ḥinukh*, pp. 227–32.
89. The *Ha-Meassef,* which appeared in 1784, was followed by other periodicals: *Sulamith* in 1806, *Zeitschrift für die Wissenschaft des Judentums* in 1822, under the editorship of Zunz, and *Wissenschaftliche Zeitschrift für jüdische Theologie* in 1834 edited by Geiger, to mention but a few.
90. The appointment of Enoch to the rabbinate of Fulda compelled him to resign the editorship of these two publications and brought about, directly or indirectly, their discontinuation—Yitzhak Raphael, *Rishonim ve-Aḥronim* (Tel Aviv, 1947), pp. 327–35.
91. *Jeschurun: Eine Monatschrift zur Förderung jüdischen Geistes und jüdischen Lebens im Haus, Gemeinde, und Schule.*
92. Heinemann, *Ta'amei ha-Mitzvot,* 2:175–80.
93. Published in Krotoschin, 1846. Graetz received his Ph.D. from the University of Jena.
94. Graetz's *History* was not published in chronological or sequential order. The fourth volume appeared first in 1853, the third in 1855, the fifth in 1860, the sixth in 1861, the seventh in 1863, the eighth in 1864, the ninth in 1866, the tenth in 1868. The first and second were published in 1874–76 after his return from a visit to the Holy Land.
95. *Jeschurun,* 1855–56.
96. Graetz's volume was also sharply criticized by Geiger and Moritz Steinschneider. Geiger maintained that Graetz wrote stories rather than history, and Steinschneider accused Graetz of plagiarism.
97. Born during the second half of the twelfth century and died c. 1230.
98. Known as the Rosh. Commenting on the Mishnah Yadaim 4:3 that the produce from the territories of former Ammon and Moab are subject to the poorman's tithe *(ma'aser ani)* in the sabbatical year as a *"Halakhah* given to Moses on Sinai," Samson of Sens remarks: "Not exactly, because it [the law] is not of biblical origin but *as if it were* a *Halakhah* given to Moses on Sinai." Asher ben Yehiel or Rosh was of the same opinion. It must be pointed out, however, that most traditionalist scholars, commentators, and codifiers interpreted the expression *Halakhah le-Mosheh mi-Sinai* in a literal sense. Rashi, Gittin 14a; Ḥullin 12b, 28b; Tosafot, Eruvin 5b, 21b; Moses Maimonides, *Introduction to the Mishnah.* Only subsequent critical scholars like Azariah de Rossi and Naḥman Krochmal advanced the metaphorical interpretation—Ḥayyim Tschernowitz, *Toldot ha-Halakhah* (New York, 1945), 1:29–36.

99. *Jeschurun* 7:196–214, 241–52, 470–91.
100. Ibid., pp. 252–69, 347–73. Frankel responded in the *Monatsschrift* (1861) but his *Erklärung* (clarification) failed to satisfy his critics. See "Herrn Dr. Frankls Erklärung," *Jeschurun* 7:437–44; Benjamin Hirsch Auerbach, *Ha-Tzofeh al Darkhei ha-Mishnah* (Frankfurt, 1851); Salomon Zeev Klein, *Mipnei Kosht, Bikoret Sefer Darkhei ha-Mishnah* (Frankfurt, 1861); S. Freund, "Nachschrift," *Jeschurun* 7:373–77. Raphael Kirchheim and Saul Kaempf came to Frankel's defense. Solomon Yehudah Rapoport's *Divrei Shalom ve-Emet* was rather feeble support. See Isaac Barzilay, *Shlomo Yehudah Rapoport and His Contemporaries* (Ramat Gan, 1969), pp. 160–79; see also Louis Ginsberg, *Students, Scholars, and Saints* (Philadelphia, 1958), pp. 207–14.
101. *Allgemeine Zeitung des Judentums* (Berlin), 1861, nos. 5, 6, 8.
102. Stein was compelled to resign after a quarrel with the leaders of his community, who insisted upon censoring his sermons and addresses.
103. Hirsch dedicated the second volume of his commentary on the Psalms to the memory of his wife, Johanna, who died in that year, 1882.
104. Hirsch wrote almost exclusively in German while other German rabbis continued to write in Hebrew. Ettlinger's and Zvi Hirsch Kalischer's major works were in Hebrew. Kalischer and Bamberger wrote even their German letters in Hebrew script—Mordekhai Eliav, *Ahavat Tziyon ve-Anshei Hod* (Jerusalem, 1970), p. 90.
105. Ibid., p. 75.
106. Ibid., pp. 75, 92–119.
107. Ibid., pp. 76–78.
108. Isaac Heinemann, "Supplement: Remarks on the Secession from the Frankfurt Jewish Community under Samson Raphael Hirsch," *HJ* 10:126–27.
109. Served as the editor of the *Allgemeine Zeitung des Judentums*.
110. A famous jurist and the representative of the directorate of the Jewish Community Council of Berlin.
111. Uriel Tal, *Yehadut ve-Natzrut be-Reich ha-Sheni, 1870–1919* (Jerusalem, 1969), pp. 17–18, 75–80.
112. Samson Raphael Hirsch, *Der Austritt aus der Gemeinde* (Frankfurt am Main, 1876); *S*, 4:295–310.
113. Jacob Rosenheim, "The Historical Significance of the Struggle for Secession from the Frankfurt Jewish Community," *HJ* 10:138–39.
114. Sammy Japhet, "The Secession from the Frankfurt Jewish Community under Samson Raphael Hirsch," *HJ* 10:118–19. Japhet was the son of the composer and staff member of the Israelitische Religionsgesellschaft during Hirsch's tenure there. His article (*HJ* 10:99–122) appeared without the author's name. Heinemann's "Supplement" in that issue, pp. 123–34, identifies the author.
115. Philipson, *The Reform Movement*, pp. 291, 307. According to the account in the *Allgemeine Zeitung des Judentums* (1871), p. 585, only eleven out of the twenty-six rabbis who had participated in the Leipzig synod attended the synod at Augsburg. The number of delegates had sharply declined from eighty-three to twenty-three. See Greenwald, *Le-Toldot ha-Reformatzion*, pp. 59–60.

116. Peter G. J. Pulzer, *The Rise of Political Antisemitism in Germany and Austria* (New York, 1964), pp. 19–21.
117. Ibid., pp. 76–126; Michael Meyer, "The Great Debate on Antisemitism: Jewish Reaction to New Hostility in Germany, 1879–1881," *LBYB* 11 (1966):137–70.
118. To counteract the vitriolic anti-Semitic campaign in Russia, which pictured the Talmud as the source of Jewish separatism, arrogance, and corruption, Hirsch published a brochure in 1884 entitled *Ueber die Beziehung des Talmud zum Judentum und zu der sozialen Stellung seiner Bekenner.* In it he endeavored to refute the contentions that the Talmud demoralized the Jews, saying that, on the contrary, it ennobled them and implanted in them the highest humanistic values. While this is significant, it points nevertheless to the fact that Hirsch was a more astute defender of Judaism than of the Jews. According to Hirsch's admirers this brochure had a salutary effect on the fate of Russian Jewry. See "Samson Raphael Hirsch und das jüdische Russland," *Israelit*, S. R. Hirsch anniversary issue, pp. 32–33. It is hard to understand how anyone with any elementary knowledge of the history of the Jews in Russia could believe and state categorically that "the pamphlet completely convinced the Tsar of the high moral standard of talmudical teachings on social virtues, civic duties, and commercial integrity; thus the danger to Russian ḥadarim, yeshivot, and to the continued printing of the Talmud was averted"—*JE* 2:155n.

The Tsar was more inclined to accept the views of his anti-Semitic tutor and head of the Holy Synod, Constantine Petrovich Pobyedonostzev, and his reactionary Minister of Interior, Nicholas Pavlovich Ignatyev, than those of Hirsch. There is no doubt that Alexander III valued more the opinions of the anti-Semitic cleric Hippollyte Lutostanski, expounded in his calumnious work *The Talmud and the Jews,* than those in Hirsch's presentation.

An abridged version in English of Hirsch's pamphlet is included in *JE* 2:155–86, entitled "The Talmud and Its Teachings on Social Virtues, Civic Duties, and Commercial Integrity."

PART TWO
A NEW APPROACH

4. The Maimonidean Mantle

1. Klausner, *Historiah*, 1:247.
2. Ibid., 1:90, 309.
3. Israel Zinberg, *Toldot Sifrut Yisrael* (Tel Aviv, 1959), 5:18–19.
4. Raphael Mahler, *Ha-Ḥasidut ve-ha-Haskalah* (Merḥavyah, 1961), p. 286.
5. Kaufmann, *Golah ve-Nekhar,* 2:370–71.
6. Hirsch, foreword to *Horeb: Philosophy of Jewish Laws and Observances* [hereafter cited as *H*], trans. I. Grunfeld (London, 1962), p. clx.
7. Introduction to the *Mishneh Torah.*
8. Hirsch, foreword to *H*, p. clxi.

9. Ibid.
10. The term *Horeb* is found throughout the Book of Deuteronomy as the site of revelation except in Deut. 30:2. It also appears once in Exod. 3:1. In the latter book, the term *Sinai* predominates.
11. An English translation of Hirsch's letter appears in Grunfeld's edition of *H*, pp. cxli-cxlv. A Hebrew translation was published in *Ha-Rav Shimshon Raphael Hirsch: Mishnato, ve-Shitato*, pp. 281–84. It was first published in *Sinai* (Jerusalem, 1947).
12. I. Grunfeld, introduction to *H*, p. xxx.
13. *CG* 22:2; also see Taanit 16a; Genesis Rabbah 55:9; *H*, p. xxx.
14. Moses Maimonides, introduction to *Guide of the Perplexed* [hereafter cited as *G*], trans. Michael Friedländer (New York, 1946).
15. Ibid., p. 6.
16. Ibid.
17. Ibid., p. 4.
18. Ibid.
19. Ibid., p. 22.
20. Henry Hatfield, "Schiller, Winckelmann, and the Myth of Greece," in *Schiller 1759–1959*, Commemorative American Studies, ed. John R. Frey (Champaign-Urbana, 1959), pp. 12–35.
21. E. M. Butler, *The Tyranny of Greece over Germany* (New York, 1935).
22. Gilbert Highet, *The Classical Tradition* (New York, 1957), pp. 367–90.
23. Translated in *JE*, 2:189–90.
24. Grunfeld combined it with the following essay, "Das Judentum und Rom." He abridged and translated them in *JE* as "Hellenism, Judaism, and Rome," 2:187–209.
25. The Talmud cites a controversy between Rabbi Judah and Rabbi Shimeon over whether or not we are permitted to suggest a rationale for a biblical law in absence of an explicit reason in the Bible —Sanhedrin 21a.
26. Ramban, Lev. 19:19.
27. Abraham Geiger, *Judaism and Its History* (New York, 1911), p. 353.
28. *NB*, p. 97.
29. Wolf, "Science of Judaism" *LBYB* 2:194–204.
30. Max Wiener, *Jüdische Religion im Zeitalter der Emanzipation* (Berlin, 1933), p. 184.
31. *NB*, p. 106.
32. Quoted and translated in Grunfeld, introduction to *H*, pp. xxix–xxx.
33. Num. 3:30. H. B. Fassel considered that the pseudonym Ben Uziel referred to Jonathan ben Uziel, who, according to the Talmud, was a leading disciple of Hillel the Elder—see Baba Batra 134a. Fassel states sarcastically that Hirsch adopted this pen name because it symbolizes zeal and militancy: allegedly when Jonathan ben Uziel "sat and studied Torah, every bird that flew over him was burned" —ibid. Fassel published his criticism on the *Horeb* under the pen name of M. S. Charbonah, *Herev Be-Tzayon, oder Briefe eines jüdischen Gelehrten und Rabbinen über das Werk "Horeb" von S. R. Hirsch* (Leipzig, 1839), p. 2.
34. Num. 3:29–31.

35. Ibid., pp. 21–26.
36. Ibid., pp. 33–37.
37. Rashi, Num. 16:1, trans. M. Rosenbaum and N. Silberman (New York, 1935).
38. Ibid., 16:28.
39. Although an analogy between Korah and the Reform movement is tempting inasmuch as this biblical rebel was considered the prototype of all subsequent insurgents against traditional Judaism, Hirsch's attitude to the Reformers during his Oldenburg period had not been that antagonistic. In the *Neunzehn Briefe* he admonished his young friend not to be vindictive toward the Reformers: "Be wroth with none, respect all, for they all feel the shortcomings which exist, all wish that which is good, as they conceive it; all desire sincerely the welfare of Israel, and if they have failed to recognize the good and have erred in their comprehension of the truth, not they are chiefly to blame; the entire past bears the responsibility together with them. You should, therefore, respect their intentions"—*NL*, p. 173. The attitude of Geiger toward Hirsch was also marked by tolerance. In a letter written to Hirsch in 1833 from Wiesbaden, Geiger stressed their common aim in spite of the emerging differences: "Since the ultimate goal of all of us is one and the same, then I should think that we should all want to further the cause of what is truly good. As long as it is earnest striving, stemming from an earnest mind and religious emotion, this should also waken, nurture, and strengthen the sentiments of true religion. Granted that orientations may differ, and that so far we have established merely those factors which will eventually lead us to the one true direction, that goal is sure of achievement in the end"—Abraham Geiger, *Nachgelassene Schriften* (Berlin, 1875–78), 5:77, trans. Wiener, in *Abraham Geiger*, pp. 101–2.
40. Gen. 30:8.
41. It is noteworthy that the character of Naphtali which he employed in his early writings did not appeal to him in his later years. It may seem amazing that he depicts his namesake in a most uncomplimentary manner. Commenting on Gen. 49:21, Hirsch states: "Naphtali does not act on his own initiative, is not self-productive, but what others have decided for the benefit of the community he quickly adopts and quickly carries out.... Neither for deed nor for thought is Naphtali original. But he knows how to adopt the thoughts of others happily both for deed and speech, knows how to carry them out speedily and present them beautifully"—*CG* 49:21. Not even his most severe critics could have formulated a more devastating attack on Hirsch based on this homiletical interpretation of the verse and the characterization of Naphtali. That Hirsch should have overlooked such a possibility is as amazing as the fact that his opponents missed such an opportunity.
42. Hirsch, *Naftulei Naphtali: Erste Mitteilungen Aus Naphtalis Briefwechsel* (Altona, 1838), p. 4, trans. Grunfeld in introduction to *H*, p. xxix.

5. An Outline of the New Guide

1. *H*, pp. cxli–cxlv; *Ha-Rav Shimshon Raphael Hirsch: Mishnato ve-Shitato*, pp. 281–84.
2. *H*, p. cxli.
3. In Geiger's review of the *Neunzehn Briefe* the prospective book is called *Miriam* by mistake: "Wie wir hören, ist der Verf. jetzt willens, eine Schrift unter dem Titel: *Miriam* und *Horeb* herauszugeben"— *Wissenschaftliche Zeitschrift für jüdische Theologie* 3 (1837): 91.
4. *H*, p. cxli.
5. *H*, p. cxliv.
6. Ibid.
7. Ibid., p. cxliii.
8. Ibid., p. cxliv.
9. Ibid., p. 4 n. 2.
10. Ibid., p. cxlv.
11. Ibid., p. cxli.
12. Bloch, *Heinrich Graetz*, p. 12.
13. Ibid., p. 13.
14. Ibid., p. 12.
15. Ibid.
16. Ibid; *Tagebuch*, 1:142ff., in *MGWJ* 62:257–60.
17. See "Jüdische Welt- und Lebensanschauungen; Versuch einer Entwickelung jüdischer Welt- und Lebensanschauung der hebräischen Sprache und der Literatur des jüdischen Volkes," *S*, 5:143–99; Heineman, *Ta'amei ha-Mitzvot*, 2:109–11.
18. *Tagebuch*, 1:142ff., in *MGWJ* 62:257–60.
19. Grunfeld, introduction to *JE*, 1:xxxi.
20. *Wissenschaftliche Zeitschrift für jüdische Theologie* 2 (1836): 351–59, 518–48; 3 (1837): 74–91.
21. Preface to *NL*, p. xxxvi.
22. Heinemann considers this "star" to be Isaac Bernays—"The Formative Years," pp. 30–31.
23. Wallach, *Liberty and Letters*, pp. 5–32.
24. Geiger noticed Herder's influence upon Hirsch's letters—see *Wissenschaftliche Zeitschrift für jüdische Theologie*, 2:353;
25. Johann Gottfried Herder, *Die Fragmente über die neuere deutsche Literatur* (1767); idem, *Vom Geiste der ebräischen Poesie* (Dessau, 1762–1783); August Boeckh, *Encyclopädie und Methodologie der philologischen Wissenschaften* (Leipzig, 1886).
26. Wallach, *Liberty and Letters*, pp. 74–79.
27. Georg Wilhelm Friedrich Hegel, *Reason in History*, trans. Robert S. Hartman (New York, 1954), p. 23.
28. Bertrand Russell, *A History of Western Philosophy* (New York, 1945), p. 735.
29. Hirsch's omission of Hegel may not be altogether accidental since he considered some of the latter's ideas and philosophic system compatible with Judaism.
30. Charles Frederick D'Arcy, *Short Study of Ethics* (London, 1912), p. 195.

31. Russell, *Western Philosophy*, p. 743.
32. Ibid.
33. Robert S. Hartman, introduction to Hegel, *Reason in History*, p. xii.
34. John Angus MacVannel, *Hegel's Doctrine of the Will* (New York, 1896), p. 39.
35. Harald Höffding, *A History of Modern Philosophy*, trans. B. E. Meyer (New York, 1955), 2:179.
36. MacVannel, *Hegel's Doctrine of the Will*, p. 36.
37. Alfred Weber, *History of Philosophy*, trans. Frank Thilly (New York, 1896), p. 514.
38. MacVannel, *Hegel's Doctrine of the Will*, p. 41.
39. W. T. Stace, *The Philosophy of Hegel* (New York, 1955), p. 73.
40. Quoted by MacVannel, *Hegel's Doctrine of the Will*, p. 90, from Sterrett's translation of Hegel's *Philosophie des Rechts* [hereafter *PR*].
41. Weber, *History of Philosophy*, p. 515.
42. J. Lowenberg, introduction to *Hegel* (New York, 1929), p. xxxv.
43. Naḥman Krochmal, *Moreh Nevukhei ha-Zeman* (Lemberg, 1851), pp. 34–41.
44. Russell, *Western Philosophy*, p. 739.
45. J. B. Bury, *The Idea of Progress*, (New York, 1955), pp. 255–56; R. G. Collingwood considers this view to be erroneous and a misunderstanding of Hegel. Accordingly, "history must end with the present, because nothing else has happened. But this does not mean glorifying the present or thinking that future progress is impossible"—Collingwood, *The Idea of History* (New York, 1956), pp. 119–22.
46. Krochmal, *Moreh Nevukhei ha-Zeman*, pp. 34–41; Guttmann, *Philosophies of Judaism*, pp. 321–44.
47. Isaac Breuer, *Moriah* (Jerusalem, 1954), pp. 53–62. Nathan Rotenstreich seems to overlook completely the external historical aspect of the Jewish people on the part of Hirsch; he maintains that Hirsch removed the Jewish people from the realm of history—Rotenstreich, *Ha-Maḥshavah*, 1:117–19.
48. Note the difference in Hirsch's attitude toward the Emancipation, which should be actively pursued and accelerated, and the messianic redemption, which must not be rushed. Aside from the difference in the theological character of these two phenomena, there is no doubt that this dual standard with respect to them was motivated by expedience. In the final analysis there was no practical difference in this respect between Hirsch and the Reformers. The latter boldly negated the concept of Jewish national restoration, whereas Hirsch relegated it to an indefinite eschatological "End of Days."
49. Höffding, *Modern Philosophy*, 2:181.
50. *Jerusalem*, p. 67.
51. MacVannel, *Hegel's Doctrine of the Will*, p. 96.
52. Höffding, *Modern Philosophy*, 2:189.
53. Ibid.
54. Ibid.
55. *Jerusalem*, pp. 71–73.
56. Höffding, *Modern Philosophy*, 2:189.

57. Ibid., 2:190.
58. On the significance of Hegelian symbolism and the difference between Greek, Hindu, Egyptian, and Hebrew symbols, see Stace, *Philosophy of Hegel*, pp. 453–61.
59. Höffding, *Modern Philosophy*, 2:192.
60. See Hirsch, *Grundlinien einer jüdischen Symbolik*, S, 3:213–447.
61. John Dewey, *Reconstruction in Philosophy* (New York, 1920), p. 19.
62. Hook, *From Hegel to Marx*, p. 18.
63. Ibid., p. 19.
64. Hegel does not refer to Kant by name but by implication.
65. Rotenstreich, *Ha-Maḥshavah*, 1:106–7.
66. Immanuel Wolf (1799–1847) changed his name to Wohlwill on October 29, 1822.
67. Wolf, "Science of Judaism," p. 201; Wallach, *Liberty and Letters*, p. 12.
68. Wolf, "Science of Judaism," p. 201.
69. Ibid; Wallach, *Liberty and Letters*, p. 56.
70. Albert Hoschander-Friedlander, "The Wohlwill-Moser Correspondence," *LBYB* 11 (1966): 262–99.
71. Ibid.
72. M. Kayserling, *Bibliothek jüdischer Kanzelredner* (Berlin, 1870), p. 49.
73. Abraham Landsberg, "Lost Traces of Heinrich Heine in Hamburg," *LBYB* 1 (1956): 360–69.
74. Altmann, "The New Style of Preaching," pp. 65–116.
75. Wallach, *Liberty and Letters*, p. 10.
76. Zunz was critical of Hirsch: "Über Hirsch und seinen *Chorew* könnte man eine *Kinoh* machen"—quoted in Nahum N. Glatzer, *Leopold and Adelheid Zunz: An Account in Letters* (London, 1958), p. 109. Zunz, however, was mindful of Hirsch's influence: "Wenn ich auch nicht auf den grossen Hirsch vertraue, so schätze ich doch seinen Einfluss auf sein Publikum nicht gering"—ibid., p. 244.
77. Quoted in Hook, *From Hegel to Marx*, p. 17, from Karl Marx's *Die heilige Familie*, p. 186.
78. S. H. Bergman, *Hogim u-Ma'aminin* (Tel Aviv, 1959), pp. 48–57; see also Kroner's introduction.
79. This assumption does not intend to minimize the fact that there were other causes that brought about the estrangement between Graetz and Hirsch, as already indicated.

PART THREE
THE RATIONALIZATION
OF THE COMMANDMENTS

6. The Quest for a Rationale

1. Shoḥet, *Im Ḥilufei Tekufot*, pp. 123–38; Eliav, *Ha-Ḥinukh*, pp. 142–61.

2. In the second part of the nineteenth century another digest gained in popularity, the *Kitzur Shulḥan Arukh* by Solomon Ganzfried. This abridgment, however, appeared after the *Horeb*. Among the popular partial digests were the *Tevuot Shor* by Alexander Shor, summarizing the laws of *sheḥitah and terefot* (it was much in demand by prospective *shoḥatim*) and *Tiv Gittin* by Zalman Margolis, a manual on the laws of divorce.

3. *H*, p. clix.

4. Eliav, *Ha-Ḥinukh*, pp. 288–310.

5. *H*, p. cxliv.

6. Ibid.

7. Zunz, *Gottesdienstlichen Vorträge*, chapter 24.

8. Confirmation was instituted in the Samson School of Wolfenbüttel on August 22, 1807.

9. Eliav, *Ha-Ḥinukh* pp. 257–70.

10. The first Jewish catechism, entitled *Lekaḥ Tov*, by Abraham Jagel, appeared at the end of the sixteenth century in Italy. Although this work was subsequently translated into other languages, it was never accepted as a school text. The Christian model after which it was patterned was alien to Jews—S. Maybaum, *Abraham Jagel's Katechismus Lekach Tob*, Report 10: *Lehranstalt für die Wissenschaft des Judenthums* (Berlin, 1892). Similarly limited in appeal were the other catechisms: *Emet ve-Emunah* by Isaac Aruvas (Venice, 1654); *Eleh ha-Mitzvot* and *Emunat Yisrael* by Gedaliah Taikus (Amsterdam, 1765); *Fundamento solido de la Divina Ley* by Judah ben Perez (Amsterdam, 1729); *Torat Emunat Yisrael* by Isaac de Moses Paz (Leghorn, 1764); and others—Eliav, *Ha-Ḥinukh*, pp. 259–62.

11. M. H. Bock, *Katechismus der israelitischen Religion: Jüdisches Religionsbuch in 13, der Jugend fasslichen Gesprächen in deutscher und hebräischer Sprache.*

12. J. L. Ben-Ze'ev, *Jessodei ha-Torah: Hebräischer Katechismus mit deutscher Übersetzung—Glaubens- und Pflichtenlehre des Judentums.*

13. *Ḥinukh Emunah: Katechismus der israelitischen Religion zum ersten Unterricht.*

14. Jakob J. Petuchowski, "Manuals and Catechisms of the Jewish Religion in the Early Period of Emancipation," in *Studies in Nineteenth Century Jewish Intellectual History* (Cambridge, Mass., 1968), p. 51.

15. Ibid., p. 50; Klausner, *Historiah*, 1:184–85.

16. *Catechismus der mosaischen Religionslehre* (Berlin, 1814).

17. *Israelitische Glaubens- und Pflichtenlehre* (1830).

18. *Die Grundzüge der Religionslehre aus den zehn Geboten entwickelt* (1826).

19. Petuchowski, "Manuals and Catechisms," pp. 51–64.

20. *S*, 1:1.

21. Berakhot 12a.

22. "Wenn nun auch euer Kind die dreizehn Glaubensartikel auswendig kennt, ist es dann ein Jude? Und wenn es die Zehngebote kennt, ist es dann ein Jude, weiss es dann auch nur annähernd schon, was es heisst 'Jude sein'?"—*S*, 1:270.

23. Ibid., p. 271.
24. Eliav, *Ha-Ḥinukh,* pp. 268–70.
25. *H,* p. clvi.
26. Ibid.
27. Ibid.
28. Eliav, *Ha-Ḥinukh,* pp. 251, 262. Benet's endorsement is puzzling nevertheless, since Homberg had explicitly declared that not all *mitzvot* can or even ought to be observed in modern times—Eliav, *Ha-Ḥinukh,* p. 243.
29. Ibid., p. 251. Similarly, Rabbi Abraham Bing of Würzburg approved Alexander Behr's *Lehrbuch der mosaischen Religion* (1826).
30. Foreword to *H,* pp. clv–clvii.
31. Baba Metzia 115a, Sanhedrin 21a.
32. Saadia Gaon, *The Book of Beliefs and Opinions,* trans. Samuel Rosenblatt (New Haven, 1951), p. 141.
33. *G,* 3:148.
34. Ibid., pp. 148–49.
35. *H,* p. clxii.
36. Ibid., p. clx.
37. *Mishneh Torah, Hilkhot Temurah,* 4:13.
38. Ibid., *Hilkhot Me'illah,* 8:8.
39. Ibid.
40. Mendelssohn, *Jerusalem,* p. 90. Ironically, Mendelssohn and Hirsch seem to have transferred Frederick the Great's dictum "Räsoniert, soviel ihr wollt und worüber ihr wollt, aber gehorcht" from Prussian politics to Jewish theology.
41. *H,* p. clix.
42. Scholem, *Jewish Mysticism,* p. 32.
43. Wolfson, *Philo,* 1:87–163.
44. Ibid., pp. 131–33.
45. Baron, *History of the Jews,* 1:202.
46. Wolfson, *Philo,* p. 136.
47. Harry Austryn Wolfson, *The Philosophy of the Church Fathers* (Cambridge, Mass., 1964), pp. 24–72.
48. Arthur Cushman McGiffert, *A History of Christian Thought* (New York, 1961), 2:241–56.
49. Ibid., p. 255.
50. Scholem, *Jewish Mysticism,* pp. 27–28; see also Yeshayah Tishbi, *Mishnat ha-Zohar* (Jerusalem, 1949), 1:144–61 (Jerusalem, 1961), 2:429–578.
51. Alfred North Whitehead, *Symbolism: Its Meaning and Effect* (New York, 1927), p. 60.
52. Rollo May, "The Significance of Symbols," in *Symbolism in Religion and Literature* (New York, 1960), p. 12.
53. Ernst Cassirer, *An Essay on Man* (New Haven, 1962), pp. 26–27.
54. Erich Fromm, *The Forgotten Language* (New York, 1960), p. 7.
55. Evelyn Underhill, *Mysticism* (New York, 1960), p. 125.
56. Cassirer, *Symbolic Forms,* 2:38.
57. Creuzer published *Symbolik und Mythologie der alten Völker,* (1810–1823).

58. Von Görres published *Mythengeschichte der asiatischen Welt* (1810).
59. Cassirer, *Symbolic Forms*, 2:38.
60. See G. W. F. Hegel, *The Philosophy of Fine Arts* (London, 1920), 2:16–19.
61. G. P. Gooch, *History and Historians in the Nineteenth Century* (Boston, 1959), p. 36.
62. Mendelssohn, *Jerusalem*, p. 74.
63. Ibid., p. 75.
64. Ibid., p. 90.
65. Ibid., p. 99.
66. Bernard Bosanquet, *A History of Aesthetics* (New York, 1957), p. 273.
67. Mordecai M. Kaplan, *Judaism as a Civilization* (New York, 1957), pp. 282–84.
68. Rotenstreich, *Ha-Mahshavah*, 1:119–22.
69. Scholem, *Jewish Mysticism*, pp. 29–30.
70. Ibid., p. 30.
71. Included in *S*, 3:213–443.
72. *Protokolle der dritten Versammlung deutscher Rabbiner* (Breslau, 1846), pp. 86ff.
73. Gershom G. Scholem, *On the Kabbalah and Its Symbolism*, trans. Ralph Manheim (New York, 1965), p. 22.
74. Ibid.
75. The cabalists, unlike the rationalists, attributed great significance to the details of each commandment and endeavored to interpret them accordingly. As a result, in the thirteenth century there had arisen a vast literature belaboring with interpretations the details and minutiae of the *mitzvot*, and it had become voluminous since —Scholem, *On the Kabbalah and Its Symbolism*, pp. 118–57.
76. *G*, 3:126–27.
77. Scholem, *Jewish Mysticism*, p. 29.
78. Avot 6:11.
79. Heinemann, *Ta'amei ha-Mitzvot*, 1:124–44, 2:237–44.
80. Mekhilta, ba-Ḥodesh, Yitro 5; Sifrei Deut., Berakhah §343.
81. According to some, the Israelites, too, were hesitant to accept it and had to be coerced. Shabbat 88a, Avodah Zarah 2b.
82. Mendelssohn, *Jerusalem*, p. 106.
83. This number is based on a statement by the Palestinian amora of the third century Rabbi Simlai and has since become universally accepted in Jewish tradition. Many scholars differed as to what constitutes a commandment to be included in that number but seemed to be in accord as to the number itself. According to Rabbi Simlai, "six hundred and thirteen commandments were given to Moses, three hundred and sixty-five prohibitions corresponding to the days of the solar year, and two hundred and forty-eight positive injunctions corresponding to the members of the human body"—Makkot 23a.
84. Ḥayyim Tschernowitz, *Toledot ha-Poskim* (New York, 1946), 1:15–16.

85. Herbert Danby, *The Mishnah* (London, 1949), p. xxv.
86. Tschernowitz, *Toledot ha-Poskim,* 1:248–51.
87. *H,* p. clx.
88. Ps. 19:8–10.
89. Any allegation that Hirsch, who admonished young men and women against "hand holding and eye winking" and married women against uncovering their hair (*H* 443), would disregard the stringent biblical and rabbinic laws of *niddah,* punishable by extirpation (Lev. 20:19), and the necessary process of purification *(tevilah, mikvah)* for the normalization of conjugal relations, is absurd. Equally unacceptable is Heinemann's explanation that prudery prevented Hirsch from discussing such an inelegant and intimate subject (Hinemann, *Ta'amei ha-Mitzvot,* 2:133). Rabbis throughout the ages were hardly less modest or less inhibited than Hirsch; nevertheless none of them ever avoided dealing with this subject candidly and forthrightly with their congregants or in their writings. Moreover, the open discussion of "family purity" was considered meritorious and imperative and constituted a most frequent major theme in the public addresses and sermons of rabbis and preachers. Should Heinemann's suggestion be correct, it would imply that Hirsch's consideration for good taste and sociopsychological squeamishness was more important than his religious commitment, a highly untenable view.

   In his work on the Pentateuch, Hirsch did comment briefly on the laws of *niddah* mentioned in the Bible *(CL* 15:19–33; *CL* 18:19; *CL* 20:18).

7. "Torot": *Fundamental Principles*

1. Mendelssohn, *Jerusalem,* p. 97.
2. Ibid., p. 71.
3. Ibid.
4. Gen. 15:6.
5. Exod. 14:31.
6. It is possible that in *Jerusalem,* which was designated for non-Jewish readers, Mendelssohn dared to translate *emunah* as trust, whereas in his translation of the Pentateuch, which was written for his coreligionists, he was more circumspect and retained the word *faith.*
7. Paul Tillich, *Perspectives on Nineteenth and Twentieth Century Protestant Theology* (New York, 1967), pp. 71–114.
8. Jacob B. Agus, *Modern Philosophies of Judaism: A Study of Recent Jewish Philosophies of Religion* (New York, 1941), pp. 5–21.
9. *G,* 1:134. Maimonides distinguishes between a person who is unable to prove incorporeality and one who repudiates this doctrine.
10. Abraham ibn Daud, *Hassagot* on Maimonides's *Mishneh Torah, Hilkhot Teshuvah* 3:7.
11. See *CE* 32:1.
12. *Kuzari,* part IV.
13. *G,* vol. 1, chapters 61–64.

14. *G*, vol. 2, chapter 25.
15. *Mishneh Torah, Hilkhot Yesodei ha-Torah*, 1:1. The Hebrew text of the first positive commandment in Maimonides's *Sefer ha-Mitzvot* employs the term *emunah*, religious faith, rather than *yedi'ah*, knowledge. In the Arabic original the word is *itikat*, a term connoting belief based on reason and occasionally religious faith. Simon Rawidowicz maintains that the Hebrew translator of the *Sefer ha-Mitzvot* was unable to find an equivalent for the Arabic *itikat*, having a dual meaning, and used the Hebrew *emunah*, which has only one. Rawidowicz also points out that Maimonides deliberately employs in his *Mishneh Torah* the term *madda* rather than *deah* in order to approximate the Arabic *itikat*—Simon Rawidowicz, *Iyyunim be-Mahshevet Yisrael* (Jersalem, 1969), 1:333–45.
16. Ibid., 1:5.
17. Ibid., 2:2.
18. Guttmann, *Philosophies of Judaism*, p. 176.
19. Paton, *The Categorical Imperative*, pp. 78–88.
20. Mendelssohn, *Jerusalem*, p. 71.
21. *Mishneh Torah, Hilkhot Yesodei ha-Torah*, 1:7.
22. Hirsch was extremely selective in his treatment of the laws concerning idolatry. Out of the many *halakhot* discussed by Maimonides, Hirsch dealt only with four. The reason for this may be the fact that idolatry was no longer a problem in the nineteenth century. Hirsch therefore selected such laws as could be interpreted as relevant to his time. Moreover, a more detailed treatment of this subject might have been misinterpreted as a veiled criticism of Christianity. Such an accusation of the *Landesrabbiner* of Oldenburg could have had disastrous consequences.
23. *Mishneh Torah, Hilkhot Avodat Kokhavim*, 2:3.
24. Num. 15:39.
25. Sifrei, Num. 15; Berakhot 12b.
26. Halevi, *The Kuzari*, p. 223.
27. Lev. 19:26.
28. *Mishneh Torah, Hilkhot Avodat Kokhavim*, 11:16.
29. Deut. 18:13.
30. *Mishneh Torah, Hilkhot Yesodei ha-Torah*, 8:1.
31. Mendelssohn, *Jerusalem*, p. 104.
32. Hirsch pointed out that Eve was punished for eating from the tree of knowledge although she did not hear the prohibition directly from God, but to her it was merely transmittled as an oral law by her husband. (*CG* 2:16, 3:3). Similarly, Isaac did not hear God's command to offer himself as a sacrifice, yet in spite of its irrationality, he did not question this oral law and went resolutely to the altar. (*CG* 22:3).
33. *Mishneh Torah, Hilkhot Yesodei ha-Torah* 2:2.
34. Deut. 6:5.
35. Deut. 7:10.
36. *G*, 3:37–38.
37. The concept of suffering as a means of elevation and testing, was acceptable to Hirsch, but repugnant to Maimonides, who devotes an

entire chapter in his *Guide of the Perplexed* to dispelling this notion. Although there are six instances in the Bible which might be interpreted in such a manner, Maimonides shows that such an interpretation is erroneous. Even the notion of *yissurin me-ahavah*, chastisement out of love, found in the Talmud, must not be considered as a theological principle. As a refutation of this notion, he quotes the talmudic concept of moral causality: "There is no death without sin, and no affliction without transgression"—Shabbat 55a. Maimonides emphatically adds: "Every intelligent religious person should have this faith, and should not ascribe any wrong to God, who is far from it; he must not assume that a person is innocent and perfect and does not deserve what has befallen him"—*G*, 3:112. Maimonides dwells at great length on the problem of the *Akedah* and proves that even this classical episode, which the Bible itself terms a test, was not so in the popular sense. He therefore concludes, "We must not think that God desires to examine us and to try us in order to know what He did not know before. Far is this from Him; He is far above that which ignorant and foolish people imagine concerning Him, in the evil of their thoughts"—*G*, 3:118. Hirsch, on the other hand, accepts the *Akedah* as a legitimate test of man's moral endurance. By withstanding a test, men like Abraham and Isaac prove their ability to reach out to higher tasks and loftier levels—*CG* 12:1.

8. "Edot": *Temporal Symbolic Observances*

1. Heinemann, *Ta'amei ha-Mitzvot*, 2:126.
2. It is possible that Maimonides included the precepts of mourning in *"Sefer Shoftim"* since death of a relative may have occurred as a result of a judgment by a tribunal or royal decree. Such a subject rightfully belonged in this section dealing with court procedure. It is also possible that since the preceding section dealt with the laws governing a rebellious son who is put to death by the court, Maimonides began his next section with the laws of mourning.
3. *G*, 2:160.
4. Ibid., 3:210; see also ibid., 3:157.
5. Ibid., 2:159.
6. *Sefer ha-Ḥinukh* §326.
7. Lev. 25:2.
8. This essay was published in *Jeschurun* during the years 1855–56. It was divided into six chapters: (1) "Der Sabbath ein von Gott verordneter Tag der Ruhe," (2) "Der Sabbath der Schöpfung," (3) "Der Sabbath in der Wüste," (4) "Der Sabbath der Zehngebote," (5) "Der Sabbath und der Tempel," (6) "Der Sabbath und die Erziehung"— *S*, 1:168–211. This essay was translated into English by I. Grunfeld, *JE*, 2:3–48.
9. Carrying is called *melakhah geruah*. See Tosafot, Shabbat 2a, 96b.
10. The following illustrates clearly Hirsch's emphasis on the negative aspect of the Sabbath: "Der Vogel, der Fisch, das Tier, die du am Sabbath *nicht* fängst, die Pflanze, die du am Sabbath *nicht* brichst,

der Stoff, den du am Sabbath *nicht* formst, *nicht* meisselst, *nicht* schneidest, *nicht* bindest, *nicht* mischest und gestaltest und bereitest, sind ebenso viele deinem Gotte dargebrachte Huldigungsgrüsse, Ihn die als den Schöpfer und Meister und Herrn der Welt verkünden; und das jüdische Kind, das am Sabbath den Schmetterling *nicht* fängt, die Blüte *nicht* bricht, hat den allmächtigen Gott lauter verherrlicht, als alle Schönredner und Dichter mit Worten und Gesängen"—*S*, 1:201–2.

11. Exod. 20:8.
12. Sanhedrin 58b.
13. Sanhedrin 56a.
14. Grunfeld, *H*, 1:273–74.
15. „שבת בראשית" קרי לשבת, משום דכל מועדות נמי כתיב בהו „שבת שבתון",
הלכך קרי ליה „שבת בראשית". „שבת בראשית", שמקודשת ובאה מששת ימי בראשית, דבשבת
ראשונה כתיב בו ב„ויכולו" „ויקדש אותו". (Rashi, Bava Batra 121a)
16. אמר ר' יודן „זכור" נתן לאומות העולם, „שמור" נתן לישראל.
(Pesikta Rabbati, Piska 23)
17. בראשונות אמר „זכור את יום השבת", לא רצה לומר „שמור את יום השבת" כדי
שלא ליתן פתחון פה לאומות לומר איך הוא מצווה אותנו על השמירה מכל
מלאכה הלא כבר נאמר לבני נח „יום ולילה לא ישבותו" ורז"ל למדו מכאן
„גוי ששבת חייב מיתה". על כן נאמר „זכור את יום השבת", לומר מי שאינו בשמירה
לפחות ישנו בזכירה, כי כל האומות חייבים לזכור את יום השבת כדי לקבוע
בלבם אמונת חידוש העולם אשר יתן עדות ה' נאמנה על מציאת הש"י, כי בכלל
שבע מצוות של בני נח הוא שלא יעבדו עבודה זרה. ואף על פי שהאומות לא
יוכלו לקבל צווי „לא תעשה כל מלאכה", מכל מקום יכולים הם לקבל עליהם
מצות הזכירה אשר גם המה חייבים בה, להיות חידוש העולם לנגד עיניהם לזכרון.
(*Keli Yakar*, Exod. 20:8)
18. It is interesting to note that Hirsch sees this connection in the climatic changes that take place during this time of the year, such as storms and the beginning of cold weather. These climatic factors, however, are not worldwide. They are characteristic of the zone in which he lived. The Torah, being in Hirsch's view universal, could hardly institute festivals having a reference only to one particular climate.
19. The horn of the bull would recall the sin of the golden calf.
20. By the *lulav* Hirsch means all four species.
21. Mendelssohn, *Jerusalem*, p. 110.
22. Jer. 29:7.

9. "Edot": Nontemporal Symbolic Observances

1. *G*, 3:267.
2. In a special volume entitled *Rabbinische Gutachten über die Beschneidung*.
3. The Verein was castigated not only by the Orthodox rabbis but also by the Reformers Samuel Hirsch of Luxembourg, Isaac Noah Mann-

439   *Notes to pp. 268–88*

heimer of Vienna, and the famous Jewish scholars Solomon Yehudah Rapoport of Prague and Samuel David Luzzatto of Padua. Similarly, the leading figure of contemporary Jewish scholarship, Leopold Zunz, denounced the Verein's assault on circumcision. Zunz's views appeared separately—included in his *Gesammelte Schriften* (Berlin, 1876), 3:191–203.

4. Although not as audacious and outspoken as M. A. Stern of Göttingen, the leader of that dissident group, many members of the Verein tacitly approved his views. The sentiment against circumcision was not only current among laymen but also among the noted Reform rabbis, like Geiger, Holdheim, and Hess of Saxe-Weimar. Holdheim and Hess expressed their views openly, Geiger in private—David Philipson, *Centenary Papers and Others* (Cincinnati, 1919), pp. 91–92.

5. Geiger, *Nachgelassene Schriften*, 5:181–83; Wiener, *Abraham Geiger*, p. 114.

6. Ibid.

7. Deut. 10:16.

8. "Nicht die Weihe des Geistes, die Weihe des Leibes steht an der Pforte des Abrahamsbundes"—*S*, 3:283.

9. Shabbat 133a.

10. *Mishneh Torah, Ahavah, Hilkhot Milah*, 2:2.

11. *Kokhvei Yitzhak* (Vienna, 1845), 1:45ff.

12. Ya'acov Levi, "Ha-Metzitzah ba-Peh le-Or ha-Refuah" *No'am* (Jerusalem, 1966), 9:285–301; Jacob H. Bloom, *Berit Olam* (New York, 1950), pp. 135–64.

13. Ettlinger, *Binyan Tziyon*, responsa 23, 24.

14. See Hirsch's letter to Moses Jonah Königshöffer of Fürth, in *Ha-Rav Shimshon Raphael Hirsch: Mishnato ve-Shitato*, pp. 345–46.

15. Ibid., pp. 347–48; Levi, "Ha-Metzitzah," pp. 295–96.

16. Ibid.

17. Gen. 32:25–33.

18. Num. 15:38.

19. Joel Sirkes, *Bayit Hadash*, Commentary on *Tur Yore Deah* §293, *Teshuvot Bah ha-Hadashot* (Korzec, 1785), §§48–49. See also *Teshuvot Penei Yehoshua* (Lemburg, 1850), vol. 2, §34; *Teshuvot Geonei Batrai* (Prague, 1816), §§1, 2; *Turei Zahav, Yore Deah* §§93:2, 4.

10. "Mishpatim": Laws of Justice toward Man

1. Paton, *The Categorical Imperative*, pp. 207–16.

2. Ibid., pp. 266–78.

3. Ibid., p. 127.

4. Huntington Cairns, *Legal Philosophy from Plato to Hegel* (Baltimore, 1949), p. 512.

5. Herbert Marcuse, *Reason and Revolution: Hegel and the Rise of Social Theory* (Boston, 1960), p. 185.

6. This expression appears frequently in Hirsch's writings.

7. Cairns, *Legal Philosophy*, p. 512.

8. Ibid.
9. Carl Joachim Friedrich, *The Philosophy of Law in Historical Perspective* (Chicago, 1958), p. 133.
10. G. W. F. Hegel, *Encyclopedia of Philosophy*, trans. Gustav Emil Müller (New York, 1959), pp. 207–8.
11. Cairns, *Legal Philosophy*, pp. 517–18.
12. Morris Raphael Cohen, *Law and the Social Order* (New York, 1933), p. 53.
13. Marcuse, *Reason and Revolution*, p. 191.
14. On a Hebrew equivalent for the legal term *property*, see Simon Rubin, *Das talmudische Recht* (Vienna, 1938), pp. 86–90; Isaac Herzog, *Main Institutions of Jewish Law* (London, 1936), 1:65–68; Samuel Atlas, "Rights of Private Property and Private Profit," *CCARYB* 54 (Cincinnati, 1944): 215. To Atlas the Hebrew term *kinyan* (property) is etymologically connected with the concept of work. Thus, the latter is the basis for possession. "The noun *kinyan* which is derived from the verb *kano*, meaning to make, indicates the relationship of the concept of property to that of making, working." Herzog considers the term *kinyan* to denote derivative acquisition. The root *kano* implies to acquire, to own—Herzog, *Main Institutions*, 1:59. To Hirsch the biblical term *kano* applies to movable goods, whereas the term *ahuzah* refers to landed property, "a possession which holds its possessor, holds him fast to the soil, so that its sale is regarded more as a transference of rights than a transference of an object"—*CL* 25:14.
15. The biblical terms *ve-khivshuhah*, "subdue it," *u-redu*, and *va-yirdu*, "ye shall have dominion," employed by Hirsch as the legal foundation of property, carry an implication of force. It would thus make the Jewish concept of ownership closer to the Roman view than to the later Lockean view. According to Rudolf Ihering, private property in ancient Rome had its origin in booty. It was personal force exerted at the time of conquest of the enemy that manifested property rights—Rudolf Ihering, *Der Geist des römischen Rechts auf den verschiedenen Stufen seiner Entwicklung* (Leipzig, 1878), 1:109ff., 2:564. To Locke, however, labor constitutes the basis of ownership of private property—John Locke, "Of Property," *Treatises on Government*, book 2, chap. 5.
16. Marcuse, *Reason and Revolution*, p. 193.
17. Ibid., p. 183.
18. Samuel Atlas maintains that the Jewish laws governing property make the latter subordinate to the sovereignty of rights. Consequently, Hirsch's almost metaphysical reverence for property seems highly exaggerated. The fact, says Atlas, "that in time of war and general emergency proprietary rights can be interfered with is rather a manifestation of the principle that private property is not an absolute domain which cannot be intruded or violated in the service of a higher good. In other words: the right of ownership can be overruled when the good of the community requires it"—Atlas, "Rights," pp. 226–27.
19. Kant maintains that property rights do not express a dyadic relation

between a person and a given thing, but constitute a relationship between one person asserting his will over the thing and other persons. The person in control of the thing to the exclusion of other persons has the unqualified right over it—see Morris Raphael Cohen, *Reason and Law* (Glencoe, Ill., 1950), pp. 108–9.

20. Cairns, *Legal Philosophy*, p. 522.

21. Alienation is the third part of the triad, the other two being possession and use. "Taking possession is *positive* acquisition. Use is negation of a thing's particular characteristics. Alienation is *synthesis* of positive and negative; it is negative in that it involves spurning the thing altogether; it is positive because it is only a thing completely mine which I can so spurn"—Georg Wilhelm Friedrich Hegel, *Philosophy of Right* trans. T. M. Knox (London, 1942 [hereafter *PR*]), p. 241.

22. On the difference between the talmudic concept of *hazakah* and the Roman concept of *usucapio*, see Herzog, *Main Institutions*, 1:154–62,

23. Hirsch's distinction between the mode of acquisition of completely ownerless property and property that has been in the possession of another person seems to follow the juridical distinction between *modus acquirendi originarii* and *modus acquirendi derivativi*. The former applies to *res nullius*, whereas the latter takes place in the transference of a given object from one person to another. This distinction did not exist in Roman law but is known in the Talmud —see Rubin, *Das talmudische Recht*, pp. 113–16. However, the talmudic distinction between *da'at aheret maknah* and *ain da'at a heret maknah* is not of crucial importance and does not involve any radical differences in the modes of acquisition—see Asher Gulak, *Yesodei ha-Mishpat ha-Ivri* (Berlin, 1922), pp. 103–5. Indeed, Hirsch's theological-juridical interpretation presents some difficulty; man's right to ownership emanates from God, who gave him the right of possession; consequently, the concept of *res nullius* is nonexistent. Logically, therefore, any *modus acquirendi originarii* is inappropriate, and all acquisitions should theoretically be the same. This difficulty, however, is only apparent, for Hirsch, like Hegel, insisted upon the concretization of the will in the act of acquisition. Unable to employ with regard to God, the original owner, even the most symbolical *modus acquirendi derivativi*, man, the possessor, had to turn to the domain of nature and there employ more primitive forms practiced toward *res nullius*.

24. Indeed, the apprehension concerning the lack of responsibility on the part of the seller, who refuses to safeguard the already-sold article still in his possession, is not limited to money. A similar indifferent attitude could be assumed by the seller if the basis of the transaction were *halifin*, *kinyan agav*, or *kinyan sudar*. In these cases, however, the seller, though free from legal responsibility, might be concerned about payment, which may be withheld by the buyer. Where the seller receives payment, there is no such anxiety on his part. Insistence upon a concrete mode of acquisition required by the Rabbis in addition to actual payment, is, therefore, practical

and desirable—see Gulak, *Yesodei ha-Mishpat ha-Ivri*, p. 107.
: 25. Regarding Lev. 25:14, Hirsch states: "In all cases of landed property not only can the acquisition be completed by legal proof *(shetar re'ayah)* but a document of transference of rights can itself be a means of such completion *(shetar kinyan)*, and with the handing over of such a *shetar*, at once, without the necessity of any further act, the property passes over to the ownership of the buyer"—*CL* 25:14.
26. In the case of *karka* any such act can be taken to have only symbolic meaning and to be of value as a public demonstration of the acquired title to rights. Hence, just as in the case of *karka*, even according to Resh Lakish, *kessef* is a means of acquiring property, so is *ḥazakah*, also according to Rabbi Yoḥanan, even *min ha-Torah*, according to the biblical law—Gulak, *Yesodei ha-Mishpat ha-Ivri*, 112–13.
27. The talmudic concept of *hefker* seems to be closer to the Hegelian concept of alienation than to the Roman concept of *derelictio*, since the latter requires a demonstrative abandonment of the object, whereas there is no such requirement in Jewish law—Gulak, *Yesodei ha-Mishpat ha-Ivri*, pp. 138–40. Alienation, like *hefker*, constitutes merely the withdrawal of the owner's will. In *hefker* a mere verbal statement of relinquishment is sufficient. Indeed, Hegel does not even require such a statement, but undoubtedly the intent of alienation ought to be communicated in some manner. According to Herzog (*Main Institutions*, 1:287), the *hefker* statement is connected with the precept of charity. Belkin explains the reason for the simple form of renunciation in *hefker* as the fact that "the owner does not transfer his property to any particular individual; his action, therefore, is not dependent upon someone else's acquisition. Since he merely renounces his own rights to the property no formal mode of transfer is required, his spoken word being sufficient to render the property ownerless"—Samuel Belkin, *In His Image* (London, 1960), p. 198.
28. Hegel maintains that Jewish law allows prosecution for crimes as *crimina privata*—*PR*, p. 73.
29. Gulak, *Yesodei ha-Mishpat ha-Ivri*, pp. 55–56.
30. Marcuse, *Reason and Revolution*, p. 193.
31. Ibid., p. 197.
32. Ibid., p. 184.

11. "Ḥukkim": Laws of Justice toward Animate and Inanimate Objects

1. Paton, *The Categorical Imperative*, p. 149.
2. Gen. 2:15.
3. Deut. 20:19–20.
4. Paton, *The Categorical Imperative*, p. 150.
5. Ibid., pp. 44, 150.
6. Collingwood, *The Idea of History*, p. 116.
7. Pesikta Rabbati; Yoma 67b.

8. In the course of time Hirsch developed a theory about the distinctiveness of the two cultures, the agricultural and pastoral. These two were so polarized that they came to represent to him the difference between the non-Jewish and Jewish civilizations—*CG* 4:1–18.
9. Hirsch himself remarked that some of these laws belonged to the *"Mitzvot"* division—*H*, §416 n 1.
10. Deut. 22:6–7.
11. Exod. 23:5.
12. Lev. 22:28.
13. Deut. 25:4.
14. *G*, 3:253–54.
15. Samuel David Luzzatto expresses a similar view: "A child who rejoices at the outcry of an animal will in the future laugh at the cry of his parents"—Noah H. Rosenbloom, *Luzzatto's Ethico-Psychological Interpretation of Judaism* (New York, 1965), p. 167, n. G.
16. Lev. 19:27.
17. Ibid.
18. Nachmanides's commentary on Lev. 17:11.

12. "Mitzvot": *Commandments of Love*

1. Deut. 13:5.
2. Sotah 14a; Sifrei, Deut. 49, 85a; Mekhilta, Exod. 15:37a; Exod. Rabbah 26:2.
3. *Mishneh Torah, "Shoftim," Hilkhot Mamrim,* 3:2.
4. Hirsch points to the reflexive form of the Hebrew term for confession, *ve-hitvadah,* which he views as confessing or admitting one's guilt to himself—*CL* 5:5.
5. "Man weist wohl mit Ironie auf diese Form hin und spricht: der Jude 'kauft' sein Weib. Jawohl kauft der Jude sein Weib, kauft sie von ihr selber, und sie bleibt sein eigenstes, innigstes, heiligstes Eigentum bis über den Tod hinaus."
6. "Der Begriff: Gott ebenbildlicher Mensch umfasst beide Geschlechter, Mann und Weib zusammen erschöpft den Begriff: *Mensch,* und beide hat Gott in gleicher Unmittelbarkeit und in gleicher, Zweck beabsichtigenden Willenstätigkeit geschaffen."
7. Deut. 23:20–21.

13. "Mitzvot": *Education*

1. William Boyd, *The History of Western Education* (London, 1950), p. 333.
2. J. Wohlgemuth, "Samson Raphael Hirsch als Erzieher," in *Israelit,* S. R. Hirsch anniversary issue, pp. 44–45, compared Hirsch with Fichte and called the former's writings "Reden an die jüdische Nation," alluding to those of Fichte. In his partisan enthusiasm he considers Hirsch's influence to be more enduring than that of the German philosopher.
3. Höffding, *Modern Philosophy,* 2:152.

4. Though aroused by the patriotic sentiments of Fichte, who saw in education a medium for the future aggrandizement of the state, Herbart rather emphasized the individualistic aspect and importance of education.

5. Concerning Hegel's educational views and theories, see F. L. Luqueer, *Hegel as Educator* (New York, 1896), and M. Mackenzie, *Hegel's Educational Theory and Practice* (London, 1949).

6. Schwab, *Orthodox Jewry in Germany*, p. 42.

7. Concerning the tendency of the non-Orthodox elements in Germany to curtail the scope of the Jewish studies in Jewish schools and concentrate on training the Jewish pupils as useful patriotic German citizens, see Eliav, *Ha-Hinukh*, pp. 209–19.

8. Max Wiener, "The Ideology of the Founders of Jewish Scientific Research," *YIVO Annual of Jewish Social Science* (New York, 1950), 5:189. Concerning Zunz's personal interest in Jewish education and his educational activities, see Eliav, *Ha-Hinukh*, pp. 213–16.

9. The original Philanthropinum was founded by Johann Bernard Basedow in 1774 at Dessau, Germany. Subsequently, the pedagogical theories and practices were adopted in many other German institutions. The latter patterned their education along the lines of the doctrines implemented in the first Philanthropinum. About the impact of this form of education upon the Jews of Germany, see Jacob Katz, *Masoret u-Mashber*, Jerusalem, 1963, pp. 302–3.

10. With regard to the history and development of the Jewish Philathropin in Frankfurt am Main, see H. Baerwald and Salo Adler, "Geschichte des Philantropins," *Festschrift zur Jahrhundertfeier des Philantropins* (Frankfurt am Main, 1904); S. Adler, "Der erste Plan zur Gründung einer jüdischen Schule mit profanem Unterricht in der Frankfurter Judengasse," *Festschrift Frankfurt-Realschule* (1928); idem, "Die Entwicklung des Schulwesens der Juden zu Frankfurt bis zur Emanzipation," *JJLG* (Frankfurt am Main, 1927–28).

11. I.e., Jewish freemasons.

12. Graetz, *History*, 5:614.

13. Mahler, *Divrei Yemei Yisrael*, 1:171–75; Eliav, *Ha-Hinukh*, pp. 142–61.

14. Some of these ideas can be traced back to the Aufklärung, particularly to Lessing's *Education of Humanity* and Herder's *Auch eine Philosophie der Geschichte zur Bildung der Menschheit*.

15. "Nicht in den Kabinetten der Fürsten, nicht auf der Walstatt der Schlachten, in den Kinderstuben, an den Kinderwiegen, auf den Mutterknieen wird das Geschick der Völker entschieden"—*S*, 1:206.

16. Mordecai M. Kaplan maintains that the Man-Israel was Hirsch's "ideal Jew," a concept related to the Nietzschean superman *(Übermensch)*—see Kaplan, *The Greater Judaism in the Making* (New York, 1960), pp. 324–29.

17. The elementary school was opened on April 11, 1853, with an enrollment of fifty-five boys and twenty-nine girls, organized in four classes—see Schwarzschild, *Die Gründung der israelitischen Religionsgesellschaft*, p. 34. Also see Schwab, *Orthodox Jewry in Ger-*

many, p. 41. The lower grades were coeducational and in the higher ones there were separate classes for boys and girls. The fact that Hirsch considered the education of girls—except for the study of Talmud—on a par with boys was unique in traditional education of the time. A traditional coeducational school was indeed revolutionary in those days. The number of students rose from a modest beginning of eighty-four to more than five hundred—see Eliav, *Ha-Ḥinukh,* pp. 231–32.

18. Quoted from Hirsch's letter to the Religionsgesellschaft of Frankfurt am Main in Schwab, *Orthodox Jewry in Germany,* p. 41.
19. Jacob Rosenheim, *Samson Raphael Hirsch's Cultural Ideal and Our Times,* trans. E. Lichtigfeld (London, 1951), pp. 40–62.
20. "Was uns retten kann, einzig retten kann, dass ist die innige Vermählung des religiösen Wissens und religiösen Lebens mit echter, wahrhaft sozialer Bildung, das ist die innige aufrichtige Vemählung der *Torah im derekh-eretz* wie es Lehre und Erbgut unserer grossen Altvordern gewesen"—*S,* 1:262.
21. Eliav, *Ha-Ḥinukh,* p. 231.
22. Isaac Breuer, *Tziyunei Derekh* (Tel Aviv, 1955), p. 137.
23. Gershom Scholem, "Politik der Mystik," *Jüdische Rundschau,* no. 57, p. 7.
24. Ibid.
25. The source of this quotation is the essay "Von den Beziehungen der allgemeinen Bildungselemente zu der speziell jüdischen Bildung" —*S,* 2:449–66, translated into English by I. Grunfeld as "The Relation of General to Special Jewish Education" and included in *JE,* 1:203–20.
26. Stace, *Philosophy of Hegel,* p. 303.
27. Hegel, *Logic,* trans. W. T. Harris (Chicago, 1895), pp. 398–99.
28. Stace, *Philosophy of Hegel,* pp. 297–317.
29. Hegel, *Logic,* pp. 398–99.
30. Collingwood, *The Idea of Nature,* p. 126.
31. Regarding the relationship of Froebel's educational theory to Hegelian philosophy, see R. D. Chalke, *A Synthesis of Froebel and Herbart* (London, 1912), p. 76; see also MacKenzie, *Hegel's Educational Theory and Practice,* pp. 146–57.
32. Friedrich Froebel, *Education of Man* (New York, 1908), p. 1.
33. Ibid.
34. Ibid., pp. 1–2. A similar monistic idea was also expressed by many thinkers at the time. Schelling, for instance, says: "Nature in its very essence is one; there is one life in all things, and one power to be, the same regulative principle through ideas"—Schelling, *Werke* (Stuttgart and Augsburg, 1859), 5:325. Krause, too, maintained such a view in *Das Urbild der Menscheit* (Dresden, 1811).
35. Chalke, *Froebel and Herbart,* p. 76.
36. Ibid.
37. Boyd, *History of Western Education,* p. 353.
38. Luqueer, *Hegel as Educator,* p. 103.
39. Ibid.
40. Stace, *Philosophy of Hegel,* p. 297. Speaking about the objectivity

of nature, Cole states: "Although they tended to regard nature as spiritual or organic to consciousness, neither Schelling nor Hegel, nor Froebel desired to detract from her objectivity, her reality or her permanence"—see P. R. Cole, *Herbart and Froebel* (New York, 1907), p. 3.

41. Maimonides in *Guide of the Perplexed*, 1:272–73, maintains that the Jews in antiquity did not negate secular knowledge. They cultivated the study of the sciences of physics and metaphysics but abandoned them only on account of suffering and persecution. Judah Halevi similarly maintains that the Jews were the original possessors of philosophic and scientific knowledge: "The roots and principles of all sciences were handed down from us first to the Chaldeans, then to the Persians and Medians, then to Greece and finally to the Romans. On account of the length of this period, and the many disturbing circumstances, it was forgotten that they had originated with the Hebrews, and so they were ascribed to the Greeks and Romans"— Halevi, *The Kuzari*, p. 109.

42. The elements leaning toward Reform rejected the view that the natural sciences or mathematics should be taught from a religious point of view. They objected to any tendentiousness even in the study of history—see Eliav, *Ha-Ḥinukh*, pp. 229–30.

43. "Einige Andeutungen über den hebräischen Unterricht als allgemeines Bildungselement in unserer Schule"—*S*, 2:433–48, translated by I. Grunfeld as "On Hebrew Instruction as Part of a General Education" in *JE*, 1:188–202.

44. Zvi Kurzweil, "Samson Raphael Hirsch: Educationalist and Thinker," *Tradition* 2 (1960): 300.

45. Ibid.

46. Simon Halkin, *Modern Hebrew Literature* (New York, 1950), p. 62.

47. Elias Fink, "Religionsphilosophisches in S. R. Hirschs Kommentar zum Pentateuch," *Israelit*, S. R. Hirsch anniversary issue, pp. 28–32.

48. *Hegel's Werke*, 16:144; *Gymnasialrede*, Sept. 29, 1809.

49. Cole, *Herbart and Froebel*, p. 93.

50. John Herman Randall, *The Making of the Modern Mind* (Boston, 1926), p. 470.

51. Stace, *Philosophy of Hegel*, p. 313, states the following: "The philosophy of nature presents us with a doctrine of evolution, a progress from lower to higher forms. But it should be carefully noted that no time element is involved here. One phase succeeds another, not in order of time, but only in logical order. Hegel lived in pre-Darwinian days and he was not aware that evolution is a fact in time as well as a process of logical thought. In fact he expressly denied the theory of an historical evolution."

52. Collingwood, *The Idea of Nature*, pp. 108–9.

53. Hirsch's attitude toward science is generally similar to that of Christian Wolff, for whom the world reflected God's perfection. Science for Hirsch therefore enlarges man's concept of the world and consequently of God's majesty—John Dillenberger, *Protestant Thought and Natural Science* (New York, 1960), pp. 166–71.

54. See also Hirsch's comments, *CE* 23:19, where he emphasizes: "The great law of *le-minehu* proclaimed at the creation of each living organism keeps every one of the tiniest and the greatest of the millions of organic creatures throughout all the ages in which the world has existed and will exist living within the prescribed form and power and material of its species."
55. Collingwood, *The Idea of Nature*, p. 131.
56. John Dewey, "The Influence of Darwin on Philosophy," *Contemporary Thought*, 1910.
57. Stace, *Philosophy of Hegel*, p. 321.
58. Note the difference between the accepted translation of this verse (Ps. 19:7) and Hirsch's version. The accepted translation of this verse reads: "His [the sun's] going forth is from the end of the heaven, and his circuit unto the ends of it, and there is nothing hid from the heat thereof." Since, however, this translation would suggest the motion of the sun, consequently Hirsch translates it in the following manner: "And yet, one point upon the heavens remains its origin and its orbit is within their defined bounds; and thus He [God] is hidden even before His [God's] sun." This peculiar form of rendering the text so as to conform with the scientific theory of his day does not imply that Hirsch attempted to read modern science into the Bible. Such a practice was frequently deplored by him. However, where it could be done so without any offense to the text, Hirsch considered it legitimate.
59. This view that "the Bible spoke in the language of men" is indeed found in the Talmud. However, this view gained credence and intellectual respectability in the expositions of Johann Georg Hamann and Johann Gottfried Herder. Accordingly, God had intentionally employed pictorial and figurative speech in the Bible, not because He wanted to hide anything or disguise certain ideas but because it was the language most comprehensible to ancient man. In his *Tagebuch eines Christen*, Hammann mocked those theologians and biblical commentators who endeavored to read into the scriptural texts the most modern and neoteric scientific theories. See Frank E. Manuel, *The Eighteenth Century Confronts the Gods* (Cambridge, Mass., 1959), pp. 283–90; see also Roy Pascal, *The German Sturm und Drang* (New York, 1953), pp. 96–97.
60. A. D. White, *A History of the Warfare of Science with Theology in Christendom* (New York, 1960), 1:158.
61. This ambivalent attitude toward the concept of miracles was not unique to Hirsch. A similar course was pursued by many Protestant theologians—see Dillenberger, *Protestant Thought*, pp. 176–79, 196–99. Mendelssohn, too, was inclined to minimize the importance of miracles as a primary source of evidence for the validity of Judaism—see Mendelssohn, *Gesammelte Schriften*, 3:-313–15.
62. Regarding the revolutionary impact of Darwinism on theology and religion, see Dillenberger, *Protestant Thought*, pp. 217–51. See also Franklin L. Baumer, *Religion and the Rise of Scepticism* (New York, 1960), pp. 146–50.

14. "Avodah": Divine Service

1. Deut. 11:13.
2. Sifrei. It is interesting to note that the term "service of the heart" is also used by Kant, although not in the strict sense of prayer—see *Religion within the Limits of Reason Alone*, trans. Theodore M. Greene and Hoyt H. Hudson (New York, 1960), p. 180.
3. Sifrei, loc. cit.
4. Berakhot 26b.
5. The various editions of the prayer book of the Hamburg Temple bore the title *Seder ha-Avodah*. This was the title of its first edition in 1819 published many years before the *Horeb* and of the subsequent revised editions from 1841 on. Many prayer books of other Reform communities had the same or similar titles containing the term *avodah*. Some later Reform prayer books were called *Avodah She-ba-lev* followed by the German equivalent *Der Gottesdienst des Herzens*—see Petuchowski, *Prayerbook Reform*, pp. 1–21.
6. Frankfurt am Main, 1895. This *siddur* was recently translated into English and published by Feldheim Publishers (Jerusalem and New York, 1969).
7. Tschernowitz, *Toldot ha-Poskim*, 3:223–31.
8. Friedrich Heiler, *Prayer*, trans. Samuel M. Combe (New York, 1958), p. xiii.
9. According to Nachmanides the institution of daily prayer is of rabbinic origin. The Torah never stipulated any definite time for such observance. Even Maimonides considers that prayer is commanded by the Bible only in a general way: neither the number, nor the form, nor the time is prescribed in the Bible. In his opening statement of *Hilkhot Tefillah* he explicitly declares:

ואין מנין התפילות מן התורה, ואין משנה התפילה הזאת מן התורה, ואין לתפילה זמן קבוע מן התורה. (Mishneh Torah, Ahavah, Hilkhot Tefilah 1:1)

See also *Sefer ha-Ḥinukh* §431.
10. *"Torot"* comprises twenty chapters, *"Mishpatim"* twelve, and *"Ḥukkim"* sixteen. Hirsch, like many other codifiers, was in need of a division dealing with miscellanea, for which the last division might have served as a most suitable place.
11. "Das Judentum sei anderwärts als in den Synagogen zu suchen, in der Synagoge liege nicht der Schwerpunkt des Judentums"—*S*, 6:142.
12. *S*, 6:131–44.
13. "In einer Zeit so arger Verirrung wie die unsrige wäre es vielleicht die radikalste und die durchgreifendste Heilung versprechende Kur: man schlösse einmal—provisorisch—auf ein Jahrhundert—alle Synagogen"—ibid., p. 142.
14. Shoḥet, *Im Ḥilufei Tekufot*, pp. 143–46.
15. Petuchowski, *Prayerbook Reform*, pp. 123–24.
16. Ibid., pp. 105–27.
17. There is a need to distinguish between rules of conduct concerned with decorum and rules of services which pertain to changes and innovations of the prayers. While Hirsch accepted the former, he

rejected the latter. Rabbis are teachers of the law but not lawgivers: "Nicht zu Gesetzgebern, zu Gesetzlehrern sind die Rabbinen berufen; es wohnt ihnen im Kreise der jüdischen Gemeinden keinerlei legislatorische Kraft inne"—*S*, 2:346. Hirsch strongly opposed the interference of the government in matter of Jewish liturgy. Such intervention by a non-Jewish authority in matters sacred and exclusively Jewish was outrageous: "Was hat der Staat und seine Regierung mit *Pittum Hakketoroth, Esehu Mekoman* und Hoschaanoth-Abschlagen zu tun! Wie sollte er sich auch nur im entferntesten die Fähigkeit zu beurteilen zutrauen, was in inneren jüdischen Kultusangelegenheiten recht und unrecht, statthaft oder unstatthaft, zulässig oder unzulässig sei!"—ibid., p. 350. See "Synagogen- und Gebeteordnung für die Israelitischen Kultus-Gemeinden der Pfalz," ibid., pp. 343–57.

18. Maimonides's designation of the second division of the *Mishneh Torah* as *"Ahavah"* (love) follows his statement in *"Sefer ha-Madda," Hilkhot Yesodei ha-Torah*, 2:2: "When a person contemplates His great wondrous works and creatures and from them obtains a glimpse of His wisdom which is incomparable and infinite, he will straightaway *love* Him, praise Him, glorify Him and long with an exceeding longing to know His great name." As already pointed out in the discussion of the *"Torot"* division, man's love of God is a direct result of his knowledge of God. The *"Sefer ha-Madda,"* the "Book of Knowledge," is therefore logically followed by the *"Sefer Ahavah,"* the "Book of Love." See Tschernowitz, *Toldot ha-Poskim*, 3:223–24. In the *Guide of the Perplexed, "Ahavah"* is listed as the ninth category and not, as in the *Mishneh Torah*, the second division.

19. See *Mishneh Torah, Hilkhot Tefillah*, chapters 7–9. See special summary at the end of *"Ahavah."* The *Shulḥan Arukh's* outline is even more extensive.

20. I. Elbogen, "Der Ritus im Mischne Thora," in *Moses Ben Maimon: Sein Leben, seine Werke, und sein Einfluss* (Leipzig, 1908), 319–31.

21. Baron, *History of the Jews*, 7:119.

22. Ibid., pp. 62–134; Ismar Elbogen, *Der jüdische Gottesdienst in seiner geschichtlichen Entwicklung* (Hildesheim, 1961). Actually, there still exist a great variety of *siddurim* dependent on various localities. There are differences between those of German, French, Italian, Rumanian, Polish, Greek, Yemenite, and Spanish versions, to mention but a few. However, fundamentally they may be divided into two categories, Ashkenazic and Sephardic. The former followed the basic outline of the Palestinian rite, the latter that of the Babylonian rite. Some, like the community of Avignon, followed a mixture of both rites—Simḥah Asaf, *Tekufat ha-Geonim ve-Sifrutah* (Jerusalem, 1955), p. 183.

23. Originally there was a prohibition against formulating any text in writing except the Bible. This prohibition applied also to prayers. Under such circumstances no *siddur*, as it became subsequently known, was possible—Asaf, pp. 181–82.

24. Petuchowski, *Prayerbook Reform*, pp. 129–30. The title of Fried-

länder's prayer book was *Gebete der Juden auf das ganze Jahr.*
25. Simon Bernfeld, *Toldot ha-Reformatzion ha-Datit be-Yisrael* (Warsaw, 1908), p. 243.
26. Ibid., pp. 240–43.
27. It was published in two volumes. The first appeared in 1817, the second in 1818 in Berlin. See Petuchowski, *Prayerbook Reform,* pp. 134–37; Bernfeld, *Toldot ha-Reformatzion,* pp. 243–47.
28. According to Bernfeld, the *Deutsche Synagogue* too was within the limits of the Halakhah—see *Toldot ha-Reformatzion,* p. 247.
29. Regarding the criticism of the Reform prayer book and service, see Petuchowski, *Prayerbook Reform,* pp. 84–104.
30. Petuchowski suggests the possibility that the "early Reformers were less disturbed by the metaphysical aspect of the angelology of the *musaf* version of the *kedushah* than by the nationalistic plea for a speedy return to Zion voiced in the Shaharit version"—ibid., p. 367. This, however, may not have been the deciding factor. While it is true that they eliminated such references to the return to Zion as "O bring us home in peace from the four corners of the earth, and make us walk upright to our land," they did not expunge such prayers as *retzei* and *ve-tehezenah* which even more heavily emphasize the hope for Jewish national restoration and the reestablishment of the Temple with its sacrificial regimen—see Bernfeld, *Toldot ha-Reformatzion,* pp. 243–47.
31. The views of the proponents were expounded in two publications, *Or Nogah* and *Nogah ha-Tzedek.* The views of the opponents were contained in a volume entitled *Eleh Divrei ha-Berit,* (Altona, 1819). The latter was followed by a refutation, *Herev Nokemet Nekam Berit* (Hamburg, 1819), and *Berit Emet.* (Dessau, 1820).
32. The title of the Hamburg prayer book was *Seder ha-Avodah: Ordnung der öffentlichen Andacht für die Sabbath- und Festtage des ganzen Jahres nach dem Gebrauche des Neuen-Tempel-Vereins in Hamburg.* Concerning the outline of the prayers and the comparison between the Hamburg prayer book and the traditional *siddur,* see Petuchowski, *Prayerbook Reform,* pp. 49–55. See also Seckel I. Frankel, *Schutzschrift des zu Hamburg erschienenen israelitischen Gebetbuchs . . .* (Hamburg, 1819), and Abraham Geiger, *Der Hamburger Tempelstreit: Eine Zeitfrage* (Breslau, 1842).
33. *PT,* pp. 5–15.
34. The root *pll.* The word *pelilim* in Exod. 21:22 is interpreted as "judges" in the Mekhilta; see also Sanhedrin 111b. In his commentary on Genesis, Hirsch defines the reflexive verb *hitpalel* as "to get oneself completely penetrated with all that is godly which should be the ruling and forming factor for mankind in every direction"—*CG* 11:7.
35. Yevamot 64a.
36. Heiler, *Prayer,* p. 89.
37. Kant, *Religion within the Limits of Reason Alone,* p. 181.
38. Ibid., p. 183.
39. Ibid.
40. Immanuel Kant, *Lectures on Ethics,* trans. Louis Infield (New York and Evanston, 1963), p. 101.

41. Quoted in Petuchowski, *Prayerbook Reform,* p. 130.
42. Quoted in ibid.
43. Num. 10:9.
44. *G,* 3:168–69. See Joseph Albo, *Ikkarim,* 4: chap. 18.
45. Kant, *Lectures on Ethics,* p. 98.
46. Ibid., p. 99.
47. Hirsch, *Siddur Tefillot Yisrael: The Hirsch Siddur, Translated with Commentary* (Jerusalem–New York, 1969), p. 5
48. Ibid., pp. 130–31.
49. Petuchowski presents a comparative schematic outline of the Sabbath services between the traditional *siddur* and the Hamburg Temple prayer book of 1819 in which the changes, omissions, abridgments, and substitutions are evident—Petuchowski, *Prayerbook Reform,* pp. 50–53. Chorin differentiated between obligatory prayers like the *shema* and the *amidah,* on the one hand, and hymns of adoration, which Hirsch termed *tehillot,* on the other. The former were ancient and essential and therefore had to be recited in the original Hebrew, whereas the latter could be abbreviated. Hence the *pesukei de-zimra,* which constitute a prelude to the obligatory prayers, could be cut and shortened—see Aaron Chorin, *Ein Wort zu seiner Zeit (Davar be'Ito)* (Vienna, 1820), pp. 33ff.
50. Hos. 14:3.
51. Yoma 86b. Though prayer was considered important, it was the last on the scale in comparison to sacrifices. Thus the Midrash states: "If a man has a bullock, let him offer a bullock, if not, let him give a ram, or a lamb, or a pigeon; and if he cannot afford even a pigeon, let him bring a handful of flour. And if he has not even any flour, let him bring nothing at all, but come with words of prayer"—*Midrash Tanhuma,* Buber ed., *Tzav,* 8:9a.
52. *Ma'ariv* was considered by some as optional since it did not correspond to any of the daily obligatory sacrifices. Some connect it with the burning of the remainders of offerings upon the altar which lasted all night—Berakhot 26b.
53. Berakhot 26b. The three orders of daily prayer were attributed also to Moses—*Tanhuma, Tavo I.*
54. According to this harmonization, the patriarchs instituted the three daily prayer services. The Rabbis in later years connected them with the order of the daily sacrifices—ibid.
55. *Mishneh Torah, Hilkhot Tefillah,* 1:5.
56. Berakhot 33a; Megillah 17b; *Mishneh Torah, Hilkhot Tefillah,* 1:4.
57. "Ohnehin liegt wohl die Annahme nicht fern, es werde ein solcher Verein der grössten Geister unseres Volkes bei der Parallelisierung ihrer Gebete und der Opfer nicht eine bloss äussere Zeitharmonie, sondern zugleich den Einklang der Gesamttendenz und des Inhaltes erzielt haben, als dessen natürliche Folge sich dann auch die äussere Einigung der Zeit ergab"—*S,* 4:211.
58. Including the *birkhat ha-minim* against informers, slanderers, and traitors.
59. The first benediction, *avot,* stresses the covenantal relationship between God and the patriarchs of the Jewish people. The second benediction, *gevurot,* invokes God's omnipotence. The third bene-

diction, *kedushah*, proclaims God's ineffable holiness.

60. The act of slaughtering the sacrificial animal, *shehitah*, is not considered as part of the sacred service. The latter begins with *kabalah*, the receiving of the blood in a vessel of ministry. This is followed by *holakhah*, carrying the blood to the altar. Finally, it was consummated by *zerikah*, the actual sprinkling of it on the altar.

61. Yoma 25a–26a; Tamid, chaps. 3 and 4.

62. The seventeenth benediction, *avodah*, is a prayer for the restoration of the Temple service. The eighteenth benediction, *hoda'ah*, is an expression of gratitude for God's kindness and mercy. The nineteenth and last benediction, *shalom*, emphasizes the prayer for peace. See also in Hirsch's *siddur* the comments on the *amidah*— *Siddur Tefillot Yisrael*, pp. 126–30.

63. "Prayers were instituted in correspondence to the daily sacrifices" —Berakhot 26b.

64. "Es dürfte aber die Beziehung unseres dreimaligen täglichen Gebetes zu den täglichen Opfern nicht eine nur rein äusserliche, die blosse Gleichzeitigkeit bestimmende sein. Schon die Parallele des Satzes *tefillot keneged temidim tiknum* zu dem andern *tefillot avot tiknum* dürfte nach dem ersten Ausspruche den ganzen Ursprung dieser Tefillot aus dem und in dem Thamidopfer vermuten lassen, wie dieser Ursprung nach dem zweiten den Vätern vindiciert ist— *S*, 4:211.

65. *G*, 3:151.

66. "Nicht als stellvertretender Ersatz, wie dies von gewisser Seite gerne dargestellt wird, um als vermeintliche Folie zu liturgischen und sonstigen Reformbestrebungen zu dienen—als Begleitung der Opfer tritt unser Gebet auf"—*S*, 4:210.

67. Concerning Hirsch's criticism of Geiger's view on the *akedah*, see *CG* 22:11.

68. See the responsum of Rabbi Moses Sofer in *Eleh Divrei ha-Berit*.

69. Commenting on the biblical verse *Shema Yisrael*, the Talmud employs the word *shema* in the sense of understanding: "Hear, O Israel —in any language you understand"—Berakhot 13a.

70. David Friedländer, *Über die, durch die neue Organisation der Judenschulen der Preussischen Staaten nothwendig gewordene Umbildung ihres Gottesdienstes in den Synagogen, ihrer Unterrichts-Anstalten, und deren Lehrgegenstände, und ihres Erziehungs-Wesens überhaupt: Ein Wort zu seiner Zeit* (Berlin, 1812).

71. Hirsch departed from the traditional rabbis who wrote their works in Hebrew. Except for a few minor writings in Hebrew, Hirsch wrote exclusively in German.

72. "Andeutungen über den hebräischen Untericht als allgemeines Bildungselement in unserer Schule"—*S*, 2:433–48.

73. *Protokolle und Aktenstücke der zweiten Rabbinerversammlung abgehalten in Frankfurt am Main* (1845), p. 22.

74. See "Schriften betreffend Dr. Z. Fränkels 'Darkei Hamischna' "—*S*, 6:322–434.

75. A. Wolff, *Die Stimmen der ältesten glaubwürdigsten Rabbinen über die Pijutim* (Leipzig, 1857).

76. *G,* 1:218.
77. Ibid.
78. Chorin, *Ein Wort zu seiner Zeit,* pp. 33ff.
79. Plaut, *The Rise of Reform Judaism,* p. 43; Philipson, *The Reform Movement,* pp. 8, 38, 86, 152, 303, 424.
80. Petuchowski, *Prayerbook Reform,* pp. 105–27.
81. Aharon Mirski, *Reshit ha-Piyyut* (Jerusalem, 1965), p. 98; Zinberg, *Toldot Sifrut Yisrael,* 1:7; Baron, *History of the Jews,* 7:89–105.
82. *PT,* pp. 98–100.
83. Describing the lack of decorum in the synagogue of Aurich, where he visited with Hirsch, Graetz attributed it to the incomprehensibility of the prayers. Nevertheless, Hirsch refused to eliminate even the complicated and abstruse Kalirian *piyyut, Atz Kotzetz,* recited on Purim. "Woher kommt das alles? Von dem vielen unverständigen Beten, von den sinnlosen *Piyyutim.* Und doch könnte man ihm *kol hon de alma* geben, ohne das er einen *Atz Kotzetz* abschaffen würde"—Graetz, *Tagebuch,* 2:143, in *MGWJ* 63:356.
84. In modern times there is a new appreciation of the poetry of Eliezer ha-Kalir and of the poem *Atz Kotzetz* satirized during the Haskalah and Reform period. See Mirski, *Reshit ha-Piyyut,* pp. 90–91.
85. Avodah Zarah 36a, Moed Katan 3b, Megillah 2a, Gittin 36b, Eduyyot, 1:5. Rabbi Moses Sofer in his responsum in *Eleh Divrei ha-Berit* applies this rule even to versions in which there are differences between the Ashkenazic and Sephardic communities.
86. Philipson, *The Reform Movement,* pp. 245, 248–49.
87. This view is expressed in Sifrei, Num. 6:27.

Epilogue

1. *H,* p. cxli.
2. Grunfeld, introduction to *H,* p. xxxvii.
3. Ibid.
4. Ibid.
5. Marcuse, *Reason and Revolution,* pp. 251–52.
6. Ibid., p. 252.
7. Holborn, *History of Modern Germany,* 2:516–17.
8. William Montgomery McGovern, *From Luther to Hitler* (Cambridge, 1941), p. 343.
9. Ibid.
10. Philipson, *The Reform Movement,* pp. 51–74.
11. Ibid., pp. 75–89; Petuchowski, *Prayerbook Reform,* pp. 54–56.
12. "Allesammt die Fackel kritischer Vernunft in der Hand"—an allusion to Kant's work—Hirsch, *Naftulei Naphtali; Erste Mitteilungen aus Naphtalis Briefwechsel,* p. 2.
13. Ibid.

Bibliography

Works by Hirsch—Selected List

A bibliography of the complete writings of Samson Raphael Hirsch is to be found in Judaism Eternal: Selected Essays from the Writings of S.R. Hirsch *(London, 1956). This bibliography is based on the bibliography compiled by H. Eisemann and first published in the Jubilee edition of the Frankfurt Israelit, issued on the occasion of the centenary of Hirsch's birth (25th Sivan 5688–June 24th, 1908).*

Der Austritt aus der Gemeinde, Frankfurt am Main, 1876. *Be-Ma'aglei Shanah: Pirkei Iyun Midei Ḥodesh Be-Ḥodsho,* translated with introductions by Jacob Rosenheim, Isaac Breuer, Yehiel Jacob Weinberg, and Yehudah Leib Orlian, 4 vols., Bnei Brak, 1965–66.

Bemerkungen zur einer Literarischen Fehde, in *Literarischen Annalen,* Frankfurt am Main, 1839.

Gesammelte Schriften, edited by N. Hirsch, 6 vols., Frankfurt am Main, 1908–12.

Horeb: Versuche über Jissroels Pflichten in der Zerstreuung, zunächst für Jissroels denkende Jünglinge und Jungfrauen, Altona, 1837.

Horeb: Philosophy of Jewish Laws and Observances, translated by I. Grunfeld, 2 vols., London, 1962.

Horeb, translated into Hebrew with introduction by M. S. Arohnson, Kovno, 1893–95.

Igrot Tzafon: Neunzehn Briefe über Judentum von Ben Usiel, Altona, 1836.

Igrot Tzafon: The Nineteen Letters of Ben Uziel, translated by Bernard Drachman, New York, 1942.

Siddur Tefillot Yisrael Israel's Gebete, übersetzt und erläutert, Frankfurt am Main, 1895.

Judaism Eternal: Selected Essays from the Writings of S. R. Hirsch, translated and annotated with an introduction by I. Grunfeld, 2 vols., London, 1956.

Jüdische Anmerkungen zu den Bemerkungen eines Protestanten über die Konfession der 22 Bremischen Pastoren. Von einen Juden, Oldenburg, 1841.

Naftulei Naphtali: Erste Mitteilungen aus Naphtalis Briefwechsel, Altona, 1838 (written under the pseudonym "Ben Usiel").

Der Pentateuch, übersetzt und erläutert, Frankfurt am Main, 1867–78.

The Pentateuch, Translated and Explained by Samson Raphael Hirsch, translated by Isaac Levy, 5 vols., London, 1958–62.

Postscripta, Altona, 1840.

Die Psalmen, übersetzt und erläutert, 2 vols., Frankfurt am Main, 1882.

The Psalms, Translated and Explained by Samson Raphael Hirsch, translated with commentary by Gertrude Hirschler, 2 vols., New York, 1960–66.

Siddur Tefillot Yisrael: The Hirsch Siddur, translated with commentary, Jerusalem and New York, 1969.

Von dem pädagogischen Werte des Judentums, Frankfurt am Main, 1873.

Zweite Mitteilungen aus einem Briefwechsel über die neueste jüdische Literatur: Ein Fragment, Altona, 1844.

Works by Others

Adler, Salo, "Die Entwicklung des Schulwesens der Juden zu Frankfurt bis zur Emanzipation," *Jahrbuch der jüdischen-literarischen Gesellschaft,* 1927–28.

———, "Der erste Plan zur Gründung einer jüdischen Schule mit profanem Unterricht in der Frankfurter Judengasse," *Festschrift Frankfurt-Realschule,* Frankfurt am Main, 1928.

Altmann, Alexander, *Moses Mendelssohn: A Biographical Study,* Philadelphia, 1973.

———, "The New Style of Preaching in Nineteenth Century German Jewry," in *Studies in Nineteenth Century Jewish Intellectual History,* Cambridge, Mass., 1968.

———, "Theology in Twentieth Century German Jewry," *Leo Baeck Institute Year Book,* vol. 1, London, 1956.

———, "Zur Frühgeschichte der jüdischen Predigt in Deutschland: Leopold Zunz als Prediger," *Leo Baeck Institute Year Book* 6, New York, 1969.

Asaria, Zwi, "Samson Raphael Hirsch's Wirken im Lande Niedersachsen," *Udim: Zeitschrift der Rabbinerkonferenz in der Bundesrepublik Deutschland* 1, Frankfurt am Main, 1970.

———, *Zur Geschichte der Juden in Osnabrück und Umgebung von der Stadt Osnabrück,* 1969.

Ateret Zwi, jubilee volume presented in honor of the eightieth birthday of Rabbi Dr. Joseph Breuer, New York, 1962.

Atlas, Samuel, "Rights of Private Property and Private Profit," *Central Conference of American Rabbis Yearbook* 54, Cincinnati, 1944.

Aub, Joseph, *Betrachtungen und Widerlegungen, book 2: Widerlegungen: Ein Dialog über Hirschs Mittheilungen aus Naphtalis Briefwechsel,* Nürenberg, 1839.

Auerbach, Leopold, *Das Judenthum und seine Bekenner in Preussen und in den anderen deutschen Bundesstaaten,* Berlin, 1890.

Auerbach, M., "Seligmann Bär Bamberger," *Jeschurun,* 1928.

Aviad, Yeshayahu, *Deyuknaot,* Jerusalem, 1962.

Avineri, Shlomo, "A Note on Hegel's Views on Jewish Emancipation," *Jewish Social Studies* 25, New York, 1963.

Ayerst, W., *The Jews in the Nineteenth Century,* London, 1848.

Ayinn, Sidney, "Kant on Judaism," *Jewish Quarterly Review* 59, Philadelphia, 1968.

Bach, Hans, "Isaac Bernays," *Monatsschrift für Geschichte und Wissenschaft des Judentums* 83, Berlin, 1939.

Baerwald, H., and Salo Adler, "Geschichte des Philantropins," *Festschrift zur Jahrhundertfeier des Philantropins,* Frankfurt am Main, 1904.

Bamberger, Bernard Jacob, "The Developing Philosophy of Reform Judaism," *Central Conference of American Rabbis Yearbook* 68, Chicago, 1958.

Bamberger, N., *Rabbiner Seligmann B. Bamberger, dessen Leben und Wirken,* Würzburg, 1897.

Bamberger, S., *Geschichte der Rabbiner der Stadt und des Bezirkes Würzburg,* Wandsbeck, 1905.

Baron, Salo Wittmayer, *The Jewish Community,* 3 vols., Philadelphia, 1945.

———, *A Social and Religious History of the Jews,* vols. 1–8, Philadelphia, 1952–58.

Barzilay-Eisenstein, Isaac, "The Background of the Berlin Haskalah," in *Essays on Jewish Life and Thought Presented in Honor of Salo Wittmayer Baron,* New York, 1959.

———, "The Ideology of the Berlin Haskalah," *Proceedings of the American Academy for Jewish Research* 25, New York, 1956.

———, "The Jew in the Literature of the Enlightenment," *Jewish Social Studies* 18, New York, 1956.

———, "Moses Mendelssohn," *Jewish Quarterly Review* 52, Philadelphia, 1961.

———, "National and Anti-National Trends in the Berlin Haskalah," *Jewish Social Studies* 21, New York, 1959.

———, *Shlomo Yehudah Rapoport and His Contemporaries,* Ramat Gan, 1969.

———, "The Treatment of the Jewish Religion in the Literature of the Berlin Haskalah," *Proceedings of the American Academy for Jewish Research* 24, New York, 1955.

Baumer, Franklin L., *Religion and the Rise of Skepticism,* New York, 1960.

Bergman, Samuel Hugo, *Hogim u-Ma'aminim,* Tel Aviv, 1959.

———, *Toldot ha-Pilosufiah ha-Ḥadashah, mi-Tekufat ha-Haskalah ad Immanuel Kant,* Jerusalem, 1973.

Berlin, Isaiah, "Herder and the Enlightenment," in *Aspects of the Eighteenth Century,* edited by Earl R. Wasserman, Baltimore, 1965.

Bernfeld, Simon, *Dor Tahapukhot,* 2 vols., Warsaw, 1897.

———, *Toldot ha-Reformatzion ha-Datit be-Yisrael,* Warsaw, 1908.

Berwin, Beate, *Moses Mendelssohn im Urteil Seiner Zeitgenossen,* Berlin, 1919.

Bettan, Israel, "Early Reform in Contemporaneous Responsa," *Hebrew*

Union College Jubilee Volume, Cincinnati, 1925.

Bloch, Philipp, *Heinrich Graetz: Ein Lebens-und Zeitbild,* Posen, 1904; Eng. trans. *Heinrich Graetz: A Memoir,* in Heinrich Graetz, *History of the Jews,* vol. 6, Philadelphia, 1945.

Blumenthal, Adolf, *Die geschichliche Bedeutung von Samson Raphael Hirsch für das Judenthum,* Frankfurt am Main, 1889.

Boyd, William, *The History of Western Education,* London, 1950.

Brann, M., "Aus H. Graetzens Lehr- und Wanderjahren," *Monatsschrift für Geschichte und Wissenschaft des Judentums* 62–63, Breslau, 1918–19.

Bresselau, M.J., *Herev Nokemet Nekam Berit,* Dessau, 1819.

Breuer, Isaac, "Hundert Jahre Neunzehn Briefe," *Nachlath Zwi* 6, Frankfurt am Main, 1936.

_____, "Lehre, Gesetz und Nation," *Wegzeichen,* Frankfurt, 1923.

_____, *Moriah: Yesodot ha Hinvkh ha-Leumi ha-Torati,* Jerusalem, 1954.

_____, *Nahaliel,* Tel Aviv, 1951.

_____, *Der neue Kusari: Ein Weg zum Judentum,* Frankfurt am Main, 1934.

_____, "Rabbiner Hirsch als Wegweiser in die jüdische Geschichte," *Nachlath Zwi* 5, Frankfurt am Main, 1935.

_____, "Samson Raphael Hirsch," in *Jewish Leaders, 1750–1940,* edited by Leo Jung, New York, 1953.

_____, *Tziyunei Derekh,* Tel Aviv, 1955.

Breuer, Jacob, ed., *Fundamentals of Judaism: Selections from the Works of Rabbi Samson Raphael Hirsch and Outstanding Thinkers,* New York, 1949.

_____, *Timeless Torah: An Anthology of the Writings of Samson Raphael Hirsch,* New York, 1957.

Breuer, Joseph, "Aus den Vorarbeiten zum *Horeb,*" *Nachlath Zwi* 5, Frankfurt am Main, 1935.

_____, "Hundert Jahre *Horeb,*" *Nachlath Zwi* 8, Frankfurt am Main, 1938.

Breuer, Mordekhai, "Prakim Mitokh Biographiah," *Ha-Rav Shimshon Raphael Hirsch: Mishnato ve-Shitato,* edited by Jonah Immanuel, Jerusalem, 1962.

Breuer, Raphael, *Unter seinem Banner: Ein Beitrag zur Würdigung Rabbiner Samson Raphael Hirsch,* Frankfurt am Main, 1908.

Breuer, Salomon, *Rede zum Gedächtniss seiner Ehrwürden, Herrn Samson Raphael Hirsch,* Frankfurt am Main, 1889.

Bury, J.B., *The Idea of Progress,* New York, 1955.

Butler, E.M., *The Tyranny of Greece over Germany,* New York, 1935.

Cahn, M., *Die religiösen Strömungen in der zeitgenössischen Judenheit,* Frankfurt am Main, 1912.

Cairns, Huntington, *Legal Philosophy from Plato to Hegel,* Baltimore, 1949.

Carove, F. W., *Über Emanzipation der Juden: Philosophie des Judenthums und jüdische Reformprojekte zu Berlin und Frankfurt am Main,* Siegen, 1845.

Cassirer, Ernst, *An Essay on Man,* New Haven, 1962.

_____, *The Philosophy of the Enlightenment,* translated by Fritz C. A. Koelln and James P. Pettegrove, Boston, 1955.

————, *The Philosophy of Symbolic Forms*, translated by Ralph Manheim, 3 vols., New Haven, 1965–66.

Chalke, R.D., *A Synthesis of Froebel and Herbart*, London, 1912.

Charbonah, M. S. [H. B. Fassel], *Herev Be-Tzayon, oder Briefe eines jüdischen Gelehrten und Rabbinen über das Werk "Horeb" von S. R. Hirsch*, Leipzig, 1839.

Chorin, Aaron, *Igereth Elassaph; oder, Sendschreiben eines afrikanischen Rabbi an seinen Collegen in Europa*, Prague, 1826.

————, *Ein Wort zu seiner Zeit* [*Davar be'Ito*], Vienna, 1820.

Cohen, Arthur A., *The Natural and Supernatural Jew*, New York, 1962.

Cohen, Hermann, *Religion der Vernunft aus den Quellen des Judentums*, Leipzig, 1919.

Cohen, Morris Raphael, *Law and the Social Order*, New York, 1933.

Cohen, Mortimer, *Jacob Emden: Man of Controversy*, Philadelphia, 1937.

Cole, P. R., *Herbart and Froebel*, New York, 1907.

Collingwood, R. G., *The Idea of History*, New York, 1956.

————, *The Idea of Nature*, New York, 1960.

Copleston, Frederick, *A History of Philosophy*, 8 vols., Garden City, N.Y., 1960–65.

Creizenach, Michael, *Shulḥan Arukh*, Frankfurt am Main, 1833–40.

Croce, B., *What Is Alive and What Is Dead in Hegel's Philosophy?*, translated by D. Ainslie, London, 1915.

Deutsch, David, *Asof Asifah: al Asefat ha-Rabbanim bi-Braunschweig bi-Shenat 5604 ve-gam Neged ha-Sheniyah bi-Frankfurt am Main bi-Shenat 5605*, Breslau, 1846.

Dewey, John, *Reconstruction in Philosophy*, New York, 1920.

Dillenberger, John, *Protestant Thought and Natural Science*, New York, 1960.

Dinur, B. Z., *Be-Mifneh ha-Dorot*, Jerusalem, 1955.

Drachman, Bernard, "Samson Raphael Hirsch: A Biographical Sketch," preface to Hirsch, *Igrot Tzafon: The Nineteen Letters of Ben Uziel*, trans. Drachman, New York, 1942.

Dubnov, Simon, *Divrei Yemei Am Olam*, 10 vols., Tel Aviv, 1958.

Duckesz, Eduard, "Zur Biographie des Chacham Isaak Bernays," *Jahrbuch der jüdischen-literarischen Gesellschaft*, vol. 5, Frankfurt am Main, 1907.

————, "Zur Genealogie Samson Raphael Hirsch," *Jahrbuch der jüdisch-literarischen Gesellschaft*, vol. 17, Frankfurt am Main, 1926.

Duckesz, Yeḥezkel, *Sefer Yivah le-Moshav*, Cracow, 1903.

Ehrmann, Salomon, *Einführung in S. R. Hirsch's "Neunzehn Briefe,"* Frankfurt, 1920.

————, "Rabbi Samson Raphael Hirsch as a Pioneer of Judaism in Eretz Yisroel and in the Diaspora," *Ateret Zwi, Joseph Breuer Volume*, New York, 1962.

————, *Rabbiner S. R. Hirsch als Wegweiser für Judentum in Lehre und Leben*, Zürich, 1960.

Elbogen, Ismar, *A Century of Jewish Life*, Philadelphia, 1945.

————, *Geschichte der Juden in Deutschland*, Berlin, 1935.

————, *Der jüdische Gottesdienst in seiner geschichtlichen Entwicklung*, Hildesheim, 1961.

_____, "Der Ritus im Mischne Thora," in *Moses ben Maimon: Sein Leben, seine Werke, und sein Einfluss*, Leipzig, 1908.

Eleh Divrei ha-Berit, Altona, 1819.

Elias, Marcus, "The Educational Work of Rabbi S. R. Hirsch: Jewish Schools in Western Europe," *Ateret Zwi, Joseph Breuer Volume*, New York, 1962.

Eliav, Mordekhai, *Ahavat Tziyon ve-Anshei Hod*, Jerusalem, 1970.

_____, *Ha-Ḥinukh ha-Yehudi be-Germaniah bi-Yemei ha-Haskalah ve-ha-Emantzipatziah*, Jerusalem, 1960.

Eloesser, Arthur, *Vom Ghetto nach Europa: Das Judenthum im geistigen Leben des neunzehnten Jahrhunderts*, Berlin, 1936.

Epstein, Isidore, *Faith of Judaism*, London, 1954.

Ettlinger, Jacob, *Binyan Tziyon* (responsa), Altona, 1868.

_____, ed., *Shomer Tziyon ha-Ne'eman*, Altona-Hamburg, 1846 et seq.

Fackenheim, Emil, "Samuel Hirsch and Hegel," in *Studies in Nineteenth Century Jewish Intellectual History*, Cambridge, Mass., 1968.

Fassel, H. B., *see* M. S. Charbonah.

Feuchtwang, David, "Samson Raphael Hirsch als Oberlandssrabbiner von Mähren," *Israelit*, S. R. Hirsch anniversary issue, Frankfurt am Main, 1908.

Fischer, P., *In seinen Spuren*, Satoraljaujhely, 1922.

_____ [Nachlath Zwi], *Über den geistigen Nachlass S. R. Hirsch*, Frankfurt am Main, 1929.

Formstecher, S., *Die Religion des Geistes*, Frankfurt am Main, 1841.

Frankel, Seckel Isaac, *Schutzschrift des zu Hamburg erschienenen israelitischen Gebetbuchs für die Mitglieder des Neuen-Tempel-Vereins nebst einer Beleuchtung des Rabbinismus*, Hamburg, 1819.

Frankel, Zachariah, *Darkhei ha-Mishnah*, Leipzig, 1867.

Frankfurter, Moses, *see* Moses Mendelssohn of Hamburg.

Frankl-Grün, Adolf, *Geschichte der Juden in Kremsier*, 2 vols., Frankfurt am Main, 1899.

Freehof, Solomon Bennett, *Reform Jewish Practice and Its Rabbinic Background*, New York, 1963.

_____, *Reform Responsa*, Cincinnati, 1960.

Freimann, A., and F. Kracauer, *Frankfort*, Philadelphia, 1929.

Friedemann, Charles, "La loi dans la pensée d'Isaac Breuer, (1883–1946)," *Revue des Études Juives* 131, Paris, 1972.

Friedländer, M., "The Late Chief Rabbi Dr. N. M. Adler," *Jewish Quarterly Review*, 1890.

Friedrich, Carl Joachim, *The Philosophy of Law in Historical Perspective*, Chicago, 1958.

Froebel, Friedrich, *Education of Man*, New York, 1908.

Fromm, Erich, *The Forgotten Language*, New York, 1960.

Gay, Peter, *The Enlightenment: An Interpretation*, New York, 1968.

Geiger, Abraham, *Der Hamburger Tempelstreit: Eine Zeitfrage*, Breslau, 1842.

_____, *Das Judentum und seine Geschichte*, Breslau, 1865–71.

_____, *Judaism and Its History*, New York, 1911.

_____, *Nachgelassene Schriften*, 5 vols., Berlin, 1875–78.

_____, "Neues Stadium des Kampfes in dem Judentum unserer Zeit,"

Wissenschaftlichte Zeitschrift für jüdische Theologie 2, Frankfurt am Main, 1836.

———, "Die 'Postscripta' des Rabbiners Hirsch in ihrem Verhältniss zu mir," in *Israelitische Annalen*, Frankfurt am Main, 1840.

———, review of Hirsch's *Horeb* and *Naphtulei Naphtali*, *Wissenschaftliche Zeitschrift für jüdische Theologie* 4, Frankfurt am Main, 1839.

———, review of Hirsch's *Neunzehn Briefe*, *Wissenschaftlichte Zeitschrift für jüdische Theologie* 2–3, Frankfurt am Main, 1836–37.

Geiger, L., *Abraham Geiger: Leben und Lebenswerk*, Berlin, 1910.

Ginsberg, Louis, *Students, Scholars, and Saints*, Philadelphia, 1958.

Ginsberg, Sigmar, "Die zweite Generation der Juden nach Moses Mendelssohn," *Leo Baeck Institute Year Book* 3, 1950.

Glatzer, Nahum N., *Leopold and Adelheid Zunz: An Account in Letters*, London, 1958.

Glueckel of Hameln, *The Life of Glueckel of Hameln*, translated by Beth Zion Abrahams, London, 1962.

Goldschmidt, J., *Geschichte der Talmud Torah Realschule in Hamburg*, Hamburg, 1905.

Gooch, G.P., *History and Historians in the Nineteenth Century*, Boston, 1959.

Graetz, Heinrich, *History of the Jews*, 6 vols., Philadelphia, 1945.

———, "Die Synoden," *Monatsschrift für die Geschichte und Wissenschaft des Judentums* 19.

Graetz, Zvi [Heinrich Graetz], *Darkhei ha-Historiah ha-Yehudit*, edited by Shmuel Ettinger, Jerusalem, 1969.

Graupe, Heinz Moshe, "Kant und das Judentum," *Zeitschrift für Religion- und Geistesgeschichte* 13, 1961.

Greenwald, Yekutiel Yehudah, *Le-Toldot he-Reformatzion ha-Datit be-Germaniah uve-Ungariah*, Columbus, Ohio, 1948.

Grunfeld, I., introduction to Hirsch, *The Pentateuch*, trans. Levy, London, 1959.

———, "Ta'amei Hamitzvoth in the Jewish Legal Philosophy of Rabbi S. R. Hirsch," *Ateret Zwi, Joseph Breuer Volume*, New York, 1962.

———, *Three Generations: The Influence of Samson Raphael Hirsch on Jewish Life and Thought*, London, 1958.

Grunwald, M., *Hamburgs deutsche Juden bis zur Auflösung der Dreigemeinden, 1811*, Hamburg, 1904.

Guddat, W., "Heinrich Heine und der 'Verein für Kultur und Wissenschaft der Juden' in Berlin 1822 und 1823," in *Festschrift zum 70. Geburtstage von Moritz Schaefer*, Berlin, 1927.

Gulak, Asher, *Yesodei ha-Mishpat ha-Ivri*, Berlin, 1922.

Guttmann, Julius, *Dat u-Madda*, Jerusalem, 1956.

———, "Mendelssohns Jerusalem und Spinozas theologisch-politisches Traktat," *Achtundvierzigster Bericht der Hochschule für die Wissenschaft des Judentums*, Berlin, 1931.

———, *Philosophies of Judaism*, translated by David W. Silverman, Philadelphia, 1964.

Halevi, Judah, *The Kuzari*, translated by Hartwig Hirschfeld, New York, 1964.

Hazard, Paul, *European Thought in the Eighteenth Century from Mon-*

tesquieu to Lessing, translated by J. L. May, London, 1954.

Hegel, Georg Wilhelm Friedrich, *Early Theological Writings,* translated by T. M. Knox, New York, 1961.

_____, *Logic,* translated by W. T. Harris, Chicago, 1895.

_____, *The Phenomenology of Mind,* translated by J. B. Baillie, New York, 1967.

_____, *Philosophy of Right,* translated with notes by T. M. Knox, London, 1942.

_____, *Reason in History,* translated by Robert S. Hartman, New York, 1954.

_____, *Sämtliche Werke,* edited by Hermann Glockner, 20 vols., Stuttgart, 1927–30.

_____, *Science of Logic,* New York, 1929.

Heiler, Friedrich, *Prayer,* translated by Samuel M. Combe, New York, 1958.

Heilperin, Pinḥas Menaḥem, *Teshuvot be-Anshei Aven,* Frankfurt am Main, 1845.

Heine, Heinrich, *Religion and Philosophy in Germany,* translated by John Snodgrass, Boston, 1959.

Heinemann, Isaac, "Gerechtigkeit und Liebe der Grundgedanke in S. R. Hirsch's Philosophie des Judentums, *Nachlath Zwi* Frankfurt am Main, 1930–31.

_____, "Meḥkarim al R. Shimshon Raphael Hirsch," *Sinai* 24, Jerusalem, 1949.

_____ "Ha-Rav Shimshon Raphael Hirsch ve-Igrot Tzafon," introduction to the Hebrew translation of Hirsch's *Nineteen Letters,* Jerusalem, 1952.

_____, "Samson Raphael Hirsch: The Formative Years of the Leader of Modern Orthodoxy," *Historia Judaica* 13, New York, 1951.

_____, "Supplement: Remarks on the Secession from the Frankfurt Jewish Community under Samson Raphael Hirsch," *Historia Judaica* 10, New York, 1948.

_____, *Ta'amei ha-Mitzvot be-Sifrut Yisrael,* vol. 1, Jerusalem, 1954; vol. 2, Jerusalem, 1956.

_____, "Ha-Yaḥas she-bein S. R. Hirsch le-Yitzḥak Bernays Rabbo," *Zion* 16, Jerusalem, 1941.

Heller, Max, "Samson Raphael Hirsch," *Central Conference of American Rabbis Yearbook* 18, Cincinnati, 1908.

Herder, Johann Gottfried, *Vom Geiste der ebräischen Poesie,* Dessau, 1762–83.

Hertzberg, Arthur, *The French Enlightenment and the Jews,* New York, 1968.

Herzog, Isaac, *Main Institutions of Jewish Law,* 2 vols., London, 1936.

Highet, Gilbert, *The Classical Tradition,* New York, 1957.

Hirsch, Mendel, *Samson Raphael Hirsch und die israelitische Religionsgesellschaft zu Frankfurt am Main,* Mainz, 1897.

Hirsch, S. A., "Jewish Philosophy of Religion and Samson Raphael Hirsch," *Jewish Quarterly Review,* 1890, reprinted in *A Book of Essays,* London, 1905.

Höffding, Harald, *A History of Modern Philosophy,* translated by B. E. Meyer, 2 vols., New York, 1955.

Holborn, Hajo, *A History of Modern Germany,* 3 vols., New York, 1967–69.

Holdheim, Samuel, *Das Ceremonialgesetz im Messiasreich,* Schwerin, 1845.

————, *Geschichte der Entwickelung und Entstehung der jüdischen Reformgemeinde in Berlin,* Berlin, 1857.

————, *Moses Mendelssohn und die Denk- und Glaubensfreiheit im Judentum,* Berlin, 1859.

————, *Das Religiöse und Politische im Judentum,* Schwerin, 1845.

————, *Über die Autonomie der Rabbinen und das Prinzip der jüdischen Ehe,* Schwerin, 1843.

————, *Über die Beschneidung zunächst in religiös-dogmatischer Beziehung,* Schwerin, 1844.

————, ed., *Zweite Mittheilung aus einem Briefwechsel über die neueste jüdische Literatur: Ein Fragment von S. R. Hirsch,* Schwerin, 1844.

Hook, Sidney, *From Hegel to Marx,* New York, 1958.

Horovitz, M., *Frankfurter Rabbiner,* Frankfurt am Main, 1885.

Ihering, Rudolf, *Der Geist des römischen Rechts auf den verschiedenen Stufen seiner Entwicklung,* Leipzig, 1878.

Immanuel, Jonah, ed., *Ha-Rav Shimshon Raphael Hirsch: Mishnato ve-Shitato,* Jerusalem, 1962.

Israelit, S. R. Hirsch anniversary issue (Frankfurt am Main, 1908).

Japhet, Sammy, "The Secession from the Frankfurt Jewish Community under Samson Raphael Hirsch," *Historia Judaica* 10, New York, 1948.

Jeschurun: Eine Monatschrift zur Förderung jüdischen Geistes und jüdischen Lebens im Haus, Gemeinde, und Schule, Frankfurt am Main, 1854–70.

Jöhlinger, Otto, *Bismarck und die Juden,* Berlin, 1921.

Jost, Isaak Markus, "Theologische Fehde des Naphtalischen Briefwechsels gegen die jüdische-theologische Zeitschrift," *Israelitische Annalen,* Frankfurt am Main, 1839.

————, *Neuere Geschichte der Israeliten in der ersten Hälfte des neunzehnten Jahrhunderts,* vols. 1–3, Breslau, 1846.

Jung, Leo, ed., *Jewish Leaders, 1750–1940,* New York, 1953.

————, ed., "Samson Raphael Hirsch," in *Guardians of Our Heritage,* New York, 1958.

Kaatz, S., *Abraham Geiger's religiöser Charakter,* Frankfurt am Main, 1911.

Kant, Immanuel, *Die Religion innerhalb der Grenzen der blossen Vernunft,* Leipzig, 1793. English version: *Religion within the Limits of Reason Alone,* translated by Theodore M. Greene and Hoyt H. Hudson, New York, 1960.

————, *Lectures on Ethics,* translated by Louis Infield, New York and Evanston, 1963.

————, *Sämtliche Werke,* ed. Rosenkranz and Schubert, 12 vols., Leipzig, 1838–42.

Kaplan, Mordecai M., *The Greater Judaism in the Making,* New York, 1960.

————, *Judaism as a Civilization,* New York, 1957.

Katz, Jacob, *Bein Yehudim le-Goyim,* Jerusalem, 1960.

———, *Die Entstehung der Judenassimilation in Deutschland und deren Ideologie,* Frankfurt am Main, 1935.

———, "Jewry and Judaism in the Nineteenth Century," *Cahiers d'Histoire Mondiale* 4, 1958.

———, *Masoret u-Mashber,* Jerusalem, 1963.

———, *Tradition and Crisis: Jewish Society at the End of the Middle Ages,* New York, 1961.

Kaufmann, Walter, *Hegel: A Reinterpretation,* Garden City, N.Y., 1966.

Kaufmann, Yehezkel, *Golah ve-Nekhar,* Tel Aviv, 1930.

Kellenbenz, Hermann, *Sephardim an der unteren Elbe,* Wiesbaden, 1958.

Kirchheim, Raphael, *Die neue Exegetenschule: Eine kritische Dornenlese aus Dr. Hirschs Übersetzung und Erklärung der Genesis,* Breslau, 1867.

Klausner, Yoseph, *Historiah shel ha-Sifrut ha-Ivrit ha-Hadashah,* vols. 1 and 2, Jerusalem, 1952.

Kley, Eduard, *Catechismus der mosaischen Religionslehre,* Berlin, 1814.

———, *Predigten in dem neuen israelitischen Tempel zu Hamburg gehalten,* Hamburg, 1819.

Kober, Adolf, "The French Revolution and the Jews in Germany," *Jewish Social Studies* 7, New York, 1945.

Kohn, Hans, *Heinrich Heine: The Man and the Myth,* Leo Baeck Memorial Lecture, New York, 1959.

———, *The Mind of Germany,* New York, 1965.

Krochmal, Nahman, *Moreh Nevukhei ha-Zeman,* Lemberg, 1851.

Kroner, Richard, introduction to Hegel, "On Christianity," in *Early Theological Writings,* translated by T. M. Knox, New York, 1961.

———, *Von Kant zu Hegel,* 2 vols., Tübingen, 1921–24.

Kurzweil, Zvi E., "Ha-Rav Shimshon Hirsch," *Sinai* 45, Jerusalem, 1959.

———, "Samson Raphael Hirsch: Educationalist and Thinker," *Tradition* 2, New York, 1960.

Landshuth, Eliezer, *Toledot Anshei ha-Shem u-Pe'ulatam,* Berlin, 1884.

Levi, Zeev, *Spinoza u-Musag ha-Yehadut,* Tel Aviv, 1972.

Lessing, Ephraim Gotthold, *Erziehung des Menschengeschlechtes,* Berlin, 1785.

Lewkowitz, Albert, *Das Judentum und die geistigen Strömungen des neunzehnten Jahrhunderts,* Breslau, 1935.

Liebermann, Eliezer, ed., *Nogah ha-Tzedek,* Dessau, 1818.

———, *Or Nogah,* Dessau, 1818.

Liebeschütz, Hans, *Das Judentum im deutschen Geschichtsbild von Hegel bis Max Weber,* Tübingen, 1967.

Liptzin, Solomon, *Germany's Stepchildren,* Philadelphia, 1944.

Lowenthal, Marvin, *The Jews of Germany,* Philadelphia, 1938.

Löwith, Karl, *Von Hegel bis Nietzche,* Zürich, 1941.

Lübgert, Wilhelm, *Das Ende des Idealismus im Zeitalter Bismarcks,* Gütersloh, 1930.

Luqueer, F. L., *Hegel as Educator,* New York, 1896.

Luzzatto, Samuel David, *The Foundations of the Torah,* translated by Noah H. Rosenbloom, New York, 1965.

MacKenzie, M., *Hegel's Educational Theory and Practice,* London, 1949.

MacVannel, John Angus, *Hegel's Doctrine of the Will*, New York, 1896.

Mahler, Raphael, *Divrei Yemei Yisrael: Dorot Aharonim*, vol. 2, Merhavyah, 1954.

Maimonides, Moses, *Guide of the Perplexed*, translated by Michael Friedländer, New York, 1946.

————, *Mishneh Torah*, 6 vols., New York, 1956.

Makower, H., *Die Gemeindeverhältnisse der Juden in Preussen*, Berlin, 1873.

Manuel, Frank E., *The Eighteenth Century Confronts the Gods*, Cambridge, Mass., 1959.

Marcuse, Herbert, *Reason and Revolution: Hegel and the Rise of Social Theory*, Boston, 1960.

Mattuck, Israel Isidor, *The Essentials of Liberal Judaism*, London, 1947.

May, Rollo, "The Significance of Symbols," in *Symbolism in Religion and Literature*, New York, 1960.

Maybaum, Ignaz, "Dubnow's Assessment of the Reform Movement of German Jewry," in *Simon Dubnow: The Man and His Work*, Paris, 1963.

McEchran, F., *The Life and Philosophy of Johann Gottfried Herder*, Oxford, 1939.

McGiffert, Arthur Cushman, *A History of Christian Thought*, 2 vols., New York, 1961.

McGovern, William Montgomery, *From Luther to Hitler*, Cambridge, 1941.

Mendelssohn, Moses, *Gesammelte Schriften*, edited by G. B. Mendelssohn, 7 vols., Leipzig, 1843–45.

————, *Gesammelte Schriften: Jubiläumsausgabe*, edited by I. Elbogen, J. Guttmann, and K. Mittwoch, 5 vols., Berlin, 1929.

————, *Jerusalem*, translated by Alfred Jospe, New York, 1969.

Mendelssohn, Moses, of Hamburg [Moses Frankfurter], *Penei Tevel*, Amsterdam, 1872.

Mevorakh, Barukh, *Napoleon u-Tekufato*, Jerusalem, 1968.

Meyer, Michael A., "The Great Debate on Antisemitism: Jewish Reaction to New Hostility in Germany, 1879–1881," *Leo Baeck Institute Year Book* 11, 1966.

————, *The Origins of the Modern Jew*, Detroit, 1967.

Michael, Reuven, "Yomano shel Graetz," *Kiryat Sefer* 37, Jerusalem, 1962.

Mirski, Aharon, *Reshit ha-Piyyut*, Jerusalem, 1965.

Moore, G. F., *Judaism*, 3 vols., Cambridge, Mass., 1927.

Morgenstern, Julian, *As a Mighty Stream: The Story of Reform Judaism*, Philadelphia, 1949.

Munk, Elie, "Rabbiner Hirsch als Rationalist der Kabbalah," *Nachlath Zwi* 3, Frankfurt am Main, 1932.

Nachlath Zwi: Eine Monatschrift für Judentum in Lehre und Tat, Frankfurt am Main, 1930–37.

Netanyahu, Benzion, *Don Isaac Abravanel: Statesman and Philosopher*, Philadelphia, 1953.

Niebuhr, Richard R., *Schleiermacher on Christ and Religion*, New York, 1964.

Offenburg, Benno, *Das Erwachen des deutschen Nationalbewusstseins in der Preussischen Judenheit,* Hamburg, 1933.
Ozer, Charles L., "Jewish Education in the Transition from Ghetto to Emancipation," *Historia Judaica* 9, 1947.
Parkes, James, *Conflict of Church and Synagogue,* Philadelphia, 1961.
Pascal, Roy, *The German Sturm und Drang,* New York, 1953.
Paton, H. J., *The Categorical Imperative,* New York, 1967.
Perlmutter, M. A., *Rabbi Yehonatan Eibeschütz ve-Yaḥaso el ha-Shabtaut,* Jerusalem, 1946.
Petuchowski, Jakob J., "Manuals and Catechisms of the Jewish Religion in the Early Period of Emancipation," in *Studies in Nineteenth Century Jewish Intellectual History,* Cambridge, Mass., 1968.
———, *Prayerbook Reform in Europe,* New York, 1968.
Philipson, David, *Centenary Papers and Others,* Cincinnati, 1919.
———, *The Reform Movement in Judaism,* rev. ed., New York, 1967.
Philippson L., *Zur Charakteristik der ersten jüdischen Synode,* Berlin, 1869.
Pinson, Koppel S., *Modern Germany: Its History and Civilization,* New York, 1966.
Plaut, W. Gunther, *The Growth of Reform Judaism,* New York, 1965.
———, *The Rise of Reform Judaism,* New York, 1963.
Posner, Akiba, and Ernest Freiman, "Rabbi Jacob Ettlinger," in *Guardians of Our Faith,* New York, 1958.
Protokolle der ersten Rabbinerversammlung abgehalten zu Braunschweig vom 12. bis zum 19. Juni, 1844, Braunschweig, 1844.
Protokolle und Aktenstücke der zweiten Rabbinerversammlung abgehalten in Frankfurt am Main, 1845.
Protokolle der dritten Versammlung deutscher Rabbiner, Breslau, 1846.
Pulzer, Peter G. J., *The Rise of Political Antisemitism in Germany and Austria,* New York, 1964.
Raisin, Jacob S., "The Reform Movement before Geiger," *Central Conference of American Rabbis Yearbook* 20, 1910.
Raisin, Max, "The Reform Movement as Reflected in the Neo-Hebraic Literature," *Central Conference of American Rabbis Yearbook* 16, 1906.
Randall, John Herman, Jr., *The Career of Philosophy,* 2 vols., New York, 1965.
———, *The Making of the Modern Mind,* Boston, 1926.
Reardon, B. M. G., *Religious Thought in the Nineteenth Century,* Cambridge, 1966.
Reissner, Hanns G., "Rebellious Dilemma: The Case Histories of Eduard Gans and Some of His Partisans," *Leo Baeck Institute Year Book* 2, 1957.
Riesser, Lazarus Jacob, *Send-Schreiben an meine Glaubens-Genossen in Hamburg, oder eine Abhandlung über den israelitischen Cultus,* Altona, 1819.
Rivals, Georges, *Notes sur le Judaisme liberal de 1750 à 1913,* Montauban, 1913.
Rosenbloom, Noah H., *Luzzatto's Ethico-Psychological Interpretation of Judaism,* New York, 1965.

Rosenheim, Jacob, "Aphorismen zur Grundlegung der jüdischen Ethik im Geiste S. R. Hirsch's," *Ausgewählte Aufsätze und Ansprachen*, Frankfurt, 1930.

————, "The Historical Significance of the Struggle for Secession from the Frankfurt Jewish Community," *Historia Judaica* 10, New York, 1948.

————, *Samson Raphael Hirsch's Cultural Ideal and Our Times*, translated by E. Lichtigfeld, London, 1951.

Rotenstreich, Nathan, "Hegel's Image of Judaism," *Jewish Social Studies* 15, New York, 1953.

————, *Jewish Philosophy in Modern Times: From Mendelssohn to Rosenzweig*, New York, 1968.

————, *Ha-Mahshavah ha-Yehudit be-Et ha-Hadashah*, vol. 1, Tel Aviv, 1945; vol. 2, Tel Aviv, 1950.

————, *The Recurring Pattern: Studies in Anti-Judaism in Modern Thought*, New York, 1964.

————, *Ha-Yehadut u-Zekhuyot ha-Yehudim*, Tel Aviv, 1959.

Roth, Cecil, *A History of the Jews in England*, Oxford, 1964.

————, *A History of the Marranos*, New York, 1966.

Rothman, Walter, "Mendelssohn's Character and Philosophy of Religion," *Central Conference of American Rabbis Yearbook* 39, 1929.

Rubin, Simon, *Das talmudische Recht*, Vienna, 1938.

Russell, Bertrand, *A History of Western Philosophy*, New York, 1945.

Saadia Gaon, *The Book of Beliefs and Opinions*, translated by Samuel Rosenblatt, New Haven, 1951.

Salomon, Gotthold, *Kurzgefasste Geschichte des neuen israelitischen Tempels in Hamburg während der ersten fünfundzwanzig Jahre seines Bestehens*, Hamburg, 1844.

————, *Predigten gehalten beim israelitischen Gottesdienst in dem dazu gewidmeten Tempel zu Hamburg*, Dessau, 1819.

————, review of Hirsch's *"Nineteen Letters,"* *Wissenschaftliche Zeitschrift für jüdische Theologie* 2, Frankfurt am Main, 1836.

Sandler, Peretz, *Ha-Beur la-Torah shel Mosheh Mendelssohn ve-Si'ato*, Jerusalem, 1940.

Sasportas, Jacob, *Tzitzit Novel Tzevi*, Tel Aviv, 1967.

Schechter, Solomon, "Abraham Geiger," *Studies in Judaism*, Philadelphia, 1924.

Schleiermacher, Friedrich, *On Religion: Speeches to Its Cultured Despisers*, translated by John Oman, New York, 1958.

Schmidt, H. D., "Chief Rabbi Nathan Marcus Adler," *Leo Baeck Institute Year Book* 7, New York, 1962.

Schmidt-Volkmar, Erich, *Der Kulturkampf in Deutschland, 1871–1890*, Göttingen, 1962.

Schoeps, Hans Joachim, *Geschichte der jüdischen Religionsphilosophie in der Neuzeit*, vol. 1, Berlin, 1935.

————, *The Jewish-Christian Argument*, translated by David E. Green, New York, 1963.

Scholem, Gershom G., *Major Trends in Jewish Mysticism*, New York, 1946.

————, *On the Kabbalah and Its Symbolism,* translated by Ralph Manheim, New York, 1965.

————, "Politik der Mystik," *Jüdische Rundschau* 57 (July 17, 1934).

————, *Shabbetai Tzevi,* 2 vols., Tel Aviv, 1967.

Schreiber, E., *Abraham Geiger als Reformator des Judenthums,* Loebau, 1879.

————, *Reformed Judaism and Its Pioneers: A Contribution to Its History,* Spokane, Wash., 1892.

Schwab, Hermann, *The History of Orthodox Jewry in Germany, 1830–1945,* London, 1950.

Schwabacher, J., *Geschichliche und rechtliche Gestaltung der portugiesisch-jüdischen und der deutsch-jüdischen Gemeinde zu Hamburg,* Berlin, 1914.

Schwartzman, Sylvan D., *Reform Judaism in the Making,* New York, 1955.

Schwarzschild, Emanuel, *Die Gründung der israelitischen Religionsgesellschaft zu Frankfurt am Main und ihre Weiterentwicklung bis zum Jahre 1876* (Frankfurt am Main, 1876).

Schwarzschild, Steven S., "Samson Raphael Hirsch: The Man and His Thought," *Conservative Judaism* 13, New York, 1959.

Seligmann, Caesar, *Geschichte der jüdischen Reformbewegung von Mendelssohn bis zur Gegenwart,* Frankfurt am Main, 1922.

Sheli, Ḥayyim, *Meḥkar ha-Mikra be-Sifrut ha-Haskalah,* Jerusalem, 1942.

Shemueli, Ephraim, *Bein Emunah li-Kefirah,* Tel Aviv, 1962.

Shoḥet, Azriel, "Beginnings of the Haskalah among German Jewry" (Hebrew), *Molad* 24, 1965.

————, "Hitarutam shel Yehudei Germaniah bi-Svivatam im Pros ha-Haskalah," *Tziyon* 21, 1956.

————, *Im Ḥilufei Tekufot: Reshit ha-Haskalah be-Yahadut Germaniah,* Jerusalem, 1960.

Simon, Ernst, "Pedagogical Philanthropinism and Jewish Education" (Hebrew), *Mordecai Kaplan Jubilee Volume,* New York, 1953.

Sombart, Werner, *The Jews and Modern Capitalism,* London, 1913.

Stace, W. T., *The Philosophy of Hegel,* New York, 1955.

Steinberg, Milton, *The Making of the Modern Jew,* New York, 1948.

Steinheim, Salomon Ludwig, *Moses Mendelssohn und seine Schule in ihrer Beziehung zur Aufgabe des neuen Jahrunderts der alten Zeitrechnung,* Hamburg, 1840.

————, *Vom Bleibenden und Vergänglichen im Judentum,* Berlin, 1935.

Steinschneider, Moritz, introduction to M. S. Charbonah [H. B. Fassel], *Ḥerev Be-Tzayon,* Leipzig 1839.

Sterling, Eleonore, "Jewish Reaction to Jew-Hatred in the First Half of the Nineteenth Century," *Leo Baeck Institute Year Book* 3, 1958.

Stern, S., *Geschichte des Judentums von Mendelssohn bis auf die neuere Zeit,* Breslau, 1870.

Stern-Taubler, Selma, "The Jew in the Transition from Ghetto to Emancipation," *Historia Judaica* 2, New York, 1940.

————, "Die Judenfrage in der Ideologie der Aufklärung und Romantik," *Der Morgen* 11, Berlin, 1935.

————, "Der literarische Kampf um die Emanzipation in den Jahren

1816–1820 und seine ideologischen und soziologischen Voraus-setzungen, II," *Hebrew Union College Seventy-fifth Anniversary Publication*, Cincinnati, 1950–51.

Tal, T., *S. R. Hirsch*, Amsterdam, 1907.

Tal, Uriel, *Yehadut ve-Natzrut be-Reich ha-Sheni, 1870–1919*, Jerusalem, 1969.

Tawney, R.H., *Religion and the Rise of Capitalism*, London, 1926.

Theologische Gutachten über das Gebetbuch nach dem Gebrauche des neuen israelitischen Tempelvereins zu Hamburg, Hamburg, 1842.

Touri, Ya'akov, *Mehumah u-Mevukhah be-Mehapekhat 1848*, Tel Aviv, 1968.

Trepp, Leo, *Die Landesgemeinde der Juden in Oldenburg, 1827–1938*, Oldenburg, 1965.

Trier, Solomon Abraham, ed., *Rabbinische Gutachten über die Beschneidung*, Frankfurt am Main, 1844.

Tschernowitz, Hayyim, *Toldot ha-Halakhah*, 4 vols., New York, 1945.

———, *Toldot ha-Poskim*, 3 vols., New York, 1946.

Underhill, Evelyn, *Mysticism*, New York, 1960.

Unna, J., *Statistik der Frankfurter Juden bis zum Jahre 1866*, Frankfurt, 1931.

Urbach, E. E., *Hazal: Pirkei Emunot ve-Deot*, Jerusalem, 1971.

Verhandlungen der ersten israelitischen Synode zu Leipzig, Berlin, 1869.

Verhandlungen der zweiten israelitischen Synode zu Augsburg, 1871.

Wallach, Luitpold, *Liberty and Letters: The Thoughts of Leopold Zunz*, London, 1959.

Weber, Alfred, *History of Philosophy*, translated by Frank Thilly, New York, 1896.

Weinberg, J. I., "Mishnato shel Rabbi S. R. Hirsch," *De'ot* 9, Jerusalem, 1959.

Weinryb, B. D., "Enlightenment and German-Jewish Haskalah," *Studies in Voltaire and the Eighteenth Century* 27, 1963.

Weintraub, Ze'ev, *Targumei ha-Torah le-Lashon ha-Germanit*, Chicago, 1967.

Wessely, Naphtali Herz, *Divrei Shalom ve-Emet*, Berlin, 1782.

White, A. D., *A History of the Warfare of Science with Theology in Christendom*, 2 vols., New York, 1960.

Whitehead, Alfred North, *Symbolism: Its Meaning and Effect*, New York, 1927.

Wiener, Max, *Abraham Geiger and Liberal Judaism*, translated by Ernst J. Schlochauer, Philadelphia, 1962.

———, "The Ideology of the Founders of Jewish Scientific Research," *YIVO Annual of Social Science* 5, 1950.

———, *Jüdische Religion im Zeitalter der Emanzipation*, Berlin, 1933.

Wilhelm, Kurt, "The Jewish Community in the Post-Emancipation Period," *Leo Baeck Institute Year Book #2*, London, 1957.

Wohlgemuth, J., "Samson Raphael Hirsch als Erzieher," *Israelit*, S. R. Hirsch anniversary issue, Frankfurt am Main, 1908.

Wolf, Willy, "Zur Philosophie Rabbiner S. R. Hirsch," *Nachlath Zwi 3*, Frankfurt am Main, 1932.

Wolf, Immanuel, "On the Concept of a Science of Judaism," translated by

Lionel E. Kochan, *Leo Baeck Institute Year Book* 2, London, 1957.

Wolfson, Harry Austryn, *Philo: Foundations of Religious Philosophy in Judaism, Christianity, and Islam*, Cambridge, Mass., 1962.

———, *The Philosophy of the Church Fathers*, Cambridge, Mass., 1964.

———, *Religious Philosophy: A Group of Essays*, New York, 1965.

Zinberg, Israel, *Toldot Sifrut Yisrael*, 7 vols. Tel Aviv, 1959–71.

Zunz, Leopold, *Die gottesdienstlichen Vorträge der Juden historisch entwickelt*, Frankfurt am Main, 1892.

Index

Aaronides, 394–96
Abel, 322
Abhängigkeitsgefühl, 270–71
Abraham, 214, 228, 266, 275, 384
Adler, Abraham, 17
Adler, Nathan Marcus, 60, 62–65, 79
Adler, Samuel, 17
Akashia, Hananiah ben, 204–5
Alexandria, ancient, 5, 199
Alliance Israélite Universelle, 110
Antigonos of Socho, 10
Antinomianism, 133, 136, 190, 192, 202, 341, 398–99
Anti-Semitism, 14, 47, 68, 117, 119, 343, 345
Aquinas, Thomas, 27
Aristotelianism, 5, 132, 193, 221, 228, 363
Aristotle, 27, 131–32, 221, 243
Ark of the Covenant, 277
Asher, Ya'acov ben, 207–8
Atonement, Day of. See Yom Kippur
Aub, Joseph, 17
Auerbach, Berthold, 35
Aufklärung (German, Enlightenment), 13, 170
August, Ernest, 76, 82
Augustine, St., 27, 197
Austria, 84–87
Austrian Silesia, 83, 88
Austro-Hungarian Empire, 83–85

Bamberger, Seligmann Baer, 103, 110, 118
Bauer, Bruno, 27
Beer, Jacob, 6
Bekhor, 280–81

Benet, Mordecai, 8, 92, 181
Benjamin (addressee of the *Neunzehn Briefe*), 126–28, 139, 143, 154–55, 340, 402. See also *Neunzehn Briefe*
Ben Uziel (Hirsch pseudonym), 125, 140
Ben Uziel, Elizaphan, 140–41
Ben-Ze'ev, Judah Loeb, 189–90
Berlin, Jewish community in, 5, 50, 79, 180
Bernays, Isaac, 56–58, 60, 63, 66, 106
Bernays, Jacob, 106
Bible
    as allegory, 196, 365
    as basis of law and authority, 81, 123, 149, 153, 213, 306, 309–12, 317, 398
    as basis of ritual, 252, 280
    Hirsch's commentary on, 48, 55, 70, 126, 133, 224, 299, 328, 399
    in Jewish tradition, 10, 47, 107–8, 367, 390
    miracles in, 366
    non-Jews, reference to, 345
    study of, 49, 51, 56, 72, 87, 189, 360, 362, 375
    translation into German, 109
    validity and values of, 7, 46, 215, 220, 352, 364, 394
    See also names of specific books
Bing, Abraham, 60
Bismarck, Otto von, 112, 115, 117
Boeckh, August, 153
Bresselau, Meyer Israel, 376
Breuer, Isaac, 167, 169, 354
Brüll, Nehemiah, 108
Bruno, Giordano, 356, 366

471

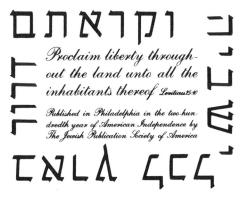

וקראתם דרור בארץ לכל ישביה

Proclaim liberty through-
out the land unto all the
inhabitants thereof *Leviticus 25:10*

Published in Philadelphia in the two-hun-
dredth year of American Independence by
The Jewish Publication Society of America